ELIZABETH DAVID
A Biography

ELIZABETH DAVID
A Biography

LISA CHANEY

PAN BOOKS

First published 1998 by Macmillan

This edition published 1999 by Pan Books
an imprint of Macmillan Publishers Ltd
25 Eccleston Place, London SW1W 9NF
Basingstoke and Oxford
Associated companies throughout the world
www.macmillan.com

ISBN 0 330 36762 5

5 7 9 8 6 4

A CIP catalogue record for this book is available from
the British Library.

Typeset by SetSystems Ltd, Saffron Walden, Essex
Printed and bound in Great Britain by
Mackays of Chatham plc, Chatham, Kent

To Marcus and Keith
with gratitude and hope

Contents

Contents

Acknowledgements

SEVERAL OF Elizabeth's friends were most kind in lending me a number of her letters for lengthy periods of time. The task of describing her life was sometimes daunting, but I was frequently aware of being privileged to listen to an older generation of people recalling their lives, often remarkable in their own right and irrespective of their association with Elizabeth.

Mrs Priscilla Longland, Elizabeth's only surviving sister, always made me most welcome and allowed constant access to her papers at Wootton, for which I am very grateful. Her daughter, Sabrina Harcourt-Smith, worked tirelessly, cataloguing newly discovered letters and family papers with extraordinary persistence and exactitude, making herself constantly available for discussion on many aspects of the family's history: this included discussions regarding Felicité, Elizabeth's younger sister. As god-daughter, Sabrina was here able to give me vital information. My thanks to her are, as Elizabeth said of Felicité, in a category of their own. Julia Caffyn (née Longland), Elizabeth's god-daughter, was always most helpful. My efforts were on several occasions assisted by Sabrina's son, Will Harcourt-Smith, whose good-natured interventions and corrections were more than once decisive. To Charles Harcourt-Smith, Sabrina's husband, I am indebted for his remarkable forbearance.

To family, friends, colleagues and associates of Elizabeth who so generously gave their time and hospitality, to whom I returned for more discussion and corroboration on numerous occasions, and who pointed me in the direction of others, sometimes proving to be of crucial importance, I owe a great debt of gratitude. Elizabeth's cousin,

Lady Anne Brewis, patiently trawled through her remarkable memory for me on numerous occasions. Doreen Thornton was a lynchpin in the story and, with her husband Colin, has been most kind in her consistent encouragement and support. Another to whose insights, humour and regular welcome I owe much, in particular one unforgettable midnight picnic, was Veronica Nicholson. Sybille Bedford's generosity and perception were most appreciated. Hugh and Judy Johnson, Viscount and Vicountess Ridley, Sir Terence Conran, Anne Scott-James, Audrey Withers, Dr Patrick Woodcock, Paul Bailey, Michael Day, Roger Eland, Ronald Latham, the late Joan O'Malley (née Warburton), Eve Durrell, Paul Gotch, Judith Lassalle, John Johnson, the late Peter Trier, his brother Stephen, Stephen's wife Caroline, Alix Coleman, the Earl and Countess of Selborne, Derek Hill, Lindsey Bareham, Frances Fedden, Sir Peter and Lady Wakefield, Peter Davidson and Priscilla Bain, were all extremely generous with their time and hospitality, often helping to disentangle much fact from fiction and clarifying old misrepresentations with care and vigilance.

Others of considerable assistance were: Lady Daphne Maynard, Sir Bernard and the late Lady Burrows, Patrick Leigh Fermor, Lord Gowrie, Mrs Humphrey Brooke (née Benckendorff), Jane Blakemore, Mrs Peter Laing, Richard Morphet, Michael Helston, Mrs Dominic Morgan, the Hon. Harry Palmer, Sir Adam Ridley, Lady Laura Easthaugh, Margaretta Scott, the late Joan Hickson, her son, Nicholas Butler, Charles Pick, Susannah Plowright, Richard Leech, Major the Reverend J. A. Croft, MC (Royal Deccan Horse), Lieutenant-Colonel A. F. Harpur, DSO (Royal Deccan Horse), Irene Gilchrist, George Perry-Smith, Martin Lam, Simon Hopkinson, Pamela Pugh, Ann Barr, Diana Athill, Marjorie and Joan Lloyd, Cherry Ripe, Pippa Irwin, Victor Morrison, Mary Fedden, Claudia Roden, Chlöe Tyner (née Chant-Communal), Professor Edward Chaney (who first introduced me to the great significance of travel literature), Giela Goldstein (previously Gibson Cowan), David Conville, Alice Waters, Judy Rogers, Hugo Dunn-Meynell, Mary Abercrombie, Betsy Udall, John Ward RA, Simon Blow, Patricia Moss, Bruce Purchase, Sam Beazley, Elizabeth Philips (née Good), Robin Weir, Michael Bateman, Diana Anderson (née Morgan), David Wheeler, Dr Lawrence Goldman,

List of Illustrations

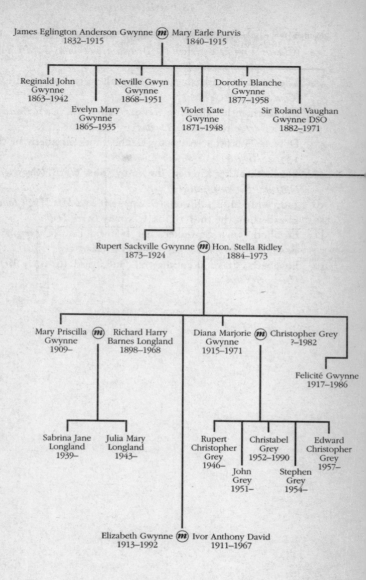

James Eglington Anderson Gwynne (m) Mary Earle Purvis
1832–1915 — 1840–1915

Reginald John Gwynne
1863–1942

Evelyn Mary Gwynne
1865–1935

Neville Gwyn Gwynne
1868–1951

Violet Kate Gwynne
1871–1948

Dorothy Blanche Gwynne
1877–1958

Sir Roland Vaughan Gwynne DSO
1882–1971

Rupert Sackville Gwynne (m) Hon. Stella Ridley
1873–1924 — 1884–1973

Mary Priscilla Gwynne (m) Richard Harry Barnes Longland
1909– — 1898–1968

Diana Marjorie Gwynne (m) Christopher Grey
1915–1971 — ?–1982

Felicité Gwynne
1917–1986

Sabrina Jane Longland
1939–

Julia Mary Longland
1943–

Rupert Christopher Grey
1946–

John Grey
1951–

Christabel Grey
1952–1990

Stephen Grey
1954–

Edward Christopher Grey
1957–

Elizabeth Gwynne (m) Ivor Anthony David
1913–1992 — 1911–1967

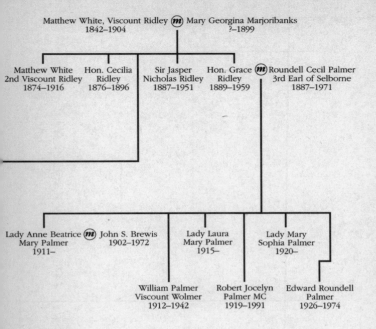

Matthew White, Viscount Ridley ⓜ Mary Georgina Marjoribanks
1842–1904   ?–1899

Matthew White   Hon. Cecilia   Sir Jasper   Hon. Grace ⓜ Roundell Cecil Palmer
2nd Viscount Ridley   Ridley   Nicholas Ridley   Ridley   3rd Earl of Selborne
1874–1916   1876–1896   1887–1951   1889–1959   1887–1971

Lady Anne Beatrice ⓜ John S. Brewis   Lady Laura   Lady Mary
Mary Palmer   1902–1972   Mary Palmer   Sophia Palmer
1911–   1915–   1920–

                    William Palmer   Robert Jocelyn   Edward Roundell
                    Viscount Wolmer   Palmer MC   Palmer
                    1912–1942   1919–1991   1926–1974

Preface

JUST OVER three years after its inception this biography was published in the autumn of 1998. Elizabeth's personality plus the efforts (mostly well intended) of those who knew her to ensure that my interpretation was one which accorded with their own visions of the truth, made the task at times a singularly difficult one.

The vexed question of biographical truth, in other words the fallibility of the biographer's material: personal memoirs, letters, diaries, and the randomness and incoherence of most lives, inclines one to impose a consistency upon it all. The temptation is to sum up and make comprehensible and consistent, relationships, unclear motives and muddle, where probably no such pattern existed. In a post-Freudian industrial age, in which life is typically perceived as dismantled and fragmented, to draw a biographical picture of an iconic figure such as Elizabeth's, apparently exemplifying personal cohesion, is attractive and restorative. However, while hers was not one of unmitigated chaos, neither would 'ordered' be an accurate description of her life. Elizabeth's real cohesiveness manifested itself through her writing.

In writing biography it is impossible to function without some bias, impossible to proceed without some preconception of what one is searching for. But as one proceeds and discovers more, it is dishonest to keep too tight a hold on prejudices and self-imposed limits. Here Elizabeth's force and complexity, the largely concealed swathes of her life, and the loyalties and enmities these engendered, meant that without myself becoming committed and involved, neither information nor insight would be forthcoming. One of the many happy compensations for the dilemmas and complications which sometimes threatened the writing of this book, was the repeated awareness that the more one gives the more one receives in return.

Elizabeth's background, the milieu in which she grew up and the crucial experiences of the first half of her life, have hitherto remained virtually unknown. In becoming familiar with these the reader will not only observe that her writing was fundamentally autobiographical, but also quite how much the motivation and essential material for it was garnered in the first, rather than the latter, part of her life. This book is a candid, yet I hope responsible, study of a remarkable and enormously influential woman. There will be other interpretations, possibly sanitized, possibly conflicting with this one. Nevertheless, faced with the shifts and alterations of perception over time, probably none can be definitive.

The favourable response to the first publication of *Elizabeth David* was a most welcome surprise. After the hours of thoughtful reflection and numerous kindnesses offered me by many of Elizabeth's family and friends, I am especially gratified that my frank portrayal of her has received so much of their sympathy and endorsement.

A number of readers, among them Bruce Wannell, have since made corrections, and encouraged me to clarify certain themes, and these have been both constructive and enlightening. I have also taken the opportunity to incorporate new information laboured over and most kindly given me by others, such as Don Chapman, Mrs Ialeen Gibson Cowan, Mrs Caroline Lassalle and in particular Patrick Lewin (nephew to Tony David). With more time than was initially available, and bearing in mind these revisions, I hope this new edition of *Elizabeth David* is now a more courteous book to the reader.

York
April 1999

Introduction

ELIZABETH DAVID, OBE, CBE, is undoubtedly the greatest English writer on food this century. After her death it seemed possible that the full extent of her influence might be forgotten. This is not to say that she has 'gone out of favour', but precisely because her influence has been so pervasive (first in the home, then beyond it in food shops, kitchen shops and restaurants) some of us, now and in the future, will be unaware of its source. This biography began as a tribute. After three years, repeatedly making the mistake of trying to forge a life of consistency and coherence – perhaps particularly tempting with a subject as enigmatic as Elizabeth – the puzzle of her life is a little closer to elucidation. With it my belief in the merits and significance of Elizabeth's art is even greater than when I began.

English cookery writer *extraordinaire*, Elizabeth died in 1992 where she had lived for over forty years, in a discreet Chelsea house filled with the spoils of a lifetime spent hoarding and collecting, particularly books. Her following extended across the English-speaking world to America and Australia – over 1.2 million copies of her books have sold in Penguin alone, and they have been translated into several European languages. At her death the obituaries proclaimed her key role in the emancipation of the post-war British palate. Exercising her beneficial influence for more than a generation, she inspired not only thousands of domestic cooks, but influential chefs and food writers, to claim her as their chief muse.

Auberon Waugh maintains that 'she has brought about a greater change in English life than any other woman this century', and his father Evelyn named her *Italian Food* his book of the year after its publication in 1954. Grey Gowrie, until recently Chairman of the Arts Council, used another of her books, *French Provincial Cooking*, in his classes for English literature students at Harvard University, for the quality of the writing. And it was as much for this reason that the novelist Paul Bailey wanted to know her. Her friend Lawrence Durrell wrote to her that a French devotee had told him she was the Jane Austen of cookery writers. Uniquely among cookery writers, Elizabeth was made a Fellow of the Society of Literature in recognition of these literary skills.

The essential appeal of her writing lies in its blend of escapism tempered with a sturdy realism. She was first a *writer*, then one whose subject was food. Linking it constantly to memories and dreams, she captured the mind and imagination of her reader, and altered perceptions and expectations of the everyday. With a steely intellect and mordant wit, her prose could move from the taut and acid to the languidly descriptive, while always exuding a refined sensuality and an estimable good sense. She was gifted with a consummate ability to evoke time and place and – significantly for the English, enticed by it for centuries – this place was predominantly the Mediterranean. Her first five books are accordingly as much evocative travelogues as they are illuminating manuals for the preparation of food.

Beginning her writing career in post-war Britain, Elizabeth was writing in reaction to both the bleak English culinary climate and a more profound legacy of repression and puritanism, represented for her and many of her travelled generation by the Protestant North. During the nineteenth century an unsavoury alliance had arisen in England between the prevailing tenets of thrift and economy and the belief that only complicated food was good food. The resulting state of affairs was characterized by the great French chef Escoffier when he complained that the English cared 'more for show than for the pleasure of eating'. By the end of the nineteenth century the Anglo-Saxon response in socially ambitious circles to simple and simply cooked food was largely one of conditioned snobbery.

Not alone among post-war cookery writers in denigrating English culinary travesties, often perpetrated with an almost wilful zeal, the high literary quality and imaginative passion of Elizabeth's rejection of these tendencies, and her authoritative espousal of something better, brought her many supporters. In journalism and books she lovingly nurtured the British passion for the South and in time turned her readership away from some of their own culinary traditions, encouraging them instead to savour the food of the sun.

Having created the audience, in 1965 she began to supply her growing readership with the *batterie de cuisine* of France and the Mediterranean in her pioneering kitchen shop (Elizabeth David Ltd), in London's Pimlico. This commercial enterprise was no marketing ploy but an extension of an avowed passion: objects relating to the kitchen interested her as much as the food itself. A discerning eye for the beauty of functional objects and an appreciation of the social traditions of rooted cultures, still connected to their non-industrial past, were what drove Elizabeth's interest in the kitchen and its objects. Much of the appeal which France and the Mediterranean countries held for her lay in the certainty that they maintained strong links with their culinary past; Britain on the whole did not.

After the opening of Elizabeth David Ltd similar shops quickly sprang up, and there is little doubt that Elizabeth's was the inspiration for them and the myriad others now catering for kitchens across the English-speaking world. Not only is her influence felt through the kitchen equipment so many of us presently use but, through the ethos of her writing, she also helped to inspire the atmosphere we often set out to create in our own kitchen-dining-rooms. Kitchens are now rooms in which, more often than not, like Elizabeth, we not only cook but eat and entertain too.

Elizabeth's earlier Mediterranean books successfully encouraged readers to react against the worst of their own culinary traditions. In her later works, however, at once stimulating recipe books and exemplary pieces of social and culinary history, Elizabeth described how English cooking could, at its best, hold its own with the Mediterranean. The more of an historian she became, the more she understood that the erosion of the English tradition had begun long ago, with the flowering of the industrial revolution. The final phase of her life was a response to this discovery and she proclaimed: 'We need to go back to the recipes of a century ago and further, when an authentic and still strong English cooking tradition flourished.'

Many of Elizabeth's devotees did not readily take her new

'English' message to heart. In the years since the Second World War Elizabeth's writing had played its part in the English embracement of 'abroad', eventually penetrating deeper into the English psyche than its reflection in the obligatory Mediterranean holiday and the production of Elizabeth's beautiful recipes for dinner parties. What England had witnessed was not simply the natural and invigorating assimilation of new ideas into its culinary repertoire through one region's contact with others. At another level Elizabeth's message had contributed towards a rejection of England's own culture, the Anglo-Saxon one, in a way which few Europeans would ever contemplate in relation to their own.

On a personal level, Elizabeth added a natural poise and elegance to her rather exotic beauty. She tried the stage when young, but was too cerebral and self-conscious to act with confidence. In keeping with a desire to reveal only part of herself, she was led to comment to the inquisitive that everything there was to know about her was written in her books. Photographs and public appearances were rare and her notorious dislike of publicity led, in her later years, to a mistaken reputation for reclusiveness. This sprang as much from the ethos of her privileged upbringing as from personal diffidence. Nevertheless, despite having no time for the cult of personality, there is ample evidence that Elizabeth regarded herself as superior to mere collectors of recipes, and possessed a shrewd estimation of her own considerable literary worth.

It is strictly true that much of what there is to know about Elizabeth *is* in her books, but one must first possess the key. Most of the early part of her life passed in a state of rebellion against her widowed mother. In her youth she spent a crucial period in France. In the company of Charles Gibson Cowan, whom her family and most friends found intolerable, she later escaped from England and its constraints shortly before the outbreak of the Second World War. In the South of France she met and befriended, with momentous consequences for herself, the writer Norman Douglas. There followed several months on a Greek island, concluding with evacuation to Egypt as Crete was being overrun by the invading German forces. Finally entering the war effort, Elizabeth worked first for the Admiralty, then for the Ministry of Information for the remainder of the hostilities. In Egypt she married, went reluctantly to India, and returned to a victorious but ration-blighted England in 1946. In 1950, at the age of thirty-six, she published her first book.

Many of these details of Elizabeth's life are already more or less known, but, during the process of their investigation and scrutinization, determining episodes, hitherto concealed from all but her oldest and closest associates, began to emerge. Family, friends and colleagues helped immeasurably, sometimes through their conflicting views, in the process of unravelling and elucidation. My path of research led, sometimes by remarkable coincidence, at others by dogged persistence, to two revealing books written by the most obscure and perhaps most important of Elizabeth's several lovers. It also turned up a cache of letters to her family, unread for almost half a century. This extraordinary material proved to be of far-reaching significance and Elizabeth was, finally, more comprehensible. Through these discoveries it also became clear that her life determined and then permeated her work, revealing her as a most autobiographical writer.

Elizabeth emerges as a highly complex and driven artist, whose razor-sharp memory and concern for accuracy at times reached obsessive proportions. She could show breathtaking disregard for others' sensitivities, was passionate, emotional, forthright and abrasive to the point of rudeness. She was also diffident and, though not inclined towards introspection, was at times self-critical and undecided. To an almost classical, pre-Christian lack of *caritas* she sometimes added ruthlessness, a reluctance to forgive, and a tendency to judgement of others which was sometimes seriously blinkered. At the same time she was cultivated, witty and at times very funny. She could also be a most encouraging, generous and devoted friend, eliciting a touching and unswerving loyalty in those to whom she was close. In her work she demonstrated an unflagging concern for truth, coupled with a note of celebration which played throughout her lucid and masterful prose. Together these gave an authority and sureness to her work, which has made of her readers thousands of grateful and devoted admirers.

CHAPTER ONE

Forefathers

CHALK-WHITE a road cuts through the brow of the hill, brick chimneys and roofs emerging above its low summit. In fields close by wild mushrooms once grew and red Sussex cattle grazed with the rare black St Kilda sheep. Nearby is the bald northern scarp of the South Downs. To one side, reaching away into a liquid blue distance is the Weald, to the other is the sea skirted by its broad coastal plain. Further on still are the sheer white coastal cliffs.

    Since earliest times this downland landscape has harboured man, and everywhere there are traces of ancient habitation. Just out of sight is the prehistoric Long Man of Wilmington, perhaps the oldest god of these islands, presenting his gigantic turf-cut shape on the steep flat slope of Windover Hill and recalling Kipling's lines:

> *I will go out against the sun*
> *Where the rolled scarp retires,*
> *And the Long Man of Wilmington*
> *Looks naked towards the shires.*

One hundred feet above his great head, against the skyline the crest of Windover Hill merges with the downland ridge running on into the distance, since prehistory used as a high causeway reaching as far as Winchester Hill, over 50 miles to the west. The Romans built fine villas hereabouts, the Normans castles and manors. Under their rule monastic orders raised new priories and abbeys, communications with the mother houses in France easy via the busy Sussex Channel ports. With Henry VIII's Dissolution of the Monasteries some of these, like

I

Battle Abbey and Michelham Priory, were turned over to private dwellings. Many of the county gentry — Howards, Fitzalans, the Bellinghams of Newtimber, the Shelleys of Michelgrove, the Gages of Firle — refused to convert and kept staunchly to the old (Roman Catholic) faith. A number of the oldest manor houses, such as Glynde and Firle Place, are still lived in by the families who had them built during the prosperous fifteenth to seventeenth centuries.

Although the building of the railways made this coast popular in the nineteenth century as a metropolitan seaside playground, agricultural Sussex and its villages continued as before, remote from industrial England. In the nineteenth century the Downs were still covered in sheep and the shepherd was king of the agricultural labourers. Well into this century he could still be seen at dawn driving his animals high up on to the Downs, following their straggling course by day and bringing them down safely to the folds at dusk. Into this century it remained customary to bury a shepherd with a tuft of wool so as to identify his occupation, and thereby explain on Judgement Day why his attendance at church had been so irregular.

Smoothed by melting Ice Age snows, the bold green chain of downland hills dominates the surrounding landscape and ends abruptly with the vertiginous chalk sea cliffs of Beachy Head. Divided into several separate massifs, the lower reaches of the Downs are sometimes densely wooded, elsewhere fields wave with billowing wheat. The upper reaches are rich in downland pasture, their majestic hilltops bared to sun and wind. In spring and early summer birds, wild flowers and herbs grow in profusion; grand beeches and ancient yews, holly and hornbeam flourish in the chalky soil. In the higher places ragwort and sometimes wild orchids grow, juniper and haw-thorn too — higher still there is only the springy velvet turf.

Once over the brow of the hill the chalky road drops steeply into a spacious courtyard set around with buildings: barns, stables, dairy, outhouses, all of soft red brick and gnarled grey flint. Through this courtyard and another, and the great rounded hipped-tiled arch leads on to the grassy oval forecourt flanked by a medieval chapel capped with a golden cockerel weathervane.

A few stone steps above the forecourt the patterned brickwork wing of the old house dictated the character of the two later adjoining ones. Kitchen offices, nursery and library lie to the south, another set of low buildings and a ballroom to the north. Everywhere the smooth mellowed brick and flint of Sussex are offset by the colour and texture of granite pavings, sea pebbles and greying oak beams. An inspired touch has every door about the forecourt painted a soft steely-blue. This imaginative use of materials fuses together the rambling assemblage in such a way that the pervading atmosphere is one of solidity, permanence – a unified, harmonious, and particularly English whole. This is Wootton Manor, childhood home of Elizabeth David.

The substantial manor house was a fitting residence for Elizabeth's father, Rupert Gwynne, the local Member of Parliament. A typical gable-fronted seventeenth-century Sussex farmhouse, Wootton's entrance surveyed the Downs and Folkington Hill, towering 630 feet to its summit. On a clear day the view from the top floor of Wootton reaches over the Downs to Firle Beacon and beyond to Pevensey Bay, where William the Norman first landed in 1066 and was met not far away at Battle by Harold, the brave and beleaguered English king. Around Wootton a series of outhouses, farm-workers' cottages, barns, stables and other buildings had proliferated over the years. Its origins are ancient, with mention of a small Saxon community there in the Domesday Book – Wootton means 'farm by the wood' – and it came under the estate of William the Conquerer's half-brother, the Count of Mortain. (Windover Hill, on which is inscribed the Long Man of Wilmington, lies on the Wootton Estate.)

Changing hands and appearance over the centuries, Wootton Manor went through a gradual process of gentrification and was eventually sold to Elizabeth's grandfather, James E. Anderson Gwynne, in 1876. Simultaneously he bought Folkington Manor nearby, a grander family residence built not long before in ponderous Victorian-Tudor style. Here Rupert and his six brothers and sisters grew up. On Rupert's marriage to the Hon. Stella Ridley in 1905, James presented Wootton to the newly-weds. He gave his daughter-in-law a choice between Wootton and Michelham Priory a couple of miles away on the large Gwynne estate. Indulging his antiquarian interests James had recently bought and restored this ruinously beautiful thirteenth-century Augustinian priory, which had been extended at the Dissolution into a Tudor manor house. Stella chose Wootton, but the atmospheric photographs in her 1905 album indicate her indecision and Michelham's appeal. With stone-vaulted ceilings and delicate gothic windows, the house was reached through a towering ivy-clad gatehouse, its only approach still an old bridge spanning the wide, protective moat.

Ten years later, in March 1915, Rupert's father died. In old age he had become bitter and isolated, leaving a will of gothic proportions and relentlessly unforgiving content. Although not the eldest son, Rupert was principal beneficiary of his father's considerable estate, left in trust to him and any male heirs. Rupert decided to stay on at Wootton Manor and it was agreed that his unmarried brother Roland and his sister Dorothy should remain nearby in the family home at Folkington. The recent history of Rupert's family was fortunate in its members' gifts of self-possession, confidence and successful ambition, but it was often marred by bad temper and sometimes narrow-mindedness of outlandish proportions. This could result — notably with Rupert's father — in hyper-sensitivity to the smallest slight and a determined vindictiveness, displayed to the end in his will.

Rupert was sent to Shrewsbury and Cambridge, not Eton and Oxford, for it was feared that they would corrupt. Rupert's oldest brother Reggie had attended both Eton and Oxford and disgraced himself by getting into debt, albeit on a small allowance: his father was wealthy but not generous. Reggie was a spendthrift. Enthusiastically munificent beyond his means at Eton, he was removed and dispatched to the recently founded Lancing. Later, after a short time up at Oxford, he was again in debt. Unable to face the fearful temper of his authoritarian father, he emigrated to Canada and, apart from short visits, never lived in England again. Poor Reggie's youthful inability to look after his money generated a train of events which led eventually to the third son, Rupert, becoming the chief inheritor of James Gwynne's considerable estates.

The first event was the making of the will. Appalled by Reggie's conduct and in accord with his own relentless and unforgiving nature, James's will stated that Reginald, although his eldest son, was not eventually to have control over the family estate. He would receive an annual income, no more. Reggie's allowance was later much reduced.

James's final will is long, tortuous and full of codicils. The changes reflect, with increasing age, a growing and wilful mistrustfulness and inability to communicate, especially with those apparently closest to him. Youthful resoluteness had hardened into inexorable implacability. Throughout James's will a desire to secure two main objectives is manifest: control of his adult children's lives (about his wife's he was already confident, not unusual for a man of his day); and the preservation of Folkington and his other properties intact, preferably via a son. This sad and vindictive document is the last testament of a man whose youthful will to succeed had initially conferred on him such sought after worldly prizes as a decorative and sensitive wife, daughters to indulge and be indulged by, and sons to enlarge the fruits of his labours and perpetuate his name.

Born in 1832, as a young man James Gwynne was full of vigour, tenacity and enthusiasm. His parents Agnes and John came from the respectable Scottish merchant classes and John had produced Britain's first centrifugal pump. The Gwynne Pump was a technological advance which eased the task of reclaiming flooded land and was to be invaluable for many years in the farthest reaches of the British Empire. With the financial assistance of a friend, the banker and tea trader Herbert Twining, John Gwynne set up a company of which James became a member at seventeen. The Great Exhibition of 1851, held in the unique Crystal Palace in Hyde Park, staged an exuberant demonstration of Victorian versatility, pragmatism and invention, coupled with the early technologists' absolute belief in progress. The youthful James was responsible for the Gwynne firm's stand. By 1855 his father was dead and James, the eldest of three brothers, was a managing partner in the firm.

At twenty-seven he fell in love with Mary (May) Purvis. James's mother Agnes was against the union and as a consequence would inflict suffering on him for many years to come. Having failed to prevent the marriage, Agnes never forgave him for acting against her wishes and according to the dictates of his heart and subsequently strove to thwart her son's progress in business. Although time now obscures Mrs Gwynne's reason for her antagonism, it probably sprang from the knowledge that her future daughter-in-law, May, was not pure Scottish, but part Dutch with exotic connections. May's beautiful mother Cornelia was the daughter of Theunis In'tveld, prosperous Dutch Resident of Padang, Sumatra, and Anna Carels, herself the daughter of a Dutch merchant and a Sumatran ranee. Thus, through Anna and Cornelia, May inherited both artistic talent and beguiling looks. In time these would re-emerge with particular originality in both May's daughter Violet and her granddaughter Elizabeth.

In the tradition of successful entrepreneur–industrialists, James completed the cycle of advancement by acquiring property. As the years passed he became less interested in his business and city life and spent most of his time on his estate at Folkington, acquiring more and more land and socializing with his landed neighbours. Despite the benefits of a country life James was neither a tranquil nor an easy man. His wife's gaiety continued for many years, but only in the company of their children. In order of seniority they were: Reginald, Evelyn, Neville, Rupert, Violet, Dorothy and Roland.

With this sketch of family background we turn once more to Rupert. Down from Pembroke College, Cambridge, by 1895 he was reading for the Bar and during this period he launched himself on a steady round of enjoyment. In the country there was shooting, hunting, weekends with friends at Folkington and nearby estates such as Lord Gage's at Firle Place, or further afield. In London his was the life of the well-connected young man with prospects. A rich man's son, Rupert was, however, bound by a set of constraints which were to determine the future course of his life.

After Cambridge he shared with his wealthy brother-in-law, Gordon Woodhouse (married to Rupert's younger sister Violet), their large Georgian house near Hyde Park. James Gwynne kept all his children on a short financial rein and Rupert, though close to Violet, lived in her London house out of necessity as well as choice, from this time until his marriage several years later. Despite his shortage of money, his looks, demeanour and name were sufficient to provide him with a constant supply of invitations to some of the smarter houses in London. Violet and Gordon's London home had its full share of entertaining company, welcoming a colourful selection of the artistic élite of the time.

Violet was gifted, extraordinary to look at and about to become one of the most celebrated musicians of her day. Her mother May had recognized early her daughter's precocious keyboard abilities and nurtured them with intelligence and care. At the same time as indulging her own taste in music, she had always taken Violet to a wide variety of concerts and opera, while the Gwynnes' London and country houses reflected May's love of music with regular entertainments. By the turn of the century Violet's own musical salon had become one of the most celebrated in London, with invitations and friendship eagerly sought by some of the most influential contemporary musical and artistic figures. Among her admirers were Bernard Shaw, T. E. Lawrence, Delius, Pablo Casals, Diaghilev and the three Sitwells.

When already quite young Violet received adulation as her due. And despite a reputation for generosity and warmth, she could be icy when treatment did not accord with her estimation of herself. Her exertion of will pervaded her private and public life in what can either be excused as the mammoth ego thought necessary to an artist's survival, or perceived as the scheming manipulation of a very selfish woman. Whichever it was, when Violet had her own way she was as charming and mesmerizing company as it was possible to be. Unconventional, even by the most bohemian conventions of the day, she lived in apparent harmony throughout her adult life with two adoring men, the Hon. William Barrington and Gordon Woodhouse. For a time the number of her consorts rose to four. Her husband Gordon Woodhouse was a retiring and pleasant facilitator who faithfully sought throughout their marriage to accommodate Violet's every wish. By whatever standards she is judged, Violet was a remarkable woman who inspired many. Her niece, Elizabeth, was to bear more than a passing resemblance to her in both character and looks, but her name would eventually outshine Violet's by far.

Whilst Rupert was now practising as a barrister, he was also socializing on a hectic scale. In 1902 a fellow-barrister and friend of his, the urbane Max Labouchère, joined the Woodhouse–Gwynne household. Unlike other members of the Gwynne family, Rupert seemed unperturbed by his sister's ménage and instead delighted in the company and sociable life-style it entailed. Gordon Woodhouse, Bill Barrington and Max Labouchère had in fact all been introduced to Violet by Rupert himself.

7

By 1903 Rupert had reached the age of thirty, and during the next eighteen months or so was to make certain decisions which would prove crucial to the future course of his life. A realist, he had undoubtedly admitted to himself that he did not have the makings of a first-class barrister. Perhaps it was with this same realism that, despite warnings to the contrary, he had chosen to embark on such a full and energetic life. While still at Shrewsbury School Rupert was warned that a severe attack of rheumatic fever had left his heart severely weakened and that if he intended to live beyond middle age he must lead an abstemious life. His youthful refusal to take the more sober path meant that he had continued to hunt, shoot and gather progressively more trophies for his equine and social prowess. His liaisons and flirtations with women had not, by 1903, produced a girl to his father's liking, or one that Rupert felt committed to. Following a terrible rift between his father James and his elder brother Neville – culminating by 1904 in Neville's banishment from the family home and disinheritance from his father's estate – Rupert was the next in line. If treated with circumspection, his father could now make him chief beneficiary of his estate. Rupert was potentially a rich and highly eligible man.

In the following year he at last made a most suitable and dignified match. His father's approval was absolute. Pressure had most likely been brought to bear upon Rupert to abandon a current unsuitable liaison, and James must have strongly hinted at what the rewards of marriage to a 'suitable' girl would be.

The Hon. Stella Ridley came from a family long established as an important Northumberland dynasty. Rich and well connected, her family would certainly not have permitted the match with Rupert without some assurance of substantial financial support on a par with that to which Stella was accustomed. The earliest reference to the Ridleys, in 1154, records their ownership of extensive lands in the Tyne valley, where they lived in a fortified manor house called Willimotswick. From Willimotswick they enthusiastically took part in the border wars and family feuds which dominated Northumberland life throughout the Middle Ages. It was in this house that one of England's more famous martyrs, Nicholas Ridley, Bishop of London, was born in about 1503. In 1555 his refusal to renounce the

Protestant faith led Henry VIII's Catholic daughter, Mary Tudor, to have him tried and condemned for heresy. Ridley's last letter was written from prison in Oxford to his sister at Willimotswick Manor. The following day he was burnt at the stake.

When young, Stella Ridley was slight. A studio photograph at about fourteen shows her pale-skinned and in her riding habit. Her dark brown hair is untied, then fashionable for unmarried girls. Still displaying the rounded contours of adolescence her face, nevertheless, hints at the qualities which were to distinguish and sustain her. She looks determined, intelligent and stubborn, with little evidence of artfulness or guile. Thoughtful dark eyes resist inquisition. Her engagement photograph at twenty-one confirms these impressions.

In the year prior to her engagement Stella's father, Matthew White Ridley, fifth Baronet and first Viscount, had died. Her mother had predeceased him, dying in 1899 a month after Stella's fifteenth birthday. Stella may have been without parents at her marriage, but she came with self-assurance as to her pedigree and standing. Her mother, Mary Georgina (Polly), daughter of Dudley Coutts Marjoribanks, the first Lord Tweedmouth, spent much time with her children. Encouraged by their mother's enthusiasm and artistic flair, they frequently accompanied her on sketching trips, showing marked ability themselves. Stella continued painting all her life, both exhibfjiting and maintaining important friendships with a number of artists.

Stella's father was Conservative MP for North Northumberland, and in 1895 he was made Home Secretary under the new Conservative administration of Lord Salisbury. After the general election of 1900 he retired from political life and was made a peer (Viscount Ridley). He spent his last years in Northumberland at Blagdon, where he had always remained actively involved in the administration of the family estate. Throughout the north of England he was regarded as a man of considerable business acumen and wielded great influence.

When his wife Polly died, his son Matthew (since the eighteenth century the eldest Ridley boy was always given this name) had reached the age of majority, but the other three children were considerably younger. Grace and Jasper, only ten and twelve respectively, were still much in need of maternal anchorage, but at fifteen

Stella too suffered intensely after the loss of her mother. At Polly's death Sir Matthew still held the post of Home Secretary. As a senior politician and landowner he was much occupied with decision-making and public responsibility. This left him little time for the private role of mother-substitute to his three younger children.

Some time later the children's Aunt Ishbel, Lady Aberdeen, made it known to Sir Matthew that she thought the present arrangements for them were unsatisfactory, and Matthew asked her to take charge. Grace was a fairly biddable child but Stella never made things easy. As a reflection of her unease everything in her power was done to disobey and antagonize the new governess, whose modus vivendi with her difficult charge was at times the stuff of farce. If, for instance, she wanted a window more open she would carefully ask Stella to close it, whereupon it would immediately be flung wider. Aunt Ishbel's reorganization had underestimated the powerful personality of the eldest of her charges, and the children were soon removed from Blagdon and taken back with their aunt to Haddo House in Scotland, where she could keep a closer watch over all that took place. Haddo was the seat of her husband's family, the Gordons, and here, before the nineteenth century they were already established as a powerful landed Scottish family.

Lord Aberdeen's distinguished political career included appointments as Governor-General of Ireland, Governor-General of Canada (1893–8) and another future Viceroyship of Ireland from 1905 to 1915. When Stella's mother died the Aberdeens had not long returned from Canada. Life at the House of Haddo was always conducted on a grand and generous scale, the Aberdeens finding it impossible to behave in any other way. Stella, Jasper and Grace became familiar with their aunt and uncle's exalted circle, which included many of the oldest aristocratic families and most powerful political figures of the day. Arthur Balfour had been uncle Aberdeen's best man, and the formidable Prime Minister Gladstone was a good friend.

Under her aunt's supervision at Haddo, however, Stella was not to fare much better than at Blagdon. Her determination, intelligence and wilfulness, all qualities possessed by Ishbel herself, did not make for easy relations between the two. When Ishbel brought Stella out in London the episode was fraught with more than the normal share of irritations and tensions inherent in these occasions. The preparations involving endless fittings for a suitably beautiful, varied and becoming wardrobe, and invitations given and received with anticipation of the impending event, sharpened the mounting nervous excitement. On the appointed day, demurely sumptuous in white silks and satins, ostrich-feather headdresses and above-elbow gloves, the girls queued for their curtsy and moment's audience with the King and Court. Filing their way out of the State Apartments at Buckingham Palace, the girls moved crabwise so as not to turn their backs on the royal couple, or fall flat on the carpet entangled in their trains. Great white tablecloths were frequently requisitioned to rehearse for the terrifying ordeal. Once the course had been successfully navigated, with mixed feelings of relief and elation, the débutantes and their chaperones went on to their first dance of the Season.

Evenings usually began at ten o'clock, but Aunt Ishbel wished frequently, and rather inconsiderately, to leave these entertainments by about eleven. Stella was having none of it and unlike the more docile Grace would refuse to leave. Stella's dance-book was quickly full. She had no desire to be a wallflower and intended making the most of these occasions, where it was finally permissible to meet and dance with so many new young men. Eventually Ishbel was forced to employ a woman to chaperone her wayward niece, sitting up late into the night long after Ishbel herself had retired to bed.

During the heady weeks of the Season Stella failed to discover any one young man particularly to her liking, the purpose of the Season being, after all, to secure a husband. But Stella's social life succeeding the Season was filled with independent social engagements, and her brown suede commonplace book and photograph albums from this period read like a roll-call of many of the country houses of the day: Tatton Park, Raby Castle, Castle Howard, Meldon Park, Belsey Castle, Beaufort Castle, Beaumaris Castle, Penrhyn Castle. A busy round of house-parties, balls and shooting weekends are recorded, with Stella's diminutive watercolour illustrations and signatures and bons mots from fellow-guests, including a revealing comment from her brother Jasper: 'Woman, I could brain you!' The sense of anticipation and excitement Stella must have felt at this new independence is palpable as one turns the crowded pages of her long-forgotten book.

The Ridley and Gordon cousins were of similar ages and had lived together in Haddo House for much of the time since Polly Ridley's death, four or so years earlier. Dudley Gordon was the second of Aunt Ishbel and Uncle John's four children and a year older than Stella. (He was later to become Elizabeth's godfather.) Dudley and Stella had much in common and became very close. Realizing the strength of their attachment, Ishbel decided something must be done before the young pair made any formal announcement. Poor Dudley was dispatched abroad for a lengthy latter-day Grand Tour, Stella pined, and Ishbel resolved to divest herself of her difficult niece.

Some months later Stella met the eligible young barrister, Rupert Gwynne. Not perhaps quite the social equal her parents might have wished for he was, nevertheless, rich; Stella had recently been orphaned and Aunt Ishbel was in charge. Besides, this older man with such striking looks was a charming and stimulating companion whose attentions were flattering to a young girl. Her father's death, in November 1904, had rendered obsolete Stella's occasional role as hostess for him at Blagdon. Another châtelaine, Rosie, now reigned there with Stella's brother, the new Lord Ridley, and in any case Stella was raring to be free of Haddo.

Rupert was invited to stay at Haddo and Blagdon and Stella came to Folkington. Family on both sides approved. Stella was very young, was falling in love and wanted to be happy. The fifth of May arrived and Society came to a grand wedding at St Margaret's, Westminster. By the summer Stella and Rupert were installed in Wootton Manor, with another pretty house in London, close by the Houses of Parliament, as Stella's dowry.

Ten years later, at the time of his father's death, in 1915, Rupert was a fashionable gentleman-farmer, taking pride in the herd of red Sussex cattle he had inherited, and in striking contrast to the flock of rare Black St Kilda sheep Stella had brought with her from Blagdon. (Family folklore held that St Kildas were a breed descended from Spanish Armada spoils.) Rupert was a fine horseman, riding competitively – a photograph shows a table filled with his cups won at point-to-point meetings – for pleasure, and with the local hunt. Stella too was a keen horsewoman, enjoying the hunt and riding the beautiful chalk Downs in sight of the sea. A popular Conservative MP for Eastbourne, with two small daughters, Priscilla and Elizabeth, and a busy political schedule, Rupert took advantage of his new inheritance and quickly set about enlarging Wootton to a standard more in keeping with his increased status. The services of a family friend, the architect Detmar Blow, were enlisted and Wootton was gradually transformed into the pleasing example of late Arts and Crafts architecture and design it remains today.

Blow added to Wootton a large staircase hall, leading off which he created the south wing. This provided kitchen and related rooms on the ground floor, nurseries on the second and a fine high-ceilinged library on the third. The library took up this entire floor and is beautifully lit by windows on all four walls, with broad views out over the Downs and surrounding parkland. By 1920 Rupert asked Blow to return and make for him another addition to the house, a ballroom. Here, repeating his imaginative handling of traditional Sussex materials, Blow created a building which admirably complemented both the original Jacobean part of Wootton and his own earlier additions. By 1922, when these final additions were complete, Wootton was a substantial house, at once traditional and interestingly contemporary.

Among political friends and associates who were regular visitors to Wootton were a number of painters, designers, and the occasional actor. The painters included Cedric Morris, his companion Arthur Lett-Haines, and Allan Walton, eventually more esteemed for his influential textile designs than his painting. The society portraitist Ambrose McEvoy came too and in 1923–4 painted a portrait of each of the by now four Gwynne children – Priscilla, Elizabeth, Diana and Felicité. These are at once pleasant and observant paintings done in the thin, transparent glazes McEvoy favoured late in life. Delicate, slightly ethereal images are intended to reflect the sitter's social niche and through skilled and precise draughtsmanship the painter has caught something of the essential nature of each girl.

A trickle of distinguished writers also made its way to Wootton. Kipling lived nearby and when not entertaining the children, loved to watch the red cattle and black sheep. Stella's brother Jasper (later director of the family bank, Coutts) was a favourite visitor and through him Walter de la Mare came too. De la Mare recorded the beauties of the garden in a poem which featured a diminutive boy statue under the trees by the water.

Under Stella's care the garden became a place of peaceful retreat. In reaction against the rigid formality of most contemporary gardens, she planted mixed borders illuminated with colour, massed and spilling over the paths, whilst roses climbed and twined through pergolas and trees. Beyond the ballroom a pleached beech and yew-lined brick path led away past lawns and vegetable garden to resolve itself in a great tree-lined paved circle, which still welcomes with its round Arts and Crafts oak table and heart-cut-out chairs. Beyond lie the sunken garden and a bluebell wood, and through a gate the open fields. Beside the stone circle Blow's round thatched summer-house provided shelter for Stella, there absorbed in her painting.

William Robinson, the garden reformer, was a family friend and lived close by at the Elizabethan manor of Gravetye. Here he had pioneered romantically informal 'wild gardens', a pattern of their kind, and written his influential books. The fiery-tempered Robinson detested the formal Victorian style of gardening; in particular he loathed the practice of 'carpet bedding'. Stella's garden was not large or grand, but with beneficial influences such as those of Robinson it achieved that quintessentially English garden atmosphere of tranquillity underscored by a balance of discipline and chaos.

Such was Wootton.

CHAPTER TWO

A Rural Childhood
(1913–1924)

DURING THE CHRISTMAS season of 1909 Eastbourne was emblazoned with electioneering posters, depicting Rupert Gwynne in grave yet becoming pose. A number of contemporary cartoons make more than passing reference to the usefulness of his looks in gaining support from women. Interestingly enough this election coincided with the period when Women's Suffrage was an increasingly public issue, something of which Rupert was not in favour. After seeing out the last weeks of the old year with strenuous canvassing, his campaign was nearing its conclusion; election day was 29 January 1910. On 27 December, in the midst of the general excitement, Stella went into labour, and after almost five years of marriage was safely delivered of her first baby girl, Mary Priscilla. Only a month later Rupert was celebrating the winning of his seat with a good majority – Thomas, Liberal, 5249 votes; Gwynne, Conservative, 7553. Stella's photograph album shows crowds lining the streets of Eastbourne in celebration and Rupert on the balcony of the Town Hall, smiling and acknowledging the cheering sea of supporters. The baby Priscilla (never called Mary) was christened in the family church of St Peter's Folkington shortly afterwards.

The next few years were filled with an escalating set of commitments for both Rupert and Stella. Rupert threw himself into the MP's life while Stella became an exemplary young political hostess. Wootton had its share of artistic visitors, but life for the Gwynnes revolved largely around politics. Stella's family background had primed her well for the role of politician's wife, which she entered into willingly and fulfilled with confidence. She also extended the call of duty to producing more children.

The Gwynne's London house at Catherine Street proved a most useful and convenient address. It was sufficiently close to the House of Commons for a bell to be installed, in order that Rupert should be alerted as the Division Bell rang for proceedings to begin in the House. Popular in both his constituency and the House of Commons, where his manner was calm, measured and purposeful, Rupert was not, however, adept at platform oratory, but in time became known for his tenacious hold on a subject and strongly held beliefs. Opponents did not relish Gwynne rising to the attack, victims of his witty jibes and thrusts. In common with other high Tories of the time, Rupert regarded the young Gandhi as a dangerous political agitator and was in fierce opposition to his objective: independence for India.

On Boxing Day 1913, almost three years after the arrival of Stella's first daughter, she gave birth to another. The baby was named Elizabeth and, like Priscilla, was christened in St Peter's, the little Downland church nearby.

In the following year war was declared on Germany. As an MP Rupert was not expected to enlist, but during the four years of hostilities he was kept extraordinarily busy, for much of it his party was in coalition government. At the end of the war, in 1918, ten million people had lost their lives and the social fabric of most of Central and Eastern Europe had disintegrated. Although England seemed less crushed by war, the country in which Rupert, Stella and their kind had grown up was in fact irreversibly changed. The general trend towards social equality had escalated as a result of the war. As a consequence conditions for the poor and the lower-middle classes had improved, whilst the rich were constrained to limit the grandness of their style.

The war came in the midst of the Emancipationists' battles for women's improved status. Meanwhile women were called upon to work in factories so as to free more men to fight at the Front. Many of these girls would previously have entered the hard and often lonely life of domestic service, but now they discovered the attractions of easier work with better wages, and also more sociable working conditions. Although this did not initially affect those, like the Gwynnes, on country estates, the immediate consequences of the war for city dwellers of their class were seen in a paring-down of life-styles, in greater difficulty in finding domestic help.

We saw earlier how, after James's death in 1915, Rupert and Stella, as yet relatively untouched by these sweeping social changes, had set about enlarging their scale of domestic arrangements with the extensions made by Detmar Blow. (In this year, when Stella gave birth to her third daughter, Diana, the Gwynnes were yet again reminded of their lack of a son and heir.) Stella's interests did not revolve exclusively around the political arena, but neither were they particularly maternal. Her own experiences of bereavement in child-hood and youth had left her with a stoic resilience, an admirable ability to cope. She was a survivor who remained impatient with weakness and vulnerability and her forte was not small children. On completion, the nursery in Blow's new wing came into immediate operation and the three little girls were removed there from the main body of the house.

In the furnishing and decoration of Wootton Stella and Rupert had become confident and knowledgeable practitioners of a lighter style than the one then favoured by most of moneyed Edwardian Britain. Both informal and uncluttered, the atmosphere at Wootton was a successful merging of the simplicity of the Arts and Crafts Movement with elements of the more decorative Art Nouveau and another love of the Gwynnes, the eighteenth century. Stella and Rupert understood the stimulating juxtaposition of old and contem-porary so that each piece was enhanced by its surroundings. And, however much the emotional tone might be set to darken at Wootton, for visitors the house retained a sympathetic atmosphere of artistry, comfort and elegance.

With the friendship of inspired and innovatory gardeners such as William Robinson at Gravetye and Laurence Johnson at Hidcote, over the ten years at Wootton Stella's interest in the garden had grown and flourished. Although at times still vivacious, by 1915 her youthful frivolity was now less in evidence and she was thought by some to be too serious-minded and reserved. As with many before and after her Stella's involvement in the garden was not only an avenue for creativity, but also a source of solace. In addition it provided a constant source of inspiration for her painting. The style of the charming but girlish watercolours from her premarital visitors' albums had become more worldly and full-bodied. Her favoured subject was now flowers, yet the most cursory glance reveals in these pictures something quite other than the customarily benign botanical tone of amateur painters. Set against mysterious dark backgrounds, the kind so beloved of seventeenth-century Netherlandish and Italian still-life artists, Stella's flowers curl and twist to a more surreal rhythm. The colours and shapes are seductively intense and there is about them a hint of the sinister.

With completion of the new nursery in 1916 and the installation of baby Diana with little Elizabeth and Priscilla, this was now the children's domain. By the following year a fourth and last daughter, Felicité, was born to Stella and Rupert. The little girls' lives revolved around the nursery and here they took their food, their lessons and their sleep. Nanny and a nursery-maid saw to their daily needs and as each girl reached the age of five so the governess introduced her to lessons in the adjoining schoolroom. Meals were sent up from the brick-floored kitchens in a small, hand-pulled lift, and until the girls reached the age of eleven they were invited to dine with both their parents only for lunch on Sundays. Unpredictable juvenile behaviour, unsettling to the smooth functioning of a busy household, was kept to a minimum. Detmar Blow's nursery was made accessible to the main body of the house, but also had its own quite separate entrance leading outside to the courtyard and garden beyond. Blow even saw to the needs of the canine incumbent with a brick-and-tile kennel in the children's entrance courtyard.

The practice of using nanny and nursery-maid to bring up the children was still followed by most families able to afford it in the years following the First World War. With that proviso the amount of time parents spent with their children was variable. Fathers were normally rather distant figures, and little was expected of them regarding the intimacies of their children's lives until the latter reached young adulthood, if then. A mother's role was more negotiable. With labour in the country still cheap, in larger houses a small army of servants was maintained to keep things running smoothly. At Wootton this meant the butler Lavender with his gammy leg, the cook and at least two to help her; then there were the housemaids, the gardener, and the groom and stable boy to keep the horses exercised and in readiness for use. As cars became more common after the war Rupert and Stella acquired one accompanied by a chauffeur.

The mistress of even smaller country establishments, such as Wootton, certainly never cooked but her attitude to the cook and her kitchens influenced the quality of the household fare. Some châtelaines of these houses were knowledgeably involved in keeping a good table. They knew and cared about food both for their family and their guests and regarded it as a reflection of their competence and success as women. They also knew the limitations and strengths of their cook and kitchen staff and went beyond the green baize door to consult on a regular basis. Discussions on what was available to hand from pantry, cellar and kitchen gardens; what could be ordered, who might be expected to visit that day, and how this would affect dining arrangements, resulted in a daily menu plan. It was noticeable too that the mistress who was au fait with the organization of her kitchens, rather than leaving it up to the cook and housekeeper, usually presided over a better table than otherwise. But this degree of attention, with the resultant high standard of cooking, was rare in England at the end of the First World War.

Writers during the nineteenth century increasingly bemoaned the withdrawal of the mistress of the house from involvement in the kitchen offices. Recognized as a form of social aggrandizement, this was often derided in books on food and fictional works. In keeping with most well-off women at the turn of the century Stella was not interested in the kitchens and she seldom entered them. Mrs Arnold, the cook, was summoned to her bedroom on most days for particular requests, but menus and the maintenance of culinary standards were mostly left to the cook. In houses comparable to Wootton, if the children were fortunate the cook might be sympathetic and give them 'house room' in her kitchens. She might possibly be a woman large in spirit (and often physique) who welcomed the overlap between nurturing and nourishment. Going about each of these tasks with ease and generosity, these women bequeathed to those in their ambit memories of childhood overlaid with a Proustian reverence for the cook's reassuring earthiness and the warm mysteries of the kitchen. Not so at Wootton. Here the little girls were not welcomed. Nor were they recompensed by delicious food pulled up to their nursery and schoolroom from the kitchens down below. With few exceptions these were meals of little cheer.

However unwelcoming the kitchens were for the children, they were a bustle of activity. Each day four separate sets of meals had to be prepared for the different members of the household: breakfast, lunch, tea and dinner for the dining room; breakfast, lunch, tea and supper for the servants' hall; added to that were a variety of meals for the nursery and schoolroom. The comings and goings of stable boys, gardener, postman, telegram boy, and delivery men bringing supplies of bread and meat from nearby Eastbourne, were rewarded with tea made from the constantly seething black kettle on a great iron range, and usually accompanied by biscuits, cake, or bread and cheese.

It was long ago concluded in English society that children must not only be largely segregated from adult company until they were civilized enough to enter it, but also required a different diet from their elders and betters. The child's régime entailed abstinence from all luxurious food and drink, as these were regarded as injurious to their moral and physical fibre. This strongly enforced set of taboos was lifted on reaching the exalted state of adulthood – permission to harm yourself was one of the perks of arrival.

What strikes us today is the degree to which children, until the recent past, were segregated from their elders. At the heart of the moral argument for this practice was the belief in Original Sin and its implication that children were born wicked, a belief already well articulated by the Middle Ages. In the seventeenth century J. Pechey could write in his *Treatise of the Diseases of Infants and Children* (1697) that 'Iniquity is connatural to Infants and they are more prone to Evil than to Good, we must not therefore indulge them too much.' At about this same period John Locke, usually considered one of our more sensible thinkers, states his belief in the value of a boy's having cold, wet feet. In *Some Thoughts Concerning Education*, §7, he writes: 'I will also advise his *Feet to be wash'd* every Day in cold Water, and to have his shoes so thin that they might leak and *let in Water* whenever he comes near it.' Mrs Gaskell tells of the half-starved Brontë daughters pleading for more to eat and being lectured by their clergyman father on the sin of caring for carnal things. No doubt those days are gone but the vestiges of this creed still linger on.

Reflecting these beliefs, earlier this century children's diet within families rich enough to confine them to the nursery was typically bland and unimaginative, and quite often downright unpleasant. Rupert and Stella's eldest, Priscilla, makes her complaint: 'The nursery food was not very nice. In fact it was disgusting.' An article in 1901 in *Queen* magazine, although more extreme than Wootton, describes the situation as the children would have preceived it:

> In many households where the dining room cookery . . . leaves little . . . to be desired in culinary ways, the nursery and the schoolroom often suffer from cooking that needs personal evidence to be credited. Many persons now a victim of dyspepsia might trace their trouble to those nursery meals, and of all the horrors of nursery fare, few can equal the disgust inspired by milky and other so-called wholesome puddings . . . and the distaste thus acquired hardly yields in later life.

Along with this puritanism in the nursery went the virtual ban on conversation about culinary matters at any 'polite' English dining table, a custom noted with such scornful frequency by foreigners. But the English thought it vulgar (some still do) to make more than passing reference to the merits of the repast. The gentlemen might discuss the wine, perhaps after dinner, but rarely the menu. By the end of the nineteenth century the enjoyment of good food in England was often confused with the old medieval sin of gluttony. Those who did pay proper attention to food were often stigmatized as decadent.

Rupert and Stella's daughters grew up in this climate and, of course, railed at the injustices of childhood. Like many before her, Elizabeth never managed to slough off her intense loathing for the culinary punishments meted out in her childhood. (Most food at Wootton, it should be said, was neither notably good nor bad for its day.) Unlike others before her, however, the inferior culinary quality of Elizabeth's childhood was to act as a gauge of avoidable defect against which she was to set her heart, her informed intelligence and her pen. Many years afterwards as a successful writer, with one or two beacon-like exceptions, she was still unreconciled and unable to feel charity towards those long-dead perpetrators of her juvenile misery. The explanation is not sufficient, but she was not speaking idly when she told a friend, Veronica Nicholson, that she had been spurred on to write, as much in reaction to this early unhappiness as to anything else. She wrote in reaction and with the passion of a reactionary. In one of her last pieces of writing, an autobiographical article for Smallbone Kitchen Designs, Elizabeth said:

> We ate a lot of mutton and beef plainly cooked, with plain vegetables. The boiled potatoes were usually put through a device called a ricer so that they came up to the nursery in dry, flakey mounds. Vegetable marrows were yellow, boiled and watery. There were green turnip tops, spinach, Jerusalem artichokes, parsnips. I hated them all. Puddings weren't much better. Junket was slippery and slimy, jam roly-poly greasy, something called ground rice pudding dry and stodgy, tapioca the most revolting of all, invented apparently solely to torment children. The obligatory mugs of milk at breakfast and teatime were a penance, although hardly one to be blamed on the cook or any of the kitchen staff. Presumably my mother, in league with Nanny, decreed those mugs of hated milk, and chose to ignore the odious puddings and vegetables dished up for her daughters . . .

Breakfast and tea were not made for the nursery by Mrs Arnold or the kitchen-maid, instead these were presided over by the nursery-maid and Nanny. Nanny Cheshire – a maiden lady of uncertain years and more sympathetic nature than the cook below stairs – held sway over the emotional life of her charges. It was with her cooking, surreptitiously carried on in the upper reaches of Wootton, that Elizabeth's first moments of culinary pleasure lay.

Nanny had a small repertoire of sweet and savoury treats made over the little open fire in the nursery which never failed to please, no doubt due in part to the illicitness of their nature. A sticky fudge-like mass, called 'stuff' by the children, was concocted and doled out to them from spare soap dishes or saucers. Mushrooms, never again to taste so perfect, were gathered at dawn by expert girlish hands in the field beyond the bluebell wood and triumphantly carried back to Nanny to cook up for breakfast in the plentiful, thick cream from the home farm. Elizabeth's recipe for Mushrooms in Cream, by no accident found in *Summer Cooking* (Museum Press, 1955), at once springs to mind: 'To make a really good dish of mushrooms in cream very fresh little button mushrooms from the field are needed . . .'

And we are at once made party to those far-off days at Wootton lingering in Elizabeth's mind's eye. 'In high summer there was the best treat of all, big fat gooseberries, redcurrants and raspberries from the garden which Nanny used to throw into a saucepan with sugar, heat over the nursery fire and give to us then and there. This hot fruit salad somehow embodied the essence of summer, and as everyone knows the summers of childhood are longer and sunnier than those of later life.' Again *Summer Cooking* reveals these benign early memories of Wootton in the shortest and simplest of entries entitled: 'Hot Fruit Salad'. 'This fashion of serving summer fruit has, to me, all the flavour and scent of a warm summer fruit garden . . . Stew the gooseberries, redcurrants and sugar together for 5 minutes (no water). Add the raspberries for 2 minutes only. Serve very hot, with thick fresh cream.'

There was much indeed to recommend Wootton as a place for the creation of idyllic childhood memories. It was a house of many levels and mellowed edges, of fine and curious collected things for feasting the eye and mind upon; a library for more when you grew older, a garden of intimate views and corners and places to nestle and hide in, and the air in spring and summer redolent with the scent of stocks, honeysuckle and roses. Outside, beyond the garden lay the wild-mushroom field, beyond that grazed their father's lowing red cattle and their mother's black, black sheep. A short walk and you reached the base of the wide open Downs, a quick breathless climb and up high on Folkington Hill, there you were alone in the stillness and quiet, with only skylarks calling and long, yellow summer grass rustling in a breeze from the sea.

Other children were brought to play, grown-ups came and went for luncheons and dinners; in summer for tennis and picnics. Memories of these picnics were stored away by Elizabeth and used later for

Summer Cooking. The picnic – at whose heart is the desire and means to step outside the quotidian, and where one shares food in pleasant company in a place highlighting the retreat from routine – has remained for centuries a favoured pastime for rich and poor alike. Its well-documented history is replete with story and anecdote from the sublime to the ridiculous. Elizabeth records a number of picnics in her writing. Some, in particular from Wootton days, show her recalling the sublime *and* the ridiculous. In *Summer Cooking* she writes:

> then there was the hospitable family I remember in my child-hood; they owned a beautiful house and an elegant garden and were much given to out-of-door entertainments, pageants and picnics. On picnic days a large party of children and grown-ups would be assembled in the hall. Led by our host and hostess we proceeded through the exquisite formal Dutch garden, across the lane and over a fence into a coppice. Close on our heels followed the butler, the chauffeur and the footman, bearing fine china plates, the silver and tablecloths, and a number of vast dishes containing cold chicken, jellies and trifles. Arrived at the end of our journey, five minutes from the house, our hosts set about making a fire, with sticks which I suspect had been strategically placed by the gardener, over which we grilled quantities of sausages and bacon, which were devoured amidst the customary jokes and hilarity. The picnicker's honour thus satisfied, we took our places for an orderly meal, handed round by the footman, and in consumption resembling that of an Edwardian wedding breakfast.

Entertainments at Wootton were got up by all who were willing. Favourite stories were rehearsed with the governess in the schoolroom and eventually performed in full stage gear; once they acted a version of *Alice Through the Looking-Glass* with Priscilla as the Red Queen, Felicité as the Mouse in the teacup, and Elizabeth, appropriately, as the Duchess. The annual Pevensey Pageant was a great dramatic excitement when children and adults dressed the part. Palmer and Hogg cousins who lived nearby were regular companions and there were always the other three sisters for company, and animals too: a succession of puppies, a favourite the irreplaceable golden retriever who grew to be Old Crocus, and cats, always Elizabeth's favourites. In adulthood she was rarely to be without one, no matter how impractical the location. Among the cats was a huge marmalade Persian named Baghdad, called Baggy; there was also a black one with white paws known as Ally, short for Ali Baba.

Nanny and the governess might confine the girls more than they would have liked but they also had time to themselves. As the girls grew old enough they enthusiastically took up country pursuits, like their parents, and each was given a pony. Each that is except Elizabeth, who was unwilling to overcome her dislike and fear of those sweating, snorting beasts, refusing ever to ride. Nor was she a great walker. This aversion to physical exertion isolated her from an important aspect of life at Wootton, and from an early age she took to reading even more than was habitually required on Stella's insistence and schoolroom dictates. Stella herself, without the benefit of either formal education or any rigorous governess-led instruction, was a well-read, informed and cultivated woman; with strong opinions to boot. Elizabeth and Felicité, as the two who indulged an appetite for literature most, were later grateful for her example, Elizabeth noting: 'We had a haphazard education but mother always made us read.'

Idyllic in some respects, childhood at Wootton was increasingly pervaded by a sense of unease. After 1917 and the birth of their last child, Felicité, Stella and Rupert's relationship became more strained. Life was busy and their many friends and acquaintances were given much hospitality. Despite these benefits and a common passion for politics, collecting and gardens, the disparity between their temperaments was edging them apart. Strongly inherited family traits were leading to increasing intransigence and with time Rupert and Stella were unable to throw off differences and disappointments and were settling into a less flexible and forgiving mode.

Rupert remained for the most part an outgoing, warm and easy-mannered man who was rewarding company and delighted in that of others. He loved his daughters, was an indulgent father, and respected and admired his wife. Together with these qualities he had inherited his father's ability for long-sighted and sometimes ruthless persistence and determination. As he had grown to adulthood his father's abrasiveness, albeit with less bitterness, had become Rupert's hallmark too. When roused his temper was fierce and his tongue sharp, making his equally formidable charm a fortunate and necessary counter to the well-known Gwynne pugnacity.

From infancy onward the Gwynne girls and their cousins, the Palmers, were often together. One of the Palmer children later became the zoologist Lady Anne Brewis, and with a clarity born of methodical scientific habits, she recalled childhood days in the years following the First World War.

In 1910, the same year that Rupert was elected MP, Stella's younger sister Grace was married. Maintaining family tradition she chose a political man. Her husband was Roundell Palmer, Viscount Wolmer, the future third Earl of Selborne. Roundell was elected (a very young) MP to a northern constituency. Stella and Grace always remained close, their relationship cemented by united suffering as children. The coincidence of marrying men with roots in neighbouring counties enabled regular family visiting. Although the Palmers found Rupert's argumentativeness and temper distasteful they liked him, appreciated his usual pleasantness, his taste, his generosity of spirit. Roundell also found him a good political ally.

The Palmers' London house was in Chester Gate, a superlative Nash terrace. Here Grace and Roundell's multiplying band of children (eventually six in all) grew up with a large complement of nannies and governesses. Over the years, at one time or another, these rooms were also to accommodate all the Gwynne girls. Out of London the Palmers often stayed at Blackmoor House in Hampshire, the estate belonging to Roundell's parents, the Earl and Countess of Selborne. During the 1920s and 1930s Blackmoor was handed over for Christmas to Roundell, Grace and the children, while the grandparent Selbornes sailed off on cruises in search of the sun. Elizabeth, Priscilla, Diana and Felicité visited during these periods, providing a lively mixture of age groups and interests for both sets of cousins. The wide oak staircase was polished to a brighter lustre as squawking children slid down head-first or sometimes commandeered baskets to fly down in. Grown-ups were gleefully spied on from behind a grille above the great hall fireplace. A game the children called 'hassock polo', using hassocks for hands and knees to emulate the horse and the *Illustrated London News* as the weapon with which to hit the tennis ball, was battled out in the long downstairs corridor, whilst other tournaments continued on the terraced lawns outside. In this imposing house, more likely to inspire fear than delight in a child, the effect was countered by parents and nannies alike untypically permitting children to be both seen *and* heard, in whatever wild games they enjoyed. Aunt Grace wasn't interested in checking hands before meals or enforcing any rigid régime. Her insistence lay instead in the enforcement of a strict consideration for one another; something the Gwynne girls had not always received.

Throughout childhood and youth the close relationship between Palmer and Gwynne cousins continued. Stella and Rupert frequently went away, leaving Grace in charge of their children and their nannies. Roundell and Grace would then gather up Elizabeth and her sisters to spend the summer with them at one or other of the houses they might take by the sea. The household moved en masse. With cook, maids and nannies, they travelled to Walcot on the Norfolk coast; other years to Hayling Island off Portsmouth. More than once the cousins were all taken on winter sports holidays to Adelboden in the Swiss Alps. At a lower altitude than some skiing resorts the snowfall at Adelboden was not always quite sufficient for skiing, so instead the cousins walked along snowy Alpine paths, or skated on the ice-covered lake.

In later years the Palmers' house became a repository for family memorabilia and here albums of old postage-stamp-sized photographs now ' recall those far-off holidays in the years following the First World War. Elizabeth seen with Palmers and Gwynnes playing 'Oranges and Lemons' on the seashore; Elizabeth holding hands in a line-up of cousins silhouetted against the brow of a hill; Elizabeth tottering uncertainly over the ice on skates with Anne at Adelboden. In all the images these two stand conspicuously taller than the other children, their future height already quite apparent. Elizabeth was called Lizard by the others for her lithe length and slimness. Her dark hair frames delicate features, her dark eyes and pretty mouth rarely more than half smile. She is reticient, intelligent, wary. She holds something back. As she grew to young adulthood Gwynne photograph albums often reveal a look of suspicion and defiance, sometimes accompanied by a precocious and unsettling allure. Elizabeth now looks the camera straight in the eye, with something inviting in her own.

In youthful letters to one another the three younger Gwynne girls approached life with a passionate intensity born of more than the passing pangs of adolescence. Interwoven with a girlishly breathless tone they lambast, dissect, ridicule; above all they *love* or they *hate*. Coupled with this intensity Elizabeth, at least, had inherited her father's forthrightness and ferocious temper. From an early age the other children learnt that they crossed her at their peril. Anne recounts a summer by the sea when they were about eight. The children were each given a pink paper-covered box for their respective collections of ephemera. There was one short, however, and Elizabeth was the loser. Anne felt sorry for Elizabeth and so gave her her own, which was to be used for shells. Later that day she regretted her magnanimous gesture when Elizabeth flew into a rage and whacked her repeatedly with her wooden spade.

Elizabeth was as impractical as Anne herself, who recalls an embarrassing occasion on the Serpentine in Hyde Park when her father had hired rowing boats with which the Palmer and Gwynne children were to entertain themselves. The other children managed the oars easily, and scooted about the water with much joking and general hilarity. Elizabeth and Anne, on the other hand, were so incompetent that they proved incapable of doing anything more than rowing round and round the lake in ever more helpless circles. Finally, in desperation, Anne's father sent out a man to rescue them and bring them ashore.

With few exceptions Elizabeth's dislike of outdoor pursuits became more pronounced as she grew older and friends later describe her notorious reluctance to take so much as an after-lunch stroll, demanding a return almost as soon as the house was vacated. The rare occasions when she would temporarily put aside her antipathy were notable.

Anne had a precocious interest in all things zoological; her father and grandfather were both keen amateur botanists, and from an early age she enlisted Elizabeth's services. Hours were spent together scouring woodland and seashore, foraging, botanizing, collecting.

Soon Anne began to sort and categorize and Elizabeth became a willing assistant. On their Alpine holidays the young botanist would take advantage of inadequate skiing snow to tramp off in search of gentians. Elizabeth went along and much later in life she recalled such episodes to her cousin Anne as some of the happiest of her childhood. Certainly Elizabeth's subsequent interest in plants as food – herbs, fruits and vegetables – was, in her writing, as much in the order of categorizing as aesthetic. Growing up with her mother's example at Wootton, she imbibed a refined appreciation of the atmospheric and pictorial qualities inherent in landscape, but was never in the least interested in the practice of gardening herself. Any number of letters were sent through her later life in gratitude for offerings of herbs made by post or in person. And although Elizabeth's appreciation of the uses and appearance of herbs was intense, her interest in growing them herself was less than passionate.

Throughout the years of Rupert's marriage a persistent disappointment for him was that Stella had not provided him with a male heir. Saddest of all for them both was the fact that before the birth of their first daughter Priscilla, at seven months pregnant Stella had fallen from a dog-cart and lost the child. The dead baby was a boy whom Rupert and Stella named Sackville and buried in the family churchyard at Folkington. Stella took a considerable time to recover her health and the episode was never referred to by herself or Rupert. (Not until fifty years later, with that liberation from constraint which sometimes illumines old age, did Stella allow herself to confide the story to Priscilla.) After the loss of her son Stella's looks became more refined, her pale English skin set off the enquiring grey eyes to better effect and her tall, slim figure moved with a new-found grace.

Marriage to Stella seems not to have constrained Rupert's flirtatiousness with other women. He combined captivating looks with a similarly compelling manner. Urbane and pragmatic, engaging and agreeable, inevitably he was sympathetic to women. Unsurprisingly, he liked to be entertained and flattered. Society was as yet more lenient regarding this predilection and Stella was required to indulge it with patience and forbearance. Many other women did so, with genuine understanding and tolerance, but probably as many became resentful if they suspected their husband had serious feelings for someone else. How tolerant Stella ever really felt towards Rupert is not known, but after a certain point her attitude hardened and she clearly became more reserved.

She may by now have regretted submitting to Aunt Ishbel's earlier manipulation of her own and her cousin Dudley Gordon's affections. She may also have realized that despite the fact that they had many mutual interests and commitments, her love for Rupert was no longer what she had believed it to be. At any rate, family anecdote had it this way. This oversimplifies the matter but any doubts must have been exacerbated by Rupert's behaviour. He became attached to another woman and over the next few years this liaison was not concealed.

Rupert was seen on public occasions with his friend on his arm. She was beautiful and less serious-minded, intelligent or artistic than Stella, but also less complex and easier company. She was brought regularly to lunch at Wootton, often after riding out with Rupert on the Downs. Rupert and Stella must have arrived at some kind of agreement over this relationship, initially perhaps amicably, either because Stella did not object or because she believed she could wait until Rupert grew out of his attachment. He did not. Over time the strain began to tell on all of them and Stella retreated more into the solace of her garden and her own friends. She took up the defiant stance she had practised in her youth. This defiance once again became her practised defence, and at the same time Stella began to establish for herself a greater independence.

From about 1920 onwards she began to travel abroad in the summer without Rupert. It was said that an operation to remove one of her kidneys had left her more susceptible to the cold of an English winter, so sometimes she escaped that too. Stella could not, or would not, continue at Wootton. Her foreign journeys became more regular, sometimes taking her away for weeks or months at a time. Letters and photograph albums show her travelling the world at a furious pace: Strasbourg, Munich, Paris, Lisbon, Rio de Janeiro, New York, the West Indies. Whether aboard a train or ship, Stella took flight from Wootton. She rarely travelled alone, and went sometimes with a woman friend – a favourite was Princess Marie-Louise, daughter to Queen Victoria. Among new friendships Stella was discovering an

affinity with intelligent and artistic homosexuals, and in her characteristically resolute fashion took little notice of the fact that Rupert
could not abide them.

During these immediate post-war years many felt disillusionment with what they believed to be the cost of victory, in terms of
shattered lives and ideals. To some, England seemed overcome by
exhaustion and lethargy and in a 'state of utter dithering deliques-
cence', as the poet Ezra Pound wrote. Even for the more optimistic
there was less security in the established order of things, the predictability of the future. But the vicissitudes of war had also left people
with the desire to embrace life and a thirst for a more frivolous and
less irksome existence. As if to bury the loss of conviction, a kind of
hectic gaiety surfaced and flourished. By the early 1920s flappers had
cut off their skirts to knee length and their hair to a boyish bob; the
Twenties were described as Roaring and everyone was learning to
dance the quickstep, the foxtrot and the charleston.

Despite the fearful prognostications heaped upon Rupert on his
youthful visit to the specialist and his subsequent refusal to be limited
by the weakness consequent upon rheumatic fever, his health had
consistently held up. After 1920 he modified the intensity of his
sporting activities, he never smoked and drank little. His hair had
turned a snowy-white but this merely gave more authority to his fine
appearance and appealing manner. Rupert's life was filled with
engagements, both public and private (he had built the ballroom at
Wootton in 1920), but by now he was socializing less than in the
past, aware that his health needed care. Nevertheless, although there
were always bottles of medicines beside him at each meal, he never
complained. Stella's own stoicism and a growing tension between the
two did not, however, make for an easy atmosphere.

Rupert was deeply attached to his daughters, but with the
arrival of each new baby girl he had been more keenly aware of his
father's will hanging inexorably over them all. Having sired no male
heir, at his death Wootton was willed to pass to the last of James's
sons. This was Roland, still living nearby at Folkington with their
sister Dorothy and aged mother May.

Although his capacity for unpleasantness was not fully developed
until adulthood, Roland seems by all later family accounts to have

matured into an ambitious, scheming and generally unlikeable man. As a child he was badly spoilt by his mother and learned young to play off one sibling against another to his own advantage. During the 1914–18 war his DSO for 'conspicuous gallantry and judgement' was not easily won, but his undoubted bravery did little to endear him to the hearts of his family.

May's death in 1922 heightened Rupert's concerns regarding his own position. Action seemed imperative. With no male heirs, not only Wootton but Folkington and the other houses and huge estate would pass to Roland on Rupert's death. Rupert's daughters would have nothing except their annuity. He consulted one of his sister Violet's 'other men', his barrister friend Max Labouchère, who suggested that they should draw up a proposal in which each potential inheritor would renounce any claim they might have on the estate in return for a sum of money. All those with a vested interest must, however, agree to this plan. Roland would retain a life interest in Folkington whilst Dorothy was to remain at Folkington Home Farm. After May's death Dorothy had been unwillingly and unceremoniously deposited there by Roland to live on her small allowance, thereby exacerbating her propensity for intensity and despair. Uprooted and thrust from Folkington, her childhood home, and with no experience of housekeeping, Dorothy had for the first time to look after herself and manage with a single servant. Her brother Roland was a spendthrift and indulged in lavish and conspicuous entertaining. On his father's death he had immediately gone out and bought a Rolls-Royce. He and Dorothy agreed to Rupert's plan; they could both use the money.

Not long afterwards Dorothy asked Rupert to help her pay for the restoration of some of her farm buildings with money from the estate. Knowing that his own debts were mounting, Rupert refused, and Dorothy's thinly veiled resentment at her mistreatment by father and brothers boiled over. She announced that she had changed her mind and would no longer agree to sign away the rights to her inheritance. Without Dorothy's consent Rupert could do nothing more to ensure Wootton for his family, but he believed that given time he would convince her. As matters turned out Rupert had little time.

In spite of attempts to scale down the pace of his life he had effectively ignored doctor's warnings, culminating the previous year in their advising him to take three months' rest. The strain of the 1924 election campaign, in which Rupert was returned for Eastbourne with a resounding majority, and the extended responsibilities of his new post as Under-Secretary at the War Office were considerable. These responsibilities were compounded by mounting personal unease apropos Stella's discontentment with his other relationship and the unresolved issue of the Gwynne inheritance. Rupert became ill and was forced to rest. The doctors informed the family that the situation was grave. It was rapidly clear that his heart was finally exhausted – his kidneys were also now failing. Contemporary medicine could do nothing, not even to alleviate the dreadful pain. With nurses in attendance, all everyone could do was endure each day until the end. Rupert was fifty-three.

CHAPTER THREE

A Taste of Abroad
(1929–1932)

WITHOUT RUPERT IN command (Uncle Top, the future Lord
Selborne, and Douglas Hogg, Viscount Hailsham, had been made
the girls' guardians) there was a diminished sense of purpose at
Wootton and energies were unfocused. Rupert's daughters had lost
their guiding spirit; they were bereft. As James Gwynne's appalling
will continued to spin out its relentless course, Roland was now
possessor of his father's estates, leaving Stella and the girls with a
tenuous hold on Wootton. They were permitted to remain there only
on condition that Stella did not remarry. Roland's presence nearby at
Folkington was overbearing, Dorothy and Stella were hardly on
speaking terms, and Violet was too far away to be of much immediate
help. Stella and she had in any case never been close. Violet was
heartbroken at Rupert's death, but she did make an attempt to
include his daughters in her orbit, and entertained them more than
previously with the help of Gordon Woodhouse and Bill Barrington
at their handsome house in Gloucestershire. Although Violet had not
wanted children of her own and would never have survived that daily
round, the perennial child and performer in her understood how to
make an occasion special for Elizabeth and her sisters when they came
over from Wootton. One memorable occasion was the visit, in the
chauffeur-driven Rolls, to the cinema in Bath. Cinema was still a
novelty in 1924 and the girls' aunt was as mesmerized as the girls
were by Douglas Fairbanks silently playing out the fantasy of *The
Thief of Baghdad*.

These lighter interludes were interspersed with increasing
unpleasantness from Roland and progressive uncertainty and insecu-

rity for Stella and the children. The eventual outcome was to be acrimonious and bitter.

Life with Rupert at Wootton had sometimes proved difficult for everyone. Without him, however, it was much more so. While bearing a full share of responsibility for the tensions between himself and Stella, he was also a unifying presence vis-à-vis the girls and their mother. This is borne out by the touching regularity of the letters and cards he dispatched to his children at Wootton. In his absence he was full of news and reassurance. Priscilla in particular, who was fifteen years old when Rupert died, and by then most able of the four to sustain a more adult relationship with him, occupied a special place in her father's affections. She appeared slower than the younger girls in recovering a sense of equilibrium and incorporating his death into her life. Felicité and Diana's suffering was no less than Priscilla's but their ages (seven and nine) rendered them almost mute on the subject, less able to voice their loss. Elizabeth, four years younger than Priscilla and equally older than Felicité, remained, as often, somehow distinct from the rest. She was old enough to articulate her grief yet having little opportunity for expressing it, set a precedent for future behaviour; she withdrew.

Searching for explanation among the bundles of letters lying hidden away for more than half a century, one sees Stella gradually emerging as unwilling or unable to give any significant support to her grieving daughters. In her own way she tried to maintain a semblance of family life but she was loath to show real warmth until age finally mellowed her. For the time being she effectively abnegated her emotional responsibilities, and in her place Priscilla gradually took on the role of surrogate mother to her bereaved younger sisters.

For nine years after Rupert's death, in 1924, Stella continued with Wootton as the main family home and Catherine Street as its London base. In letters between the four girls during this period it is amply clear that Stella was the scapegoat for most of their woes. When apart their letters to one another railed against the tedium of their mother's friends, her changeable moods, severity of judgement, unfairness, lack of warmth. Their feelings of anger and disappointment were at times extreme. They became well practised in unity against their mother, referring to her with biting regularity as 'The

Hon. Lady', and contrived strategies for withstanding her authority. With their sense of loyalty to one another sharpened by loss, the girls made increasingly formidable adversaries for Stella who, nevertheless, inspired a kind of awe in her daughters and seems to have ruled Wootton with an iron hand. A younger acquaintance recently described her as 'Severe, haughty, grand, remote'. An anecdote from Elizabeth in the article for Smallbone Kitchen Designs reveals the child's point of view:

> On one unhappily memorable occasion the family's golden retriever [Old Crocus] found his way into the larder and was discovered gobbling down the remnants of what had been an entire chocolate cake, fresh from the oven. Who had left the larder door open? Recriminations and arguments raged for days, the younger children were, as always, suspected, and the kitchen regions were more strictly than ever out of bounds to us.

A rare light note is sounded in Elizabeth's memories of this period when, in the same article, she recalled her transition from the austerities of nursery food to adult fare in the dining room downstairs.

> Yet as each of us in turn grew old enough to be promoted to grown-up tea, we discovered a rather different world [from the nursery]. True to English country house usage at the time, tea at five o'clock was presided over by my mother sitting at the head of a long table, the silver hot water urn set over a spirit lamp and the silver teapot in front of her. There was a jug of milk, of course, but that was for visitors, because once we were out of the nursery my mother, who was nothing if not consistent, considered that it was wrong to put milk, not to mention sugar, into her fine China tea. Lemon, yes, but nothing else . . . I at least was more than thankful for the release from the odious tea-time milk. Five o'clock tea was nice too. I don't remember anything spectacular, but there was always a spread of simple wholesome things like thin bread and butter, scones, home-made jelly – crab apple, quince or blackberry – cucumber sandwiches, a sponge cake. For special visitors there was usually a cake with

delicious orange-flavoured icing, one which must have been a house speciality, passed on from cook to cook. At any rate, I have memories of it all through my childhood and school holidays. Today it is still a source of wonderment to me that anyone contrived to cook such faultless and delicate cakes in the oven of that old coal range . . .

The little girls' letters to one another at this time are sad yet angry documents. They are also forcible reminders of Stella's own anguish and anger at her mother's death and its aftermath at Blagdon a quarter of a century earlier. Again, in her daughters, that same sense of juvenile frustration and powerlessness acted as a uniting force, with Stella this time the adversary. So too in Priscilla and Elizabeth's early letters an echo of Stella's youthful obduracy and disregard for opinion is apparent. A significant reason for the clashes between Stella and her elder daughters was that her own stubbornness had not mellowed but instead ripened into an autocratic and unselfconscious eccentricity. Accurate descriptions of family events and relationships are hazardous enough at the time they take place but, in the case of Stella and her daughters, the emotional accretions and distortions of vision over time make decipherment of their relationship near impossible. Whoever was to blame, Stella found her daughters too difficult to manage on her own. Within months of his death Rupert's belief in governess education for girls was abandoned and Priscilla and Elizabeth were sent away to school.

Although Stella kept up with a number of political friends, her own family was still in the thick of politics, Wootton was no longer a household where political matters were the dominant influence. With a wide circle of friends and relations ranged about the country, she also comfortably maintained friendships with many of the more exalted members of local Sussex society. Visits were made to Wootton by her sister Grace and by her brother Jasper, now chairman of Coutts, and married to Countess Nathalie Benckendorff, daughter of the last Russian ambassador to England before the 1917 revolution. Stella's widowed cousin, the first Viscount Hailsham, Douglas Hogg, made Elizabeth's guardian on Rupert's death, lived nearby and was another Wootton habitué. His sons Quintin (the future Lord

Chancellor) and Neil were of similar ages to Stella's girls and their paths were to overlap with one another on into adulthood.

During this period Stella also made or sustained a number of friendships with artistic figures whose lives and work were to support and influence her own, and thereby contributed substantially to the ambience in which her daughters were growing up. Prominent in this group of friends were the painters Arthur Lett Haines and Cedric Morris, Allan Walton, painter and textile designer, and Stanford Holme, the entrepreneurial actor-director who was later to play a part in Elizabeth's life. Stella had met Cedric and Arthur before Rupert's death, but his dislike of their life-style had not always made their visits to Wootton comfortable. Cedric and Arthur (always referred to as Lett) had lived together since their first meeting at a party on Armistice Night, 1918 (Lett was married at the time). Despite numbers of liaisons with other men and women, the stormy yet remarkably creative partnership of these two men survived for the remainder of their lives.

Lett Haines was himself a painter and sculpter, but his profound belief in Cedric's abilities set him early on the path of evangelizing agent for his more retiring companion. Cedric's main subjects were people, birds and plants. Elizabeth came to possess several of his paintings and one of them, *The Eggs*, illustrated the cover of her penultimate book, *An Omelette and a Glass of Wine* (Robert Hale, 1984).

Through friendship with Cedric and familiarity with his work and ideas, Stella's own painting broadened in outlook and style. In addition, through identification with friends such as this colourful and exuberant pair of outsiders, she was reassured in her own singularity. As a widow she was also at greater liberty to explore a wider variety of friendships and with them the milieu at Wootton grew more varied, more unconventional. Stella was not only independent in her opinions but had no fear of voicing them. Years later a younger friend, Judith Lassalle, said, 'I have never come across a woman who was so much her own person as Stella.' That Stella's artistic associations were not always approved by agricultural, conservative Sussex was of less and less concern to her.

More than once in these years Stella set sail for Jamaica on a banana boat with her friend the eccentric Princess Marie-Louise, a talented painter who, within the confines of her upbringing and heredity, carried on the semblance of a normal life. As well as travelling incognito on banana boats with friends like Stella she was also in the habit of leaving Buckingham Palace and travelling around London on a double-decker bus.

Stella acquired her friend Allan Walton's work for her houses. At first a painter, his experience in textile and interior design led him to set up Allan Walton Textiles in 1931. One of his earliest design successes was carried out for the colourful French writer and entrepreneur Marcel Boulestin's unique restaurant, Boulestin's, in 1925. Commissioning an article from Virginia Woolf, *Vogue*'s editor Dorothy Todd agreed with Boulestin that the details should be discussed over a lunch prepared by himself and his partner Robin Adair in their apartment. Allan Walton and a wealthy friend were also invited. The lunch was so successful that Boulestin was asked why he did not start a restaurant where others could come and enjoy his delicious food. He agreed. The rich friend put up the money whilst designs by Walton created the perfect backdrop for Boulestin's authentic French food.

The litany of daughters' complaints against Stella took little account of the socially privileged and cultured climate to which she introduced them. They took this for granted, wanting warmth and security before interest and aesthetic education. Stella was no doubt unconcerned about the girls' opinions. Both Felicité and Elizabeth later recalled how as children they were rather intimidated by Lett's large presence and weren't interested in the conversations about art. But in just a few years Elizabeth's appreciation of Cedric and Lett and her friendship with them and their large circle at Benton End would grow. Lett's gossipy forthrightness and Cedric's concentration on the essence of a matter would early appeal to her own sensitivities.

Despite her daughters' adult lives strongly reflecting the legacy of Stella's taste, their appreciation, always grudging, only came much later in life. At the last Elizabeth finally had the good grace to admit this when writing to a friend, Maudie O'Malley (an ex-Benton End student) after Stella's death many years later. She conceded that although she could seem alarming and her personality was so strong, her mother really had been a very remarkable person. Stella had not been a good mother in the conventional sense, but she possessed extraordinary qualities in other ways. None of her daughters had inherited her talent for gardening, but the furniture in all their houses, their very surroundings, came from her. Elizabeth added that the influence she had exerted upon her children was great and would endure.

Stella's haughtiness kept many at a distance; she made no attempt to put others at their ease nor to subdue her own eccentricity. This same eccentricity extended to her dress, which was at once deliberate and utterly unconscious in its very individual stylishness. Veronica Nicholson, in conversation with the author, said of the Gwynne style, 'Oh they were very "Greenery Yallery". Although superior about the Bloomsburys, they dressed in a way rather similarly. Colours, textures, they were always doing things with them which were interesting. And jewellery. When others of their kind were mostly still wearing precious stones they were forging ahead in semi-precious.' A later story, illustrating Stella's dress and blithe unawareness or insensitivity to opinion, is told of an occasion when she was in retreat from her second husband Major Hamilton (abandoned for good in Jamaica because she had grown exhausted by his drinking). Met off the train by a relative at a country station, far from being inconspicuous Stella stepped out of the carriage stately and resplendent in a huge brimmed hat hung all around with little tinkling bells.

Stella's own education by governesses, themselves badly educated, had been a failure. This was no great matter since little more was expected of her than to take on the mantle of gentility and confine herself to the domestic sphere. But then she also had the conflicting precedent set by such formidable female members of her family as Aunt Ishbel. Ishbel had contributed to Stella's restlessness and dissatisfaction with the Victorian triad of responsibilities, given to women from families with the slightest of social pretensions: produce as many children as possible, organize the servants, and look pleasantly decorative. Stella was not an intellectual, nor did she set out to destroy the traditional position of women, nevertheless she possessed considerable natural intelligence, which resulted in her becoming more wide-ranging and better read than many of her social counterparts. She was unwilling to mask this forceful intelligence and at times was branded a blue-stocking, then as now generally disapproved of by men. She did not practise much the ancient female arts of subtlety, compromise and accommodation and her development (however unconscious) of the English habit of individuality did not always make her an easy woman to be with.

In spite of remaining conventional enough to put her daughters through the same social hoops as those through which she had jumped herself, with the concomitant expectation of good marriages, other factors were also at work in the decisions regarding her charges. To her credit, in sending the girls away to school Stella was not simply ridding herself of an irksome responsibility. She was reflecting both dissatisfaction with her own education and the rapidly changing expectations for women in the 1920s. It is also worth noting that having revoked Rupert's decision about education at home, the school to which Stella planned handing over her daughters, Wycombe Abbey in Buckinghamshire, was as much concerned with the academic training of a new generation of thinking women as with the training of young ladies in social accomplishments. Priscilla and Elizabeth, however, were aware of Rupert's views on their education and were reluctant to leave the home where they had spent their childhood. When ordered to pack their lives into the hard school trunks, they did so with resentment and foreboding. Stella decided to keep Diana and Felicité at home under the tutelage of their governess, Miss Spencer, for a short while longer.

Priscilla was the first to leave Wootton, sent to Wycombe in January 1925, only four months after Rupert's death. Elizabeth was not yet old enough to enter the senior school and so, in September 1925, she began her own life away from home at Godstowe, the preparatory school for Wycombe. Experiencing those pangs of early days at boarding school, Priscilla and Elizabeth felt thrust from home. However much their anger might be projected at Stella while living at Wootton, away from it their sense of belonging drew them back. All four girls also felt the pull of separation from one another for the first time in their lives. Priscilla was not to last out long. Having completed only one term she was so unruly and unhappy that she was sent back home, in quarantine. The school was relieved by the excuse that she had contracted whooping cough, then more dangerous than today. Elizabeth, meanwhile, had not yet gone to Godstowe, for she too was ill, recovering from appendicitis. It was feared that in her weakened state she would be more receptive to Priscilla's whooping cough, resulting in abortive attempts at Wootton to keep them apart.

Elizabeth spent the next two years at Godstowe, with journeys back and forth for school holidays at Wootton or with the Palmer cousins if Stella was away travelling. Elizabeth's reports of this time are mixed and sometimes contradictory; a postcard to Felicité at Wootton in July 1926 from Godstowe thanks her for the 'letter and silver paper. Exams are over. Have you been on any picnics? Isn't it lovely weather. Love from Elizabeth.' But she did, like most others, remain steadfast in her hatred of mealtimes at school. The food, she said, was atrocious, 'terrible boiled fish, awful meat'.

Ill and sent home early in the spring of 1927, she missed what should have been her last term. In the lazy warm days of May Elizabeth wrote to Felicité that her enforced absence from Wootton had kept her from savouring its beautiful gardens at that season for two years.

After recovering from her whooping cough in 1925 Priscilla had never gone back to Wycombe. Her dislike of the school was intense and her refusal to return was so vehement that Stella had relented and sent her every day with the chauffeur to school in Eastbourne. Under the same roof again, Stella and Priscilla found each other's company no easier than before, but this was soon relieved when Priscilla was sent off to Paris with her cousin Vivien Ridley.

By now Stella had decided not to make the mistake of having Elizabeth at home too. During 1926 Felicité had begun at Moira House in Eastbourne, and after Elizabeth's recovery from appendicitis, instead of going up to Wycombe Abbey she too was probably installed at school in Eastbourne, where it seems she remained for only one academic year. Family tradition has it that Elizabeth was so piqued at not being given a major part in the school play that Stella was obliged to remove her, sending her further away to board at St Clare's Ladies' Private School in Tunbridge Wells. The principal, Miss Despree Vickery, had extended and developed her own property as one of the many small private educational establishments which flourished for only a few years earlier this century. After two terms, and just as Elizabeth was preparing to sit School Certificate exams at sixteen, Stella decided her daughter should leave the school. In later life Elizabeth seemed undecided as to whether or not she resented this move on Stella's part. Probably divided between resentment of Stella's prerogative and subsequent gratitude for its effect on her life, her reminiscences on the subject reflect this when she says at one time that she was 'torn willingly' from her school and at another, that, although she liked it, Stella thought she was 'becoming too hockey-stickish there and sent me off to France'.

Resentful or not, Elizabeth went to Paris. Here she boarded out in the company of two other English girls with a family whom she called 'Robertot' in the rue Eugène Delacroix, while studying at the Sorbonne. One of her fellow-boarders was Marian Butterworth, an unassuming, sweet-natured girl with whom Elizabeth had made friends at Godstowe. Like Elizabeth she was intended for Wycombe and although she too had ended by going elsewhere, the two girls remained friends and were now to spend most of the next year and a half in each other's company in Paris. Their friendship was cemented by this first youthful period abroad together and they remained close for much of the remainder of their lives. Elizabeth's more forceful and dogmatic nature found the perfect foil in Marian's unassuming and simpler one. Her acceptance of Elizabeth as the dominant partner set an early precedent for many of Elizabeth's female friendships. And to these relatively subservient friends, despite repeated lapses of sensitivity, she remained devoted and loyal.

The curriculum at the Sorbonne covered French language, literature and history. Study was hard and not very inspiring but gave Elizabeth a lifelong attachment to French literature and enabled her to become a fluent French speaker. While in Paris she led a fairly cloistered and hard-working existence, a sharp little flavour of which comes with a card to Felicité on Shrove Tuesday: 'I was going to write to you the other night but then I upset a bottle of ink all over my room and by the time I'd finished mopping it up with one piece of rather thin blotting paper and a hanky . . . it was time to go to bed. Did you have pancakes for lunch?'

Like most people Elizabeth was unaware of the artistic turmoil to which Paris was then subject and from which was being carved a new set of principles for the century. The latest in the hectic parade of artistic movements to emanate from the city was André Breton's inauguration of Surrealism in 1924. Elizabeth, however, followed a time-honoured Parisian route for the young foreigner and took more conventional painting lessons in a private studio. Influenced by the milieu in which she had grown up, she wanted to paint, always referring to it later as her 'first love'. Accordingly, after about eighteen months in Paris, Stella sent her to Munich not only to learn German but also to further her painting studies. Veronica Nicholson says: '. . . she was far too realistic and honest with herself not to admit when she couldn't do something though . . . and she realized she couldn't paint. Elizabeth *had* to do something artistic, it was almost pre-ordained. If it was not to be painting then there were only so many other things she could try her hand at. She took time to find her *métier*.'

Music was not a possibility. Unlike her sister Priscilla, Elizabeth had no ear, no real need for music. A friend of later years, Gerald Asher, recently wrote, 'She was bored by music.' She felt no affinity with her extraordinary Aunt Violet's musical craftsmanship. Ever alert to the merest trace of foolishness in others, Elizabeth would instead lampoon Violet's musical crusade in a series of comments and letters in days to come.

The discovery of a satisfactory form of self-expression for Elizabeth took time, but the foundations, in both negative and positive senses, were laid down early. In later years she would record a crucial part of this foundation in her famous retrospective tributes to the bourgeois Norman-French 'Robertot' family with whom she boarded in Paris. Their great greed was refined by an overriding concern, amounting almost to reverence, for the quality of their table. After several years of writing and with her wide knowledge of French food synthesized into the magisterial *French Provincial Cooking* (Michael Joseph, 1960), Elizabeth was able to register her appreciation for the gift given her by the 'Robertots': the taste of food which did more than simply fuel her body. Not responsive at the time, she subsequently realized that through French cooking it was not only her body which had been nourished, stimulated and soothed, but her emotions and spirit too.

The rather stifling routine in this most proper of Parisian households reached its weekly climax on Thursday afternoons, when Madame presided over her 'At Home'. This comprised a gaggle of female relations and friends dressed always in funereal black. Accompanied by a recitation of the previous week's calamities, which befell the assembled company with unerring regularity, they ate the choicest selection of cakes and *petits fours* the gifted young cook Léontine was capable of providing. Obliged to attend these excruciating social occasions, the three English girls remained unmoved by their culinary merits. Elizabeth was restless and impatient and she and her fellow-boarders learned to devise other commitments to avoid the following day's lunch. Friday meant boiled salt cod and this the girls simply could not stomach. In her book *French Provincial Cooking* Elizabeth wonders at this aberration of otherwise impeccable culinary taste, which allowed the family to eat, with such regularity, the 'Grey, slimy, [fish] in great hideous flakes, it lay plonked on the dish without benefit of sauce or garnish of any kind.'

In reaction to Madame Robertot's slimy Friday lunches the philistine young English mesdemoiselles would treat themselves. The wicked bad taste of a minimal plate in a cheap student canteen, or ham or an orange disgorged from gleaming chrome self-service cabinets in a Latin Quarter restaurant, were as exciting, because forbidden, as any of the quiet masterpieces which emerged with such unfailing certainty from the patient Léontine's kitchen.

A few years later while on enforced stay in the South of France for several months, Elizabeth discovered what she believed were more enlightened Provençal ways with salt cod and recommended it to Priscilla in ration-blighted wartime Britain. She told her that it was impossible to buy haddock, which was annoying, but that they did have dried salt cod – she wasn't that keen on it, however, if soaked for about two days, it became quite all right to eat.

With too many unpleasant memories of unimaginative and bad

fish cooking served up at Wootton and at school, even at the beginning of the war Elizabeth was still not keen on fish. Writing again to Priscilla from the South of France, and beginning to suffer the first inconveniences of living in a country at war, she said that she wished they owned a South Seas island and were dependent upon coconuts and fish, much as she hated these foods, and to which she could escape. She saw a large octopus caught and killed in the harbour at Marseilles, a sight which made her feel quite ill. She outgrew this distaste and realized, ten years on as a fledgling author, that her readers might not hold with such aversions. Thus, again on the subject of cod in her first book, *A Book of Mediterranean Food* (John Lehmann, 1950), she describes *brandade de morue* – garlicky, creamed cod – as 'a triumph'. She gives another way with salt cod when she describes its accompaniment *aïoli*, that notable Provençal garlic sauce of such earthy pungency.

Oddly enough, for someone who began with such an aversion to fish, one of Elizabeth's most affecting memories of food, from the first months of war spent in France, was associated with another variety. The 'Robertots' owned a small farmhouse at Bieville, near Caen in the Calvados region of Normandy, and during Easter or summer holidays Elizabeth sometimes stayed there with them. Set amidst rich green pastures away from the roar of Paris and the French exodus from town to country *en vacance*, the family's pretty farmhouse exuded a reviving atmosphere of calm. A traditional kitchen garden gave them all the fresh vegetables they could use and the farm supplied perfect Normandy cream and butter, normally sent to Léontine in Paris for her delicate cakes and creams.

Away from Paris Madame 'Robertot' let Léontine return for a spell with her own family in the country, while the 'Robertots' were looked after by a young girl from the village, Marie, with the help of her very small brother. Marie herself was little more than Elizabeth's age, yet she unfailingly produced meat and vegetables dishes of a refined delicacy and simplicity. Little could she have guessed that the plate of *moules à la crème* or *mouclade*, mussels in their creamy herb sauce, which she served up one day, were to be such a revelation to the young English mademoiselle.

Elizabeth had neither heard of nor tasted mussels before and when recollecting their effect upon her in *French Provincial Cooking* she calls them 'mysterious and extraordinary'. The small black shells harbouring such curious, seductive contents send her into a reverie on another fleshy food: Wootton field mushrooms cooked with nothing but cream and served up illicitly by Nanny in nursery days. 'So those Norman mussels which reminded me, for whatever reason, of our secret childhood feasts, became forever endowed with the mystery of far off and almost unobtainable things.' In tracing the lineage of what was to become a personal rite she tells us that other mussel dishes eaten over the years had often been good, some even perfect, but they were ultimately 'more evolved, less innocent'. And in her obeisance to a memory and its habitual re-creation she describes how 'to this day' the first dish she tries to eat on arrival and the last before departure from France is a dish of those 'mussels, sweet small mussels'. In her youthful innocence Elizabeth had believed the mussels special to the Robertot family or Marie and was amazed to discover the same dish on the menu at the great Walterspiels restaurant in Munich not many months later.

After concluding her stint at her Eastbourne school Priscilla had been sent to Paris to learn French, to acquaint herself with a wider social circle. In other words, to be 'finished'. Stella's daughters were sent away to become gentlewomen; in practice by the 1920s this had often been reduced to little more than perfecting ones languages and acquiring a cosmopolitan gloss. Priscilla was sent to France with her cousin Vivien Ridley, after which they went on to spend some months in Vienna together. Elizabeth followed suit and after Paris her 'civilizing' was completed with a period in Munich, where she would also continue with painting studies. Between the two world wars Germany and Austria were still regarded as suitable for the 'finishing' process. The Ridley and Palmer families had connections in both countries where Diana and Felicité later took their turn.

Attractive, sophisticated, with money enough to indulge their passion for beautiful clothes, and connections with which to distract themselves, the Gwynne girls each spent an intensely social time in these two countries. Entertained by wealthy and well-connected young men and their families, there was plenty of scope for forming attachments. Shortly after Elizabeth's stay Vivien Ridley married a

Baron von Bebenburg. Felicité too fell in love – unsuitably as it turned out, he was married – and recovery was slow, perhaps never complete.

Elizabeth spent a hectic six months in Munich with an aristocratic German family, accompanying them in their progress from town to country. Following a strenuous round of house-parties, balls, opera (notable in the light of her increasingly pronounced 'deafness' to music), gallery visiting, clubs and restaurants, it is doubtful that Elizabeth spent much time with her paint-brushes. Certainly on returning to England she launched herself into an entirely different career and made no further reference to her 'first love' for some time.

Munich was a brief episode in Elizabeth's life and she wrote next to nothing about it, once saying, misleadingly, that the food not the place was enjoyable in Germany of the 1930s. She records that her host family's Austrian cook was particularly adept at those rich cakes and puddings so much loved by wealthy Germans and Austrians. Sunday breakfasts often meant a delicious 'sweet buttery bread' whilst evening meals might provide venison from the forests outside Munich with 'a mysterious wild red berry sauce'. The cakes and puddings delighted Elizabeth: rich, tempting, sophisticated and quite different from those more homely English offerings at grown-up Wootton teas or the subtle and refined productions of young Léontine in Paris.

Wary of the unsympathetic post-war attitude to Germany, Elizabeth was circumspect in her later pronouncements, but her own experience of the place remained forever associated with her final emergence from adolescence into young adulthood. She needed little encouragement, and gave herself up to an orgy of distraction. Her forte was never to capture the crowd, but in more intimate social gatherings she began to test the power given her by the development of her sparkling wit and sinuous dark looks. In Munich her concerns, therefore, were more likely to be with whether the stuff and cut of a modish new dress fell to her advantage, rather than any considerations on a larger scale. Simultaneously her sharp eye was vigilant and her prodigious memory was storing up the sights and sounds of the great European city which was Munich.

Elizabeth returned to Germany and Austria on a number of occasions. In the spring of 1934, for example, she travelled to Munich and met up with Felicité, Priscilla and her new husband Richard Longland, to spend a few days there together. The reunion was not an entirely successful one and Elizabeth realized that with the change in family dynamics she should not really have expected otherwise. When neither Felicité nor Richard appreciated Munich as she did, Elizabeth became cross. She was not inclined to notice the disadvantages of the place, because for her it was 'almost sacred', permeated with a charm and a beauty so powerful that nothing could spoil it. Despite the fact that when she returned she found that everything had changed and all the people she knew were gone, Elizabeth remembered only that she had been happy there, and so its magic was preserved.

Consequently, when Felicité wanted to leave a few weeks later, unhappy with the von Stengel family in Munich, Elizabeth wrote to her: 'I think you would be mad to go there [Innsbruck] when you can be in the most interesting and beautiful town in the whole world, when you can hear the most perfect operas and concerts, and see the most lovely pictures and meet the most charming people. Munich in the spring is simply too lovely for words – I would sell my soul to come back at Easter – only no one wants to buy it.'

Probably the last visit Elizabeth made to Munich was in August 1937, two years before England was to declare war on Germany.

CHAPTER FOUR

The Stage
(1932–1934)

AFTER HER SIX months in Germany, in 1932 Elizabeth was back in England. Her freedom from the confines of Wootton, Stella and serious schooling had initiated her into the independent life she now intended to lead. But Stella was adamant that in June it would be Elizabeth's turn to go through the gruelling process of presentation at Court. Elizabeth was not sure enough of what she wanted and had neither the single-mindedness of conviction, nor a large enough allowance, with which to reject Stella's plans. Elizabeth's coming-out dance was to be held at Aunt Grace and Uncle Top's No. 3 Chester Gate. The dance was shared with Karen Harris, a girl whose family were friends and neighbours of the Gwynnes in Catherine Street and Sussex. Sir Austin and Lady Harris's country house was on the Isle of Wight, where Karen had grown up with these her eccentric parents – her mother Cara quite remarkably so. (Karen was soon to marry Osbert Lancaster, who became one of the most influential cartoonists of his generation.)

In the midst of the Season Elizabeth had been sent down from London to Wootton; in quarantine with measles, still a feared disease, and wrote to 'Dearest Pris' staying with Nathalie and Quintin Hogg at Middleton House in Oxfordshire. She complained that Stella had written to her 'to the effect that in her house people don't do things without her permission and that I've given measles to the whole of London'. And in her frustration she continued to characterize Stella with her typical volleys: 'Really you'd think she was a Queen Elizabeth for power and Helen of Troy for looks the way she goes on – actually she's more like Catherine of Medici for both looks and abuse of authority, although she's not got a tenth part of that lady's wits.'

Elizabeth listed some of the young men whom she had suggested Stella might invite for her dance: 'Eric Cudder, Hearty Henderson, Desmond, Rag Shackleton, Stephen Bull, Norman Molle, Clydesdale, Philip Chetwynde, Tommy Martin, the Tivertons, Ridgeways, Alec Pilkington.' This was in the hope of forestalling Stella who might otherwise 'go and ask some bloody growth she is pleased to call Bohemian'. But then Elizabeth declares that 'You can't think how heavenly it is here – the garden looking too lovely, and not a soul to be seen and nothing to do except walk about and pick flowers and breathe in the perfect peace.'

Elizabeth had two pretty, adjoining beamed rooms as bedroom in the older part of the house, overlooking flower borders spilling on to lawns and the great paved circle and bluebell wood beyond. 'Wootton devoid of Mummie is like Paradise . . .' And further on in the same letter she is wailing: 'I wish to goodness I could stay here in peace. I'd rather be here than going to all the parties in the world – I'd sell my soul to be able to give the 2nd a miss. The thought of all those people makes me sick and giddy. I've got about 14 more dances till the end of the Season. I can only pray I don't get asked to any more as long as I live . . .' She concludes with a revealing threat: 'And . . . very soon if she isn't jolly careful I shall become some man's mistress and live with him.'

Nevertheless, having survived her presentation at Court on 11 May 1932, and despite saying to friends in later years that she was a wallflower and loathed it all, she also survived the dances of the Season. With her delicately smouldering looks, her shyness shielded by a steely coolness and barbed tongue, she must have been a daunting prospect for many of the equally self-conscious young men in need of as much reassurance as herself.

Meanwhile Elizabeth had made up her mind that with painting rejected as unrealistic, she would become an actress. The stage was still not regarded as a reputable place for a girl of her background but, with Gwynne–Ridley wilfulness already a well-defined trait, the alarm it might cause was unlikely to affect her decision in the slightest. There were fierce and prolonged arguments back and forth with Stella, but at the end of it all Priscilla remembers Elizabeth walking off down the drive with her suitcase. Although she couldn't then know it, this was to be the last time Elizabeth would spend any length of time at Wootton.

Stanford Holme was a maverick actor-manager who already knew Stella from a period spent acting in Sussex. Stanford had recently taken over joint direction of the enterprising Oxford Repertory Company, and Elizabeth had turned to him for advice. This procured for her an invitation to come and work for the company as assistant stage manager-cum-trainee actress in Oxford. The Repertory Company was based at the Playhouse, then a small building in Banbury Road more reminiscent of a village hall than a theatre with ambitious intent. Undeterred by their unprepossessing building and position off the city's centre, the players were full of enthusiasm, and several had a good measure of talent.

The Playhouse's reputation for undemanding plays appealing to both an undergraduate audience and townspeople alike, was maintained and developed. Stanford drew his cast and stage managers from a wide range of promising actors, mostly professional but some also from the set of undergraduates keen to be involved in the theatre. One of these, George Devine, later founded the prestigious English Theatre Company. Meanwhile a high proportion of the professionals succeeded, many of their names subsequently reading like a roll-call of the most sought-after actors of their time.

Stanford was one of that breed of actor-managers more common in the days before the profession was made softer and safer by the institution of Equity. Work was hard, insecure and yet carried on with the cheerfulness of the amateur. Stanford was a capacious drinker and incorrigible philanderer, and saw to it that his young cast kept up their relentless schedule of dramas. Here he was abetted by the public school system from which many of the company had sprung, and which had schooled them in a similar ethos of discipline and intensity combined with a determined lightheartedness.

The Oxford Rep made up for lack of money with inventiveness, and everything was done at breakneck speed. Assistant stage managers like Elizabeth were regularly sent careering off round the town in search of props to augment the company's own meagre collection. A market scene was one day ordered by the director, resulting in a first-night stage aglow with bright yellow posters announcing 'Fyffes Bananas'. During Christmas of 1933 Elizabeth was organizing the publicity for the pantomime, tearing around Oxford with posters, handbills and programmes, and making it known abroad that on Boxing Day, at the Playhouse, there would be 'glittering scenes, exquisite singing, gorgeous girls and lovely music – and the Cat (it's Dick Whittington)'.

She found the producer 'particularly difficult and annoying', and told Felicité she was having such an awful time doing the shows, rowing with everyone, that she would never stage-manage again.

An invitation arrived from Aunt Violet at Nether Lypiatt and in her Christmas letter to Priscilla, Elizabeth was in 'a savage temper about it'. Violet had made a gothic set of arrangements for collecting Elizabeth from Oxford, involving out-of-date train timetables and an obscure collection point in the Rolls. Elizabeth said that Violet could come half-way to fetch her. Another series of convoluted suggestions from her aunt followed, and Elizabeth agreed to be collected at Moreton-in-Marsh, about twenty minutes from Oxford.

After further complications Violet suggested yet another meeting place. Elizabeth, who had to work and didn't really want to spend a weekend with Aunt Violet and 'all her old men', delivers damning judgement to Felicité. 'It makes me absolutely furious. That woman has never done anything in her life except drive about the country in a Rolls-Royce with Lalique mascots and filled with rugs and sweets and adoring men, and occasionally earn £1000 by Tinkling on a Toy instrument. It's never occurred to her that anybody could have anything better to do . . .' Then she relents a little. 'Really I'm very fond of her and I'm always enormously entertained when I go and see her but she will not realize that there are people in the world who have a spot of work to do now and then.'

Elizabeth's sharp characterization of her aunt is a good one, containing as it does kernels of real truth, but equally it reveals her own self-absorption. She appears both oblivious to Violet's great diligence and application to her music and quite insensitive to its merits. Working at her first job, at times gruelling and not very glamorous, Elizabeth's jealousy of her aunt's 'leisure' is clear; but the particular irritation she feels at her capriciousness, her demanding and imperious manner, hints that these were nascent qualities of her own.

Later she experienced a vindictive pleasure when seated at Violet's dining table, and told Priscilla: 'Poor Aunt V. had her work cut out preventing any of us talking to any of her men, except Gordon, for longer than 3 minutes — Laurence Johnson was there — he is a perfect angel. [Johnson owned Hidcote Manor and was a good friend of Violet and Bill Barrington.] He motored me half-way back to Oxford and showed me his house and perfectly lovely garden on the way. Aunt V. was rather annoyed with him because he said: "Good." when I said I was on the stage, and she said: "Oh no Johnnie it's not good."

'And Denis said: "It depends if *she's* good . . ." (general roar.)'

The Rep usually did each play for a fortnightly run and in that time lines for the following production had to be learnt, props and stage managed, and the cast rehearsed. It was customary for the company to share digs in houses run by landladies in various parts of the town. Among the first people with whom Elizabeth shared digs was a girl already launched into lead parts. She was a little older than Elizabeth; a cheerful, hard-working girl experienced at living in lodgings and fending for herself. Her name was Joan Hickson and she became a steady, reliable actress. Always in work, her career recently concluded on a high note when her elegant, wry and sympathetic interpretation of Agatha Christie's Miss Marple made her a family name.

Without any hint of malice the late Miss Hickson told the author how Elizabeth's ignorance of the kitchen in those first Oxford days was so extreme that 'I even had to teach her how to make a cup of tea'. Until then Elizabeth's accommodation had been accompanied by servants, and young ladies were not expected to come into the kitchen. Her first attempts at cooking are recounted to Felicité in a flat and slightly bemused tone, and although she seems to expect little of the food itself or of herself as cook, it is worthy of comment that she says anything at all.

'I cooked my own lunch today. I had sausages, and tomatoes and fried onions and green peas. Then loganberries and cream and then cheese and celery and then coffee. Only the onions were burnt and they stank the place out. I shan't be able to have onions often. Or fish.'

Post-rehearsal high teas, in one of the recently opened chain of Cadena Cafés, provide no evidence of gourmandise, with tinned fruit salad for a sweet.

On another occasion Elizabeth described the supper she had just eaten in her digs: '3 sardines on 1½ bits of toast, one very tired sponge cake, 2 digestive biscuits, 2½ cups of tepid tea, and smoked 9 cigarettes' before drinking her tonic, putting her hair in curlers and going to bed.

With Elizabeth in Oxford, Priscilla now uneasily back at Wootton, Diana and Felicité undergoing their final stages of schooling and 'finishing' in England and Austria, the four girls maintained a regular and affectionate flow of letters back and forth. Priscilla and Elizabeth's busy social calendars were interwoven between family and friends and, nurturing their close relationship, they kept each other constantly abreast of the latest concerns and fears about the Hon. Lady, family, friends and men.

At twenty-three 'Dearest Pris' continued in her role as chief confidante and adviser to her younger sisters, and both she and Elizabeth exercised considerable thought over the welfare of the young Bulgies or Bolsheviks, as Diana and Felicité were tagged. Elizabeth and Felicité were forming a particular bond through their literary tastes and although all four girls sent each other books as presents, literary discussion between these two was more thoughtful. For Christmas 1933 Elizabeth was very pleased with some Shaw from Felicité. Already owning a volume of his criticism she said that she had wanted to read him for a long time. A year later Felicité made her a rather more extravagant present of two Shaws, one of which, *Back to Methuselah*, Elizabeth had particularly wanted to read. 'My collection of Shaws is gradually getting longer . . . thank you a thousand times.'

Meanwhile, in January the Rep was about to put on Shaw's *Arms and the Man* in which Elizabeth thought she would not have a part. She could not leave Oxford because caught up, as she says to Felicité, 'working on this paper we're supposed to be going to publish —

you've probably heard about it from Diana – it's going to have her design on the cover.' (Diana, unlike Elizabeth, began and continued to paint.) Revealingly, in the light of her own future, Elizabeth says, 'I'm supposed to be sub-editor of *Repertory* I believe – *but I can't write at all* [author's italics] so other people will have to do all the articles, write the jokes etc.' She then asks if 'Wicked Uncle [Roland] has given us the usual £9 to be divided between the four . . .' She asks Felicité about her Christmas presents and rounds off on a typically wry note: 'I also had a very singular piece of clanking chain from Aunt Violet, did you get one too? What are they meant to be?'

By the following year Elizabeth was taking more parts and living in new yellow and blue digs in Banbury Road, by the Playhouse. The Rep were doing *The Cathedral* and *The Taming of the Shrew*, in which she played Bianca; for once the notices were good and she was relieved at her reviews. She considered herself quite lucky to have the part of Bianca as it was the only other woman's role, and the other five girls in the company were furious.

Elizabeth's 'luck' in truth coincided with her relationship with the Playhouse's director, Stanford Holme. Stanford's wife, Thea, was a beautiful and respected actress who had long since learnt patience with her husband's frequent liaisons. Some preferred Elizabeth's sister Diana's cooler grey-eyed English beauty, but Elizabeth's dark mercurial looks hinted at the exotic in her ancestry and were well suited to the drama of theatre life. She now carried herself with a poise which rarely deserted her, and a certain reserve, at times haughtiness, added to the allure. Although her sharp temper and wit were not modified by a desire to please, Elizabeth's humour often did. She was challenging, unbiddable, compelling, and not surprisingly Stanford Holme was smitten. It was fortunate that Thea understood forbearance, because any objections would have made little difference to Elizabeth, whose cast of mind is clear when advising Felicité about a year later.

Chafing at the frustrations of her attempts to holiday in Norway with her love of the moment, Felicité complained to her sister about her guardian Mrs Headlam's refusal to permit the journey. (Mrs Headlam was a family acquaintance with whom Felicité stayed in Durham for several months in order to learn secretarial skills and be introduced to local society.) Elizabeth wrote to Felicité and told her to go to Norway and be damned to everybody. Felicité must do what she wanted to about these sorts of things, because if she didn't now, then she never would. 'How do you think I shook off interfering people who wouldn't let me do what I wanted?' Elizabeth said that if she were in her place, she'd go, whether it was over Mrs Headlam's 'dead body or not'. If it had been Stella who had forbidden Felicité to go, it would have been different, because she was her legal guardian, but Mrs Headlam had 'nothing to do with it whatsoever'. Felicité had asked Elizabeth to come up to Durham to make peace between her and Mrs Headlam, a suggestion that Elizabeth unequivocally rejected: 'You might as well ask Hitler to marry a Jewess as me to make peace with Mrs. H.'

Prior to this episode, by the summer of 1933, Stella and her daughters' lives had been irrevocably altered. Stella had felt so beleaguered by the wrangles with her brother-in-law, Roland, at Folkington, that at one point an inventory of everything she and Rupert had collected whilst at Wootton was given to Roland to ensure that if the day came when she must leave, at least it would not be without her possessions.

Roland had spent prodigiously on entertaining and maintaining a grand style at Folkington over the years, and by the early 1930s he was in debt. Letting Wootton would go some way towards remedying his problems, and as a consequence the more pressing his financial problems became, the more his unpleasantness and obstructiveness towards Stella had increased. To add to her sense of insecurity she knew that recent developments in her own life could leave her in just the position Roland wanted.

Stella's visits to Jamaica had been sociable and productive and she found the brilliance and fertility of the island a stimulus for her painting. She felt at ease among the expatriates and old landed Jamaican families. Life was conducted at a leisurely pace. Stella loved Wootton and its gardens, but its memories, combined with the difficulties presented by her daughters and Roland, made for tensions which grew rather than diminished with time. Far away from Europe she felt freer, soothed by the languid balm of this beautiful tropical island.

Major John Hamilton, ADC to the Governor of Jamaica, owned

a plantation and a large house and grounds in need of care. On a recent visit to England Stella had invited him down to Wootton. And in between the filial tirades, Diana had written to Felicité recounting a light-hearted lunch spent with Stella and 'Ham' – his inevitable Gwynne nickname. Stella was in good spirits and amused Diana and Hamilton with tales of childhood conspiracy and wickedness together with Grace and their brothers at Blagdon. Life once again held possibilities of a more creative kind and Stella was happier than she had been for a long time. Sadly, her own increased sense of well-being did little to make relations with the girls easier.

The crisis which had been looming for so long finally came to a head with Stella's announcement of her forthcoming marriage to Major Hamilton. Her decision must have been tinged with relief at the prospect of escape from a brother-in-law whose lack of sympathy and bullishness she now found intolerable. For Wootton she was substituting a Jamaican plantation, a house with no electricity or running water and a garden surrounded by bush. (Within a year Stella would impose her will on the landscape and transform it into one of the most impressive gardens in Jamaica.) The girls' awareness of their mother's weakening hold on Wootton had grown with her increasing attachment to 'Ham' and their animosity towards both Roland and 'Ham' escalated accordingly. Even more bitterness, however, was reserved for Stella, whose marriage would lose them Wootton. Not only was she replacing their father, but as a consequence they were to be ejected from their childhood home. Added to this, Priscilla had announced her own intention of marrying.

Elizabeth had already left home. Albeit feeling as rooted in Wootton as the others, she avoided too much involvement in the family's last fraught years there. Committed to her new life, after 1931 she no longer returned to Wootton for Christmas, and wrote wit-spiked grumbling letters for several years about the dutiful periods spent with the Palmers or Aunt Violet during the festive season.

Before leaving England Stella asked her sister Grace and brother Jasper to act *in loco parentis* to her daughters. The arrangements were not ideal for anyone, but the feeling was that, as Grace told her daughter Anne, 'Stella has had little happiness; she deserves some now.' Priscilla and Elizabeth were to be based at Chester Gate with Grace and Uncle Top, whilst the other two would spend more time with Jasper's wife Countess Nathalie Benckendorff's brother and his family at their houses in London and Suffolk. By the summer of 1933 Wootton was packed up, Roland had moved in a Miss Hudson as tenant, and Stella had fled.

At this point Felicité was sent to learn secretarial skills with Mrs Headlam in Durham and Diana went to the Benckendorffs at Marlborough Hill, St John's Wood. When the Rep had no work for her Elizabeth moved back and forth between Oxford and London, staying with the Palmers or sometimes Aunt Violet, whilst Priscilla now took on in earnest her role as surrogate mother.

In a letter to Felicité the following year the girls' old drawing mistress, Miss Harrison, wrote: 'Hated to hear of Wootton desecrated like that . . . I loved the place – it was all just perfect and in keeping. I always wondered what Elizabeth would do – for I thought she would branch out some time. I thought at one time she would take up painting, but not acting. I was amused at your remark, "Sometimes with a job but more generally without." What a scattering of family you are now.'

In the spring of 1933 Priscilla had, like her mother, been making choices and decided against the more forceful dynamic of one of her present suitors in favour of a pleasant young officer called Richard Longland. Richard was a passionate Francophile, knowledgeable about French food, and devoted to its literature. He was particularly fond of Proust. Elizabeth tendered her congratulations from the Playhouse on Priscilla's 'somewhat staggering' piece of news. She thought Priscilla would be very happy with Richard, and agreed that he was utterly charming. She added a rather world-weary caveat to the effect that his mother should be dispensed with if at all possible, as she undoubtedly worshipped her son. She asked after those whom Priscilla had rejected and said: 'We're going on right through the Vac . . . Do come down for a week-end – this week we're doing *The Faithful Heart*, next week *The Sign on the Door*, then a farce, *Almost a Honeymoon*. I'm appallingly busy – our stage manager has gone on holiday for a month so I've got all her work to do – it's appallingly nerve-racking – never have a second to do anything. Let me know when you're coming and I can get you a room in my digs. Unless I am sacked I don't suppose I shall get a holiday in months.'

The company travelled when Oxford students were down for vacation, and the following year Elizabeth was acting and stage-managing for a month in Sussex at the Pavilion Theatre, Peacehaven. Here she played in Frederick Lonsdale's *On Approval* alongside Joan Hickson, Stanford Holme, Harald Norway, Prudence Khan and John Boxer.

Uncle Top gave Priscilla away from Chester Gate in November 1933, with her sisters as bridesmaids and Ismay Crighton-Stuart and Nathalie Hogg as maids of honour, all in shimmering satin. Society came and afterwards Violet wrote to Roland saying how satisfied she thought Rupert would have been at his Pris's happiness, and added: 'Yes, I did notice Elizabeth's poise.' The bride and groom spent the first night of their honeymoon with Aunt Violet at Nether Lypiatt, then sailed from England bound for Malta and Dar Ida, the house Richard had bought in Guardamangia. Her sisters soon yearned for Priscilla's companionship and mothering and within weeks Diana was writing a distraught letter saying she was so lonely without her that life was unbearable.

This was one of the Christmases Elizabeth spent with Violet at Nether Lypiatt and complained about it beforehand to Pris in Malta. Elizabeth knew she would have to go, because, if she did not, there would be a terrific family row and a reconciliation brought about by Roland. She was most disparaging about his Christmas gift to her, a pair of sham diamond and glass earrings; she said she disliked jewellery, never wore earrings and, even if she did, they wouldn't be of that kind. She thought it high time Roland learnt not to buy cheap-looking expensive jewellery.

Elizabeth went on to say that she should like to put Roland, Aunt Violet and Dorothy 'into a Siberian prison camp picking oakum 18 hours a day and have them shaken up in a sack together for the remaining six. Even then I doubt if any sense could be drummed into them.' She ends her tirade against the Gwynnes with enough self-knowledge to add that next time she writes no doubt it will be the Palmers or the Ridleys who are out of favour with her.

Although Elizabeth was apprehensive at the prospect, Christmas with Violet and her 'old men' at Nether Lypiatt proved better than expected. Laurence Johnson was there and the Blows came over on Christmas Day. 'Green Line Bus' (the Gwynne girls' name for Detmar's wife, Winifred, Elizabeth's godmother) asked a great many questions about Stella and was, Elizabeth believed, altogether far too 'cock a hoop'. Violet gave her a 'perfectly heavenly' turquoise jumper, and Denis and Bill an attractive scarf. Violet and her men dispensed presents to one another from Fortnum's and Spink's, whilst from the moment she arrived at Nether Lypiatt to the moment she left, Elizabeth suffered from indigestion.

Stanford rang asking Elizabeth to do the publicity for the pantomime already mentioned. Accordingly, on Boxing Day she rushed back to Oxford and was left exhausted by spending what seemed a fruitless day's work with a demanding producer, Leonard Gibson Cowan. By evening he had relented and asked her out to dinner – it was her twenty-first birthday. She told Felicité that 'Uncle Top has given me £20 for my 21st! Isn't that incredibly sweet of him? . . . And they're so hard up too.' She reminds her sister that at least they will spend part of the Christmas period together, with the Palmers at Blackmoor. She was dreadfully tired and in need of a rest, and also a proper job.

Elizabeth was, as always, worried about her finances, but still protested to Pris that the five pounds she had sent her for her birthday was too much. The following year Elizabeth told Pris that she must stop giving her money, especially as Pris was without a job. Elizabeth thought it pitiful that she was the only member of the family with a job and yet she practically lived on charity. Nonetheless the precedent was set and although not particularly well off herself, Priscilla continued contributing to Elizabeth's and her other sisters' finances for many years to come.

More significantly, Elizabeth was suffering from the intense and insecure nature of her relationship with Stanford, and confided to Pris: 'Things seem fairly alright with Stanford again. You know I can never stay away from him or from Oxford for very long. It'll always be the same – I can't exist without him for long – I feel so lonely and miserable and bored, and the other men I meet mean less than a spit in the eye to me. I wish I could have married him – or perhaps if I had or did I should have a row and kill him with the frying pan or something sordid.'

During the last days of winter, while relations between herself and Stanford became more strained, letters flew back and forth as the sisters negotiated those previously mentioned few days' holidays together with Richard in Munich in early spring. (Felicité was already there.) Having survived an 'excruciating' train journey in third class, Elizabeth spent a frantically social week in Munich. She stayed on until the Saturday, going to more hectic parties, where she continued 'baby-snatching'. She soon grew very tired of it all, however, and wished Pris had stayed longer. Apologizing for going off somewhere before Priscilla's departure she added that it all seemed so different now that her sister was with Richard. She had previously refused to accept that Pris belonged to him, and not to her family: 'When there are two or three Gwynnes gathered together, nobody else has much of a look in, much as they may try.' And yet she sympathized with Richard managing three Gwynne sisters at a time and in spite of everything, was terribly glad Pris came.

Munich was only a brief respite from the complications of Elizabeth's peripatetic and emotionally tangled life and she complained that it was 'perfectly frightful' when she got back to Chester Gate. Diana's perpetual absentmindedness and scattiness were annoying Elizabeth, and relations with Aunt Grace and the Ridleys were at a low point, their concern about her present life-style fuelling her irritation with them. She told Pris that the next morning at breakfast Grace was savage with her for taking the butter with the same knife that she was using to spread the marmalade. 'When I explained that I was used to economizing on washing up and that compared to the magnificence of her household I lived in comparative squalor, she snorted "Yes, Bohemian squalor" and turned me out of the dining room in order to say prayers. After that crowning insult I packed my things . . . and betook myself to Oxford.'

Stanford, however, was not welcoming; his coldness threw Elizabeth into confusion and she decided the best thing was to leave. She would finish it all at once and go away. Having packed up and on her way to the station, Stanford suddenly said: 'Don't go.'

And she couldn't.

'It's the same old story. We want to get away from each other and can't.'

For the moment they were reunited, and Elizabeth wrote to Pris, unself-consciously delighted. Stanford gave her a good part at once and said she was to have roles in the rest of the plays that term. With this encouragement she moved into new digs and said she was coping with everything. But these brave words were hollow. In a letter to Priscilla Elizabeth was miserably aware that things were hopeless between them. The sympathy they had felt for one another was gone. Elizabeth could not foresee what would happen, and her only remedy for the situation was to work desperately hard.

Blunting the edge of emotion by burying herself in hard work was to become a self-preserving mechanism for Elizabeth. She did an hour's work before breakfast every morning and stained and polished her three attic-room floors in spare moments during the day. To replace the green which she 'loathed' she had ordered some undyed linen curtains and a sofa cover to complement the pale blue sitting-room walls. And in the letter about Stanford she gave Pris instructions to have some napkins made up and embroidered: 'And tell the hag to send them immediately or I shall have left here before I get them.' Elizabeth's imperious tone was already well established; if they felt any resentment her sisters, nevertheless, always acquiesced.

Looking down from her attic rooms: 'A lot of drunken undergraduates have just gone by singing "Night and Day". Sometimes I do wish life was more peaceful.' But it was not to be. Work once again became intermittent and Elizabeth's pretty rooms brought only a temporary consolation. Her cousin Anne Palmer was up at Somerville (she was one of the first college students to read zoology), exactly opposite the Playhouse and she saw Elizabeth on stage a number of times. She told the author 'No, she was not a good actress.' Elizabeth never learnt the actor's knack of flinging off self-consciousness at the stage door, of giving herself up to instinct and intuition, of temporarily suspending the rational self.

CHAPTER FIVE

London
(1934–1938)

ON HER TWENTY-FIRST birthday Roland had wished Elizabeth a very happy future, as she deserved it and he believed she would get it. Her acid comment to Pris reflected her low expectations: 'I cannot think how or why he should have been led to believe anything so improbable.' By late 1934 she was driven, through hopelessness, finally to extract herself from Stanford Holme, and left Oxford for London and a brief period with Aunt Grace and Uncle Top. She quickly found a flat not far away in Primrose Hill, at 112 Regent's Park Road and moved in with her old schoolfriend Marian Butterworth.

Their rooms were in one of the large houses in Primrose Hill, no longer as grand as they had been and now divided up for a more reduced life-style. In this area, however, reduced did not mean small and Elizabeth had an enormous, high-ceilinged living room with huge windows overlooking the garden, a bedroom and a bathroom, albeit with a kitchen space carved out of a landing. Here she 'installed a gas cooker, one of those old food safes with perforated metal sides which nowadays you see only in junk shops and eventually a biggish refrigerator'.

Although the great chef Alexis Soyer had installed gas cookers in the Reform Club as early as 1841, it was not really until after the First World War that most new London homes had one. There were, though, many more who hung on to their coal-fired ranges and the gas industry worried away at this reticence by exploiting the desire to be up to date. With servants more difficult to come by and many more women working outside the home, tools for labour-saving were quickly taken up and contemporary cookery books sing the praises of recipes which are 'efficient and labour-saving'. If Elizabeth's gas cooker shows her desire for 'modern convenience' in the kitchen, her purchase of a refrigerator in place of the ubiquitous old wire-meshed meat safe was almost avant-garde in its forwardness; in the 1930s fridges were still the exception.

She may have told Aunt Grace she lived in 'comparative squalor', but Elizabeth's expectations were still such that even if there was no cook, there was a maid to come in from time to time to clean and keep order in her rooms and a wardrobe chosen with a sharp and discerning eye to the higher reaches of fashion. (Letters between the four Gwynne sisters from various parts of the world, for many years to come, were filled with ideas, advice, requests and orders for 'stuffs' to be made up.) In a permanent state of 'just managing' at the upper limits of her allowance, Elizabeth was bolstered by regular handouts from Pris and the occasional one from older and richer relations.

In a small social gathering Elizabeth could shine but on the larger scale of theatre life, where many ambitious, talented and pretty girls battled for position, she did not always make that instant impact necessary to catch the eye of a director. Still determined to act, she did what she could to get work, but continued to spend more time 'resting' than acting. If her particular allure was too subtle for the relatively exhibitionist methods of the theatre, pulling a few social strings was not something Elizabeth would balk at in order to get what she wanted.

In 1932 an impresario businessman, Sidney Carroll, had put up the money for an Open Air Theatre at the Inner Circle Gardens, Regent's Park. Initially the company performed on a slightly raised stage, with the audience perched on green deck-chairs on the grass. The plays were a success and stage-managing grew more ambitious. With lighting by the young Carol Reed, the stage made grander and actors dressed in costumes of striking brilliance, the Open Air Theatre drew some of the most sought-after performers of the time.

A beautiful and promising young actress, Margaretta Scott, had recently played Ophelia to the legendary Henry Ainsley's Hamlet and was taken on straight from a season at Stratford. In conversation with the author she remembered that the Open Air 'had a sylvan quality to it, a fresh spontaneity which was enthusiastically picked up on by the audience'. Miss Scott recalled how every performance was introduced by an elderly actor: 'And a little eight piece orchestra down right accompanied the performances. The situation demanded movement so, as well as other playwrights, much of Shakespeare was perfectly suited. *As You Like It, Twelfth Night, Midsummer Night's Dream* – many others. We changed costumes in a large tent, and if it rained we moved inside to a marquee, which the audience liked because they were closer to us.'

Each play ran for two or three weeks, with Robert Atkins the company's first producer. 'Matinées were always popular with schoolchildren, and nannies and their charges. In the evenings there was a normal theatre-going audience. Quite large, several hundred people to a performance. As we got bigger we used microphones, but it lost some of its simple quality then.' The company was a large one. Sidney Carroll was noted for his ability to spot talented unknowns and to persuade established actors to play for him: John Laurie, Jack Hawkins, Leslie French, Agnes Lockwood, Greer Garson, Joan Hickson, Jack Carlton and many more.

Elizabeth asked her Uncle Jasper if he would say a word on her behalf to Sydney Carroll; she wanted an audition. Carroll said she could have a walk-on part. A girl called Doreen Brownlow was there at Elizabeth's first rehearsal: 'Sydney Carroll was mad keen on titles and knew her family were rather smart, so he let her in. I shall never in my life forget it. The rehearsal was taking place underneath somebody's vegetarian restaurant just off the Strand. We were all sitting there in jeans and sloppy clothes when in walked Elizabeth. She was wearing a *huge* black hat, and a black summer suit with white organdy cuffs and white here, and white there. She was so elegant and all of us just – *looked* at this apparition . . . Anyway, she learnt how to dress, or how not to, after that.'

In spite of her connections Elizabeth never landed more than those walk-on parts and money remained continually short. Initially this did little to stop her using her Selfridges account with abandon. The refrigerator she installed at No. 112 was bought with her twenty-first birthday money from Uncle Top and, as she still knew little about cooking, it was regularly filled with pre-cooked food ordered from Selfridges Food Hall. In her article for Smallbone Kitchen Designs Elizabeth later wrote: 'I had only to pick up the telephone for roast chickens, smoked salmon, butter, fruit, cheese, cream, eggs, coffee to be delivered next day. It wasn't till the monthly accounts seemed to be adding up to much more than I could afford that it dawned on me that having a roast always handy in the fridge was rather an extravagant way to entertain friends.'

Since the bills from Selfridges were too much for her allowance and meagre earnings, she was obliged to take greater care. The two girls had to eat and Elizabeth began to teach herself to cook. In about 1934 Stella had given her daughter a cookery book, one of her first, and instead of simply reading it she now began to use it. In spite of Stella's own complete lack of interest in cooking, with her sure artistic touch she had found a little book which could not have been better calculated to inspire a girl of Elizabeth's temperament and inclinations. *The Gentle Art of Cookery* (Chatto and Windus, 1925), by Mrs Hilda Leyel and Miss Olga Hartley, was a book to which Elizabeth much later devoted almost the entire introduction of her own *Spices, Salt and Aromatics in the English Kitchen* (Penguin, 1970), she mused:

> Come to that, I wonder if I would ever have learned to cook at all had I been given a routine Mrs Beeton to learn from instead of the romantic Mrs Leyel, with her rather wild and imagination-catching recipes ... I am recalling ... the reactions ... of a young woman quite ignorant of cooking techniques but easily ... beguiled by the idea of food as unlike as could be to any produced by the conventional English cook of the time.

Elizabeth continued with the observation that she was uncritical of Mrs Leyel's vague attitude to quantities and paucity of technical instruction because, in her ignorance, she didn't even notice the lack of them and would probably 'not have believed anybody had they tried to tell me'. She came to the conclusion that Mrs Leyel's 'greatest asset was her ability to appeal to the imagination of the young'. And that the young and the 'totally inexperienced will usually prefer a book which provides stimulus to one which goes into technical details, makes strenuous efforts to keep the reader on the straight and . . . the main roads of established cookery.'

Hilda Leyel was that extraordinarily dynamic woman who had founded the Society of Herbalists and the Culpepper herb shops as well as writing over half a dozen books and editing the encyclopaedic *A Modern Herbal* (Jonathan Cape, 1932). Unlike most English cookery books of the 1930s which give instructions for economical, labour-saving food – cookery as domestic science – *The Gentle Art of Cookery* is indeed an alluring little book, which evokes with a quirky charm the strange and the mysterious.

In her own introduction Mrs Leyel makes a bold claim: 'There are seven different ways in which this cookery book differs from all others.' Amongst these differences is a chapter containing 'a unique collection of flower recipes' and another with recipes for the dishes conjured up in the *One Thousand and One Nights* and about which Elizabeth writes, 'No doubt because of its vagueness and brevity [it] contained the true essence of magic and mystery.' She recalled that: 'When I first had Mrs Leyel's book nothing and nobody on earth could have sold me an English rice pudding, but a rice cream made with lemon and almonds and served in a silver dish, well, that gave one something to think about . . .'

In this same vein of rebellion against the prosaic, Elizabeth lauded Mrs Leyel's separation of mushrooms and chestnuts from the more ordinary potatoes, beans and sprouts and approvingly recorded her love of fruit, vegetables and salads. She described 'her treatment of them almost as dishes to which meat and fish and poultry were little more than incidental accompaniments, or scarcely necessary adjuncts to a meal'.

The Gentle Art abides by traditional (French) culinary principles. Exactly those which Elizabeth had witnessed Madame 'Robertot' practising daily when she returned from the Parisian markets, laden with the produce of the day for her greedy family and those reluctant young English lodgers. Thus, another of Mrs Leyel's 'seven ways in which this cookery book differs' is that the recipes 'are arranged under their principal ingredients, because it is more economical to do as the French do, shop first, then arrange the dinner according to what is most plentiful in the market, than to go out and buy for a pre-arranged menu'. In using this book Elizabeth, however unconsciously at first, began slowly to imbibe both French principles and Mrs Leyel's advice that *The Gentle Art* was 'not intended to be an elementary handbook on cookery, but has been written for those who appreciate the fact that good cooking is one of the obtainable amenities of life if extravagance is eliminated'.

Stimulus, the quality Elizabeth claimed so abundantly for Mrs Leyel, was also provided for her by another book published at about this time. In her Smallbone article she described seeing piled high in Selfridges' window copies of a Countess Morphy's *Recipes of All Nations*: 'At 2s 6d or 3s 6d. for a version with a thumb index. . . . The book seemed amazing value for money. One day I carried home a copy with me on the bus and began reading it. It was fascinating – it still is – but Countess Morphy . . . threw little light on such matters as quantities, timing, temperatures and other technical details.'

Unusually for the period, and in spite of her shortage on detail, Marcelle Morphy had a keen eye for good food. In the Thirties and Forties she put out a stream of cookery books for 'bright young things'. With books like *Lightning Cookery* and *Picnic Snacks*, she epitomized that conflict between the time-conscious kitchen sensibilities of the age and the (unresolved) problem of making what were often essentially grand dishes, without the grand back-up to go with them. 'Still,' continued Elizabeth, 'with the help of Mrs Leyel . . . I began to teach myself to cook nice food.' And in *Spices, Salt and Aromatics in the English Kitchen* she says that *The Gentle Art* 'turned out to be almost the equivalent in cookery of [that old family friend] Walter de la Mare's unsurpassed poetry anthology *Come Hither* which had enlightened my childhood.'

This was all very much a beginning for Elizabeth, who simultaneously persevered with a liberal use of the plethora of tinned goods by then available. With methods improving during the nineteenth century, at its conclusion canning was used largely for luxury goods. Although more basic foods were flooding the market, inexperienced upper-class housewives and girls like Elizabeth – with a shortage of servants – were still turning to tins for much labour-saving and problem-free food. Fortnum and Mason, for instance, sold tinned Scotch salmon, mulligatawny soup and chicken gumbo, and it was to be some time before Elizabeth applied herself to anything more than erratic uncoordinated essays in the kitchen.

Looking back in *Spices, Salt and Aromatics*, to her mind, Mrs Leyel's 'Arabian way of cooking red mullet . . . sounded irresistible, so much so that even if you barely knew whether a red mullet was a bird, a flower or a fish, you quickly set about finding out'. *The Gentle Art* 'certainly took one very far away indeed from the world of grapefruit and Scotch eggs to which a bed-sitter cook so easily succumbs'. And so far this had been Elizabeth's style. She was writing about Scotch eggs from experience, for they were one of her first [and abortive] attempts at cooking anything much more than 'fry-ups' and things on toast since moving into No. 112 Regent's Park Road.

Among the actors playing at the Open Air Theatre were several Elizabeth already knew from the Oxford Rep, including Joan Hickson. The Open Air players were a relatively amicable group and Elizabeth made friends with several of the other performers. One of those was the young Leslie French whose rendering of the part made him for many the quintessential Puck. Another new friend was a striking redhead, Doreen Brownhill, the girl who recalled with such vigour Elizabeth's melodramatic entrance to the 'vegetarian' rehearsal. A young woman of spirit and cheerfulness, Doreen was determined to have a good time. She put on no airs, knew her own mind, and was a match for Elizabeth. Although fascinated by her, Doreen was not going to be dominated. In conversation with the author she described Elizabeth: 'Oh, she was desperately intolerant. Always. Even from our youth. If people disagreed with her they were out. Yes, Liz and I fought.'

Disagreements failed to diminish the girls' youthful energy and they were imbued with a sense of *joie de vivre* which propelled them along. A close friendship quickly formed and was to remain intact for the rest of their lives. Doreen recalled the dish to which, Elizabeth later wrote, 'a bedsitter cook so easily succumbs': 'One crazy day Liz decided we would make Scotch eggs. Don't imagine she was doing any *real* cooking then. We'd got this recipe and went to the butcher's and asked for a huge quantity of sausagemeat; we hadn't really an idea how much to get, or really what to do with it. I do remember her making broad beans in pasta sauce – that was lovely. And then there were those delicious things from the Selfridges account. She was hopeless about money, she'd be forever saying, "Oh, put that on my account." '

When they had a part, however small, work at the Open Air was hard work for the two girls: 'After a wretched day rehearsing at the theatre – from ten in the morning till eleven at night – or on other days when we weren't working, we'd go to the Lyons Corner House in the Strand, often with Dickie Kerr [Richard Kerr Carey] and Gar Greerson' [the future star, Greer Garson].

'We'd sit around drinking coffee for hours and hours, because it was only 4d a cup. And *then*, when it was late, I'd say to Liz, "Oh, you come back" . . . and we'd listen to records and look at magazines and read the agony columns together in my flat [in Chelsea]. And by now, in the middle of the night she'd say, "Let's go back to *my* flat," and we'd walk through the night right across London from Chelsea to Camden Town. Can you *imagine* it, Liz walking those distances?'

The Open Air Theatre's Shakespeare seasons were popular, and one performance which unfailingly held the audience until the last words had died away on the balmy evening air, was the pastoral comedy *As You Like It*. In the play's outdoor setting the famous wrestling match was 'staged to such advantage that the audience were on the edge of their chairs until the very concluding moment', recalled Margaretta Scott. In the summer of 1935 the scene was fought with great panache between a young, and as yet unknown, Jack Hawkins and the fight's choreographer, Leonard Gibson Cowan. Gibson Cowan, who had recently adopted the name Charles, was an actor-producer who wrote plays and occasional journalism. A one-time tramp and beggar he was to assume a crucial role in Elizabeth's life. In 1928–9, at the age of twenty-four, Gibson Cowan had written a book which he called *Loud Report*. Its journey of escape from responsibility and routine had initially been inspired by the romance of W. H. Davies' *Autobiography of a Super Tramp*. *Loud Report* itself is more representative of that genre the likes of which, George Orwell in *Down and Out in London and Paris* and Joseph Stamper in *Less Than the Dust*, would expand on during the 1930s. In a disingenuously simple style, and masquerading under the same guise of candid observation employed by these writers, Gibson Cowan writes purposively, one aim being a description of the appalling social conditions of the underprivileged.

Nevertheless, the close relationship between fiction and travel writing, whose claim to authenticity *appears* to rest with actual places and events, has long been recognized and sometimes questioned. With the author portrayed as a shocking anti-hero, like all writers of travel and fiction Gibson Cowan is selective when something does not fulfil his purpose. This and other such devices are described by another skilled practitioner of the travel-writing genre, Norman Douglas, when he says, 'One suppresses much . . . what is boring or unprintable', and . . . 'Why not add a little later?'

To the generation of the Twenties and Thirties travel (and its literature) had an aura of the sacred about it and some travelled unrelentingly, to the point of neurosis. Within this milieu the romantic figure of the wanderer, the vagabond, the gypsy, was not a new one; George Borrow's *Lavengro* (John Murray, 1881) was popular, so too was W. H. Davies' book, never out of print since publication in 1908. (Lionized by literary salons, both sociable and retiring, W. H. Davies, whose poetry is now almost forgotten, was befriended by the Sitwells and Elizabeth's Aunt Violet – he lived near her in Gloucestershire until his death in 1940.) Between the wars the vagabond theme was given new life with books like Helen Waddell's *The Wandering Scholars* (Constable, 1927), about medieval itinerant clerks, Orwell's *The Road to Wigan Pier* (Gollancz, 1937) and, in the same year, Robert Byron's *The Road to Oxiana* (Macmillan). Similarly, Charles Gibson Cowan's memoir reflects the roving, questing mentality of the inter-war generation. Charlie Chaplin's cinema tramp epitomized on screen the man Cowan sometimes depicts himself as having become: a past master of the shrewdness, cynical evasiveness, self-reliance and initiative necessary for the open road and, by implication, for life itself. However, it is clear from both *Loud Report* and later events that Charles is a far more complex and sympathetic character than this would suggest; there is a naïveté in him too. Often he is emotionally honest to his own detriment, trying to reconcile conflicting drives at just those times which most demanded the persona of a con-man.

A world of difference existed between Charles Gibson Cowan and George Orwell. Orwell's Eton education made him part of that class for whom the worker was still 'quite foreign'. He was seen as a specimen for anthropological study, the subject of missionary zeal, or as one whose sufferings should be shared ... sometimes all three perspectives together. (These attitudes of mind were in the air. Across the Channel another gifted middle-class intellectual, Simone Weil, driven by similar forces, had worked for a time in the Renault car factory.) By contrast Cowan is at one with W. H. Davies in coming himself from that foreign land; he writes about territory with which he is entirely familiar. However harrowing the 'down-and-out' life Orwell encountered, he had chosen it himself, just as Simone Weil had opted to endure what was for her the nightmare of a giant mass-production factory. However grim, it was still a kind of game, an experiment from which they could extract themselves at any time. For Charles it was not a game, it was a central reality. He *was* an Outsider, whereas George Orwell was playing at being one.

Although it is clear that in *Loud Report* Gibson Cowan exaggerates, even fabricates, nevertheless the persona he creates is, at least in part, that same one he would convincingly project at Elizabeth and her friends. Charles wrote in old age that *Loud Report* had little to recommend it 'beyond youthful enthusiasm'. However, ten years after its creation, in 1938 at the age of thirty-four, he still identified sufficiently with the essentual matter and radical tone of the book to publish it, written in the first person and under his own name.

Of his parents Gibson Cowan wrote in *Loud Report*: 'My father was a Jew, my mother the daughter of an English mother and a Dutch father. We were lower-class. My father was the only man I have ever heard admit he was lower-class.' According to the picture he drew of them in his book, Charles's family were a ramshackle, feuding, cheerful and intense lot of Portuguese Jews. His great-grandfather was a rabbi, and of this detail the family were inordinately proud. Work, as coalmen, costermongers, booksellers' assistants, boot-clickers, tappers, fortune-tellers or itinerant musicians, was precarious and their lives were often lived close to the edge of wretchedness. Some Jews, like Charles's father, had married out of the faith, but more retained their Orthodox religion and sociable European ways in the midst of London's teeming, impoverished, raucous East End. Charles recalled his very Jewish grandmother who 'lived in Merchant Street and was a wizened little woman . . . with a foreign lilt of phrase. When she was eighty she still went to the theatre, alone.

'She remembered all the great actors and actresses. Marie Lloyd, Vesta Tilley, Lottie Collins, Bernhardt, Duse, Irving, Tree, were all names to me; they meant nothing, but stuck in my memory. She went to the films once or twice before she died. She could not bear Chaplin. "Chaplin! Tch! He makes himself silly." '

Charles tells us that, summoned to her bedside the doctor said she would probably die. She wanted to see *Ruddigore* at the theatre, but Charles's father would not let her get up. She evaded their surveillance, nevertheless, and was later found in the front row of the auditorium, where Charles's father and his brother watched her from the back of the gallery. They 'followed her home travelling on top of the same bus. That night she fell asleep quite normally. In the morning she was dead.'

Charles was born on 29 May 1904 in Guildford, his father having taken a job outside London. By the time the young Gibson Cowan had reached secondary-school age the family were once again living in London. According to *Loud Report*, Charles went to the local high school where 'The boys were all snobs, the masters, if anything, worse than the boys. Anti-Semitic feeling was openly upheld and I had no means of redress. I was called Jew and Sheeny even by the masters, but I did not complain to my parents.' Charles left his next and final school at eighteen with records revealing good behaviour and an unremarkable academic record, except in chemistry. Working for a year as a clerk in a jam factory where he described himself as utterly miserable, having devised a superior form of calculation, he either handed in his notice or was dismissed. Now nineteen Charles took to the roads. Living rough for six months provided him with the basis for *Loud Report*, eventually written five years later.

Charles tells us that: 'On the road consists of incidents, connected only by dreary walks through the rain, or sleeps under haystacks when the weather is warm enough to stop moving. It is

74

difficult to estimate time . . . Once a goal, however futile, was in sight, each day gave the illusion of progress.'

We are treated to a series of apparent adventures, including living off fish and beggings in a dugout shelter on the coast while he entertained himself with a local servant girl; walking 200 miles to Wales, clothes and shoes falling apart, and returning to London to live in a series of insanitary, unsavoury lodgings, with actresses, prostitutes, pushers and hustlers for companions. Portraying himself by now as a masterly beggar, Charles describes his apprenticeship in a selection of underhand occupations before becoming a barker for a travelling circus sideshow. Although the narrative of *Loud Report* is interspersed with a flagrant manipulation of the chronology of his early life, bearing in mind others' accounts of Charles's demeanour during the following decade and beyond, the exploits he describes often have a convincing ring to them.

Disenchantment with the vagrant's life sent him back home and to a job. His grandmother's love of the theatre had eventually surfaced in Charles and from this point he seems to have found his métier. Within a few years he was acting and producing for the likes of the avant-garde actor-playwright Miles Malleson. By the following year, 1927, a volume of stories, *Fantoccini* (Danegeld Press) had also been completed and published.

We are told in *Loud Report* that Charles was asked to complete a play begun sometime earlier and called *Eastside, Westside*. This may have had at its heart an examination of the inequalities of those living in London's East and West ends. The rapid expansion in population and sharp decline in prosperity of the East End during the nineteenth century had given rise to the truths and myths of sweatshops, vagrantism, and a plague of deviancy, traditionally creating fear in the hearts of every prosperous West-ender. Charles's experiences at the seamy edge of existence had fitted him well for the transient world of the theatre, where security is non-existent, where you take what you can while you may and where reality and illusion are only loosely distinguished.

Over the next few years he read, wrote and laboured at establishing himself as playwright and producer by working in rep, the Oxford and Cambridge Dramatic festivals, and the prestigious Oxford University Dramatic Society, OUDS. Charles was tough and demanding; rehearsals frequently went on until well after midnight, and the students gave him the epithet 'back-on-it-Gibson'. Then, in 1933, he acted in *As You Like It* at the West End's Phoenix Theatre, where he played Charles the Wrestler and made the role his own. Henceforth he only used the name Charles.

Elizabeth had met Charles on the occasion when he annoyed her so much while producing for the Rep at Oxford in that same year. After her move to London they met again. Charles had worked on his part in *As You Like It* for Sydney Carroll at the Open Air Theatre in the summer of '34, and the following year his and Elizabeth's paths crossed once more.

At thirty-one Charles was now a rakish and enigmatic figure whose slight aura of danger added to the attraction for Elizabeth, and his was a type for whom she would retain a weakness. Charles's magnetism notwithstanding, Elizabeth's friend Doreen was unimpressed and always kept him at a distance. Exhilarated by his company, within a short time Elizabeth was intimately involved with this man about whom not only her family but also her friends were alarmed. Whatever her own doubts may have been, Elizabeth acquiesced in Charles's 'open' life-style, which now included an actress wife and a baby. She ignored warnings and appeals and, faced with her usual self-willed determination, there was little anyone could do.

It is worth remarking here that the family did not object to Elizabeth's associating with Aunt Violet and her four men; did not fear contamination from her aunt's life-style, which was in effect more deviant than that of Charles. It was a matter of social class, race and money, rather than one of sexual morality.

Neither was there much anyone could do when Elizabeth's determination was exerted in coming to someone's aid. A case in point was her involvement with the proceedings for Diana's apprehensive visit to Stella in Jamaica. Felicité, in Durham with Mrs Headlam for six months, told Pris in Malta that she was appalled by Elizabeth's current behaviour, which had left herself and Diana wounded and exhausted. Elizabeth had attempted to organize Felicité seeing Diana off from Bristol, and a series of phone calls followed. Elizabeth found all concerned intolerable and Felicité wrote to Pris that she ended by 'ringing Diana up in one of her ghastly storms of rage ... and a fearful scene ensued' during which she abused Diana, and later Mrs Headlam, 'violently'. Eventually Aunt Grace felt obliged to intervene and rang Mrs Headlam to apologize for the 'ill-mannered' behaviour of her niece, while Felicité was left in Durham to live with the consequences: a very disgruntled landlady who had 'made everything so marvellous for me and now L has wrecked it for the time being'. She continued bitterly: 'Liza is making everything go wrong ... You know, Pris, much as I like Liza, I think she can make herself more unpleasant than anyone I know. It's desperately despairing.' Felicité noticed too that 'really she's quite changed. She looks such a sight, goes about with a face like a shiny ball of light, never particularly clean ... hair ... with no vestige of ever being combed ... And ... takes no notice of anyone. Besides she gives such a very slovenly impression, clothes creased, dirty shoes.'

Writing to Pris in Malta the following spring, 1935, Felicité felt more positive about her sister when describing the terrors she had recently encountered in her presentation at Court. 'The strain was altogether too much for me – and I'm relieved that the fans and feathers and trains are carefully laid away in their boxes again.' With a distinctive Gwynne gift for acerbity, Felicité nevertheless does not practise the same level of forthrightness or defiance as Elizabeth, revealing herself in her letters as more retiring and modest. She was 'highly surprised' when Viscount Hailsham – Quintin Hogg's father and at that time Lord High Chancellor – recognized her in the crowded and tense spectacular of a Court presentation, and noted that he 'was very affable to me'. Overcome by the splendour of all the uniforms and the great numbers of people; 'when it came to my turn to curtsey I was rooted to the ground with terror and could hardly see the Royalties without my glasses.' Afterwards she 'forgot to curtsey to the Duchess of York. I don't ever recognize her'.

Elizabeth joined in the celebration dinner at the Savoy afterwards and Felicité was now pleased to tell Pris that 'Liza seems quite flourishing,' but added, 'though as far as I gathered with no prospects of a job at all – and she doesn't even seem to be looking for one,'

In fact Elizabeth was making more concerted efforts in other directions and thus by the end of the year she could tell Pris, after thanking her for a typically generous birthday cheque, that she hadn't bought a single item of clothing since her elder sister had left England. With her inexhaustible delight in clothes (And despite her 'slovenly appearance') this predicament was probably an exaggeration. She later added that some blouses had been the exception, made up from 'bits of stuff' that she'd had for years. But the point underlying the sartorial comments was that for now Elizabeth wanted to use Pris's cheque to finish decorating and furnishing the house. Any such 'house beautifying' had been at a standstill for months, lack of money making basic necessities more pressing. Instead Elizabeth had been concentrating on how 'to obtain three meals a day for about four people for thirty bob a week'.

In the absence of Marian who was with her parents, and Diana and Felicité who were abroad, Elizabeth was again at Blackmoor for a 'pleasant Christmas', although bursting with indignation at both Stella and Uncle Top who seemed 'to absolutely loathe me these days. Either it's that people have been doing too much talking about me or else it's that infernal H. L. [Stella] telling him I'd frittered away his £20 which was an absolutely malicious lie seeing that I spent it on the flat, and as that's the thing that it gives me most pleasure to spend it on I can't see that anyone should complain. Pesk them all!' The money (for her twenty-first) was that which had recently gone towards the purchase of the fridge.

Elizabeth gave Aunt Violet a beautiful set of enamel buttons found in an antique shop. It broke her heart knowing full well that they would only go into the 'bottomless pit' of Violet's knick-knack box, but Lily (the maid) had instructions to retrieve them after a decent interval had elapsed. Elizabeth cooed with pleasure over a pair of long suede gloves from Fortnum's given her by Violet, and she then lambasted Uncle Roland for sending her yet another unsatisfactory present. Instead she was given a tiny mirror on a stand with very dirty drawers and the mirror as black as her 'best hat, most probably turned out of her room by the under-housemaid at Folkington'. Diana and Felicité received the usual pink and green beads, which they immediately gave to the servants. None of the girls gave Roland anything. Elizabeth had sent a Christmas card, and thought even that too good for him. 'Dirty old bastard . . .'

At Blackmoor 'We had the usual Christmas Tree orgy, the stairs are as slippery as ever and the cover of the silver breakfast dish still comes to pieces in your hand, and there is as usual a spider in one's bath in the morning.' This was so unfailingly the case that the family called it 'the spider bathroom'.

Back in the city Elizabeth was oblivious to the possibility of her sisters' disapproval of Charles Gibson Cowan. She was excited by life in the shadow of such a colourful lover, whose friends included a mixture of figures from London's underworld and members of the left-wing avant-garde. Charles had engineered a contract to translate some Russian plays and was paid fifty pounds in advance, much to everyone's astonishment. Elizabeth and Marian earned 'a nice little windfall' by doing some 'shady business' with cut-price cigarettes for a friend of his just before Christmas. Elizabeth told Felicité that she'd be going to a party with him on New Year's Eve – 'what the H. L. would call a Bohemian Party' – where there wouldn't be many men with flowers in their hair, but quite a few with beads. As she hadn't been to a party for six months, she hoped it would be worthy of her. It undoubtedly was.

Despite these defiant immersions in London's avant-garde; symptoms of Elizabeth's reaction against her family, she was sufficiently bound by an ingrained sense of etiquette to be appalled at Aunt Violet's dawn phone call on New Year's Day. Elizabeth was completely 'blotto' and Violet was asking her to lunch. She felt she 'had to go'. Having been entertained by Aunt Violet to that lady's satisfaction, Elizabeth was sent home in a taxi when she proved too ill to remain any longer. On ringing Violet the next morning to thank her, her aunt proceeded to ask her to lunch *again*. Once again she 'had to go'.

Charles was a vital and stimulating companion for Elizabeth and she was happy for the moment to lead a double life. Unwilling to relinquish the benefits her privileged background had conferred upon her, her social values remained, finally, intact. She was questioning art rather than politics and in the process took on certain mannerisms which her sisters found distasteful. Felicité, writing to Pris of her distress about Elizabeth's 'fits of passion', described how she now 'throws her hands about all over the place and casts her eyes to heaven and ruffles her hair'. Felicité thought it 'altogether very stagey . . . it's silly and affected'.

Charles scraped a living together through a variety of sources. He was producing and acting fairly regularly, had written a couple of plays and found the odd commission for pieces of journalism. Although hampered by a certain lack of application, he was increasingly determined to make his living as a writer. Elizabeth had made no such serious decision, but her appetite for books was no less voracious. Books, both classics and contemporary, are constantly referred to in letters.

An important part of the attraction Charles held for Elizabeth was that their talk ranged at length over literary matters, and before the year was out they were writing a book together. After a few months Elizabeth told Pris that nothing had yet happened about it. Charles later wrote: 'The idea was a good one, but it was not a success.'

Elizabeth and Charles's lives gradually became firmly interwoven. Initially Charles's wife and the baby were in evidence. They lived in a beautiful down-at-heel Georgian house Charles had discovered near the pierhead at Wapping. In the heart of the East End, it had a view of Tower Bridge from the window, with the sirens of steamers and the whistle of tugs in the air.

Unmoved by children, Elizabeth was certainly not interested in babies and Doreen Thornton remembers an isolated journey across London on the tube one day, with the baby unwell and in their care. 'I wasn't going to have anything to do with it, so Elizabeth had to carry it. She didn't want to.' At about this time Elizabeth informs Pris that it is a good thing their cousin Anne is not yet having a baby because 'she and John seem extremely happy'. By implication, a baby would diminish rather than enhance their happiness.

Charles eventually separated from his wife and he and Elizabeth spent the following three years, on and off, sharing a succession of London flats. Elizabeth made several trips abroad, including the final visit to Germany. It was the journeys to warmer southern Europe, however, which were soon to crucially alter her perceptions of England.

Just before the Christmas of 1935 she excitedly told Felicité that Dorothy Goodwin had invited her to stay in Cairo, as soon and as long as she liked, with her cousin Kit, Neville Gwynne's daughter. They would travel on to Malta afterwards. She intended to go at the beginning of March and to stay for about three months. Dorothy and Teddy Goodwin were old friends of Stella's and Teddy worked for a firm with a post in Cairo.

Elizabeth soon informed Pris about her ideas for the trip and indicated her impatience with any form of restriction. Coupled with this impatience was a tendency to be easily bored if people did not adapt quickly enough for her. She thought she would wander over to Malta 'on some old tub or other', remain a fortnight, and then take the first cargo boat that presented itself to Cairo or Port Said. Elizabeth couldn't bear the idea of having her trip planned out weeks ahead – she wanted to go out and return when she chose, and avoid at all costs 'such abominations as P&O boats and changing for dinner on board'. Elizabeth's comments quickly establish her attitude to travelling. Although some were willing, many women still felt uncomfortable travelling alone. But Elizabeth was well equipped with the necessary independence, unafraid of the solitude it might bring, and relished the prospect of the encounters along the way.

Elizabeth did make the journey to Egypt with Kit, probably late in 1936, and seems to have spent an energetically social time with the hospitable Goodwins in the thick of Cairo expatriate life. This trip did not, however, coincide with the prospective one to Malta.

With Elizabeth's dislike of restraint, despite the tacit agreement of 'freedom and openness' between herself and Charles, there were often difficulties. She remained intrigued by him yet, always wary of being wounded, was both reluctant to commit herself and also impatient if her demands were not quickly met. Meanwhile, Charles's regular infidelities neither deterred Elizabeth nor meant Charles had lost interest in her. Aware that something was lacking, and propelled by her need to be in a state of either stasis or incessant movement, Elizabeth set off for Malta during the spring of 1936.

Felicité saw her off and Elizabeth's subsequent letter – 'still on this rotten old tub plodding through the Mediterranean' – barely contains her frustration. Her independence as a traveller never stretched to a capacity for enjoyment of uncomfortable surroundings unless these were counterbalanced by a high degree of visual satisfaction. She complained that the boat was dirty and her cabin right over the engine room – for the first few days the noise almost drove her mad. She wrote that she was sick, couldn't eat so much as a dry biscuit for days, the food was more or less uneatable when she could, and her cabin was so uncomfortable that she had to survive almost without sleep. The weather through the Bay of Biscay was passable, but down the coast of Portugal high winds rose to gales of over a hundred miles per hour, and the sea became so violent it washed right over the ship and smashed one of the life boats. As they moved south the weather improved and Elizabeth began sunbathing on deck and ate with the officers who were all 'charming' despite coming from Yorkshire and speaking with 'terrific accents'.

Wireless contact aboard ship was lost for a time, and they eventually arrived two days late. Elizabeth was greeted by Priscilla and Richard and taken to their beautiful house, Dar Ida, overlooking the sparkling blue of the lapping Mediterranean Sea.

Pris and Richard spoiled and cosseted Elizabeth and she luxuriated in the straightforwardness of their cheerful and busy social round on this small but cosmopolitan island. Malta was a refreshing and stimulating retreat for Elizabeth and she stayed for the full three months, leaving only reluctantly, in a flurry of flowers and telegrams from new friends and admirers. Pris as usual helped her by organizing and paying for her ships berth back to England. The three months had done her an enormous amount of good and on return she wrote saying she felt encouraged and revitalized.

In contrast with Charles and his friends, the social background of her recent associates in Malta was on a par with her own. As a major British naval base several regiments, such as the Rifle Brigade, were stationed on Malta and most of Pris and Richard's friends were in either the military or the navy. Pris herself had gone out because

Richard was there with the Royal Engineers Corps and several of Pris's and Elizabeth's friends who had enlisted were also now stationed on the island. Political convictions among these Malta friends were also in strong contrast to those of Charles, they did not lean to the left.

In the manner of expatriate communities, social life was hectic and sometimes intense. Far from home, with its perfect climate and sometimes spectacularly beautiful scenery, Malta made an idyllic backdrop for liaisons of all kinds. However illicit some of these may have been, Elizabeth's time there was simpler than the complexities of her recent London life. (Although she was defiant and quite open about her intention to do as she pleased, family disapproval of Charles had remained undiminished.) So invigorated and cheered was she by her stay in Malta that the following year she returned for another long spell of entertainment under Pris and Richard's care.

Not only had Malta been a place of extended respite from the realities of London, its Mediterranean bounty had the effect of sending Elizabeth into Priscilla's kitchen in a spirit of enquiry which she had never previously displayed. Angela, Priscilla's cheerful, absent-minded and gifted cook, was the person responsible for Elizabeth's present interest, and she gave her her first cooking lessons. A Maltese who had always worked for military and naval families, Angela was unschooled yet instinctive. Both inspired by the possibilities of the kitchen and at ease with its demands, she served up unfailingly delicious meals. Elizabeth more than once accompanied her to the market on her forays for food and was amused and impressed by her competence, noise and scattiness. Once the cat managed to leave a dinner party for that evening short of a vital quail. 'Piercing wails rent the air . . . the council that followed was one of desperation.'

Years later, in 1951, shortly after her first book, *Mediterranean Food*, had been published, Elizabeth wrote an article without recipes, entitled 'Two Cooks', for the inimitable André Simon's quarterly, *Wine and Food*. In keeping with the style of this élite and influential journal, Elizabeth's essay was a true piece of gastronomic literature. For one so relatively inexperienced, her sense of concision and humour were already beautifully honed. And with these as tools she used the vehicle of her own experience of a small Mediterranean island to give the outlines of a philosophy of taste.

In those days food was remarkably cheap in Malta, drink was untaxed and entertaining was easy, and immense fun. Marketing was carried on with an Oriental approach to the delights of haggling . . . In the market you could buy a variety of boned, dressed meat and game at ridiculously small prices . . . there was a prodigal supply of fruits and vegetables grown on the neighbouring island of Gozo; the local oranges were sweet and delicious; there were figs, grapes and exquisite wild strawberries.

In the summer of 1937, when Pris and Richard returned to England and a cottage on Salisbury Plain, they brought Angela with them. For a while she was 'blissfully happy in that damp and clammy atmosphere: she thought the little red bungalows on the road to Andover the most beautiful houses in the world and she continued to cook like an angel. On English mutton and most un-Mediterranean vegetables her talent thrived.' But Angela's Southern temperament and love of her little island got the better of her. 'You cannot [in England] haggle with a village grocer, and she began to pine for the shouting and the disorder of Valetta's market, the incessant gossip, and the fun of preparing immense quantities of food for the parties which had been an almost everyday occurrence in Malta.' Angela returned home, came back to Pris, and eventually went back for good to the island of her birth.

If a gastronome's message is about choice and discrimination, then in the short space of a page and a half 'Two Cooks' succeeds with admirable skill. Elizabeth inspires the wish to emulate the culinary style, the tenor of Mediterranean life; describes the minimum required to be a good cook and hints that England would be the richer for a turn in this direction.

As the narrative unfolds, in the reflection of Angela's lovable personality Elizabeth conjures up the noise, vibrancy and sparkle of a bustling Mediterranean town. Here one has the impression that food, without necessarily being luxurious, is in 'prodigal' supply. The quality of fruit and vegetables is the best, whilst inexpensive cuts of meat are not considered drawbacks, because the cook is one for whom things like 'stringy birds' can be transformed into 'creamy soufflés and mousses'. Everything is cooked with a simplicity and sureness of touch which has at its heart the assumption that food is a matter for celebration. By contrast a picture of a grey and overcast England emerges in the essay. It is judged a place ruled by an unbending obedience to order, where a sense of largesse is absent and where the natives fail to cook even their national dishes with any flair or distinction.

Homeward bound from Malta, the thought of London appalled Elizabeth and on arrival her worst fears were confirmed, for she found it 'simply awful' and was thrown into a depression. Lyrical in her praise of Pris and Richard and all the trouble they had taken, she surprises by recalling her huge enjoyment of one of Pris and Richard's favourite pastimes, sailing: 'The [sailing] and bathing were absolutely divine . . . all the parties and . . . your lovely house and all the flowers . . . and lovely food were miraculous.'

The state of No. 112 Regent's Park Road and the negative response it provoked in her now seemed symptomatic of her rejection of London, England and much of what it represented. On return she found the flat filthy and untidy, in fact exactly as she had left it — empty jars of face cream and bath salt jars were everywhere, and a kitchen grimy with dirt. She was very annoyed with Marian's lack of domesticity in her absence and, as the maid was not as available as she would have liked, Elizabeth launched into cleaning up as soon as she arrived. Wishing she could return immediately to Malta, despite the unlikelihood of finding such grand rooms again, the only answer was to leave. She told Pris she would find a smaller flat for which no one but herself was responsible and added that she would have to get somewhere with more modern conveniences. Elizabeth shared houses and spent much time in the sociable company of any number of people over the years, but her childhood habit of retreat, of hiding away with a book, remained a passion it was not wise to thwart. Literature was a restorative, a means by which she replenished herself and this retreat remained essential throughout the course of her life.

For the moment, however, Elizabeth wanted company in the awfulness of London. She needed to reinstate herself in the metropolis in order to justify returning there, but it was Whitsun and everyone she knew seemed to be out of town, frustrating her attempts. Doreen was still working with a rep company in Ireland, Marian was about to go up to her family in Kendal, Felicité was away at Folkington, and Elizabeth couldn't find Diana, or Arthur Watkins. One person who did prove to be around was Charles, and any hopes Pris and the others might have had of Elizabeth giving him up were quickly shelved.

The holiday in Malta had filled her with a new purposefulness, and she announced to Pris that she was full of energy, desperate to find a job and equal to facing 'a regiment of foul beastly Sydney Carrolls and film agents and pimply theatre managers and I have a feeling that perhaps I'll get a job this time'. Concurrently with these good intentions Elizabeth was facing up to the unlikelihood of finding any acting work that could be called a living, and told Pris that if nothing appeared within the next two months she would give it up altogether.

Pris would soon be home on several weeks' summer leave and Elizabeth promised to set about finding a cottage in Wales where the four sisters could spend some time together. The Welsh origins of their name seemed an inducement to indulge what became something of a fixation with this beautiful and still unspoilt part of Britain. Between 1935 and 1938 the sisters took at least two or three houses together there. One such, Glys Andreas, was a cottage at Talybont, which Felicité described as a 'lovely lonely place' in the winding, leafy Usk river valley. Friends came to stay and Doreen remembers one year when 'Elizabeth threw herself into learning Welsh'. Although it can hardly be claimed typical of anything Welsh, during the Thirties Elizabeth also spent the first of several holidays at Portmeirion in North Wales, on that occasion with Stella, Cedric Morris and Arthur Lett Haines. The mix of diminutive and grand ice cream-coloured baroque splendour set amidst a very un-continental Welsh landscape appealed to the quirky and at heart metropolitan sophisticate in Elizabeth. Many other artistic figures had also been captivated by Portmeirion since its opening in 1926. Its designer-owner was the remarkable Clough Williams-Ellis, a friend of Cedric and Lett. Elizabeth's fascination with Wales took her back many times over the years to a succession of houses for holidays and work and a restaurant near Abergavenny, The Walnut Tree, was eventually to become her favourite outside London.

During the war, abroad and worn out with it, she nostalgically recalled to Priscilla a little house they had seen near Machynlleth on their first Welsh holiday together. It was found along a path by a river, which ran through the garden, and nearby was an odd-looking sugar loaf hill. Elizabeth always regretted that she hadn't rented it and longed for its beautiful rooms and the little garden pool.

Back in London and still finding only the odd acting assignment, Elizabeth took up a recommendation from Cedric Morris to his friend Madame Chant-Communal, the gifted chief designer for the influential fashion house, Worth. Worth prided itself on the social prestige of its clients, many of whose dresses were made for Court occasions. The girls who assisted clients with fittings were required to have not only something of Elizabeth's social clout but, for all her delight in clothes, considerably more knowledge of design and materials than she could then muster. Her meeting with Madame Chant-Communal led to a brief new part for Elizabeth as a junior Worth vendeuse.

After leaving No. 112 Regent's Park Road Elizabeth lived in a flat in John Street, most of the time with Charles, and not doing very much. Doreen was out of work and her father insisted she took a typing course at Pitmans, only a few streets away from Elizabeth and Charles, but her resolve was not very fixed. 'I used to pop into Pitmans for about half an hour then I'd abscond to their flat. We'd lounge around, listen to records, spend the rest of the day there. We didn't seem to *do* anything much.' This inactivity failed to bring peacefulness for Charles and Elizabeth. Their life appears to have had little tranquillity about it and when not 'lounging around' Elizabeth continued with her incessant activity.

By July 1937 she had decided to quit Charles once and for all and set off on her final pre-war visit to Germany recuperating with friends. Diana wrote to Felicité in the Tyrol on the eve of her departure: 'Saw Liza last night – had supper with her and we went to the flicks – she's looking very well now . . . and C. [Charles] has produced – in his usual way – a little black kitten from under the wheels of a tram . . . It's called Alexander and I think it makes her feel much less lonely ... C. you will be glad to know is definitely off. I think there is something new.'

Elizabeth and her family's repeated attempts to extricate her reveal that she was not as independent of Charles as she believed, and that his ability to reinstate himself with her was unnerving. Stella, now returned from Jamaica, summoned Doreen to her house. During their friendship Doreen recalls that she had 'got Elizabeth out of many fixes' but this time, despite feeling intimidated by Stella's haughty manner, when commanded to 'do something about Elizabeth and that most *unsuitable* man', she was obliged to reply 'Mrs Hamilton, there is *nothing* I can do.'

By August, when Elizabeth had returned from Germany, Diana wrote again to Felicité from the Benckendorffs' house in St John's Wood: 'I am rather worried about Eliza – she went off with Charles on his bally boat for the weekend – said definitely she was going to be back on Wednesday ... and now it's Thursday evening and she still isn't back. I hate her going out on that rickety boat. Mania [Constantine Benckendorff's wife] says the engine is permanently wrong.' Diana concludes by observing that Elizabeth 'seems very restless'. On another occasion Diana had said to Felicité that Elizabeth 'has taken Selma's flat instead of her own – and is now choosing the colours in which to have it done. I really think she's a bit mad – all this money spent on moving house every year – and immediately it's completed and made liveable in – moved out of.'

The same restlessness had taken Elizabeth on trips to the South of France with Doreen, once together with another friend, Diana Morgan (later Anderson). Their route usually took them down by the Blue Train to the South where they stayed in *pensions*, hotels or friends' houses. These were trips for sun-bathing, sea-bathing and assignations, with as much inebriation as their youthful constitutions would allow. Once they chanced on several of Diana Morgan's university friends (she had been up at Oxford) and the girls spent about a week in their company; during the day on the beach and in the evenings playing at casinos and dancing in clubs, or nude-bathing in the moonlight off secluded sandy beaches.

During the nineteenth century the South of France and Italy were normally visited in the winter, but after the First World War a complete volte-face occurred and it became fashionable to travel during the season of sun. The nineteenth century was obsessed with the implied wealth, privilege and 'refinement' of pale skin. Now, spurred on by a new generation of writers, such as E. M. Forster with *Passage to India* and D. H. Lawrence with *Lady Chatterley's Lover*, taking the power of the sun to incite and affect as one of their central themes, England succumbed to the heat. The notion that the sun made naturally hypocritical Englishmen and women from the cold North more passionate, sincere and true to their real, instinctive nature was always implied and often articulated. Typically, Evelyn Waugh reacted to the craze for sun-bathing and wrote an article hating it and entitled 'The Sun-bathing Business'. Friends like Peter Quennell up at Oxford had formed the Cicada Club, the sole purpose of which was for members to cook themselves on the beaches of the Riviera.

During the Twenties and Thirties the route to sun and South began at Victoria Station. Here, like Henry Green's South-bound *Party-Going* crowd, you boarded that magnificent Blue Train in the evening, enveloped yourself in its blue velvet upholstery, ate its exotic food – a tank full of writhing eels was exhibited in the dining car – bedded down in the luxurious cabins while the sleek blue and gold locomotive sped you, sleeping, or perhaps not, south to Marseilles, Toulon, Cannes, Nice, Monte Carlo and further afield. 'Sleep your way from the city's fogs to the Riviera Sunshine' ran the seductive advertising posters. The grey of London left behind, next morning you awoke 'to the sight of mimosa and orange trees . . . the red rocks of the Esterel on one side of the line, and the blue waters of the Mediterranean on the other', wrote Patrick Howarth. The Blue Train came to symbolize everything about holiday, freedom and frivolity. Diaghilev's *Le Train Bleu* enshrined it in a ballet with costumes by Coco Chanel and scenario by Jean Cocteau, Agatha Christie set a murder mystery on board, and any number of other writers used it in their fictions. This was the post-war world of international travellers for whom holidays that no longer proved attractive in remote places of stillness and quiet, were now being replaced by urban glamour and ritz.

Elizabeth's attention, however, could be diverted from physical pleasures and direct itself to literary ones with knowledge, feeling and conviction. Her confident intelligence and energy may have reinforced her tendencies to impatience and fits of boredom, but they also endowed her with a prodigiously accurate memory and an ability to leap nimbly from observation to judgement and thence to characterization. In strong contrast she was frequently complacent, incurious and insensitive to others. She suffered also from an unwillingness to analyse her own motives and avoided introspection; she was often hampered by a debilitating indecisiveness, aimlessness and lack of purpose.

In some ways Elizabeth now typified the non-political fast living of so many clever young Society people of the Twenties and Thirties. Nonetheless, after four years of living a life beyond her means and in busily pointless ease, this life-style was proving insufficiently rewarding and Elizabeth began to tire of the demands it incurred. She was no longer able to convince herself that success awaited her as an actress, nor had her joint efforts with Charles proved the written word any easier. Charles was also struggling. Writing later (1946) in another book, *The Voyage of the Evelyn Hope* (Cresset Press), he regretted the eclipse of theatre by the ascendancy of the cinema. He believed that: 'Nobody stays in the theatre if they are good enough for the film,' and continued with prophetic accuracy:

> Only a handful of stars stay in the theatre . . . It's the same story with the dramatists; make a list of the promising playwrights of the 1920s and . . . you'll see the names of most of them . . . on the subtitle of some film. Soon the theatre will exist only as some museum piece. The Old Vic will be turned into a national theatre for Shakespeare . . . Already the film has all the brain and all the blood. Five years ago I would have had enough enthusiasm to start all over again in a new medium. Five years more and I'll be content to scrape a living where I am, but at the moment, what I want to do is get out.

Since his youth Charles had been fascinated by boats. He not only loved their endless physical variety but was seduced by their power of suggestion: places far away, mysterious and unknown. And for several years before his meeting with Elizabeth he had owned a succession of small boats, teaching himself how to sail and maintain them. Elizabeth's own experience of sailing had given her too a love of being out on the water. There one experienced a sense of freedom. So, as Charles put it: 'We decided to leave England. We decided to buy another boat. We decided to go to the Mediterranean: Marseilles, Nice, Naples, Piraeus, and the Isles of Greece.' A lack of purpose was the simplest and strongest motive spurring Charles and Elizabeth's exodus. They had found an answer to their present malaise, escape. Just when war in Europe had become almost inevitable.

CHAPTER SIX

Beautiful Evelyn Hope

(1938–1939)

BETWEEN THE TWO world wars in Britain a shift of emphasis occurred in the collective artistic and intellectual sensibility. Where previously the Englishman who had gone abroad was often enamoured of what he saw on his travels, few were driven on return to denigrate their homeland. Since the 1920s, however, when for some travel had become almost a cult, dislike of home had become the prime incentive for many to travel abroad. This distaste for the homeland encompassed dissatisfaction with the political system (the Spanish Civil War of 1936 concentrated the minds of left-wing sympathizers), a perception of intellectual and artistic stagnation, and a general feeling that England was at best dismal, moribund, graceless and dull, and at worst mean, joyless, desolate and sordid. For many, such as Elizabeth, foreign travel also offered an escape from family censure about one's personal life-style.

The list of writers who fled the country is a long one and several, like Robert Graves, 'resolved never to make England ... home again'. D. H. Lawrence, Norman Douglas, W. H. Auden, Aldous Huxley and Lawrence Durrell intended not to return; Graham Greene too. Cyril Connolly spoke for many when he wrote that he was 'tired of England ... I do feel it is a dying civilization – going stuffy and comatose instead of collapsing beautifully like France'.

On the physical plane, these themes were reiterated when decrying the appallingness of English food, the puritanism of the drink laws and the hellishness of the weather. The cold and badly fed English were enticed abroad with images of ships and trains sailing and puffing their way into balmier sunsets. In *The Rock Pool* (Obelisk Press, 1936), Cyril Connolly talks of a 'scabby winter landscape that seemed to cover; a thin soup under a greasy tureen'. In *How About Europe?* (Secker and Warburg, 1930), Norman Douglas rants about the disgusting food, and in *Coming Up for Air* (Gollancz, 1939), Orwell has George Bowling say that when he found the frankfurter he ate was filled with fish 'it gave me the feeling that I'd bitten into the modern world and discovered what it was really made of . . . Rotten fish in a rubber skin.'

Despite criticisms like these and however much they may have been confused about other issues, Orwell and most other literate English travellers went armed with a sure sense of who they were: British. With few exceptions, notably D. H. Lawrence, Gerald Brenan and Charles Gibson Cowan, their privileged backgrounds had made them secure in their values and sense of implicit superiority. (A striking inconsistency is noticeable with these writers' denigration of their homeland.) This did not mean that these young travellers necessarily had much money, but abroad the Anglo-Saxon had the initiative and drive to make the most of journeys where one didn't really quite pass muster unless one had suffered discomfort and inconvenience. When seen in the context of contemporary attitudes such as these, Elizabeth and Charles's projected voyage falls squarely into place as a journey in accord with the zeitgeist.

After three months' searching, according to Charles they found a boat 'in a mud berth at Hamble [near Portsmouth on the river leading into the Solent and the sea] on a wet day. It cost just twice as much as we had decided to spend, and . . . needed extensive repairs, but it was what we were looking for. We stood in the mud, heedless of the rain, for the best part of an hour, and agreed that it was a ship . . .' They bought it. Elizabeth paid, and in the certainty of their disapproval refused ever to quite clarify this point for her family. 'We went back to London full of enthusiasm for the first time for months.' The ship was called the *Evelyn Hope* (undoubtedly a reference to Browning's poem about the young girl, 'Beautiful Evelyn Hope is Dead', and one whose significance would not have been lost on Charles and Elizabeth). On the third day of the New Year of 1939 Elizabeth wrote excitedly to Felicité that she had been down to see the boat, and that it would be very comfortable when finished. 'You will *have* to come . . . and stay on her sometime.'

Charles had worked for several weeks repairing the boat before he was one day appalled to discover dry rot hidden in the timbers. In desperation he called in a small firm of shipbuilders. 'They tried to pose as hard-bitten businessmen, but it was a sham; their sole interest was ships. They tore out planks with vicious enthusiasm and settled down to build me a new ship out of the remains.'

Months went by. Charles continued to work in the theatre as a producer and finally, just as work on the *Evelyn Hope* was nearing completion, Elizabeth was unexpectedly asked to play a very small part in a GPO film. She wouldn't be able to help with the boat until the beginning of July and planned to relinquish her flat altogether at the end of that month. With little apprehension of the magnitude of the journey she was about to embark upon Elizabeth commented that she was unable to afford the flat during her absence.

Whilst preparing to move out of John Street Elizabeth and Charles went 'on an orgy of spending' for the voyage. Elizabeth found bed and table linen, materials for mattress covers, curtains and cushions. She searched out a medicine chest and cheap china (to be replaced in France) in the Caledonian Market; Charles bought compasses, a camera, tinned food, tools; they spent a day in Woolworths. Whatever her living conditions, Elizabeth was not satisfied until she had not only made the place habitable, but had also stamped it with her own easy brand of elegance, usually involving significant expenditure. They found they had 'hopelessly overspent' and Elizabeth suggested paying guests. A girl was found. Elizabeth in her letters and Charles in his book always referred to her as 'the paying guest'. She wanted to make the journey as far as Marseilles and was willing to pay a cheque immediately for the full amount. With this new source of finance the rest of the ship's restoration and provisioning could proceed.

Elizabeth had enthusiastically given Felicité a profile of the little ship. Several years later, in 1946, Charles published an account of their journey as *The Voyage of the Evelyn Hope*, dedicated 'TO E. G. [Elizabeth Gwynne] WITH ALL MY LOVE'. In his telling of their remarkable story Charles carefully records his own description of the

Evelyn Hope. In combination Charles and Elizabeth's two accounts leave us with a vivid image of the little craft. Charles loved any excuse to 'talk ships', so he gave details of the Certificate of British Registry, including the information that it was 'built in 1906 . . . that the number of decks is one, of masts two: that it is carvel built, rigged as a yawl . . . and is described as a wood pleasure yacht.'

Elizabeth's description made it a 'black fishing boat-looking sort of craft, with a lot of teak and not too much brass; a small cockpit, a roomy saloon which, with a lot of alteration, could be made fit to live in; a cabin aft with washbasin, one single and one double bunk . . . a toilet that you could at least stand up in; a forecastle, which . . . would make a fairly decent galley; and an engine amidships which looked quite clean and seemed out of the way.' She told Felicité that much needed to be done.

Just into the New Year of 1939 Elizabeth is writing excitedly to Felicité from the 'Beautiful *Evelyn Hope*' then moored at Hamble. Her description of the boat and its enhancement is deftly conveyed in two sketches: one a bird's-eye plan from above and the other a profile. Typically she takes care with all details, showing her sister the exact position of bunks, washbasin, lavatory, bookshelves, cooking area and sink.

As the end of July approached, in the frenzy of last-minute activity Elizabeth had made a complete list of the things she was packing off to Pris for safe keeping. It amounted to a quantity of boxes, trunks and pieces of treasured furniture, rather more than she had described to her sister. In addition she appends instructions to hang up clothes and take out her precious silk paisley shawl. She gives Pris permission to use her lacquer tea chest if she would like to but then, in characteristically commanding tone, gives strict orders that on no account is anything ever to be stood on top of it; 'I never allowed people even to put their hats on it.' Priscilla's favours must stretch to Richard taking a 'filthy' carpet to be cleaned in Bristol (where he was then working for the BBC). The removers had sent inadequate help, so Elizabeth remonstrated with them and ordered more men. In the midst of this débâcle Diana and her new man, Christopher, arrived to see how events were progressing.

Elizabeth stayed just a few more days in London, finalizing

preparations before her departure. She told Pris that Diana Morgan had arranged quite a good impromptu leaving party, apropos of which Elizabeth revealed an inclination which was later to become notorious and established practice: the segregation of her friends. Despite her intention of being away from England for several months, she asked only the friends she had in common with Diana, saying that she really couldn't cope with more.

After the party they went with her sister Diana and Christopher to Smokey Joe's and didn't get home until five o'clock. Christopher was 'well away by the end of the evening, in fine form and refusing to go home.' Elizabeth thought he drove like a maniac but was still 'quite safe'. Marian was due to spend the weekend on the *Evelyn Hope* with Charles and Elizabeth before they set sail for France, but a severe hangover on the morning following the party put off the moment and they would leave instead at break of dawn the next day.

Charles described Elizabeth's arrival at Hamble in *The Voyage of the Evelyn Hope*, 'with half a dozen suitcases and a trunk-full of clothes, a small packing case and two kit bags full of books, two cases of assorted dried and tinned provisions, several parcels containing curtains, mattress covers and various oddments and armfuls of . . . cushions; the result of an extra week's shopping and the paying guest's cheque'.

Her propensity for collecting books was well established and Elizabeth would not submit to their ejection from the ship either by persuasion or argument, even when reminded that there were already about 400 on board and shelf space for only a third of that number. A place was found for them and they were stowed away. Charles gave a partial list of titles. It is long and tantalizing for what is omitted, and is clearly meant to impress the reader. Nevertheless it gives a remarkable impression of the breadth of Charles and Elizabeth's reading and implies that books are a requisite for (shipboard) life. There was no doubt in their minds that travelling was not an isolated event. A literate traveller had always set out with other men's (and women's) travels in mind. Undoubtedly then, some of the thrill was in transposing one's own present journey on to the experiences of other travellers, taking the same routes as those from the past.

The half-dozen desert island books had long ago been agreed

upon, according to Charles, 'in the order named as: *Pears Cyclopaedia* [years later Elizabeth's high opinion of Pears remained unaltered], a Shakespeare, the Bible, one or two Alice books, a Marlowe or a Milton, and either the *Decline and Fall* or Boswell's *Johnson*, for bulk'. With these as a nucleus Charles had added: 'the *Oxford Book of Verse*; the poems of Rupert Brooke; a Byron, since we were going to Greece; *Dead Souls*; *The Enormous Room*, *War Birds* and *Le Feu*; Crane's *Red Badge of Courage*; *Love and Mr Lewisham*, *Kipps*, *First Men in the Moon* and two or three more early Wells; a complete O. Henry; Hardy's *Jude*; Huxley's *Antic Hay*; Rabelais, and a couple of dozen, mostly Greek, dramas, a few Shaws and some Anatole France. I took most of the Penguins . . . a few Everyman and a Hoyle.'

Elizabeth's selection included '*The Seven Pillars*; Doughty's *Arabia Deserta*; the entire works of Conrad; Flecker's *Poems* and *Hassan*; the plays of Jonson and Ford . . . a second Marlowe (in case mine was not complete); a *Golden Treasury*; Mather's *Arabian Nights*; a Tchekov; the remaining works of Anatole France; the *Odyssey* and the *Iliad*; several Baedeckers; *Robinson Crusoe*; some of the Barchester novels (because neither of us had read Trollope), Percy's *Reliques*; *A Short History of England*; two C. E. Montagues [a writer to whom Elizabeth remained singularly attached]; two Mark Twains; three odd volumes of Hakluyt; and about a hundred paper covered thrillers, which she said could be thrown over the side as soon as they were read.'

With her final words of farewell to Pris written on 8 July 1939, Elizabeth had thanked her again for the handsome present of a camera and the loan of her binoculars. She promised her a postcard as soon as they were across the Channel, trusting that it would not prove a long ordeal. Set to leave England, Elizabeth was twenty-five and Charles had just turned thirty-five.

A couple of days later they were at last under way. The sun shone through the clouds and it was warm. Passing out of Southampton Water with the Isle of Wight to the leeward, they slipped out into the English Channel. Sitting along the bowsprit watching 'the stem cutting the sea', Charles mused over their final departure and the voyage to come, and was elated. By nightfall, with Elizabeth taking her turn at the tiller, the wind was freshening up and the ship began to make good headway. Charles sent Elizabeth and the 'paying guest' down below to sleep and kept watch for the rest of the night. By dawn they were in sight of the flashing Havre Lighthouse.

Anchored in the outer harbour they intended leaving the following day, but slept long and stayed on board until the evening when they went ashore and ate, appropriately, large soup bowls of *moules marinière*.

It rained the following day and they decided they would not be able to reach Paris for the Bastille Day celebrations so stayed on in Le Havre. Elizabeth wrote her promised postcard to Pris saying that all was well, and on the 15th they weighed anchor and set off down the Seine estuary bound for Paris. At Rouen ocean navigation ceases and the Seine river technically begins. They moored, the *douaniers* came on board and after a most cursory inspection handed them clearance to proceed. With the mast taken down and rolled they slowly manoeuvred the great river, sluggish and swirling by turn as they passed through the locks. It rained consistently for days and visibility was poor but the novelty of the undertaking was still enough to keep fretting at bay.

On reaching Paris they shopped and did some sight-seeing. Unlike Elizabeth, who knew it well, Charles had not seen Paris before and was dazzled. He wandered through streets and museums, then went with Elizabeth to the Louvre. They met friends and found that all the talk was of war, which later on Charles said he had been prophesying for years. The day before leaving Paris Elizabeth and Charles 'took [friends] for an evening on the river and everybody got drunk'.

In 1936 Germany had remilitarized the Rhineland; that same year the Spanish Civil War commenced and the Italians had invaded Abyssinia. With the Japanese, German and Italian axis developing apace, in February 1938 Hitler had assumed supreme command of the armed forces. By March he had occupied Vienna and declared Austria an annexe of the German Reich. By March 1939 Czechoslovakia was overrun by Germany. That month the fragmenting left and centrist forces in Spain finally succumbed to the Fascist rebels. It was a turbulent Europe, rapidly preparing for a gigantic orgy of self-destruction, through which Elizabeth and Charles now began to make their leisurely, escapist way.

Avoiding the great working Seine barges they proceeded along the river to Melun. It was cold and they spent half a day in a café playing a trivial game on a pinball machine. At Montereau they branched off the Seine along the Yonne to Sens where they passed a day drinking *vin gris* at Tonnere. They entered the Canal de Bourgogne and followed its 150-mile length with over 200 locks, all kept by women. These locks allow the canal to rise gradually until it passes under the summit of the Côte d'Or, the line of hills running south to Chalon-sur-Saône. Here, in this beautiful central part of Burgundy which has always been celebrated for the pleasures of its table, the food was hearty, the wine full-bodied to match and the travellers sampled both with gusto.

Dropping down the canal lock by lock they reached the great medieval city of Dijon, capital of the old dukedom of Burgundy, its splendour amply reflecting the magnificence of its rulers. Later Charles and Elizabeth would regret the brevity of the ten days spent en route through the rich and fertile surrounding land. Charles recalled that 'We wished we had lingered where once, even at seventeen hundred feet, we were among the clouds, where the red earth and dark forests of Burgundy were spread out below us, and where we sailed on top of the world.' At Dijon, revered as one of the greatest gastronomic centres of France, they ate at the city's famed Trois Faisans and Charles concluded that the meal 'came as a climax to ten days of the best food that France can produce'.

On 23 August the Soviet–German Non-Aggression Pact was signed. This sinister alliance at once launched the British government into preparations for war.

Along the river Saône at Lyon Charles and Elizabeth were irritated by French mechanics, bad weather and the 'paying guest'. Consequently they did not bother to see much of this ancient town, with its Roman ruins and cathedral. After Lyons the Saône joins the great swift-flowing Rhône and here they took on a pilot to help navigate them south. Passing Valence they went on through the valley of the Rhône past Montélimar and into one of the earliest settled areas of France: the Midi, Imperial Roman Provence.

Here were the immense broken arches of the Pont d'Avignon, still reaching half-way across the river. The beautiful city of Avignon was long home to the exiled poet Petrarch and still holds the vast palace refuge of the schismatic Popes, for a hundred years rival to the throne of St Peter. The *Evelyn Hope* continued past Montélimar; past Beaucaire, the castle standing precipitously above the river, where Aucassin and Nicolette played out their tragedy; past Tarascon and finally to ancient Arles lying at the head of the Rhône delta and at the entrance to the great river valley along which the Romans had advanced northward their domination and culture.

At Arles the voyagers ate in a restaurant where, Charles wrote, 'we obtained an excellent five course dinner with wine and coffee for five francs'. In this labyrinth of winding streets, the strangest of which is Les Alycamps, a straight 'miraculous' tree-edged avenue of marble tombs, they did little more than speed through the most famed sites. Even in a hurry these remain fabulous: the cathedral of St Trophime, a Romanesque beauty, one of the loveliest in Provence, and the Roman amphitheatre, comparable in size to the Colosseum. Elizabeth later told Felicité that she saw only the Roman remains and the cathedral, which she thought marvellous. They remained in Arles for only one day, and were 'hampered by the awful paying guest, who walked about in shorts and sea boots, and carried several bottles of wine in a net slung over her shoulder'.

They had by now navigated the 200 and more miles along the lower course of the Rhône valley from Lyons to the Mediterranean. The vegetation grew more Southern, grey-green and parched as they passed the tributary valleys, catching glimpses of the snow-clad Alps to the east and the lower volcanic hills to the west. The last stretch took them along the Great Rhône to the sea. Here the river's broad eastern delta forms the mysterious, shimmering salt marshlands and lagoons of the Carmargue; whose pastures nourish beef and fighting bulls for the arenas of the South, whose glistening waters harbour wild ducks, egret, ibis and flamingo. To the west lie the flatlands of Bouches-du-Rhône, bordered by Aix, once glorious, still beautiful; capital of Provence, site of a great university, seat of Count René and birthplace of Cézanne.

By early next morning the *Evelyn Hope* was once again out on the sea. As the little black yacht crossed the Golf de Foy from St Louis to Port de Bouc, Charles wrote, 'It was our first taste of the Mediterranean, and it wasn't blue, it was brown with the muddy waters of the Bouches-du-Rhône.' By the afternoon they had crossed the edge of the vast salt lagoon, the Etang de Berre, and passed Martigue, the thriving little fishing port so favoured by the Impressionists and still an artists' haunt. With fish-trap nets sinking to allow them passage, they left the Etang de Berre and entered the enormous, busy watery subterranean thoroughfare, the Tunel de Rove, final section of the Marseilles–Rhône Canal. Out of the lengthy cavern of muffled light, they passed Cap Janet and finally dropped anchor in the Vieux Port of Marseilles. One of the oldest and largest seaports of the Mediterranean, its influences and atmosphere are often as much Levantine as French. Arriving in Marseilles, the *Evelyn Hope* had completed the first leg of her journey to those distant 'Isles of Greece'.

Elizabeth and the 'paying guest' went ashore and gathered food at the bustling Italian market, piled high with an abundance of glistening Southern vegetables, while Charles sat on board and marvelled. He had never before been South, and was enchanted. The 'painted fishing boats, with stumpy masts leaning forward to support the yards of lateen sails came alongside to sell their loads of black mussels, purple sea urchins, blue crayfish and green and white oysters. I watched them until it became dark.' Nearby was the broad Canebière, with its strolling promenaders and little bars and restaurants, the urbane yet explosive life of the South.

As night fell and Elizabeth returned through the Italian quarter laden with food, all the city's lights were kept extinguished in accordance with the new directives and Charles wrote: 'The war scare had already overtaken us.' They ate that evening in a 'little Italian restaurant where in an open fire the chef turned strange vegetable pies with an immense baker's peel . . . and the embers filled the room with a steady red glow. We drank large quantities of Algerian wine.' At table in the Italian quarter of this sometimes garish, often squalid, but always exhilarating port; with its ancient tradition of learning and commerce amongst a melting-pot of races from the four quarters of the Mediterranean, the three travellers were indeed far from England and the concerns they hoped to have left behind.

CHAPTER SEVEN

By the Shores of the Mediterranean
(1939–1940)

AT DAWN ON 1 September Hitler attacked Poland and the mobilization of British forces was immediately ordered by the Prime Minister. Charles heard the news from a crowd as he admired the streets of Marseilles. He made his way back to Elizabeth and the 'paying guest'. Although not a surprise the actuality of war stunned them and for a short time Charles and Elizabeth were uncertain about what to do.

The 'paying guest' rapidly decided to return to England; they helped her pack and saw her off at the station. On 2 September Elizabeth sat down and wrote to Pris in Chipping Sodbury, telling her that the Germans had marched into Danzig and bombed Warsaw. She was doing her best to remain calm, and to make arrangements; as far as she and Charles were concerned, everything depended on whether Italy came into the war – in that case they would go somewhere inland immediately. Meanwhile Chamberlain was making last-minute efforts to preserve peace.

In need of repair the *Evelyn Hope* was now in dry dock at the Bassin de Carenge. When finished it would be in a condition fit to be left in the water for some time. Charles and Elizabeth had intended sailing to Spain in order to leave the boat in a neutral country, but this was now doubtful. Elizabeth felt that 'not a soul' in France was anxious for war, any more than in England, and that there was very little anti-German feeling. She told Pris to write to her at Cook's, 'as if I left here it would probably be in a hurry and I wouldn't know exactly where'. Letters would probably take a long time to arrive, so Pris should not be alarmed if she didn't hear from them. Elizabeth said she had a small suitcase already packed enabling her to leave at a moment's notice. The reason she gave for not returning immediately was that she hoped things might become more settled. On 3 September Chamberlain broadcast to the nation and said that Britain was at war with Germany. There was no longer any question of anything being 'settled'.

Elizabeth said to Pris that Charles had not tried to keep her there, but that she felt the boat was now in some sense her home, and that she wasn't inclined to leave Charles alone 'to deal with everything'. She wanted to see things resolved, and their belongings taken ashore before leaving France. A Danish ship's chandler would store their possessions and look after the boat. Meanwhile Elizabeth told Pris that if she needed any help Marian was a reliable person in 'times of stress' and would be at Melrose Place in Kendal where she was going to join her family.

By early October, after the initial uproar caused by the declaration of war, Poland's fall and France's entrance into hostilities, life in the South settled down into an edgy normality. Charles and Elizabeth swam in the dirty waters of the Vieux Port and fished for the little bony things ideal as practise for *bouillabaisse*. Elizabeth wrote back to England saying that she was unable to return as companion to Stella because for the moment she couldn't afford it. (Having returned from Jamaica in the late 1930s, Stella had bought the Old Grammar School in Dedham, near Cedric Morris and Lett Haines, and here launched herself into the antiques trade with considerable success.) With the family's income growing smaller each year Elizabeth said she was desperately trying to pay off her debts. She did intend to 'come back sometime', but refused to tie herself down to a particular date. Elizabeth was hedging here; she had little intention of coming back 'for the duration' and gave her habitual answer to requests for obligation: 'I don't want to tie myself down.' Escaping the ordered round of stability and structure as Romance does, with Charles Elizabeth had worked hard to achieve it, at least for a time. And she was not about to abandon it because of the small matter of the declaration of a world war.

She grew to know Marseilles and its environs well, sometimes shopping for the pretty Provençal prints – she sent some home for

Pris, about to give birth to her first baby, and her other sisters – and chafing at 'the unspeakable monotony' of staying in one place for so long. Elizabeth's friend Doreen had gone to live in Rome with her new husband in 1938. He was working there for a tourist firm, but at the outbreak of war they had returned to England. Her husband now had a commission in the Navy and Doreen was 'sitting at home again with her family right back where she started' whilst Pris had lost Richard back to service in the Royal Engineers.

Charles and Elizabeth were suddenly given permission by the authorities to move the ship out of Marseilles and spent a number of days sampling the beauties of the coastline between Cassis and Hyères. November came and the impending treacherous mistral 'spelt certain disaster to a yacht'. They decided, without permission from the authorities, to make for Antibes where Elizabeth had friends and they could remain for the winter in the sheltered harbour. The journey was not a long one but the nervousness of French officials, and the information that ships would be fired upon if they sailed at night, involved making short hops along this wild and lovely coastline. They stayed for a week at St Raphaël while Elizabeth made excursions into St Tropez to see friends and shop for pieces of the brightly coloured local pottery to replace their Woolworths china. As she later wrote for *The Times*, 'The charm of St Tropez is apparently indestructible.' The mistral, combined with the war, was beginning to hold them up, but finally Mike Cumberlege was there waiting on the quay as they sailed into the port of Antibes.

Elizabeth knew Mike and his wife Nan well. She had met them while holidaying on Malta with Pris and Richard. Mike wore an earring, was cheerfully high-spirited, the less conventional member of a distinguished naval family – his father was an admiral – and could not keep away from ships. His grandfather kept a house near Antibes, where Mike and Nan were presently staying; Mike was captain of a 60-ton yacht, the *Landfall*, left at Venice at the outbreak of war. He had little to do and spent time on board the *Evelyn Hope* giving Charles tips and new ideas about boats. He was a member of the RNVR and hoped to be called up for the volunteer services' spying missions around the Mediterranean, part-organized by his and the Gwynne's mutual friend, Henry Denham.

Pris's baby arrived on 10 November and Elizabeth described her name, Sabrina, as 'most beautiful'. She supposed Pris had been reading Milton's *Comus* and then – in case she hadn't – tells the story. Here for a brief moment Elizabeth evokes a feeling of contemplation and ease, so rare in all her letters. 'As you know ... Sabrina was the nymph of the Severn, and as she was born in Bristol it's most appropriate. The Spirit in Comus sings the most exquisite song to Sabrina, summoning her from the cool translucent waves to come and save the lady who is under the spell of the wicked Comus. It's the most lovely bit in *Comus* which is one of my absolute favourite poems.'

Mike and Nan saw much of Elizabeth and Charles, introducing them to friends. This was the Riviera, the Côte d'Azur, where until late each year the skies remained intensely and cloudlessly blue, where a luxurious vegetation threw up flowers sometimes gaudy in their brilliance in gardens surrounding terracotta-roofed and white-walled towns, and luxury villas overlooking a sea almost always warm. Since Lord Brougham popularized the Riviera in the nineteenth century, famed or notorious as the pleasure-ground of the rich, one came to see and be seen, a refuge from stern northern winters; the resorts of Hyères, St Raphaël, Cannes, Antibes, Nice, Menton and more. The Riviera is bordered by the Alps: the Maritimes to the east rise at points to almost 7000 feet, snowy and magnificent; Provence to the west, sometimes parched grey-green and arid, was the land where olives, wine and garlic had been transformed over 2000 years into some of the best food in the world. Socializing was hectic and very bibulous.

In November there was talk of Mike and Charles making the journey by train to Venice and sailing back on Mike's boat. Elizabeth would spend the time while they were away on shore with Nan. Although Mike's changeability made the venture seem unlikely, the men had set off before the end of December. They were not well suited. Charles was assertively pacifist, a conscientious objector, whereas Mike, whatever his surface self-presentation, was essentially patriotic. Later in the war he was to distinguish himself in more than one episode of bravery and heroic endurance. Their differences of political opinion quickly emerged and the rest of the journey was not particularly amicable. Charles, nonetheless, did acknowledge his envy and admiration for Cumberlege's seamanship when he masterfully sailed the retrieved yacht back to Antibes.

The tension between these two was typical of Charles's relations with the men of Elizabeth's milieu. They belonged to the ruling class, whereas Charles was an outsider. They were the beneficiaries of the present system and, for most of them, when it came to the test patriotism was both instinctive and reasonable. For Charles it was neither. He had nothing to be grateful for, no reason for loyalty. He had been sneered at and maltreated too many times in his formative years to offer England that. On balance Charles's attitude proved more his loss than gain. It provided him with limitations, and his life would have proved happier if he had been able to transcend some of his resentments. He had educated himself to move among more privileged classes than his own, but in general the men he met there did not have the largeness of vision and imagination to reach out to him. He was always on the fringe, his presence tolerated, not welcomed.

Elizabeth was a rebel, not an outsider. She sometimes felt misplaced, but she was not a misfit like Charles. The problems of feeling oneself either misplaced or a misfit seem naturally to suggest the life of a nomad, a wanderer; a form of escape the response. Before they met Charles and Elizabeth had both done their share of restless wandering and were now at one in their plan of escape to the Isles of Greece. Their difficulty in living together was a social difficulty. They were united in their love of literature; they felt no incompatibility of sensibility, the incompatibility lay in social style and expectations. Charles's social malaise was effectively curable, whereas Elizabeth's was not social at all. Charles had spent years at the rump of society, unsure where the next meal was coming from, or where he would sleep that night. Elizabeth was Anglo-Saxon (still, in the 1930s, the world's dominant race) and at the upper end of the social scale. However much she went in for slumming she always assumed that in times of trouble she would be rescued. And frequently she was.

In some fashion Elizabeth was aware of this. Charles records her words as follows:

'Always live on a ship. Never wear anything but a blue jersey and an old pair of flannel trousers. Never wash the salt out of your hair.'

'Why?'

'Then perhaps I shall stay in love with you.'

In confining him to shipboard she was telling him that their liaison could only hold in a context outside the everyday, away from land – outside time.

While the two men were away Nan and Elizabeth had spent Christmas together and Elizabeth told Felicité that she hadn't had time for anything except drinking or sleeping. In fact, she hadn't been sober for ten days. If she thought she could get back, she would go home for a month or two, but knew she couldn't face England for the duration. 'God knows it's bloody enough here and I feel pretty well suicidal, but I should hate to cause the family the caper of a funeral in unconsecrated ground.' They had a party on New Year's Eve, 'which was quite fun, except that nothing now is fun', and she had to get drunk to find anything at all amusing.

The busy aimlessness of this socializing was interspersed with news of friends and their activities as the war progressed. Many from Malta had joined up or been promoted and Elizabeth wrote to Pris that she couldn't imagine Mike Edwards as a Major. What amused her more than anything else was 'old Hiles' joining a unit of the Rifle Brigade. 'Trust Hilary to get himself into good company.' (Hilary Magnus was a family friend.) The Gwynne girls' cousin Quintin Hogg, a close friend of Hilary's, was also in the Brigade and Elizabeth thought him less suitably placed there.

Leonard Watkins had offered his services to the army but had not yet been called upon; meanwhile his brother Arthur was an ARP warden in Eastbourne. He had already practically killed a man by suffocation during a bandage test and set light to himself in the process of extinguishing a fire in a shed. He told Elizabeth that Stanford Holme was a fireman in Oxford. 'After these two pieces of information nobody can say that the local authorities are devoid of a sense of humour.'

Mike Cumberlege had finally been called up and was now, Elizabeth wrote, second in command of the 'English Contraband doings at Marseilles'. He had in fact taken up spying for them:

'quietly seeking information on Italian defences in the Mediterranean', as Henry Denham later wrote in his book *Inside the Nazi Ring* (John Murray, 1981). Elizabeth said, 'He is a lucky devil.' Although she was annoyed at the nonchalance with which Mike seemed always to fall on his feet, she had the good grace to add that he did work damned hard on board the *Landfall* when he was there.

Early in the spring of 1940, when Elizabeth and Charles had been in Antibes for several months, Elizabeth enthusiastically wrote home of meetings with a new friend, Norman Douglas, under whose spell she had recently fallen. Douglas's erudite travel-novel-writing of books such as *Siren Land*, *Old Calabria*, *South Wind* (with their remarkable disquisitions and diatribes on food) had by this time achieved cult status with the travelled Englishman. Elizabeth was enthralled.

She introduced Norman and Charles, who recorded an evening spent together at the kind of place Douglas thrived in – a 'dirty' Italian restaurant. Norman was his inimitable self: gracious, his fine manners concealing a well-developed arrogance; witty, pragmatic, learned, following his gruff habit of *ex cathedra* utterances with: 'It stands to reason', a favourite justification, then forestalling further argument with, 'Take or leave it.' In *The Voyage of the Evelyn Hope* Charles captures something of the Douglas style, but his account is noticeably less adulatory than Elizabeth's. Unsurprisingly, there appears to have been a mutual wariness and Douglas was ultimately disapproving of him. Any negative response Charles might in turn have had to Douglas was not going to deter Elizabeth, who told Felicité that she very much enjoyed the time she spent with the spry 72-year-old. She described him as full of fun and wit, not 'caring a hang' for anyone or anything. He had taken her up to some of the little towns and villages in the hills, and utterly charmed her. Elizabeth had read only two of his books, one of which, *South Wind*, she hadn't liked; she asked him to lend her some more, and managed to borrow one. It seemed to Elizabeth that he knew Europe 'from end to end', and almost everyone in it as well. Two years later, again writing to Felicité about Douglas, she said that she regretted ever having left him all alone in the South of France – she would have been quite happy to have stayed with him. He was such good company that hearing about places and things from him was as good as seeing them with one's own eyes.

The burgeoning friendship between this unlikely pair grew into a relationship which was to affect Elizabeth profoundly, maintaining its influence upon her long after Douglas's death on Capri in 1952. Although she didn't recognize until much later quite how momentous the occasion of her meeting with him was, at the time she certainly felt mentally revived and inspired by Douglas's company, and now sought it out whenever possible.

Elizabeth was relatively familiar with the Riviera from those pre-war holidays, and the novelty of this visit for her had been as much about living there, and on a boat. After six months, however, she was exhausted and made restless by inactivity and the lightweight nature of most of those with whom she socialized. Her friendship with the Cumberleges, on whom she had been so dependent, was becoming strained too. Writing to Priscilla, she complained that Nan Cumberlege and her sister Nora were clothes snobs, and jealous of her because she had clothes from Worth and Maggy Rouff. They indignantly asked why she wasted money on them, and she felt her own indignant and justified reply might well have been to ask why they wasted their money drinking champagne all day in the most expensive bar on the coast. Elizabeth also complained that Nan had changed: 'always arrived late for dinner'. Despite her criticisms Elizabeth did add that Nan had been kind to her and that Priscilla must not breathe a word of these indiscretions to anyone.

She maintained that although the English community on the Riviera was 'peculiar anyhow', the worries engendered by the war and too much leisure are 'now making people odd'. This was the recognizable frustration of living in a provincial, albeit sophisticated, goldfish-bowl expatriate society and, accustomed to a larger stage, she recounted the minutiae with a sharp but weary eye. She told Pris that 'the gossip is something staggering here. Malta was *nothing* to it. One never has to tell anybody where you've been the day before because they always tell you *first* and if you forget what day someone has invited you out you've only to ask the first person you meet in the town and they'll be able to inform you.' She did not care what the gossips would try and invent about herself and Douglas. 'Probably that I'm his illegitimate daughter, or that we sacrifice goats up on the hills – anything for a story.'

When Elizabeth met Douglas in Antibes early in 1940 he was living in rented rooms with little money, but enduring an enforced exile from Florence with the famous Douglas equanimity, bite and humour intact. He had spent many years living in Florence, maintaining friendships with most of the remarkable group of expatriate English who lived in and around the city. Atypically for these self-imposed exiles, Douglas also befriended Italians. A number of these had always been young boys, for whom his predilection had necessitated his flight from England to Italy in 1917. In 1937, however, Douglas was again in trouble, this time for his alleged affair with a little girl. After seducing two brothers he had in fact bought their little sister a new set of clothes. When questioned as to their origin she revealed her patron, and Douglas was immediately ordered to leave Italy.

In Norman Douglas Elizabeth found a man of great charisma and charm who, at the age of seventy-two, was fascinating to her without representing any threat of sexual predatoriness. (Always attractive to women and retaining many as friends, Douglas no longer had physical relationships with them after the age of about fifty.) The writer Sybille Bedford, who later became a close friend of Elizabeth's, had also fallen under the Douglas spell before the war and describes him as 'very masculine, very attractive . . . robust, but so gracious'. Intelligent and sensitive women were often drawn to Douglas, responding to his robust humour, his quirky, wayward, yet ultimately scholarly methods, and beguiling way of dealing out his vast knowledge to those younger and less informed than himself.

Elizabeth's relationships more often than not involved something close to exploitation, indeed her friend Doreen Thornton says, 'Oh, she always had slaves.' She wasn't often inclined towards anything in between, unless the other party stood up to her, and then Elizabeth frequently came off best. Usually charming about it, and often grateful, she nevertheless took it as her due to accept favours rather than dispense them. In like manner she inflicted more pain than she received, and if she recognized her will to make others subservient to her she chose not to comment on it. In her relationship with Douglas for once there was no doubt who was master. To Elizabeth, Douglas clearly represented something of the father lost in childhood. She had found a kind of soul-mate. His effect on her was complex; most significantly she was inspired, fascinated by his erudition and manner of presentation, and touched and flattered that so distinguished an author should find her acceptable company.

In cast of mind they were very compatible. They both respected, even worshipped the Fact — what *is*. It was a respect for what is simply *because* it is. This was a matter of temperament even more than doctrine, of unconscious presupposition rather than explicit theory. In Europe seen as peculiarly British, this is given the name of empiricism. The predominance of this temperament would seem to account for the enduring talent of the people of these islands for natural science, engineering and the useful arts. Writings about Douglas usually claim that he was a scientist as well as a travel writer and novelist. This is misleading, for he was a natural historian, not a natural scientist. Like Elizabeth he had little feeling for the abstract, for explanation, for the poetry of analysis; was perhaps even contemptuous of such things. And in this lies the key to both his strengths and his weaknesses.

Regardless of being separated in age by almost half a century, the common elements in Elizabeth and Norman's lives helped to bind them in an unlikely friendship. Both were familiar with Austria and Germany (Douglas grew up in Austria and was one-quarter German, three-quarters Scottish, but German was his first language). They were social equals; each a part of that vast, intricate web of social and family ties which extended amongst the European upper classes, making it rare for one to meet a person to whom one was not either related, however distantly, or who at least knew someone who knew someone whom one knew oneself. Both Elizabeth and Douglas had reacted against their backgrounds, yet had a strong sense of social order; both were at heart diffident, but were also robustly individual and capable of ruthlessness and arrogance.

There is no doubt that Douglas — older, more experienced, learned without being in the least academic — was better able than

Elizabeth herself to articulate what she was fumbling towards in her journey South away from England.

The educated British resonated to the cities, the ruins, the landscape; to the golden light and warmth of the South. It was all so familiar from history, literature and art. This was the classical world, the root of their civilization. Once South they were emancipated from the web of Northern constraints. More than one such visitor wrote that on his first visit to the Mediterranean it was all so familiar it was as if he had arrived home. Here, where man was seemingly more practised at harnessing and living in harmony with his surroundings than in any other part of Europe, the traveller was able to reconnect with what Norman Douglas called those '. . . elemental and permanent things . . . Casting off outworn weeds of thought they escaped to a world . . . removed from the wilderness of our ever-changing circumstances.' In *Siren Land* Douglas says, 'Many of us would do well to *mediterraneanize* ourselves for a season, to quicken those ethnic roots from which has sprung so much of what is best in our natures.'

Douglas's was a complex and refined aesthetic hedonism, based on a deeply felt antipathy to what he had experienced as Christianity, and for which he substituted, with a real knowledge of the classical world, his own form of morality – some would call it amorality. His escape into exile from Northern Europe and his rejection of much of what it represented, had not landed him by accident in the region which lay close to the centre of the ancient Greco-Roman world. His mode was nearer to a modern Hellenism than to anything from further north. The first people to become intoxicated with ideas, the Hellenes set out to examine how we learn and to develop the concept of suspended judgement. If the Mediterranean had been no more than the region of empirical and temperate hedonism which Norman Douglas portrays, it would never have served as the origin, the focus, of what has become the nearest to a world-culture that mankind has ever developed.

Without being as yet aware of it, Elizabeth had within her a similar strain of anti-Christianity to Douglas's and warmed to the hedonistic spirit of the Mediterranean. (As well as the better qualities she was also to demonstrate some of the worse ones characteristic of the pagan mentality – most notably in her unwillingness to forgive.) In her erratic way she had tried to throw off 'outworn modes of thought' without sacrificing her deep feeling for truth. Here also Douglas was the right model for her, with his precise observation, empirical exactitude, his knowledge of literature and capacity for accurate scholarship. With minor differences they were at one, both in how they set about it, and to where they had chosen to escape. Underlying all this was the consistent theme of escape which permeated both Elizabeth's and Douglas's vision.

For centuries the South had enticed and beckoned educated Englishmen, so much so that Dr Johnson could write: 'The grand object of travelling is to see the shores of the Mediterranean.' They had gone in the Middle Ages as pilgrims to holy sites, later in search of education, health, and finally in the eighteenth and nineteenth centuries as 'aesthetic escapists'. With the growth of the railways and the middle classes, the nineteenth century saw the Grand Tourism of the seventeenth and eighteenth centuries gradually eclipsed by mass tourism and the eager customers of Thomas Cook.

It is hard to find a Victorian poet, painter, novelist, philosopher or historian who didn't make the pilgrimage South at least once. So much had been written on Egypt, the Levant and the Mediterranean by the end of the century that some thought there was nothing left to say. By 1845 the traveller and collector Robert Curzon was already complaining that, for example, 'The public were overwhelmed by little volumes about palm trees and camels and reflections on the Pyramids.' But the allure of the South did not diminish with familiarity, nor did the voracious appetite for literature feeding every aspect of this allure. Apart from the great travellers of earlier centuries, during the nineteenth century and into this one there was a host of literary figures: Thackeray, Robert Louis Stevenson, Dickens, Henry James, George Eliot, the Trollopes, Samuel Butler, Gissing, Belloc, Ford Madox Ford, Forster, Lawrence, Osbert Sitwell, Robert Byron, Patrick Kinross, Cyril Connolly, Lawrence Durrell, Patrick Leigh Fermor . . . and the list continues.

Returning to Elizabeth and Charles, relations between them had become strained since before Christmas. By now Elizabeth was spending time away from Charles and the *Evelyn Hope*, either with friends such as Norman and the Cumberleges, or helping a rich American, Stanley, in a soup kitchen he had set up for the local poor. This he had recently enlarged by the costly addition of a huge dining hall panelled in oak, and one senses Charles's ultimate isolation from Elizabeth and her privileged friends when he succinctly conveys his scorn at the rich man's 'war effort'. He notes that the interior of Stanley's hall now has 'refectory tables, Jacobean chairs, and an assortment of china and cutlery which would have frightened away the poor had they not been too hungry to notice'.

Elizabeth wrote to Priscilla in early January of her work in the soup kitchen and said there were a great many very poor people there, mostly Italians with huge families. If a family had a soldier home on leave they would be given extra food. She described how galling it was for the soldiers to come back from the trenches to be fed by charity. It is worth noting that Douglas, like Charles, would have been contemptuous of these efforts. Helpful and generous to friends and individuals in need, he had no time for organized welfare, for charity in the abstract, or away from home.

Into the New Year of 1940, and on the same theme of wartime deprivations, Elizabeth wondered what Pris's staple food now was – she supposed it to be bread and cheese without butter, and potatoes. In these enforced months on the Riviera she had now spent many hours wandering the markets on her own. More recently she had luxuriated in the company of Douglas, whose knowledge on the foods and traditions of the region was boundless. In spite of feeling some guilt, in her letters Elizabeth cannot hide an unceasing delight in the sumptuous variety and quality of produce available on this paradisia-cal coastline. Back in September she had already remarked to Priscilla on how impossible it was to believe in the war there, under sunshine and blue skies, and with piles of brilliant fruit, rainbow fish and straw-covered wine jugs in the markets. To Elizabeth on the Riviera, the whole idea of the war was like a Hollywood extravaganza by Cecil B. de Mille.

A few months later the list of foods Elizabeth recites to Priscilla is striking in the variety still obtainable compared with the sparsity in rationed Britain. She found meat and butter expensive but said that cheese was cheap and of a great variety. Vegetables cost little, and salads — lettuce, endives, etc. — were never more than about 1½d. There were ravioli, gnocchi, and ready-prepared foods, all of which were inexpensive. She and Charles existed mainly on stews, because they could be cooked on the coal stove that heated the cabin — a more effective way of cooking that also saved paraffin. Elizabeth recommended to Pris 'a very good dish' that she found in a French cookery book; cheap and nourishing, the recipe was later quoted with minimal alteration in *Mediterranean Food*:

> 1 lb liver (calves', or pigs' or ox, I use ox because it's the
> cheapest and quite as good done this way)
> 1½–2 lbs of carrots
> 4 onions
> about ½ pint of Espagnole Sauce

Cut the liver in the usual long slices, salt and pepper then wrap them up in the caul (like Angela used to do for beef loaf, or greaseproof paper I think would do), and fry lightly in margarine with the onions cut up. When they are golden take them out of the pan and make an Espagnole sauce (see recipe below).

Put the sauce through the sieve, put it in a big casserole, bring it to the boil; put in the liver wrapped up, the onions, and the carrots peeled and cut into rounds. Put in the herbs, salt, etc. and cook in a very slow oven or over a very low flame for about 2½ hours. When it's done take the liver out of its bag and serve it in the same dish.

*Espagnole Sauce   In the butter and gravy which is in the pan from frying the liver and onions, put some more butter (margarine I mean), add 1 teaspoon of flour, let it fry for a minute or two till it goes brown, add 1 small chopped onion and one small chopped carrot, let it fry two minutes more, add about ½ pint of stock if you have it, otherwise a cube of Bovril or Oxo melted in water (which is what I always use). Let it cook slowly for about 5 minutes adding salt, pepper, thyme, bayleaf, and water if it gets too thick, then stir in about a tablespoon of tomato pureé (Heinz Tomato Soup or ketchup would do) and when it's cooked about 3 more minutes strain it, put it into the casserole in which you're going to cook the liver.

Actually this is an excessively simple dish to make and is excellent . . .

The Espagnole Sauce should be a good dark brown, so I always put in some gravy salt, which is dark brown and colours it – I expect Connie [Priscilla's cook] uses it. In the ordinary way you have to cook Espagnole Sauce for about 30 or 40 minutes very slowly, then put in the tomato and put it through the strainer. I find it very handy for all kinds of things, and it's quite good with spaghetti as a change, or you can put in some blanched pieces of orange peel and orange juice with a little red currant jelly and it makes an orange sauce which is very good with escalope de veau or with chicken, duck, etc.

Another thing we have quite often is dried haricot beans soaked and then stewed with small pieces of gammon (what they call bacon here) and a few sausages. Of course you can't get smoked sausages in England except at a vast price . . . If you add a spoonful of ginger to the beans it improves its taste enormously. [And here she makes a comment which in the future would become a dictum.] The secret of all these things is to cook them dead slow. You could put them at the side of the fire and let them cook for hours – the less they boil the better . . . What makes even boring food like spaghetti eatable here is that there's such a variety of things to make sauces with – olives are very cheap, so are mushrooms, you can even buy a little tin of truffles for 6d. and of course you can always put wine into anything without being extravagant . . .

Elizabeth described the variety of fish and said a sort of Pilaff with mussels, pimentos and other shell fish made a wonderful dish. She complained that the coffee shortage was a great blow, the tea disgusting, and the olive oil exorbitantly priced, which was hard on the people there, as they cooked everything in oil.

This remarkable letter illuminates Elizabeth's present level of knowledge and working practices. Despite the recommendation of 'Oxo cubes melted in water . . . and Heinz Tomato Soup or ketchup', a change has taken place since those first tentative days at the stove in Regent's Park Road. The recipe may initially have been culled from a book, but more importantly it is the annotations and instructions to her sister which reflect her growing knowledge and confidence.

Apparently this was not Elizabeth's first offer of culinary advice. Quite recently a little manuscript book in her hand was offered up for sale. While sharing the flat with Marian Butterworth in London, Elizabeth had written out a selection of recipes, for interest and use, as a present for her friend. In an attached note of authentication (1979) Elizabeth said that she had them from several sources, all but a few of which she could remember. Some came from the inspirational Angela, Pris's cheerful Maltese cook who had given Elizabeth those first instructions in cooking; next there was the Countess Morphy's *Recipes of All Nations*, Elizabeth's trophy from Selfridges; then others were from *Farmhouse Fare* (a little book she recommended forty years on in a list of favourite cookery books) and finally, some from Mrs Leyel's *Gentle Art*.

These four books mentioned in her choice of recipes for Marian remained well used and were among those she took with her on board the *Evelyn Hope*. We are fortunate in knowing that these made up the core of her little shipboard collection, because they and several others were subsequently lost. Elizabeth later wrote in consternation asking Pris to find duplicates for her.

I'm terribly sorry to bother you with such details at such a time but one has to live all the same . . . All my cookery books are of course lost, including the ones I collected myself. Now could you ask Dillon or someone to order me the following, I will tell the bank to pay her bill [she refers here to Miss Dillon in the early days of the bookshop], and ask her to send them to you, to keep them for me until I come home or until after the war – I think it better to get them now because after the war these things might be out of print . . .

| *The Recipes of All Nations* | (can only get at Selfridges) |
| *The Finer Cooking* | Marcel Boulestin |

The Gentle Art of Cookery	Phoenix Library
The Farmhouse Cookery Book	(Published by the *Farmer's Weekly* I believe)
Good Savouries	Ambrose Heath
100 *Ways of Cooking Eggs*	Adair and Boulestin
Hors d'oeuvres and Savouries	Boulestin
French Wines	Paul de Caragnae . . . ?
The Epicure's Companion	Edward Bunyard, Dent

Albeit a brief list, we can glean a fair idea of where her interests lay: with the likes of Boulestin. She was instinctively drawn to his crusade for fresh, subtle and simple food. What she later described in an article on him for the *Wine and Food* quarterly in 1965 as: 'Boulestin's intelligence, sense and taste' and 'that feeling for authenticity which alone is true luxury'. Along with Marcelle Morphy and Hilda Leyel, Marcel Boulestin's delightful and approachable books do not stress the accuracy of quantities or the detail of instructions, but Elizabeth was already feeling confident (or as she later said, ignorant) enough to forgo the dry detail of more technical works in favour of inspiration and character. (Not that Elizabeth despises accuracy or detail – quite otherwise – but she expects her readers to be attuned to these necessities, and wants to avoid the dampening of individuality and the constraint attendant on over-specification.)

Although under straitened circumstances Elizabeth had by now ample time and opportunity to sample the foods of the South. As anyone will know who has experienced them, it is the markets of the South which first enthral. Most extravagantly in the vast arenas of Marseilles, Nice or Naples, but any smaller town has its own and striking version. Here, with the animated bustling backdrop of clatter and chatter Elizabeth had been enticed by the careless profusion of vegetables, many almost unheard of in England. She had marvelled at the glowing purples, pinks, scarlet reds, acid yellows of apricots and peaches, colours of the same intensity as the unfailing sun under which they flourished alongside myriad lettucy greens. The market air was heady with the musky, ripe scent from great bunches of glistening basil, silvery-grey wild thyme, marjoram and rosemary, brought down from the parched grey-green olive mountainsides.

Matthew White (1842–1904),
5th Baronet and 1st Viscount Ridley,
Stella's father

Mary Georgina (Polly), d. 1899,
Viscountess Ridley, Stella's mother.

Blagdon Hall in Northumberland, Stella's birthplace. The lake was designed by
the celebrated architect Edwin Lutyens. His daughter Ursula married the
3rd Viscount, Elizabeth David's cousin.

Wootton Manor, Elizabeth's childhood home. Detmar Blow's library and kitchen wing are to the right, the ballroom to the left.

A meet at Folkington Manor where Rupert grew up. Stella is far left, beside her stands the architect Detmar Blow. Centre left are Dorothy (Rupert's sister) and Grace (Stella's sister). Far right is Rupert.

Rupert's parents May and James (Stick) Gwynne shortly after their marriage in 1862.

James Gwynne in old age.

The Hon. Stella Gwynne (1884–1973), Elizabeth's mother.

Rupert Sackville Gwynne (1873–1924), Elizabeth's father.

Pre-election Gwynne family photograph, 1923.
Rupert was to live only a year longer. Back: Priscilla and Rupert.
Front (left to right): Felicité, Stella, Elizabeth and Diana.

The four Gwynne sisters at Wootton c. 1923–4.
Left to right: Priscilla, Diana, Felicité and Elizabeth.

In the garden at Wootton, *c.*1923–4.
Back (left to right): Elizabeth and
family friends.
Front (left to right): Felicité and Diana.

A rare photograph of Elizabeth (left)
caught smiling for the camera.
With Priscilla (centre) and
Stella at Wootton, *c.*1930.

At Wootton in 1931. Back (left to right): a friend of Stella's, Priscilla, Stella,
Felicité. Front (left to right): the Gwynne girls' cousin, Neil Hogg, and Diana.

Doreen Thornton, Elizabeth's spirited friend from Regent's Park Theatre days, in the 1940s.

Richard Longland and Priscilla at Guadamangia, their house on Malta where Elizabeth spent several idyllic holidays in the mid-1930s.

Elizabeth said of this blouse in which she posed for the society photographer
Dorothy Wilding: 'It looks terribly nice with my black suit and the maid (the only
person who has gazed upon my beauty today) said, "It looks sweetly pretty."'

Above: Charles Gibson Cowan,
the pacifist with whom Elizabeth
escaped England.

Above right: Felicité, Elizabeth's
youngest sister, at about seventeen.
They were to share a house for over
thirty years.

Right: The writer Norman Douglas
at Capri in 1951, the year before his
death. His outlandish style and
quirky scholarship influenced
Elizabeth and her writing,
though she ignored his advice
to leave Cowan.

Elizabeth had seen the fish, whose variety promised such possibilities: fresh sardines, spiky sea urchins, *poulpes*, tuna, red mullet, oysters and any number of shellfish; and other spiny little creatures ideal for the garlicky aromatic Provençal stews, blended with such skill and assurance after centuries of practice. In the cooler months there were still fruits and vegetables and by then rabbits, game birds and those tiny flying mouthfuls, figpeckers, and other wild birds still sold by the trayful and so beloved of all the peoples of the South.

Elizabeth had eaten in the grand restaurants of the Riviera serving their lofty, emasculated menus. But she had also spent better hours in restaurants where the food served up was the true *cuisine à l'huile* – the cooking at whose heart is a refined blend of garlic and olive. She had eaten in expensive Provençal restaurants like Isnard's in Marseilles and Félix in Antibes, with reputations to keep up and Provençal wines like Châteauneauf-du-Pape to match, where the much-abused bouillabaisse – the fish dish with garlic and olive oil – was prepared to perfection. She had eaten in many more modest establishments too, restaurants and cafés around the markets and quaysides where local specialities could often be found for very little.

With these experiences in mind, although writing that they existed mainly on stews, she had nevertheless carried back the abundance of the markets to the galley of the *Evelyn Hope*, and there tried her own hand. Her cookery books were in regular use and new French finds were also added. Elizabeth did not spend her whole time bent over the galley stove, but she was experimenting and learning, picking up ideas and hints from those about her: a market stallholder, a fisherman cook, a friendly restaurant proprietor; taking down recipes and adding to her growing repertoire. Neither must it be forgotten that Charles's untutored, slapdash, yet inspired attitude to cooking had a significant influence on Elizabeth at this time.

Most intriguing of all, in the letter requesting Pris to find duplicates of her lost books, was the brief and tantalizing reference to her misery at the loss of 'my precious cookery book'. From those earlier letters written in the mid-1930s when she was living with Charles, we know that Elizabeth had already begun to write, probably fiction. But here we have the earliest reference to her intentions. Although she may never have spoken about it to her friends, long before her first publication her future path was already half antici-pated. At the time of its loss in mid-1940 the collection of recipes she had slowly put together had grown large enough for her to have been contemplating publication.

The stormy weather was nerve-racking and Charles remembered Douglas's advice: 'If you want to see Europe it is your last chance. There won't be any Europe left after the war. I envy you . . .' Charles wrote to the authorities in Nice for permission to move the *Evelyn Hope*. No reply came so he went in person. After a day spent waiting in corridors with worried Italians seeking repatriation, he was told to put his application in writing. He wrote again and again received no reply. Finally he realized that although the French would not categor-ically deny permission to a British ship to move freely around their waters, by stalling they indicated that this was in effect their intention. He decided that when the time seemed right, they would have to leave in secret.

Meanwhile Elizabeth was apologetic for not having written to Pris for so long but said she'd had flu and that the boat was ashore being painted, and altogether she felt unable to do anything at all. Not doing anything does seem to have included regular meetings with friends, and she felt that she spent the entire day cooking, eating, washing up, marketing and meeting people for drinks.

Elizabeth was enormously relieved that soon some money would be forthcoming from an insurance company sorting out the aftermath of a previous theft at their London flat, at which time many of hers and Charles's possessions had been stolen. She had written to Felicité in irritation and impatience at the procrastination of the insurance company's broker, Jewell, a friend of Stella's. Elizabeth's method of dealing with the situation highlights her expectation of respectful treatment for herself, and her impatience with those who either didn't cooperate or wasted her time. Among other tactics was her intention to write a weekly postcard reminding the company of their obligations to her, the desired effect being to exasperate them into finishing the business with speed; to get rid of her as quickly as she wished to get rid of them.

This money had been so eagerly awaited that upon its arrival Elizabeth told Felicité she felt as if there was no longer anything left to look forward to. In view of the present state of relations between herself and Charles this statement was probably not an exaggerated description of her feelings. Typically, Elizabeth did not dwell on the subject, and was soon talking about sending pretty materials found in Cannes for Felicité and Pris (these were the Provençal prints that remained in vogue for years to come), with advice on lengths, possible styles and instructions to dressmakers. In an earlier letter she had bemoaned the fact that without the insurance money she was unable to buy any new clothes. On the Riviera in the 1930s, just as now, this was a serious drawback to fashionable self-respect. Everything she had left after the robbery was in such a 'disreputable' state from being constantly worn that she felt she could hardly be seen out.

Descriptions of Elizabeth's appearance throughout her life usually reveal as much about the portrayer as Elizabeth herself. There were some who were won by her dark, un-English prettiness hinting at her exotic ancestry, and others who were not seduced. They preferred instead the paler, less predatory, sometimes asexual English look, with its implications of good breeding and refinement. Some found Elizabeth at times threatening in her seriousness and directness. Nevertheless, she also possessed a genuine self-consciousness and diffidence, for instance, when she looks away from the camera in the fine studio photograph later taken of her in Egypt.

Having decided on escape from Antibes, Charles was advised by the Greek sailor Costa, who had returned with Mike and himself from Venice, that although they were still beset with heavy winter storms, the beginning of May would bring the mistral. A herald to the light winds of summer, this stormy wind was exactly what was needed and Charles now intended to harness its strength to carry them across to Corsica. Elizabeth meanwhile was writing to Felicité on headed writing paper from one of the best Provençal restaurants, Grand Café-Restaurant chez Félix au Port Antibes; she was obliged to write on land because the gales of the past month made the boat 'rock like a shell'. Charles decided that they would sail on the third day of the first mistral in May.

With the arrival of May Charles spent his days watching the mountains, waiting for the little puffs of cloud that would signal the coming of the wind. He wrote: 'Just before midday on 17 May it began to blow, gently at first, rippling the water of the bay, and then suddenly with gale force, bitterly cold, out of the north. The few fishing boats in the outer harbour doubled their mooring lines. It settled down to blow steadily from the north-west.'

On 10 May the Germans had finally begun their long-awaited attack on the Low Countries. Only the previous night Germany had professed its friendship, but now soldiers had crossed the Meuse and were pouring into Belgium and Holland, without pretext or warning. The Dutch had opened their dykes and were flooding their little country to stem the invading troops, but their desperate attempts proved useless. By 15 May the Germans had swiftly crushed Belgium and Holland and would now break through French lines and move forward into France at terrifying speed. French official documents were being destroyed; the evacuation of Paris had begun.

Charles said that Viscountess Astor epitomized their feelings about the war better than anyone when she declared that it was 'not only dangerous, it was dull'. Charles sums up the way in which these feelings of monotony changed to bewilderment when the Russians invaded Finland and the initial incomprehension of most people regarding the significance and magnitude of this war. 'As far as we could see, to all intents and purposes we were at war with Russia, Russia was at war with Germany and Germany was at war with us; whilst somewhere to the East and somehow remotely connected to it all, the Chinese were fighting the Japanese. For the first time it became apparent that the war would last very long.'

CHAPTER EIGHT

Escape
(1940)

─────────────

CHARLES WROTE that with the fear that something might stop them they 'told nobody that we were leaving but gave a cocktail party at five o'clock' on the eve of 19 May 1940. 'Even Norman overcame his dislike of boats and was on board.' Early the next morning, with the mistral blowing strongly and no possibility of turning back, they weighed anchor and the *Evelyn Hope* slipped quietly out of the harbour. After a few miles under power they caught the full force of the wind in their sails and went full speed ahead, neither of them sleeping during that night. The next day they discovered that, 15 miles off course, they were nearing Corsica.

On 20 May Elizabeth wrote to Pris with the news that they had left Antibes and arrived in Corsica after twenty-six hours. She said it was terribly difficult to get permits and dangerous to tell anyone where you were going. She was careful not to give away any details of their plans, only saying she didn't know how long they would stay or when they would leave. Should Italy enter the war, they would have plenty of warning and time to get back to France – an optimistic belief on Elizabeth's part, as the invasion of France was in progress. To Elizabeth, sheltered in that calm sea, it seemed impossible that the Germans were pounding into France and that an 'absolute battle of Armageddon' was taking place in the north.

Amongst these comments there were hints as to what their real intentions were: perhaps to go to some other country. She claimed not to know exactly where, but was finding it impossible to live in a boat in those regions. They had become 'so sickened by the war that the only way to retain a sense of proportion was to get away from it for a bit.'

Elizabeth told Pris that on her last visit to Corsica she didn't get to see Bastia and was now glad to be there. It was an attractive little place, dilapidated, like most Corsican towns. 'The last visit' refers to the journey down France with Doreen Brownhill and Diana Morgan during the mid-Thirties, when Elizabeth had come across to Corsica on her own. Doreen and Diana's parents would not give permission for their visit, but at the time Elizabeth's mother was in Jamaica and, according to Doreen, 'didn't have much say as to where she went, or appear to worry about it that much either'.

Elizabeth revealed that her only sadness at leaving the Riviera was in the loss of Norman Douglas, who had heaped innumerable kindnesses on her and was one of the most fascinating people she believed she could ever hope to meet. She then recommended Priscilla to look at *How About Europe?* by Douglas because it was very stimulating. In fact the book is a weakly argued diatribe, which has been called 'a sort of pink Nietzscheanism', written in protest against the awfulness of conditions in England: the puritanism of the licensing laws, the food, hotels, cooking, the misery of the climate. Douglas calls the British 'a pack of masochists' and maintains that they are weighed down by duty and sobriety. Although something of a political embarrassment to Douglas's followers, it does reveal some of his most heartfelt aversions; namely the 'plague of repression' which he saw as infecting England.

Another Douglas book to be searched out was *Alone* (Secker and Warburg, 1921) – Elizabeth preferred his travel books to his novels. And next she delivered a dream: that if the war were to end, they could all come out to the Mediterranean. None of them would have a farthing, but it would be better to be penniless in a warm climate than in England, and one could 'always line in fish, and [there is] maccaroni'.

Leaving Corsica after several days of regal treatment, Charles and Elizabeth set sail for Greece. A storm forced them to shelter in the harbour of the tiny island of Giglio (now a major tourist resort, then little more than a rocky outcrop with a few people surviving by quarrying). Again they set out for the South and finally Elizabeth informed Priscilla that they had intended going straight from Corsica to the Greek port of Piraeus, but were held up by bad weather. She still hoped to escape from the war on a 'paradise' island and maintain her exile from England to which she felt little allegiance.

'By the time you get this we shall probably have sailed. We shall go to Athens where I know one or two people and then possibly go to the islands. Our plan is to try and find some little house somewhere and keep it ready in case any of you want to come out. In any case when the war is over it will be impossible to live in England and I really feel I may be of some use to you all if you have somewhere to come to . . .' The boat was full of provisions, the engine working perfectly — 'with luck we should be in Greece a week or so from now'. Little could Elizabeth have imagined quite what dramas were in store for them as they set off once more.

Weeks later Elizabeth wrote a long letter to Pris from Athens, outlining all that had recently befallen them. She described how for the first time they had been compelled to seriously confront the difficult conditions of war. She did so with both an admirable resilience and a self-centredness which must at times have seemed quite breathtaking to those back home.

She began with their halt on the island of Giglio in Italy, where they had put in during a fearful storm. The bad weather kept them there for five days. The people, even the officials, were more than friendly, giving them gifts, inviting them to meals, and seeing to all their needs. On the morning they were due to sail, one of them came down and told Elizabeth and Charles that the news was bad, and warned them to leave as soon as they could. By this time it was obvious that Elizabeth's optimistic hopes of returning to France if necessary could not be realized. Their only course was to stay completely out of territorial waters, while at the same time keeping the coast of Italy in sight; watching to see if the lights were on at night; if not they intended making a dash right round Sicily.

On the first day the wind was very good, and in twenty-four hours they were past Ostia. After this they encountered nothing but light winds and flat calms; perfect weather for sailing, but the situation caused too much anxiety to be enjoyable. They were also becoming 'dead tired because we didn't dare heave-to much at night because of the desperate hurry'. Off Ischia they were stopped by an Italian warship, which then followed them all night across the Bay of Naples and past Capri. Elizabeth wrote, 'That morning was the most beautiful dawn I ever saw in all my life, with Vesuvius in the distance and Capri behind us.'

It took the *Evelyn Hope* five days to reach Stromboli, and at five o'clock in the morning on 10 June, with Stromboli in sight, an Italian cruiser passed them. They dipped the ensign, and the ship replied to the salute, giving Elizabeth and Charles the impression that England was not yet at war with Italy. They were enormously relieved. Later that day they would be through the Straits of Messina, and then into the open sea, with Greece the next land they would sight. As they passed Stromboli, they stopped a fisherman and bought a lobster from him; Elizabeth called it 'exquisite, the last decent meal we were to have for weeks'.

Late that afternoon the wind ceased altogether, and it was necessary to start up the engine in order to enter the Straits that night. A fast Italian coastal motor boat raced out from Messina, but took no notice of them. As they approached the entrance to the Straits, the signal station signalled them to hoist their colours but was unable to see the *Evelyn*'s ensign; Charles ran another one up the main mast. The station then asked for their name and they signalled back *Evelyn*. They progressed into the Straits and saw a dozen large warships from Sicily and Italy. Despite these they carried on unhindered through the Straits. 'Suddenly the warships began to dash in every direction, signalling, hooting & simply hurtling past. Then we saw that the decks were all cleared for action, sandbags round the gun turrets and all the rest of it & realised that something serious was up'.

A patrol boat ordered them into Messina harbour without revealing what was afoot. When another ship came up and towed them in, they saw that Messina was under blackout. A young officer came on board once they were in the harbour, and Elizabeth asked him if Italy had declared war: he wouldn't answer. A captain came alongside on the quay and Elizabeth repeated the question. 'Have you no radio on board?' She answered 'no' and he said: 'I regret to tell you that Italy declared war on the Allies at five o'clock this afternoon.' 'That moment,' wrote Elizabeth to Pris, 'was the worst of my life, without any exception. No need to tell you the horrors that passed through my mind,' not least the idea that if they'd been twelve hours earlier they would have escaped. Two officers immediately came on board and took away every scrap of paper with writing on it: charts, log book, letters, Charles's manuscripts, address books. The officers, whom Elizabeth found unfailingly polite and considerate throughout, then allowed them to stay on board for the night.

The next morning the officers came to collect them for questioning in the Admiral's office. The first thing they were asked was: '*Vous êtes de l'Intelligence Service, n'est ce pas?*', to which Elizabeth giggled in reply. They could hardly have been spies, 'cavorting into Messina & not even knowing they'd declared war'. They were told to return to their ship and pack their things, for they were to be taken to the police in two hours. Believing that they might be sent directly to a concentration camp, they threw together and tied in bundles clothes, books and other bits and pieces. Charles just had time to take down the sails and stow them below before the naval officers returned and ordered them to leave the luggage behind. While waiting, in their panic Elizabeth said they had polished off an entire bottle of apricot brandy.

They were kept at the police station for three hours, during which time, they discovered afterwards, the chief of police had been fighting with other authorities to prevent them from being thrown into prison. Finally, 'after writing down when our grandmothers were born & all the addresses we had had in England for the past 10 years', they were informed that they would be sent to a hotel, to be paid for by the Italian government; they had no Italian currency. Charles and Elizabeth were now told there was no question of them returning to the boat to collect their things. Someone was sent, and left behind half of what Elizabeth had requested, including two pairs of her spectacles. Someone else was dispatched, and this time returned with nearly all of their books and 'a mass of perfectly useless clothes including C's dinner jacket, but without the things we really wanted, such as the typewriter, the coffee, the wine, brandy, etc. And they absolutely refused to go back again.'

'The so-called hotel was a hovel of the worst kind, crawling with bugs, fleas and cockroaches as big as mice, I am not exaggerating, so you can imagine how big the mice were in proportion.' It was full of Italians who had fled from Egypt, Tunis and other French and English colonies, and who were as unhappy as Elizabeth and Charles to be in Italy. The proprietor's wife was Austrian, 'the meanest dirtiest harridan ever I saw'. They had a very small room, with a bed, a chair and no window, and a partition dividing it from the kitchen. The washing and sanitary arrangements were beneath Elizabeth's contempt. With the exception of the proprietor and his wife, everyone was kind and generous to them, even though Charles and Elizabeth had no money. The food was appalling, and so meagre that they were constantly hungry. The evening meal consisted of bread, half a dozen black olives, and very little else; no butter and no coffee (Elizabeth longingly recalled all the marvellous French coffee left on the boat). She then 'kicked up such a shindy' that they started giving them soup (pasta and water) as well.'

During the day Elizabeth found a secluded corner of the roof and spent all day sun-bathing. Whenever she wanted anything she staged a 'fortissimo scene of hysteria' in English, German, French and Italian, in order to ensure that she was understood by everyone. She discovered that the Italians 'crumple up astonishingly when confronted by a screaming woman.'

After two weeks in the hotel the police informed them they were no longer regarded as suspicious and were free to travel on to Greece – without the boat. Elizabeth and Charles did all they could to retrieve their papers – 'the log book and Charles' half written novel, my address book, full of addresses and notes for Greece given me by Norman and others, & my precious cookery book & the typewriter'. This they were absolutely forbidden to do but were reassured that the war would surely be over in two weeks, when they could return to Messina and retrieve their boat, along with everything on it. This proved to be the attitude of all the Italians to whom Elizabeth spoke: 'they were so pulled up by the French débâcle 3 days after Italy entered the war that they thought England was going to capitulate at the first sight of an Italian warship'.

The detainees were told they would be taken to Venice and there put on a ship for Greece; this was the first of a long series of lies which were to drive Elizabeth almost to distraction. Two guards arrived to escort them to Venice and promptly informed them that they were allowed to take only one bundle each; Charles and Elizabeth had eight bundles between them. Elizabeth categorically refused to leave without her luggage, whereupon they were told that without the money for a taxi to the station, they would not be allowed to take their possessions – and that was that.

Charles threw himself upon the generosity of three destitute Greek sailors and asked them to carry their bags to the station. The sailors were so shocked by the behaviour of the Italians that they lent them eight lire for a taxi; the maid in the hotel gave them ten lire to buy cigarettes. Despite having to leave behind quantities of books, they were now finally on their way.

Messina to Venice was a journey of two days, with a five-hour stop in the waiting room at Rome. Ill-fed they asked to be taken to the American Consul; the reply was that there was no American Consul in Rome.

In Venice they were taken to a hotel for the night. The next day, after countless questions, Charles was thrown into a cell at the police station and Elizabeth was left in the gaoler's room all day. By this time they'd had nothing to eat for two days.

Elizabeth found out later that Charles was told she had been sent to Yugoslavia, and that he would be kept in prison for another week or two and then sent to a concentration camp. She again asked to see the American Consul only to be told he had gone. They were to leave for Trieste that night, so were given permission to see a yacht agent Charles had met in Venice when he was there with Mike Cumberlege.

At the station they bought wine, but ran out of time before they could get any food. Upon arrival in Trieste they were given bread and a cup of coffee, despite having the money for food and a hotel after which they were both thrown into police cells. These were crawling with bugs and stank. During the night two well-dressed young prostitutes, caught in a street brawl, were thrown into Elizabeth's cell. The only place to sleep was a sort of sloping shelf with filthy blankets and Elizabeth found it impossible; she talked to the girls instead, and was grateful for the company. Charles and Elizabeth heard subsequently that Trieste had been bombed by the English, which undoubtedly accounted for their treatment, so much worse than that which they had received at Messina.

The next morning after more complications they were eventually taken to the American Consul. Elizabeth thought him charming and the consulate a haven of peace. At nine o'clock they got the train for Posthonia, a frontier town. Arriving at midnight, they were told there was no train for Yugoslavia until six thirty the next morning. The night was spent in the waiting room with about thirty Italian soldiers who kept all the doors and windows locked. By this time Elizabeth felt she hadn't really slept for at least three weeks; her stomach was also in a 'fearful state'.

The following morning they were in the train 'like a flash' and to their huge relief were over the border in ten minutes. In Zagreb they saw the British Consul, who paid their hotel bill for three days and their fares to Athens. Yugoslavia seemed 'excessively Germanic' to Elizabeth after the Latin countries they'd been in, with 'thin sausages & beer & enormous meals & Ruritanian uniforms. Zagreb is a dull new & very teuton town'.

With very little money, no boat, no 'suitable' clothes, and obliged to live in hotels and restaurants in the boiling heat, Elizabeth now felt caught in Athens. Luckily, she still had the address of a friend of Norman, Jimmy Roan, an amusing homosexual concerned, according to Charles, that under the financial constraints of war he might become too conventional; Elizabeth described him as a 'godsend'.

Elizabeth was shocked by her first sight of Athens. Despite ample forewarning the noise, the trams, the crowds overpowered her. She was unable to do any sight-seeing owing to the lack of proper shoes and the discomfort of walking on city pavements 'after a whole year of espadrilles'. The food she pronounced 'unspeakable, although if one did one's own cooking one could live like a millionaire on £1 a week'. The system she described as prevailing in all the restaurants entailed cooking large quantities of rice, spaghetti, stuffed aubergines, stuffed tomatoes, fried fish and potatoes, after which they were left 'in large pans soaking in oil for the next 8 days'. It was only with the greatest difficulty that Elizabeth could persuade them to heat the food up. 'And when you cannot even read the language, let alone speak one solitary word of it, hope of survival is small.'

She wrote that there was some chance of Charles getting a job with the British Council in Athens, because 'all their boys went off to Cyprus but never got further than Alexandria owing to the Italian declaration of war' and would now probably not return. She said that without jobs the Consulate would be obliged to keep them. It was also clear that they were most unlikely to recover the *Evelyn Hope*. Elizabeth thought that even if it had not been blown to bits, it would undoubtedly be in a terrible state, with rotting ropes, peeling paint, a ruined engine and water flooding in. She remembered that she *had* said she was thoroughly tired of living on board, but she 'didn't intend getting rid of the boat in quite that way'.

Elizabeth fantasized to Pris about taking themselves off to a small cheap island and living in a hut or tent and eating octopus: 'it can be delicious, although a year ago I should have fainted at the idea'. She was resigned to taking a flat in Athens if it turned out that they must stay, but was finding a large city 'hell' after living on the sea for a year.

'How I regret France,' she wrote to her sister, despite knowing full well that if they had remained they would have been in much the same predicament that they found themselves in now; forced to flee the Germans and without the boat. She realized they were extremely lucky to get out of Italy at all – if they had been imprisoned there she believed they might very well have died of starvation or gone quite mad.

Elizabeth detailed to Pris what she considered their most serious losses had been: the typewriter, Charles's manuscripts and her cookery book, 'which was getting to be such a good collection that I was thinking of writing it up properly and trying to get it published in America'.

Worrying about the family, Elizabeth asked Pris to send a wire, if she could afford it, telling her they were all right. Her letter was to be passed round and then given to Marian, who would give it to Diana (Anderson) to read. She asked after Stella, saying that she hoped she had left Dedham for somewhere safer but acknowledged that nowhere was particularly good. Her letter is full of advice to Pris about how best to survive: always have money ready, and buy jewellery; 'if I'd had even so much as one little diamond ring I'd have been in a better situation than I am now'. She also details requests for clothes to be sent out to her for the winter. She apologized for bringing up such trivial matters, but said that there were no 'good shops' in Athens, and that all she had for the winter was her black suit, red jacket and old clothes from the boat. She was perfectly serious about this need for her wardrobe, and pointed out that her clothes could be sent care of Cook's by way of India and Turkey. 'If by the time you get this England is not in chaos & you have time & courage would you consider the matter?'

Elizabeth expressed concern about her friends in France, especially Norman. Two letters from him awaited her, but they had of course been sent a long time ago. She fretted about how little news they received, no English newspapers despite the presence of quite a few English people who had been very kind to them.

Desperate for money she had wired to her bank from Zagreb to send a hundred pounds; to break her trust if possible and sell the shares, regardless of how much they realized. It was better to get what one could rather than 'let it go down the drain when the crash comes, as it must, whether we win or lose'.

Elizabeth includes few political reflections in her letter but does express disgust with 'the whole bloodstained business'. She believed the Italians were going to be very sorry that they had ever entered the war. There was little to eat, with the coffee ration at about two ounces a month and sugar half a pound a month; there was no soap for washing clothes and only the rich could get butter. The Italians, she said, would be 'done out of' all the colonies they hoped to acquire. And if they got Corsica, then 'God help them . . . the Corsicans hate their guts & there'll be wholesale murder of them if they ever set foot on the island'. They would soon see that things were not to be as easy as they imagined; the Italians were so frightened of each other at the outset that she couldn't imagine what would happen to them if ever they came into contact with the British Fleet. The Italian newspapers had been full of the damage they had done in Malta, but Elizabeth knew this was an exaggeration – Malta would have been under the sea if it had been bombed as much as they claimed.

The letter concludes by asking for news of friends and family, and for the first time perhaps, there is a hint of genuine alarm, genuine concern: 'I am thinking about you all the whole time.'

Far away in Greece which seemed so alien after Southern France, Elizabeth's concerns for those at home were edged with new sentiment, for she was feeling cut off and tired. Still set in her determination to stay away from England, her recent experiences through Italy and Yugoslavia had brought about a change in her. She remained confirmed in her intention not to have any involvement with the war effort, but some of the realities of this war were no longer avoidable. The tone of her request for news of friends' movements – she had heard nothing from anyone since the middle of May – reveals a note of fear not previously there. Her loss of papers, books and home, as the *Evelyn Hope* had become, now began to extend to human loss for Elizabeth in this war which gradually encroached.

In the Athens letter Elizabeth inquires after 'Chan'. This was Chandos Hoskyns, one of the Gwynne sisters' greatest devotees on Malta during the Thirties, and himself universally admired. A Lieutenant-Colonel in the Rifle Brigade, he was a sparkling figure who charmed all whom he met and was often at Priscilla and Richard's dinners. Elizabeth liked Chan, and it was he whom she enshrined in her first piece of non-recipe-based writing, 'Two Cooks'. Chan was the 'honoured . . . guest coming for dinner' to eat 'one of his favourite dishes . . . Angela's way of doing quails, boned and stuffed with sweet corn and wrapped in bacon', the quail which Angela so endearingly and carelessly lost to the cat. Back in May, as the Germans relentlessly pushed forward towards the French coast, with the British army before them, Chan had been killed in action while commanding the 2nd Rifle Brigade. This was part of the crucial and sacrificial defence of Calais, without which Dunkirk would certainly have fallen and the great exodus of men could never have taken place.

At first Elizabeth and Charles found themselves ill at ease in the Levantine atmosphere of Athens. As Elizabeth complained to Pris, after so long on a boat wearing espadrilles (and sea clothes) the noise and crowds and pavements of the city were almost too much to endure. Despite saying she loathed Athens – the English colony were just Malta all over again – she maintained that now she simply couldn't return to England. Now that Italy had joined in the war and Mediterranean sea routes had been cut off, the journey back home was a mammoth undertaking. One had to go to Turkey and from there to Karachi and 'practically around the world', or to Egypt, Syria and Palestine, plane to Durban and boat from there. Elizabeth had had enough of being stranded in strange countries without money and captured by enemies. She recounts the story of the British Consul in Athens who informed a girl intending to make the journey back to Britain that if she had been his daughter, he would have locked her up in the gaol rather than let her make the trip alone. The physical results of war were now a legitimate excuse for Elizabeth not to return to England. Equally important, she was not yet sufficiently moved to make that journey, she was not ready to return.

It was in this letter that Elizabeth asked Pris to try to replace her lost cookery books at Miss Dillon's. She bemoaned the loss of all her other books but said it was useless to think about them, they couldn't be ordered again. Many were irreplaceable because she'd had them all her life. Her most treasured ones had been left in England; she wondered if their fate would be very different. Letters from friends and family were beginning to get through to her and she wrote that she had received news from Norman, who remained in Antibes. She thought he must be wretched and lonely, as everyone had gone. The Cumberleges, he told her, had left in their car and been heard of in Gibraltar. She presumed Mike had left in a battleship. (Mike Cumberlege was in fact continuing his spying missions around the Mediterranean and beyond.)

Regardless of their disillusion Athens was a Mecca of sorts, and Elizabeth and Charles decided, as he put it, 'as we had left England with the express purpose of seeing Greece . . . to make the most of it'. Before using Norman Douglas's introductions, however, they thought it best to familiarize themselves with the city. They made valiant attempts, searched almost in vain for a route up to the Acropolis, hindered by knowing not a word of Greek, were surprised at the dirt, the dust, the mess, the neglect of the past, out of ignorant disregard or a ramshackle grasping for the future, and decided that Greece was the salvage dump of Europe. Everything, including ships, trams, anything mechanical was apparently made from the discards of other countries. Elizabeth described the clothes shops as provincial and overpriced, and shopping generally as one long pain in the neck. She could never get anything that she wanted, and had to bargain for everything down to the smallest packet of pins.

The days spent reluctantly in Athens were not entirely barren. They could sit with all the foreign newspapers on the terrace of the grand King George Hotel looking out, Charles wrote, 'watching the changing light on Hymettos . . . We sat in the tavernas at Phaliron, eating grilled fish – slightly burned, over-salted and covered in cold oil – while the boats with acetylene lamps to attract the fish to the nets, moved like fireflies on the Bay of Salamis'. They explored the ancient silver mines at Lavrion and spent nights in the Turkish quarter at the base of the Acropolis . . . exquisite against the garish architecture of modern Athens. 'We visited (finally) the Parthenon.' They saw 'the Theatre of Dyonisios, and the Temple of Poseidon at Sunion, where we searched in vain for initials of Byron carved on the stone; we visited Eleusis and Daphne'.

In fine form, Elizabeth described the rituals of food in Athens to Priscilla. Having grumbled that kitchen utensils were colossally expensive, and that when she got a flat of her own it would cost a small fortune, she berated the Greeks for their inability to make utensils with lids, which may have accounted for the food in restaurants being stone cold. Her next statement was uncompromising. 'In a hundred years I could never get used to Greek food.' She told Pris that she had eaten the food of almost every country in Europe, but that in Greece she had met her Waterloo.

Pris, Elizabeth thought, must be glad of her vegetable garden now. She continued her letter, gradually more withering as she warmed to the task: she found it difficult to get sugar, there was only brown bread, meat only two days a week. Vegetables were plentiful, but they consisted of tomatoes, aubergines, small marrows, potatoes,

ochra, cucumbers and pimentos. There was no green salad, or anything remotely like it. 'There is a kind of spinach muck which they
boil to shreds, chew up and then spit out into an enormous pan full
of oil where it stands for a fortnight and is served under the name of
green salad.'

'They say one gets to love Athens in time but the report is
exaggerated . . . the islands and the Peloponnese are different . . .' It
was difficult to get around without boat or car and Elizabeth clearly
dissociated herself from the contemporary traveller into unknown
regions à la Robert Byron in Persia, or Peter Fleming in China and
Brazil, and neatly characterized that style with her usual touch of
irony. 'I never was one for packing ten days' supplies in a basket,
hanging it on the back of a mule and tramping off into the wilds.'
Nonetheless she saw things for what they were and added, 'This
method is the only way to see Greece.'

Charles and Elizabeth preferred the islands to the mainland and
Elizabeth told Pris that they had been taken to several. The Greeks
were frightfully hospitable and they had been asked aboard practically
every yacht in Greece. She described the extrordinary luxury exhibited
by these wealthy Greek sailors and laughed at their meekness and
Mediterranean *sprezzatura*. She thought the people who owned yachts
there a 'perfect scream' – with 80 and 100 ft yachts they sat all year
in the harbour, venturing out occasionally in the summer to the
nearest island five miles away. They gaped when told how big the
Evelyn Hope was, and thought Elizabeth and Charles were like
Christopher Columbus. In spite of cynicism about the Greek yachts-
men's showy use of their wealth, they took advantage of the snobbish
collecting of English friends, accepted the unsophisticated generosity
of the newly rich and the occasionally stifling but boundless hospitality of the Greeks. One of their hosts, Embiricos, was the owner of a
shipping line whose bounty included the island of Andros where he
was happy for them to borrow a house.

Elizabeth had a chance to observe customary Greek behaviour.
Although, as we have just seen, her vision could be limited – she did
not tend to look inward – her outward eye was exceedingly sharp,
especially for any signs of pretentiousness or absurdity. In one of her
letters to Priscilla she describes a custom rigorously maintained in

Greece, what she calls 'the jam and water party; an ordeal one sometimes has to go through'. The piece is such a fine example of Elizabeth's style and the high level of writing she has already attained when on her mettle that it is quoted here almost verbatim. She already succeeds at something her mentor Douglas was a past master at, namely description with an eye for accuracy, for objective truth. Yet at the same time making the description personal, letting the reader know — mostly by implication — her own opinion, all set down with most effective understatement.

Among all the less Europeanized Greeks of all classes, at whatever time you call on them, or even if invited to a party you will find a number of people sitting in a circle right round the room. After you have been introduced and given a chair you sit bolt upright and don't speak to anyone until you're spoken to. Presently a maid arrives with a tray on which is a small dish of jam (very sweet and syrupy) and a large glass of water for each guest. On top of each glass is poised a spoon. The technique, which it takes some time to master, is as follows: you take the spoon, dip it in the jam, take a mouthful, put the spoon in the glass, take the glass off the tray and drink the water, trying to avoid knocking your teeth out with the spoon. If you stay a long time and if you're lucky you may get a tiny cup of coffee and a piece of Turkish Delight ... (the Turkish Delight is excellent here but now they have stopped making it for lack of sugar.)

She then appends to the story another example of Greek hospitality, with timing and variations.

Just before I left Athens I went to a party — 10.30 I took my place in the circle, round an immense room with parquet floor, marble statues and 18thc. furniture (the sign of enormous wealth in Greece) and we had coffee, jam, water and little sweet cakes. At 12 o'clock I had not moved off my chair, and nor had anybody else ... and then a lot of cocktail party food was handed around, little bits of ham on bread, little clams (delicious shell fish) nuts and so on. At 1.30 we were offered a whisky or brandy and soda and at 2 o'clock the party broke up – voted by everyone a riotous evening.

Money became desperately low, eaten up by hotels and restaurants. Charles was attempting to get work in Athens, preferably at the newly founded British Institute – Elizabeth comments wryly, 'Institute for teaching English culture (!) to Greeks' – but, in spite of promises, neither Charles's obligatory work permit nor the job materialized. They now went out as little as possible to avoid spending money. Throughout the whole period in the South of France Pris had, whenever possible, sent Elizabeth sums of money. Each was gratefully accepted, and spent. Now finances were worse than ever before and Elizabeth had written asking for a loan and the release of her trust fund. Richard was away and Priscilla was on her own with the baby, Sabrina, intermittently with Felicité or Diana, in the Old Vicarage, Chipping Sodbury.

In straitened circumstances herself by now, Priscilla must have asked her mother for advice. This elicited a revealing outburst giving vent to Stella's exasperation with Elizabeth. It is a harsh and wounded letter giving a valuable insight into the way Elizabeth was perceived by Stella. It was written in July 1940 from Dedham where Stella, with the hazard of regular air raids, was struggling on with her antiques shop. The Old Grammar School was very large and here she was alone except for a maid whom she wished would leave (but felt unable to throw out) so that she could save the money. A student from Cedric and Lett's school, Maudie O'Malley, remembers Stella 'working away there all on her own. She stripped pine before anyone else did, all those things she did on her own.' Stella said she no longer took any notice of the raids, that she refused to hide in the cellar with her furniture, felt encouraged by 'our own Fighters overhead' and 'existed'. Cedric Morris and Lett Haines were nearby and they also doggedly kept on with work. Stella writes:

My dear Priscilla,
I am answering at once, tho I do *not* know what to say re E. My own experience is that she does her best to flout and annoy me,

138

always has. She is still owing me £250; the arrangement made
by the bank that she was to repay me £20 a month having come
to nothing. Remember she has no morals re money – like Eva
and Violet & will roll you till your last [farthing] ... without
any feeling or gratitude – So whatever you do you will be the
loser. & she is I imagine keeping that Pacifist and the £100 is
probably for him too. I never realized the implication when she
decamped like that before the War – jolly clever ... to find a
person like Elizabeth to support him – I shd let the Bank do
whatever they think best.

Stella asked Pris if she could not persuade Elizabeth to return, and
'could you tie her down to a furnished room and a job? What does
Richard say?' Stella is sure that Athens must be cheaper than London.
'and I feel sure she only asked for the £100 to keep the party
[Charles], so that if getting her home wd get her away from him, I
shd be in favour – because the more you help her the quicker will
you have nothing left. I'm sorry to appear so hard but I have bitter
experience of Gwynne morals . . .

'I think E. ought to come home and live in a British place – but
one can't do anything and it is so involved with that awful worm –
one can't call him a man . . . I'm thankful Daddy is not alive I cannot
imagine what he'd say to E. going off with a Pacifist.'

This was not the first letter Stella had written about Elizabeth's
present activities. Pris had sent on to the family the long letter from
Athens describing Charles and Elizabeth's capture and their eventual
journey to Greece, and this elicited a fiery response from her mother
regarding Elizabeth's war effort. 'She's alright, but how *can she* sit
there idling when the Athens hospitals are shrieking for helpers of all
kinds. And if ever she returns to England what sort of reception will
she get from everyone who is working in every possible way. She'll
never never get a job. However – nothing can be done. Love Mummie.'

Meanwhile, after three months in Athens a more serious proposition than hanging around waiting on the British Institute was
made to Charles: teaching English on one of the Cyclades islands. He
went ahead to look. There were complications but it appeared likely
that he would be able to muster a few students. Better than nothing

in Athens. Within a fortnight Elizabeth was packed up and on her way to meet him. Charles had rented a small cottage on the island of Syros. Under circumstances quite other than planned they were at last to come to a halt for a time, on a small island in the midst of this sea of which Elizabeth's future friend, Lawrence Durrell, wrote: 'The Mediterranean is an absurdly small sea; the length and greatness of its history make us dream it larger than it is.'

CHAPTER NINE

A Kind of Idyll
(1940–1941)

SYROS (Syra is the name of the principal town) is one of that strung-out group of harshly beautiful seductive islands in the Central Aegean, forming a chaplet around Delos and from whence comes their name, the Cyclades. Long inhabited, their rounded forms burnt by the searing Greek sun, each island is quite distinct in character: Syros, Andros, Tinos, Paros, Naxos, Kynthos, and more, their names ring out back beyond Homer into prehistory. Most are rocky, at times spectacular; several are arid and waterless. Some, like Naxos, were famed in antiquity for their wines and fertility. Delos, really no more than a great granite rock, was the birthplace of the god Apollo, and the vast sanctuary which grew up there became one of the holiest and most revered sites of the ancient world. At the maritime crossroads between Greece and Asia and the Northern Aegean and Egypt, this tiny island also became one of the great commercial ports of the Mediterranean.

Syros was not illustrious but until its displacement by Piraeus at the end of the nineteenth century Hermoupolis, or Syra as it was renamed, was the first port of Greece. Approaching by steamer through the indigo sea, two hills rise steeply to the left and right of the town, each terraced with the brilliant white houses so character-istic of these islands. The hill to the left holds the Roman Catholic community, the cathedral of St George at its summit, whilst the hill to the right is the Greek Orthodox quarter. The entire town of Syra was built of marble, glistening a sparkling pure white, from the gleaming waterfront upwards along the winding stairways to the Old Town on top of the Catholic hill. The shipyard was famous for its building of caiques, the brightly painted merchant boats seen across the Eastern Mediterranean.

Beyond the town the vine and the olive grew well on this arid little island. There were also vegetables and some orange groves in the valley. The low, winding stone walls were marble – stones cleared from the fields – and led towards the sea. Charles found a place for them to live in the tiny hamlet of Vari, a few miles out of Syra. Charles describes the hamlet and the house they were to live in for many months thus: 'A cluster of cottages overlooked the bay, narrowing between high broken cliffs to seaward . . . It widened to a stretch of shingle, upon which, side by side, were built two small tavernas. Beyond them a strip of flat, white sand led from a shallow side of the bay to a pink rock at the foot of a thorn-covered hill. In the angle between the rock and the hillside, overhung by a willow tree, was a white marble cottage.'

After they had settled themselves into the cottage on the edge of Vari, Elizabeth wrote home, but in the knowledge that her letter might take months to get there. She now comprehended the magnitude and the implications of this war, the truth of Douglas's prophecy that Europe would be ineradicably altered, and her lines are weary with a sense of endurance when she says to Pris that what will happen to them all is no longer a matter that they can decide for themselves. Elizabeth is becoming resigned to the idea that for many years to come life will be little more than just a dreary scrabble for a bare existence. 'The less one thinks about the future the better,' she tells Pris, because for their generation she believes there is none. She recalls Bryan's words at the famous party in Malta, after which they had dinner on *The Delhi*: 'I b-b-believe that our g-generation is g-going to be b-blown to p-pieces.'

They were, for the present, on the island of Syros. Not the most interesting or beautiful of the Greek islands, but the one on which there were likely to be more people wishing to learn English. Elizabeth told Pris that because they were exhausted with life in hotels and restaurants their failure to rent another house, 'absolutely new and fully equipped with everything, including a small sailing boat', had led them to their small furnished cottage in the village of Vari. It was five miles from the town on a lovely bay. There were no communications with the town, and they had to walk in or borrow a donkey or horse from one of the local peasants. They were, however, when not cut off by the tide, only five minutes' walk from the tiny hamlet with its tavernas.

In *The Voyage of the Evelyn Hope* Elizabeth is identified as Caroline. Charles here describes their first night in the cottage:

Tootosi took us out to Vari in his car. We managed to find an excuse to get him to leave us at the road, and the two of us went together across the shingle to the house. Unasked, the fisher-woman and her son followed us, carrying our bags. She placed them just inside the doorway and slipped timidly away. Caroline ran after and shook her hands. I undid the padlock of the inner door. The house was barely furnished; a chair and a bed in each of the bedrooms, four broken cane chairs, a small table and a kind of settee in the living-room and in the kitchen, besides the small charcoal brazier stove, a large table and four bentwood chairs. I walked out on to the large stone balcony and waited. Caroline came up behind me and put her arm on my shoulder. We looked at the nine little houses, washed pink or yellow, each with its flat square roof of mud, and the small walled balcony leading down three or four steps to ground level.

'I like it,' she said.

'The lavatory is outside, and is just a hole.'

'I've seen it. It's luxurious, it's got a roof.'

'It's not going to be too terribly comfortable.'

'It's all marble, even if it's whitewashed. There are not many people who can boast a lavatory in marble.'

'You haven't seen the best of it, the view. Now is really the time to see it, or are you too tired to climb the hill?'

'No,' she said. 'I'm not too tired to climb the hill.'

I helped her up the rough ground, jagged with marble outcrops, and covered with clumps of thorn.

'That is what you use to light the fires. They burn charcoal, and they are good to cook on, once you get used to them. You have to keep them going with a fan. I've had an idea to get a girl here to help you, who speaks French. The *papa* says that there is an Italian woman about half a mile away, she speaks French, too. I'm afraid she'll be your only intellectual neighbour.'

'I liked the fisherwoman.'

We stood on the top; around us was the purple circle of the Cyclades, lifted slightly from the sea: Kythnos, Seriphos, Siphinos, Paros, Mykinos.

That night we slept together, without proper sheets, and with a lumpy mattress, in a shaky iron bed.

In the morning we were awakened by a soft tapping at the door. Outside stood the fisherwoman, timidly holding a plate of fresh fish.

Caroline spent the day cutting some cheap material she had bought in Athens into covers for the chairs and for curtains. I walked into Syra and came back with a few necessary pots and pans. At dusk we had our first visitor, a short, cheery-faced peasant with an almost Chaplin moustache and a twinkling eye. He introduced himself.

Kala Speras! Josipi.'

We offered him a chair. I had brought a bottle of cognac from the town, and I poured three glasses, while Caroline cut some small pieces of bread, and a little cheese; the conventional offering of food and drink to a guest. He raised his glass and clinked it against ours.

'Issigean!'

It seemed that something was required of us. We repeated it after him.

'Issigean!'

He laughed, a soft musical laugh. A few minutes later he pointed to the large hooked briar pipe which I was smoking. I handed it to him. He put it to his lips and puffed before handing it back.

'Sibouki.'

'Sibouki.'

We began our first lesson in Greek.

The next day I arranged with the girl to help in the house for one thousand drachmas a month. In the evening Josipi arrived again, with a bundle of sheets, blankets, cushions, and a

collection of cutlery, china and glasses. He had quietly noticed
what was missing and had supplied all the deficiencies. We
attempted to refuse the gift, the girl interpreting.

'But he says that you have no sheets, and that you must
have sheets, also you have not sufficient knives and forks. If
friends come to stay with you, you will need knives and forks. If
he does not give them to you, where else will you obtain them?'

Josipi laughed away our protests, refused a second glass of
cognac, and settled down to our second lesson. He turned up
punctually every evening at the same time.

On the island of Syros, for once, Charles and Elizabeth's different
social origins were forgotten. They were accepted hospitably and
judged only by the most ancient and elemental criteria, that simple
moral code which scarcely varies throughout the Western world. As
far as one can judge, from Charles's writings and Elizabeth's letters,
they seem to have stood up quite well. Syros brought out the best in
each of them, and for a few months they were mostly happy, probably
happier, the evidence suggests, than either was ever to be again.

Elizabeth's description of her life on Syros – the house, the
neighbours, her daily round – is confirmation of a change taking
place in her over the last few months. The arena of war was initially
in Northern Europe, which meant that staying South, on the Mediterranean coast, one was left reasonably unaffected. As Italy entered
the combat and the German forces pushed down through France,
Elizabeth and Charles had fairly inevitably become involved. Their
retreat further South on to this little island allowed them to settle
down for a time.

Undoubtedly it was the most uncomplicated milieu Elizabeth
had ever experienced, in both a physical and an intellectual sense.
And at times her 'civilized' irritation at the simplicity and lack of
sophistication she now encountered was palpable. Before leaving
France she and Charles had been subjected to no more than the
'dullness' of war, as Lady Astor had put it; after Italy and Yugoslavia
they understood better the fear and danger it creates. Athens was
ultimately a period of anxious and deteriorating tediousness. In
combination the experience of Athens and Syros wrought a change in

Elizabeth's writing. The first Athens letter describing their capture by the Italians is a narrative of concision, sharpness, coherence made out of chaos; but her present pared-down existence completed the sacrifice of her old life, and this is reflected in her letters. They become noticeably less effusive, less sprinkled with the gushing hyperbole of a 'bright young thing', and are a more accurate reflection of that self which was at heart motivated by the austerity of truth.

In several letters to her sisters and mother from Syros a vivid picture of Elizabeth's island life emerges which complements Charles's descriptions. Their little house was 'rather dilapidated, badly in need of painting, with holes in the floor (thank God none in the roof) and furniture was of the scantiest. One bed, one mattress, five wicker chairs, two tables and a charcoal cooking stove.' The sea was at their door. She had two blankets from the boat and a hot-water bottle; Elizabeth always found it difficult to live without one. Water was brought from a distance of a hundred yards.

The cooking stove was a 'sort of brazier', then common to most country houses in Greece, and Elizabeth was thankful that as far as food went they were pretty well off. Compared to heavily rationed Britain the level of choice was luxurious. They had stores of rice, macaroni, flour (brown, mixed with some bran) and small quantities of sugar, coffee and dried beans. Everything else was obtained locally. In spite of butter being very expensive, it was almost inedible – 'margarine would be a treat after it', Greek cheese was 'impossible', coffee, sugar and tea almost unobtainable, 'olive oil so bad that it ruins the taste of anything cooked in it'. No spices were obtainable, but there were compensations.

Every morning they had fresh milk and newly laid eggs from a local peasant, the Josipi of Charles's book; he also brought them the fresh things that he grew for market: tomatoes, onions, potatoes, aubergines, turnips; and fruit, including pomegranates, oranges and lemons. Although prices had risen she said that the two days a week when meat was sold, it was cheap. The fishing was not very good, but she was not particularly worried by this. Occasionally they had an octopus, which she found delicious when properly cooked. Chickens could be had from their market gardener although Elizabeth baulked at killing them herself. After three months of hotels and terrible restaurant food it was a great relief to have her own dwelling, however modest.

We are made party to the routine of her 'existence' as she called it with a résumé of her day, sufficiently predictable to be written as an hourly timetable: '7.30 a.m. get up and go for a swim, 8 o'clock breakfast, 8.30–10 cleaning up, getting dressed etc., 10–12 out in the garden reading, endeavouring to knock a few Greek verbs or sentences into my head, writing letters etc., 12–1 cook lunch, 1 o'clock lunch – 2.30 go for a swim, walk or row in borrowed dinghy, general pootle around, 5 o'clock cup of excessively weak tea and piece of toast, 5 to 7 more reading, or local café for a glass of wine or oozoo, the national Greek drink, or call on our local Catholic priest Père Pedro who speaks French, 8 p.m. supper, 9.30 bed. A somewhat aimless life – but better than swanning around Athens drinking and spending money I haven't got – and as I said before one merely exists nowadays.'

She bemoaned her inability to travel around exploring the other islands of the Cyclades visible in the distance, but commented that two years ago if she had found herself in such a hovel without electric light, bath, water, carpets, armchairs, and in a kitchen without gas or electricity, coffee, butter or tea, she wouldn't have remained there two minutes. Now she took what she could get, ate what there was, and considered herself lucky to have it.

Elizabeth and Charles's home comforts extended to a tiny flea-infested white kitten brought to Elizabeth by the 'crazy one', the village simpleton, and named Asphodel after the lily-like flower of the underworld in Greek legend so hated by Norman Douglas. In fact there were fleas everywhere and the locals thought Charles and Elizabeth quite touched in their persistent efforts to be rid of them. Clothes, besides the utterly basic, were impossible to buy and Elizabeth regretted her oilskin lost with the *Evelyn Hope*. She told Pris that the lack of rain in Greece was a myth and that when the South Wind blew the sea came right up to the door of their cottage, cutting it off completely from the village.

This she did not at first entirely regret because it gave them some respite from the inquisitive eyes of the local peasants. Quite unabashed, they would walk right into the house or simply stand in the doorway, watching. They didn't expect to be spoken to or entertained, but would simply sit down and 'gape for an hour at a time'. Elizabeth and Charles grew accustomed to these visits, however, and when they made Sunday suet pudding their neighbours continued to drop in as if by accident, and now brought gifts of their own food specialities in return for their hospitality. An old horse pulled round the windlass for their neighbour Josipi to irrigate his fields; the fisherwoman, whom Charles sometimes helped, continued to throw her nets, and the two foreigners became accepted and welcomed and invited to the little feasts commemorating a child's birth or the killing of a pig.

On 28 October, after they had been on the island for about a month, using his best divisions Mussolini invaded Greece. A few days later Elizabeth wrote to England and said that she did not now know what would happen, or for how long they would be able to remain on Syros. She knew she might have to 'get out of here pretty damn quick'. They had heard no further news after the bombing of Patras, nothing certain except that everyone had been called up. This was the third time she had been in a country at the moment war began, the men mobilized, the women weeping, the lights all out. As usual there were requests from Elizabeth to Pris to negotiate with the bank on her behalf and also immense gratitude for money. 'I can't thank you enough for this . . . with all the expenses and worries you have on your own account and I owe you so much already I wonder if I shall ever be able to pay it back.' Coutts had telegraphed Elizabeth the money to Athens and asked her her intentions, saying that her family would prefer her to return. 'Please give all my news to Marian, Di, Doreen, Arthur – Mummie, D & F. No news of Richard in D's telegram. Where is he?'

She realized that it was unlikely any more letters would now get through and worried about Norman, from whom she had received several missives; he was still in Antibes and trying to get to Portugal. France was now in a bad way; in fact very close to famine conditions. Elizabeth had written to their cousin Neil Hogg, Under-Secretary at the Embassy in Lisbon at the time, asking him to help and he had responded generously with an invitation to Douglas to stay. This Douglas eventually did and spent almost a year in Neil's apartment

before finally returning to England (with great reluctance) for the
remainder of the war. Elizabeth ended her letter to Priscilla days after
the Italian invasion of the mainland of Greece with the news that for
the moment they were still peacefully there.

Nonetheless men of military age had already gone off to the war
and Charles chronicled the melancholy occasion:

> Barely distinguishable in the half light, the village gathered
> outside Jorgos' before dawn. We watched from the balcony.
> Slowly they dispersed. A small group remained standing on the
> shingle. Against the white road the figures were clearer; twenty
> men walked slowly towards the town.
>
> I took a footpath through the canes, and met them at the
> bottom of the hill.
>
> 'Josipi, for you! The English pipe to bring you luck in the
> war.'
>
> His eyes were already wet. He held me in an embrace for a
> moment, and kissed me on both cheeks. I bade him the
> traditional Greek farewell:
>
> *'Kalo molivi.'*
>
> Without speaking he thrust the pipe in his mouth at a
> jaunty angle, and swaggered after the retreating men.

Elizabeth wrote that they were very out of touch with things
and were living almost like hermits. They did, nevertheless, give a
Christmas party for their neighbours who remained, including the
young village priest. In the town and their little hamlet of Vari the
bells and fireworks were absent except on days of great victories. It
was still cold, but not exceptionally so by English standards. The
fields were full of narcissi and wild anemones, oranges and mandarins
were plentiful, and they managed quite well for food.

Most of the islands were casually bombed. News of the progres-
sion of the war began to filter through to Syros. The Greek army,
often under severe winter conditions, was holding back the Italians in
a series of victories; the capture of Koritza, the annihilation of an
Italian division, the Italian retreat from the Kalamas river; for months
the Greeks kept twenty-seven divisions hemmed into Albania with

only sixteen of their own. This heroic Greek resistance kept the Balkan countries in optimistic mood. Meanwhile Churchill and his War Cabinet had acted on their immediate realization (following the Italian invasion) that at all costs Crete must be in British hands: as a strategic airfield and naval refuelling base it would be invaluable in the defence of Malta and Egypt. On 31 October the best harbour in Crete, Suda Bay, was occupied by British forces at the invitation of the Greek government.

By the end of January General Metaxas, the Greek dictator, had died after an unsuccessful operation and although he was replaced immediately, Greece felt itself effectively without a leader. Steamers no longer visited the islands and sailing boats were once again used to ferry food secretly at night from island to island. British, Australian and New Zealand forces had been sent into Greece to prevent German invasion, but they were heavily outnumbered. On 6 April German armies invaded both Yugoslavia and Greece from the north and south. Newspapers ceased to arrive from the mainland; what news Elizabeth and Charles received on Syros was from brief radio reports broadcast from loudspeakers in the square in Syra. Salonika was lost, the Allied armies were fighting a rearguard action; they began a retreat. Korysis, the new Greek Prime Minister, committed suicide, unable to bear the stain of failure to save his country.

Greece surrendered on 24 April while the King and his family retreated to Crete, the last foothold for the government and a brief haven for evacuated troops. Under appalling conditions of attack, over 50,000 men had to be evacuated, by night, from mainland Greece. A huge operation was set in motion and, aided by the Greeks, many thousands were saved. On 28 April Charles and Elizabeth watched from the hillside as Syra was bombed. The island was in chaos, and surrendered. Having refused offers of protection in the hills from the villagers, Elizabeth and Charles packed and left for Syra in Josipi's cart, to search out a boat to get them off the island and away to Crete. Now they were fleeing a pursuing enemy and at times this escape made their experience of Italy seem almost trivial by comparison.

A Palestinian soldier with a 40-foot caïque hidden on the other side of the island, invited them to take passage with him to

Crete. They would leave that night. The company grew and by nightfall there were six or seven, including Charles and Elizabeth. The *Agios Marco* left as darkness fell. Charles wrote that 'The plan was to make it to Crete in three hops, travelling at night, and stopping during the day at lonely island anchorages where ... we ourselves would scatter against possible machine-gunning from the air.' First halt, just before first light, revealed that the navigator was not an expert after all. They discovered they were now mistakenly on Mykonos, 25 miles due east of Syra. Crete lies due south. In the ensuing debate, heightened by anger and fear, it transpired that the boat was stolen. Eventually a Greek army sergeant, a Cretan soldier and Charles took command of the *Agios Marco*; Charles was now at the tiller.

In the pre-dawn light of the following day the boat crept in along the shores of Ios and the company on board quickly disembarked to hide for the day – they were still 90 miles from Crete. Walking inland they were soon met by weeping village women who told them that all the men, except for one old one, had gone and they must not stay outside, because enemy planes flew over every day searching out retreating boats and any figures they could see. Divided up between the village houses, they were fed and despairingly requested news of the war.

The old man who had remained advised them on a possible route to Crete: very dangerous but they had little choice. After an intensely nerve-racking voyage in a ship whose motor was failing and whose sails were falling apart, they finally entered Heraklion harbour in broad daylight, while three German dive-bombers were attacking the town. A British naval officer swore at them from the quay and ordered them to drop anchor immediately and get ashore under cover. It was Mike Cumberlege, not seen for almost a year since the time when Charles and Elizabeth had sailed out of Antibes harbour determined to reach Greece.

Elizabeth took up the story of their flight from Syra in her subsequent letter to Pris from Egypt, saying that those at home must have been dreadfully worried about her, but it had been quite impossible to communicate with them. The escape to Crete had taken four days and they'd had a 'perfectly wonderful' view of the Cyclades.

They stopped at Ios and as they passed Santorini flames came out of the volcano. Elizabeth said that Santorini was where she wanted to live when 'this foul business' was over. She thought Crete beautiful. In contrast to the aridness of Syra she responded to the fertility of Crete, its vines, its fruit trees, 'real rivers and snow-covered mountains'.

Having encountered Mike Cumberlege in the midst of the bombing raid on Heraklion, they heard his latest news. It is here, for the first time, that Elizabeth and Charles's descriptions of events markedly diverge. Either Charles's story is blatant fabrication, or Elizabeth is aware that her letters may be opened and in her wish to protect Cumberlege, acting as a Navy spy, gives a very edited version of events. From the safety of Alexandria her desription of the next few days is tantalizingly brief and to the point. 'We were there about 10 days. They had already started heavyish night bombing when we left – in a comfortable and uneventful convoy.' Later she adds: 'While wandering around the port of a certain town in Crete who do we see . . . on the battered deck of a . . . ship but Mike – he has done wonderful work I believe.' 'We were just that minute going off to the other end of the island in an Army lorry which couldn't be kept waiting so we only had about ten minutes conversation.' (In the light of what other survivors of Crete have written Charles's chronicle of events is the more credible, whereas that of Elizabeth makes little sense.

Charles's version filled the last ten pages of the *Voyage of the Evelyn Hope* with a remarkable and terrifying escape story. It began by stating, contrary to Elizabeth, that they spent *two* days with Mike Cumberlege, who 'left us liberally supplied with cash'. The 'cash' was certainly a fact, although it became confused in family myth. Trying to piece together this escape, it does appear to coincide with the known events of the battle for Crete, one of the great disasters of the war, and which began with the terrible German bombardment on 20 May. Whitehall and Middle East command between them had realized the possibilities for months but were quite unprepared. As a consequence of changing commanders too many times, lax forward-planning and unimplemented directives, the force of the onslaught was so overwhelming that many more lives were lost than might otherwise have been the case. As the soldier-poet John Manifold later put it, in laconic Australian style: 'Muddle tall as treachery.'

According to Charles, he and Elizabeth spent time sightseeing at the recently excavated palace of Knossos (near Heraklion). Here they wandered through the Minotaur's labyrinth, and two Australian soldiers good-naturedly cleared sandbags for an hour, enabling them to see the famed king's throne. In addition to the troops recently sent in, Crete was already awash with the remnants of units of different nationalities fleeing from the mainland; one of these sheltered Charles and Elizabeth, and a café nearby cooked them basic food.

One night, with bombs falling unceasingly around them, the Cretan captain walked with them 2 miles out of the chaos into the hills to eat their first proper meal for days at a taverna hidden in a ravine: roast chicken, a dish of stuffed peppers, tomatoes, eggs and a quantity of retsina. From these extraordinary Cretan days Elizabeth later drew – with remarkable sangfroid and the sure touch of the true artist's ability to synthesize experience into art – some of the recipes for *Mediterranean Food*. To the innocent reader they are already redolent with the smell and taste of the wildly beautiful mountains of Crete. Knowing more of their provenance, one almost begins to believe that, like so many others in the book, these short and to-the-point recipes have such a weight of experience and history behind them that part of the spell they work upon us is at the level of the subliminal.

ARNÍ SOUVLÁKIA (lamb on skewers)

Cut a piece of lamb from the leg into inch cubes. Season with salt, pepper, lemon juice, and marjoram.* Thread the meat on to skewers and grill them. Serve them on a thick bed of parsley on the skewers, with quarters of lemon.

Eaten on the terrace of a primitive Cretan *taverna*, flavoured with wood smoke and mountain herbs, accompanied by the strong red wine of Crete, these kebabs can be the most poetic of foods . . .

*In Greece wild marjoram is used . . . *Origanum* means in Greek 'the joy of the mountains'.

Before the conclusion of the ferocious German assault and the last desperate evacuation of Allied troops by the Navy twelve days later, the largest-scale airborne attack ever mounted had been directed at Crete by the German Air Corps. Utterly regardless of heavy losses to their own forces soon after landing, and almost unopposed from the air, thousands upon thousands of highly trained German troops, in wave after wave, were relentlessly parachuted on to the island. In spite of gallant and sustained back-up from the Navy and the outstandingly valiant and continued defence of this beleaguered little island by Greek, New Zealand, Australian, Polish and British troops; accompanied by a Cretan population mostly unarmed, yet bitter and ruthless in their island's defence, the task finally proved hopeless. The Allied and Greek losses were huge in a battle which had from the start, through lack of information and communication difficulties, proved confusing, quickly disheartening and ultimately in vain. Those remaining could congratulate themselves, nonetheless, on having inflicted enormous (almost equivalent) losses and practically destroyed 7th Airborne Division, one of Hitler's élite fighting forces.

Charles tells us that he and Elizabeth were caught on the edge of this terrible battle. For days they tried to make their way towards Suda, then retreated, informed that the last civilians had left ten days ago and evacuation from there was now impossible. Constantly caught up in enemy gunfire, with bombs dropping incessantly, men dead and dying all around them, they gradually made their way with exhausted, retreating and wounded troops, towards Sphakia, where boats and ships were desperately evacuating thousands to naval vessels waiting offshore. Here they were finally hauled on to one of the ships, and sailed away from the battered island in the last days of its defence to safety in Egypt. If Charles's story is true, in only a few more days they would have been among the thousands reluctantly left to the mercy of the crippled but victorious German forces now occupying Crete.

According to Charles, they acknowledged the end of their romance just before they waded out to the waiting boats.

'It hasn't worked, has it?'

'No,' she said. 'It hasn't worked.'

'I know, it went wrong in Antibes, but it came back again. It would have survived Italy, but it went wrong again in Athens. I thought we had found it again in Vari, but if we get out of this, it will go wrong again. You can't live in a world of your own, you have to live in other people's worlds.' Charles's description is essentially true, but a précis of events, for their final separation was neither immediate nor painless.

CHAPTER TEN

War and the Levant
(1941–1946)

ELIZABETH AND CHARLES, without quite knowing it, were
in a state of shock. They were disoriented, bemused and found
the teeming, ancient Egyptian capital city of Cairo, now the centre
of Middle Eastern Operations for the British and Allied forces,
almost unmanageable. The contrast between their present conditions
and the life they had so recently relinquished was extreme. Elizabeth
bitterly regretted her island, saying to Pris that she was broken-
hearted to leave. For six weeks it had been 'brilliant Spring', with
breakfast on the verandah and all-day bathing. It was all the more
lovely for the knowledge that it couldn't last. They had lost more
books and clothes but above all their peace and quiet. Elizabeth
had become so used to leaving places at a moment's notice that
possessions 'now mean nothing to me. One is lucky to get out with
one's life.' She was writing in June 1941, two weeks after the fall of
Crete.

Complaining of only 'one cotton frock' in Cairo's boiling heat,
it appears that Elizabeth was finally about to enter the war effort. She
begged for communications from home and huffed that the authorities
wanted to evacuate her to India, but she absolutely refused. One thing
she had learnt after being a refugee for a year was to put her foot
down and keep it there, a trait already rather well developed.

As a result of her determination to stay put she was sent to work
as a cypherene for the Navy at the Ministry of War Transport in
Alexandria, leaving Charles job-hunting in Cairo. Her job was not
particularly exciting, yet although the hours were inconvenient it
wasn't particularly demanding. Some of those with whom she worked

'could hardly read or write'. Not being a member of one of the forces, Elizabeth was always paid on a civil servant's scale, in other words less than those in the army. Lodgings were in a *pension* with an air-raid shelter so Pris was not to worry about bombs, and anyway Elizabeth told her that she didn't yet venture out far at night. Her talk was of the 'fantastic' life of Cairo. Here little appeared to have changed since her previous visits back in the Thirties when her sister Diana said Elizabeth had written home with 'some incredibly funny stories about the Goodwins and cousin Kit, and all her expeditions across deserts with pashas in Shell cars . . .'

'Except for the hordes of officers in Shepherds', one would hardly know there was a war on; no food shortages, people out dancing, gossiping, as if nothing had changed. Elizabeth visited her mother's old friends the Goodwins, her hosts on those previous visits to Egypt, both frantically doing war work. She found other old friends and was grateful for the sight of so many familiar faces after so long. She had also come across several mutual (Malta) friends of hers and Priscilla's, now stationed in Egypt, and gave news of their positions and advancements. Charles in Cairo told her that one of those from Malta, Mike Cumberlege, had just arrived slightly wounded. Elizabeth was not troubled about his safety, 'even after the Crete business', as Mike was the sort of person who would get 'into and out of anywhere and everywhere'. The Gwynne girls' friend from London days, Hilary Magnus, now a Lieutenant-Colonel, was around but Elizabeth couldn't track him down. She asked Pris to try and discover where he was, as she would be glad to see him. She continued in ambivalent mood, saying that it was in many ways a relief to be back in civilization, with coffee for breakfast, and hot baths, and able to buy what she wanted but that she missed her island. She felt it a mockery to look at the sea and not be able to bathe; there was no beach near the town and she could bathe only 'if taken out by someone who has a cabin'. When she first arrived in Cairo, Elizabeth went into the food shops just to look at the array of provisions – the last few weeks in Greece they had been unable to get anything at all. This letter concluded with instructions to 'take care of yourself and little Sabrina and Little Stranger no. 2'. Pris had recently given birth to her second baby girl, named Julia, and was still trying to manage in her vicarage in Chipping Sodbury with little help and regular war work – she drove an ambulance.

Elizabeth later recounted that on her arrival in Egypt, for the first time since leaving home ten years earlier, a vision of Wootton as a rare oasis of calm sprang into her mind, and for a short space of time gave her a kind of succour. During the last few weeks, in surviving the ordeal of escape from Syros and then Crete and the 'general ghastly misery of everything' in the present frenetic and tense climate of war, her childhood had begun to reassert itself as a place symptomatic not only of anger and sorrow, but also of isolated pools of light and hope. 'When I arrived in Cairo and just couldn't think what I was going to do I suddenly had a conviction for about three days that if only I could find myself for a few moments in the bluebell wood at the end of the garden I should find the answer.' This conviction was accompanied by 'visions of the daffodils round the summer-house, a wooden seat in the little hole where the hops grew, a summer evening on the grass by the snapdragon borders, and I came in to find a party in progress in the Ball Room – the memorable party of Edward [Hogg (Marjoribanks), the favourite cousin who had died] and Basil Taylor and "Mind the Step".'

For over a year Elizabeth was to live in Alexandria, a place of such ancient memories that by the time of the doomed Antony and Cleopatra it was already well established as one of the most cosmopolitan cities encircling the Mediterranean Sea. Alexandria is a maze, lying low against the shoreline. A city without hills, it lies at the mouth of the Nile's great green delta with flatness stretching out beyond, to the west the Libyan Desert and to the east the Arabian one. Built by Alexander the Great 300 and more years before Christ, Alexandria quickly attracted scholars and artists of the highest rank, and shortly after Alexander's death the greatest library in the world was gathered together there.

'Five races, five languages, a dozen creeds . . .' wrote Lawrence Durrell in *Justine*, one of the *Alexandria Quartet* novels set in the city. It is at once a kind of microcosmic Durrell vision of the Middle Eastern world and the seamier aspects of the psyche; one version of the East. Later, in *Balthazar*, Durrell's narrator tells us that these parallel Alexandrian communities 'still live and communicate – Turks with Jews, Arabs and Copts and Syrians with Armenians and Italians and Greeks . . . ceremonies, marriages and pacts join and divide them . . . it is a great sprawling jellyfish.' From its founding Alexandria was a polyglot city whose culture and atmosphere were, nevertheless, above all Greek.

The Second Secretary at the British Embassy in Cairo was then Bernard Burrows (later Sir Bernard), and in conversation with the author he recalls being stirred by the knowledge that 'In the Middle East one was surrounded not only by the war but also by the Classical world. This evidence of that past world, it brought it home . . . very much. Before the war I travelled in the Eastern and Western Deserts. In a remote oasis you might find a long Greek inscription on a great stone lying there. And then in the Eastern Desert, going on in time you found the place where the Romans quarried granite for columns and floated them down the Nile, and then a broken one left there before they got it out. This continuity with the Classical tradition should not be underestimated . . . Egypt was such a puzzle; a great melting pot, culturally and politically . . . In the first war we in Britain had a greater empathy with Egypt, it was an Arab-European war with people like T. E. Lawrence and Gertrude Bell fostering that alliance. In the second war this had gone. We had written them [the Arabs] off, let them down really; it was an inter-European war. In the First War we had sought to build up the Arab States to use them against the Turks; in the Second War SOE [Special Operations Executive] was building up the Greeks, the Albanians, to use them against the Germans.'

Sir Bernard continued: 'As well as the soldiers and the diplomats, during the war there was this great inrush of intellectuals into Cairo and Alexandria, a number of whom were not really much interested in Egypt as such, but rather the literary life of London, of Paris. With the English, they were either at the Egyptian University or they'd been with the British Council in Greece. All intellectuals or at least semi-academics of one kind or another. These different strands all added to make a very potent mix. A good part of one's conversation was attempting to unravel that, to relate one part to another. But one thing which one shared with many of these people was an acquaintance with the Classical World.'

With his future wife Ines (née Walter), Sir Bernard later became part of that group of officers, diplomats and writers from whom Elizabeth was to derive stimulation and support. Many of them, like her, felt in some sense marooned by the war in a land where their European education made them more familiar with its Graeco-Roman past than either the ancient Egypt of the Pharoahs or the fast developing modern country. Since the early nineteenth century it had become prosperous again through a commerical revival – the cultivation of cotton.

Elizabeth's job in cypher was initially dull, hard work, and necessitated 'the most ghastly hours, all-night watches and suchlike antics'. It also made her terribly tired and hurt her eyes. (She had appalling sight, possibly brought on by the attack of measles suffered as a girl, and always needed glasses.) After several months, by March 1942 Elizabeth had changed her job for the better, although she was still working for the Navy in the Ministry of Transport. She was relieved to report to her sister Diana that the work was more interesting, no longer requiring sitting out night watches, and her hours were now civilized. She worked from 8.45 until one o'clock, and 3.45 until 6.30 in theory, but rarely got away before 7.30. She had two free afternoons a week but worked Saturday and Sunday. Her eyes improved and she was feeling 'in fine form and walk backwards and forwards to the office and am also frequently known nowadays to walk even when I don't need to. This country does most queer things to people.'

Elizabeth remained only a short time in the 'ghastly *pension*' after her arrival in Alexandria, moving out to share a flat with Mike Cumberlege, now based in the city. Apart from its cooler climate and the possibility of sometimes getting to the sea for bathing and sailing, she thought 'Alex in every other way a shocking dump'. Nevertheless, the re-affirmation of her friendship with the more grounded Cumberlege was to prove soothing and encouraged her re-establishment in society. She afterwards wrote to Pris that he helped her, probably without knowing it, over the first few agonizing weeks of war and town and office life, having lived in a remote place for so long without contact with civilization. Even to wear shoes was painful to her at that time, and she was convinced she could never again exist 'without the sound of the sea in my ears as I went to sleep'.

Cumberlege himself was in a dreadful state owing to his cousin's recent death in battle and his own experiences in Crete; he couldn't be left alone and needed the society of women. Elizabeth supplied this for him without any complications, which he did his best to avoid, feeling as he did about his wife, Nan. Elizabeth, with some relief, said that they succeeded in living in the same apartment for six months without 'sex rearing its ugly head'. In this mutually supportive atmosphere she began to 'feel connected up again' and to take her part in the hectic gaiety of Alexandria and Cairo.

Already exotic to those from the West, under conditions of war Alexandria and Cairo became, for Europeans, something like Western frontier towns in the Gold Rush years. Men would return there from terms of duty in the Eastern or Western Deserts, having lived for weeks on end on bully beef and tea rations cooked up in the dreadful sand-filled jerrycans. In gruelling, parched-dry alien landscapes where the engulfing sands relentlessly infiltrated every possible secret part of the body, the convoys could travel for mile after mile over sands with as few landmarks as the waves of an ocean; finally to encounter minefields or the enemy, in the air or on the shifting, mirage-ridden land. Those fortunates who survived returned to the cities for respite, with pay in their pockets and a desperate will to enjoy themselves if it was the last thing they did before returning to the desert and a good chance of maiming or death.

As Elizabeth told Pris, the bars, cabarets and restaurants were always full, everyone had plenty of money, and any girl who was at all presentable could go out every single night if she chose.

To her old friends and relations passing through or based in Cairo or Alex (among them cousins Bill Palmer and Quintin Hogg, 'covering himself in glory', and whom Elizabeth now found 'easier to talk to and . . . an extremely nice individual'), she added a growing collection of new friends and admirers. The apartment she shared 'thanks to the kindness of Mike' was large, cool and comfortable and ideal for entertaining. They employed Kyriakou as a cook, a sympathetic and poignant figure who was to be enshrined, like Priscilla's

Angela, in Elizabeth's beautiful essay for *Wine and Food* entitled 'Two Cooks'. With minimum fuss, in evocative and disingenuous prose, the piece captures something of the essential nature of both herself, her cook and his homeland. The reader's imagination is swiftly captured, and we pause for a moment to listen as Elizabeth draws us into her cameo vision of another, far-off world. In the first part of the essay, Priscilla's cook Angela is open, enthusiastic, noisy, comprehensible, out there in the clear bright sunlight. Whereas this gentle man, though quite as vivid and passionate, has an aura of contemplation, mystery; the Mediterranean sun which is his natural element is of a mellower, more melancholy kind.

Kyriakou was a Greek from the Dodecanese island of Simi. He was a sponge fisher and he had escaped twice from the Italians, for whom he had a boundless contempt. When they declared war he had sailed his boat to Mersa Matruh, and when Mersa Matruh was captured he sank his boat in the harbour rather than let the Italians get it, and escaped with the British Navy, carrying with him a sack of electrical equipment he had looted from an Italian store. How he came to be a cook-general in our absurdly grandiose Alexandrian flat is no longer very clear, and, devoted and charming as he was, a dedicated cook I cannot claim him to have been. He was not entirely of this world, perhaps it was being so much under the sea that made him so dreamy when he was on land. He would sweep the carpet with his gaze fixed on the ceiling, as if he expected any minute to swim to the surface.

The Greeks are the most democratic people in the world and a Greek servant is in every sense a member of the family . . . every detail of expenditure is discussed with the same passion as politics. Together, conversing in unlikely French and fantastic Greek, Kyriakou and I went shopping.

Kyriakou's grief as the cost of a bottle of olive oil crept up . . . was tragic to watch, and he often had to be consoled with a stiff drink of *ouzo* in the market after spending my money in this reckless fashion. The rising cost of living was considerably

augmented by the alarming quantity of breakages in our hideous
but lavishly appointed flat. This turned out to be due to the fact
that poor Kyriakou, already affected by the disease which finally
gets all deep sea divers, would sometimes have a spasm of
terrible pain ... most often when he was carrying a laden
tray ...

Even this did not account for the number of teapots which
he managed to get through in a few weeks; going into the
kitchen one day at tea time I found him in the act of putting
the tea pot, in which there was half a pound of tea and a little
cold water, straight on to the gas.

Kyriakou took some of the responsibility of entertaining into his
own hands, and sometimes invited those of Elizabeth's and Mike's
friends he preferred to a dinner he thought fitting. 'Not unnaturally
the people he favoured [the garrulous, passionate Lawrence Durrell
was one of them] were usually Greek-speaking or connected in some
way with the Greek cause, so it happened that now and again the
chromium and mirror bar, the road-house splendour of our flat, took
on the atmosphere of a taverna. Kyriakou would sit and drink with
us, pouring out the drinks and fetching clean glasses with the grace
of a host which is instinctive to every Greek ever born.'

When Kyriakou heard one day that his wife and children had
escaped from their island to Palestine, his jubilation was such that a
celebration was called for: a party for Elizabeth and her friends.
'Nothing would stop him and we were not allowed to buy a single
bottle of wine or contribute in any way to the expense. When a Greek
sets out to give a party there is no cheese-paring.'

Elizabeth was unable to discover from where her 'cook-cum-
lady's-maid' Kyriakou procured his booty for the celebratory dinner.
But he 'returned home with a bucket of shellfish the like of which
had never before been seen in Alexandria; from this he concocted a
pilaff which would have made a Spanish *paella* seem positively penny
plain. It was a fish dinner, for as well as the pilaff there were
mountains of fried fish (in Greece they like fried fish cold)'. There was
a shift of emphasis here – previously Elizabeth had railed at the Greek

taste for cold food. Kyriakou produced 'a great basin of skordalia, the Greek garlic sauce, and the masterpiece of the evening was an octopus stew'.

Although by early 1942 Elizabeth told Pris that she was preparing for limitations with the 'appalling goings-on' in the Far East, she had never ceased to be amazed by the quantity and variety of food available in Egypt. The corner shops and vegetable stalls were piled high, there was no rationing – although they were without meat for three days running a week, and without white bread, these were the only inconveniences she noticed. In Greece she said they were 'only able to buy meat once a week, the bread was as black, and as hard, as coal, and towards the end it was virtually impossible to get butter, cheese, chocolate, rice, tea, coffee, sugar or anything except vegetables'. In Alexandria one could get almost anything if one had the money – 'even TCP!'

She told Diana that she was almost 'sickened' at the amount of food available and was disdainful of those, like Hilary Magnus, who complained because they couldn't get Camembert or pâté de foie gras. Elizabeth was later to concede that a spell in the desert on army rations had made Hilary less decadent and better company. Her disdain was forcibly projected at her indolent maid, given short shrift by Elizabeth when she complained of eggs and macaroni three days running. The maid was somewhat chastened when Elizabeth asked her if she'd prefer to go to England, where she would be allowed one egg a month and no macaroni at all, and would have to really work instead of doing a bit of dusting, cooking and ironing, for which Elizabeth had to pay the 'colossal' sum of four pounds a week.

Elizabeth's published writing often presents the reader with a set of descriptive images arresting in their delineation. We are frequently aware of omissions; never so much that we cannot follow the story, but enough to leave us intrigued, wanting that little bit more. Practising this latter quality – never revealing all – with such consistency in her own life, Elizabeth instinctively understood its virtues and the methods by which one goes about it in writing. Her letters, although frequently long and full of news and events, are (aided by her persistent resistance to introspection) consummate examples of the partially revealed self. A consequence of this same trait made Elizabeth choose with a well-honed instinct the friends to whom she revealed those different aspects of herself, always maintaining her habit of compartmentalizing their friendship.

In December 1941 after six months in Alexandria Elizabeth's friendships were many and varied and included a wide spectrum of those then in Egypt, both foreign and native. As to herself and Charles Gibson Cowan, without benefit of any comment she told those at home that he had left Egypt in October 1941 and was bound for America. The circumstances surrounding Charles and Elizabeth's separation are not clear, but looking ahead at what we know of subsequent events we can make out something of the story.

Among those whom Elizabeth would later meet was a young man called Paul Gotch, who had made his own remarkable pre-war journey south with his wife Billy (on bicycles) on their pilgrim way to Greece. Paul took up employment with the infant British Council in Athens in 1940, on the same day as the writer Lawrence Durrell. Although they were both sent to different outposts, when the Germans invaded Greece, Paul Gotch, Billy, Durrell and his then wife Nancy were amongst the English exiles who escaped to Egypt. Paul taught English to wealthy Egyptians for one of the Council's Institutes at Tanta on the Delta and together with Billy – and sometimes others – in 1943 began sharing their large villa apartment with Durrell.

Recently separated from his wife Nancy, Lawrence Durrell had been loaned by the British Council as one of the Press and Information Officers to the Ministry of Information. At first in Cairo, Durrell was transferred to Alexandria in 1943. Here he utilized his remarkable grasp of Levantine languages, in combination with his garrulousness, to consort both with those of rank and to infiltrate any low dive; thereby gaining insight into the underbelly of the Middle East, to the advantage of the British government.

Durrell soon told Paul that he had encountered an interesting fellow whom he wanted him to meet; this was Charles Gibson Cowan. Whether Elizabeth's report of Charles's departure for America in 1941 was mistaken or deliberately misleading is unclear. Whichever it was, he had in fact left Egypt by the beginning of September.

The truth of the matter was that in 1941 Charles had sailed

from Port Said bound for Mombasa as bosun aboard the *Samothrace*, a large but ill-maintained luxury yacht owned by absentee American millonaire George McFadden USNVR. At Mombasa Charles joined the crew of another sailing vessel but decided to find work ashore. After briefly working in a factory he became Welfare Officer to the Port of Mombasa and, somewhat to his surprise, excelled at the task of giving assistance to visiting seamen, which included visiting and advising those in prison. During his eighteen months or so in Mombasa Charles remained in contact with Elizabeth. He also began and completed a good part of *The Voyage of the Evelyn Hope*, in effect an elegy to their affair. In 1943 McFadden asked Charles to take charge of the *Samothrace* as captain and sail her back to Alexandria, and Charles willingly accepted his offer.

The *Samothrace* reached her destination at the beginning of August and, apart from short breaks for unpublished missions, remained in the port of Alexandria, with Charles on board as caretaker, until sold to King Farouk early in 1945. In the meantime, apparently at a loose end with a luxury yacht at his disposal, Charles sailed on more than one undercover assignment culminating in his civilian attachment to MEF with the title of Chief Advisory Pilot Eastern Mediterranean.

Paul Gotch recollects an outrageous incident which occurred at this time. With the intention of giving some assistance regarding employment, he told the author that he had invited Charles to give a public lecture on the English theatre, at the British Institute in Alexandria. Public lectures at the Institute were events attended by some of the more prestigious members of Alexandrian society. True actor that he was, Charles waited in the wings until the 200 or so members of the audience had arrived, before mounting the stage and seating himself casually on the edge of the table. For the space of several minutes, and in complete silence, he proceeded to give a thorough demonstration of the art of picking one's nose, after which he began his lecture.

Paul was horrified but also amused. Later, taxing Charles with his behaviour, he was given the reply: 'Well, they didn't give me a job, did they?' (He was referring to the refusal of the British Council in Athens to give him work prior to his and Elizabeth's months on the island of Syra.) Paul described Charles as: 'an East Ender, a wide boy; a very bright, tough courageous fellow but, let's face it, to those who were, he was simply not quite a gentleman.'

Another member of the Villa Ambron household was Eve Cohen, who later married Lawrence Durrell. She had recently escaped from her repressive background into what at the time she felt was the luminescence of Durrell's vision. Eve's mother was proud Spanish-Jewish and her father an impoverished Egyptian-Jewish moneylender. Eve may have been untutored and clung to Durrell's superior knowledge, but there was no doubt regarding her natural intelligence and qualities of perception. She had an instinctive understanding of the languid decadence of her city, where, she told the author, 'You can do anything, be anything you want. Everything is too easy. Once you are out in the streets and breathe the exquisite air, you are in an atmosphere of sensuality and live for the moment, and tomorrow is another day. It is a city of the mind, but it is a sensual intellectuality. People become either self-indulgent and slothful – or ascetics. There is no middle path.' Eve's own integrity mitigated against these extremes and she was gradually to reject the city of her childhood. This questioning of a Middle Eastern essence, combined with her beauty, Durrell found irresistible.

Elizabeth sometimes came out to Alexandria to see Durrell on Ministry of Information business and he would ask her to stay overnight at the villa. As to Eve, Elizabeth did not regard her as existing in the same social orbit as herself. Elizabeth may have apparently rejected England, but her preconceptions remained for all that patrician English, amounting at times to a failure of imagination and an intellectual and social complacency. Not untypically, her interest in a less exalted class than her own extended only to a few, like Charles, with whom she felt she had a cultural bond; and Eve was conventionally unlettered. Durrell's 'Gypsy' remained quiet: 'At this time I hardly spoke,' nevertheless she observed more than Elizabeth was aware.

Charles became friendly with the members of the Villa Ambron household. By Christmas of 1943 he had finished the first draft of *The Voyage of the Evelyn Hope*. He asked for Durrell's comments on his writing but Durrell was not particularly enthusiastic. Whether or not it was this work Charles showed Durrell, by November of the following year he had signed a contract with the Cresset Press.

Paul Gotch believes Durrell was sometimes irritated by Charles. Eve believes he was sometimes jealous of his undeniable charisma and says, 'Oh, Charles always took centre stage; Larry was – half of him – keen to torture Charles, and envious of him.' With a luxury ship at Charles's disposal, Eve and Paul both remember extended parties on board at which he excelled himself at the stove. 'Charles was a very good, confident, and completely slapdash cook,' says Eve. (Apropos this when Paul was on a British Council posting to the island of Menorca after the war, his wife Billy set up a hotel. One day Charles appeared from nowhere, and in recognition of his skills as a cook Billy gave him the job of chef. Charles was a success except that, as Paul remembers, 'He would come into the restaurant dressed only in shorts and tell the clients with some force what they should choose from the menu.'

Eve Durrell says she found Charles at times histrionic, a buffoon with an endlessly mobile face: 'He had the flavour of the East End about him. He was enigmatic, a loner; a man always performing – well – and never revealing all. But he was not a shallow man. He dared to trust people, unlike Larry. Sometimes Charles made me cringe.'

Whilst Charles made it clear that he did not want his own visits to the Villa Ambron to overlap with Elizabeth's, it seems that his reappearance provoked feelings of regret in her concerning their earlier separation, which she confided to Durrell with Eve present. Despite her flat, non-committal announcement to Priscilla of Charles's departure for America two years earlier in 1941, and her subsequent negative comments about him, Elizabeth seems to have hidden from her family, and most friends, the significance of her experiences and emotions in relation to the man whom her family had censured for so many years. Above all she successfully hid her feelings from herself.

Something of the significance of Elizabeth's affair with Charles is more convincingly captured in the letter from herself to Charles, written some time after they had separated and quoted by him (anonymously) on the dedicatory page of *The Voyage of the Evelyn Hope*:

We'll both think often of the things we have done together; of
the canals, and the wine, and the red rocks of my beloved France;
of the sea white with nautilus off the coast of Corsica; of dawn
in the Bay of Naples; of a certain lobster mayonnaise we ate
between one life and another; of mountains of golden oranges in
Josipi's garden, and those purple islands lying all around us from
the top of the hill behind our house. Thank you for the lovely
experiences you have given me, and remember that you made
the Isles of Greece more than just a beautiful name for both of
us . . .

Whatever the tangled sequence of events, and the vexed question
of who had left whom, Charles and Elizabeth never lived together
again. A postscript highlights the inconclusiveness of both their
feelings. Eve Durrell and Paul Gotch remember that on several
occasions at the Villa Ambron Charles would speak about Elizabeth
and say, 'She was the woman of my life and that is why I left her.'

Back in England and several years after the war, Elizabeth went
to stay with her friend Doreen Thornton (née Brownhill), who quickly
regretted her misguidedness in putting a copy of *The Voyage of the
Evelyn Hope* in Elizabeth's room. She was enraged, in tears, and tore
up the book.

In January 1945, through Lawrence and Eve Durrell, Charles
met an Israeli girl, Giela. They soon left to live in Cyprus, and
eventually married. Years afterwards in the 1960s, and back in
England, Paul came across Charles running a successful restaurant in
Kent called High Rocks. Charles had long since been out of touch
with Elizabeth. He had married for a third time and died not long
after Paul's visit to his restaurant.

Returning to October 1941, the month in which Charles and
Elizabeth had separated, she was writing from Alexandria about her
pleasure at receiving letters from Norman Douglas again. She was
relieved at his present safety with her cousin Neil in Lisbon, and
announced her approval of her sister Diana's August marriage to the
young doctor Christopher Grey. By December Elizabeth and Mike

Cumberlege had amicably decided it was time to move on and find themselves separate accommodation – he was frequently out of Egypt on secret Naval missions – and Elizabeth had found a tiny flat of her own. She gave Felicité a bitingly funny characterization of that ponderous aspect of Middle Eastern taste and conjured up a whole world. The flat was covered with brown wallpaper and filled with aspidistras, plush curtains and huge mirrored sideboards. She threw them all away and painted the flat cream, keeping only a few pieces of furniture. She described her bedroom furniture as 'Tottenham Court Rd modern', of a 'hideosity' rarely seen, but said the bed was comfortable and the wardrobe large with a long mirror. There was a minute bathroom and a fairly good kitchen.

And, although she was immensely grateful for the companionship and support that Mike Cumberlege had given her and the highly sociable life of their flat, she said, 'I'm really happier living on my own.'

Elizabeth was self-conscious about the burdens and the impoverishment of life at home in England while she lived in Egypt with an abundance of food, drink and cigarettes, and regularly went out, nonetheless she explained that if she didn't occupy her mind with other things, the war and Egypt would get her down completely. For a good part of the time Elizabeth's need to retreat from her own thoughts or unresolved emotions had been kept at bay with a very full social life, and the insecurity of war made this frenetic life-style even more seductive. She said, 'I feel I simply have to go out to parties and fall madly in and out of love and beat up the town from time to time.' Surprisingly, she added that she was no longer able to read, she lacked concentration and was always too tired after leaving her office. She then referred Pris to the perpetually worrying question of money and succinctly described what always seemed to be her position: 'I am extremely sorry to be such a pestering nuisance with my finances – I keep trying not to spend money & it just goes like mad.'

References to her social life, sometimes exhausting, and emotionally precarious, grew more and more frequent as the months passed and her circle widened. Amongst new friends she met old ones from London and Malta. She joined Hilary Magnus, now a Major in the

Rifle Brigade, one evening in one of the grandest hotels, aptly described as the Shepherds of Alex. On the subject of Magnus Elizabeth was in fine form; irritated by his habits and tastes, she produced a good vignette for Felicité. She found him in the bar of the Cecil, 'consuming champagne cocktails at about 30/- a time', red in the face and looking quite extraordinary in what appeared to be a floor-length captured German overcoat. She had dinner with him, and for once he had the money to pay the bill without having to borrow it, but he made her promise to buy him five pounds' worth of marmalade, which he would return to collect in a week's time. Fortunately Elizabeth ignored this, because when Magnus came back he announced that he'd bought it himself. He annoyed her so much she made up her mind not to go out with him that evening. She gave him an excuse but Magnus outdid her, saying he'd had no intention of asking her anyway, he felt too liverish. 'In spite of this I'm always pleased to see him.' On another occasion he was 'the old wretch . . . had a new pose . . .' and was evocatively described as 'like a breath of Lincoln's Inn, the Ecu de France, The Café Royal and No. 16 John St' (Elizabeth's last flat before leaving London).

She was not unusual in her sensuous responses to the glimpse of a face, a curve outlined, an arresting movement, a colour, a scent; the taste of another time and place. Where Elizabeth differed from many, aiming at Proustian effects, was in her wish to describe these sensuous responses and in her ability to achieve it. She was not to begin writing professionally for several years, but in her war letters all her faculties and sensitivities are at work: collecting, sifting, rejecting, criticizing, discerning. She also displays an endearing lack of punctuation, reinforcing one's impression of her in private: smoky silences, or thoughts and feelings spilling over one another so quickly her pen cannot keep up. These early characteristics are ironic in the light of her subsequent grammatical punctiliousness as a writer — so extreme that she once tried to have a young sub-editor on a magazine sacked for 'mis-editing my work'.

A sensuous delight in clothes was a constant theme of her letters. A friend from Malta, Lindsey Jackson (later an admiral), had brought back with him from a recent trip to England a magnificent parcel of favourite clothes, jewellery, photographs and letters; collected together by Priscilla for Elizabeth and delivered to her office. Elizabeth thanked Priscilla ecstatically for everything, including the organization of letters from everyone she cared about in England. As soon as she arrived home she tore open the parcel, to find clothes 'reeking' of John Street and the existence they now thought of as 'before the war'. The first item to emerge was her blue coat: she remembered trudging through the snow with Pris, in woollen stockings and snowboots, on the way to her first fitting for it; and sitting in the flat during that dreadful winter, the pipes frozen, two enormous fires blazing, cutting out penny-plain twopence-coloured prints for Christmas cards. Next out was a little black taffeta jacket, new when Elizabeth first went to Malta; it reminded her of Pris's sitting room, pale blue armchairs, striped curtains, bowls of freesias, Angela in a panic about a quail that the cat had eaten. A blouse threaded with coloured ribbons, worn at the party for Felicité's twenty-first birthday: the flat pandemonium, people running up and down the stairs with food and champagne, while Elizabeth frantically made asparagus rolls. Twenty-five people came to dinner that night instead of the ten expected, including a Romanian whom no one had invited. Evarts had carved turkey like one possessed, and Elizabeth was still painting her nails as the first guests arrived. With a 'wild yell of joy' she seized her scarlet woollen dress, and felt she could almost 'live through again two years' of her life, so often had she worn it. And then the black dress she wore the winter she worked at Worth, and a studded belt. And finally, 'in the midst of all this . . . past', some mysterious little parcels with exquisite bracelets, brooches, and beautiful old buttons that she had never seen before.

Elizabeth's friend from schooldays, Marian Butterworth, had recently married and Elizabeth hoped she would be happy. Felicité was working as a secretary in the Admiralty (organized by Uncle Top) and Pris struggled on with the little girls in Chipping Sodbury, while continuing in the role of surrogate mother to her three younger sisters.

By March 1942 Norman Douglas's welfare was again concerning Elizabeth. He had returned to England. She was immensely grateful to Neil Hogg for having looked after him so well in Portugal: 'One couldn't help being of course [grateful] . . . he is the world's darling and my life's love, but it is so nice of Neil all the same.' Felicité was thanked for writing to him, but Elizabeth was really concerned about Douglas because he hadn't been in England since 1917, hated the climate and was bound to be very miserable. She asked her sister to look him up in London and told her that she would find him most interesting. Elizabeth next asked Felicité if she had read his *Old Calabria*. Elizabeth preferred it to *South Wind*, and thought it first-class writing; although *South Wind* was 'good fun to read', first-class writing it was not.

Although Elizabeth had now held down a job more consistently than ever before, her habitually erratic *emotional* pathways were not easily altered. Her need to blot out the insecurity produced by war or her own unwanted thoughts, were not conducive to an emotional state of greater equilibrium. She was hard on herself; hard in that she abused her body with too much alcohol and her emotions in relationships with men who were likely to hurt her. She was self-destructive, and at a profound level was untrusting. Nevertheless, she leapt into the more existential levels of experience and had the courage to face up to the consequences of her own actions. This pattern of behaviour was already well established, and would remain more or less unchanged for the rest of Elizabeth's life.

Her judgement of others was equally severe, but this severity sprang from self-centredness combined with a vein of austerity, rather than the austerity of a moral vision. She was a realist and a pragmatist, yet endlessly hopeful and passionate; she was not a romantic but nurtured intense likes and dislikes regarding both people and ideas. A friend of many years, Patrick Woodcock, recently said of her, 'I think she always liked pleasing men. But I don't think they ever came up to scratch for her. I don't think she was very perceptive about them. She had passionate friendships. What she really wanted was friendship.' This comment is instructive in the light of Elizabeth's romantic attachments. There are many factors at work here, but the most significant relate to her limited ability to accept men for what they were.

Meanwhile Elizabeth wrote to Pris that she had 'an occasional racket around the town when a particular friend turns up out of the blue'. Elizabeth's normal reaction to her own excesses was a complete withdrawal: going home from the office, resorting to her old habit of unhooking the telephone, refusing to answer the door bell, ignoring dinner engagements, and behaving rudely to her friends. In this mood she did not emerge until she felt human again. She even went 'for long walks at strange hours of the day and strode along the Corniche Road in the heat of the afternoon, gaping at the sun and oblivious of passers-by'. Behaving, in fact, rather like her Aunt Dorothy, her maiden aunt still living on the home farm at Folkington.

She wondered if she wouldn't end up in similar circumstances. She told Pris that there might be many worse fates, and reminded her that she never could abide the idea of marriage. She never liked any man sufficiently to want him hanging around her all the time; and when she did 'lose her head' in that respect, six months was always more than enough time to cure her. Elizabeth knew this, she said, when she left England; Charles knew it; they had a good life all the same, although she had no intention of it ever becoming permanent. If she were to marry now, it would be for money, and only to someone extremely rich. She was perspicacious enough, however, to realize that hers was not the type that appeals to millionaires. She thought she would probably continue to exist in her current state. Pris was told that their childhood had completely put Elizabeth off having children of her own. Of course she never knew what she might do in a 'moment of aberration', because one of the 'main conditions of continued existence is that life should always be full of changes and surprises'. It certainly always had been for Elizabeth.

Only some of Elizabeth's new friends were mentioned in letters to her family and old friends. In part this was because her instinct for a good story led her, in letters back home, to refer to those whom they could recognize and identify. More importantly this was a reflection of Elizabeth's inclination to keep the elements of her life separate.

One of the new friends whom she did mention was a young woman she had met not long after her arrival in Alexandria, Renée Catsaflis. Renée was half Italian and half Greek. From an old and wealthy family of Alexandrian lawyers, Renée moved amongst that cosmopolitan upper echelon of Alexandrian and Cairene society where Jews, Copts, other Christians and Muslims tolerantly overlapped. These were people for whom French was the first language and who were perfectly familiar with Europe, often wintering in Switzerland, Paris or on the Riviera. Beautiful, intelligent, cultivated, Renée had been sent to school in France. She was both enigmatic and outrageous, reticent and forthcoming. She was also devoted to her twin brother. Renée and Elizabeth became close friends and spent many of Elizabeth's free days together, in the summer months often spending the whole day by the sea, or going 'for some sort of totter around in the winter – one can't call it going out to the country because there isn't any sort of country here'.

By May of 1942 Renée's company was helping to lighten the load of Elizabeth's present employment. Working every day, always distasteful to her, had become a daily burden, and she counted the hours until her day off. Without her weekly break she felt she would sink into 'sheer robotism'. Through friends like Renée Elizabeth came to know some of the more exalted members of Egyptian society, including Baron Georges de Menasce, a Jewish financier and one of those whom Elizabeth eventually regarded as the kindest to her during her years in the Middle East.

She told Felicité at this time that she was bored and frustrated by her work in cypher at the Admiralty, 'being harried about by jumped up shipping clerks, forever typing out lists, cyphering a lot of rubbish, sitting in an office with a lot of clods smoking stinking pipes and having practically to ask permission to go to the lavatory'. This was soon to come to an end. Elizabeth was too intelligent, self-willed and independent to flourish under any kind of bureaucratic discipline. However, the events of war would once again be responsible for a sudden change in her circumstances.

On 20 June 1942, when Rommel had relentlessly pushed the Allied Forces forward along the coast and in the desert, after enormous bombardment and desperate resistance from the troops, Tobruk fell. In Egypt and Britain the loss was regarded as a disaster. The Eighth Army was in retreat from Rommel, but at El Alamein Rommel's exhausted forces stopped, only 60 miles from Alexandria. This terrifying proximity, combined with what was mistakenly interpreted as the withdrawal of part of the Allied Fleet from Alex, led to general panic and a grand exodus of civilians from both Alexandria and Cairo. This was known as 'the Flap'. Rommel was in fact subsequently driven back and Alexandria and Cairo were never occupied. Churchill nevertheless, changed his Commander in Chief in the Middle East, Auchinleck, unceremoniously dumped back in India, and Montgomery began his leadership of the Desert War which would make him a national hero.

On 1 July, when the British Embassy and GHQ in Cairo began burning documents, Elizabeth and her colleagues had already been evacuated to Suez. She wrote to Pris telling her not to worry. She had become accustomed to speedy evacuations and by this time her sister 'ought to have confidence in my ability to extract myself from these tiresome situations'.

In due course the office was returned to Alexandria. Elizabeth had to stay in a makeshift hostel, which she referred to as 'the Haggery'. She was, of course, scathing about the other women with whom she shared the hostel, saying that they were all 'flapping like crows'. At the time she was suffering from a severe skin infection on her foot, picked up at the beach, and was almost unable to walk, both feet done up in yards of bandages. In fine acerbic form, she gave a revealing picture of self-awareness and her ability to manipulate. Surrounded by battered cases, 'waiting for someone to come and help me or lean heavily on someone's arm looking as brave and splendid as any wounded hero while four or five other people follow carrying my fantastic pieces of baggage – the system has its advantages'.

After two months of 'encampment and borrowing (for three weeks) a house outside the city right on the edge of the sea, where a continuous wild party was in progress', Elizabeth was moved to Cairo. She was reluctant to go. Most of her friends were in Alex; Cairo was noisy, full of people, hot and sticky, and she could never find her way about and spent a fortune on taxis. A friend, her cousin Kit Ayling's husband, Alan, had recently said to her that she would soon be fed up with 'racketing around', but Elizabeth thought England a 'difficult proposition' and felt fatalistic about her own destiny. Making plans, she believed, was an utterly futile pastime, one she indulged in 'only when in reckless mood'.

In Cairo she was at first in lodgings, bed and breakfast with a 'ghastly landlady in the centre of town' although it was clean and well furnished. Having overcome her distaste for landladies, she was relieved not to have dealings with 'beastly servants, the everlasting meals . . . the marketing which although I love, doing it takes a fearful time – and all the rest of the business . . . I know that . . . whoever I share a flat with it's always me who does the housekeeping. As you know I love entertaining and so am led into fantastic expense . . . I really cannot bear to share a flat with droves of people and that's the only way one can afford to exist . . . as living conditions in Cairo are so absolutely impossible . . . one considers oneself lucky to have anywhere to live at all.'

Naturally Elizabeth could not survive for long in the despised lodgings and so found herself a flat. It was small and like a little oven in summer but it was her own. And she could luxuriate in the knowledge that when she was too tired to speak she could indulge in her favourite and 'indescribable pleasure of coming home, locking the door behind me and settling down in bed with a pile of books'. She quickly made a great many friends in Cairo and for the first time in years actually had a job that she liked.

Elizabeth was now working as Reference Librarian for the busy office of the Ministry of Information, part of GHQ Middle East. J. M. Richards, since 1931 the influential and ambitious editor of the *Architectural Review*, was about to take over as Director of Publications and he and Elizabeth soon became friends. The MOI was a department of the Ministry of State in Britain, set up as an information and propaganda machine with three sections: Publications, Library and Reference. The Ministry had any number of Press Attachés and Information Officers situated throughout the Middle East at embassies or high commissions, constantly feeding in information which might be useful in the exercise to persuade the Middle East that it was better off with the British than the Germans. These Press and Information Officers were an enormously varied group, recruited from all types of peacetime occupation; several were academics or writers of one kind or another. Amongst this particular group were a number who became good friends of Elizabeth's.

Reference librarianship was probably not a job Elizabeth would have sustained well for a lengthy period of time, but for a while, with her natural curiosity and formidable memory, it suited her perfectly. Teaching her a considerable amount about gathering material, about

precision and concision in writing, it also gave her first-hand knowledge of the workings of a library. Her job was to read newspapers,
books and magazines, write summaries of the comments, and pass the
important issues on to the people who could best use them. After her
boredom in the Navy the job seemed wonderful, although what she
had to read was not what Elizabeth would have chosen for herself.

She also revealed her relative lack of interest, or certainly lack of
sophistication, in the workings of politics. She had scarcely read any
papers since the outbreak of war; her present job was a far cry from
the days when the only newspaper she ever opened was the *Sunday
Express*. The outpourings of journalists and propaganda writers were
not her idea of mental stimulus, but it was another matter when she
was paid to read them. Her office took all the daily papers and most
of the weeklies, and she had to read them all. Speeches, battles,
figures and statistics of losses, production, notes on well-known
personalities, activities in occupied countries – all must be carded up
and distributed. Added to this, Elizabeth had to deal with people
dropping into the office all day long asking for articles, cuttings,
books: 'what Eden said at Anapolis, how many planes the Germans
lost last month'. She had an unerring nose for anything with a whiff
of the absurd: 'what date the Germans first took so and so, when the
Russians retook it and when the Germans took it again'.

Two further references are good indications of her future self and
what would become her established methods of working. 'I can never
see over the pile of stuff waiting to be read . . . I go nearly mad
sometimes, and as I can't bear to appear inefficient I sometimes spend
whole mornings looking for some footling date or other – to be quite
honest *I really love the job* and wouldn't change it for anything.' Later
she wrote with relish to Felicité that as far as books were concerned
she was in a better position than most people, because one of her jobs
was ordering them for the library in her office. This suited her down
to the ground, because, although she couldn't order exactly what she
would have liked, the library consisting mainly of reference books and
propaganda, she was still able to buy most of the new Penguins and
all the books reviewed in the English papers.

One of Elizabeth's friends who regularly turned up at the library
was a tall, dusky young man, with lustrous eyes as brown as her own

and an equal attention to self-presentation. According to his second wife, Judith, George Lassalle and Elizabeth had met in 1932, or thereabouts, while he was up at Oxford and she was acting at the Playhouse (although by George's own account in *The Fish in My Life*, published in 1989, they did not meet until 1942, in Cairo). George was sent to Oxford by his father to read Forestry, changed to Law and ended by taking a degree in Modern Languages. Strict Catholics, the Lassalle family appear to have arrived from Trinidad in 1914. George was born there in 1911. After Oxford, having been given an allowance for France, instead George went off to the Greek islands where he perfected his fishing technique, refined his wit, collected eccentric friends, got himself in and out of dramas and a marriage, and returned to run a jazz music business in Soho. Having remarried, he was called up, entered the Royal Sussex Regiment and was sent out to Egypt. Here, partly as a result of his French and Greek, George was transferred to Intelligence in the Greek section; ideal for someone to whom subterfuge was second nature.

Always charming, dedicated almost as obsessively as Lawrence Durrell to his conquest of women, George had long since begun an affair with Elizabeth. They had few illusions about one another, but remained friends, and sometimes lovers, for the rest of their lives.

All those whom one should know – those, that is, who graced the bar at Shepherds, Groppis and the parties at Zmalek and Bulaq Dacrour – often passed through the doors of the Ministry of Information Library to give and receive information and gossip. Two of Elizabeth's closest friends in Egypt were the aforementioned Lawrence Durrell, and Robin Fedden. A conscientious objector, Fedden had followed the course often suggested by pacifist beliefs; working as an ambulance driver, before taking a lectureship in the English department of Cairo's Fuad El Awad University. He was soon to marry Elizabeth's friend Renée Catsaflis and lived with her and several others in a large, cool house in Bulaq Dacrour across the river, to the west of Gezira Island and the Sporting Club. During their stay, for the summer months the house became a favourite venue for the literate and stylish to gather, and parties there made it one of the most sought-after places at which to be 'seen'. John Brinton (American Military Attaché) and his wife, Bernard Burrows and his future wife, the beautiful Ines Walter, David Abercrombie (later Professor of Linguistics at Edinburgh University) who also taught at Cairo University, and his wife Mary made up the household. Elizabeth came there to escape the heat of the city and after the drinking and the dancing one could always cool off in the welcoming pool.

Elizabeth had met Robin Fedden before the war in Egypt, when she first visited the Middle East and when Fedden was already living there. In 1939 he had published *The Land of Egypt* in which he gives due credit to the classic works on Egypt and adds some resonant descriptions of the country and its classical remains. He was an open-minded and cultivated man, a true European, who mixed with both the wealthy and more scholarly of Egyptian society; yet, despite cautious hopes for a future, emancipated non-fundamentalist Egypt, he was unable to disguise his distaste for aspects of the country, and a clear preference for the land, the culture and climate of Greece shines through *The Land of Egypt*.

The regret and nostalgia of exile are palpable through Robin Fedden's description and rejection of modern Egypt in his introduction to the literary quarterly, *Personal Landscape* (privately printed 1942–5, then by Editions Poetry London, 1945). This he founded with his friends Lawrence Durrell and the poet Bernard Spencer. For those who contributed to the magazine the identification was the same. They were, however, like Fedden referring in their lamentations of exile not to England but to an adopted country – Greece. And, like religious converts, those who adopt another country often do so with a fervour never accorded to their native land. In the case of Greece it was the country which most Europeans between the wars still felt was their cultural Mecca. Even for devotees of Italy, Greece was the source of Western civilization; still accessible enough for those who had the cultural resources to understand how to summon up its past.

Robin Fedden and Lawrence Durrell were both men for whom the ideal of Greece was very real. Elizabeth might not have benefited from the rigorous classical education of Spencer or Fedden, but like Durrell she identified entirely with their sense of exile and was party to many late-night conversations emanating from the same principles inspiring *Personal Landscape*. (Burrows recalls that some believed Durrell's lack of a classical education made him not quite 'pukka'.)

Overlapping socially with this diplomatic and literary group of Elizabeth's friends was another set which fought its war with arms. Several of its members may afterwards have written good books, but in keeping with the best-known of them, Patrick Leigh Fermor who remained a good friend of Elizabeth's, they were men of action as much as writers. That Leigh Fermor became one of the most revered of post-war *travel* writers is, then, no coincidence. With his friend 'Pint Pot' Xan Fielding, Leigh Fermor was in and out of Cairo on one mission or another. With others of their circle they had taken a house of grand Italianate proportions and ageing elegance at the northern end of Cairo's Gezira Island.

In February 1943 Elizabeth was writing to Pris about her worries of the moment. Back to her 'old habits of regular entertaining', she fussed over arranging the flowers, sewing buttons on her clothes and her servant—cook who was giving concern. She found it impossible to explain to a cook who could not read or 'speak any known language', and who 'couldn't cook anyway', what she wanted for dinner.

For this cook, Suleiman, Elizabeth came to feel great affection and, as with those other cooks, Angela and Kyriakou, she recorded his sympathetic nature and abilities for posterity at regular intervals for the rest of her life. In *Mediterranean Food* Suleiman's Rice Pilaff became famous; in 'Fast and Fresh', an article for the *Spectator* in 1960, she characterized his talents and charm; again, ten years on, when Elizabeth launched her rediscovery of the East, in *Spices, Salt and Aromatics in the English Kitchen* and in the article she wrote for Smallbone Kitchen Designs, one of her last, he was lovingly remembered. The following extracts give brilliant, swift evocations of the food of the Levant. Most cooks employed by the English were convinced that the only proper food for them was nursery fare with Middle Eastern overtones. In 'Fast and Fresh' she wrote:

My own cook, Suleiman, was a Sudanese who had previously only worked for Italian and Jewish families. He was erratic and forgetful, but singularly sweet in nature, devoted to his cooking pots and above all knew absolutely nothing of good clean, English schoolroom food.

The description of Suleiman and his cooking was refined for the Smallbone article and as the story develops we are charmed and amused as he:

> performed minor miracles with two primus stoves and an oven which was little more than a tin box perched on top of them. His soufflés were never less than successful, and with the aid of a portable charcoal grill carried across the road to the Nile bank opposite (the kitchen was so small it didn't even have a window, and if he had used charcoal he'd have been asphyxiated) he produced perfectly good lamb kebabs. The rice pilaff I named after him . . . became part of quite a few people's lives at that time.

Besides entertaining Elizabeth was above all preoccupied and tense about her present lover; an ex-Oxford student from North America, at present in the 9th Queen's Royal Lancers and lying wounded in a hospital outside Cairo. She told Pris in April 1945 that he 'had been in the thick of battle and terribly wounded at Mersa Matruh in November'. For the past five months she had gone out twice a week to the most 'god awful' hospital she had ever seen, which was forty minutes outside Cairo. 'All the worst things that could have happened to him have happened to him and he never uttered a murmur of pain or discouragement.' Elizabeth was thankful she was in Cairo, and able to attend to him.

Meanwhile she told Pris that she was 'terribly grateful to a friend, Guy Charvet (head of Shell), for lending his car twice a week for the purpose. 'The whole business has been very heartbreaking – I haven't mentioned it before because we've all got our own hells to cope with . . . I have been so glad to have had my flat and he has been able to come out of the hospital and have meals with me.' During this period her cousin Neil Hogg, who had recently looked after Norman Douglas so well, dashed through Cairo on his reluctant way up to the Embassy at Baghdad. He wrote from there to Priscilla and their similar style explains something of his and Elizabeth's attachment to one another: 'Isn't it hell being sent away like this? I was bundled off in a flying cattle truck and just contrived to reach here alive a week ago. Now I shall roast and rot here for two years at least ... Liza was in pretty good form, looking rather Persian I thought ... We had dinner on the roof of an Arab restaurant — kebabs and rice and eggfruit — and talked of you and ourselves and the family ...'

This oriental touch in Elizabeth's appearance is also noted by her friend Leigh Fermor who told the author: 'She wore caftans of rather nice material, with many buttons down the front. But then it didn't look affected to dress up, we all did.' He noted too her 'beautiful voice'. This merely hints at that feline quality Elizabeth possessed and which some found so striking. Her voice has been described by certain friends as 'quiet', by others 'breathy', still others 'actressy'. But perhaps the most evocative description is given by the journalist Alix Coleman, who became a friend of Elizabeth's and who told the author: 'She had an expiring voice. Very femme fatale ... She could, without doing anything, make a man feel good. She used to turn her nose up or give a little gasp — or the way she put a cigarette out — she did it in a sexy way. Once there were some workmen across the way at Halsey Street, one look from Elizabeth and they would have been right over and through the door.'

In the same letter to Pris describing her wounded lover's suffering, she also mentioned having written to Aunt Grace and Uncle Top about their son Bill's recent death. Another cousin, Jasper Ridley, her Uncle Jasper's son, was killed in 1943. 'Not that there is anything to say under the circumstances. Tragedy is part of one's everyday existence and one thinks less of it than what one is going to order for lunch — it sounds callous but that's the way it is.' Perhaps these are truisms of the brutalizing consequences of war, but this was not the only response made by survivors and reflects Elizabeth's capacity for insensitivity. In contrast to the solace she had given Mike Cumberlege after his cousin's death, on these other occasions her unwillingness to reach out emotionally and soothe those facing the starkness of this reality is quite striking. With no belief in an afterlife, death for Elizabeth was complete oblivion: utter finality and nothing less. Its immensity was such that for the moment Elizabeth saw no point in wasting time over it once it had happened.

By July she was writing that her lover Peter Laing was much recovered and had gone back to North America. Certainly at the time she believed herself very much in love with him and was bitter a year later when she said that he had forgotten her. (Peter Laing was extremely attractive and women were apparently smitten by him with unerring regularity.) This man wounded Elizabeth and continued to do so for a number of years; having resumed the liaison after the war. In not marrying her he had presumably recognized (no matter if unconsciously) what Elizabeth never properly faced: that she would have been unable to sustain the relationship.

In addition to her very full working day, combined with entertaining friends and going out, Elizabeth somehow fitted in 'a little acting for ENSA', the organization which produced entertainment for the troops. But she was feeling worn out and pining for friends no longer in Egypt. One of these was Mike Cumberlege, gone missing on one of his secret missions in the Mediterranean. It was subsequently discovered that Cumberlege had been captured by the Germans. Refusing to talk under torture he was incarcerated (sometimes in solitary confinement) for twenty-one months in Saxonhausen, one of the worst German prisoner-of-war camps; then taken out and shot just as the Russians moved into Berlin in 1945. Cumberlege was posthumously awarded two DSOs, 'a rare honour', as his wife later wrote to Pris when asking her to pass on the final confirmation of his death to Elizabeth.

Elizabeth found some solace in her work. It was a pleasure to immerse herself in this instead of 'spitting' at everyone as she had in the old office. This repeated and very evident sense of fulfilment in her work reflects a subtle, but extremely important shift in her attitudes and sensibilities. Here in Cairo Elizabeth was for the first time carrying out a job which she cared about enough to do consistently well. Her regular and increasing familiarity with the unpleasant details of war also now made her own war effort (namely her job) more a matter of commitment than, as previously, mere necessity.

Time passed and a year later, on 5 July 1944, Elizabeth wrote in weary tones to Pris, and later her mother, with a startling piece of news. 'In fact what with one thing and another Cairo has so worn down my spirit that I am thinking of getting married.' She asked Pris's absolute confidence over this, not yet having decided whether she could face giving up her liberty, and continued in the same mode: 'The man in question is not at all the man I intended to marry, but he seems to love me very much and is apparently able to provide for me in modest comfort.' Her astoundingly practical and imperious tone throughout this and a subsequent letter to her mother was tinged with the usual tongue in cheek. 'He has been in the Indian Army, poor man, most of his life and as a result is practically illiterate . . . He likes dancing and drinking. I rather suspect he is given to riding, and reading P. G. Wodehouse, but one can hardly expect anyone in the Indian Army to do anything else . . . However as all my intelligent and more irresponsible boyfriends are always penniless it would seem wiser to keep them as friends and marry someone who can look after me.' (Owing to Tony David's tendency to do things 'in style' Elizabeth possibly believed her future husband to be richer than he was.) She again insisted on no presents, saying that Tony was very generous and would give her whatever she wanted, 'barring mink coats and Packard motor cars'. One of the most revealing aspects of this letter is Elizabeth's consistently objective tone. In her determination to protect herself from being hurt again she is choosing a relationship over which she believes she will have more control; possible with Tony because she is not captivated. Elizabeth has not yet learnt, however, perhaps she never did, that this control will only be partially effective, because those aspects of herself which she refuses to address will always manage to surface in unexpected ways.

To her mother she said, 'I am beginning to feel the need of a prop'; and told her that although she would probably be horrified to hear Tony David was in the Indian Army, 'I think he has spent most of his career dancing attendance on Governors and Viceroys rather than flogging the natives . . .' Elizabeth's comments here are, typically, pretty accurate. Tony David was ADC to the Governor of the Punjab and later also to the Viceroy. 'I have told him that I don't see myself sitting in some compound or other watching people play polo for the rest of my life, and I think he wants to get out of it anyway.'

Elizabeth instructed her mother and Pris to tell only Diana and Felicité. Friends and family were not to make a fuss or spend money on presents. Neither did she want anyone at home to be offended at her secrecy, but said that it would all be over quickly and, with a revealing piece of self-knowledge, that anyway they knew her well enough to expect anything she did to take place in a 'shady' manner. On Tony's return from a term of duty in the Allied advance pushing up through Italy, she would make her final decision. They planned to marry at the Consulate and Elizabeth insisted that her dislike of formal weddings was so great that, as her large number of friends would 'insist on a demonstration of some kind', she had decided to tell almost no one in Cairo until after the event. She had threatened Tony with calling the wedding off if he disobeyed her instructions. For all that, Tony was apparently friendly with John Brinton, American Military Attaché, and Sir Miles Lampson, Britain's Ambassador to Egypt, so Elizabeth supposed they would have to have a small party. She said she would keep on her flat and job after the wedding.

Aware that her wedding announcement sounded as weary as it did, she explained herself. 'The glamour boy I was so attached to . . . has apparently forgotten my existence and at my age . . . I have no intention of being led a dance by anybody, I simply don't care enough. I'm afraid this letter doesn't sound a very happy one, but don't get a wrong impression. I like the man very much and get on well with him . . .' She added that he was kind, competent and intelligent enough to accept her as she was; would not try and make her into something different, and that she would probably be able to lead quite a reasonable life with him. Her final comment admirably sums up her attitude: 'It is only the realization that I am so tired of living this haphazard life, never having enough money and never being able to do what I want and that marriage is the only answer has depressed me somewhat.' Elizabeth's desire for a protector is understandable, but her calculation is more startling.

Ivor Anthony David was born in Bristol in 1911 and was, most probably, taken out to Ceylon with his mother not long afterwards.

His father, Ivor Edward, was Inspector General of Police in Ceylon, but died of lockjaw in 1913 when Tony was only two. Having buried her husband (given a state funeral), we can assume that Beatrice brought Tony and his other siblings, Yvonne and Richard, back to Britain before the beginning of the 1914—18 war. The David family home, the Hendre, was in the ancient Welsh city of Llandaff where the Davids have been recorded for several centuries. It was here that Beatrice brought her children to live for a number of years.

Beatrice's own ancestry had established wider family horizons: she was French and Spanish and claimed descent from the house of Bourbon. Her belief that children's upbringing should be varied and cosmopolitan meant that, accordingly, her own became familiar with the countries of Europe. It is likely that Tony shared some of his brother's and sister's fluency in European languages, but whether he travelled with his mother quite as much as they is not clear. Yvonne and Dick were, respectively, ten and nine years older than Tony when he went up to public school in 1925 and although very fond of him they were already young adults when he went away to school.

During the holidays time must have dragged for a young boy in London, where Beatrice now lived when not abroad. Soon a solution appears to have been found which pleased both Tony and his mother. At Bradfield College, although not in the same house, Owen Llewelyn was the same age as Tony. It would seem that Beatrice's concerns at his lack of company and her own habit of spending time abroad, encouraged her to accept Owen's mother's open offer that Tony should come and visit. As a consequence, for several years a good part of his holidays were spent in the Llewelyn's hospitable household. Owen's mother was not only beautiful, she also possessed a generous and sparkling nature. Tony became devoted to her and obviously found with these friends some of the sense of home otherwise missing from his life. Owen's younger sister Daphne (now Lady Maynard) modestly recalls that Owen and their elder sister Hermione were as dynamic as their mother, and describes how they became for Tony a permanent source of enjoyment and stimulation.

According to Lady Maynard Tony was 'a slightly lonely character, a loner, but always a very comforting person all the same . . . He tended perhaps to attach himself to "stars", and both my brother and sister Hermione were this.' An admired and charismatic young man, in 1933 while still very young, Owen was killed in an air crash; and Lady Maynard remembers Tony's solicitous visits to the three Llewelyn sisters when they were sent away to 'recover' by the sea. Hermione, later the Countess of Ranfurly, was to become a highly experienced and discreet personal assistant, which, combined with her connections and determination to stay on in the Middle East during the war, kept her at the heart of its highest level politics. Her younger sister Daphne, meanwhile, had come out to Cairo as a secretary for Special Operations Executive and would soon utilize her own similar skills as Fitzroy Maclean's (and later Dudley Clarke's) personal secretary. In this way she met up with Tony again in 1943. Here Lady Maynard makes another pertinent comment regarding the man Elizabeth was contemplating marrying. 'My means of transport to work every day was on the back of a truck and Tony had a car. It was out of his way, but he insisted on collecting me every morning. He was the kindest possible person at doing those most boring things.'

Tony David was commissioned from the British Army into the Scottish Rifles at Lucknow, four months after arriving in India in February 1934. A year later he was attached to the Royal Deccan Horse, a distinguished cavalry regiment of the Indian Army. According to Lieutenant-Colonel Harpur who served together with him: 'Tony joined us because he was some kind of relation to our 2nd in Command, later Commanding Officer, Frank Tinley. He came from Oxford and Cambridge, not Sandhurst.' Tony had in fact been up at Cambridge.

Originating as a body of cavalry maintained by the Nizam of Hyderabad on behalf of the East India Company, by 1903, with a confirmed reputation for bravery and fine horsemanship, the Royal Deccan Horse was incorporated into the Indian Army. In 1940 Tony was made Captain and for a time was ADC to the Governor of the Punjab; he was also ADC to the Viceroy, a recognition honour. In 1941, although remaining with the Deccan Horse, he became attached to the Indian Ordnance Corps. By mid 1942 he had left India for the Middle East and in 1943, now based in Cairo, was made Assistant Director of Ordnance Services and granted the rank of Lieutenant-Colonel.

He was by all accounts a gifted horseman and belonged to Cairo's magnificent Gezira Sporting Club. The club owned a vast acreage: landscaped gardens, croquet lawns, tennis courts, golf and race courses and polo fields engulfing the southern end of the Nile's Gezira Island situated, effectively, in the midst of the city. In the welcoming cool of a newly built club-house heat and dust were left behind; here British officers, rich Egyptians and their female companions came to play. Although devoted to polo, according to Lieutenant-Colonel Harper, 'Tony David's main interest was racing and he was an accomplished amateur jockey.'

Most of Elizabeth's friends who met Tony thought them most unsuitably matched. Some believed Tony to be a fool, others, more astute, realized he was not. When he was brought out to Alexandria to visit Durrell, never mind his undoubted good looks, Lawrence and Eve found Tony 'wooden' beside Elizabeth. It was simply that he was unable to keep stride with her knowledge and appreciation of literature, her restless curiosity about those things which interested her, her particular intellectual vigour. Nonetheless at present Elizabeth found him soothing and entertaining. 'They had this rather annoying habit of giggling together,' says a friend. And anyway, Elizabeth was never given to taking advice.

Shortly before Tony's return to Cairo, and Elizabeth's decision to marry him, she was taken to meet the elderly Bishop Gwynne, a long-time resident in the Middle East. Although she found him 'a sweet old thing', she didn't relish his lecture on the 'sad moral tone of Cairo. He's heard rumours about me I expect.' (No doubt correct.)

In his autobiography, *A Sparrow's Flight* (Collins, 1990), Quintin Hogg recalls the Bishop:

One of the curious features of Cairo at this time was the enormous attendance in the English Cathedral at Evening Service every Sunday. I always went . . . You had to be there at least half an hour in advance to get a seat, and there was a very large standing congregation of all ranks. The Cathedral was big, and when it was constructed under the auspices of old Bishop Gwynne it was already treated as a sort of *folie de grandeur*. Now the old Bishop's vision was fully justified and filled a great spiritual need, both for those on leave from the theatres of war and for those in residence in the capital. We were all far from home, and on these occasions all ranks worshipped together with an immense sense of purpose. The Cathedral is now no more, having been bombed by fanatics after the war in an outburst of anti-British and anti-Christian feeling. I have not seen its successor, but Gwynne's great church had already justified its existence.

Tony returned to Cairo from his service with Combined Military Forces in Italy and, despite having written to Pris three weeks earlier that she thought marriage 'perfectly ridiculous', Elizabeth concluded that 'as it's one of the things I've never done I might as well try it for a time'. She added, 'Poor Mummie, her daughters marrying regular soldiers *and* Indian Army.' Accordingly, amidst 'tremendous speculation here about the end of the war', Elizabeth signed away her 'liberty' at the Consulate on 30 August 1944, sending a telegram to Priscilla that afternoon. It read:

> Married Tony David today. I am very happy.
> My dearest Love to you Elizabeth David.

Elizabeth wrote to her friend Doreen in England saying, 'I have married an English Colonel.' Doreen remembers her first thought was: 'Oh *no*.' Tony's connections with Kenya must have inspired him to suggest taking their honeymoon there, for it appears that this is where they spent the month of September.

By November 1944 'Tony has gone off again to the war and Cairo goes on.' She heard from him 'nearly every day – he is cold and uncomfortable' and longing to return to his bewitching bride and proudly walk out with her on his arm. Felicité was hoping to go to Europe to carry out relief work and Elizabeth said that if she hadn't had to wait on Tony's next posting she would have applied too. 'If there is a chance of him going to the Balkans I shall be there pretty quickly, otherwise I shall stay in Cairo, where I now live a life of comparative comfort. My work is still very agreeable and plenty of it.'

Elizabeth's friend Renée, now married to Robin Fedden, had

come to work in the Ministry of Information and so the two saw each other with more ease. Renée's cool, patrician sophistication was in strong contrast to another lifelong woman friend Elizabeth made at this time. Lesley Pares was the daughter of an academic, Professor Pares, and began the war as a semi-trained nurse before being recruited to Bletchley Park, the seat of British Intelligence Operations, by the art historian Cecil Gould. Lesley went through a brief training and was then sent out to Cairo to work in the Ministry of Information as a cypherene. With dark hair, milky skin and a beautiful figure, Lesley was pretty, dressed elegantly in clothes she skilfully made herself and, as Sir Bernard Burrows says of her, 'She gave the impression of being delicate, a little fragile.' In combination with her utterly feminine manner this of course made her extraordinarily attractive to men. But Lesley's attraction lay as much in her gentle personality as in her looks, her 'great capacity for friendship', as Sir Bernard and Lady Ines Burrows and all who recently recalled her wished to stress. 'She wasn't fundamentally an intellectual in the academic sense, though very well read; or perhaps particularly creative', says Sir Bernard. 'She was essentially receptive.' These qualities were a perfect foil to Elizabeth's more demanding and forthright intensity. They soon became intimate friends.

During the latter stages of the war the fighting moved northwards and Cairo became less important as an active centre, but Elizabeth remained there for many more months.

Tony's next posting was finally decided. It was not, as Elizabeth had hoped, to the Balkans where her friend Durrell *was* sent, but instead back to New Delhi, GHQ in India. Tony was obliged to leave Elizabeth in June of 1945 and was still without her at the end of the year. Contrary to her vows that she would never set foot in India, Elizabeth was persuaded to relent and early in 1946, having packed up several years of life in Egypt, she had arrived. Writing to England in February she said that she had been harassed in her last few weeks moving, handing over her job and wrangling with the removers, who were determined to put her on a ship, while she was equally determined to get an air passage. Elizabeth won of course, and she flew to India, stopping in Baghdad for a 'hilarious evening with Neil' (Hogg) on the way.

Shortly before leaving Cairo she had also managed to get herself sent to Greece for a week on a mission for the MOI. To her delight she ended by spending almost two weeks there and reaffirmed her love of the country. In Athens she met up with old friends and, in contrast to her previous opinion, now decided it was the best capital in the world in which to find one's self, never mind present difficulties. 'The people are alive, it's a lovely city and the countryside of such indescribable beauty. I shall go back again.' To be reminded of the attractions of Greece so shortly before Elizabeth's first impressions of India was indeed unfortunate.

CHAPTER ELEVEN

India and a Marriage
(1946)

ON ARRIVAL IN India's vast and confusing subcontinent Elizabeth reacted in her customarily passionate manner. She loathed it. And here a point made by Robin Fedden in his illuminating introduction to the magazine *Personal Landscape* is relevant. He reminds the reader that for the European in Egypt, there is above all a cultural isolation.

> It is possible to travel almost anywhere in Europe without quite getting off a familiar cultural beat: whatever the country, Christianity – whether the inhabitants like it or not – is at the back of the way they think and act. Once you cross to Islamic Africa . . . the current of thought sets towards Mecca and the European is inevitably swimming all the time against the stream . . . he cannot hope to find his own life and . . . efforts seconded and strengthened by unconscious community with . . . the life and efforts of people around him.

She may have felt herself cut off from Europe in Egypt, but Elizabeth at least had the Mediterranean Sea on Alexandria's shores, the resonance of the Classical past if one chose to look, and friends, exiled like herself from Greece, for whom that past mattered. India was so much worse. And here Robin Fedden's comments on Egypt are effectively underlined by E. M. Forster's Cyril Fielding in *A Passage to India*. Returning home via Venice, for centuries one of the centres of Mediterranean life and thought, Fielding is struck by 'the harmony between the works of man and the earth that upholds them, the civilization that has escaped muddle, the spirit in a reasonable form, with flesh and blood subsisting'. Fielding's vision proclaims 'the Mediterranean as the human norm. When men leave that exquisite lake . . . they approach the monstrous and extraordinary.' For Elizabeth there is no doubt, India was monstrous: utterly removed from the Mediterranean arena, where the old conflicts between Christianity and the Classical world, Apollo and Dionysius, the spirit and the flesh, had inspired scrutiny and struggle for the last 2000 years, and out of which had arisen some of the greatest works of man.

In 1911 the British government concluded (King George V himself announced the decision) that the British Raj was to move its seat of Empire from Calcutta and set up in the ancient city of Delhi. Built, fought over, destroyed, rebuilt; there had been no fewer than eight New Delhis over the centuries before this last and lavish display was completed in 1931. Under the auspices of two English architects, Herbert Baker and Edwin Lutyens, there arose beside the medieval forts, mosques and bazaars of Old Delhi, a set of vast administrative buildings, a viceregal residence, and other noble monuments all set along enormous avenues and surrounded by huge planned gardens. There are many who regard New Delhi as a pompous, cumbersome piece of blind folly, whilst others believe parts of it Lutyens' masterpiece. It remained the Imperial seat of government for only fifteen years; India was granted independence in September 1947.

Robert Byron, whose highly praised travel book *The Road to Oxiana* had been in many ways a plea for the virtues of Islamic art, thought the new city flawed but magnificent. (Asked after his death why, as someone who was friend to so many homosexuals, she had not taken up with him, Elizabeth's response was that: 'He was just too queer for me.') Her opinion of the new city was far more negative. As usual a reaction like this spurred her to some of her most pointed and witty writing and her letters from India are a discriminating howl of horror.

She spoke little of it after her return to England, but one anecdote in particular serves well to exemplify her experience. On her arrival in India Elizabeth had to wait for Tony and booked into a hotel for the night, not realizing that the large room she was shown to was the only one. Exhausted from her journey, she fell soundly asleep but was awoken some time later by disturbances in the room.

She sat up and, peering about the darkened space, discovered that she was not alone. Her room was filled with 'a *massive*' number of people asleep or settling in, all over the floor. She was horrified and said she had never been so frightened in all her life. In India the concept of privacy has almost no meaning, while for Elizabeth lack of privacy was an appalling deprivation.

Tony had done his best to find suitable quarters for his new wife, but in writing to Felicité she found Delhi 'terrible beyond all expectations and description'. She slated the vast and stagelike conceptions of Lutyens and Baker, saying they had 'large ideas and a pretty good idea that they were supposed to put up something imposing and triumphantly Imperialistic but were evidently unaware that you can't have a city comprised entirely of palaces and parliament houses with the result that you have to drive for hours up and down processional avenues, interspersed . . . with the very charming domed tombs of Moghul Emperors and . . . with the less charming monuments to the glory of The Great White Queen and her successors, and when you get to the centre of the town what do you find? A great circus called Connaught Place round which are arranged the whole of the Delhi shops, round and round you go, incapable of differentiating one . . . street from another because they all look exactly alike in their sterility and hideousness.' This was the notorious centre, designed as the regal hub of the city, from where roads radiate out like the spokes of a wheel, and where getting lost is almost inevitable.

Elizabeth complained that after you had finally located the place you were looking for and couldn't buy what you wanted, 'Do you think you can drop into a café or bar to revive yourself with a drink? No. Because in *all* New Delhi there are no cafés and no bars and because for all their grandiose visions those two ridiculous architects could think of nothing better than to model the capital of a great continent on the town of Cheltenham . . . and nothing has ever been done about it because the British were all brought up there and the Indians wouldn't think of making the place more attractive because they're praying for the day when we'll bloody well get out anyway – so am *I*.'

Elizabeth and Tony were living in one of six newly completed blocks of flats near a main avenue, Kingsway. Elizabeth told Felicité the buildings were as inefficient as they were ugly: 'a livid crimson'. But at least their flat was comfortable, chiefly owing to Tony's industry in getting it into a habitable state. Although the building was new, the flat had no bath until Tony installed one and with it a hot-water heater. This was unusable, however, because the building didn't yet have any power. Elizabeth described how the 'hordes of servants heat up buckets of water and pour them into the bath'. And any deviation from this custom, practised all over India, would cause the most terrible unemployment.

As an officer's wife she was not expected to work and in fact did nothing about finding any, being 'unwilling to start again as a dogsbody'. As a consequence she was burdened with more time than she had been accustomed to for years. In spite of her unerring ability to find willing hands to run errands for her, the numbers of servants in India disturbed and irritated Elizabeth. Also unable to accept that the memsahib did not take part in kitchen activities, she was indignant at the resentment this caused and told Felicité she had sacked two cooks within a couple of months of arrival. Her attempt at introducing her primus stove from Cairo had caused such panic amongst the staff that she had given in to the Indian habit of cooking entirely on charcoal fires. This didn't overly worry Elizabeth because she had become accustomed to this method of cooking on her Greek island where conditions were much the same as in the Indian capital. 'If only my God the compensations were as good. There are in fact *no* compensations in Delhi.'

She waged battle with her Indian cooks over their refusal to understand that she did *not* want the 'nice clean English nanny food' they were accustomed to providing for their English employers. She wrote years later in *Spices, Salt and Aromatics in the English Kitchen* that they produced 'cakes festooned in spectacular spun sugar work, attempts at French dishes savagely flavoured with hot green chillies ("I make a French a-stew as good as you," one of my Indian cooks remarked defiantly, and untruthfully) and, oddest of all, Edwardian fantasies of the school which liked to present food in any form except its own (mashed potatoes got up to represent a roast chicken, mushrooms made out of meringue and the like).' How could they, poor men, possibly know that this was part of the very reason Elizabeth had finally ended up in India — she was trying to stay away from that very England which the Raj was concerned to uphold more desperately with each passing year. The food served up by Indians to their British masters was a fundamental reflection of the Raj ethos and, as despising a large proportion of the customary elements of Britishness had long ago become an integral part of Elizabeth's life, she was not likely to thank anyone trying to thrust them down her neck.

There was nonetheless, as she later told Judith Lassalle, fascination and amazement at the capacity of her Indian cooks to produce 'incredible food out of what were really no more than tin cans' (for cooking pots). In an obvious sense the exotic food of India appealed to her, but again she was disappointed. This was of course inevitable; not only because Elizabeth did not remain in India long enough to discover the enormous variety, complexity and subtlety which exist in the cooking of that remarkable country, but because she was unwilling to make the modification of opinion necessary to its discovery. Having said this, with typical honesty she was aware that there *might* have been an India other than the one of her own experience. Her comments are etched with deadpan wit. 'Indian food is perfectly frightful, or at least what I have seen of it. The curries always look simply delicious, and one is presented with dozens of different little dishes, but when you come to taste them you find they're all so drenched in chilli peppers that you can't taste anything else for three weeks.'

Many years later, when writing *Spices, Salt and Aromatics in the English Kitchen*, Elizabeth knew more about Indian food but hadn't changed her mind about curries. Later still she would arrive at a stage where one of her favourite types of restaurant was the Indian. Her interest became sufficiently pronounced that on being asked to propose a venue for the launch of her friend Richard Olney's cookery book, *Simple French Food*, she suggested an Indian restaurant!

With her intense curiosity, in a new town Elizabeth would normally have set about discovering those areas which for her were particularly interesting, the markets. But here in India she complained that the teeming hordes of people were frightening and 'The ugliness and death-like barrenness of everything to be seen strikes horror and despair into anybody accustomed to European civilization, however degraded.' After a time she did of course venture from their 'livid crimson' flat and with some trepidation explored both the markets and bazaars of the city, more especially the old city. But she did not often go alone.

Although Elizabeth said that Tony had 'wisely kept away from . . . local society, the majority of which is as dreary as you would expect', there was probably a certain amount of wishful thinking on Elizabeth's part here. It appears that Tony did socialize with friends in his regiment and rode often at polo and horse-racing. They went sometimes to watch the races, a favourite pastime of many in Delhi. 'But Elizabeth thought it *absurd* to go to the races, and *stand up* and eat and drink there, but of course there were many hands to do it for you,' says Veronica Nicholson (then Meagher), a woman of humour and charm who came into Elizabeth's life soon after the first shock of her arrival in 'this desert of a place'. Veronica described to the author how, having given up her job on *Vogue* to enter the war effort, she had come out to India some months before Elizabeth on a secretarial posting with the War Office. 'It was a kind of Renaissance to go to India – the black hole that was England in those days – and come by way of boat which took a month from London via Scotland.'

Unlike Elizabeth, Veronica 'had never been outside England before and the difference was dazzling. It was lovely . . . I never did anything really. I was a terrible Flapper of the Thirties – was awfully unserious. My department became rather fed up with me.' This may have been true but Veronica was also more than simply a Flapper. With the background of a large, close and comfortably off family she was less intense and endowed perhaps with less wit, but more humour than Elizabeth. Not uncritical of British life in India and quite capable of mocking its pomposity, Veronica was of a more open nature, more willing to find a place for herself in this new milieu. She was soon sharing a house with the charismatic Biddy Carlisle and enjoyed socializing with the Commander in Chief of Indian forces Auchinleck, and his entourage. This included Tony, relegated there from Cairo. It was a group similar to the 'suave and sprightly ADCs who helped to conjure up the atmosphere of a court', which, in his

More Memoirs of an Aesthete (Methuen 1970) Harold Acton refers to surrounding the more austere Viceroy, Wavell. Veronica was immensely feminine, beautifully dressed, well read, funny, and light-hearted; as a consequence her social life was very full.

'Oh, but it was so unlike Elizabeth. She wouldn't have *lent* herself to it all — she was totally uninterested in that kind of man [Auchinleck]. And the Army wives, she was so much more greenery yallery than they. Hers was not in the least like a military family . . . She made it pretty clear that she found them boring . . . She was so much more intellectual than most people at GHQ at the time. I think she did keep herself to herself. Not that she didn't adore conversation more than anyone I have ever known. But it had to be *good* conversation or else she would do without. She wasn't doing what we were doing.' Veronica added that the commanding Biddy Carlisle and Elizabeth did not become friends. 'They were each too prima donna-ish for that.'

No less thoughtful than Elizabeth, Veronica was probably more perceptive, certainly more sensitive to others' feelings. She was fascinated, nevertheless, by Elizabeth's biting wit, her observations, her very literate company; saw her difference, realized it was quite unlike anything she had known before. She found Elizabeth retiring, prickly, disdainful. But Veronica also made it clear from the outset that although Elizabeth's wish for her friendship was mutual, she would not be dominated.

The two shared the same Italo-Indian hairdresser. At the hair-dresser's expense, of course, Elizabeth was hilarious. 'He gave her the most marvellous hairstyle, Apollo-like with tight curls, for a particular outing. Very fashionable. At first I wasn't impressed by her looks. She had very pale coffee-coloured skin, brown eyes and very nice regular features and, as she remarked herself once, pretty hands.'

Veronica and Elizabeth visited the markets and bazaars together, watched Tony and other officers at their games of polo, and some-times, with him, joined a party of two or three other army and War Office friends for dinner at one of the beautiful colonial hotels such as Maidens, set amongst elegant acres of lawns in the old city. 'Tony brought people into her life here, but I was sorry for him. It wasn't that he was unintelligent, he simply wasn't her weight intellectually at all.'

There was a certain coolness to Elizabeth. She was quite capable of maintaining a haughty distance, remaining reserved to the point of iciness. And yet behind the ice lay an intense and passionate nature. Increasingly too she reflected her mother's disregard for some of the niceties of social convention. She certainly didn't bother much with its more onerous aspects and felt no compunction about showing her boredom or irritation in public. Her preference at a dinner table was for the more intense, intimate and therefore isolating Anglo-Saxon dialogue between couples, rather than the French regard for more general conversation. This tendency was to become more developed. Veronica adds: 'But she was very good at being a friend too. Elizabeth was much more evolved than most people one met.'

Tony David was one of the few to have a car, and although rationing of petrol meant that a profligate use of vehicles was impossible, occasional excursions out of the city were still possible. Picnics were a favoured excuse for leaving town and one such event was famously recorded by Elizabeth (one of the few personal references she ever makes to India in her writing) in her book *Summer Cooking* several years later. This was to be a night-time picnic beside one of the marvels of India, the Qutb Minar. About 10 miles south of Delhi, this soaring round tower of sandstone and marble rose as a victory monument to celebrate the Muslim defeat of the last Hindu king as long ago as the twelfth century. Its five beautifully balconied storeys set amongst scrubby land are awash with Koranic inscriptions (the traveller Robert Byron thought them too Indian and painstaking). Nearby stands the very earliest Indian mosque.

The party had driven out late in the cooler air of evening, and Veronica remembers that 'We had settled ourselves down. The moon came out and we were all engaged in conversation when we were quite surrounded by Pi dogs.' Elizabeth takes up the story in *Summer Cooking*. She gives no recipe. Her piece is simply one of those at which she excelled, perfectly conjuring a small drama and its setting, leaving the reader anticipating the rest, always building enough tension to keep him just on edge, the ensemble carried along by the drive of Elizabeth's prose.

There was nothing wrong with the transport, the food, or the moonlight; we had merely reckoned without the hordes of half wild dogs which are a familiar feature of Indian outdoor life. Scarcely had we had time to draw the cork of a bottle of . . . Australian hock . . . than we were surrounded; literally surrounded. They did not apparently want food, or at any rate not our food; they simply formed a circle round us at a respectful distance and stared and howled.

First we pretended not to notice, then we shoo-ed them away several times. They returned immediately, with reinforcements, re-formed their dreadful circle, and howled and stared and sniffed again, until they forced us to get into our cars and return to the city.

Although maintained on a reduced scale, social life for British society in these last days of the Raj was still in full swing. Nonetheless Elizabeth found it resonant with a sad gaiety. There was, she told Felicité, plenty of food and drink but parties were mostly formal and dull, and there appeared to be no spontaneous entertaining. To her amazement one was expected here to change for *drinks*. Neither was there any theatre and the only films available were of the order of propaganda exercises, such as *The Way Forward*. Others, more attuned to her tastes, were occasionally put on in someone's house. She regretted Cairo and her 'hundreds of friends', where 'not a week ever passed without some old friend turning up. People were continuously arriving with introductions from England, from Greece, or other parts of the M.E.,' and she bemoaned the loss of her job where there was 'contact with a great many interesting people. So obviously Delhi is deathly dull after all that and I know nobody.' Attempting to console herself, she acquired two cats, having been without one for all her years in Egypt.

'Elizabeth didn't work, she was a wife,' recalls Veronica. 'That meant you could stay in bed all day if you wanted to – which Elizabeth might well have done, but she'd be up all night instead if she had. Yes, she always kept odd hours.'

After a short time Elizabeth's lack of friends weighed heavily upon her and Tony's charm and pleasantness were insufficient recompense. She was never a romantic and as her letters to her mother and sisters made abundantly clear, was highly dubious about the whole conjugal enterprise. With a combination of cool-headed pragmatism and weary disappointment Elizabeth had, nonetheless, made a marriage. She was ultimately, however, unwilling or perhaps unable to follow through her decision with the hard work necessary to sustain any marriage, let alone one made with such apparent calculation. Initially Elizabeth's instinct was to make herself attractive to men, and she succeeded, but her relationships with them were usually uneven. She was so often more intelligent than her male companion that the rather mysterious and alluring woman who was also part of her nature seemed after a time almost to have been a disguise. When the relationship was more than a casual fling – on such occasions Elizabeth was capable of fairly ruthless usage – her intelligence would gradually displace her emotional attachment.

This force of intellect and personality could not content itself with feminine compliance for long. 'It was impossible to sit on Elizabeth,' says Doreen Thornton. She hungered for an equivalent force to counteract and complement her own, but for all her sophistication and intelligence, didn't really know how to nurture it when it presented itself. Tony was an attempt to convince herself that she could manage with a man who would make things work by *his* compliance and willingness to serve. For all her realism it was as if for a time Elizabeth were wilfully suspending her beliefs. As she said to Veronica Nicholson: 'Well, everyone else was marrying.' It was as if she was half hoping that by marrying, the future would see to itself, and besides which she had reckoned without her own impatience and capacity for boredom when people didn't stimulate her. Elizabeth needed a subtle yet authoritative man but went about acquiring one in the wrong way. A string of men had already retreated, but most hurtful was probably the rich 'glamour boy' officer wounded so badly at the battle of El Alamein. As much through her own behaviour as the inadequacy of the men she met, Elizabeth found 'they rarely came up to scratch for her'.

Idle in India, Elizabeth's old restlessness, for years in Egypt kept at bay with hard work, now had little outlet and she was 'praying I shan't have to stay'. Unfortunately books, which were a vital part of her life, were almost unavailable in Delhi. This was because any packages, let alone the latest books from England, were very hard to come by. For the moment Elizabeth was furnished with a stash brought with her from Cairo and wrote to Felicité (working for the Allied Commission in Vienna) that 'As long as they last I will be all right. After that I cannot say.'

She told Felicité she had read a few Trollope novels in Cairo, but Elizabeth's main escape in India was Henry James. She read Proust, twice, Osbert Sitwell and the Greeks. In the same letter, in sharp contrast to what she felt was her present intellectual stultification, Elizabeth recalled her recent visit to Greece where she had sat in a café with a friend 'over a bad bottle of Cypriot wine talking Balkan politics, Greek literature, Shakespeare and other gossip'.

Her present choice of reading was revealing, in its appreciation of those writers at the turn of the century, and Sitwell into this one, whose work did not reflect the more destructively experimental aspects of Modernism. Elizabeth identified with that artistic vein of thought which was, nevertheless, intent on reflecting the effects of the modern age, and with those writers for whom, paradoxically, this was achieved by an uninterrupted avenue of communication with the values of the past. Although Elizabeth doesn't mention writers like Eliot or Joyce – for whom this endeavour was their *raison d'être* – her great appreciation of another modern, Proust, is confirmation of where her sympathies lay. These writers were all committed to the present and lived it to the full, but they were also firm traditionalists in remaining constantly aware of the past. This attitude was at the heart of Elizabeth's essentially high Tory stance. It is exemplified in T. S. Eliot's essay 'Tradition and the Individual Talent' (reprinted in *Selected Essays*, Faber and Faber, 1952): 'The historical sense involves a perception, not only of the pastness of the past, but of its presence; the historical sense compels a man to write not merely with his own generation in his bones, but with a feeling that the whole of the literature of Europe from Homer . . . has a simultaneous existence.'

Elizabeth's 'main escape', Henry James, was disdainful of the vapidity, the determined anti-intellectualism of the English country-house set, whose mentality Elizabeth was familiar with and had herself largely rejected. But central to James's observations was

something which concerned her too: civilization and its mani-
festations.

Veronica eventually left India to work in Rome. 'After six
months of friendship, then I went on to Italy.' Having written earlier
to Felicité from India that 'the majority of English here treat their
employees in the manner one always supposed to have been invented
for the stage', Elizabeth added that everything her sister had ever read
about life in India appeared to be true and wondered how much
longer it would all last. Meanwhile the country was preparing 'for the
hottest summer and the most disastrous famine for hundreds of years
. . . Everyone is running around getting fans, mosquito nets and loose
muslin dresses.' Elizabeth concluded: 'I hate the Orient.'

Writing letters of frustration and boredom to friends and family
she stuck it out for a while longer. But fortune was on her side.
Having persuaded Tony that he did indeed wish to leave the Army
and that they should return to England, she was struck down with a
bad case of sinusitis; she was advised that the climate was exacerbating
the problem. Elizabeth was given the excuse she needed. She must
leave. Now. Tony would have to follow later when he had managed
to extract himself. from the Army. After years living away from
England, but less than a year with her husband in India, Elizabeth
was at last to return home. She was almost thirty-four.

Much to her sadness, only weeks before this Norman Douglas
had finally managed to flee from London, 'this benighted hole', and
with it his experience of penury and misery suffered during the last
years of the war. He told his young friend Harold Acton, just back
from India, that but for a small circle, including loyal friends such as
Nancy Cunard, Faith Mackenzie and Viva King (wife of Willie,
curator at the Victoria and Albert Museum), the last couple of years
in England had been the unhappiest of his life. He had written to the
Italian authorities asking permission to return to his beloved Italy.
His request was unexpectedly granted because an official was moved
by his statement that he wanted to return, not to live in Italy but to
die there.

CHAPTER TWELVE

No More Talked of than Love or Heaven
(1946–1949)

IN AUGUST 1946 Elizabeth David came back to England, the land of her birth. She had been away continuously for seven years. And although she was to live abroad again for shorter periods, these were mostly a natural outcome of her work. For the rest of her life, then, England was Elizabeth's home. In 1939 she had escaped from her homeland with an appropriately disreputable character, Charles Gibson Cowan. Sometimes disgruntedly and with the application of all her wit, Elizabeth would now make a stand. Instead of a wild, distraught departure away from the inadequacies of her own culture she was to use her remarkable gifts to remedy these inadequacies by showing how we can learn from those abroad.

Her return was to prove far more significant than simply the initiation of another chapter. In any account of Elizabeth's life we can make out two clear and distinct phases. The first was spent filled with a variety of busyness, activity and adventure: the second half was also active but it became more focused; increasingly, in the form of writing. She would continue to travel, but this was more circumscribed than her relatively impromptu voyages of discovery in the Mediterranean and Middle East before and during the war. For a number of years Elizabeth refined her escape as a synthesis in her writing. Eventually this satisfied her less, and finally she would focus her writing in a different direction: history, and with it a greater propensity for contemplation.

Meanwhile, in 1946 with rationing still very much in force – ration books were even required at restaurants and hotels – provisions for meals were nothing like the relative plenty which Elizabeth had known in war time. There are many examples and records of life under rationing – one in particular, in Vere Hodgson's *Few Eggs and No Oranges* (Dobson, 1976), demonstrates the types of meal being eaten by the average family in 1944; in 1947 things were no different.

> Meat ration lasts only for three evenings. Cannot be made to go further, that is, Saturday, Sunday, and Monday. Tuesday and Wednesday I cook a handful of rice, dodged up in some way with curry or cheese. But the cheese ration is so small there is little left. Thursday I have an order with the dairy for a pound of sausage. These make do for Thursday, Friday and part of Saturday. Don't taste much of sausage, but [they] are of soyabean flour. We just pretend they are the real thing ... All rather monotonous, but we are not hungry.

This is really the operative phrase for the condition of England's diet in 1947. Food was monotonous but people were not hungry. It is ironic, but strictly correct, that the British population as a whole was better fed during the war than before it. (Better, that is, from the viewpoint of nutritional science.) The failures of the First World War had taught subsequent politicians important lessons about the management and supply of food, so that by the Second World War a coherent plan was evolved focusing on the nourishment of the nation as a whole. The Minister for Food, Sir Fred Marquis (Lord Woolton), a successful businessman and natural communicator and his chief adviser, the gifted biochemist Jack Drummond, had between them set up a national system based on sound nutritional principles. This included the development of allotments and the re-introduction of brown bread to a nation of white-bread consumers. The success of these policies meant that many people understood more about basic nutrition at the end of the war than they had at its commencement.

Preparations were put in hand for rationing well before the 1939–45 hostilities and by August of 1939 – a month before war was even declared – ration books had been printed and deposited at depots around the country. Implementation of the measures for conserving the nation's food supplies were avoided until January

1940, when Elizabeth was forced to remain in Antibes but not suffering hardships.

At the same time bacon, ham, butter and sugar were put on ration in England. By March meat was added to the list and in July cooking fats, margarine and even tea – indispensable to the working of the English nation. Tinned foods, already used by the English in vast quantities, were more relied upon than ever and during the war dehydrated foods, loathed by most people, became much more common. Writing to Felicité in Vienna in early 1947, Elizabeth asked her when she was 'coming back to dried egg land'. Eggs had been rationed for years – a blow to any self-respecting cook, forming as they do such a vital part of most Western cooking. And, although their dried substitute was used for all the normal egg recipes, it was unsatisfactory and universally disliked. Many of those who had the space, even in the cities, kept hens in their back gardens. A sad anecdote forcefully illustrates the situation.

Judith Richardson's mother followed this practice in Onslow Square, an elegant South Kensington haven. Judith, who was later married to Elizabeth's friend, George Lassalle, and whose brother John became the noted art historian and biographer of Picasso, was then about seventeen. She told the author how the artist John Minton, who lived nearby, came round one day. 'He looked so sad, awfully thin and half-stoned, and said, "Do you think you could spare me a couple of eggs if I give you this sandwich for your chickens?" He was holding an envelope and inside was a dried up old sandwich. My brother said, "Don't give Minton anything." But I boiled a couple of eggs and gave them to Johnny anyway.'

For those like Elizabeth who could afford it, an important dehydrated substitute for rationed tea was instant coffee, first manufactured by Nestlé as Nescafé in Britain in 1939. Elizabeth was never a tea lover and, interestingly, in Egypt before her return home she had already tried Nescafé and been converted. Eve Durrell remembers Renée Fedden offering it to her there and thinking it delicious, 'But after the war it was never so good, it had changed.' Nevertheless, in a remarkable and endearing lapse of taste, Elizabeth remained a devotee of instant coffee all her life. 'I don't know what all the fuss is, about the real stuff.'

Spices, lemons, blue cheese, dried salt fish such as anchovy, all stimulants to the palate and vital in small quantities to enliven a meal of otherwise nondescript ingredients, were almost impossible to find in England. Rice had disappeared fairly early on in the war, but rabbit was not rationed, nor was game or fish. And for those living in London there were the possibilities offered by Soho, then the only part of the city with shops selling 'foreign' produce in any quantity. Vegetables were not rationed but restricted. Cooking fats were limited, even lard was rationed. Elizabeth's future friend, the novelist Paul Bailey, told the author: 'You could only find olive oil in a chemist's — with a doctor's prescription. You weren't meant to eat it, to use it in *cooking*.' Although few would agree with Bailey over the prescription, there is general agreement that olive oil was hard to find.

Lord Gowrie, in the previous administration Minister for the Arts, recently Chairman of the Arts Council, first met Elizabeth as a young man in the 1950s. He described the post-war situation to the author: 'Farming was efficient. Woolton had sorted out diets, but one chafed against the controls after the war. After all, we had won, but we looked as if we had lost, with the persistence of powdered egg and synthetic custard, imported tinned Spam. Growing up in austerity was incredibly nasty from a culinary point of view. I mean, the food was really disgusting. You've no idea how nasty it was.'

The question arises: Why? Rationing was a necessary measure during wartime, but did it have to continue for so many years afterwards? Explanations deriving solely from national financial constraints are insufficient. There is one convincing conclusion: the food was 'really disgusting' because most people in England did not sufficiently care that it was.

England was the pioneer industrial nation. Industrialism, which harmonized so well with puritanism, completed the job of destruction of the peasantry and peasant culture, chronicled in the melancholy novels of Thomas Hardy, and reiterated later by Flora Thompson. Chapel replaced Church and the urban barns of the town-dwelling Baptists and Methodists frequently displaced the beautiful parish churches. A single statistic is a salutory reminder. By 1893 the English folklorists had collected 140 'fairy tales'; between 1870 and

1890 France and Italy had yielded over 1000 each. Puritanism and Industrial Capitalism had been replaced, by 1945, by Socialism and Scientism, but the underlying spirit was much the same. And these were the principal reasons why Sir Stafford Cripps was enabled to be quite as effective as Cromwell's Major Generals at stamping out premature rejoicing when the British thought they had won the war.

Celia and John Herbert were friends of Doreen Thornton and lived in a top-floor flat in John's mother's large house behind Barkers, in Kensington. They were going away and were happy to hand over the flat to Elizabeth in their absence (Tony was still in India). Elizabeth at once installed herself in this Kensington eyrie, and in the conditions then prevailing in England, did her best to bridge the chasm between her previous and present life-styles and survive. With no job and nothing forthcoming, Elizabeth took up again her habitual entertaining. Most of her friends, abroad during the war, had also returned.

After years in the Mediterranean and the Middle East there were few restaurants whose English atmosphere these friends found congenial, and whose food they were willing or could afford to eat. Even bread was rationed in restaurants. Those like The Ivy and L'Ecu de France, frequented by Elizabeth and her kind before the war, remained open and carried on a semblance of the style and sophistication which had made them famous. Their old clientèle continued to frequent them, but this was as much for the social cachet, the atmosphere and predictability of interesting companions while you ate, as for the quality of the food. Gallati of The Ivy described in his autobiography (*Mario of the Caprice*, Hutchinson 1960) how: 'I used to make a kind of mayonnaise with flour and water put into the mixing machine with vinegar, mustard and a bit of powdered egg. It made me shudder to serve it.'

Elizabeth's new flat was equipped with one of those ridiculous kitchens, not then uncommon in converted English houses, in which a work table doubled up as the cover to the bath. This necessitated a tidiness to which Elizabeth was neither accustomed — servants had seen to that — nor naturally inclined. Nevertheless, with her gas cooker she began to try out some of the dishes eaten in her years of wandering. Few other than her most intimate friends, literary or otherwise, realized how passionate was her interest in food. And neither then nor later did her sense of good taste permit her to indulge her passion with anyone, unless they showed particular interest or were in some way professionally involved.

Elizabeth's experience of cooking and eating places was by now enormously varied, both in a geographic and a gastronomic sense. This experience included running a ship's galley, with primus stoves, managing a primitive kitchen on a Greek island, in Egypt – and, to a lesser extent, India – becoming familiar with the world of Eastern food. Before the war this would have been unknown to her but for the beguiling Mrs Leyel and *The Gentle Art of Cookery*. Elizabeth's experience included eating in some of the best restaurants – both costly, modest and unknown – in all these countries. Throughout her travels she had learnt the art, essential for both travellers and good cooks, of pragmatic adaptation and accommodation to circumstance. Notwithstanding her youthful tendency towards extravagance, necessity had encouraged her to develop a sense of thrift and had driven her to use her intelligence and ingenuity. She had written to Priscilla from Egypt: 'I feel that one of the main conditions of continued existence is that life should always be full of changes and surprises,' and we are reminded of her own determined and consistently creative response to these changes and surprises.

With parental example from early childhood at Wootton, Elizabeth had an imperative need for her surroundings to reflect her own aesthetic. She cared deeply about the look of things, always including her own appearance. This applied to whatever she was doing: writing during the war lengthy screeds on 'stuffs' and colours and designs for clothes sent or ordered from her sisters and mother; 'redoing' the digs in Oxford, the flats in London, the *Evelyn Hope*, the cottage on Syros, her apartments in Egypt, and most recently 'new covers and curtains' for her latest move. Using her knowledge and ingenuity to create edible meals for her friends was in part an extension of this discernment. Without ever being effete, Elizabeth had an unerring sense of taste. It was never outrageous, it was instead taste at once fastidious, traditional, catholic and bohemian. She had an instinctive ability to apprehend and develop the potentialities in the tone of the present. Her detection of the pretentious, which became keener with time, was reflected in both her own appearance and the atmosphere she created in her surroundings.

Although Elizabeth's collection of recipes was lost when the *Evelyn Hope* and most of her own and Charles Gibson Cowan's belongings were confiscated by the Italian navy, she had not returned from her travels empty-handed. In the years abroad she had been alert to all aspects of food: watching, listening, eating and preparing dishes herself. She had kept notes of recipes wherever she was. Back in England she confidently set about re-creating the remembered dishes of her travels, saying later, 'With whatever I could get I cooked like one possessed.' In London there was one undoubted luxury: bookshops, and Elizabeth began to replace what she had lost and buy unfamiliar books too.

Meanwhile, in 1944, André Simon and Louis Golding had brought out an anthology for the readers of the Wine and Food Society. Aimed at giving hope to the down-hearted upper-middle-class reader, entitled *We Shall Eat and Drink Again*, the stress of course was on '*Shall*'. The differences between what one eats and how it is perceived, borne out by countless records of this in action during the war years, remind us that a nutritionally adequate diet can be close to torture, especially to those accustomed to a more than adequate one. The English did not starve during the war, but for the better off particularly, accustomed to more meat, cream, eggs and imported fruit, the war and its aftermath was a grey landscape indeed.

During the war years Elizabeth's diet, by comparison with those left at home, had been anything but monotonous. And despite the war's end her return to English rationing provoked in her a feeling akin to deprivation of the spirit. This was as much in reaction to English attitudes as to the physical dearth.

It took her another fifteen or so years to write at length about the effect of the Levant upon English cooking and herself. It eventually emerged in a piece written originally for the *Spectator*, then reprinted as the introduction to her book on *Spices, Salt and Aromatics in the English Kitchen*. Here she gives credit to Hilda Leyel, founder of Culpepper's, for probably first inspiring her to cook. As importantly, she describes how on re-reading *The Gentle Art* she came to the realization that here was 'Yet another manifestation of the English love affair with Eastern food and Arabian Nights ingredients'.

Knowing as we do the volume of personal history behind Elizabeth's lilting description of Levantine food in *Spices, Salt and Aromatics in the English Kitchen*, it now reads both as an evocative exposition and a masterly display of reticence.

> . . . circumstances had landed me in Alexandria and subsequently in Cairo. In my turn I fell under the spell of the beautiful food of the Levant – the warm flat bread, the freshly pressed tomato juice, the charcoal-grilled lamb, the oniony salads, the mint and yogurt sauces, the sesame seed paste, the pistachios and the pomegranates and the apricots, the rosewater and the scented sweetmeats, and everywhere the warm spicy smell of cumin [we learn in the same book that this was an indispensable spice in her store-cupboard].

In a *Spectator* article of three years previously (9 December 1960) she had reminded us that while in the Middle East her menu consisted of the above, combined with 'rather rough, but highly flavoured colourful shining vegetable dishes, lentil or fresh tomato soups, delicious spiced pilaffs . . . The Egyptian *Fellahin* dish of black beans with olive oil and lemon and hard boiled eggs'.

What Elizabeth said she found on returning to England and 'the awful, dreary foods of rationing was that while my own standard of living . . . had perhaps not been very high, my food had always had some sort of life, colour, guts, stimulus; there had always been bite, flavour and inviting smells'. In 1947 she felt that 'These elements were totally absent from English food.'

In those first months of re-acclimatizing herself to England, with no job and nothing forthcoming, Elizabeth was depressed but launched herself back into London life. Many of her friends were, like herself, intent on reinstating themselves in England and maintaining the coterie they had formed in Cairo. 'Elizabeth rather liked to be part of a group of people, a clique, and didn't care much for those outside it,' says her friend Patrick Leigh Fermor. What he did not add was that Elizabeth always maintained a position in more than one clique at once. Included in the comings and goings were: Robin Fedden, now curator of Polesden Lacey for the National Trust, and his wife Renée; Xan Fielding; John Young, future Oxford zoologist and his painter companion Ray; Betsey and John Udall, phoneticists; Lesley O'Malley from the MOI (left by her unbalanced husband in Cairo but still suffering the frequent despair this caused her for several years to come); Cecil Gould the art historian; George Lassalle; J. M. Richards the architectural historian; Doreen Thornton; Mary and David Abercrombie, future professor of phonetics, whose description of Elizabeth as 'a myopic black swan' captures well her extreme short-sightedness, her reticence, her sinuous grace and that hint of the predatory about her.

Judith Lassalle recalls how for some time after the war 'They all, these people, came and went at a furious pace. Again in England they were trying to get things back to the way they had been before the war – but they could never quite get it back to how it was ... Elizabeth would have a few drinks and warm up and then she would always say, "I must tell you, I must tell you." You could always say something to Elizabeth to make her laugh. Even when she was miserable you only had to smile at her and she would smile back.' 'Yes,' says Patrick Woodcock, a future friend and later Elizabeth's doctor, 'she was a great sender up but she knew how to be so funny.'

Autumn that year soon turned to one of the nastiest winters in living memory; everything and everyone froze. Diana and her husband Christopher (working as a doctor in St George's hospital) were living not far from Elizabeth in Abingdon Road. Diana, expecting a baby, was having a difficult time and everyone was concerned. Towards the end of winter Elizabeth wrote to Felicité in Vienna saying that London had been 'vile' for the past few weeks and that she had been 'chained' to the stove, making meals for friends or for Christopher and Diana, going out only to Abingdon Road to bring them nourishing soups and other dishes wrapped in napkins.

She made the most of rationed ingredients, ignoring the powdered and dehydrated foods to which the English had become so conditioned. With a sense of passionate urgency she scoured Soho; found garlic, searched out lemons, olive oil, bootleg butter, in typical

vein sent a young friend back to Harrods when she arrived with
something misdescribed as butter, saying, 'Get me the real thing.'
Visitors always came with contributions: 'Unexpected ones sometimes. A wild goose. Snails from Paris ... Mock liver pâté from
Fortnum's ... One of my sisters [Felicité, back for a visit] turned up
from Vienna with a hare which she claimed had been caught by hand
outside the State Opera House.' That autumn and winter of 1946–7
was a good one for game, which was not rationed and was cheap.

In an article written for the *Spectator* in 1963, entitled 'John
Wesley's Eye', Elizabeth praised her post-war landlady, Mrs Herbert
down below, for her long-suffering patience at the 'cooking smells,
the garlic, the onions, those eternal bacon bones simmering in the
stock ... about the heating she was, with the best will in the world,
powerless. Literally. And gas-less.' Doreen Thornton says that in fact
Mrs Herbert 'who should have been scandalized by Elizabeth and her
friends, actually found her fascinating. She was intrigued.'

Tony was planning to take 'longer leave' in England to be with
Elizabeth, herself already feeling tetchy at the prospect. In her dislike
and rejection of freezing, ration-blighted England (vegetables that
winter were sometimes only recoverable from the ground with pneu-
matic drills, animals froze and died, fuel was in short supply) she had
attempted to organize a passage to 'the island', Syros. Here she
wanted to reinstate herself in the little house with Tony, his journey
to England forestalled for a while; but this proved impossible 'because
Tony was being very tiresome about returning straight to England'.
With acid pen Elizabeth regrets her failure to return 'before the
Americans arrive in their hordes to preserve Greece for the Mid West'.
Frustrated at the loss of her beloved Greek island she adds, 'Feeling
desperately in need of a change, respite from the telephone and some
fresh air I have heaved myself up and am spending a few days in a
place called Ross-on-Wye, don't ask me why and that's not meant to
be funny.'

When Elizabeth later wrote about this episode it was deftly
transformed and became the passage in 'John Wesley's Eye' mentioned
above; and justly famous for her passionate response to the bleakness
of post-war England. It is a heartfelt piece, moving in itself. But for
anyone who knows Elizabeth's writing and has mused over, or made

a more methodical search for an explanation as to why she began to write, it appears that here one has found some kind of an answer. She sets the scene with apparent nonchalance; in fact it is a careful crafting of a series of minor crescendos culminating with the final dénouement; the inception of her first book.

With the gas in her flat all but giving out, she wrote: 'At this moment somebody put into my head the idea of going to stay, at reduced all-in rates, in a hotel in Ross-on-Wye,' the little town on the Welsh border, perched above the wide, leafy valley of the river Wye. Exploring, encountering the many pubs en route, Elizabeth came across one of those wildly unreconstructed places, with châtelaines as unorthodox as their contents, few of whom any longer exist.

'An interesting looking antique shop. A very large shop, with immense windows. These were filled from floor to ceiling with a fantastic jumble of every conceivable kind of antique. Lamps, china, glass, bedsteads, curtains, Sheffield candlesticks, desks, pictures, books, bookshelves, bronzes, Georgian silver, coffee pots, horse brasses, corner cupboards, whole services of dinner plates, soup tureens, sauce boats, statuary. The lady inside the shop was as unusual as her windows . . . If you asked to look at something she pulled it out from the morass regardless.' Elizabeth keeps the tension taut, building on our growing sense of the reckless disregard 'Miss D.' exhibits for her wonderfully various and insanely balanced merchandise. Several near misses and an avalanche or two of collapsing valuables later Elizabeth described how she would extract herself from the shop with a sense of triumphant relief that her purchases were intact. On this particular occasion she had just rescued a 'Leeds dish and put it in my basket before Miss D. had a chance to knock it flying. The friend I was with rescued from under the lady's foot, and gave to me, a frail white jug . . . As Miss D. took my cheque her elbow jogged the tap of a copper tea urn perched on top of a model four-masted barque in a heavy box frame. It knocked over a solid silver clock representing General Gordon sitting on a horse, which fell against a scrap screen, a japanned tray and a tortoiseshell and silver-inlaid musical box . . .'

To Felicité Elizabeth complained of the weather and that she was 'constantly reminded of my one disastrous expedition to The

Hills in India. For all one can see through the blanket of snow Kanchenjunga might easily be in the background.' This refers to Elizabeth's unsuccessful holiday with Tony; escaping from the heat of Delhi by train to the cool clear air of Darjeeling, that exquisite hill-station high up on the Eastern edge of the Himalayas. Darjeeling, little town of labrynthine steps and terraces, of exotic village and hill people, of bazaars and markets, glowing, intense and fantastic, ringed around with pine forests and snowy mountain peaks, had been a favoured British Raj retreat since its nineteenth-century creation.

Following her rest on the Welsh borders Elizabeth was planning a visit to Priscilla in 'Chippers' (Chipping Sodbury) in Gloucestershire en route back to the austerities of London, but extensive flooding of the surrounding towns and villages marooned her in Ross-on-Wye. The terrible cold of that winter had progressed to flooding of disasterous magnitude. Root crops were destroyed, thousands of sheep and cattle died, the smell of burning corpses soon floated on the air. Elizabeth meanwhile told Felicité that the horrors of English hotel life had not lessened with the years. As she elaborated in her *Spectator* article: 'I stuck it out. It was an effort. By this time I was finding it very difficult indeed to swallow the food provided in the hotel. It was worse than unpardonable, even for those days of desperation; and oddly, considering the kindly efforts made in other respects, produced with a kind of bleak triumph which amounted almost to a hatred of humanity and humanity's needs.' We are treated to a sample of 'flour and water soup seasoned solely with pepper; bread and gristle rissoles; dehydrated onions and carrots; corned beef toad-in-the-hole. I need not go on.'

The aspect of this perfectly judged essay which contains the greatest biographical import follows immediately on this little dia-tribe; when the reader believes he is witnessing Elizabeth's conversion of frustration and longing into her first piece of writing. The essence of what Elizabeth tells her reader is usually true and correct. Her omissions are in the name of a respectable desire for privacy (she is writing about *food* after all, not herself), concision, clarity, and as importantly; her instinctive appreciation of what was artistically relevant and what superfluous to a piece. Here, however, we are presented with one of those rare examples where an omission is outstanding, following to the letter the implication of her friend Norman Douglas's dictum: 'One suppresses much' – because there is something to hide.

The passage evokes with exemplary accuracy Elizabeth's thoughts and feelings at that time; her discovery that England provoked as much animosity in her as when she had escaped it seven years earlier. Temporarily unable to leave the country, or even this small provincial town, the words she began to write were a perfect synthesis of her attitude: a wail of longing for what she had lost; and a description, penned in vitriol, of what she had found in its place.

> Hardly knowing what I was doing, I who had scarcely ever put pen to paper except to write memos to the heads of departments in the Ministry which employed me during the war, I sat down and started to work out an agonized craving for the sun and furious revolt against that terrible cheerless, heartless food by writing down descriptions of Mediterranean and Middle Eastern cooking. Even to write words like apricot, olives and butter, rice and lemons, oil and almonds, produced assuagement. Later I came to realize that in the England of 1947 those were dirty words I was putting down.

And here we come to Elizabeth's omissions; two important facts which she was disinclined to tell her reader, but which are fundamental to an appreciation of her development as a writer. First, she was not alone; second, the friend accompanying her was responsible both for the journey to Ross *and* for encouraging her at this moment to pick up her pen. The friend was George Lassalle.

Having married as his second wife the cousin of his first, George had been sent on a posting from Cairo to Istanbul, and here he carried on, with admirable subterfuge, his work for Intelligence. George left the Army and returned to England in 1946 and for a short time continued his intelligence work in the Press Office of the Egyptian Embassy. Struck down by a series of health problems he was sent to hospital. Failing in his ambition to become a journalist, George eventually took up market trading in books and antiques, for which he discovered he had a real talent.

Some time after Elizabeth's return from India, and probably just into the New Year of 1947, the two resumed their old liaison. This they maintained, intermittently, for the next few years, remaining in regular contact with one another for the rest of their lives. George had been the 'somebody' who had put it into Elizabeth's head that before Tony's arrival in England they should escape to a place where they were unknown. George was a keen fly fisherman and a knowledgeable consumer of all fishy things from fresh and salt water. As a boy, at a London Benedictine Priory school, his initiation into the rites of fly fishing had taken place while on holiday in Ross-on-Wye, with the benevolent Father who also supervised his French and choir studies. George subsequently described this holiday as a semi-visonary experience; both Ross and fish were special elements in his past, hence his recommendation of the town to Elizabeth. Ironically, we see in the autobiographical *Spectator* article that Elizabeth *also* claimed her stay in Ross as something of a road-to-Damascus conversion.

The appalling weather turned the occasion into more than a brief interlude, but George was his habitual entertaining, ebullient self and refused to take the situation too seriously. Hardly to be trusted further than he could be seen, for him the occasion would have been a great joke. George and Elizabeth knew one another well; remaining fascinated, each recognized something in the other which went some way towards consolation. Amongst George's many and varied interests was not only a concern for fish but food generally: initiated by his first trip to Greece three years before the war, when he had taught himself to cook. His war experience was, like Elizabeth's, predominantly a Middle Eastern one, and he too was dismissive of the food to which they were now subjected. In spite of his disreputableness Elizabeth remained fond of George and spoke of him often. At different times they both said that if they 'hadn't each had a touch of the tarbrush we would have married'. However, in 1947 they were also both already married to someone else.

With time to fill in, waiting for the floodwaters to subside, the conversation again turned to Elizabeth's shortage of money and means of procuring some. Here George was the ideal adviser, he was always short of it, yet, a natural hustler, he somehow always managed to extract himself from tight corners. One is reminded here both of

Charles Gibson Cowan and of Elizabeth's unerring ability to associate herself with men who could be relied upon for unreliability. (An old friend recently said with sadness, 'Oh, she was attracted to people in the most indiscriminate way.') Having dabbled with outsiders, Elizabeth would always remain interested in similar types. Generally the point at which she identified with someone was the point central to their own exclusion.

Meanwhile Elizabeth needed to find some employment. She had long since rejected the possibility of acting, but was unwilling to take on the other role in which she had gained valuable experience – librarianship. It was too unglamorous and besides, as Patrick Leigh Fermor recently said of her, 'Liz chafed so under discipline, she was a terrible handful.' So it was that here in Ross-on-Wye, at this comfortable, friendly hotel serving up its atrocious food, George encouraged her to write. He may sometimes have been a rogue but he was an intelligent, literate and multilingual one who was also endowed with generosity and enthusiasm. The retrospective *Spectator* passages in which Elizabeth outlined the origins of her writing career, tell us how she 'had hardly put pen to paper', but this was patently incorrect – the traditional disclaimer to patron and public at the beginning of so many good books.

In the very letter from the Oxford Playhouse, in 1934, where she had claimed that she couldn't write, we saw evidence of her nascent abilities. She had, anyway, been writing in a small way for years. We remember the juvenile recipe manuscript written for her friend Marian Butterworth; more importantly the mysterious book with Charles Gibson Cowan; then the building of her collection of recipes which she had hoped to publish, lost with the *Evelyn Hope*. Most recently, her work as reference librarian for the MOI in Cairo had provided ideal practice for concentrating the mind and discarding extraneous material. We recall the description of her activities there, which entailed her 'reading newspapers, books and magazines, writing summaries, distributing material where it could best be used'.

The essence of Elizabeth's statement, that she had hardly put pen to paper, was that not until now had she addressed the problem with any purposefulness; *how* would she go about writing? Perhaps her association with the very literary (mainly male) authors of criticism and fiction in Cairo, as well as stimulating her, may have smothered her own literary beginnings. She did perhaps for a time harbour the idea of writing fiction, but the confidence and élan of friends like Lawrence Durrell and Robin Fedden possibly intimidated her. Ultimately the reason she did not finally take up fiction was because she did not want to. Perhaps, like the novelist Olivia Manning, in Cairo at the same time as Elizabeth, she realized her inspiration did not come from the imagination – Manning managed quite well nevertheless. But as Elizabeth's future friend the writer Sybille Bedford astutely observed of her in conversation with the author: 'She cared too much about truth. A novelist must be prepared to make things up.'

At George's encouragement then, in that ration-blighted hotel in Ross-on-Wye, Elizabeth sat down and made a beginning: a record of her Mediterranean experiences and memories of dishes eaten along the way. Together they had concluded what it was she must write about, and the obvious subject was food.

With Tony's arrival imminent, Elizabeth eventually returned to London with those first notes, while George went off for a time to pick up labouring jobs around the country. One of these was organized for George by Elizabeth on her uncle Top's Hampshire estate. This she did despite the fact that their stay together in Ross had ended in argument, and it took her some time to forgive him – but then she always indulged George.

Tony David's return to England at the end of April 1947 appears to have been a relatively insignificant event in the larger scheme of Elizabeth's life. For the moment, however, she essayed the role of married woman; introducing her husband to the family and taking him to stay with several of them. They were above all enormously relieved that Elizabeth had had the good sense to 'rid herself of that terrible actor and marry a man who could at least ride a horse'. Stella, still at Dedham near Cedric and Lett, thought him a decent young man and felt the two seemed well suited. One can hardly imagine the artists Cedric Morris and Lett Haines being so enthusiastic about Tony, whose abilities as a good-looking, pleasant socialite and 'butler' would no doubt have been enlisted for their entertainment. Priscilla thought him 'absolutely charming'. So too did some of Elizabeth's female friends, but they also had more than an inkling that Tony and Elizabeth might be mismatched.

However distasteful Elizabeth may have found her Uncle Roland, she visited him several times at Wootton with Tony. Having squandered old James (Stick) Gwynne's money on years of lavish entertaining, Roland had found it impossible to remain at Folkington. Ousting the tenant forthwith (a Miss Hudson, who had entertained Virginia Woolf to tea there and been credited as 'frightfully chi-chi'), he had moved into Wootton. Here Roland was sufficiently impressed by Tony's horsemanship that he permitted him to ride his favourite black horse out on the Downs nearby; Tony was reputedly the only person who achieved this honour.

Tony and Elizabeth entertained frequently and drinking carried on, as ever, at a furious pace, but Elizabeth managed to weather the hangovers. 'She never admitted to having one,' recalls George Lassalle's future wife, Judith. 'She would always say: "Oh, I feel terrible, so ill – I feel absolutely as if I'm going to die." And she would mix up some sort of hangover special. She smoked a lot. Always.'

Elizabeth's cooking was beginning to reflect something of her own travelled sophistication. Soho was then really the only place in London where some of the ingredients for the Mediterranean dishes she was trying out were obtainable; and under the stringencies of rationing these were still in severely short supply. Keenly interested in food and apparently not a bad cook, Tony was interested and useful in the experiments to which Elizabeth was now devoting considerable energies. Her limited patience, particularly with those not as quick-witted as herself, was, however, easily abandoned. Concurrent with her growing expertise at the stove was an expanding collection of books on cookery: needless to say Elizabeth's literary interests were by now far too well developed for her to marginalize them in favour of an exclusive interest in cookery writing.

In the summer of 1947 Elizabeth, Tony, and Doreen Thornton, now separated from her husband, set off in an old Rolls for a holiday in the South of France. 'Tony always did things in a grand way, so he took a day cabin – they were up on the deck – just for going from Dover to Calais. We sat and drank champagne for the crossing . . . Tony and I shared the driving, because Elizabeth never could. The

Rolls was lent by Chris Grey, a terrible old thing. It was like driving a tank. Liza and Tony were getting on very well most of the time – perhaps the only time – which made it a bit difficult for me. I do remember one day, though, going round the ramparts at Avignon and we were all not speaking to one another.

'We went right on down to Italy, but it was hard going because we had this awful fifty-pound limit on expenditure abroad. We met up with Veronica [Nicholson, now working for *Harpers Bazaar*, and in France to review the fashion shows] in Paris on the way down. We had to go there so Tony could do some shady deal to get money. Veronica took us out to a fabulous meal at Plaza Athénée on her expense account.' Dior's cinched-waisted, swirling-skirted New Look had been launched that year; and whilst many marvelled at the seductively feminine image its use of yardage created, others railed at the unseemly abandonment of sense this necessitated when clothes were still rationed. Fashion, as always, overcame political stricture and the style was a wild success.

Paris after the war was almost without petrol and painfully short of food, yet, despite Occupation, or because of collaboration, many Frenchwomen had maintained a high level of interest in clothes throughout the war. Audrey Withers, then editor of *Vogue*, had made a post-war trip to report on the designer shows and like others from Britain, marvelled at the remarkable clothes. In the streets as much as on the catwalk she saw outrageous hats and high platform shoes; made of wood in the absence of rubber, and worn for walking and bicycling in the almost carless streets.

The occasion of Elizabeth's visit is vivid in Veronica's memory because on one evening when they all met up for drinks, Ernestine Carter, then editor of *Harpers*, was part of the group. Ernestine was a formidably ambitious American journalist (small and not particularly attractive), who reached the heights of English journalism and would later feature in Elizabeth's professional life. Elizabeth proceeded to ridicule her size and appearance to Veronica and Tony almost within Ernestine's earshot, and Veronica afterwards regretted not having chastised her. 'But the awful thing was that Elizabeth could be so funny, never mind that it might be at someone else's expense . . . Yes, somewhere there was that feeling with Elizabeth that she had a chip, was defensive, and so would always rise to the attack before it might happen to her . . . which of course it rarely did.'

Another woman who remembers being slighted by Elizabeth at this time was the young wife of Elizabeth's lover, the 'glamour boy' Peter Laing so badly wounded in Egypt during the Battle of Alamein. It seems he was unaware of, or insensitive to, the depth of Elizabeth's attachment to him, for there is no doubt she had hoped he would marry her. After the war he brought his new bride to meet Elizabeth and Tony, and Elizabeth made the young woman feel distinctly uncomfortable. From a family of considerable wealth, she was, nevertheless, relatively inexperienced and unaffected in manner. 'Elizabeth was very smartly dressed and with a friend did an awful lot of giggling. I felt it was at me.' No doubt it was. Elizabeth was uninhibited about bearing grudges and quite capable of setting someone up as the butt of her ridicule if she thought it was deserved; never mind that in this case the party may have been unaware of her crime. Elizabeth's strong sense of justice was often selective, consequently not always aimed in the right direction. 'She was very unforgiving, very temperamental. Very severe in her standards,' says her friend Sybille Bedford.

During the course of the years Elizabeth was happy to resume this affair on Peter Laing's periodic visits to Europe. Noteworthy here are the conflicting statements Elizabeth made towards the end of her life: that she had been relieved at his return home during the war, and her subsequent comments to a select few stressing that he had been the most important man in her life.

Some time after holidaying in France with Doreen, Elizabeth must have persuaded Tony not to return to India. During the latter part of 1947 he must then have formally extracted himself from the army, for he never returned.

Elizabeth's mother, Stella, had been feeling the strain of running a house as large as the Old Grammar School at Dedham, and in 1948 she made the decision to move. Priscilla and Richard had recently separated and Priscilla moved with the little girls to a house in South Kensington. In the following year Stella bought a fine Georgian town house in Brighton, and with the dealer Hugh Schooling's help proceeded to fill it with another remarkable and eclectic collection of strange and beautiful things. By the time the Old Grammar School was sold it had become clear to Elizabeth that Tony did not have anything like the money she had needed. Knowing almost nothing about him at the time of her marriage, neither had she been particularly curious to discover more.

Tony's mother, Beatrice, had, like Elizabeth, been stranded on the French Riviera at the fall of France. She was subsequently able to make her way to Kenya where her daughter Yvonne had lived with her husband for several years. Beatrice eventually moved to Durban where she died a few years after the war. The Davids were not poor but the Welsh puritan family ethos apparently dictated that Tony would not have expected, nor been given, handouts. His natural desire to do things stylishly for his wife may, nonetheless, have been wilfully misread by Elizabeth as a sign that he had more capital than was the case. However that may be, using some of this capital, Tony had soon become the managing director of a company which (legitimately) sent luxury parcels of British-only food to people in Britain, paid for by friends and family abroad.

Elizabeth may have been disappointed in her husband, but was realistic enough to see that she would have to do something about their finances. She asked for Stella's assistance and it was agreed that Elizabeth would be bought a house with the proviso that, because Stella regarded her as financially untrustworthy, it was to remain in her [Stella's] name and Tony was gradually to repay her. By 1949 Elizabeth and Tony were installed in their pretty four-storeyed Georgian house in Halsey Street, a quiet Chelsea street lying almost equidistant from four of London's most fashionable and elegant shopping thoroughfares: Brompton Road to the west, Beauchamp Place north, Sloane Street east and the King's Road to the south, with property in the vicinity correspondingly valuable. In the triangle nearby, where Brompton Road and Sloane Street converge, lies the vast acreage taken up by Harrods, at that period probably the most fashionable Mecca in the Kingdom; in 1948 it had lavishly celebrated its centenary.

Elizabeth set to and furnished her house in a style now confirmed as her own, English with touches of the Mediterranean. Most of the furniture (and the fridge from Uncle Jasper) which she had left behind in England before the war was lost; destroyed by a bomb, so almost everything had to be replaced. Notwithstanding her ambivalent feelings about Stella, Elizabeth always respected her taste and had a number of pieces from her with which to furnish Halsey Street. In this context she went round one day to visit Maudie O'Malley, now living close by. Maudie had been a student of Cedric Morris and Lett Haines at Dedham Art School and like many students had bought things from Stella at the Old Grammar School nearby. Elizabeth looked at some chairs Maudie had from Stella with a view to buying them herself. With their mutual friendship with Cedric and Lett and an almost equal fear of Stella in common, they began 'a fair amount of to-ing and fro-ing' to each other's houses.

Maudie, so named by Cedric Morris, was living and painting in London with her husband Peter and later did some drawings for Elizabeth. 'Oh, Elizabeth knew several of the painters from Dedham, she would go and visit Cedric and Lett. Robert Buhler, who had been a student at Dedham, did a portrait of her. Her mother was such an autocratic old thing. Very grand. She was always shaking her head and had large dangling earrings, and they went up and down – everything tinkled.' Elizabeth now exhibited the same kind of confident mixing of objects at which Stella had always excelled. Amongst other oddities which Elizabeth had acquired, perhaps through a theatrical contact, was an enormous bath. The journalist Alix Coleman remembers going to the bathroom on her first visit to Halsey Street a few years later and asking Elizabeth why she had such a vast bath.

'"Oh, that belonged to Dame Marie Lohr," said Elizabeth with a smile. And we both laughed. Marie Lohr was one of those great old stage actresses. Played alongside people like Leslie Howard in the film version of *Pygmalion*. She had those sweet small features in a face now large, and a voice like cut crystal. She was *huge*, and hence the bath.'

A high four-poster bed was acquired for upstairs (for which many years later a friend, Andrew Patrick of the Fine Art Society, had steps made so that Elizabeth's ascent was facilitated) and she began her usual ordering of stuffs for curtains and covers. No. 24 Halsey Street followed the standard pattern for small Georgian town houses; a long hall off which led a sitting room to the front, a dining room to the back and behind that a kitchen-scullery. Downstairs was a basement with rooms similar to the ground floor. The stairs led up to two more floors of bedrooms.

Visitors from the early years, and later, remember the chill at Halsey Street in winter. 'Oh, Elizabeth and Tony kept it cold. She would turn on the oven in the kitchen to warm it up. Downstairs was the perfect larder temperature.' Veronica Nicholson then described Elizabeth's New World cooker bought at the purchase of Halsey Street as: 'one of those great machines'. Ubiquitous by the early Fifties, in 1949 its rounded edges, were in reaction to the starker geometry of Thirties and Forties Art Deco. As time passed and cookers changed in efficiency and design, Elizabeth hung on to the style; in fact a version of it remained in her kitchen until her death forty-three years later. Long ago grown accustomed to cooking stoves of the most primitive order she was unperturbed by the inconveniences involved. But, for the moment, her cooker was the height of modernity.

The prevailing atmosphere of Elizabeth's kitchen was, nonetheless, at some variance to the design of her cooker. Hers was not the austere, deathly modernity increasingly promoted by most women's magazines throughout the Fifties and Sixties and reflecting the post-war advance of the streamlined 'kitchen as laboratory, food as efficiency and technology' ideal. (The same ethos gave the appalling title 'domestic science' to the well intended, in practice usually sterile, school and college cookery lessons for girls.) In the new 'ideal' kitchens without servants, a practical linoleum floor, stainless-steel sink and rash of post-war labour-saving domestic appliances would become necessities for a fulfilling life. A 'dream' kitchen, shining clinically from the pages of magazines, sported ever-larger refrigerators in which to keep the rapidly multiplying range of processed and frozen foods, whilst the desirable fitted look was soon given even greater unity by smothering every available surface under acres of the new Formica in a rainbow choice of patterns and colours. A heatproof, wipe-clean material, Formica was in perfect harmony with an age now increasingly addicted to hygiene and thrilled by the wonders of technology.

Although more women now worked than before the war the domestic ideal was still a wife at home with one or two young children, mindful of her role as 'home-maker'. In 1949 most young women were aware of their shortcomings in home management and cooking: the better off because they found themselves without servants; the less well off because they had been deprived of practice by the dislocations of war and rationing, now subject to the consequent loss of the last of an oral culinary tradition passed down from mother to daughter. At all levels cookery classes became popular. So also did women's magazines and cookery books and their popularity as organs of domestic instruction, inspiration and advice had soared by the early Fifties. Just as the rapid expansion of the middle classes during the nineteenth century had left them unsure and greedy for instruction in everything from recipes to etiquette, from the likes of Mrs Beeton, so now another age of expansion needed more of the same assurance.

Elizabeth's kitchen was a different sort from those pictured in magazines, including those for which she wrote. In 1949 and 1950 her taste was eclectic, essentially an amalgam of English and Mediterranean *country* living. Floors were of oak woodblock, her walls painted pale colours, in part to counteract the lack of light in a long lowish room – it had been extended in the 1920s, not too well, and was always a bit damp. She had found a farmhouse dresser on which she displayed much of her (unmatching) collection of pottery and china: old, English (much blue and white) and some brought back from her travels abroad. A large old pine table was set in the middle of the room and around it farmhouse chairs. An old china sink, like those still in place in many English sculleries, was left *in situ*, its cupboard not to be updated for another thirty years or so. This was flanked by the New World cooker and beside that another painted early nineteenth-century dresser for more china and containers. On the end wall, beside the pretty porthole window leading on to her tiny yard, was a dark and voluptuous French *armoire* in which were kept glasses, cups, preserves, cake tins, pans. At the other end of the room was a Georgian cupboard with sliding doors where spices and more pots were stored.

At this time, for the majority in England and the rest of Europe the kitchen, often small, was for cooking. It was not a room in which the family relaxed or entertained their guests, kept beyond it in the dining and drawing room. The designers of houses and arbiters of social etiquette had not yet faced up to the actualities of contemporary life. The post-war situation which prevailed, certainly when entertaining guests, demanded that the housewife prepare the meal, then bring it into the dining room with the kitchen shut off from view. That way, by implication, there just might be someone helping her out of sight.

Only in rural farmhouse kitchens had an older tradition been sporadically maintained; here master, servants and farm-workers had never become separated by proliferation of 'the green baize door' and sometimes still sat together at table. Most farmhouse kitchens were large enough to accommodate numbers of people who could still benefit from the use of the old range or Aga, painted or scrubbed pine cupboards, dresser for display of china, and a large pine table at which much of the meal was prepared and then sat up to by the family.

In keeping with these traditions and the largely Mediterranean and unpretentious food which she prepared, Elizabeth asked her visitors into the kitchen, where they almost invariably stayed. 'Elizabeth had made it such a pleasurable room, and so conducive to the consuming of good food and the making of good talk, that we rarely got round to moving,' says Veronica Nicholson. Elizabeth wrote from experience and heartfelt belief in the introduction to her second book, *French Country Cooking* (John Lehmann, 1951), that: 'Some sensible person once remarked that you spend the whole of your life either in your bed or your shoes. Having done the best you can by shoes and bed, devote all the time and resources at your disposal to the building up of a fine kitchen. It will be, as it should be, the most comforting and comfortable room in the house.'

Elizabeth and Tony gave good parties. Veronica recalls an early occasion in Halsey Street when Elizabeth gave a cocktail party (the word was unfortunately again in vogue after its demise during the war) and the drawing room was still occasionally in use for its designated purpose. Quite a collection of people was there: Stella, the Feddens, Walter Baxter, Stewart Perowne (briefly married to Freya Stark), and a number of Elizabeth's other homosexual friends and acquaintances, such as Brian Howard, for a few years the narcissistic exquisite par excellence, whose renowned elegance with language gradually succumbed to drink and drugs.

In describing the occasion Veronica remembers being struck by the incongruous way in which Elizabeth and her mother behaved at this sparkling social gathering. 'Everyone was in evening dress and there Stella was seated on the sofa. She had soon to catch a train back to Brighton and Elizabeth brought her a tray, almost as you might when ill in bed, but not in quite such a gathering. She had made a boiled egg and cut the toast up as you would for a child – into soldiers – and Stella sat and ate. Quite oblivious.' Meanwhile Brian Howard was getting into his stride by loudly insulting the gentle Walter Baxter: 'Why aren't you in evening dress, everyone else is?'

Afterwards Elizabeth said to Veronica, 'I'm *never* going to give a drinks party again.'

Tony's presence was becoming irksome to Elizabeth and he would sometimes absent himself: 'She was getting so bored by him' says Veronica Nicholson. George Lassalle was often at Halsey Street. Since 1948 he had been living with Judith Richardson at her mother's Onslow Square flat while she was away in Monte Carlo. Judith's father had run the then prestigious Army and Navy Stores before his death. 'Oh, everything came from the Army and Navy when we were young, including my mother.' Judith's mother had in fact been a popular society photographer based at the store. During the war and just afterwards Onslow Square was almost empty of its eccentric inhabitants except for a few such as Daphne du Maurier and the Venns. It was still a fairly quiet neighbourhood when George brought Elizabeth to be introduced to Judith in 1949. She had made a meal and Elizabeth's tart response was, 'Well, George, at least she can cook.' When the two were married in 1950 Elizabeth said to Judith, 'There's one thing you've got to remember about George, he can't face up to anything, he'll always run away from things. He's a terrible coward.' It so happened that the date of their wedding, 10 May, coincided with the marriage of Elizabeth's cousin, Robert Palmer, to the Hon Anne Cooper, so Elizabeth was unable to be present at the Lassalles' celebration. Judith remembers that in characteristically generous style Elizabeth nonetheless came round in the morning 'with a huge salmon for our party, all beautifully cooked. She couldn't come, but made up for it by getting away from her family as soon as she could. She arrived when we'd all drunk a lot – so had she – and the party was breaking up. She didn't want to leave. George said, "Someone has to take you home," and we had to get Mark Culme-Seymour, an old boyfriend of mine, to take her.'

Contemporary descriptions of the monotony, leadenness and lack of skill demonstrated in English cookery during and immediately after the war are too frequent for their testimony to be doubted. But it is worth remembering that the same was also true during the 1920s and 1930s, when there was little feeling for the sensuousness of food, either in cookery books or in practice. The novelist (and gourmet) Ford Madox Ford could write, sententiously but accurately, that: 'Nowhere is our English inattention to a proper appreciation of the intrinsic values of life more conspicuous than on matters appertaining to the domain of the table.' In 1926 in *A Mirror to France* (Duckworth) his disquisition on the merits of modern French cooking concludes that: 'Food in Anglo Saxon countries is no more talked of than love or Heaven.'

One is left with two overriding impressions from books and personal accounts of the first half of this century: an obsessive concern with economy and efficiency, and the assumption that cookery is a burden to be dealt with as quickly as possible. This prevails whether it is the working woman of small means who has no time and little money (or skill) with which to feed her family; or her better-off counterpart who, not working, has time at her disposal, but no inclination to spend it in the kitchen. These richer women, until recently protected by a bevy of servants from the unseemly and distasteful business of preparing food, were left relatively helpless after the First World War and utterly so after the Second, when servants had almost disappeared.

With few exceptions, there were two kinds of food. For those who could afford it there was what amounted to bastardized versions of haute cuisine, where more often than not the appearance of a dish was more esteemed than the subtlety of its taste. On the other hand there was 'plain wholesome food', based on the use of suet and dripping rather than butter and oil. 'Wholesome' meant heavy main courses, accompanied by vegetables stewed until soft; this was then reinforced with the ubiquitous boiled, baked or steamed puddings. (An undoubted English skill did still endure in the domestic tradition of sweet baking; cakes, pastries, biscuits.) English cooking practice was in strong contrast to the French one where cookery books and women's magazine articles took it as their premise that not only did the French housewife *enjoy* cooking, being prepared to devote lengthy periods of time to its perfecting, but she had also inherited from her forebears a certain degree of basic culinary skill.

Of course some enthusiasts in England had been labouring for years, before, during and after the war to inculcate an appreciation of good food and a consequent demand for it. Knowledgeable essays were produced by cultivated and cosmopolitan writers such as Philip Morton Shand who, in *A Book of Food* (Jonathan Cape, 1927), both appreciated the best of our food and produced the well-rehearsed argument that 'for the last hundred years our national cuisine has provoked the world's grimace'. In 1948 Romilly Fedden (Robin's father) was reiterating these sentiments in *Food and Other Frailties*. The cookery book writers continued the struggle. Amongst their offerings were Hilda Leyel's *Gentle Art*, her little books on salads, Elizabeth Lucas's *Pretty Kettle of Fish* (Chatto and Windus, 1925) and another on vegetables, André Simon's numerous publications with the Wine and Food Society, Constance Spry and Ambrose Heath's endless flow of material to inspire; and not forgetting the Countess Morphy and Marcel Boulestin.

Ambrose Heath's *Good Food* of 1932 (Faber) was already using an extract from Norman Douglas's *South Wind* as its epigraph, reflecting the spread of Douglas's influence amongst a travelled and literate minority. 'The ideal cuisine should display an individual character . . . a menu reflecting the master's alert and fastidious taste.' Heath then launched into his introduction with the argument: 'First, to show how easy good cooking can be; and second that it need not be expensive . . . it is often cheaper in the long run, for many of the famous dishes are derived from peasant and bourgeois kitchens, where it is essential that everything should do its full duty, and a little always went a long way . . . There are two essentials, however; the giving of a little time and a little trouble. Food that is worth eating cannot usually be flung together . . .'

He adds that those appreciating his book will be 'ready to give up some time and thought and care to the preparation of their meals'. Alert to the now servantless wife from Elizabeth's background, 'Those whom our present distress has forced to take, shall we say, a more active interest in the affairs of the kitchen', Heath's principles are commendable (even if the dated combination of ornament and tasteful restraint occasionally make his language verge on the comical). And his intention of introducing the reader – via a calendar layout – to the best and freshest foods available at all times of the year is a useful one. 'Good things out of season are but a ghost of their true selves.' Mr Heath recommends his book also to those who 'possibly from sentiment . . . would like to taste again . . . some of the dishes which they remember having eaten with delight in a restaurant, on a holiday abroad'. Finally, his little volume came with a dust-jacket and decorations by one of the most astute, humorous and stylish artist-illustrators of the day, Edward Bawden; whose other illustrations included the famous Shell advertisements, fabric designs, posters for the cinema and decoration of the prestigious Fortnum and Mason catalogues.

The man whose work most influenced the eating habits of the younger artistic and literary circles of the Twenties and Thirties and whose message is clearly disseminated in Ambrose Heath's writing, was Boulestin. A vital culinary influence upon Elizabeth, Marcel Boulestin was the latest in that tradition of colourful French chefs and gastronomes who first adopted the English and then encouraged them to care more about their table.

The culinary dialogue between England and France was an ancient one, set in motion as long ago as the Norman Conquest of Britain in the eleventh century. It appears that the links between European courtly food at this period, and on into the later Middle Ages were much closer than hitherto recognized; meaning that what appeared as the culinary conquest of Britain was not such a simple matter. England was not as barbaric as some have thought and competition between French and English court cooks was an openly waged battle. With skirmishes flaring up over the ensuing centuries, references to the French victory are occasionally observed by the late Middle Ages. There were many cooks and writers in England, nevertheless, who staunchly maintained their English ground until the restoration of Charles II in 1662. The returning royalist court, bringing with it the sophistication and refinement of Versailles, for a time made everything French the vogue. Henceforward all self-respecting aristocrats kept a French cook, often a religious (Protestant) refugee; although pastry-makers were preferably Italian. French recipes became ubiquitous in cookery books and this vogue extended to bills of fare, frequently done out in French.

Even one of the new eighteenth-century breed of acclaimed English domestic cookery writers, Hannah Glasse; whose fame derived in part from staunch English rejection of 'fancy' French food and the overblown notions of male cooks, was less 'patriotic' than she would have us believe when she wrote that much-quoted passage from *The Art of Cooking Made Plain and Easy* (London, 1747):

> If gentlemen will have French cooks they must pay for French tricks . . . I have heard of a cook that used six pounds of butter to fry twelve eggs; when everybody knows (that understands cooking) that half a pound is full enough or more than need be used. But then it would not be French. So much is the blind Folly of this Age that would rather be impos'd on by a *French* Booby, than give Encouragement to a good *English* Cook.

It transpires that Hannah in fact lifted a number of, as it happens, inadequately understood French recipes, directly and indirectly, from at least two monoliths of French cookery literature: La Chapelle and Massialot.

This reaction against what was perceived as French extravagance (a misconception of French cooking based on courtly books and courtly émigré cooks) took hold in England. But France would once again find itself in the culinary ascendant early in the nineteenth century, this time partially instigated by an influx of French refugees in the aftermath of the French Revolution. By the end of that century this French influence was properly understood by few. The omnipresent nineteenth-century tenets of thrift and economy gradually merged with the misconceived idea that only *complicated* food was good food, and drew the exasperated complaint from the great nineteenth-century chef Escoffier that the English cared more for show than good food.

With his grace, good humour and sound French principles Escoffier's compatriot, Marcel Boulestin, set out, in his restaurant and his writing, to purge the English of the parsimony and misjudged attempts at: 'What they think is "French" cooking, which results in strange concoctions and alarming sauces, either simplified or elaborated with names equally vaguely French.' To readers like Elizabeth he became something of an icon.

Opened in 1925, Boulestin's restaurant had not only served beautifully prepared, unpretentious and authentic dishes from the French bourgeois cooking repertoire, but also provided delightful regional ones passed on by word of mouth from generation to generation and as yet uncommitted to paper. The spirit of the times was in reaction to what many felt was their parents' empty Victorian formality. Boulestin's message was perfectly in tune with the growing desire for (sophisticated) simplicity, reflected in the rapid success of his restaurant. More truly French than almost anywhere else in London, Boulestin's attracted the élite of the Twenties and Thirties; the rich, the artistic and the travelled.

CHAPTER THIRTEEN

A Cooking Book
(1949–1950)

SHORTLY AFTER ELIZABETH and Tony's move into No. 24 Halsey Street Veronica married John Nicholson, a solicitor. Tony and Elizabeth went round to their mews flat off Kensington Church Street and made up the marriage bed. (During the commotion they met Walter Baxter, a neighbour and future proprietor of the influential Old Brompton Road restaurant, the Chanterelle; a place Elizabeth would often visit in the Fifties.) Universally liked, John Nicholson was a gracious man of principle and humour and he and Veronica were to remain good companions throughout a long and harmonious marriage. His relationship with Elizabeth was maintained, however, for the sake of his wife. John was mystified at Veronica's attachment to her, his own reservations remaining intact.

Veronica was working at that time on the staff of *Harpers Bazaar*, the quality magazine which competed on fairly equal terms with Condé Nast's *Vogue*, the international oracle of style. Towards the end of 1948 Veronica had persuaded Elizabeth that she should be introduced to *Harpers*' editor, Anne Scott-James, with a view to writing for her. A tall and elegant young woman, Anne Scott-James's cool and refined English beauty complemented her incisive intelligence. Her editorship of *Harpers* had established her as part of that brisk, well-educated, increasingly powerful, yet still rather embattled breed of women journalist-editors. Several of them came, like Anne Scott-James, from families noted for their literary and cultivated inclinations.

Anne Scott-James told the author she found Elizabeth 'reserved' but realized too that 'she obviously had a lot new to say'. After discussing possible ideas for articles, she asked her to write one for the magazine. Elizabeth's first attempt was accepted – she was asked for more – and in March 1949 her maiden article was published. It was entitled 'Rice Again' and the reception from editor and readers was such, that she continued contributing to *Harpers* in her capacity as cookery columnist for the next six years. In this time she passed from the position of unknown journalist to sought-after writer of four successful books.

The article for *Harpers* was a modest single column, a standard 1000 words, whose introductory sentence led off with the information that rice was again available after years out of circulation, 'and with it come possibilities of pilaffs, risottos, curries – all those beautiful savoury dishes, snowy white, pale yellow with saffron or fried golden brown, spiked with scarlet of lobster, or black of *truffe*'.

Noticeable for the self-conscious stylishness of phrases like 'scarlet of lobster' and 'black of *truffe*', a flourish which seems to have little to do with her inexperience as a writer, and occurring as it does at intervals throughout all but her final writing; from the outset we see Elizabeth in characteristic mode: authoritative, practical, tart and evocative. In contrast to so many cookery writers now or then, she made the reader aware of the taste that the dish should have. She told them that as the rules for cooking rice, which are very simple, seemed to be 'insufficiently known', she made 'no apology' for stating them again. The notoriously difficult subject of rice cooking, in which each person claims the infallibility of their own method, was glossed over. Elizabeth's way was correct 'and that is that', as she would say.

Four recipes followed, each using rice: a pilaff, a *riz en salade*, a risotto and a rice stuffing. Elizabeth's Cairo cook Suleiman was immortalized, with his pilaff the first recipe of this debut article, although here she calls it Turkish. A year later the pilaff was honoured with Suleiman's name and had become 'one of the most comforting dishes imaginable'. Here one is presented with one of those elusive statements typical of Elizabeth and inducing in any reader alive to the hints in her prose the desire both to lie back and muse *and* to sit up and think. 'Comforting' is a word more often applied to the hot, warming soups and slowly matured, unexotic meat stews associated with cold northern climates, than to the pilaff, a dish so redolent of the spice-filled savour of the Far and Middle East. Did Elizabeth mean comforting to herself in the heat and sometimes despair of Cairo, or to herself and her readers as a reassuring reminder of lightness, brilliance and sun here in these cold northern wastes to which she felt at present confined?

Her first article was not a dazzling piece of prose, nevertheless, she included so much that was herself, it can be read as an understated exemplification of what her writing would come to represent. The quality, presentation and style of recipes and writing exhibited those features which remained her trademark to the end. Admittedly the qualities are easier to see with the hindsight of later writing, but the series which followed bears out Anne Scott-James's judgement of her work that: 'It was as if her prose sprung fully formed from her pen.' The one feature, so characteristic of her, which Elizabeth did not yet quite have the confidence to display, was her wit, but that she would remedy quite soon.

For her second article in April, she was again given 1000 words and dealt with the possibilities of 'Easter Lamb'. Once more none of the recipes (except the last) was English: Anatolian Kebabs, *Tranches de Mouton Sauce Catalane*, *Gigot à l'Infante*, and for accompaniments she added Potato Kephtedes, *Concombres à la crème* and Mint Chutney. But neither were they tired French fare; rather, when not recipes from Greece or the Middle East, they were examples of a mellow southern earthiness like the *Gigot*, a leg of lamb marinated in olive oil for twelve hours, 'well seasoned with salt, pepper and herbs, including rosemary and marjoram. Put the *gigot* into a braising pan with half a pint of *malaga* or *marsala*, a quantity of small onions and 1lb of small sausages. Cook it in a very slow oven for several hours.' In conversation friends and relations remember the private version of this frequently voiced dictum: 'Cook it dead slow.'

In June Anne Scott-James was confident enough – her magazine staff were as impressed with the articles as the public – to unleash Elizabeth; she extended her to three columns for 'Gourmet Picnics'. The more expansive style this permitted meant that her entire first page was without a recipe and Elizabeth was now well into her stride. In urbane, informative prose, subtly her own, she described the rules pertaining to the complicated game of make-believe; sophisticated rusticity, which we call a gourmet picnic. Two menus followed, each with a page of recipes. The note of authority, tinged with that caustic humour familiar from her letters, made it clear that the writer had actually partaken of the picnics she described. The reader need have no qualms about the efficacy of the recipes, all that was now required was to get up and try them.

For all but the most wealthy or resourceful and enterprising cooks amongst the magazine's readership this, however, was impossible. Owing to a combined lack of demand and rationing, the ingredients: courgettes, green and red peppers, aubergines, garlic, olive oil, olives, anchovies, fresh pasta, pitta, almonds, raisins and garlic; were virtually unobtainable anywhere except in a very few shops, situated almost entirely in the capital. Nonetheless, in those bleak post-war days Elizabeth made little concession in her recipes to the current dearth and gave only the occasional recommendation to her reader, such as 'chopped chives, or the green top of an onion or leek' instead of basil, and 'grated cheese' in place of Parmesan. 'A lot of the food she was talking about was like fiction,' says Joyce Molyneaux, an early devotee and now a renowned chef; 'because it was food that you had never seen or thought you were ever likely to see.'

But this deterred neither *Harpers*' editor nor Elizabeth herself, who continued to provide this delightful 'fiction'. To those of the well-heeled young wives who read *Harpers Bazaar*, who were as yet unfamiliar with the attractions of the Mediterranean and its table, her writing provided a certain exotic stimulation. The rest, au fait with the Mediterranean's 'blessed shores' from Riviera holidays pre-war, were propelled into reminiscence; the anticipation of adventure while speeding southward on that luxurious Blue Train.

Recently Anne Scott-James was surprised on being reminded that Elizabeth was born in the same year as herself, saying: 'When we met she seemed older. I have no memory of her dress. She didn't strike me. But she was very grande-dame, very sure of herself; there was an egoism of quite an advanced kind. I thought she was pretty formidable and didn't instantly warm to her.' But personal feelings were unimportant when the magazine's editor had discovered such a contributor and she let Elizabeth largely dictate her own material. 'She knew exactly what she wanted to do. The article would always be about a particular subject, for example vegetables. She was quite poetic about them.'

Elizabeth was soon demonstrating the breadth of her reading on her subject with confidence and flair. At a glance her writing made it abundantly clear that here was no culinary novice with a sentimental attachment to the 'shores of that great lake', as Forster had described the Mediterranean Sea. Although many may not have recognized it, readers were being presented not simply with good recipes, but with a synthesis; a distillation of Elizabeth's varied experience knowledge and understanding of the development of European (but particularly French and English) cooking. In 'The Presentation of Food' she briefly outlined a history of what, to her mind, had been the misguided fashion for display. She launched in with a lengthy quote from the absurd and facile marathon which describes how to make *Lobster à la Newmarket* 'in a book called *A la Mode Cookery* published in 1902. It is typical of the inanity of fashionable cooking at that period. Mrs Brook . . . even went so far as to suggest that flowers, food and yes, wine should be chosen to match the hostess's gown.'

We are then treated to a passage of historical information, smoothly incorporating wit as a device to inform us effortlessly of her opinion. She describes how the First World War had called a halt to most of these 'preoccupations . . . and I suspect that most women who have the time and talent for this form of self-expression prefer to exercise it on the devising of lampshades. The inspiration for this upholstered food had come of course from France. Mid and late nineteenth century French cookery books abound with engravings of elaborate dishes carried out in the grandest possible manner.' This custom, initially so favoured by the great French chefs, was questioned by Prosper Montagné who, according to André Simon, 'originated the movement to put an end to the extravagance and waste of time and materials which all this fancy work entailed'.

Elizabeth's style of delivery: accurate information, opinion couched in wit, with enough conjuring and mystery calculated to intrigue and inspire; already evident in the very earliest pieces of her writing, was much in the spirit of her beloved mentor Norman Douglas. In the South of France at the outbreak of war, with his erudite talk of the Classical past and the Mediterranean present,

Douglas had both concentrated Elizabeth's mind and expanded its vision. She had imbibed the essence of his message; the ethos of elegant simplicity and authenticity shared by some of her favoured cookery writers, Leyel, Boulestin, Pomiane. But she was never a copyist. Elizabeth had already arrived at a voice uniquely her own.

Anne Scott-James's confidence in Elizabeth's writing sprang from two sources. 'She struck the exact right moment. With freedom again and the expectation of holidays once more, without ghastly restrictions or bombs.' She also recognized that Elizabeth 'wrote beautifully. Right from the start. You could smell the shrimps, hear the fishwives talking on the quay. She was old enough to write well, and it was quite clearly not run of the mill. There was this feeling that she wasn't thinking how to do it, but was always associating it with places, always with places – with mountains, with ports, with beautiful villages. There was a Proustian quality about it.'

By December of that year Elizabeth was writing another long piece, entitled 'Style in the Kitchen', in which she hinted at principles and intent. She described types of cook and cooking to be fostered and avoided in the amateur arena. Anathema: the flamboyant, ostentatious, or 'false chic style of cookery advocated by certain classes of cookery school. Sausages in jelly mould decorated with carrots, sponge cakes topped with tinned peaches and whipped cream . . .' Although they 'may be well executed with professional skill'; just as with the 'pompous *Poulet à la Lucullus* of the International Palace Hotel, you may be able to disguise inferior ingredients, but not the wrong outlook on food'.

Esteemed was the style of cooking practised by those who often, like herself, had unconventional culinary backgrounds. Writers such as Edouard de Pomiane, the son of Polish émigrés to France, who became one of France's most popular cooks. Sometimes scorned by the contemporary exponents of the Grand Tradition, Pomiane's cheerful disregard for the sacrosanct and pompous aspects of French haute cuisine, combined with flair and a knowledgeable enthusiasm for food, enamoured him to many. Of his *Cooking in Ten Minutes* (Bruno Cassirer, 1948) Elizabeth told her readers that 'His recipe for skate in black butter is almost the perfect example of a delicate, rapidly prepared dish for these days.'

She writes that the experience necessary to make the perfect gratin or soufflé was 'hard to acquire nowadays, for it entails a certain recklessness in the matter of cream, eggs, and butter, plus a searching knowledge of your cooking stove, to achieve the perfect degree of creamy smoothness and the inimitable crusty golden coating of a successful gratin'. Who better to tell her reader how to achieve it than the great Prosper Montagné with his recipe for *Gratin Dauphinoise* (although Elizabeth's own far simpler version, given in *French Provincial Cooking* ten years later, is much better).

Only 'slavish attention to the rules' laid out by her dear Marcel Boulestin in *Finer Cooking* will save the amateur food-rationed cook from 'the ghastly anxiety endured by the hostess who has flung caution to the winds, entombing a month's butter and eggs and the last of the Grand Marnier into a soufflé'. In that dramatic image of eggs and butter 'entombed' this *Harpers* piece bears out Anne Scott-James's judgement on the fully fledged nature of Elizabeth's earliest writing. From the beginning she manifested a style of great economy and elegance.

Elizabeth was interested in analysis only to a limited degree, and although highly intelligent, was not an intellectual. She was most adept at classification but was not interested in the abstract. Her approach had already given her a firm (eventually profound) grasp of both the historical and aesthetic principles of her chosen subject. This approach was determined, at times stubbornly so, and passionate. Equally important, she had the imagination and peculiar discipline of an artist. Her synthesizing and refining intelligence and her formidable memory were often at their sharpest in her work. But this dedication and passion with which she approached her work, could cloud her judgement when it came to other people. In this context the length of her contributions was a recurring problem in the years she spent as a journalist.

'Oh, she was a very tetchy contributor, there would always be difficulties. One page, 1200 words, was what she had. But she never fitted in with you in any way.' Anne Scott-James would say to her: 'Elizabeth, I can't make the magazine bigger for you.'

'As a journalist you have *got* to give, there is no one too grand not to be able to accept changes and alterations. I'd say, "Elizabeth, there are too many words, you've got to cut them. Are you going to do it or shall I?" She wouldn't come in and I had to do it. She was unbending, couldn't see it, nothing mattered but her piece. In August I asked her to do me a Scottish article. '"I don't know anything about Scottish food." She thought Scotland was barbarism.'

With time Elizabeth would come to think differently about Scottish traditions, but for now 'Everything was Mediterranean. She sort of compromised with the Scottish number by putting a whole lot of other people's recipes in. She was very exciting, but very rude, you know. She was confident her work was good, and it was. I was rather frightened of her. It was hard, for women particularly, to like her, but with that knowledge, that imagination, you couldn't not respect her.'

Anne Scott-James had advised Elizabeth to hang on to her copyrights, then unusual for a cookery writer, and from the outset Elizabeth utilized her literary labour to the full, making it bring in the best possible rewards. Practising this right (and insisting on it for all her subsequent journalism during and after the *Harpers* pieces), she was able to incorporate as much *Harpers* work as she chose into her other present endeavour. Before the end of 1949 she had put together a coherent collection of recipes in such a way as to feel she could call it a book. Veronica, George and Felicité were asked to read it through and had a number of comments to make. Apart from the benefit of George checking over the Greek pieces, they were all three at pains to stress that there was too much of Norman Douglas. They told Elizabeth that much of him would have to go.

After persuasion Elizabeth grudgingly made the cuts and the manuscript was shown by a friend, Robin Chancellor, to several London publishers. It duly came back with the rejection notes. They said food wasn't a good subject at the present time. But one, the entrepreneurial John Lehmann, publisher of the adventurous and prestigious Penguin New Writing was, almost in spite of himself, to become involved. His own brief résumé of events is the best.

'One day there came into my office a disreputable piece of paper – several pieces of paper – typewritten, which said they were a cooking book.' Later, Lehmann and Elizabeth were to become friends and he told her that the manuscript was the untidiest he had ever received. She had been using it to cook from.

'I couldn't make very much of it myself, not being a cooking expert, but I had Julia Strachey with me and asked her to report on it. She came back and said, "I think this is a masterpiece."'

Now intrigued, Lehmann read it again but still needed persuasion. Julia Strachey later told Elizabeth that it was with the recipe for Turkish Stuffing for a Whole Roast Sheep that she had finally cajoled Lehmann into a realization of the book's strength and strangely alluring appeal: 'Imagine, a whole roast sheep, and the meat ration a few ounces a week.'

Lehmann continued: 'I was very thrilled at this and went through it. Though not an expert I (now) saw that it was a very remarkable piece of work. That was the typescript of *A Book of Mediterranean Food*.'

Without Julia Strachey, that small pink and brown linen book, encased in its enticingly vivid dust-jacket, may well never have become the icon it did for a generation of upper-middle-class readers. However, in Julia Strachey it could not have found a better ambassadress. As the niece of Lytton Strachey, the enemy of the Victorians with his *Eminent* ones, she had grown up at the centre of Bloomsbury life. For all Elizabeth and her family's dismissal of the inhabitants of Monk's House, Charleston Farmhouse and their charmed circle, what she propounded with such conviction was very much to their taste. Through her evocative descriptions of unpretentious peasant and bourgeois Mediterranean food and its places, Elizabeth championed, with a singular literary grace, the ethos of Marcel Boulestin: 'Faites Simples.' This had already, by 1927, been exemplified in Virginia Woolf's sensual description of the *Boeuf en Daube* dinner in her novel *To the Lighthouse*. The Bloomsbury Group and others of the artistic and social élite, such as Cedric Morris and Lett Haines, had identified with this ethos such that their devotion had helped make Boulestin a success.

On the subject of *Mediterranean Food* John Lehmann continued: 'I always, perhaps not justifiably, believed that one of the causes of its success was a misprint in the first impression. In those days it was difficult to get eggs. Elizabeth had written take 2 to 3 eggs for a particular recipe and the printer had put "take 23 eggs".

'Well, I pretended to myself that that fascinated and excited people very much. And so I left it. I was struck by the imagination and knowledge of what she was writing about, and her style. Her command and subtle use of English, and only then did I begin to see her importance in a general sense.'

Without any particularly well-articulated understanding of its merits beyond its quirkiness and Mediterranean escapism, after years of uniform war-time puritanism, Lehmann nonetheless sensed something of the book's potential appeal. Summoning Elizabeth to his office, he laid out his proposal for publishing her book. He would pay her an advance of £100: £50 on signature of contract and £50 on publication, but he did not like Elizabeth's title and asked her would not 'The Blue Train Cookery Book' be better?' Elizabeth demurred, suggesting that the train had never reached Egypt. She was privately reluctant to have her book associated with a life-style which she felt had ceased with the war, and with which she didn't anyway particularly wish her labours to be linked. She was correct that that life had gone for ever; and as Norman Douglas had predicted to her and Charles Gibson Cowan, Europe was irrevocably changed, however, this was the very core of the audience to whom her evocative nostalgia would appeal. Elizabeth was in a sense writing for herself, and her past self had some of its roots in that life. She was always ambivalent about this and never publicly professed it.

Elizabeth's persistence paid off. Having instructed her to think about the title, as would he, Lehman asked her to write an introduction. A few days later he wrote to her saying, that on reflection she was right, the title 'should stand'. Being right was something Elizabeth was rarely in doubt about, but she 'admired the good grace with which John, a man who – as I was to discover . . . was far from easy-going, conceded that I must have my own way over that *Mediterranean Food* title. Now of course it seems unthinkable that it could have been anything else.'

In spite of her confident prose, flowing as it does with such apparent facility, writing was never easy for Elizabeth, and for every finished page there were a number of false starts. An introduction called for a distillation of thought which she was later to make out hadn't been given much, when calling the result 'pretty perfunctory'. This is the judgement of hindsight, of a more experienced writer. In essence, what she had arrived at was a synthesis of those first 'agonized cravings' put down in the Ross-on-Wye notes, and her more measured versions of them written out in the articles for *Harpers Bazaar*. It purports to be an introduction, and it is. It is also a challenge and a battle cry.

But first Elizabeth paid her friend Veronica the tribute of dedicating the book to her, and years later, in her thanks for an honorary doctorate from Essex University, she described how Veronica 'chivvied me, coaxed me, badgered me, in fact bullied me into writing about cookery at all'. As we have discovered Elizabeth's motivation to write sprang from more powerful sources than a coaxing friend. Veronica was nevertheless, like George Lassalle, undoubtedly one of those significant few who recognized in Elizabeth something unique which needed airing. In musing over it Veronica has recently said: '*Mediterranean Food* was a very reserved book.' She felt that Elizabeth's passion and intensity and that shattering yet invigorating wit, were here too modified and 'her own voice didn't entirely come over'. Her friend was understandably disappointed in the loss of the 'person' Elizabeth. But Elizabeth had transcended the personal, had (like any artist) transformed real life and herself. With her unusual combination of romance and utter practicality Elizabeth had reached out to her audience with the instinct of the born communicator.

Her introduction begins with these words: 'The cooking of the Mediterranean shores, endowed with all the natural resources, the colour and flavour of the South, is a blend of tradition and brilliant improvisation. The Latin genius flashes from the kitchen pans.

'It is honest cooking, too; none of the sham Grande Cuisine of the International Palace Hotel.'

' "It is not really an exaggeration," wrote Marcel Boulestin, "to say that peace and happiness begin, geographically, where garlic is used in cooking." '

The inclusion of Boulestin's outrageous hyperbole in her first page clearly demonstrates Elizabeth's own standpoint. The message she had purveyed for several months in her articles for *Harpers Bazaar* was here thrown down gauntlet-like at the feet of her unsuspecting English readers. But Elizabeth is concerned with evocation, she is not really interested in persuading: she is an artist, a myth-maker, not at heart a propagandist. Names flow one after another as an incantation, and within moments she has conjured images of those distant lands encircling the shores of the Mediterranean. In her mind's eye, and now ours, their significance resonates as we recall her journeys of discovery. These countries, to most readers mysterious and strange, were to her also vivid and real. As the book unfolds, one is reminded constantly of Charles's diary of their voyage on the *Evelyn Hope* and Elizabeth's letters to her family. The letters where food was described almost incidentally but was actually at the heart of a celebration which was Elizabeth and Charles's life together: along the Rhône to the sea and the South of France, on the Riviera at the outset of war, and on into Greece and the harsh, isolated beauty of life on the 'Isles of Greece'; and afterwards the more voluptuous, worldly years of Middle Eastern living in Alexandria and Cairo.

At a level only half understood by Elizabeth herself, this book rejoices in the romance of her life with Charles (inextricably bound to her experiences of the Mediterranean) and is a lament for all that she has lost. The essential core of the vision she is conjuring in *Mediterranean Food* is found in the poetry of her life on the lost 'Isles of Greece'. The dream is central to her vision, yet so intimate that she was never able to refer directly to it in her writing. Only much later does she make oblique reference to aspects of this period, and then only because with time she had buried and de-mythologized its significance for herself.

Elizabeth traces the routes: 'From Gibraltar to the Bosphorus, down the Rhone Valley, through the great sea ports of Marseilles, Barcelona, and Genoa, across to Tunis and Alexandria, embracing all the Mediterranean islands, Corsica, Sicily, Sardinia, Crete, the Cyclades, Cyprus . . . to the mainland of Greece and the much disputed territories of Syria, the Lebanon, Constantinople . . .'

The ever-recurring elements in the dishes of these countries of the Southern and Eastern Mediterranean were, as she later described them:

the oil, the saffron, the garlic, the pungent local wines; the aromatic perfume of rosemary, wild marjoram and basil . . . the brilliance of the market stalls piled high with pimentos, auber-gines, tomatoes, olives, melons, figs . . . the great heaps of shiny fish, silver, vermilion, or tiger-striped, and those long needle fish whose bones mysteriously turn green when they are cooked. There are, too, all manner of unfamiliar cheeses made from sheep or goat's milk; the butchers' stalls are festooned with every imaginable portion of the inside of every edible animal (anyone who has lived for long in Greece will be familiar with the sound of air gruesomely whistling through sheep's lungs frying in oil).

Of course, almost no one in England reading this in 1950 would have been familiar with that sound, or the dish which was its end, and the image is both unexpected and powerful. During the war in England some had attempted, without too much success, to utilize those (unrationed) parts of animals for food which had before the war already fallen out of favour. Even these were hard to come by. If anyone – such as the writer Theodora FitzGibbon, who asked her butcher if their scarcity meant that animals were no longer born with 'tongues, tails, hearts, kidneys, livers, or balls' – succeeded in obtain-ing the odd trophy it would have been unlikely to include the lungs of a sheep. Writing about such things, Elizabeth added to that hint of the exotic and unattainable evident in her descriptions and recipes which followed. E. M. Forster said of Virginia Woolf: 'The passages in her books describing food were a sharp reminder that here was a woman alert sensuously.' Unquestionably this also applied to Elizabeth.

With descriptions of the strange and mysterious places of her experience she takes her reader beyond the kitchen and into the realm of the traveller and the allure of the unknown. In the grey aftermath of war she tells her English reader that in the Mediterranean 'There are endless varieties of currants and raisins, figs from Smyrna on long strings, dates, almonds, pistachios and pine kernel nuts, dried melon seeds and sheets of apricot paste which are dissolved in water to make a cooling drink'. These and the other seductive ingredients she chronicles, 'make rich and colourful dishes. Over-picturesque, per-haps, for every day; but then who wants to eat the same food every day?' And here Elizabeth is reiterating one of Norman Douglas's typical maxims on food: 'The longer one lives, the more one realizes that nothing is a dish for every day.' For Norman Douglas, unlike most, had no fear of life, only death.

What Elizabeth stresses next is that although 'the variety and quantity of ingredients called for in some of these dishes seem, at first sight, alarming, it is because I preferred to give the authentic recipes and leave it to the resourceful cook to improvise her own substitutes when necessary'. With these words and the following ones she has distinguished what will be the essential tone of her book: 'I hope to give some idea of the lovely cookery of those regions to people who do not already know them, and to stir the memories of those who have eaten this food on its native shores, and who would like sometimes to bring a flavour of those blessed lands of sun and sea and olive trees into their English kitchens'. Whatever difficulties the reader might find in reproducing the recipes, the book's authentic voice was abundantly clear.

In part because at that time publishers did not employ specialist editors for cookery editing, and also because John Lehmann had recognized the quirkiness of the text, Elizabeth's manuscript was left intact with few alterations. The war had, by necessity, conferred on many English housewives a more French-Mediterranean resourceful-ness in matters of food. Some of them were intrigued enough to try recipes for dishes such as: Soup Basque, and Iced Beetroot Soup made from baked beetroots whose 'resulting delicious flavour happily bears no resemblance to the bloodless things sold ready cooked by the greengrocers . . .' Avgolémono (*The* Greek Soup); Soupe au Pistou, vegetables and vermicelli, with the addition of *Aillade*, that fierce Southern paste made of pounded garlic and basil.

There is, inevitably, more than liberal use of garlic throughout *Mediterranean Food*, including, famously, the recipe for *Gigot à la Provençal* left in the original French and whose author, 'rather severely remarks, this dish is supportable only to those who are accustomed to the cooking of the Midi'. Instructions are to lard the leg of lamb with a dozen cloves of garlic and serve with another litre of them blanched.

How this must have shocked the English reader in 1950, when the attitude of most towards garlic differed little from that of Tobias Smollet; the querulous eighteenth-century traveller who remarked that in France 'I am almost poisoned with garlic, which they mix in their ragouts and all their sauces; nay, the smell of it . . . perfumes . . . every person you approach.'

The insertion of the Provençal *Gigot* recipe is also a forceful reminder of the transformation of Elizabeth's attitudes. In her letter to Priscilla regarding preparations for the 1935 journey to Munich by train, she had said they were to travel third class, although it would be uncomfortable. She discovered they could stay the night in Cologne, which would prevent them sleeping on 'hard benches smelling of garlic and disgusting tobacco'. From the South of France after the outbreak of war, she wrote again to Pris that she had 'taken to garlic, which went into absolutely everything – they lash it into salads here, and I hate to think of having to cook without it.'

When it came to the Savoury Omelette Elizabeth could see no better possible way of describing the method than to 'quote "Wyvern's" wholly admirable views on the subject' from his book *Fifty Luncheons*. 'Wyvern' was the pseudonym of the nineteenth-century Indian Army colonel Kenney-Herbert, whose *Culinary Jottings for Madras* (first published in 1878, later Higginbotham and Co., 1948) went into several editions and of whom Elizabeth was later to write: 'His recipes are so meticulous and clear, that the absolute beginner could follow them, yet at the same time he has much to teach the experienced cook.' There follow three pages of instructions on the cooking of an omelette.

Rognons Braisés au Porto . . . How many of her readers could lay their hands on a truffle? Never mind, they could at least salivate and imagine the day when it would be possible to try out 'the beauty of this dish', depending 'on the aroma of the truffle permeating the wine'. Or *Pissaladina*, that lusty onion, olive and anchovy Southern French pizza, 'one of the delights of Marseilles . . . where it is sold in the market places and the bakeries in the early morning and can be bought piping hot, by the slice off big iron trays.' *Anchoïade Croze, Grenouilles Provençales, Fish Plaki*: 'this is a typical Greek way of doing fish and appears over and over again in different forms.' *Arní*

Souvlákia, 'eaten on the terrace of a primitive Cretan taverna, flavoured with wood smoke and the mountain herbs, accompanied by the strong red wine of Crete, these kebabs can be the most poetic of foods'.

'Octopus and Cuttlefish': in Robert Byron's Greek mountainside banquet, from *The Station*, 'We learnt what is meant by a Feast of the Church,' with his gothic descriptions of the gargantuan octopus feast presided over by a bishop, 'recently of Asia Minor, at a table set for seventy'. Each of Elizabeth's chapters was introduced and sometimes interspersed thus, with instantly evocative passages from writers who were, like herself, reminiscing on their love of France and the Mediterranean. None of them (except Douglas, and then it was for a joke) wrote cookery books. Rather these cameos, sometimes taken from novels, more often from travel books, were observations and memories by the literate and educated for others of their kind. Such was Elizabeth's book too, the food of her travels.

She gave us Henry James on the exquisite simplicity of fresh boiled eggs, bread and butter; Tobias Smollett on the variety of fish on the Côte Niçoise in his eighteenth-century travels; an eighteenth-century exotic, the vastly rich William Beckford, on an ecclesiastical feast in Spain; D. H. Lawrence on the abundance of vegetables – 'Piles of white and green fennel, like celery, and great sheaves of young, purplish, sea-dust-coloured artichokes, nodding their buds, piles of big radishes, scarlet and bluey-purple, carrots, long strings of dried figs, mountains of oranges . . .' from his *Sea and Sardinia*; Compton Mackenzie on responding to the exquisite selection of ices in an Athenian café; Osbert Sitwell in *Great Morning* lunching on truffles, Pecorino cheese, grapes, pasta and red wine of the neighbourhood at his Tuscan castello, Montegufoni.

And finally we come to Elizabeth's beloved Norman Douglas in a passage from his *South Wind*; which to the generation after the First War had proved liberating in its challenge to modern morality and manners. 'All culinary tasks should be performed with reverential love, don't you think so? To say that a cook must possess the requisite outfit of culinary skill and temperament . . . The true cook must have not only these externals, but a large dose of general worldly experience. She is the perfect blend of artist and philosopher . . . If she drinks a little, why it is all to the good . . . It proves she possesses the prime requisite of the artist; sensitiveness and a capacity for enthusiasm.'

Elizabeth's identification with these tenets was of course absolute. Only rarely, and then expressly stated, were recipes for dishes included in her writing which had not been tried out by Elizabeth herself. Simply making a dish, however, was not enough, it must *work*, be completely understood, before Elizabeth would include it. Many friends over the years had a dish given them once, twice, three times. 'I want to see if the soufflé needs 14, 15, or 16 minutes,' she might say. But this concern for accuracy came more from attempting to get the 'feel' for a dish so that she could then communicate it; she watched the clock and weighed and measured, but only to understand the principles, not for their own sake. Apropos Elizabeth's concern for the 'rightness' of food she said to Judith Lassalle, 'I'd rather cut myself in half than a potato. You find the right-sized potatoes and cook all the same size together. You don't cut them, you just find the right size.'

Mistakes and failures were carefully noted; friends were not resented if they didn't like the dishes. Judith Lassalle remembers 'an awful cold Greek soup she would insist on doing. And a thing made of dried apricots, it was a complete flop. Sometimes we would laugh. Oh yes, she could, she could be so relaxed and jolly. George and she always had so much to talk about. He was very well read, he spent all his time reading, they both liked the French. And his languages were always a help to her. But it was often food. She loved finding out about it. When other people had a portrait on the wall Elizabeth would have a picture of a fish.'

Amongst the literary and artistic coterie of homosexuals whom John Lehmann patronized and befriended was the young John Minton. Minton was a painter, one of whose outlets, like many of the best of his generation, was book illustration. Lehmann had sent Minton with a friend, Ian Ross, to write up and illustrate a holiday in Corsica. Published by Lehmann as *Time Was Away, A Notebook in Corsica* (1948), it subsequently became a post-war classic of travel literature and book illustration; capturing the feeling of sultriness, the heat, the elemental timelessness and brooding history of the island. Elizabeth did not know the book and neither had she heard of John Minton when Lehmann showed it to her and proposed Minton as the illustrator for *Mediterranean Food*.

With typical flair Minton captured perhaps the most important aspect of this book for the post-war audience: escapism. On a brilliantly eye-catching dust-jacket he used his by now well-established repertoire of images and the free-script lettering in vogue at the time, to create an intense Mediterranean image; of food laid out on crisp white cloths, wine, boats on a blue, blue sea and, somewhere up above, a blazing sun. Throughout the book his stylized pictures of Mediterranean largesse; by the sea, on rustic tables, in simple kitchens, with their setting often seen through a window, are skilfully integrated with the text.

On the Sunday following publication Elizabeth Nicholas, the noted *Sunday Times* travel writer, wrote her unqualified praise of *A Book of Mediterranean Food*. To Elizabeth's delight she had appreciated the author's unwillingness 'to make any ignoble compromises with expediency' and was entirely in favour of a serious book which made no concessions to suit 'present, we hope transitory, weaknesses in our own victualling service'. She praised Minton's illustrations and Elizabeth's choice of quotation and, almost as importantly to Elizabeth, she noticed the absence of Brillat-Savarin's rather tedious strictures on the 'culinary art', then almost ubiquitous in any work on food.

With the completion and publication of *Mediterranean Food*, Elizabeth had reached the end of a lengthy period of gestation. Paris is claimed by others – and for simplicity's sake by Elizabeth herself – as the locale of its conception; the Paris of months of girlish academic exercise and good bourgeois food twenty years before. But effectively her whole life had been a preparation for this synthesis of beliefs and ideals. Elizabeth's writings *were* her beliefs and ideals, those lost and those still cherished. What she later wrote of herself in reference to prying eyes and pens is quite true: 'All there is to know about me is in my books.' What she did not add, though, was that so much of it was so cryptic as to be indecipherable unless one had the key. Her statement should be rewritten: 'All I understand of myself or *want* you to know about me . . .'

Elizabeth's 'life's love' and a vital aspect of her biography about which she was quite open, even proud, was her relationship with

Norman Douglas. In *Mediterranean Food* her tribute to him was simple: 'Above all I owe a debt of gratitude to Mr Norman Douglas, whose great knowledge and enchanting talk taught me so much about the Mediterranean.' Douglas had, from the time of their earliest meetings, given Elizabeth greater confidence to be herself. Hence her oft-quoted Douglas maxim in her essay on him 'Have it Your Way', after his death: 'Always do as you please, and send everybody to hell, and take the consequences.' Like Douglas, albeit sometimes with less gusto, Elizabeth had done just that and, like him, she had reaped the benefits and the sorrows which this had so far entailed.

As often with Elizabeth the qualities of some of those she admired, perhaps above all Douglas, were frequently attributable to herself. This in no way implies emulation, rather an admiration for superior knowledge and a confirmation of what was already her own approach to life. Mark Holloway, in *Norman Douglas: A Biography* (Secker and Warburg, 1976), quotes him writing of the South: 'I am only dreaming through the summer months to the music of the cicadas.' Holloway adds: 'Dreaming perhaps, but sharply aware, and weaving scholarship, impressions, fact, and fantasy into an intricate fabric . . . enchantingly entertaining . . . This atmosphere is created without fuss, with economy and elegance, with style and verve, with measure and serenity, eminently considerate to the reader, good-mannered, enticing, satisfying.' It shall be left to the reader to judge how much fantasy or serenity Elizabeth's writing demonstrates, but most of the other qualities Holloway ascribes to Douglas are also eminently hers.

CHAPTER FOURTEEN

The Only Real Paradise is the One We Have Lost
(1950–1951)

FROM THE COMMENCEMENT of her daughter's writing career Stella took an intelligent and appreciative interest in her progress. Despite her history of defiance, Elizabeth did want this approval. A feeling of mutual respect grew on both sides and gradually tended to balance Elizabeth's resentful youthful judgements. This improvement is reflected in Priscilla's recent comment: 'Mummy was better company, took more interest in us when we were grown up.' This mother whom many of her friends were given to believe Elizabeth disliked, was in fact the dedicatee of her daughter's second book. Although there is consensus on Stella's fearsomeness, friends and family are not consistent in their estimation of Elizabeth's relationship with her mother. Dislike is too simplistic a word here. A certain fear which Elizabeth never entirely outgrew, a certain sense of inadequacy in relation to her; resentment combined with a grudging but real admiration, might be a more adequate description. (Ironically, of Stella's four daughters there is no question that Elizabeth became the most like her as she grew older.)

An anecdote from some years later reflects something of Elizabeth's attitude. Veronica and John Nicholson were living at that time at Glynde Place, a beautiful Sussex house not so far from Wootton, and Elizabeth had been driven down from London for a large party they were giving. The following day Veronica and Elizabeth were due at lunch with Stella in Brighton. Driving towards their destination Veronica became hopelessly lost and by the time they finally arrived in Brighton, over an hour and a half late, Elizabeth was very agitated at the prospect of facing Stella. 'Oh, it was a rather awful lunch, and all my fault; Stella was not amused,' said Veronica. 'We arrived so late that there was nothing of the day recoverable really. Elizabeth did remain in awe of her mother.'

After her return to England, notwithstanding disagreements of sometimes volcanic proportion, Elizabeth maintained regular contact with her mother. One particular event, whilst highlighting the tensions of any parent–child relationship, also illustrates Elizabeth and Stella's inadequate methods of resolving them. The event occurred several years later, by which time Elizabeth was an established authority on food.

Stella would come up to London, go round the auctions, see one of her daughters for lunch and return to Brighton on the evening train. On this occasion she and Elizabeth were having a meal at Halsey Street. Elizabeth made her mother cauliflower cheese and Maudie O'Malley remembers: 'They had a frightful row about it. Liz said that there was "no goodness in it whatsoever", and her mother said, "I totally disagree with you."

'Stella wasn't much of a cook, she could cook an omelette and cauliflower cheese and that was about it. Well, they started knocking back the whiskies and having this terrible row at the same time, and then Stella finally left in an awful huff. She stomped off down the road to Sloane Square underground going to get a train back to Brighton and fell down the steps and broke her leg and ended up in hospital. They had such arguments, quite tremendous.'

Tony David's food parcel business was probably not lucrative enough and he was now concerned to make something more of his capital. Apparently he and Christopher Grey's brother came up with the idea of an up-market club and with this as their purpose, bought a property in Herbert Crescent. Doreen and her small daughter stayed there for a time in a top-floor flat. Simultaneously with these negotiations Elizabeth was spending money having Halsey Street divided up into three more or less self-contained apartments to accommodate tenants, as it already had done on an informal basis. Although not without offers Felicité had so far refused marriage and the two sisters arranged that she would take one of the apartments. Felicité agreed to Elizabeth's terms, paid her a lump sum for the tenancy and contracted to move into the top flat by late October 1950.

In the letter thanking Felicité for her cheque Elizabeth said that it did seem quite a lot of money. She hoped Felicité would consider the flat as 'apart from the family in every way – you must do as you please and live as you choose, and I will continue to do exactly the same.' Elizabeth wrote with conviction when she said she would be delighted when Felicité moved in. She also told Felicité that her cheque had enabled her to send off dozens of her own, and added with that hint of the expiring actress which she never really lost: 'The relief of paying the bills has been so great that I feel dreadfully light-headed and I have retired to bed to recover.' Already a favourite place of respite for Elizabeth, in future it would become more so. Finally, she complained to Felicité about a recent appreciation of their Aunt Violet (she had died in 1948). She didn't think very much of what Sir Osbert Sitwell had written on Violet, as it gave 'no real idea of her at all, except the colours she wore and the "mulish" expression of obstinacy that we all knew only too well.

The tenant moving out before Felicité's imminent arrival was 'Denis' with his then companion. Elizabeth related to her sister the 'drama' of the ex-tenants' departure: some of Stella's furniture was being removed, but was immediately returned when Elizabeth telephoned to say she was observing the proceedings 'through her periscope'. With both her wit and territorial antennae here finely tuned and impressively displaying her determination not to be pushed around, one is reminded of Elizabeth's resoluteness in negotiation with the broker, Jewell, when recovering the insurance money after the pre-war robbery at her flat in London.

Another tenant at Halsey Street was the art historian Cecil Gould (known by Elizabeth and her friends as Goldilocks) whom Elizabeth met in Cairo while he was in cypher with the other Cecil, Robson. Patrick Woodcock says of Gould: 'Oh, Cecil's cooking was appalling. He gave a dinner to which Ivy Compton Burnett was invited. Champagne and cherries, it was absolutely awful. He was terribly pretentious and it was agreed that Elizabeth would give him cooking lessons, and she got her wires crossed with him as she often did with men. She really rather fell for him but it was useless. He was not that way inclined.'

It was Gould who had recruited Lesley O'Malley to Bletchley

Park, the seat of British Intelligence, early in the war. Lesley, Elizabeth's close friend from the MOI in Cairo, was also back in England looking for a job. After a long and worrying search she eventually found work with Royd's advertising agency, where she remained for many years. Some time in the early Fifties Elizabeth offered her the basement flat in Halsey Street and Lesley's acceptance marked the beginning of a stay which would last for another thirty years. The flat shared its stairs with Elizabeth's central part of the house and also, with a typical touch of eccentricity, a fridge at the top of these stairs.

Felicité and Lesley's presence and relative 'positions' in her house were significant factors in a subtle shift of Elizabeth's allegiances emerging during this period. Lesley was an intelligent and literate friend and Elizabeth would always value her advice. Nonetheless, allowing for her periodic absences abroad – for several weeks, sometimes months, almost every year until her death forty-two years later – she was to develop a particular dependence on her sister Felicité. And, just as her reliance on and identification with Felicité grew, so her dependence upon her elder sister Priscilla diminished. Priscilla's life (and Diana's) had become more absorbed with the time-consuming responsibilities of motherhood. Sisterly loyalties were relatively unchanged, but Priscilla simply had less time to devote to the role of surrogate mother. In England again, Elizabeth was once more faced with her mother and sisters and the rest of her family after the years of emotionally less fraught communication by letter. Before and during the war, when Pris could always be relied upon to get them out of a fix, either financially or sometimes as go-between, she had represented a figure of permanence for her sisters. The pressures placed upon them during the war had left Elizabeth's sisters remarkably uncritical of her. Despite their consistent contribution to the war effort they would always judge *Elizabeth* by different standards. For all their own individual force of personality Elizabeth's sisters never quite overcame the slight awe in which they held her, and as she grew older and became more of a 'personage', as the family would have said, she herself did little to modify this response.

With two small daughters to care for, it was not easy for Priscilla to reshape her life. Here, Elizabeth's relative lack of interest in children would soon become more apparent, extending to a greater or lesser degree to Diana's family too. Although feeling few qualms about favouring one above another, as her nieces and nephews grew and developed Elizabeth was a fond aunt, although never a motherly one.

Elizabeth's position regarding children was not a simple one and the complexities of her character were revealed in her attitude towards them. From youth she had stated that she did not like them or want any of her own. In the light of these convictions, on more than one occasion when Elizabeth found herself with an unwanted pregnancy, her decision was to terminate it. Nevertheless, as she grew older Elizabeth grew more ambivalent regarding both her earlier boast to Priscilla that she couldn't bear any one man hanging around her after the first six months, and her determination never to have children. Already by 1952, when she came to see George and Judith Lassalle on the arrival of their first child, her response at seeing the baby was to burst into tears, saying to Judith: 'Oh, I don't want to see your children.'

When her love affairs were failing Elizabeth was quite capable of inflicting wounds, but neither did she always escape unscathed herself. With her feline sensuality and her magnetism Elizabeth instinctively knew how to treat a man. However, the sheer force of her intelligence, sometimes thrusting and impatient, and her flights of temperament and wilfulness, were not ultimately calculated to support the fragilities of a male ego. Her forte lay more in the arena of courtesanship than in the sometimes duller but more enduring one of conjugality. Nonetheless, with each renewed search for a lover, she was also reasserting her belief in the possibility of companionship and fulfilment.

After her years abroad, during which time all four Gwynne girls had developed more defined and adult personae, with resumed proximity to her sisters Elizabeth now found Felicité's unmarried and childless state one with which she could identify most closely. To an extent this happened because Felicité was never subject to the emotional and time-consuming strains of child-rearing, but it was also because she remained, like Elizabeth, someone for whom literature was an utter necessity. Her library grew on a par with Elizabeth's, until Halsey Street became a house weighted down with books.

The publication of *Mediterranean Food* extended Elizabeth's audience, its enthusiastic reception alerting John Lehmann to a greater realization of her earning potential as an author. His immediate approach to her for another book on 'escapist' food was then, only natural. But 'This time I was ready for him,' Elizabeth later wrote. 'I had a small collection of French recipes which hadn't been suitable for the Mediterranean book.' This collection would be published a year later, in 1951, as *French Country Cooking*. With her monthly articles for *Harpers* and other pieces of journalism now being commissioned, Elizabeth was in demand. Amongst the first of the professionals to recognize her value was André Simon, the grand old man of the Wine and Food Society. And it was he who had the foresight to commission her first non-recipe-based article for the Society's journal, her brilliant essay already mentioned, 'Two Cooks'.

While working in Allan's bookshop, and before moving into Halsey Street, Felicité had already been helping Elizabeth with her new book. Elizabeth's boast to her sisters from Cairo of her newly learnt typing skills was premature. After *Mediterranean Food* (much of which was typed on a machine borrowed from Richard Longland) almost all Elizabeth's writing, both articles and books, was done in long-hand and expertly typed by Felicité.

As Elizabeth wrote in her introduction to this most usable of little books, *French Country Cooking* was not another work seconding the 'nonsense . . . talked about the richness of the food to be found in all French homes'. Not wishing to appear ungracious, nor debating the higher standard of French middle-class cooking compared to its English counterpart, she described 'the proportion of rather tough *entrecôtes*, rolled and stuffed roast veal, and *sautéd* chicken' in French homes as 'exasperatingly high . . . Those who care to look for it, however, will find the justification of France's culinary reputation in the provinces, at the riverside inns, in unknown cafés along the banks of the Burgundy canal, patronized by the men who sail the great petrol and timber barges to and from Marseilles, great eaters and drinkers most of them . . .'

As always Elizabeth was writing from experience. She knew at first hand about those barges along the grand North–South French artery, from Burgundy to its culmination in the salty Carmargue marshlands and the Rhône delta beyond Aix-en-Provence. The cooking she described was that encountered in 'hospitable farmhouses of the Loire and the Dordogne', the Auvergne, and the Normandy known since her youth; 'in sea-port bistros frequented by fishermen, sailors, ship-chandlers and port-officials'. This was the cooking experienced and enjoyed with such savour along the route she and Charles had followed in the French section of the voyage of the *Evelyn Hope*. When, however, she wrote: 'In such places the most interesting food in France is to be found,' she was not only recording her own opinion but also aligning herself (however unconsciously) with a well-established tradition. This was represented by that small group of travelled English men and women – most recently by writers already mentioned, such as Ford Madox Ford, Morton Shand and Romilly Fedden – for whom wayside France, its table and wine, was a place of infinite discovery.

A few passages from Romilly Fedden's *Food and Other Frailties*, well known to Elizabeth, illustrate the theme. Elizabeth had probably known the Feddens since before the war, initially through Romilly's son, Robin, possibly staying as a guest in their Brittany house, Chantemeusle. When, years later, Elizabeth told her god-daughter Frances, Robin and Renée Fedden's daughter, that she had been engaged to Robin, Frances surmised that 'This must have meant an affair.'

Referring to the inter-war period Romilly wrote: 'On another occasion we were touring, in a car . . . and we had lunched and dined and slept at many international caravanserais. Be it known, you cannot eat superbly at any of these tourist-ridden hotels. There is a sameness about them, something standardized. You eat passably . . . but not with bliss . . . Perfect food is to be found rather in the out-of-the-way corners of Europe. Both in the country and in small market towns where you shall eat exquisitely.' He continued with the reminiscence of a fine small village inn 'renowned to a few initiates for its cooking', and described the lunch given by 'Madame' to himself and his party of friends in the garden, 'where a rough lawn led down to apple trees and a bubbling stream'. They ate 'perfect' melon from the garden, 'delicious' *quenelles de brochet*; a 'perfect' foie gras, chicken *à la broche* with a consummate salad, and the whole complemented by an Auberdière Vouvray and 'a Bourgeuil of 1902'.

Romilly described another superlative meal of sole, pheasant, a chicory salad, a fondue 'the succulence of which still steams in memory', taken at the invitation of an elderly commercial traveller in an insignificant country town, at a resturant down a side street through an arch and a courtyard 'painted a sickly green'. Thence they passed through the enormous kitchen 'backed by a vast range and endless pots and pans in brass and copper. The chef, a huge person all in white, was bustling with his three subordinates . . . We passed into the *salle à manger*,' where, after they had finished with a fine house brandy, the waiter bawled out the *addition* across the room to 'Madame, fat and placid at the desk'.

In the same idiom Elizabeth wrote in *French Country Cooking*: 'the shopkeepers, the lawyer, the doctor, the curé, the gendarme and even those stony-faced post-office officials are exceedingly addicted to the pleasures of the table; and, being thrifty as well, you may be sure they know where the cheapest and the best of everything is to be obtained.' She maintained that as the peasant farmers were prosperous and thrifty too; 'Every scrap of food produced is made use of in some way or another, in fact in the best way possible . . .' We are told that it was in the depths of the country that one learnt about the variety of foodstuffs and ways of preserving them; meat products, charcuterie, sausages, smoked ham and pâtés. (A friend later commented that Elizabeth loved all pork products so much that she could have written a book about them, and indeed the section on charcuterie in *French Provincial Cooking* is inspiringly written.)

> The cheeses and creams, the fruits preserved in potent local liqueurs, the fresh garden vegetables, pulled up before they are faded and grown old, and served shining with farmhouse butter, the *galettes* . . . the mushrooms . . . gathered in the forest, the mountain hares, pigeons, partridges and roebuck . . . the fried trout straight from the river, the sustaining vegetable soups enriched with wine, garlic, bacon and sausages, the thousand and

one shell-fish soups and stews, the *fritures du golfe* . . . of France's
lovely prodigal coast . . .

As we have seen Elizabeth's proclamation of the virtues of the food of
France was not in itself original, but her own experience and particular
voice had a singular relevance and enormous appeal to those of her
generation and class who had recently survived the war and were
presently surviving the dreariness and boredom of its aftermath. Her
introduction to *French Country Cooking* continued: 'Rationing, the
disappearance of servants, and the bad and expensive meals served in
restaurants, have led Englishwomen to take a far greater interest in
food than was formerly considered polite . . .' She identified her
readers as those who in the country had grown and produced much of
their own food, and those in the city, who 'take trouble over their
marketing, choose their meat and fish carefully. . . . keep a good store
cupboard' and are 'equally interested . . . in good and interesting
meals . . . [as often with Elizabeth there is more than a hint of the
prescriptive] which derive from French regional and peasant cookery,
which, at its best, is the most delicious in the world . . .'

In the same year as the publication of *French Country Cooking* and
in sharp contrast to it, *100 Meat-saving Recipes* was published by Anne
Robbins (Nicholas Kay, 1951). In spite of its genuine efforts to
provide an interesting post-war cookery book, its very title, *Meat-
Saving Recipes*, revealed that underlying mentality of compromise
Elizabeth was reacting against and attempting to counteract in her
own writing. Although Anne Robbins tried her best to give 'tasty
and flavoursome' dishes (unappetizing words), one is left remembering
comments such as: 'The recipes . . . do not require endless time and
pains' and are for 'the housewife who wants to prepare really good
meals with a minimum of fuss and trouble'. Of course she does, who
doesn't often feel the same? But with a little culinary experience one
is reminded of Elizabeth's introduction used both as exhortation and
inspiration, words which could well be described as her creed:

> Good cooking is honest, sincere and simple, and by this I do not
> mean to imply that you will find in this, or indeed any other
> book, the secret of turning out first-class food in a few minutes

with no trouble. Good food is always a trouble and its preparation should be regarded as a labour of love, and this book is
intended for those who actually and positively enjoy the labour
involved in entertaining their friends and providing families
with first-class food.

Elizabeth's introduction ended with the reminder that it is not so
much the merits of cuisines which are most important, but 'the spirit
in which cooking is approached; a devoted, a determined spirit, but
not, it is to be hoped, one of martyrdom'. Commendable ideals, but
her readers might have argued that Elizabeth David, with an accom-
modating husband and no children interfering with her 'labours of
love', could easily talk. However, although those who became her
devotees may not always have achieved such a high standard, it was
that *spirit* which they were inspired to emulate.

Martin Lam, now chef-patron of Ransome's Dock in London,
became friends with Elizabeth more than twenty years later. In
describing one of her great strengths as a writer on food he says, 'As
a teacher she was able to impart ideas very clearly, without always
going into great detail.' Others have criticized this aspect of her
writing but those like Lam see it as a virtue.

'She won't always give specific quantities, but she was the most
precise person where precision was important. She will presume a
certain amount of knowledge and understanding about a style of
cooking and then describe a particular recipe that will fall into that
style or method. Other times she will be quite specific. Being of that
frame of mind she was able to talk about food generally and convey
an awful lot – without going into pounds and ounces, without going
into specific measurements.' And here Martin Lam makes an observation central to Elizabeth's ethos: 'Cooking is more than responding
to ingredients.'

Referring to what was an essential part of Elizabeth's credo,
implied in her introduction to *French Country Cooking*, Lam points out
that 'She knew what the best was and wasn't going to accept second
best, not in any sense of being élitist or wanting the most expensive,
but just knowing.' In reference to this theme Elizabeth's friend
Sybille Bedford says, 'Liking what is best is different from what is

snobbish.' Elizabeth herself had written in a *Harpers* article entitled 'Windfalls':

> Sometimes the simplest luxury proves the most delectable. Last October a friend brought me fresh Normandy butter and new-laid eggs. Anxious that those eggs should lose nothing of their fresh bloom, and wanting to share the feast with a favourite guest, I decided it should consist simply of perfectly boiled eggs, and fresh brown bread spread with that lovely butter, to be followed by a pound of English field mushrooms, grilled, buttery and black, their flavour unmatched during the brief autumn week of their season. After the mushrooms we had Comice pears, which were at their wonderful best that particular day. A meal which heaven knows was nothing an Englishman would not have taken for granted a few years ago, but it was the startling simplicity of the fare and the quality of the ingredients which made the occasion a memorable one.

Martin Lam continues: 'She liked a particular restaurant because they had fresh crab salad. It was nothing but boiled crab, but they did it well and she would go there for that thing only, which in many ways would typify her approach to food. It didn't need to be five processes of cooking to achieve some very fine dish. She would be as happy with the best raw ingredients treated interestingly and sympathetically. Something which comes over time and time again with her – the ability to arrive at simplicity. But you have to go through several processes to get to the simple result.'

This attitude, sometimes explicit, always implicit, was evident throughout the whole of Elizabeth's work. This was what she meant when she wrote that 'Good food is always a trouble,' later expanding on this with the comment: 'Even more than long hours in the kitchen, fine meals require ingenious organization and experience *which is a pleasure to acquire* [author's italics].' She added several other points, by now fundamental to her approach to food and appreciated by few English cooks at this time: 'A highly developed shopping sense is important, so is some knowledge of the construction of a menu with a view to the food in season, the manner of cooking, the texture and colour of the dishes to be served in relation to each other.' These strictures were those understood by any ordinary Mediterranean housewife. They had little to do with fancy ingredients and were something for which the French of course were renowned. Although still as alien to most English cooks in 1951 as in her youth, Elizabeth's own familiarity with these principles had begun with Mrs Leyel's *Gentle Art* even before her adult sojourns in France.

She had written in *Harpers Bazaar* in 1949:

> How pitiful that a generation is now growing up which has scarcely known what good cooking is; which has never made a sauce with real eggs, never eaten parmesan cheese on pasta, never heard of *Cèpes à la bordelaise* or seen ham and Cumberland sauce on a breakfast table . . . Unless young people learn now about the art of cooking, and eating and drinking wine, one of the great pleasures of life will be lost to them, and how can they learn to cook if they don't know how food should look and taste and smell?

French Country Cooking again followed Mrs Leyel by concluding with useful lists (actually nuggets of comparative social history) of foods, 'preparations' and proprietors to be relied upon; some in France, most in London. Again it is interesting to note that where those shops recommended by Mrs Leyel still existed, Elizabeth recommends the same, and we are reminded that her familiarity with these exotic oases of 'foreignness' extended as far back as her reading of Hilda Leyel in the Thirties. We are recommended by both Mrs Leyel and Elizabeth to that Mecca of food, Hediard's, in the Place Madeleine in Paris – the shop about which Elizabeth wrote, 'Every exotic product in the world can be obtained [there], with particular emphasis on the French Colonies.' We are then given a hint of the passionate interest she already had, not simply in the recipes and their ingredients, but also in their social history. 'The firm was inherited from Hediard by his son-in-law, an Englishman, members of whose family are still in the shop, and who take great pleasure in explaining the origin and uses of the wonderful foodstuffs they sell.'

Elizabeth next sent her reader on to the Marché St-Honoré for 'cheaper foods unobtainable in England', where 'It is a fine sight to see, and the Parisian housewives doing their shopping provide a notable lesson in the art of marketing.' Remembering the dearth of such produce in England a vividly contrasting picture to it here emerges: 'Soissons, the good white beans for making cassoulet, fresh Norman butter and cheeses, baby courgettes . . . aubergines which will *not* cost 2s. 6d. each or whatever ludicrous price one pays in England, dandelions for salad, sorrel and all manner of simple and forgotten delights.' (Here and elsewhere, she already reveals her acute awareness of an English heritage so buried in this period as to have become almost lost.)

Continuing with her recommendations of where best to find these basic ingredients, it is noticeable that almost all are foods which now sit on any supermarket shelf: lentils, split peas, haricot beans, rice, macaroni, spaghetti, etc., dried mushrooms, salami sausages, olives and their oil, good-quality dry biscuits, lemons, garlic, shallots, almonds, figs, other dried fruits, good jams and preserves. Noticeable too are the recommendations for buying and growing herbs in pots in the garden, at a time when their absence was then so conspicuous from most English shops. The purchase of spices was apparently most reliably to be done at Harrods and Selfridges food halls, Whiteleys, and an Italian family shop which occurred repeatedly in Elizabeth's (and Mrs Leyel's) references to all sorts of foods – Parmigiani of 74 Old Compton Street – and several more of their shops along the same street. Other recurring names were Roche, Delmonico and King Bomba.

Yet these shops, which were frequently Italian, had not previously been so unusual in larger cities as Elizabeth's text might here imply. Arising as they had from the tradition of the Italian warehouse-men, they had been established in England since the early eighteenth century. Italian warehousemen or oilmen had sold a variety of Italian provisions: olive oils, anchovies, salami, pasta, parmesan, as well as those other foods which we now associate with high-quality grocers and delicatessens. Their stock later included some of the earliest tinned goods and many bottled sauces, pickles, chutneys, jams, dried fruits, almonds, pistachios, chocolate, coffees, teas and spices without which no sophisticated household could function.

The introduction to *French Country Cooking* preceded sections on *batterie de cuisine*, wine in the kitchen and the construction of a menu, each again exemplifying Elizabeth at her confident best. Terse, acerbic, opinionated, useful and accurate. But more, where this vital material could be made dry and dusty, here it was replete with perspicacious observation of physical and human detail infused with touches of wit; the whole meanwhile elevated to a cameo on the fine art of living. This, the art of living, was the whole of which food was a fundamental part. The *batterie* section proclaimed her visual sensibilities as much as registering her good sense: the appearance, the shape, colour, design as well as function of everything in the kitchen was always of the utmost interest and concern to her, finally, as important as the food itself.

Elizabeth's practical and very English soul responded to the deeper significance of objects. Here it is worth remembering that her forebears were experienced engineers: both the Ridleys with their coal-mining successes and the Gwynnes with their pump. Elizabeth's nephew Johnny Grey (son of Diana and Chris), now a noted kitchen designer, remembers her fascination with, for instance, ironmongers' shops. 'Aunt Liza loved all those things: knobs, gadgets, hinges, hooks, handles. Walking along the street we *couldn't* pass an ironmonger's by, would always have to go in and look. Even a metal grating on the pavement fascinated her.'

Elizabeth maintained: 'One thing is quite certain, and that is that if Englishwomen paid more attention to having the right equipment in their kitchens, we should hear a great deal less about the terrible labour of good cooking. How many times have I been told: "Oh, I haven't time to fiddle about with that kind of thing," just because a recipe called for putting something through a sieve or chopping up a few vegetables.' On the subject of knives she said: 'Take the greatest care . . . keep your kitchen knives in a special box or compartment of the knife drawer [she was eventually to keep her own on one of those magnetic blades on the wall]. Let it be understood by all members of the household that there will be serious trouble if your knives are borrowed for screwdriving, prising open packing cases, cutting fuse-wire or any other purpose for which they were not intended.' One trembles at the thought of the reprisals for such crimes in Elizabeth's own kitchen.

Sybille Bedford describes this 'largish, longish room' in Halsey Street with its 'very long table, on which you could make and eat food. Everything was open, all the shelves. The stove, the sink, everything was in order, but a working order.' Reinforcing this subtle comment on Elizabeth's superficially disordered house, many friends have said that with the passage of time it became more likely that in order to sit down at her table you sometimes had to move a pile of books off a chair or papers to one side. But the overriding impression was of the most 'artistic' clutter: a bowl of purple plums, a plate of salted almonds, a bottle of white wine in a stoneware cooler, jars of gleaming fruits and preserves on the dressers, olives black and shiny against a terracotta dish, placed with apparent nonchalance but always with a painter's eye.

Elizabeth never had a study, working mostly from that large kitchen table and always in longhand. Latterly she almost always wrote in green ink and, with her knowledge of army hierarchy, probably with wry awareness that this usage was permitted only to those of the highest rank. The kitchen functioned as the hub of her house: as her workroom, here she cooked and experimented; as her study, here she wrote; and finally as her room for socializing, here visitors were made welcome, dined and were entertained. In this kitchen she increasingly kept her utensils outside of cupboards. They sat in earthenware pots, on the dressers, many others eventually hanging (like arcane pieces of metallic sculpture) on the walls – as was in fact the tradition with old ironmongers' shops – and note-worthy in this period when it was thought unsightly by the majority to display anything which indicated that a kitchen, even less a dining room, was actually a room in which to prepare or to eat food. Elizabeth wrote in *French Country Cooking*:

As time goes on you accumulate your personal gadgets, things which graft themselves on to your life; an ancient thin-pronged fork for the testing of meat, a broken knife for scraping mussels, a battered little copper saucepan in which your sauces have always turned out well, an oyster knife which you can no longer afford to use for its intended purpose but which turns out to be just the thing for breaking off hunks of Parmesan cheese . . . an

earthenware bean-pot of such charm that nothing cooked in it
could possibly go wrong.

And later: 'Earthenware casseroles and terrines for oven cooking
should be in every household.' The early nineteenth-century expansion
of the china clay potteries in the Midlands and the subsequent
development of enamelled tinware, had put an end to the extensive
use of earthenware in most metropolitan English kitchens. 'For some
of the French farmhouse and peasant dishes described in this book
they are essential; with time these rustic clay pots acquire not only a
patina but an aroma all of their own, which in the course of long,
patient simmering communicates itself to the *cassoulets, choux farcis,
daubes* and *civets*, onion soups, and terrine of game which would lose
something of their flavour and a good deal of their charm if cooked
in an ordinary saucepan.' Elizabeth was here saying something novel
for post-war England. Her plea for those cooking pots was a heart-felt
cry for the agrarian-based, pre-industrial Europe of the South, a state
long since lost to England. She was mourning this (and paid homage
to it in her own pot collection) when she later wrote: 'Look at the
friendly browns, and warm terracottas, the ivories and greys and the
pebbles-on-the-beach colours of old English earthenware and stoneware.'

Significantly for future events, she recommended purchase and
retinning of copper pans at Cadec's of Greek Street and Jaeggi's in
Dean Street – both in Soho and then frequented largely by the
catering trade. There were at this time no 'kitchen' shops as we now
know them, only ironmongers, hardware shops and specialists like the
above or the larger company, Ferrari of Wardour Street, for the trade.
'A very heavy copper sauté pan . . . is the most convenient pan in the
world for braising a whole chicken or duck on top of the stove . . .
They [copper pans] are fairly expensive and their upkeep takes time,
but they look lovely.' Again regarding appearance, 'A long platter for
serving fish is important; the appearance of a fine salmon is ruined by
being brought to table on too small a dish . . .' And elsewhere she
would write: 'You see that utterly plain unadorned long white fish
dish? On that dish a whole pink and silver salmon trout [a favourite
fish] is unimaginably elegant.' These qualities, a 'painterly' eye and a

passion for the products and seasons of agriculture, were central to Elizabeth's writing.

Following the section on *batterie de cuisine* was an exemplary short essay on wine in the kitchen, that most intimidating of subjects to the English housewife.

On the composition of the menu she wrote: 'I should be surprised to hear that anybody had ever followed any cookery book menu in every detail; all that is needed to design a perfectly good meal is a little common sense and the fundamental understanding of the composition of a meal.' (This last was of course precisely what a good proportion of several generations of Englishwomen no longer possessed.) Referring to the present dearth of knowledge Elizabeth wrote: 'The restrictions of years of rationing have been the cause of some remarkably unattractive developments in the serving of food in restaurants, but if some ignorant or careless restaurant managers still serve chips with spaghetti or boiled potatoes and cauliflowers heaped up in the same dish with curry and rice, there is no need for us to do likewise at home . . .'

The precedent had long ago been set for cookery books with advisory sections like those Elizabeth incorporated into *French Country Cooking*. But hers were successful because they encapsulated several of those elements which made her writing so appealing: at once intimate in its detail, it enabled the reader to feel party to the experiences she described, to be inspired by her enthusiasm and intrigued by the sense of mystery she purveyed. She had both the common touch necessary for communication and an aloofness calculated to provide allure. And although no one element of this writing was outstandingly original, it was the manner in which Elizabeth put together these elements which singled out their totality. As with any artist of merit this elusive touch lay both in reflecting something of the spirit of the time, and being just sufficiently ahead of it to stimulate question and change. In interview with the novelist Paul Bailey he made an astute observation regarding Elizabeth's writing: 'And the tone of voice I liked. It was accessible to the reader, but not bending over backwards to them. It wasn't treating the reader like an imbecile . . . Hiding herself behind her prose . . . There is another message there to do with Art and the whole seriousness about life. She was so reticent, she would never talk to me about her private life . . . she uses style as a way of hiding something, which is a time-honoured tradition. It really was a case of *le style c'est l'homme*.'

There were contemporary and near-contemporary cookery book writers who had offered advice on marketing, the store-cupboard, the hazards of composing the 'right' menu (this had after all been one of the prime functions of Mrs Isabella Beeton's writing for an aspiring nineteenth-century middle class). Others had held forth authoritatively on many of the same French dishes as Elizabeth; few on the Middle Eastern, Greek or Italian ones. Authors in more literary genres had written inspired and erudite travel books on France, the Mediterranean and beyond; many writers had colonized and created their art from the same territory as the wistful, sometimes obsessive, semi-melancholic Proust's *À la recherche du temps perdu*, 1915–27. (Elizabeth would no doubt have concurred with Lesley Blanche's statement in one of her books: 'Yes, Proust was right . . . the only real Paradise is the one we have lost'). None of them, however, had organized such a finely wrought and potent mix of all these elements in cookery books, which spoke to a generation of English men and women in search of relief from a lack-lustre drabness, loss of purpose, and the insecurities of a society still reeling from the aftermath of war.

Grey Gowrie remembers the effect of Elizabeth's writing 'on one's parents, who had gone to war. (Elizabeth had known Gowrie's parents in Cairo and in fact later told a friend that she had come across his father much earlier, dancing with him at her coming-out.) They looked upon her work as part of the Liberation that had gone on afterwards, an indication that civilization was going to restore itself. There was an element of pornography about it, when you were living in Austerity and you were reading about sun-kissed peppers . . . it had an immediate dynamic . . . I think there was this tremendous feeling of joy when one read her books, of hope.' Growing up in Ireland, Gowrie subsequently met Elizabeth at the house of a mutual friend, also from Ireland, the painter Derek Hill, and was 'very amused by her, which I did not expect. She was salty, witty, sometimes shocking. She had what would now be called politically incorrect habits.' He remembers a later occasion when 'I was watching her cook a paella whilst chain-smoking and some of the ash dropped in. She didn't care and just shoved it on. She drank reasonably, and she wasn't a precise cook. To follow her work well you need some basic knowledge of cooking.'

In a subsequent preface to *French Country Cooking* Elizabeth wrote that she was 'anxious to stress the fact that this little collection gives no more than an indication of the immense diversity and range of French regional cookery. It is a subject of such scope that half a dozen large volumes of recipes would scarcely exhaust it.' She added that as French regional cooking was so 'very much alive', and therefore perpetually evolving, it would be 'almost impossible ever to compile a complete collection'. Nevertheless, she was to make her own significant mark in this field nine years later with the publication of *French Provincial Cooking*. Not only a major contribution to the subject, *French Provincial Cooking* was a masterly work of cookery and literature. In one sense *French Country Cooking* reads like a sparkling trial run.

Among those seeking Elizabeth out after the success of *Mediterranean Food* were the editors of two magazines then in their infancy. One of these, *Contact*, described itself as a 'Magazine of Pleasure' (a title now assured to raise eyebrows); it commissioned an article from her on Spanish food. Another, *Go*, 'The International Travel Magazine', was edited by Elizabeth Nicholas, who had reviewed *Mediterranean Food* with such enthusiasm and who had recently commissioned Elizabeth to contribute a long section to *The Sunday Times Travel Guide to the Continent* (1951). This book, for the educated tourist, included distinguished writers such as Georgina Masson, Lina Waterfield, Denys Sutton and Tamara Talbot Rice, noted for their interest in cultivated travel.

Elizabeth's contribution of over fifty pages included potted histories of the more interesting towns, information on hotels, shops, wine and restaurants of note throughout the whole Riviera and Provençal region. A feat of concision, as Elizabeth once again visits some of her pre-war haunts, her piece offers us glimpses of her past. At St Tropez, 'In spite of trippers who crowd in at weekends, noisy film stars . . . in great yachts, millionaires in Packards, and Existentialists from Saint Germain des Prés . . . there is nothing to stop one bathing by moonlight, a most exquisite Mediterranean pleasure.' At

Marseilles, 'to the right of the Vieux Port . . . are a number of small cafés and restaurants where one can eat Italian and Provençal food in noisy but characteristic surroundings'. At Antibes she refers the traveller to '*The Ship Bar* and says 'it is a pleasant drinking place; Rudolf, who has presided there for years, knows everything that goes on and . . . serves . . . the best steaks on the Côte d'Azur.'

This is the same Rudolf Elizabeth referred to in a war-time letter to Charles Gibson Cowan when he was collecting material for *The Voyage of the Evelyn Hope*. Despite previously breathless comments to Priscilla that she had seen 'Mistinguett doing the marketing . . . and this morning Lillian Harvey was in the bar, and once I saw the Windsors' car but I don't think they were in it', she had written to Charles that Antibes was for her, 'Norman Douglas, and champagne cocktails'. The Riviera people, she said, made almost no impression on her. They may have made an impression on Charles, because that was the first time he had encountered the type but she advised him against including them, they were too well known. For Elizabeth Rudolph the international barman had been the most interesting. She had told Pris before leaving Antibes in 1940 that she would above all rather listen to Norman's conversation or spend the day with him, aged as he was, than fifty of the 'warped and sodden sea kales who have made the Côte d'Azur a sort of *White Man's Burden*'. She thought the men there mostly resembled the 'Man who Stayed' in the play *White Cargo* (in which Elizabeth had acted): 'The character in the play who, quinine-soaked and gin-sodden, warns all the young men against going native and finally sends them home when they start babbling in delirium of green fields . . .'

In Elizabeth's *Sunday Times* piece, another of the frequent covert references to her war-time stay in the South of France occurs a couple of lines after the Rudolph comment: '*Chez Felix au Port*, on the harbour in a lovely setting, has been famous for years for bouillabaisse, langouste and soufflés; it has become very expensive.' It was here, in 1940, that Elizabeth had written the letter to Felicité in which she said the gales of the past month had made the boat 'rock like a shell'.

Aix, Arles, Avignon, Biot, Nice: 'The great food market is a spectacle calculated to drive the English visitor into a frenzy of envy . . .' And 'the flower market in the Rue St François de Paul in winter

. . . and in summer is another sight to dazzle English eyes.' Elizabeth had first marvelled at this demonstration of Southern fertility (just as had Van Gogh half a century earlier) on one of those treasured days spent with Norman Douglas in the early part of the war. She had written enthusiastically of it to Felicité from Antibes. The country, she said, 'was very beautiful, the flowers glorious: wild hyacinths and tulips, daffodils and anemones, in profusion; when the sun came out it was marvellous. The flower market at Nice seemed to stretch for a quarter of a mile, and was stocked with the most glorious flowers: marigolds, narcissus, fruit blossom, mimosa, daffodils, violets, hyacinths – pink, purple, blue and white – all for practically nothing. One day she went in and bought thirty-five francs' worth of flowers; she couldn't carry them all and had to bring them home in a huge basket, then had no idea what to do with them all.

When the restaurants were to be dealt with she was using her sharp and discerning eye as well as the ability to evoke. Of one in Le Lavandou she said: 'the entrance is through the kitchen where Madame Loulou Rossi is to be seen bent over her cooking pots, stirring a great pan of Langouste à la Provençal, all the perfumed aromas of the Mediterranean cooking issuing from the scarlet orange stew . . .' At St Raphael, 'After the host of "little" restaurants, furnished with gingham curtains, decorated with hideous pottery, and serving pretty indifferent food that have become a positive plague along the coast, it is with a sigh of relief that one enters a serious restaurant, where one knows at once by the smell of the place that the food is good.'

From France in the following year, 1951, Elizabeth wrote to Felicité saying she had been offered the job of going to Rome to write a 'sort of guide' for *Go*. She had told Elizabeth Nicholas that she would accept it if the pay were large enough, however, as she neither knew Rome nor spoke Italian, it was unlikely to be an easy job. This publication appears not to have materialized, possibly because Elizabeth's 'pay' demand was too large but also, and more significantly, because the magazine folded during that year.

The above letter to Felicité was written soon after Elizabeth had given the manuscript of *French Country Cooking* to Lehmann, and for which he commissioned another striking and flamboyant Minton cover. This time, both herself more experienced and having greater familiarity with Minton's style, Elizabeth knew what she wanted the illustrations for her book to do. She later said that she had encouraged 'a theme which recurred in all, or nearly all, of my subsequent books. I wanted the illustrations to convey information not just atmosphere.' Hence we see that the food in these pictures is better integrated into its surroundings than in *Mediterranean Food*. For instance, the cover shows the interior of a provincial kitchen ready for work and the frontispiece portrays a woman inside her kitchen surrounded by the food she is about to cook.

After the exertions of finishing *French Country Cooking* Elizabeth was, as so often, short of cash, wanting to get away from England, and implementing plans for future publishing ventures. She had packed up her favourite valuables and thrust these and a number of her books and other belongings into Felicité's custody upstairs – 'I trust the books are not falling out of the wardrobe on to your head' – and decamped to a huge draughty house in the South of France. By this manoeuvre she was establishing early what would remain standard practice; continuing her peripatetic habits. For some months of almost every year she would let Halsey Street (at a good price owing to its desirable location) and rent somewhere abroad, thus enabling her to have a holiday with money left over for living. Always maintaining her journalistic obligations, and keeping notes with historical references, recipes and practical observations – all of which were subsequently used in future books – these periods away from England were usually successful in lifting Elizabeth's bank balance out of the red.

'How you would laugh your head off if you could see me in this tumbledown old Castle of Otranto, with Romney [Summers] stacking logs on a great open fireplace as large as the town hall, and carrying his little khaki bag down to the village every day for the shopping. The weather has been a disgrace, the place as cold and wet as Charity. A fog comes up from the valley (or down from the hills) every night and in the morning you can't see out of the windows.'

This had been Elizabeth's introduction to several months in the rambling Provençal house, its grandeur that of a semi-fortified *manoir*. As she wrote, first in a *Harpers* article of 1955, later in a powerful passage in *French Provincial Cooking*, the house at Menerbes was set in a 'crumbling hill village opposite the Lubéron mountain', where the 'relentless screaming' of the mistral brought herself and her friends 'perilously near to losing our reason'. In her letter to Felicité she provided more detail. The gas worked only spasmodically, and on the first day there was a tremendous explosion that blew off Romney's eyelashes; 'since when it has been difficult to whack him into lighting it'. Her bedroom housed bath and toilet, and Romney's the gas geyser. The whole arrangement, she wrote, might well have been 'invented by Emmett' (a popular contemporary cartoonist).

Romney Summers had become a friend to Elizabeth, George and Robin Fedden and other more exotic social luminaries, such as Edward Gathorne-Hardy, in Cairo during the war. Harold Acton said of this languid friend in his *More Memoirs of an Aesthete* (Methuen, 1940) that he was: 'perhaps the only undergraduate who had a private house instead of lodgings when we were at Oxford . . . and received . . . in princely style . . . He maintained the same hospitable tradition at Gezira . . .'

Elizabeth's complaints to Felicité about bad weather were modified, when the sun came out it was warm enough to eat outside and even to lie on the terrace. 'The wine is 1/9 a bottle, new laid eggs 3d each, butter alas is 6/- a pound, and meat pretty expensive too.' The charlady was not too expensive, the cooking arrangements, surprisingly, fairly adequate, and the people in the village charming. Although the rent 'Mrs Bootface is extracting from me is sheer banditry', Elizabeth felt confident it would be 'delicious' there in two or three weeks' time.

The village of Menerbes in the *département* of the Vaucluse is in the heart of Provence. Set back inland from the towns of Aix, Cavaillon and Manosque, the beautiful, high, wooded Lubéron range with its string of fortified villages was in an area then frequented only by more adventurous travellers. Elizabeth took the house with two or three other friends. Apart from the other woman, Georgina (who paid rent to Elizabeth), being replaced for a time by Lesley O'Malley, this group remained fairly constant throughout the months Elizabeth was there.

Far away in her Provençal retreat, Elizabeth taxed Felicité back home with her financial arrangements. Always paying lip-service to the social niceties of gratitude Elizabeth was nevertheless demanding, and now worried about the lack of her rent from the Boultings; tenants she already knew socially (Mrs Boulting's twin sons were to become film directors of some note). 'I have written to beat the agent about it . . . I hope all is well in that quarter and that they are not flinging my favourite lamps on the floor and grinding them underfoot.' For all her ability to appear disorganized Elizabeth was in fact very much the disciplined artist. Periods of hectic activity and concentration were followed by periods of intense relaxation, usually lunches and evenings of entertaining and drinking. She was also most particular, almost neurotic, about the care of her possessions, giving rise to the occasional scene in the future which, if she had not taken it so seriously, would have been comical.

By May the weather 'continues perfectly appalling' and Elizabeth was writing under some strain, her letter prefaced by an apposite quote from the nineteenth-century poet Flecker: 'They knelt on the rotting Poop to Pray.' She told Felicité it stopped raining about 'once or twice' a week, at which time the mistral started to blow with deafening force. The sun, when it did come out, was hot, but that was a rare occurrence. She was tired and disaffected with her Provençal retreat, saying that she never seemed to have a moment. Cooking two meals a day for four people on two gas rings without much in the way of resources, while at the same time trying to do her writing, took up all her days. These commitments had included 'plodding through' a 1500-word article on cheese for the *Children's Encyclopedia*, her monthly articles for *Harpers*, '& odd bits for French C. C. [*Country Cooking*] . . . I shall be grateful for a small amount of typing now and again.'

The 'daily' seemed 'continually in poor health and finds herself quite unable to walk up the hill', so wasn't much use to Elizabeth who had to do 'a good deal of washing up and general organizing . . . Romney bosses around and does a lot of shopping, Hamish doesn't get up till lunch time and most of his working hours are occupied fetching wood for the fire and doing the flowers. (Hamish was Hamish Erskine, son of the Earl of Rosslyn, whom Nancy Mitford made the hero in her novel *Highland Fling*; and had hoped to marry. He was, according to Doreen Thornton, 'very sympathetic'.) Elizabeth continued, 'Georgina is a dear, and very good about helping but the poor wretch is supposed to be on holiday and paying heavily for the privilege of sitting in extreme discomfort on this dripping hilltop . . .' In reference to passing friends who couldn't 'resist coming to see my Provençal Paradise', she said, 'such arrivals are invariably the signal for a tremendous blind, the guests are then incapable of driving their cars away and have to spend the night. Bedlam then breaks loose, with Romney giving up his room to everybody in turn, a general shambles, and the whole company waking up still tipsy. However as 7 or 8 people can drink themselves into a stupor for 36 hours for the sum of about £2 one can hardly complain.' (She had previously apologized to Felicité for cleaning her out of gin before leaving Halsey Street.)

Doreen was one of the 'passing friends' who remained for a time and remembers that the house was full of people, so she was 'given the *dépendence* to stay in. Hamish walked me down the garden each night in the dark. One day I found a scorpion in my shoe and that was it. I refused to stay there any longer and moved into the main house. The dining room was very large with an *enormous* table, rickety like the rest of the house. The weather was terrible and we sat about all day at that table, with a barrel of awful wine. What you could get then wasn't always very good.' (Writing later of wine in Avignon in an essay first published in T. B. Lanyon's *Besides*, 1959, Elizabeth said that 'The wine of our own village *was* notable though: the worst I have ever consistently had to drink.')

Doreen continued: 'The house was dreadful, in the most gorgeous position. Hamish loved flowers. He knew a lot about them, and we would go out looking for things like wild orchids.' Elizabeth had 'tried going for a walk one day, and bore up very well, but upon our return collapsed in tortures of backache' and again later she was 'bent double with appalling backache . . . so shan't try again'.

In the *French Provincial Cooking* piece Elizabeth said: 'It does not do to regard Provence simply as Keats's tranquil land of song and mirth. The melancholy and the savagery are part of its spell.' This response to the elemental, sometimes threatening aspect of a land as ancient as Provence goes well beyond the comforting tourist's vision.

The grumbling house, the appalling weather, in combination with too much bad wine – and 'it was the kind of wine it was wisest to drink out of a tumbler so that there was room for a large proportion of water' – succeeded in rousing Elizabeth's demons so carefully kept at bay. She much later wrote a witty postcard to Doreen illustrating the *Castellet* in which they were staying, describing local events whose harsh discord reflected and confirmed her own sense of gloom:

'The butcher took to drink, kept 4 mistresses & was murdered by his brother-in-law in self-defence. The café proprietor's wife died 4 years ago, the proprietor of the little hotel committed suicide, the curé & his mother both dead, Madame Fernende had a stroke – How did we all escape? Love E.' Meanwhile Elizabeth described herself to Felicité as experiencing 'such a bout of depression I was convinced death was imminent and have in fact made a new will, which I had better tell you about'.

She regretted not being able to leave Felicité her flat due to the fact that the house was not in her name. Nevertheless she had made ample provision for her sister, both for the lump sum Felicité had paid her and in case she might need to move should the house be sold. Elizabeth made out a letter giving personal items to friends and said to her sister, 'If I fall off the precipice I'm afraid all this will be a bore for you, but you are the only person competent to cope.' Her previous reliance upon Priscilla in all these matters had now been largely diverted to Felicité. She continued: 'My collection of cookery books is to go to Veronica, but you will of course get all the rest' (Felicité's interest in food and its literature was of a limited nature). Elizabeth ended, typically, with no further explanation, 'Enough of gloomy goings on.'

When the landscape was visible through heavy mists and Welsh rain it was becoming more beautiful every day. Three weeks previously all the gardens had been full of the most exquisite lilac she had ever seen. Elizabeth told Felicité that the household was getting hard up for reading matter, particularly 'tecckes' (detective stories, which Dorothy Sayers called 'the sport of noble minds'). She requested any new Penguins or Pans, or anything else Felicité thought she might enjoy. She 'adored Scott Fitzgerald', especially 'The Diamond as Big as the Ritz'; described the latest Ada Leverson [reprint] as having been 'locked up with Georgina and Hamish and I can't wait to get my hands on her', and wanted Evelyn Waugh's novels soon coming out in paperback.

A friend arrived in a sports car and 'We were all very envious of him,' Doreen remembers. 'We had to go everywhere on buses, it was awfully hard to get about.' Elizabeth wrote to Felicité that there were some lovely villages there, and that in one of them they found an excellent restaurant, very cheap; there were probably more but communication was 'fearfully complicated'. Almost twice weekly Elizabeth, with one or two others, would take the bus the twenty or so winding miles into Avignon to shop for provisions on market days. Here they found one of those 'totally unpretentious' little French restuarants which Elizabeth loved and subsequently mourned the loss of in a more 'modern' France.

This little restaurant and its omelettes were to be enshrined in the title essay of Elizabeth's most popular later book, *An Omelette and a Glass of Wine*. This late collection of her journalism contains not only some fine essays but also some vital clues to her personality and her thinking about food. *An Omelette and a Glass of Wine* is an insight into both how she perceived her own work and how she wished to control this perception for posterity. The book was published in 1984 when Elizabeth was seventy-one, and in the essays which she chose to reprint, in addition to her editorial comments which preface them, she came as close as she ever did to extended autobiographical writing. In the title piece she wrote:

'Physically and emotionally worn to tatters by the pandemonium and splendour of the Avignon market, tottering under the weight of the provisions we had bought . . . we would make at last for the restaurant Molière to be rested and restored.

'. . . the proprietors had always been angelically kind [how Elizabeth hung on to a few of those vapid words so beloved of Thirties socialites], welcoming and generous' and often plied Elizabeth and her companions with a fine after-lunch *marc de Champagne* before return to 'the rigours of our mistral-torn village'.

Having outlined the story of Madame Poulard's rise to fame on account of her omelettes of 'exquisite lightness and beauty', Elizabeth admits that 'cookery after all does contain an element of the ritualistic

. . .' She concedes that each must observe their own rituals – citing her own favoured pan in which she cooks her omelettes – but says that 'As to the omelette itself, it seems to me to be a confection which demands the most straightforward approach.' She wants the taste of fresh eggs and butter and 'visually, a soft bright golden roll plump and spilling out a little at the edges. It should not be a busy, important urban dish but something gentle and pastoral . . . And although there are those who maintain that wine and egg dishes don't go together I must say that I do regard a glass or two of wine . . . as an enormous enhancement of the enjoyment of a well-cooked omelette.' The accompaniment of a fine cheese omelette with a glass of wine was indeed to be had at that little Avignon restaurant.

Provence was that part of France with which Elizabeth was most intimate and about which she gives us the most detail and insight. Nonetheless, her practice of only partially revealing herself persisted when telling us about Provence. Her 'art' lay properly in the arena of the impersonal, and she herself remained only partially knowable until the last.

Elizabeth had no plans after the end of June when the lease was up on the Menerbes house and by which time she would have finished the proofs of *French Country Cooking*. If the Rome venture for *Go* materialized she would travel on to Capri to see Norman Douglas and, finally in August, return to England. Always needful of money Elizabeth didn't plan on reinstating herself in Halsey Street if Mrs Boulting and her brood still wanted it. Her plans were very fluid, including the possibility of returning to stay with 'Sib, Veronica, some rich American Friends in Cleveland Row or if I find some other house in these parts, less broken down and less expensive, I might stay here until September'. She in fact did spend June 'in frenzied despair correcting proofs' for her book, but by July was in Capri to visit Norman Douglas.

After leaving the Vaucluse Elizabeth told Felicité she was held up in Naples, 'in a state of utter collapse and had to stay in bed two days before I could totter on to the Capri boat'. The heavy drinking and late nights of her youth had not significantly diminished and despite a constitution robust enough to withstand the punishment she had meted out to it, now close to forty years old her hard usage of herself began to tell. She already tended towards a preoccupation with her health, combined with a good dose of English stoicism. Barbara Doxatt, someone Elizabeth had known from schooldays, says: 'she was a bit neurotic, hypochondriac,' but Elizabeth's reference to 'utter collapse' is an early indication of ill-health, eventually to become a chronicle of physical mishap and decline. In Naples and now Capri she succumbed to 'something called water on the ankle', which had become chronic. Capri is composed entirely of steep hills, so she could hardly have gone to a more unsuitable place. She told Felicité that 'as long as I spend the day boiling up compresses and staying in bed, all is well; but as soon as I put my foot on the ground it swells up like a bolster'. Apart from the inconvenience of being unable to walk and the exasperating pain, she was distressed by having her ankles look worse than they normally did – her legs were, by common admission, not her best asset. She contemplated asking Diana's husband, Chris, a trusted doctor and friend to Elizabeth and several members of the extended family, to engage a room for her at St George's hospital for the second half of August.

On Capri Elizabeth had taken a room in a private villa, large and cool, where she could work a little and put compresses on her foot. She said she hadn't much to do there but was catching up with her sleep, which she badly needed. Menerbes had been enjoyable but exhausting for the last few weeks. She had certain vague commitments which included some pieces for Elizabeth Nicholas at *Go*, and told Felicité that she agreed with her judgement of the magazine – which was soon to fold. Elizabeth hadn't heard from them for a while and had no idea whether they were going to publish her articles or not. Having been asked to write a piece for them on housekeeping in France she had no will to begin it. She then makes what is an accurate and damning judgement on the present attitude to food in England. 'Mrs N [Elizabeth Nicholas] seems to be quite sold on that technicolour food, & if that's what the public cares for who can blame her.'

Elizabeth was on Capri to see Norman Douglas, but told Felicité with irritation that she couldn't afford to stay very long on 'this preposterous island . . . full to bursting with Neapolitan grocers and Americans. The piazza in the evening is a perfect nightmare of noise and screaming.' Complaints notwithstanding, and contrasted with a

Britain still labouring under rationing, she described shops stuffed with all manner of agonizing temptations, particularly the shoes, which she reluctantly admitted were not really for such as them, particularly with water on the ankle.

'The stuffs are lovely too, and the food, as long as one sticks to fish and vegetables & pasta, is not at all bad.' In the light of John Lehmann's future suggestion and subsequent commission the following year; that she should write a book on Italian food, these and similar comments elsewhere are a surprising revelation of her relative lack of enthusiasm for it. With her sharp eye for the heart of the matter and the Gwynne memory for slights, Elizabeth still harboured memories of Italy's fickleness during the war and her own mistreatment when 'imprisoned' with Charles at Naples in 1940. In writing her 1963 Penguin introduction to *Italian Food*, the ambivalence Elizabeth felt towards the country in the 1950s was clarified as springing from a profound source. 'Italy was a country to which I had come long after Provence and Greece had put me under their lasting spells. Towards Italy I felt more critical, my emotions were less engaged.' This is one of those statements Elizabeth makes from time to time which are so condensed as to reveal little more than a fraction of the truth. Consequently, the full significance of this comment can only be understood when recalling how seminal had been her experiences in Provence and on her 'beloved' Greek island in those early years of the war.

Since 1947 a rather infirm Norman Douglas had been settled and surrounded by his library in the ground-floor flat of Kenneth Macpherson's large and comfortable Villa Tuoro, some distance above the main town of Capri. This small and mountainous island, inhabited first by the Greeks, was already famed in Roman times, the magnificent and profligate emperor Tiberius retiring there. With a view of mainland Naples the island rises up precipitously out of the sea, its perilous cliffs making the coast almost inaccessible; while caves and extraordinary rock formations are both beautiful and forbidding. For at least the last century and a half the island has been home to a succession of expatriate artists, writers and eccentrics, some of quite exotic proportions. The endless sunshine and skies of exquisite blue, extraordinarily lucid air and luxurious vegetation – fruit and olives grow in abundance – have long attracted those in search of an earthly paradise.

Under the benevolent and watchful eyes of Macpherson and his companion Islay Lyons, Douglas was to spend his last years at the Villa Tuoro. Emerging daily to wander the town, often in the care of his young friend Ettore, he would talk to old friends, both local and those from abroad, and in company at favourite trattorias. Something of a cult figure for many short-term visitors, Douglas weathered this, at times revelling in it, but his general attitude to post-war Capri was critical. He wrote that 'At this moment Capri is in danger of developing into a second Hollywood, and that, it seems, is precisely what it aspires to become . . . roads blocked up by lorries and cars [until this period there had been almost none], steamers and motorboats disgorging a rabble of flashy trippers at every hour of the day.' Amongst this heaving mass of humanity it was still possible to slip into less frequented haunts and Elizabeth and Norman happily entertained themselves in each other's company.

During those first meetings in Antibes in early 1940 Douglas had been as much taken with Elizabeth as she with him and he had shown consistent concern for her welfare during the course of the war. After his escape from the South of France to Portugal and the safety of Elizabeth's cousin Neil Hogg's Lisbon apartment, by June of 1941 Douglas was fretting to Felicité about Elizabeth's whereabouts. 'I write to ask whether you have any news of your sister Liz, of whom I was very fond. I used to know her in Antibes and the last letters I had from her were from the Island of Syra (Greece). Since then – nothing!' (Douglas means Syros; Syra was the name of the main town.) Felicité soon told him what she knew of Elizabeth's recent escape from Syros and her present location in Cairo. Douglas, by early July, having left Portugal for his 'exile' in London, responded quickly. 'I was so glad to get your letter . . . with the – relatively – good news of your sister. If you hear anything more from her, would you please drop me a line? Neil and myself are going to send her a wire, as letters are quite uncertain' (he had received one from his brother [Quintin] in Egypt two days ago; sent off in March!).

Ten years later, in 1951, Elizabeth told Felicité that Norman was still very spendid but not at all well, not liking the heat and grumbling because he couldn't drink as he used to. Nevertheless he would issue forth from his house at six o'clock in the evening, when she would go to meet him at one of the cafés. Afterwards they might eat together and, in an article for *Gourmet*, written in 1969, Elizabeth lauded Douglas's approach to food in and out of restaurants. Harold Acton, who had known Douglas for much longer than Elizabeth, recalled that his culinary habits were wayward well before this period. Elizabeth's respect and fondness for Norman were not so coloured that she could not see his foibles, however it is an idealized Douglas that Elizabeth presents. His understanding of food was more idiosyncrasy than taste, often astonishingly so. Although eccentrically knowledgeable about it Douglas was sometimes so erratic as to be merely puzzling to those with a wider range of understanding. Her writing on Douglas is an example of both Elizabeth's generosity of spirit and her creative sureness in concentrating on the best that a remarkable man could give. Writing for her super-refined *Gourmet* readers, and quite aware of the toes she might be bruising, Elizabeth revealed that 'His way was most certainly not the way of the wine sipper or of the grave debater of recipes . . . Authenticity in these matters was of the first importance to him . . . Cause and effect were eminently his concerns, and in their application he taught me some unforgettable lessons.' In demonstration of these she continues:

> Once during that last summer of his life . . . I took him a basket of figs from the market in the piazza. He asked me from which stall I had bought them.
>
> 'That one down nearest the steps.'
>
> 'Not bad, my dear, not bad. Next time you could try Graziella. I fancy you'll find her figs are sweeter.'
>
> He knew, who better, from which garden those figs came; he was familiar with the history of the trees, he knew their age and in what type of soil they grew; he knew by which tempests, blights, invasions, and plagues that particular property had or had not been affected during the last three hundred years; how many times it had changed hands . . . that the son now grown up was a man less grasping than his neighbours and was consequently in less of a hurry to pick and sell his fruit before it

ripened . . . I may add that it was not Norman's way to give
lectures. These pieces of information emerged gradually, in the
course of walks, sessions at the tavern apropros a chance remark.
It was up to you to put two and two together if you were
sufficiently interested.

Elizabeth's assimilation of these lessons had already been integrated into her work with the completion of *Mediterranean Food*. One
of the qualities which she singles out in her tribute to him (above)
and often glossed over by the English reader, but so fundamental to
an understanding of the Mediterranean; was an appreciation of the
'variations in climate and soil' as she succinctly put it in *Mediterranean
Food*. With this, and his profound respect for the seasons in mind,
Elizabeth describes the famous Douglas habit of rarely eating in a
restaurant unless he had 'first, in the morning . . . looked in; or if he
felt too poorly in those latter days sent a message. What was to be
had that day? What fish had come in? Was the mozzarella cheese
dripping, positively dripping fresh? . . . Giovanni's wine will slip
down all right my dear. At least he doesn't pick his grapes green.'

These attitudes of mind were to prove invaluable to Elizabeth in
the following year and helped to bring about her complete conversion
to the food of Italy. In talking about her work recently Grey Gowrie
said: 'The writing had a sense of optimism and hope and the old
Mediterranean world was still there. One of the consolations of being
in my fifties is that we can remember the Mediterranean world before
the age of tourism.'

That summer on Capri Elizabeth and Norman might have been
forgiven for believing in the irreplaceable loss of an older world, but
as they ate and drank and talked and listened, they were in fact
experiencing a culture which (like much of Italy) was in some ways
still in touch with its Graeco-Roman past. Elizabeth's friend Sybille
Bedford also saw a good deal of Norman in these last years and he
would regularly drag her off on the famous post-prandial walks. 'He
liked to walk for two hours after lunch. He liked his food and drink,
he would talk about food, but he was not a gourmet. The moment
you walked for a few minutes out of the piazza there is a rock path
and we would make our way along it out into the country. He knew

a vast amount about nature, he knew something about everything. He was very tough, very virile, he had beautiful manners. He always liked a woman with him. He was violently atheistic, was very much afraid of dying.'

Norman's penultimate book, a final autobiographical work of 1946, entitled *Late Harvest* (Lyndsay Drummond), was a disappointment to him for its 'austerity' production on 'authorised economy standard' paper. To some of his friends its content was similarly insubstantial. They had hoped for a more organized and coherent account of his life, but this was hardly realistic with someone as difficult to categorize as Norman. On her departure in late August Douglas gave Elizabeth a copy inscribed: 'For Liz. Farewell to Capri.'

CHAPTER FIFTEEN

Italy

(1951–1954)

HALSEY STREET WAS still full of Boultings, and Elizabeth's need for money kept them there until the following year. Returning to London at the end of the summer of 1951 she needed somewhere to stay beyond a few days here or there with friends. George and Judith Lassalle had moved to a basement flat at No. 14 Eccleston Square a few months after their marriage in the previous spring and, quickly re-establishing contact with George, Elizabeth was soon set up next door to them. (The two basement flats in fact took up Nos. 14 and 16, and No. 16 was temporarily vacant.)

Judith Lassalle describes the accommodation: 'It was another of those flats with the cooker in the bathroom, or you might say the bathroom in the kitchen. Anyway, the bath doubled, with a lid on it, as the kitchen table. She would knock on the door [which divided the two flats] if she wanted to borrow something or say something. She was in a way very polite. In her kitchen she had hardly any facilities to cook on. It was camping gear really. She cooked a lot of bacon bones and Continental lentils. After she'd come through the connecting door and been with us for a while, talking, she'd often say, "Well, I must go and eat my lentils." She'd eat them cold or hot. Other times she would bring a bottle of wine and say, "I can produce this, what have you got?" and that way we'd spend the evening together.'

That autumn and winter in Eccleston Square Judith noticed how 'Elizabeth already sounded knowledgeable. She could take a teaspoon of something and analyse it, tell you what *wasn't* in it and what should have been in it. She and George talked a lot about food. She was writing about what we were eating . . . Then, and later in Halsey

Street Elizabeth was always having people round. But she was someone you didn't just pop in on.'

Elizabeth's now ingrained habit of dividing up her life, and accordingly her friends, is something which most of them have commented upon. As Alix Coleman says: 'She didn't keep open house, but people came often as guests, frequently they came separately too.'

Judith Lassalle remembers that during the Fifties and early Sixties, when they saw much of each other, 'We were rarely there with anyone else. Friends would wait to see Elizabeth in The Australian, the pub round the corner from Halsey Street. As we arrived someone would often leave . . .' One of her most distinctive qualities was this habit of separation, so extreme as to amount to a disciplined schizoid behaviour. This is the 'compartmentalization' of her life so frequently referred to by colleagues and friends. There are many who thought they were intimate with Elizabeth, indeed were, and yet knew nothing about whole strands of her experience. 'George said that Elizabeth needed a drink to get confidence. And she smoked like mad, tipped Gauloises. She was very shy, often put out a tough front to cover this up. If she didn't want to hear something she would just turn around to the wall or take her glasses off or put them on and screw up her eyes so that she couldn't see them . . . She never got into an argument, she would simply shrug her shoulders and walk away.' Other friends have not only commented on Elizabeth's extreme short sight but also noticed her habit of putting her glasses on and off. George once said that 'when Elizabeth answers the door to you [without her glasses] she smells who it is'. One is reminded of that description of her as 'a myopic black swan'.

Audrey Withers, editor of *Vogue* and for whom Elizabeth would eventually write for a number of years, had great respect for her writing. She has said of Elizabeth herself: 'She was, I think, the most private person I have ever known. I had the feeling she had drawn a line around herself and it would be unwise to cross it without invitation.' The markedly different aspects of Elizabeth's personality were managed by existing in the different regions of herself at successive times. These regions were skilfully kept apart, just as she kept separate many of her friends. This type of existence, not uncommon in anyone of any complexity, and particularly artists, was in Elizabeth's case extreme, and the distinctness and sharpness of the separations she engineered necessitated a high degree of practical management and self-government.

In her earlier life Elizabeth's ceaseless movement, her unsettled nomadic life-style, usually made unnecessary any serious management of these different selves. The boredom and satiety which she so easily experienced were kept at bay, avoided by change; whether of occupation, associates, her milieu or her physical environment. Back in England after the war the problem became more pressing but in the short term she did her best (unconsciously) to keep moving, frequently changing her place of abode, launching herself feverishly into cooking, entertaining and trips abroad whenever possible. When young Elizabeth's sheer vitality sustained the most bizarre juggling acts, but with age the resource of raw energy diminished. To her own future cost she avoided the difficult emotional work of integrating her disparate and often warring selves, work so necessary for her long-term equilibrium. Increasingly these unintegrated parts of herself demanded some kind of attention and she managed them in two ways: through anaesthesia (alcohol-induced oblivion) and by a meticulous manipulation of scene.

Several events took place early in the New Year of 1952 which keenly affected Elizabeth. First came the untimely death of the King, George VI. This upset her considerably and she repeated to the Lassalles, 'Why did he die? He shouldn't have died, it's so sad.' Despite her rejection of aspects of England she was at heart deeply English and her high Tory background made her monarchism entirely predictable. She dabbled with being an outsider, but at heart Elizabeth was a traditionalist, not a radical.

Another event shook her further. 'On a dark drizzling February day . . . news came from Capri of Norman's death.' With his going Elizabeth lost her revered mentor and friend and she was deeply moved. His paternalistic friendship had been one of the most significant features of her adult life and unquestionably one of the chief spurs to her writing. His life and writing remained a model for the rest of her days, and she truly mourned him. Before Norman's death Elizabeth had taken up John Lehmann's suggestion and agreed to write a book on the food of Italy. Looking through the resulting book it could almost be seen as a kind of tribute to Douglas and the Classical land in which he had spent over forty years of his life. Elizabeth now began to research her new subject with thoroughness. Judith Lassalle remembers Doreen (who had come to know Italy while in Rome before the outbreak of war) and Elizabeth 'poring over maps and planning routes for Elizabeth and what presents to take for the journey. They decided she should stock up on tea and coffee, France still being very short of them. They were even short of gas.'

Tony was currently not very much in evidence although there was nothing formal about their degree of non-cohabitation, and he and Elizabeth continued to see each other for some time yet. Judith says that 'in this period Liz was broke and unsure of herself. Ian Erskine [the future Lord Rosslyn, brother to Hamish who'd stayed in the house in Menerbes], amongst others, used to take her out.' A close friend from around this period (1951–2) was to become more prominent in her life and would eventually have one of her books dedicated to him. This was Peter Higgins.

By March Elizabeth was writing to Felicité from her apartment in Rome and the tone is reminiscent of those earlier letters to Pris, who for a great part of her youth and early adulthood had 'managed' so many of the mundane details of Elizabeth's life. 'A million thanks for all your coping. The newspapers have started to arrive, for which blessings to you.'

Though not always conscious of it, in transferring this role to Felicité Elizabeth was allocating her younger sister to a subordinate role in their relationship. Although they had literary and aesthetic interests in common, and her knowledge of these matters was as impressive as Elizabeths', Felicité did not have her sister's drive; the demon was not there. Felicité was not weak but in comparison with her sister she was more malleable, a sweeter personality who ultimately complied with Elizabeth's assignment of her role. Elizabeth's appreciation of her was genuine – as it had been with Pris – but she also had an instinctive understanding of how to use the willingness of others. Judith Lassalle recalls a scene in Halsey Street which illustrates this trait. 'Elizabeth must have been without a cleaning lady at the time because she said to George, "I've got no one to wash my floor."

'"I'll do it for you in return for a meal." And he did! Oh,

Elizabeth could get people who didn't do things for others, to do things for her.'

One recalls Elizabeth's knowing comments from Egypt during the Flap of 1942 when, with bandaged foot as ploy, she had people carrying her baggage, and noting that: 'the system has its advantages'.

Her Roman apartment was in the Palazzo Doria and she wrote that she was very comfortable in her little attic; was on good terms with her landlady, yet only too aware of how briefly that might last. Her rooms were small but pretty, with a good view over the rooftops of Rome. The kitchen was primitive, she had, philosophically, long ago given up supposing that she would 'discover a decent kitchen anywhere but in my own house'. Considering that Elizabeth had spent so much time out of Halsey Street and was planning more months away in Italy, the use of this 'decent kitchen' was not possible in the foreseeable future.

She had moved to the palazzo from a 'gloomy' *pensione* and had concluded like so many before her and since, that Rome was a very noisy city. Elizabeth spoke little Italian and although some of her friends were extremely knowledgeable about the country, most of her contacts were in fact English people; exiles of one kind or another. Friends such as Archibald Lyall from the Ministry of Information in Cairo during the war and Archibald Colquhoun, recently acclaimed for his translation of the most notable Italian novel, Alessandro Manzoni's *I Promessi Sposi* (The Betrothed). In writing about Italy, Elizabeth began with a disadvantage in that she simply did not possess the same ease and familiarity with place and language as she had with France.

This knowledge, that she was less au fait than usual, made her uneasy and was reflected in her general feeling of malaise. She was not at all happy about her book, or her finances. Money was always a problem for Elizabeth because of her incurable tendency to overspend, even when she was being careful. Unfortunately her 'Irish Signora [landlady]' was fairly grasping, and Elizabeth had to pay her almost twenty pounds a month for the two rooms. Elizabeth was also preoccupied about her prospects of reaching most of the places she wished to visit. Several of those to whom she had introductions had taken her out, but this would not be sufficient. Her next comment is consistent with her general opinion of Italy: 'So far I have found the food only fair and Italian wine disagrees with me.' In these negative comments Elizabeth is still careful. She knows that she doesn't yet have enough information with which to make an overall dismissal of the cooking as she almost does with the wine. Despite profound concerns about her writing, concerns which never left her, however 'magical' her final prose might have appeared to her readers, she responded to Rome itself with an understandable enthusiasm; saying it was lovely and that she would have enjoyed it enormously if she had friends there. She then reveals that panic which constantly beset her, 'the fearful agonies of writing and finance hanging over my head'.

Elizabeth's need to surround herself with a group of friends at whose centre was a clutch of intimates, was more persistent than it might be for most normally sociable people. And her carefully constructed mechanisms to avoid more than a minimum of self-reflection would inevitably be less effective in a strange environment, especially where she didn't have the language with which to locate herself. She ends her letter by asking after Felicité, soon due to have an operation and also regularly indisposed with migraines. Ill-health disregarded, in Elizabeth's absence Felicité continued dealing with house bills, ensuring that all went as smoothly as possible with the Boultings downstairs, sending on Elizabeth's newspapers and mail, keeping her up with the latest in interesting book catalogues and dealing with the resultant orders from Elizabeth who said she couldn't thank her enough 'for all your help and good works on my behalf'.

In a few weeks she was writing more happily about Rome while on a short visit to Capri: many people had been kind and hospitable, and if she went on eating at her present rate she would have to go and take the waters at Montechatini, the famous Italian spa town. She now apologized for having left London in 'rather a shambling kind of way, but I really felt dispirited (and also too poor) for any sort of festivity'. News of Norman's death only days before her departure had added a great extra burden of gloom to her sadness over the demise of the king. 'Nobody wanted, quite rightly, to give a ball. The time for that will be when & if my book is finished, & when that will be it is hard to say.'

Having read more on her subject and moved about Rome and its environs she felt she had partially organized her task, saying that although she had collected enough material, she would not be able to cook it while in Italy. This illustrates that thoroughness we have already noticed which was one of Elizabeth's trademarks as a cookery writer, and for which she was at times feared by those who knew her. Confusion and inconsistency, common enough in her personal dealings, were rigorously excluded in the description of recipes. Recipes which felicitously combined, on the one hand the daily round and that within it which is universal. In her writing she could bring all her knowledge, intellect, honesty, clarity, sense of poetry, history and the romantic, to work simultaneously. One of the important reasons Elizabeth stood above her contemporaries, still does above most who write about food, was that without in any way relinquishing her personality she transcended the personal. As a result her recipes are authentic, authoritative cameos of Truth.

Elizabeth said to Felicité that she would have to do her experimenting on her return to England when, with Halsey Street still rented out, she would 'go and stay alternately with Doreen and Sib, & make free with their kitchens'. She wrote retrospectively that she 'had been naggingly aware . . . that a tremendous task still awaited me when I should return to England'. In a letter to Felicité she said the book was due for delivery at the end of November, but she would soon have to break it to John Lehmann that there was no hope of having it ready by then. Most of the rest of 1952 was spent in Italy and in 1953 she was back in England, reading, cooking and writing. It was a long and arduous task but one whose outcome she seemed generally to prefer to her other literary achievements. She commented on this in the Penguin (1963) issue of *Italian Food*. However, on careful reading one is left unsure of what she actually thought about the *merits* of the book as apart from her *feelings* about it. Elizabeth's lack of clarity here reflects her own ambiguity on the whole Italian venture. It is only with recourse to later comments that it becomes clear, she did think it her best book.

'Writing of the feelings of authors towards their own work, Mr

Raymond Mortimer . . . observed that they usually prefer, perhaps wrongly, the book which has given them the most trouble. That this book was uncommonly troublesome cannot be denied.' She also said that she 'felt . . . less detached from it than any I have done before or since'.

Writing from Capri, Elizabeth told Felicité that George Menasce – the wealthy Egyptian banker who had befriended her in the war – turned up in Rome the day before she left for Capri, and that it was 'nice to see a familiar face'. A familiar face which she mourned in Capri was Norman's and she wrote that she had so far not been down to the Piazza, and didn't much want to, knowing she would not find him sitting there. She knew that V. S. Pritchett had written something about him in the *New Statesman and Nation* – 'any good?' – and that Brian Howard had written an angry letter about Harold Nicolson's article in the *Spectator*. Harold Acton had last seen his old friend Norman only days after Elizabeth left Capri the previous autumn. He wrote that 'The meal was punctuated by bursts of laughter and arteriosclerosis was sent to blazes. By the time we reached the funicular [by which Acton would descend to the steamer bound for Naples] Norman was almost buoyant.' And Acton sums up his last impressions thus: 'Standing there in his loose overcoat and shabby beret, he had the elegance of a Scottish Jacobite in exile. He was the most sanguine of the octogenarians I knew [Acton knew many]: his physique, like his intellect, belonged to the eighteenth rather than to the twentieth century.'

Over the years Elizabeth was to write several tributes to Norman herself. One, for *Wine and Food* in 1964, was built around a denunciation of a posthumous publication of Douglas's. A spoof on aphrodisiac cooking, *Venus in the Kitchen*, with an introduction by his friend and summer resident of Capri, Graham Greene, and 'decorated' by Bruce Roberts. 'Defacements would have been a more accurate description,' spits Elizabeth, whose anger and disappointment provoked her to bemoan the emasculation of her friend's 'instructive and entertaining little collection of recipes, mainly . . . of ancient Mediterranean origin . . .' She said, 'What makes this . . . anthology notable is not the recipes. It is the characteristically irreverent Douglas spirit which imbues them . . .' On the banal illustrations which so trivialized the tone of the book she was at her attacking best: 'Anything more anaphrodisiac than [Roberts's] simpering cupids (in Bathing trunks), his bows and arrows and hearts, his chefs in Christmas cracker hats, his amorphous fishes and bottles and birds, his waiters in jocular poses, sexless couples seated at tables for two, it would be hard to imagine.' Elizabeth's criticisms are just, nonetheless, for all her wit and waspishness, the adulatory tone of her comments about Douglas does sometimes begin to verge on the schoolgirlish.

Obviously she could not have been party to his friendships with other homosexuals, and those with men such as Pino Orioli and Harold Acton sometimes give glimpses of a life so much more sexually forthright than the one his good manners allowed Douglas to reveal to Elizabeth. When Elizabeth wrote, for instance, that John Davenport's portrait of Douglas was 'beautiful, lucid and truthful' some might not entirely agree; Acton was obviously one of them. She wrote, 'We made friends easily. He reinforced my own growing love for the Mediterranean shore. Our shared enjoyment of wine and food had a certain reckless quality.' With admirable succinctness she then described her own position vis-à-vis the whole subject upon which she was now acclaimed as a distinguished authority. (Here Elizabeth is capitalizing, as often, on having kept her copyrights by reworking and expanding on something she had previously written; the passage usually improved each time.) 'We had in common a dislike of meanness, and an aversion to fuss, interference and pretension. Solemn sippings and grave debatings were not for Norman, nor were or are they for me.

'What Norman taught me above all else was to distinguish between the second-rate and the authentic in matters of food and wine.' This was a generous credit to Douglas but Elizabeth could not have imbibed his message with such certainty if he had not touched something there in her already.

Some time after the publication of *Mediterranean Food* she had been at a dinner where the publisher André Deutsch was also present. Elizabeth was already sufficiently well known for him to ask if she would act in an informal way for the firm, as a kind of roving editor. If she came across something she thought worth publishing it would be a recommendation to them, and similarly if they were sent something upon which they needed advice it would go out to her. In this way a number of early Fifties André Deutsch cookery books were described by them as being under the general editorship of Elizabeth David.

Diana Athill shared editorial directorship with Deutsch. She was only four years younger than Elizabeth but says: 'She was a very formidable person. I was a little bit frightened of her. She made you feel inadequate . . . but she was invaluable in teaching me how to get the really authentic in a work of cookery, and avoiding the sham . . . My position in charge of commissioning and editing the cookery books was a joke really because when I started out I could hardly boil an egg. But food was always given to women. Elizabeth would never have done as an editor herself, her hair sieve was much too fine for the more everyday books which we also did. But she was extraordinarily scrupulous and one could always trust her judgement, which came with admirable speed.'

Elizabeth talked to Diana Athill about the difficulties of being regarded as a cookery expert, saying that: ' "It wasn't taken seriously." We would laugh over what she called "the tinkling mandolin syndrome".

'What I got from Elizabeth was how one should approach food. Her sensuous and aesthetic appreciation of it. She always remained a touchstone for me long after she had become too big for us . . .'

The Deutsch cookery series consisted of genuine little books with unpretentious workable recipes and a few quite unusual ones. Some of those Elizabeth recommended to Deutsch included: two books by Gertrude Mann, on berry cooking and apples, one on mushrooms by Garibaldi Lapolla, one on Indian food which Elizabeth (ironically) particularly liked, *German Cooking* by Robin Howe and another by her on *Italian Cooking* published in 1953, a year before Elizabeth's own *Italian Food* came out.

In attempting to discourage her from taking on Lehmann's commission Elizabeth's friends were reflecting the general English attitude: 'All that *pasta* . . . We've got enough stodge here already; you won't find much else in Italy. You'll have to invent.' More than forty years on, when the English love affair with all things Italian shows little sign of abating, it is hard to realize that in this period when rationing still hung over England, Robin Howe's *Italian Cooking* would have been quite unusual. Indeed under the auspices of Diana Athill it was not a bad little book. Howe recommends the use of those still scarce Italian ingredients, but all now so familiar we often take them for granted: olive oil, garlic, 'zucchini and aubergine . . . dried beans of all descriptions, a dozen or more different kinds of pasta and the Roman and Parmesan cheeses without which you can hardly begin Italian cooking'. She doesn't encourage substitutes and, if rather short on explanation for the uninitiated, is certainly not 'sham'.

Why was *Italian Cooking* then, not received with the acclamation of Elizabeth's book one year later, in 1954? The answer is that Robin Howe's book simply lacks Elizabeth's weight, inspiration and sheer dazzling prose. She does not summon up readers' imagination, transporting them to another world. Describing her 'voyage of discovery' in Italy as 'far from easy', Elizabeth wrote that gradually 'the sense of discovery that Italian food brought me was . . . potent. As recipe after recipe came out and I realized how much I was learning, and how enormously these dishes were enlarging my own scope and enjoyment, the fever to communicate them grew every day more urgent.' That was Elizabeth. On returning to England after the war she had 'cooked like one possessed', eventually producing *Mediterranean Food*. Now she was 'feverish' to let her readers know what she had discovered: that Italy was, after all, extraordinary.

> Of all the spectacular food markets in Italy, the one near the Rialto in Venice must be the most remarkable. The light of a Venetian dawn in early summer – you must be up at about four o'clock in the morning to see the market coming to life – is so limpid and so still that it makes every separate vegetable and fruit and fish luminous with a life of its own, with unnaturally heightened colours and clear stencilled outlines. Here the cabbages are cobalt blue, the beetroots deep rose, the lettuces clear pure green, sharp as glass. Bunches of gaudy gold marrowflowers show off the elegance of pink and white marbled bean pods, primrose potatoes, green plums, green peas. The colours of the peaches, cherries, and apricots, packed in boxes lined with sugar-bag blue paper matching the blue canvas trousers worn by

the men unloading the gondolas, are reflected in the rose-red mullet and the orange *vongole* and *cannestrelle* which have been prised out of their shells and heaped into baskets. In other markets, on other shores, the unfamiliar fishes may be vivid, mysterious, repellent, fascinating, and bright with splendid colour; only in Venice do they look good enough to eat. In Venice even ordinary sole and ugly great skate are striped with delicate lilac lights, the sardines shine like newly-minted coins, pink Venetian *scampi* are fat and fresh, infinitely enticing in the early dawn.

The gentle swaying of the laden gondolas, the movements of the market men as they unload, swinging the boxes and baskets ashore, the robust life and rattling noise contrasted with the fragile taffeta colours and the opal sky of Venice – the whole scene is out of some marvellous unheard-of ballet.

Such a lilting and evocative description of the sheer wonder of an Italian market has rarely been accomplished. And that shimmering, watery marvel of a city, with its 'blissful . . . respite from trains and traffic . . . the most gorgeous city in the world' had so captivated Elizabeth that she leaves her reader, too, longing for '. . . the light of a Venetian dawn in early summer . . . so limpid and so still'.

It was in Venice that Elizabeth met Renato Guttuso, who was to do the drawings for *Italian Food*. Archibald Colquhoun, like Guttuso a Communist, was the intermediary (Lehmann, who had met Guttuso in about 1950, was also a one-time party member). In his second volume of autobiography *More Memoirs of an Aesthete* Harold Acton remembers him: 'Archie Colquhoun . . . had been a liaison officer with the Italian partisans, who had converted him to Communism. His conversion had been more emotional than intellectual, for he told me they were more handsome than the bourgeoisie and entirely free from middle-class prejudice. "The salt of the earth and the honey." So far so good: I was glad he had enjoyed his war experiences but my temper rose when he remarked: "How lovely it will be when your villa and garden are handed over to the proletariat!" [Harold lived in a very large and beautiful fifteenth-century villa on the hills above Florence.] I could picture them stoning the statues, wrecking the flower beds, killing the goldfish and running bicycle races through the box hedges in the public garden . . . at the foot of the hill. "But you would be employed as a caretaker," he said to soothe me, "if you behaved yourself." '

Elizabeth wrote to Felicité from Venice: 'I found all kinds of fascinating characters assembled here for the Biennale . . . John Lehmann in most cordial mood . . . I had a great talk with him about the illustrations, for I really do feel very strongly the necessity for a change . . . He is doubtful about dropping John Minton, but has at least conceded that if I find someone suitable he will consider the matter.'

Elizabeth told Alix Coleman that she and Archie Colquhoun had been sitting together in Venice after a party when Guttuso walked by; Elizabeth had already admired his paintings in the Biennale exhibition. Colquhoun said, 'There's Guttuso – we'll ask him to do the pictures for your book.'

Moving on from Venice, Elizabeth became 'oblivious' to the cacophony of Genoese traffic because in the market she was 'spellbound by the spectacle of the odd fish which come up from these waters', Elizabeth takes us 'Along the coast at Santa Margherita' where 'the fish market is famous; here the fish are less forbidding and savage of aspect, but their brilliance of colour is phenomenal'. And finally, in this admirable scene-setting for the chapter on fish, we are at 'Cagliari, in the island of Sardinia'. Elizabeth wrote later that 'when planning my Italian venture I had for some reason become interested in Sardinia – perhaps D. H. Lawrence's *Sea and Sardinia* was partly responsible'. Elizabeth had already quoted Lawrence's book in *Mediterranean Food* and one sees in *Italian Food* the influence of his luminous descriptions.

In a letter to Felicité referring to her curiosity about Sardinia she said that people had been mystified: 'What on earth can take you there?' She was determined to see it – the island being unknown to tourists and D. H. Lawrence so 'grumpy' about it, she thought there must be something attractive to be found.

In *Italian Food* she wrote of Cagliari market:

Spread out in flat baskets large as cartwheels are all the varieties of fish which go into *ziminù*, the Sardinian version of fish soup:

fat scaly little silver fish streaked with lime green; enormous
octopus, blue sepia, mauve and turquoise, curled and coiled and
petalled like some heavily embroidered marine flower . . . silvery
slippery sardines; rose-red mullets in every possible size, some
small as sprats, like doll's-house fish . . .

Before this joyous display of sensual delight might topple over
into an orgy of purple, with consummate timing Elizabeth draws the
passage deftly to a close. She makes one of those agile transitions at
which she excelled, from the *genius loci* to the cooking stove and
sound, practical advice.

The mullet, the slices of fresh tunny, the little clams, seem to
have been washed straight from the sea to the frying pan, so
fresh and tender is their flesh. In such conditions there is no
necessity to create complicated sauces and garnishes; and, indeed,
for the cooking of fish Italian cooks are mainly content to
concentrate their skill on the arts of frying, grilling, and
roasting.

She fell for the island, calling her two-week stay there 'bliss . . .
And I have decided to go back there, often . . .' Elizabeth enjoyed her
time on Sardinia as much as she did because she imbued it (however
unconsciously) with a dimension beyond its obvious attraction as a
wild and beautiful island. She clearly experienced there something of
that sense of remote simplicity found only on her now mythic 'Isles
of Greece', and which remained for her a kind of shining inner light.
As time passed this light grew dimmer, but anything which rekindled
memories of the purest happiness she ever experienced – on Syros
with Charles – was inevitably close to her heart. On Sardinia she
described 'a wonderful beach, miles of soft white sand, and clear, clear
sea . . . How unlike the refuse strewn and stuffy little playgrounds of
Capri, Positano, Sorrento, & all the International Southern Blackpools
of Italy and the Riviera.'
As she watched and ate and read Elizabeth recognized one of the
fundamental differences between Italian and French cooking. 'What
the Italian kitchen misses in the form of concentrated meat glazes,

fumets of fish and game, the *fonds de cuisine* of the French, it makes up for in the extreme freshness and lavishness of its raw materials.' Should her English reader have mistaken these words for a call to outrageous luxury (the book was published in 1954, rationing ended only in that year), she was at pains to establish the fact that Italy too had fared badly in the last few years, 'and since the war Italian cooks have had to learn to make a little go a long way'. The purpose of her comments was to show how the Italian reaction to dearth is so unlike our own and that we could learn from it. We 'attempt to produce an imitation', whereas in such circumstances when an Italian wants 'to cook one of the traditional extravagant dishes . . . her method would be to produce some attractive and nourishing little dish out of two ounces of cheese and a slice of ham, or a pound of spinach and a couple of eggs. A hefty *pizza* made of bread dough and baked in the oven with tomatoes, cheese and herbs costs very little and is comforting, savoury food.

Here one remembers some of those simple, inventive Italian variations on the theme of eggs, cheese, ham and spinach. The recipes Elizabeth gave included: *Uova al Tegame al Formaggio* (Fried Eggs with Cheese), *Uova Stracciate al Formaggio* (Scrambled Eggs with Cheese), *Fonduta* (Piedmontese Cheese Fondue), *Crostini di Provatura* (Cheese Croûtons), *Spinaci con Uvetta* (Spinach with Sultanas), *Piselli al Prosciutto* (Green Peas and Ham), *Maccheroni alla Carbonara* (Macaroni with Ham and Eggs), *Crochetti di Spinaci* (Spinach Croquettes) . . ., all delicious and none hard to make. A mixture of spinach, ricotta, eggs, Parmesan and nutmeg to taste, favoured in Tuscany and called there ravioli, but perhaps better understood as gnocchi, is fiddly but infinitely worth the trouble. As Elizabeth rightly said, 'The most delicious of all the tribe.' The above is hardly a hint of the good Italian food the book contains, but in answer to those who believed that Italy's repertoire was a limited one, she later said: 'Invent indeed. I had so much material that a vast amount had to be rejected.' And it is true, her book covers a fraction of what there is.

Back in Rome after her visit to Capri, Elizabeth's plans were coming to fruition. She had told Felicité that the Italian Tourist Board had promised free tickets on a number of trains which, if they materialized, would be quite a help to her. Despite understandable wariness at the *sprezzatura* of such an Italian undertaking, they kept their promises and Elizabeth was treated 'royally'.

With the details of living wearing away at her, she resents the time taken to organize them. Whereas in Halsey Street much was undertaken for her by Felicité, here in Italy where such matters can become quite tortuous, there was no such factotum. Nevertheless, the recounting of it is tinged with a weary wit. 'I can't say my path here is very smooth, my landlady although quite an endearing old trout, is so dotty that no servants will stay, so my fine arrangements about laundry and so on have broken down, & life is a long struggle to keep a clean white blouse.' (As long ago as her years in Cairo Elizabeth was noted for her slightly mannish white shirts.)

At this point she had already searched out enough to be saying that eating and drinking were exhausting her to collapsing point. To make matters worse, the Italian Tourist Board had fulfilled their promise and the following week she was 'leaving to eat my way through a gruelling marathon': Perugia, Bologna, Florence, Venice, Milan and Genoa, at the expense of the Italian state. The Tourist Board had organized an itinerary with some thought and care and she wrote to Felicité that they had fallen for her 'hook, line and sinker, but their enthusiasm will I fear be the death of me, for they are laying on 36 meals in 15 days, travelling in between so that as someone very rightly said I shall come back like a stuffed turkey. If I come back.'

Friends then in Rome included Archibald Lyall, and Elizabeth asked Felicité to continue in her role as book scout by finding for him 'the Augustus Hares about Rome'. (Augustus Hare was one of those remarkable literate and travelled Victorians whose books on Italy remain some of the best in an illustrious genre.) In requesting Felicité to search out these two volumes for her friend, she demonstrates both her own memory for a book and the pains she expected her sister to take over the task.

'I am almost certain I saw them, and a lot more besides, in that good bookshop near South Ken . . . not the Beauchamp — the one with the books outside. Or perhaps you have them in Allens [the bookshop where Felicité worked]. If so, or if you can lay hands on them do send them to him . . . He might prove a nice customer to you. He is doing something about selling books for English publishers in Rome. (He wrote that book called 25 languages, without which I never move) . . . The Augustus Hares to go on my bill — a way of returning hospitality . . . Do tell Mrs Boulting that her friend took me out to dinner & was perfectly charming. And tell Tony, Diana and so on that I will write soon. Joyce Murchie has been . . . in Rome. So it has been cheerful to see her & a good deal of drinking.' (Joyce Murchie was a lively friend who lived near Elizabeth in Halsey Street.)

Elizabeth returned to Rome and her little attic rooms overlooking the endless variety of terracotta roofs, common to all Italian towns but in Rome almost an undulating sea. Before her return she had visited many of the major cities, 'pilgrim routes' as she called them, of Italy. In July she wrote to Felicité from Verona, saying that Aunt Violet's gondola would have been just the thing there. She was being royally entertained and had worn out six pairs of gloves shaking hands with officials. She also made the revealing comment that: 'In Verona had to exercise considerable tact to avoid the toils of a haggard, dissolute but still handsome character, just my cup of tea but it would scarcely have done.' Elizabeth had not changed much; she still hankered after the echoes of a Charles Gibson Cowan.

To Priscilla she wrote a summary of her experiences: 'Rich living in Bologna and Venice, Milan, Como, Genoa and the Italian Riviera to follow in rapid succession. Oh for a boiled egg on a tray!'

In Florence Elizabeth visited Derek Hill, the painter friend of Lesley O'Malley in Italy since 1948. In 1952 Hill had been invited to stay in the Villino, the exquisite *dépendance* in the garden of the art historian Bernard Berenson's villa I Tatti, while he painted the grand old man. Set amongst the cypress slopes of Settignano, above Florence, I Tatti was Berenson's masterpiece: a dignified Cinquecento house, Italian art and a library, where he entertained and was entertained by some of the most artistic and articulate of America and Europe for almost half a century. Derek Hill also painted Harold Acton, who lived nearby and was a close friend of Berenson. When asked if he liked the painting Acton said: 'Like it no, but it is exactly like me.' Amongst other things he disliked his premature baldness.

Derek Hill's cook Giulia, who had been maid to Berenson, impressed Elizabeth with her elegance and delicacy. Years later she wrote of her: 'In bearing she was more the fastidious aristocrat than the sturdy peasant.' Elizabeth felt that her cooking followed the same principles. 'Subtly seasoned, but with unexpected contrasts, as in the cold, uncooked tomato sauce which she served with hot dry rice. Conversely, *riso ricco*, or rich rice, consists of plain white rice left to cool until barely more than lukewarm, when a hot cheese sauce resembling a fonduta is poured over it. Not an easy dish to get right.'

Elizabeth's comments on the cook Giulia were put together with two others as an essay entitled 'Mafalda, Giovanna, Giulia' in *Petits Propos Culinaires* in 1980. The Mafalda piece is one of those glimpses of personal recollection which make her writing at times so intriguing. It demonstrates too the dedication and persistence Elizabeth needed and was prepared to give in order finally, and triumphantly, to secure a recipe. 'Come back in the summer and I will show you,' Mafalda had said when Elizabeth asked about her delicious bottled pimentos. Mafalda and her husband ran a small restaurant in Anacapri where Elizabeth stayed briefly on that visit down from Rome. In the summer she returned, also to Mafalda. A good part of the research for the book now completed, she removed herself, as do all Italians who can possibly afford it, from the summer heat of the city, and withdrew to Capri.

That summer Elizabeth paid her only visit to Norman's grave and wrote in an article on him for *Wine and Food* in 1965, entitled 'South Wind through the Kitchen': 'I had never shared Norman's rather melancholy taste for visiting churchyards. A more fitting place to remember him was in the lemon grove to be reached only by descending some three hundred steps from the piazza. It was so thick, that lemon grove, that it concealed from all but those who knew their Capri well the old Archbishop's palace in which was housed yet another of those private taverns which appeared to materialize for Norman alone. There, at a table outside the half ruined house, a branch of piercingly aromatic lemons hanging within arm's reach, a piece of bread and a bottle of the proprietor's olive oil in front of me, a glass of wine in my hand, Norman was speaking.

For the second time Elizabeth was the guest of Arthur and Viola Johnson, who normally lived in Rome and kept a summer villa on the island. Elizabeth had been introduced to Arthur and Viola by

Norman Douglas and they soon became close friends. The Johnsons were cosmopolitan, discerning – Arthur was an international lawyer and authority on modern art; both he and his wife were knowledgeable about wine – and appreciated Elizabeth. Viola later commented to her son John that in a way she found Felicité a more interesting person than Elizabeth. John recollected in conversation with the author: 'Mother and Father avoided at almost all costs having their friends staying *in* the villa. The form was to stay close by, as Elizabeth did, and take all meals with them at their Casa Molino a Vento.' Elizabeth's 'cool room' was five minutes' walk from the bottom of the Johnsons' garden.

Viola and Elizabeth would make early-morning assignations together: 'Oh, I remember they would go out very early. At five a.m. they'd be off to the market and come back conspiratorially with mountains of aubergines and other things. I used to think they were completely dotty', says Viola's son John. That first summer they met [1951], on leaving Capri my mother had asked Elizabeth to look after Norman for her while she was away.' The Johnsons were close to Douglas and young John too found him 'delightful', in spite of being 'a very naughty old man . . . He once got me drunk at a café, I was about twelve, and my parents forbade more visits, but of course I went all the same. I pretended I was going swimming. He was a great charmer. He said that if he married again he would marry my mother. I would go round there often. He had a huge bronze pot filled with all the visiting cards collected during his life and we would play this game of "Looking Back" over his life. His stories about people were so interesting. It was great fun.'

Elizabeth was to spend six weeks on the island. Knowing that 'these pimientos were rather a speciality of Mafalda's and . . . were by far the best I had ever tasted' she made repeated visits to the restaurant in the hope of securing the privilege of watching her bottle them.

John Johnson describes Mafalda as a 'tiny little lady, she was wonderful'. Wonderful maybe, but not to be hurried in her bottling of pimentos. So Elizabeth went off with the Johnsons for a week or so, travelling around the Gulf of Salerno to some of the ancient towns of the Italian South. They went to Sorrento, Salerno, and down to the coastal village of Agropoli. 'An awful flea-bitten little town,' says

John, who accompanied his parents and Elizabeth. He recalls an episode revealing the grip of superstition under which most of Southern Italy still functioned; about which Douglas had written so descriptively in *Old Calabria* and of which Elizabeth was uncomprehending. 'Liz and I were going for an early morning swim there and some little boys clamoured at us that if we didn't cross ourselves before we entered the water we would turn into devils. Of course we didn't and so when we emerged from the water they were terrified because they thought we *must* be devils.'

They visited ancient Paestum on its wild and lonely plain of whispering sun-bleached grasses. The city was famous in Greek antiquity for roses and violets even before its domination by the Romans, but the population gradually dwindled owing to the ravages of malaria, and was finally sacked by the Saracens in the ninth century. Not until the classically minded eighteenth century were its majestic golden Doric temples marvelled at and fully revealed, making it a place of pilgrimage almost as moving as Athens. 'At Paestum we clambered about,' says John. 'My father had read classics at Oxford and was intrigued, wanted to look at everything there. We spent ages going round it. We had a picnic. It was a beautiful, strange place and we went back again a few days later whilst staying in a converted Carthusian monastery in Positano. I remember Liz met in Positano by chance a friend of hers. He was boiled lobster red. He was very suave, a well-known homosexual photographer of the fifties.

'Another suave man friend I remember. One day an enormous luxury yacht came into the harbour whilst we were at the Marina Grande at Capri, and Liz knew this chap in the party on board. We went to lunch on board the yacht and the Yugoslav captain was very taken with her and kept asking her to take off her sun-glasses so that he could see her eyes. But she wouldn't of course because she wouldn't have been able to see without them. Liz insisted that I must go for a trip on a yacht and so it was arranged that I should go off for a few days on this great luxury ship.'

At Ravello in the hills above the coast the Johnsons and Elizabeth ate and drank better than for days. As Elizabeth wrote, 'In the south, it is true, careful cooking is not common.' Her caveat that apparently food in Calabria – she didn't travel that far south – had improved a good deal since Douglas's First World War denunciations of it, is still only partially true. Elizabeth's hopes of visiting Sicily were dashed as her finances were in poor shape. She had recently written to Felicité that her finances were 'worse than they have ever been (*not* to be passed on to *anybody*)'. Owing to Elizabeth's practice of rarely putting recipes into her books unless she had seen them *in situ*, there are few from the island. This was a pity because it made some of her judgements about Italian food less balanced than they would otherwise have been. Sicily has a fascinating culinary history, if sometimes lacking in finesse. Its location, and consequent invasions, had made it for a time one of the most cosmopolitan and cultivated places in all the Mediterranean.

One of the recipes, *caponata*, which Elizabeth did include from that beleaguered and beautiful island, she described as only 'interesting'. She is mistaken. Why she also gave a Frenchman's version of it is obscure. When done well and well in advance, it is a powerful and memorable hors d'oeuvre with true echoes of the Graeco-Roman civilization of which Sicily was a part. When she wrote: 'Considering that aubergines have been cultivated in Italy since the fifteenth century, it is odd that the Italians should never have evolved a dish of aubergines half as good as the Balkan *moussaka* or the Greek purée of aubergine with oil and garlic . . . or the Provencal *ratatouille*,' one must take issue with her. *Caponata* is more odd, but at least as good as *ratatouille*.

A dish from the South, *crespolini*, which she appreciated and took down from the chef at that 'comfortable' hotel at Ravello was one which she said became 'a lasting favourite of my own as well as being much taken up by later cookery writers'. One detects here that wail of 'plagiarism', to which cookery writers have always been so ruthlessly subjected, and about which crime Elizabeth was to become so sensitive that it occasionally verged on zealotry. If sometimes mistaken and misplaced, her sensitivity was understandable.

Another unexpected pleasure of the hotel at Ravello, 'far above Amalfi and the coast', was their own 'unusual' *Gran Caruso* red wine. Elizabeth enjoyed two other wines with the Johnsons in Rome. They owned a vineyard at their fine eighteenth-century villa outside the city at Grottaferrata, and here was produced a wine which Elizabeth described as: 'red and heady and one of the treats of the months I spent in Rome.'

On return to Capri Elizabeth writes to Felicité with more book orders. As gifts for hospitality: *The Romantic Exiles* [E. H. Carr, with notes on the English who had lived in Sicily] is for Arthur Johnson, the Beerbohm is for *Mrs* Arthur Johnson. For that matter they can both go in the same parcel if you have them at the same time.' She next asks Felicité to organize supplying *another* Mrs Johnson with Tony's tea coupons: he never used his, and Mrs Johnson wouldn't be in England for long.

'At last Mafalda relented: the weather was fine, the moon no doubt was in the right quarter, the peppers were fat and fleshy, the price was as low as was compatible with the goods being in their prime. As it turned out it was well worth waiting for, because year after year I have used Mafalda's method of bottling peppers with great success. A number of people have questioned whether it is possible to do this preserve without oil . . . yes it is, I think it is because of this that they are so good, for the addition of oil tends to make the peppers soggy. [The roasted peppers Elizabeth loved so much, and reproduced several times, appear in a little booklet she wrote for the Le Creuset cast-iron ware company in 1969, one of the rare occasions on which she wrote for a commercial enterprise.] The acrid-sweet smell from the roasting peppers fills the kitchen with what is, to me, a most potent evocation of a warm October day in the Abruzzi and the unforgettable scent, all pervading, of charcoal-charred *peperoni* in an inn on the mountain road down from Aquila to Ascoli Piceno and Ancona on the Adriatic Sea.'

Before the middle of October Elizabeth was back in Rome for the last time. Just returned from Sardinia and the final two-week phase of her Italian journey, she eventually included many recipes from that large and culturally remote island which Italians still don't really regard as Italian. The Sards would agree. Elizabeth tells Felicité on 11 October: 'Books arrived – many thanks. Leave Rome 16th to Turin, Paris; London 25th. See you soon. Love E.'

*

Back in England, with Halsey Street still let to the Boultings, Elizabeth did indeed 'make free' with Doreen's kitchen as she had planned from Italy. The money from the Boultings' tenancy was crucial and Tony had been unable to remain at Halsey Street in Elizabeth's absence. Where he did stay is not clear. Anyway, Tony and Elizabeth's enforced separation whilst she was in Italy appears to reflect the present pattern of their relationship; they now spent less time together than apart. Tony may well have been troubled by these arrangements; Elizabeth clearly was not.

Elizabeth stayed with Doreen and her husband Colin Thornton for over three months, experimenting, cooking, writing. 'This was fine,' says Doreen, 'but what wasn't was that when we had people to dinner Liz would invariably say "I'll cook" and she wouldn't produce dinner until eleven o'clock at night. Once my step-father was staying and it was awful. He needed to eat and Liz had hardly started by nine o'clock. She'd have spaghetti hanging all over the kitchen chairs to dry and everything in general disarray. Everything in *Italian Food* was practised on us. She'd make the most lovely food. There was a chocolate cake she made, the most divine thing imaginable, uncooked and made with layers of chocolate and biscuits.' (This is *Torrone Molle*, which came from Lina, the Johnsons' fine Tuscan cook.)

Elizabeth was using all her practical and synthesizing abilities to make coherent the food of Italy. To achieve this would be difficult for someone *familiar* with Italy's great variety. Beginning in relative ignorance, despite her abilities Elizabeth's task was formidable. Whatever the book's shortcomings it did nonetheless accomplish most of Elizabeth's professed objectives. One of these had been to describe her joyful discovery of the regionalism still very much intact after Italy's relatively recent unity. At the end of the nineteenth century, in attempting to symbolize and encourage this new unity, many towns had ripped down their still near-perfect medieval walls, and Elizabeth wrote in the introduction to *Italian Food*:

> Whereas only the very credulous would suppose that Italians live entirely upon *pasta asciutta* and veal escalopes, the enormous variety of their local dishes is quite unappreciated outside Italy, and the highly regional aspect of the food is not grasped at all

... The term 'Italian' used in relation to food would in fact mean very little to most Italians. To them there is Florentine cooking, Venetian cooking, there are the dishes of Genoa, Piedmont, Romagna; of Rome, Naples and the Abruzzi; of Sardinia and Sicily ...

Elizabeth continued:

It is not yet a hundred years since the creation of United Italy. Not only have the provinces retained their own traditions of cookery, but many of their products remain localized.

In London or Paris can be found ... the best of everything which England and France produces. In Italy the best fish is actually to be eaten on the coast, the finest Parmesan cheese in Parma, the tenderest beef in Tuscany ... Everyone has heard of the *mortadella* sausage of Bologna, but how many hurrying motorists drive past the rose and ochre coloured arcades of Bologna quite unaware that behind modest doorways are some of the best restaurants in Italy?

Forty-five years later many Italians will still tell you first the province from which they originate, before informing you that they are Italian. This regionalism has long been recognized in Italy as a problem as much as a virtue. Its days may be numbered.

Jane Grigson, who would become a friend of Elizabeth's and one of the few cookery writers of a younger generation who was as literate and as fierce against fuss as she, said of *Italian Food*: 'Elizabeth was the first person to tell us why Italian food works in certain ways. She points out that ... Italy is dominated by regionalism in a way that France isn't ... When you begin to see Italian food like that the whole picture clears and you begin to understand how it works and why you put certain things together. She did the same for French food; she taught us about the background to eating.'

In her introduction to *Italian Food* Elizabeth continues: 'In Italy, therefore, it is always worth finding out what is to be had in the locality in the way of wines, cheeses, hams, sausages, fruit, and vegetables. They should be asked for ...'

A vignette, written as Elizabeth's sensuous response to the unerringly successful Italian combinations of colour, shape and taste, was put into one of her articles for *Vogue* a few years later.

> A handsome round white dish, quite flat, entirely covered with slices of pale rose Parma ham, cut so thin as to be almost transparent, with edgings of opaque silky white fat; in the centre a little pyramid of purple figs fresh from the tree, their honey-sweet flesh bursting here and there through their skins; a glass of fresh, cool white wine.

She called this the 'most perfect of all hors d'oeuvres'. And in the chapter on Hors d'Oeuvre and Salads she wrote that: 'Among Italian *antipasti* (hors d'oeuvre) are to be found some of the most successful culinary achievements in European cooking.'

An anecdote incorporated into the *Vogue* piece attests to Elizabeth's stubbornness and insistence on what was 'right' in food. Little did the 'magisterial assistant' of the 'celebrated store' realize with whom he was contending when he told her that to cut the Parma ham 'in doorsteps', as she said he was doing, was correct. 'I left him in undisputed possession of his massacred ham and his individual notions, wondering what would have been the reaction of the Italian friend who was so frequently my host in Rome and whom I had known to send her cook back to the shop with the *prosciutto di Parma* because it was only as thin as writing paper, whereas, she maintained, it should be perfectly transparent.' Viola Johnson was capable of being almost as formidable as Elizabeth.

In direct relation to the regional nature of Italian food Elizabeth mentions something which is central to the message of her book. 'But at the same time it should be borne in mind that as in any country which relies largely on its own agricultural produce, the seasonal character of the food remains intact.' On revising the book in 1963, she believed that this was still largely the case. As a similar consideration for the seasons in cooking was already one of Elizabeth's tenets, its discovery at the heart of Italian cooking was a happy one and something she tried to convey throughout *Italian Food*.

There are dishes which are made in certain seasons or for certain festivals and at no other time of the year. Heavy winter dishes such as the *polenta pasticciata* of Lombardy, the *lasagne verdi al forno* of Bologna and the brown bean soup of the Veneto give way after Easter to lighter dishes of *pasta in brodo*, or *antipasti . . .* of raw vegetables, or little *crostini*, fried bread with cheese and anchovies.

Together with her descriptions of 'how to get the best out of Italian food in whichever province one happens to find oneself', these were messages taken to heart by many readers on visits to Italy. And Elizabeth wrote: 'This is reward enough for the work I put into the book.'

For the first time, in this book she was permitted to give a (brief) bibliography and demonstrated how she had made herself conversant with the Italian literature on the subject, both ancient and modern: She combined her reading of all these to give, in two succinct, useful and elegant pages, the history of Italian food. In 'The Italian Store Cupboard', she tells the reader with her usual practical and (increasingly) historical thoroughness what is essential to Italian cooking. For the 1963 revised edition, at the end of the chapter she attached the whereabouts of purveyors of Italian produce in Britain, there now being a sufficiently large number to give 'a cross-section'.

In 1963 she wrote that 'On the whole I think it is easier to find the best Italian cooking in Italy than to come by its English equivalent in our own country.' The tide in favour of all things Italian, which Elizabeth described as turning between the publication of *Italian Food* in 1954 and its first revision in 1963, did not abate. In the last thirty years it might even be described as having grown to a tidal wave. The best of the myriad eating houses which now serve menus based on Italian food can be excellent; the majority, however, still produce Italian food which runs from the mediocre to travesty.

After months of labour *Italian Food* was nearing completion, and Elizabeth made a trip to Scotland for a couple of weeks to write up the index with Lesley O'Malley's help. She and Lesley set off for a working holiday in a friend's borrowed bungalow on the West Coast of Scotland. 'On their way up to Plocton they stayed with us,' Mary Abercrombie told the author. Her husband David (then running the newly formed phonetics department at Edinburgh University) was an old friend from Cairo. 'David had once left a party with Elizabeth when she had said: "If you're not doing anything come and have pot luck." Pot luck turned out to be roast suckling pig!'

It rained solidly for two weeks and when they got back to Edinburgh they greeted the pavements with joy, put on their 'walking shoes' and spent the day doing the antique shops of Edinburgh. During that same visit 'We ran out of mayonnaise at lunch. My son and I fled to the kitchen and made some on the spot, winding the egg beater. We felt very daring giving Elizabeth mayonnaise made with a metal spoon. She said it "wasn't bad", and we breathed again.'

In the Penguin introduction to the book there are some hints which, on careful reading reveal their barbs. Elizabeth felt she had suffered from shabby treatment at the hands of her publishers during the making of *Italian Food*. And, justified though her complaints were, one notices the litigious side of her asserting itself again. Once Elizabeth felt that she had been wronged her sense of outrage would rarely allow the matter to rest. During 1953 and the writing of *Italian Food* John Lehmann's ailing publishing firm had ground to a halt. In spite of being one of the most entrepreneurial and prestigious contemporary publishing names Lehmann was making a loss, and the printers Purnell told him they couldn't subsidize him any longer. The final insult came in a meeting of directors when Lehmann was told: 'What we need, Mr Lehmann, is a few rattling good yarns,' at which he left in frustration and fury.

Another more aggressively market-orientated and hence financially successful firm under the Purnell aegis was Macdonald. They had been offered Lehmann's list of authors by Purnell but agreed to take on only two. One of these was the American Paul Bowles, already synonymous with Morocco, and acclaimed for his novel *The Sheltering Sky*. The second was Elizabeth. She was furious, but could do nothing to extract herself from what she felt were Macdonald's clutches. (Bowles, much cannier than she, quickly escaped from his contractual obligations to Macdonald.)

As a result of these developments *Italian Food* was not published under the John Lehmann imprint but instead that of Macdonald. Elizabeth's ire was still sufficient for her to vent some of it in her Penguin introduction ten years later. She was good enough to call Macdonald 'endlessly patient and generous in the matter of production' but she let it be known that they had 'looked at it coldly. I had been a long time about it – it was twice as long as they had been led to expect . . . paper shortage . . . printing costs . . . they hoped the expenditure would be justified.'

Macdonald's chief director, Eric Harvey, was a ruthless operator whose foremost interest was sales. As a consequence, on delivery of her manuscript he said, 'Do you mean to say that Mr Lehmann contracted to pay you £300 for this book? For a *cookery* book? No wonder his firm wasn't paying. Ah well, let's hope we get our money back.' As it turned out they did, many times over. Harvey's treatment of Elizabeth *still* rankled more than thirty years on and so she recorded more of the details in the final edition of *Mediterranean Food*, published in 1987, saying that Macdonald had 'certainly proved a sorry exchange for John'. Elizabeth knew how to use her pen in reprisal and never hesitated to do so. She was a formidable opponent.

While she was writing *Summer Cooking* Macdonald approached her to ask if she was interested in an offer Penguin had made them to publish *Mediterranean Food* in paperback. Rather to Macdonald's surprise and in spite of indignation at the meagre 50 per cent of the royalty she would be given, Elizabeth jumped at the chance of extra circulation. She both wanted to spread her message and needed the money. She was always keen to see her books in as many venues as possible and complained about her publisher's unwillingness, or inability, to do this better. As well as the 'vastly increased readership' she knew Penguin would bring her, Elizabeth always wanted 'a younger one which would include students, young married couples and many professional women sharing flats or living on their own but still needing to cook for themselves and to give the occasional dinner party . . . the paperback was to be 2/6, a price within the reach of nearly everybody'.

Perhaps most significant of all was the fact that *Mediterranean Food* would be one of the very few paperback cookery books on the English market. This was thanks to the enlightened efforts of Eunice Frost at Penguin. The only woman director, with the support of Allen Lane, the firm's founder, she had stubbornly pushed through the offer to Macdonald.

Interestingly, the biographical details of the author on the back cover of the Penguin book take careful account of the contemporary anti-German climate of opinion: Elizabeth went to school 'in Switzerland' rather than her actual residence with the aristocratic German family in Munich in the Thirties.

The reviews for *Italian Food* could not have been more gratifying, with praise from culinary luminaries such as Margaret Lane. More impressively, the grand old man of wine and food, André Simon himself, wrote: 'It is the pattern of what a cook book ought to be which introduces the fare and wines of a land foreign to its readers; it is informative and reliable without any traces of pedantry; it is valuable because of the first hand knowledge and original appraisal passed on to the reader with ease and grace.'

But *Italian Food* was more than an exemplary cookbook and this was reflected in the praise the book received from writers of more literary genres. These were critics who saw in Elizabeth's books the writer as much as the cook, and this refers to more than her style alone; here was no mere collector of recipes. The distinguished traveller and writer Freya Stark was amongst this group, but most pleasing of all was the accolade from Evelyn Waugh. In the Penguin revised edition Elizabeth wrote that 'When Mr Evelyn Waugh, a writer whose books have given me more pleasure than I have powers to acknowledge, actually named this book in the *Sunday Times* as one of the two which in the year 1954 had given *him* the most pleasure I was, and still am, stunned by the compliment and by Mr Waugh's tolerance of my amateur's efforts.'

Ingratiating herself didn't sit well with Elizabeth, and knowing her personal style the reference to herself as amateur is irritating, however much it falls into a respectable rhetorical tradition. She was no amateur, and no one who knew her or her work would have thought her one; certainly Waugh recognized that that was precisely what she was not. However, as he was for many of her generation arguably the greatest living English writer – she had recently crowed with delight at having wheedled a proof copy of his latest novel out of her friend Archie Lyall in Rome – the praise could not have been more gratifying.

CHAPTER SIXTEEN

Summer Cooking *and Consolidation*
(*1955–1960*)

DURING THE COURSE of 1954, while waiting for *Italian Food* to go through the first stages of production and printing, Elizabeth had been at work on a new book; one which she later described as 'less taxing'. So incensed had she been by Macdonald's treatment of her that this time she would publish with another firm, the Museum Press. Called *Summer Cooking*, this little book was another attempt to encourage the English to look at the principle which Elizabeth had seen at work around the Mediterranean and France and again repeatedly in Italy during the previous year: that the preparation of the right food at the right time and in the right place was the most desirable way to live.

In her introduction to the revised Penguin edition ten years after the book's first publication in 1955, Elizabeth's argument is substantially the same, but with an enormous increase in the English consumption of frozen and convenience foods, she makes her point more forcefully this time:

> As I understand it, summer cooking means the extraction of maximum enjoyment out of the produce which grows in the summer season and is appropriate to it. It means catching at the opportunity of eating fresh food freshly cooked. It means appreciation of treats such as new peas, fresh little carrots, the delicate courgettes now home produced and to me as delicious as the finest asparagus. There are ... omelettes flavoured with fresh green chives, chervil, tarragon, parsley ... a few heads of purple-sprouting broccoli or a pound of tender little string beans cooked

for just seven minutes, to be eaten cold – as a separate course, with an olive oil and lemon dressing – but quickly, almost before they have cooled.

She explains that because many think summer is for cold food, this does not mean that it should be 'over-refrigerated lifeless food'.

After the months of financial worry and what had often seemed like gorging herself in Italy – 'Italians are on the whole abstemious drinkers but big eaters' – Elizabeth could enjoy writing a little book which had no obligation to tourist boards or magazines. *Summer Cooking* is a lovely varied collection of pieces from around her travels. A good number of course are from France; several here could have gone into *Italian Food* ... Some are from her years in the Middle East, others still are from the English tradition.

Accompanying the usual sections on soups, fish, meat, etc., there are also chapters on 'Jams ... and Other Preserves', 'Buffet Food', 'Improvised Cooking for Holidays' and 'Picnics'. There is also a chapter on eggs and an instructive and well-judged little essay devoted to fresh herbs, then sorely needed in England. The following comment reveals in its necessary description how uncommon pizza was in England.

> ... wild marjoram ... is an essential ingredient of the Neapoli-
> tan pizza, that colourful, filling, peasant dish of bread dough
> baked with tomatoes, anchovies and cheese ...

With reference to those dishes whose use of herbs reflect 'an essential rather than an incidental flavouring', Elizabeth says that this is something to which she wishes to

> call attention, for it is this aspect of cookery which is passed over
> by those writers who enjoin so much caution in the use of herbs.
> Sometimes it is a good thing to forget that basil, parsley, mint,
> tarragon, fennel, are all bunched together under the collective
> word 'herbs' and to remember that the difference between leaf
> vegetables ... and herbs is very small, and indeed at one time
> all these plants were known collectively as 'salad herbs'. Nobody

tells you to 'use spinach with caution', and neither can you be 'discreet with the basil' when you are making *pesto* sauce, because the basil is the essential flavouring . . .

'How one learns to dread the season for salads in England.' Perhaps at last, close to half a century after Elizabeth wrote this, we can safely declare that there are many in England who now know how to make a good salad. There are also many who do not, but in 1955 Elizabeth's dread was even better founded, for these latter made up the majority. The following diatribe has a grim ring of truth to it: 'What becomes of the hearts of lettuces?' (One is reminded of Theodora FitzGibbon's search for animals' 'tongues, tails, hearts, kidneys, livers, or balls'.) Elizabeth continued: 'What makes an English cook think that beetroot spreading its hideous purple dye over a sardine and a spoonful of tinned baked beans constitutes an hors d'oeuvre?' She acidly questions why we make the cold salmon, already beyond its best by the summer season, 'look even less appetizing than it is by serving it on a bed of lettuce leaves apparently rescued from the dustbin?' Anyway, Elizabeth preferred salmon trout, finding it 'one of the most delicate of all fishes'.

Dispensing with the endless instructions for lettuce salads in cookbooks she says that: 'it seems to me that there are only three absolutely essential rules to be observed: the lettuce must be very fresh; the vinegar in the dressing must be reduced to the absolute minimum; the dressing must be mixed with the lettuce only at the moment of serving'. An admirably precise and succinct description of a much mangled task. Her friend Sybille Bedford noticed that 'she always mixed salad with her hands, saying that this was the only way that every leaf was properly covered in dressing'. As for dressings; 'however mild the vinegar, I prefer lemon juice, and very little of it'. Elizabeth next makes a swingeing attack, concluding with a typically tart finale: 'The grotesque prudishness and archness with which garlic is treated in this country has led to the superstition that rubbing the bowl with it before putting the salad in gives sufficient flavour. It rather depends whether you are going to eat the bowl or the salad.'

On the same theme she gives an invaluable list of instructions for the care of lettuces. Amongst these she advises that: 'Porothone food bags, which are now sold in most large stores and in stationers are excellent for keeping greenstuff fresh.' Elizabeth was always fascinated by any kind of simple new gadget or container and, knowing that her readership was now considerable, she enthusiastically mentioned them in her journalistic pieces. Judith Lassalle recalls her excitement at the advent of tin foil. 'She loved all those new things as they came out. I remember her holding up a Pyrex dish and saying, "You can actually hold something up and see when it's done."'

Regarding the preparation of summer food Elizabeth gave that same advice which had become her hallmark: keep the dishes simple, don't mix things when they can be left separate. Accordingly: 'The simplest hors d'oeuvres are the best, looking clean and fresh ... When devising a mixed salad be careful not to overdo the number of ingredients ... one of the nicest of country hors d'oeuvre is the Genoese one of raw broad beans, rough salame sausage, and salty sheep's milk Sardo cheese; each of these things is served on a separate dish ...'

She gives A Summer Hors d'Oeuvre:

A dish of long red radishes, cleaned, but with a little of the green leaves left on, a dish of mixed green and black olives, a plate of raw, round, small tomatoes, a dish of hard (not too hard) boiled eggs cut lengthways and garnished with a bunch of parsley, a pepper mill and a salt mill, lemons and olive oil on the table; butter, and fresh bread. Not very original perhaps, but how often does one meet with a really fresh and unmessed hors d'oeuvre?

From the chef of one of the most understatedly elegant establishments in Italy, the Gritti Palace Hotel in Venice, fillets of *John Dory Marechiaro* shows Elizabeth's ease with unpretentious grandness. Her next recipe for the earthy *Routes à la Provençal*, or the utterly simple herring – 'A plain grilled herring really fresh is one of the most delicious of fish' – shows the skill with which she could migrate from complex sophistication to total simplicity.

Her Spiced Grilled Chicken, a variation on the Indian 'kubab' chicken, is a refreshing and interesting change from the simpler European ways of grilling the bird. In 1955 when recommending this recipe, chicken was a sought-after meat which had not yet been transformed into the tasteless, drug-packed battered thing turned over to millions of supermarket customers in suffocating polystyrene packaging. Elizabeth could then write what now only pertains for free-range varieties: 'A grilled chicken is perhaps one of the nicest foods at any time . . . and although expensive . . . it could be much less rare than it is.'

A stock made from old grouse can be used in several delicious ways, 'notably for stewing mushrooms', and in the vegetable chapter we find Mushrooms Cooked in Grouse Stock; but for Mushrooms Cooked in Cream we must turn to 'Improvised Cooking for Holidays'; as much because of Elizabeth's association of this dish with the idyllic aspects of her childhood at Wootton as because any holidaying reader might really find them out in the fields: 'To make a really good dish of mushrooms in cream very fresh little button mushrooms from the field are needed.'

'Sweets' is replete with light, simple, enticing little dishes redolent of English summer days and evenings at their best; fresh fruit purées, mousses, creams, fools and ices. The traditional open French fruit pies are there, as are melons stuffed with raspberries, Sugared Nectarines, and Crémets d'Angers to be presented in those little heart-shaped moulds. There is Chocolate Chinchilla with its earliest of chocolate's accompaniments, cinnamon, and that quintessential English dish Summer Pudding: 'Although nearly everybody knows of this wonderful pudding, authentic recipes for it are rare . . . Thick cream is sometimes served with summer pudding but it is usually served without.'

'Cold Spiced Beef, Shooter's Sandwich, Bacon and Lettuce Sandwiches, Figs and Cream cheese'. From one of her earliest articles written years earlier for *Harpers Bazaar* Elizabeth extracted and expanded a little essay wittily instructing the reader on how to make the perfect picnic. These instructions, followed by the few recipes, are a dialogue with her own past and are here to inspire, to stimulate the reader's imagination as much as any precise rules which can be followed: 'As for the food, preparing it always seems to me half the fun. The possibilities are almost without limit, and fantasies can be indulged.' She tells us that on the whole elegant food is to be eschewed in favour of the rustic. 'The simpler charms of salame sausage, fresh cheese, black olives and crusty French bread are enhanced when they are eaten on the hillside or the seashore.'

Summer Cooking concludes with six pages of extracts from those who have written on the art of the picnic, a pastime the English have always approached with particular thoroughness. Elizabeth excelled at the practice of using other authors. She was able to select with an informed mind, knew who to turn to, where and when, and one only wishes for more. From the start, in both her *Harpers* articles and *Mediterranean Food*, she appreciated how to surround the atmospheric prose she was creating, with passages which added to the texture and weight of her own writing. Here one is reminded of that presumption pervading her work and essential to the reader's understanding of her art: that we will share through our own experience a knowledge of at least some of her material. Likewise the passages of quotation, sometimes only tenuously related to the topic, will find a sympathetic and eager audience in many of her readers. Henry James tells us that a perfect picnic must be 'not so good as to fail of an amusing disorder, nor yet so bad as to defeat the proper function of repasts'; Ford Madox Ford picnics in pre-war Provence, William Hickey (*père*) with the Archbishop of Canterbury, and Mrs Beeton gives us her 'Bill of Fare for Forty Persons'.

Indian picnics are recorded for us by one of Elizabeth's favourites, the redoubtable nineteenth-century Colonel A. R. Kenney-Herbert ('Wyvern'). From his *Culinary Jottings from Madras* come: 'A nice piece of the brisket of beef salted and spiced . . . is a very handy thing for a tiffin basket; and a much respected patron of mine recommends . . . a really good cold plum pudding in which a glass of brandy has been included.' This naturally leads into Elizabeth's own experience of Indian picnics and she regales us with the disastrous evening beside the Qutb Minar outside New Delhi.

Next she tells us about the *fellucah* party:

> An agreeable form of picnic taken in Cairo . . . on board a hired
> Nile sailing boat Arab servants would carry the food; there were

copper trays of pimentos, small marrows [courgettes, such favourites of Elizabeth's] and vine leaves stuffed with rice, large, round shallow metal dishes filled with meat and spiced pilaff, bowls of grapes and peaches and figs and melons cooled with lumps of ice . . . there would be music and the wailing of Arab songs as the boat swung rather wildly about, the crew made Turkish coffee and we drank the odd . . . red Egyptian wine . . .

Elizabeth is recalling for us here, one *fellucah* party in particular spent out on the Nile; reclining on cushions with George Lassalle, Romney Summers, and Robin Fedden 'prancing up and down [according to Lassalle] like an elegant monkey in the rigging'.

The release from the quotidian, the sophisticated game of make-believe necessary for picnics to succeed, was a fantasy in which Elizabeth loved to indulge. Her sense of irony, her wit – not infrequently a masquerade, the protective shield of the sophisticate – she held always at the ready. The conclusion to *Summer Cooking* is made by Bernard Berenson's brother-in-law, Logan Pearsall Smith. Elizabeth selects the piece on 'The Ideal Picnic' from his *All Trivia*, in which he expresses both his exasperation with England (he was settled here, an Anglophile American) and his projection of a vision only partially ironic. Pearsall Smith has returned, disillusioned, from a day's wet picnicking and says: 'If I had dreamed a dream incompatible with the climate and social conditions of these islands, had I not, out of that very dream and disenchantment, created, like the Platonic Lover, a Platonic and imperishable vision – the Ideal Picnic . . . the wonderful windless weather, a Watteauish landscape, where a group of mortals talk and feast as they talked and feasted in the Golden Age.'

In her writing Elizabeth creates a unity out of a huge range of social and cultural elements. She presumes that the elements of food which she singles out . . . the bottled pimentos on Capri, the octopus of the Greek islands, the wild mushrooms of her childhood . . . these and their like will have some resonance for others; as will also the people whose characters come briefly and vividly alive for us as individuals or types: Norman Douglas, Kyriakou the deep-sea diver cook in Alexandria, and Mafalda of the red peppers on Capri. Finally we have the context in which the food and people are set; the places, the countries themselves. These are the building blocks Elizabeth uses in creating that single ongoing work of art which is — far more than with most writers — her whole body of writing.

During 1954, while *Italian Food* was going through the press and Elizabeth was writing *Summer Cooking*, a young man, Terence Conran, was launching himself into a related venture, a King's Road coffee bar-restaurant which he called The Orrery. An orrery is a clockwork model of the solar system whose name derives from the seventeenth-century Earl of Orrery; one of them hung from the ceiling of the restaurant. Conran has said subsequently that he was much influenced by Elizabeth's books. The coffee bar in 1950s England — with modern furniture, an Italian espresso machine and its appeal to the now more solvent young — was sufficiently novel and prevalent for the *Architectural Review* to run a feature on the phenomenon. The Orrery, with its young proprietor, was included in the article. Conran's aim was to serve not only espresso coffee, but also a small menu of good simple food, including a few soups, omelettes, perhaps a fruit flan, good French bread, and all at reasonable prices.

Conran had trained at the Central School of Art as a textile designer, but under the democratizing influence of the Bauhaus he rapidly extended his vision beyond simply designing materials to the concept of complete interiors. His *métier* was the marketing of simple, effective and affordable designs for the high street rather than élite artistic salons. His creative genius lay in the area of public communication: he was selling a vision, a way of life, not a collection of items. So was Elizabeth, but Conran, as befitted the next generation, was more clear-headed about what he was doing. From the outset he was aware that he was appealing to the rapidly growing mass middle class ... middle class in taste, whatever their professed opinions and however modest their incomes. *Mediterranean Food* was originally addressed to an élite; nevertheless, by the publication of the first Penguin paperback edition in 1955, Terence Conran and Elizabeth were speaking to the same, loosely constituted, but large social group.

In 1953 Conran had travelled for the first time to France with several friends and stayed in a cottage in the Dordogne owned by Nancy Cunard, Thirties socialite and eternal rebel. Talking and drinking 'the roughest red wine' he had ever tasted, Conran told the author, 'She was finishing her book on her old friend Norman Douglas and talked about him a good deal.' Conran was struck by 'the plenitude of France compared to grey England. For someone who had grown up in England during the war, going across the Channel, and the further south you went, where there were piles of aubergines, lemons, peppers, garlic – nobody had *heard* of it in England. The ordered disorder of masses of cooking equipment muddled up with hammers and saws, nails, everyday things you could see all around you in the markets and iron mongers. Simple, wonderful, practical, durable designs in the little shops and markets as well. Piles of porcelain and flowers and plants.' The more robust life-style of rural France, with an easier sensuality than could be found in England, was something Conran was trying to suggest in his coffee shop. This holiday and his subsequent visits to the cafés, little shops and markets of Paris made a lasting impression upon him.

Since those first ventures Conran had prospered, and when Veronica Nicholson's friend and neighbour Walter Baxter needed a designer for his new restaurant, the Chanterelle, Conran was the young man he chose. The restaurant was credited by the *Architectural Review* with having an instant air of 'sophistication and solid comfort . . . by the use of natural woods and finishes combined with a warm but subdued colour theme'. Throughout the Fifties the Chanterelle remained one of the best and most favoured restaurants in London. Patrick Woodcock remembers that it was at the Chanterelle in the later 1950s that he met Elizabeth one day with friends.

'She was wearing a beautiful black dress and was very pulled together. We were all sipping away and we got on well, so I asked her to dinner with the councillor to the French Embassy, Gerard André. It was because of him that she got the French order of the onion.' (Patrick Woodcock refers here to Elizabeth's being honoured as a Chevalier du Mérite Agricole some years later.) Patrick and Elizabeth became close friends and she later stayed in his house in the South of France. Patrick is generous and perceptive, with a talent for friendship, and his observations on Elizabeth are some of the more enlightening of those made by her friends. Patrick was friendly with a number of the better English artists of the time, including Keith Vaughan, John Craxton, Robert MacBride and John Minton, illustrator of Elizabeth's first two books. 'She was this curious academic figure, too. In her way she knew herself to be a great comic figure. She was a great sender-up, had such a sense of humour. She was awfully funny.'

Summer Cooking was published with illustrations and dust-jacket by Adrian Daintrey. Daintrey, never more than a moderate artist, turned out some truly mediocre work for *Summer Cooking*, and the portrait drawing he did of Elizabeth, used on the inside of the dust-jacket, is similarly uninspired. Nevertheless, the book's content was acclaimed as another fine Elizabeth David achievement, confirming her position not only as one of the foremost cookery writers of the day, but also as someone to be read on the Mediterranean – as useful abroad as a good travel writer.

In the summer of 1955 Elizabeth was asked by Leonard Russell, long-standing Literary Editor of the *Sunday Times*, if she would join the paper as a cookery columnist. She agreed. Despite Elizabeth's liking and respect for Leonard Russell, her column in the *Sunday Times* brought her up against someone who proved to be one of her most unpleasant adversaries and whom she grew unreservedly to hate.

Ernestine Carter was that formidable journalist, by now editor of the *Sunday Times* women's pages, with whom Elizabeth had already crossed swords in that Parisian hotel just after the war. One might assume that Mrs Carter's attempts to decapitate Elizabeth's work were a sustained effort of reprisal. It seems, however, that she applied the same tyrannical methods to all her contributors. More than one talented female journalist has observed, as Alix Coleman says; 'as soon as you began to do well Ernestine began to cut your work'. Suicide for the paper, one would have thought, but there were always those prepared to step in when others, defeated, had left.

Elizabeth had herself been a 'tetchy' contributor when Anne Scott-James was editor at *Harpers Bazaar* (by 1951 Eileen Dickson had taken over and Anne had gone on to the *Sunday Express*). As she had observed, not only Elizabeth's prose seemed to have sprung from her fully formed but her sense of 'being someone too'. Clearly, from the beginning Elizabeth commanded respect — albeit sometimes qualified by irritation or fear — but her insistence that her work should remain unaltered made more than one hard-working editor's hackles rise over the years. Her inability to function comfortably in a team arose because to an extent she lacked the imagination and the ability to stand outside herself. Protecting The Word, her art no less, inevitably made writing journalism problematic both for herself and any editor who employed her. She enjoyed the power journalism gave her to disseminate her message, but was not happy for this message to be constrained by the relentless demands of a page layout.

After six years under Ernestine Carter, however, although never in the least servile or manipulable Elizabeth had become a little more willing to accommodate herself to the needs of an editor. For the thirty years that she wrote journalism, some of it very good and much of it influential, she was never truly comfortable in the role. She was too much the innovator, the maker, whereas the good journalist remains a purveyor of messages, not (in his journalism at least) the creator of them. Elizabeth was too much of an artist to be satisfied by simply purveying her own message, she also needed time to create it.

Through her journalism and the popularity of her books Elizabeth spoke to more and more people. Her initial audience was that fairly small élite, with whom her writing had in a sense been a group collaboration of responses to shared interests and social background. As time passed, as The Word which was the Mediterranean was spread by Elizabeth's books, the circle of her élite devotees began to extend until gradually her converts came from a broader audience, the same audience which Terence Conran had quickly identified. The lively middle-class young of post-war England may not have experienced that passionate pre-war contact with the Mediterranean which Elizabeth expressed for her generation, but others like Conran shared enough — travel abroad to France and beyond — to find her books a practical means to an expansion of themselves.

By 1956 Elizabeth had agreed to two other journalistic commitments. Audrey Withers had been up at Somerville and after Oxford had made the rapid transition from 25-shillings-a-week girl at Bumpus,

bookshop to the rich and aristocratic, to editorship of English *Vogue*.
A discerning and hard-working editor of the magazine since 1940,
Audrey Withers had long been an admirer of Elizabeth's writing. She
told the author: 'In 1956 we got in touch with her. She was
immediately recognizable as a person you couldn't push, so we wooed
her.' Audrey's advances succeeded and Elizabeth left *Harpers* to write
a monthly article not only for *Vogue* but also for another of Condé
Nast's sister publications recently brought to England, *House and
Garden*. For the next several years Elizabeth's energies went into
journalism: with the *Sunday Times*, *Vogue*, *House and Garden* and other
pieces here and there she became a skilled professional with a
flourishing and mounting following. Her trips abroad, even when not
directly on behalf of a journal, usually ended by finding their way
into her writing. In that sense she was deeply autobiographical, she
never wrote about what she hadn't experienced.

Remembering a trip to France in 1955 with her husband,
Audrey Withers reminds one how Elizabeth's articles for *Vogue*, about
the largesse of France and the Mediterranean, were as uplifting to her
readers as her first articles for *Harpers* had been in 1949. 'We went to
a food fair whilst in the South of France and it was so extraordinary
seeing all that agricultural produce. And butter, still so rare in
England. We could have bought mountains of it. We had so little
spending money compared to the rest of Europe that on that holiday
we could hardly afford to buy a cup of coffee.'

When Audrey Withers had asked Elizabeth to write for *Vogue*,
they agreed she would begin with a series of twelve articles, one each
month, on 'the finest foods in season'. The first one, 'Food at its Best
in May', set the precedent. 'It was', said Audrey Withers, 'a straightforward account of what she considered met the title description and
how it should be cooked. It occupied a full page in the centre of the
magazine . . . continued on two turns, and was faced by a full-page
colour photograph by Anthony Denney . . . illustrating one of the
dishes she described.' Elizabeth had initially said to Audrey, 'You
can't do colour pictures of food. I think they're bloody awful.' (And
so they were at that time.) Elizabeth was emphatic that the photographs wouldn't work in studio conditions and at her insistence they
were all done at Halsey Street. 'Audrey gave it such a lot of room . . .

Audrey was the first to put my articles in the middle of the magazine with a picture.' Elizabeth felt she was being treated as her work deserved. There was of course, as Audrey Withers knew, something less than straightforward going on in Elizabeth's articles. They were not simply well-written recipes got up in pretty prose; Elizabeth's writing was, throughout, a crusade, a cry to the English to make more of life. And here her considerable skill as a writer was revealed. Bearing in mind her temperament, it is notable how she refrains from the temptation of easy victories by deploying her acerbic wit: instead it is a sustained crusade of seduction, not one of assault.

> According to tradition it is in the month of May that all the spring vegetables come in; duckling and green peas, followed by green gooseberry tart, should be the Sunday treat, and the scents of mint and buttery potatoes fill the kitchen. The opportunity to enjoy these first fruits of summer is to be seized with both hands . . . Tiny broad beans, baby peas, miniature carrots and early asparagus are best prepared in the plainest and most obvious way, cooked in the minimum of water and served with butter melting over them as they come to the table.

The basic ingredients she has described here are English; they have to be because the point she is making is one about 'catching the moment as it flies', something she once told her sister Priscilla from her Greek island that she was so good at. Freshness from each season and in spring and early summer . . . 'the tenderness of very early youth' . . . is the basis of her food. In her *Vogue* articles the elements she uses to make a more complex picture are more often than not from abroad, especially France or Italy. The salami for the Genoese hors d'oeuvre she loved, with its requirement of the pungent sheep's cheese, Sardo, were imported, but so long as they came from a reputable shop they could be almost as good as in their homeland. The third and simpler element, broad beans, came fresh from the reader's local English greengrocer; respect for freshness is at the heart of her message.

The recipes themselves throughout the first *Vogue* articles are for dishes mostly French, sometimes Italian and English, occasionally other. For June there is Cucumber and Prawn Salad, French Beans and Tunny Fish; July offers Iced Sorrel Soup (Russian), *Langouste en Brochettes*, Herb Gumbo (Creole); for August: 'Holiday Cookery in hired houses, the picnic season, huge breakfasts for hungry children, are upon us . . . Cold ham, or bacon and spiced beef in the larder is invaluable because it is acceptable to children and grown-ups, whether for breakfast, luncheon, tea, supper or picnics . . .'

Times have changed and Elizabeth's words here read almost like something from a previous age, but her justified fascination with things like spiced beef remained. It was she who inspired the Harrods master butcher, Mr Ducat, to make it again from the recipe she gave him and printed in the Christmas number of *Vogue*, in 1958. Its popularity was instant and the beef sold in vast quantities. Elizabeth described it as 'one of the very best in the whole repertory of our national cookery'.

September has *Ratatouille Niçoise, Poulet Sauté aux Olives de Provence*, English Field Mushrooms, Blackberry Water Ice and the extraordinary Buttered Grouse, for which she says: 'Have the courage to serve . . . quite alone in its beauty, for any salad, sauce, watercress or other accompaniment would simply get in the way.' For years to come Elizabeth continued to berate the English for their suspicion of the admirable French habit of eating dishes unadorned, in splendid isolation. Related to this was Escoffier's guiding principle, 'Faites Simples', which in turn produced Elizabeth's article for the *Spectator* in 1961 entitled, 'Letting Well Alone'. As an inspired young cookery writer, Jane Grigson, said of the English: 'They always love to gussy things up.'

In October's *Vogue* Elizabeth is talking of late harvests and partridge, grouse, hare and the first pheasants of the season. 'English autumn vegetables and . . . imported aubergines are still abundant, the first chestnuts, onions bought from the Breton onion boys' (in the days when they sailed across the Channel and rode around the English countryside selling them from their bicycles). She sings of 'home-grown Comice pears' and celebrates the quince, 'that curiously scented and beautiful fruit, hanging golden and ripe in English orchards, ready to be made into jellies and marmalades, creams, pies and preserves'. Elizabeth always loved the quince and wrote often about this singular fruit, associating it as other Europeans do with some of the best-loved traditions from each of their homelands.

In December she says: 'As to the more substantial part of the Christmas cooking, the turkeys and goose must go to their inevitable fates in the oven. Every year . . . the thousands upon thousands of English women cooking, for one week of the year, as if for their very lives, patiently chopping and pounding . . .' Elizabeth tells us that these women, skinning, mixing and stuffing, with their 'mountains of brussels sprouts, cannot but command respectful admiration'. Lukewarm praise for those gargantuan efforts. Elizabeth cannot hide her distaste for English Christmas fare and in confirmation gives recipes entirely untypical: pâtés and terrines. The fact was that she hated Christmas turkey, loathed Brussels sprouts, and had said before and was saying again, by implication, that English women would do better to look to the quality of their simpler daily fare rather than this impressive annual burst of effort. Many years later in her beautiful book *Spices, Salt and Aromatics in the English Kitchen*, she used some of this article to vent her real feelings on the subject in a delightful piece describing the dinner she prepared for her Greek neighbours on Syros with Charles for that Christmas of 1941.

In May 1957 Elizabeth began another series for Audrey Withers. This came about because 'during the course of the previous year Elizabeth and I had often discussed her contributions. Early on she had only wanted to give us recipes. It was only when we began talking that I realised how interesting, how witty she was and how varied was her experience of France. I felt that if her recipes incorporated the story of how she came by them her articles would be even more popular. I was wary but began to suggest that she could think of writing them in that way.'

Revolutionary though Elizabeth's *Vogue* articles were in having much more discursive material than recipes, even with this greater freedom under Audrey Withers than was permitted to other cookery writers, she was still obliged to follow what she called, 'the strait-jacket of convention'. Elizabeth described the convention thus in *An Omelette and a Glass of Wine*: 'The old routine had been to open with a short introductory piece relevant to the products of the season, or to one particular type of dish . . . or it might deal with the cookery of a specific region of France or of Italy, or perhaps it might be a little moan . . . about the poor quality of something or their rarity in the shops. Whatever it was, once the opening piece was dutifully concluded, you filled the rest of your space with appropriate recipes and that was that.'

In a posthumous tribute to Elizabeth, Audrey Withers wrote in *Convivium*, a quarterly dedicated to 'good eating', that she found her the most private person she had ever encountered. Audrey told the author 'I just knew that I mustn't intrude. I have never felt it so much with anyone else, but understood I had to tread so carefully, had to be very, very cautious. One had to respect her or it seemed she might bolt. I felt that there was such a protective fence around her. I can't therefore call her a friend.' These perceptive observations made by Audrey Withers were put into practice; she was a sensitive and facilitating editor. This sensitivity first paid off when Elizabeth agreed to write the French Regional Cookery Series on the 'more intimate personal lines' *Vogue*'s editor had suggested. She says: 'I felt the thrill of success.' These articles, combined with some from the *Sunday Times* written during the next four years, were eventually to form the heart of Elizabeth's next book, *French Provincial Cooking*.

The articles for the *Sunday Times* and for *Vogue* were the result of specific trips to France taken in these years. Elizabeth never drove, and when enlisting the help of someone who did, it was often her old friend Doreen Thornton whom she asked to accompany her. From the first the *Vogue* articles and those Elizabeth wrote for *House and Garden* were accompanied by photographs. Her earlier writing had been complemented by the illustrations of artists, such as John Minton. When she had some say over the matter, however, as with the illustrations for *Italian Food*, it was Elizabeth who had chosen to drop Minton, not the publisher Lehmann. Her liking for Minton was immaterial in her judgement that he picked up too much on the escapist theme present in her work. And although when 'decorating' *French Country Cooking*, Minton had put a little more emphasis on the informative aspects of the book, rather than simply conveying an atmosphere, this was still not sufficient for what Elizabeth believed to be her purposes. She did not want the fantasy decoration of the

Mediterranean but instead more of the reality. Guttuso's unromantic 'drawings' with their almost monumental quality were much more to Elizabeth's present taste. (Note the change of nomenclature under Elizabeth's influence. Minton's illustrations, like so many illustrations in books at this time, were described as 'decorations'.)

Notwithstanding that a certain level of fantasy was precisely what Elizabeth was purveying, she was also doing more than that. Part of her early achievement lay in the fact that she was also translating that fantasy, that illusion, into a working reality; her recipes were, increasingly, to be used. Accordingly she wanted the illustrations to her work to be as much about information as atmosphere.

When Anthony Denney began taking the photographs to accompany Elizabeth's magazine articles, they had already been friends for a number of years. Denney started out as a painter, but after Audrey Withers had 'acquired' him to work for *Vogue* he became one of Condé Nast's major photographers. *Vogue* and *House and Garden* were full of his work. 'He was absolutely top of the tree, he was the best,' said a former *House and Garden* editor.

Denney was married and had three children before he divorced in 1950, after which his flamboyant homosexuality became common knowledge. During this period he graduated to interior designing; he knew 'everyone who was anyone in London society'. Denney's photographic assistant was the young Anthony Armstrong-Jones, later Lord Snowdon; clients included Jacqueline Kennedy and Aristotle Onassis – Denney decorated his yacht. His position as one of the arbiters of contemporary taste was sufficiently established for his houses to be photographed in some of the earlier books on 'style' to emanate from this period. He began to amass a large and valuable collection of modern art.

Denney's photographs for Elizabeth's articles are amongst his quietest and finest work; some of the best food photographs of the time. The problems of food photography had long been appreciated by magazines and book publishers but few had yet understood how to solve them; Denney instinctively did. Their friendship was an important factor in the success of his and Elizabeth's partnership, and their shared visual sensitivity made for a considerable bond, a partnership then unique. Denney's ability to capture, enhance and assist in the dissemination of Elizabeth's message, is without doubt during this period. It is also noticeable that as photographers like Denney gradually became more 'artistic', the worth of their images decreased. Too much soft focus, too much reliance on faux still-life compositions, corporate designer-led book imagery; all have trivialized much recent photography of food. Be that as it may Denney's photographs for Elizabeth in the Fifties and Sixties avoided these pitfalls and were often unlike anything seen before.

When Doreen drove Elizabeth on her French trips for *Vogue* and the *Sunday Times* Anthony usually came too, accompanied by his boyfriend; like Elizabeth, Anthony didn't drive. 'Anthony and Alex went in another car, neither did we drive in convoy. We'd arrange to meet up at some place for lunch or the hotel where we were going to stay for that night ... Elizabeth and Anthony would spend ages talking about what to photograph, and then Anthony would take hours and hours doing it or get something in a flash that had happened by ... A market stall piled up with things, waiting at some odd angle for the light to be just right, a sudden flock of geese walking past, a table after lunch.' The discussion of photographs for Elizabeth's articles was equally thorough when Denney was to take shots of made-up food. The arrangement was that Elizabeth prepared the dishes in Halsey Street, and they would then set about displaying them. Denney's photographs of food for Elizabeth were almost invariably taken *in situ*, a practice whose importance photographers and designers, then and since, have tended to underestimate.

In France: 'Oh, there were ructions,' says Doreen. 'They would sometimes forget to photograph something and have to go back and do it. It could be chaos ... And Anthony would take those wonderful photographs. Once, after a morning's wait for the right shots, we'd driven to the next place and Anthony wailed, "Oh no! There was no film in the camera." Liz and I'd share a room. One day in the South of France we arrived at the hotel and she was hurling suitcases about. There was no calming her like that. And I said to Anthony, "*I* can't deal with her, you do it." *Something* was wrong. So Alex and I left them to it. We went in the car to the beach for a swim, it was lovely, and they were stranded.' There were few like Doreen who could withstand Elizabeth's real furies. But over the years Doreen remained consistent in her down-to-earth devotion to her friend; she remained equally determined not be to dominated by her. As a result not many knew Elizabeth so intimately and there were few whom she respected so much.

'Like her mother Stella, Elizabeth never minded in the least showing if she didn't like someone . . . her behaviour could be appalling . . .' says Doreen. And one recalls Elizabeth's near-vendetta with Ernestine Carter; obviously an unpleasant and difficult task-master, but Elizabeth's nature was not a forgiving one. Her need for revenge continued beyond the grave, in her posthumous page of diatribe against Mrs Carter's loathsome 'cutting shears'. In fairness to Elizabeth this strain of vindictiveness was particularly active with regard to her work. The spirit which drove her, and in spite of her reticence, also made her believe absolutely in her writing, fired her to defend it with messianic vigour. 'Elizabeth was different from *all* the other people,' says Doreen.

CHAPTER SEVENTEEN

French Provincial Cooking

(1960–1965)

WITH THE BIRTH of their first child in 1952 George and Judith Lassalle had moved out of London to a large house in Sandwich, while George retained a stall in Bermondsey Market selling antiques and books. Judith, who had bought and sold since she was very young, came up to London to run the stall two or three days a week. 'Sometimes we would go to Elizabeth in Halsey Street; she came down to Sandwich too. She and George often talked about her work. "Can you describe what I'm trying to say better than me?" she'd sometimes say to George. He found her books. Once he had a Wycliffe bible, had it for nothing and sold it for £500. He knew a lot about books and with his languages he did well. But he was so unscrupulous. Once he borrowed some cookery books from Kitty Gaunt, wife of William Gaunt, the editor of the *Studio* magazine, and gave them to Elizabeth. She was very pleased. Kitty Gaunt kept asking George: "When am I getting my books back?"

'And he'd keep telling her some story. She was furious, but he never told Elizabeth, and Kitty never got her books back ... Elizabeth once said to him: "You'll either be in prison or dead in twenty years' time, George."

'George always had an effect on Elizabeth, and she was the only person who could keep *him* in hand.'

Elizabeth's circle grew as she became well known, but she always remained close to a number of friends like George made before and during the war in Egypt. If it turned out that she didn't quarrel beyond reconciliation Elizabeth could be a devoted friend. Amongst the closest of this group were Robin and Renée Fedden. Of their two children the younger, Frances, was Elizabeth's god-daughter. Robin had continued his advancement within the National Trust since returning from Egypt after the war; his associations and friendships were legion, his affairs frequent. As Veronica Nicholson said: 'Yes, Robin *loved* women, often had an attachment, usually pretty. Renée took it in good part and had her own friends.' Staying the night once after a drunken party, Robin said most graciously to Veronica in the morning, 'I'm *so* sorry, Veronica, I forgot to seduce you.'

To his wide interests – he wrote books on suicide, Egypt, skiing, the National Trust – and gift for friendship he also added great knowledge and a passion for buildings: he was Secretary of the Historic Buildings Commission for many years and an honorary RIBA. James Lees-Milne wrote in his obituary of Fedden that 'He was very hard to define. He had numerous interests, and many accomplishments . . . everything he did seemed effortless . . . He moved in many worlds and shone conspicuously in them all. He was alert, witty and informative . . .' There was a steeliness there in Fedden too. And this, combined with his 'elegance' and 'vitality', had attracted Elizabeth from the first. Lees-Milne said: 'He was no ordinary man.'

Neither was Renée any ordinary woman, but she was a more private figure than her husband, and only those who knew her well realized quite the force of her personality. Veronica Nicholson says of her, 'She seemed somehow wooden, perhaps even dull at times.' Elizabeth would insist that this was not Renée. Renée was intelligent, vital and to some beautiful. But like Elizabeth she could be very reserved. Their intimate and long-standing friendship was to have significance for them both in this latter part of their lives.

In the late Fifties Priscilla had moved to Catherine Place, Stella's London house, where she entertained and cooked her way through many of Elizabeth's recipes. Although Elizabeth now usually turned to Felicité as her closest adviser and advocate, Priscilla appears once again the lynchpin of the family. So, although they might eat at favourite places like the Chanterelle, it was at Priscilla's that Stella, on her weekly visits to London, would be most likely to see Felicité and Elizabeth for lunch. On a typical occasion Priscilla invited their old family friend, the painter Lett Haines, with the young, as yet unknown, Robert Carrier, Stella and Elizabeth.

As well as looking at an auction Stella usually visited the dealers' stalls at Bermondsey Market. Judith Lassalle looked forward to her visits. 'She was so eccentric and didn't care a bit. She wore sand-shoes and a long white Fair Isle knitted coat and a blue veil. She'd always pick out the *one* thing on your stall that was unusual, tell you something interesting about it, never haggle and get out her Coutts cheque-book. The other stallholders loved her for it. I loved her *telling* me things. Elizabeth was quite sniffy about me dealing with her. "Oh, you see her, do you?" 'As if it wasn't quite the thing to do.'

Judith 'met Stella in the V&A once with a young man in his twenties. She said, "Oh, how nice to see you," and introduced me to the young man, her nephew. "This is Nicholas Ridley, your next prime minister!"

'She told me once that she'd been round the Queen's Gallery with the director [the distinguished art historian Oliver Millar]. "That man Millar, he'd got the captions on the paintings wrong, so I put him right" [knowing Stella she may well have had one or two significant contributions to make].

'I thought Stella was great fun,' Judith concludes.

Elizabeth liked Judith Lassalle and 'was always so generous. Whenever you arrived she'd immediately open a bottle of wine. She was tall and slim and would sometimes give me her clothes; they were always beautiful, made by fabulous people like Worth, Maggie Rouff, Hardy Amies. She wore superb clothes . . .'

From the beginning of George and Judith's marriage he and Elizabeth sometimes went out together. 'And Elizabeth would always ask: "Is it gracious living, George?" '(Her way of gauging the formality of the invitation.)

'On Saturday nights when George came down from London he'd often bring some food sent down by Elizabeth after he'd been working at Bermondsey. Elizabeth would ask me now and again: "Has he given you any money recently?"

' "No."

'And she would say, "Well, you'd better have some then." ' At that point Judith was bringing up three small children and George sometimes left her with no money.

Elizabeth's sister Diana, still in London with her doctor husband Chris Grey, had by now four more children: Johnny born in 1951, Christabel in 1952, Stephen in 1954 and Christopher in 1957. Sometimes one or other of them would be brought to visit 'Aunt Liza'. For Johnny, and later Stephen, these visits were to prove especially significant.

Meanwhile, despite Elizabeth's finances frequently causing her concern, her reputation as a writer was growing apace and friends like Patrick Woodcock remember that in the late Fifties 'She was an icon for many of us.' With her steady journalistic output this status amongst that first élite group was spreading out so that by the end of the decade Elizabeth was something of a cult figure. And, although she complained about the pains journalism caused her – 'the dreaded deadline' – she had now become a true professional. In so doing she had completed a vital shift of orientation. As we can see she had made the transition from writing for an élite to writing for a mass audience, from writing for a few people whom she knew or could imagine, to writing successfully for a wide range of distant, anonymous individuals.

The ability to make this shift – not an easy transition – sprang from the same source which had enabled her to appreciate and live with Charles Gibson Cowan. This was the reason Elizabeth was a greater artist than her Aunt Violet, whom in several ways she resembled. Violet could not transcend the gap between a refined and privileged élite and a less exalted but still discerning mass. Violet had no desire in fact to make herself available to a wide audience, hence her great artistry is now remembered by few.

Elizabeth's management of her increasing status reveals much that was typical of her. At heart it was a use of public power deriving from a private style; a distaste for publicity inherent in her social background. From the start Elizabeth treated her celebrity with an almost Garbo-like reserve, somewhat easier then than now. She was aware of her growing power to sway opinion, nonetheless her response to the comparative success of her campaign to teach the English how to live – and it really was no less than that – was mixed. She did not always approve of those who were, in however remote a fashion, her followers. Perhaps they themselves were not always aware of the degree to which Elizabeth David was the bearer of the *Zeitgeist* which they themselves reflected.

Others were writing good cookery books and articles at the time: Elizabeth Craig, Ambrose Heath, Constance Spry, Sheila Hutchins in the *Daily Express* and Philip Harben in *Woman's Own* and on television (Marcel Boulestin, the first television chef, had died during the war and was followed by Harben). They were all influential and popular, partly because they were willing to make concessions in their food to the Englishness of their audience. In a different category was André Simon, the spirited advocate of a fine Gallic palate, through his Wine and Food Society and its Journal, and whose members and readers remained predominantly upper class. Elizabeth's writing would in some sense straddle these two categories; the social élite and the burgeoning middle class.

Alan Davidson, one of the most distinguished writers on both cookery and its historical significance, stressed to the author that: 'Nothing can detract from Elizabeth's position as the leading public figure in all this. Her books became the standard-bearers of these changes . . . they were emblems for people who were taking a fresh look at food and cookery . . .' But Alan believes that 'It must be remembered that to an extent this would have happened anyway. She was not the only force. There were all sorts of invisible ones at work. These shifts were going on in post-war Britain and even if Elizabeth hadn't taken up writing on food they would have continued anyway. Books like Patience Gray's [Patience Gray and Primrose Boyd, *Plats du Jour*] were, for instance, influential. But it's hard to overemphasize Elizabeth's importance. The main thing she did was not to influence people to "Keep it simple" but to "Lift up your eyes to the Continent and take an interest in exotic ingredients."

'I can still remember olive oil being a tiny bottle you only bought in the chemist (for medicinal purposes such as unblocking ears) and people would have been astonished if you had suggested it had another use. That was the kind of world Elizabeth was operating in in the 1950s. She often referred to shops in Soho and I remember it because working in the Foreign Office then, I used to go up there in the lunch hour and bring things back for the evening. Soho was a showcase for good European ingredients: Italian, Spanish, French . . . They had all you would want and you could explore the whole subject by shopping there weekly. There was an Italian shop which had a dazzling array of types of pasta. Up and down the streets of Soho you would have salamis and charcuterie which you wouldn't have anywhere else at that time. The ripples spread out from there.'

Elizabeth wrote over and over with only minor variations, sometimes almost ad nauseam, to the effect that we are a nation which has 'a curious distrust of the primitive and simple in food, and so carefree a way with the specialities of other countries that while retaining names, we have no inhibitions about complicating, altering, travestying and degrading the dish itself'. Despite her crusade against these habits, Alan Davidson may well be correct: that Elizabeth's greatest success lies simply in having encouraged people to look abroad at different foods.

A new development in Elizabeth's writing occurred soon after she began working for the paper with a request from Leonard Russell of the *Sunday Times*. In the introduction to *An Omelette and a Glass of Wine* she recalled Russell asking, '"Would she review a book?" Appalling me with a task I had never before tackled,' Russell 'proceeded to cajole, coax, persuade' until Elizabeth agreed. 'I don't think he found me very good at reviewing, and given that among his regular reviewers were Cyril Connolly and Raymond Mortimer, it took some courage to even accept the few books he entrusted to me.' Elizabeth reprinted all but one of these pieces in her *An Omelette and a Glass of Wine* collection. These few reviews plus one or two later ones from the *Spectator* which she put in the book are good, concise pieces of criticism. Interestingly, almost every one of them is in some way related to interests which were to preoccupy Elizabeth in years to come: the restaurant in France, Middle Eastern food, and English food.

A related interest was highlighted by the first book she was sent. This was a slim volume called *Home Baked* (Faber, 1954) by Celia and George Scurfield and Elizabeth found that 'The book is a sympathetic one.' So it is, right down to the pleasing, unpretentous exuberance of the yellow and black dust-jacket; the kind of book design Faber

Elizabeth at twenty-two in a publicity photograph. She wrote her credentials on the back: 'Work. 5ft 6ins. Fluent French and German.' She was more than 5ft 6ins.

Lawrence Durrell, writer
and *enfant terrible*.

Tony David 1911–71, Indian Army
Cavalry Officer, married Elizabeth
in 1944.

Elizabeth at her desk at the Ministry of Information in Cairo in 1943.
Note the cigarette in hand and the glasses – always removed for photographs.

Veronica Nicholson, the dedicatee
of Elizabeth's first book, in Italy
at the end of the war.

Anne Scott-James, editor of
Harper's Bazaar, in about 1949 when
she published Elizabeth's first article.

Viola Johnson. She and her husband
Arthur looked after Elizabeth in Italy.

The painter Derek Hill,
photographed by his friend
Cecil Beaton in the 1970s.

The Eggs by Cedric Morris
was donated by Elizabeth to
the Tate Gallery.

Right: The first edition
of *French Country Cooking*,
designed and illustrated
by John Minton.

The first edition of *A Book of Mediterranean Food*, published in 1950.
The jacket was again designed and illustrated by John Minton.

The Provençal 'Castle of Otranto' where Elizabeth stayed in 1950.

George and Judith Lassalle on their
wedding day, June 1950.

The photographer
and interior designer
Anthony Denney in 1960.
He collaborated with
Elizabeth for many years.

The window of Elizabeth's shop with a display designed by the artist
Gilli Gretton. Elizabeth called her 'a genius' for it.

Elizabeth in her drawing-room,
photographed by Cecil Beaton.

Doreen Thornton, Anthony Denney
and Elizabeth in the mid-1970s.

Elizabeth in her kitchen, drawn by John Ward RA in 1958.

Judy and Hugh Johnson.

Elizabeth photographed by
Derek Hill in the mid-1960s.

Above: Elizabeth with Squeaker, her beloved cat, photographed by Cecil Beaton.

Elizabeth's grave in Folkington churchyard. The tombstone was designed and carved by Geoffrey Aldred.

In
fondest
memory
of

ELIZABETH DAVID
C.B.E.
26. Dec. 1913 – 22. May 1992

Daughter of
Rupert Gwynne M.P.
& the Hon. Stella Gwynne
of Wootton Manor. Folkington

Her books on cookery brought joy
and enlightenment to food-lovers
all over the world

excelled at. Elizabeth wrote an enthusiastic review and 'a little research into the history of English bread-making proved instructive'. She said: 'For at least 250 years the bad quality of English bread has been notorious' and cited a nineteenth-century writer, Eliza Acton – who was beginning to take on heroic status for her – saying that our bread was noted 'both at home and abroad, for want of its genuineness and the faulty mode of preparation'.

Elizabeth agreed with the Scurfields that 'the only remedy for those who rail against the travesties of ' "genuine wholesome bread" sold by bakers is the same as it has always been. It must be made at home.' As it turned out, her review helped to sell many copies of the little book on bread. Writing about it again in 1984 she said, 'It has gone into many editions since, is still in print . . . and must have helped thousands of readers to learn how to make their own bread.' She added the generous comment: 'For me the book eventually opened up a whole new field of study and of cookery.' Although this little volume triggered off in Elizabeth a serious interest in bread-making, it was to be several years before it became an obsession, and finally a book.

Long before these events were to take place, in 1960 Elizabeth brought out another book, by far her longest so far; the culmination of much travel, research and thought. Published by Michael Joseph, it was called *French Provincial Cooking* and in the opinion of many is Elizabeth's masterpiece. The book is undoubtedly a very fine achievement for its great knowledge of French culinary developments and provincial traditions, thoughtfully and beautifully written down. Indeed, probably no other English person had ever managed to convey these matters with such authority and enthusiasm. This was the considered development of what Elizabeth had begun in *French Country Cooking* nine years earlier. The French too regard the book with respect. While in England France's self-appointed gastronomic respresentative, André Simon, hosted a lunch in Elizabeth's honour at the book's publication.

French Provincial Cooking was based on years of familiarity with French food – eating in France, living and cooking in France – and a deep knowledge of the cookery literature; the bibliography is exhaustive and demonstrates Elizabeth's impressive range. She describes the success of the French between the world wars at rescuing their regional cooking, initiated by such men as Curnonsky, Marcel Rouff and Austin de Croze. But she also makes the salient point (of which these dedicated men were aware), that this would have turned into an exercise in nostalgia if there had not existed in the provinces of France the wherewithal to effect their task of preservation. Elizabeth writes here with coherence and understanding about something which was an essential aspect of her motivation and had been an essential, albeit unarticulated, spur to her writing from the very beginning. What she says about France applies, more or less, to all the Mediterranean countries about which she had written in reaction against the depredations which the industrial revolution had wrought upon the traditions of her own land.

> France is still largely an agricultural country and the right conditions for the preservation of their traditions still prevail. These traditions are constantly being renewed from within; the professional cooks and the housewives adapt the old methods to changing tastes and altered conditions without thereby standardizing all the food ... the tourist organizations work hard to foster their own local products and cookery magazines publicize them in a sane and sober way, so it is not so surprising that the regional cookery of France is a profitable and flourishing industry as well as a beneficent one.

Although she says that good food is not always as good as it was, for those prepared to look: 'One of the great points about the cookery of France is that it is so extraordinarily varied.'

With this in mind she continues: 'To compile a comprehensive volume of French regional recipes would take a lifetime of work and research', and she concludes that it would still be impossible 'because ... cookery is continually evolving'. Elizabeth tells her readers that she has selected recipes 'which have pleased me and which can be reproduced in English kitchens without too much difficulty'. Although 'difficult' is a relative term, her judgement is a true one for those with care and time to give. She creates possibilities where before there were none; she describes, draws pictures, instructs, until the regions of France become a manageable and comprehensive map across which her reader is drawn with that enticing sensual prose, and the desire to make these dishes becomes an urgent and pressing need.

'We ate all the way through *French Provincial Cooking* over the late Fifties,' says Judith Lassalle. 'Elizabeth would invite us all around for endless meals. She would come herself or send things down to us at Sandwich too. We were guinea pigs – "It's for four or six" she would say. "Let me know how far it goes round . . ."' Pies, prunes, plums, apricot things. A woman came down to do drawings of the things Elizabeth made. (These are some of the drawings of unpretentious clarity by Juliette Renny which head each section of the book. Kitchen equipment: pots, tians, marmites, mandolins, knives, ramekins, fish kettles and much more are illustrated.)

It is in this book that Elizabeth describes her first and subsequently revelatory experiences of French food, as a teenager in that claustrophobic Parisian household practising such exquisitely refined greed. It is here that she gathers together her *Vogue* articles and gives us a beautifully clear résumé of the food of each region of France. Amongst those she discusses: Paris, the Ile de France, Normandy . . . its beautiful northern fish . . . Breton artichokes, 'shining leeks; and fluffy green-white cauliflower . . . Carefully bunched salad herbs' and with them all we recall the memories of the France of her youth: Brittany where there is fine salt-marsh lamb, 'Nantais ducklings served with the tiny green peas or the baby turnips of the district . . . the delicious fresh cream cheeses called *crémets* which are eaten with sugar and fresh cream. . . . At restaurants in Nantes, Tours, Angers . . . Amboise and many other places along the banks of the Loire,' she describes 'the unique speciality of this country, the famous *beurre blanc* . . . Anjou's great contribution to the regional cookery of France.'

It remains clear that Provence still holds a special place in her heart. She is sufficiently aware of this to write: 'If I seem to be biased in favour of the food of the South, it is because the country itself has for me such a very powerful appeal.' It could not be otherwise when so much of her own development was bound up with this plenteous, beautiful, at times parched, sometimes 'bleak and savage' region. A single card to Felicité from Alsace in May 1957 sums up her feelings: 'Terribly cold, country rather like Switzerland. Otherwise all going well, plenty of good food, but would rather be in Provence.' Her piece on Provence in the book is close to a creed, the nearest she gets to monotheism:

> Provence . . . to which I am always returning, next week, next year, any day now, as soon as I can get on a train . . . now and again the vision of golden tiles on a round southern roof, or of some warm, stony, herb-scented hill-side will rise out of my kitchen pots with the smell of a piece of orange peel scenting a beef stew . . .
>
> But to regard the food of Provence as just a release from routine, a fierce, wild riot of flavour and colour, is to oversimplify it and grossly to mistake its nature. For it is not primitive food; it is civilized without being over-civilized. That is to say, it has natural taste, smell, texture, and much character. Often it looks beautiful, too. What it amounts to is that it is the rational, right and proper food for human beings to eat.

Lorraine, its capital the beautiful Nancy, launches Elizabeth into a superb example of her Proustian-style reveries; beginning with the bakeries and pastry shops whose enticing smells beckon her inside to buy early-morning croissants. Here she is beguiled by the counters piled with 'flat round orange and gilt tins, glinting and shining like little lamps in the pallid sunshine'. Filled with the *Bergamottes de Nancy*, 'little boiled sweets, scented with essence of Bergamot . . . one of the oldest specialities of Nancy . . . and as I walked away carrying my pretty little tin of childish sweets I thought how often some trivial little discovery colours and alters in one's mind the whole aspect of a city or a countryside.'

With Proust already in our minds she next tells us: 'At the little town of Commercy originated the small, fragile, shell-shaped cakes called *madeleines* so beloved of French children, and which have become celebrated in French literature because it was the taste of a *madeleine* dipped in a cup of [lime] tea which Proust used as the starting point of his long journey back into the past.' A signpost to

Epinal triggers another of her own childhood memories 'of primitive coloured pictures and sheets of brightly uniformed soldiers, the *images d'Épinal* which have the same primitive charm as our penny-plain twopence-coloured prints'. And one travels with Elizabeth in her mind's eye to the decorations she made from the same little paper soldiers for the cabin of the *Evelyn Hope*; and further back still to the Wootton nursery of her childhood.

This and many more such interludes, along with the evocations of markets and shops, are the passages which support the recipes; the essential core of the book. Elizabeth later called these fine pieces 'informative background material, local colour and general chatter'. A shift of orientation has taken place here, and also a degree of unawareness on Elizabeth's part. It was these passages as much as the recipes themselves which gained her devotees. For them she was not only creating a recipe which they could replicate in their kitchens, she was describing a world which could be imagined and summoned up amidst the cooking pots. This is several steps on from *Mediterranean Food*. Elizabeth, like her first readers, has had to face the world and with it become more of a realist. The talk now is often of reliability, good reputable restaurants, as well as the apparently delightful little discovery down a back street, which may turn out a disaster. Elizabeth now describes these establishments: their dishes, their wines, their quietly remarkable fare; whether a local speciality or a house favourite, with poetry, confidence and authority.

Many of the trips to France for *Vogue*, *House and Garden* and the *Sunday Times*, during the late 1950s, were made with the purpose of discovering more about places with which she was not already familiar. These were the trips taken at the suggestion of 'the original and enlightened Audrey Withers . . . provided with £100 . . . to help cover restaurant meals, hotels, petrol and so on'. Journeys often taken in the company of Doreen and Anthony Denney and: 'even though these trips were very much France on a shoestring, the knowledge I derived from them was valuable'. So also was the dedication with which Doreen supported Elizabeth during these years. In return Elizabeth concluded her acknowledgements by thanking 'my friend Doreen for driving me, with much patience and care, on many rather arduous journeys around and across France in search of good food . . .'

She could not make the central dedication to Doreen because this had already been given: 'To P.H. with love.'

Peter Higgins was a man whom Elizabeth had known for some time. Indeed when he was given the dedication of *French Provincial Cooking* their liaison was already several years old. Nonetheless he was to be another of those doomed to disappoint her. Some friends have said that, even more than the lover who returned to North America after being injured in Egypt during the war, this was the man whom Elizabeth most deeply cared for. He was a wealthy importer, of conventional good looks, whose pleasant personality nevertheless seems to have been sufficiently vague beside Elizabeth's for her friends to be unable to describe him with any particular verve. Some say he doted upon her, others say that he was undynamic and boring. More than one friend thought the reason he did not eventually marry her was that his liking for money and the life-style a richer woman could bring him was greater than his love for Elizabeth.

In conversation Peter Trier recalled: 'I did think it a bit odd Elizabeth being attracted to a man like that . . . Liz was far too intelligent for most men, she could run rings around most of them intellectually. She was frightening, because she was both intelligent and intellectual.' Perhaps, like the lover in America, it was not only a matter of money but also the comprehension that he was not strong enough to prevent Elizabeth consuming him that kept Peter Higgins from marrying her.

The dedication of her book to this man is particularly poignant because in this same year, 1960, she was also finally divorced from Tony. Ironically, he was an old friend of Elizabeth's present lover; they had in fact been fellow-soldiers in India. In 1960, in order for a divorce to be granted it was necessary to prove that there were 'sufficient grounds'; one of the parties must be deemed to be at fault. As it was Elizabeth who took out the divorce petition, she had to prove Tony to be at fault; this involved detailed descriptions of his errors, probable adulteries and other misdemeanours. However true the criticisms levelled at Tony may have been, to a large extent this was an academic exercise necessitated by the requirements of divorce law.

Elizabeth and Tony's marriage had ceased to be a real one years earlier; Elizabeth certainly had maintained longer and short-term affairs for the whole of this period, and the two had not effectively lived together for several years. Above all it should not be forgotten that Elizabeth was as quickly bored by poor Tony as her friends predicted she would be. Pleasant though their short conjugal interludes may afterwards have been, their marriage did not really last for many years beyond India. Elizabeth was irritated by Tony's inability to keep up with her and his failure to maintain her. But here she was playing a game of double standards. She wanted a marriage of convenience yet couldn't support the consequences of it for herself longer than she had whilst in India. Elizabeth was quite conversant with what Tony was and was not; nonetheless, pragmatism for her was not sufficient. Her mistake had been to pretend to herself that she had enough self-discipline both to successfully manage Tony and herself into the bargain. It was too much to ask and in her heart Elizabeth knew it wouldn't work, as more than one of her letters had revealed in those weeks of indecision before her marriage.

According to his nephew Patrick Lewin, Tony now owned a club, The Thousand and One Nights in Tangiers, with a livery stables attached and patrons such as Barbara Hutton. Increasing restrictions became too irksome and he sold up. He married again and with his wife Létie lived on Ibiza, where he owned another club/restaurant. Eventually Tony and Létie settled on the Riviera and here he died in 1967. Elizabeth and Tony appear to have remained in some contact with one another; on at least one buying trip for the shop Elizabeth and Renée visited Tony and his wife Létie for lunch.

There seems little doubt that with her divorce and the dedication of her book to him, Elizabeth was in a sense offering herself to Peter Higgins. Their liaison continued for some time after 1960. Needless to say, it was not Elizabeth to whom Peter Higgins made an offer of marriage; but instead the other woman who had been in the background for some time. Elizabeth and he continued seeing each other for several years, although less frequently following Higgins' marriage. When it finally came to an end Elizabeth felt heartbroken. 'She rang me in tears, she said Peter is gone, she rang everybody,' says Alix Coleman.

'Oh, Elizabeth was so fond of him; she was devastated when he went,' says another friend.

Although Elizabeth was always responsive to men her drive to control and manipulate worked against her when she provoked their sense of self-preservation, sending them into retreat. In the process Elizabeth was sometimes undoubtedly used. Coupled with her undoubted attraction to men, Elizabeth clearly also felt ambivalence toward them. This other response to men, sometimes verging on dismissive, was noticed by some women as quite pronounced. Caroline Trier remarked to the author: 'She liked intelligent men but there was this feeling that women were really much more interesting and ultimately worthwhile. She was always very pro-woman which was unusual for then . . . she used to say: "I think that a woman's position is terrible."'

Women have repeatedly remarked on how extraordinarily supportive she was to them in times of stress. On reflection they are inclined to agree that the support was strongest when it involved conflict with a man. 'Oh, if you had a bit of a moan about your husband, she was *absolutely* behind you. One had the strong feeling that men were the inferior breed.'

In common with any number of other women Elizabeth appears to have believed that they were ultimately more respect-worthy than men. Whether from greater respect, or simply an identification with an expansive and unprejudicial life force, at different times during her life Elizabeth appears to have entered into a lesbian relationship with another woman. These relationships appear in no way to have been mutually exclusive and should probably be described as one element of her complex personality rather than an *essential* part of it. Elizabeth could never, for instance, be described as having an aversion to men, her response to them was much too sincerely and consistently positive for that ascription to apply.

During the first five months of 1960 *Vogue* published a discursive series by Elizabeth on the markets of France, in which she combines again more of the detailed practice, the whereabouts of the produce, as well as the romance. Cavaillon, Yvetot, Montpellier, Martigues, Valence; under Elizabeth's mellow pen the names of these great centres for the buying and selling of local produce and foods ring out, as she said herself of 'the little towns round about Valence . . . like peals of bells compelling you to go and look at them'. And the reader was further intrigued and enticed by the accompanying pictures. The research for this series had been done on a two-week marathon with Doreen across France, with Anthony and Alex in tow to take photographs.

Doreen had been permitted 'to jump the queue for one of the first Triumph Heralds if I promised to write an article for their magazine'. And so it was that she featured Elizabeth's and her journey around the French markets in an article entitled 'Woman Driver's 2300 miles in a Herald'. One of the most fashionable new sports cars, the Herald created great interest as they sped through France. Doreen knew little about cars but satisfied her regular male interrogators with the statement that 'It was the first British car produced in any quantity to have independent suspension on all four wheels. Whilst the other members of the party were taking photographs of the market, the farmers and market police were gathered round the Triumph . . .'

Elizabeth's article in September *Vogue* on autumn fruits and preserves, a subject always dear to Elizabeth's heart, is accompanied by one of those sumptuous Denney photographs set in her Halsey Street kitchen. Anthony and Elizabeth always discussed how the photograph would be set up and, with their combined instinct for the best image for the moment, they unerringly succeeded. Denney's photographs accurately reflected Elizabeth's work in their contrast between the absolute simplicity of white plates and terracotta dishes of olives, radishes, fresh butter, new bread, golden and white halved boiled eggs, a green salad or a bowl of fruit; or the impression of autumnal largesse, here with an enormous *galette* of glistening jewel-like fruits on the table. As a backdrop, on the wall is a strange and Surreal image: a painted fish, cutlery and red plates stuck on to a canvas. Just as Surrealism's unsettling Alice-through-the-looking-glass displacement of reality would have a predictable appeal to someone of Elizabeth's personality, so this picture by the modern Surrealist Coetze (also collected by Anthony Denney) was one of her favourite possessions. Shortly after the publication of *French Provincial Cooking* Elizabeth very reluctantly agreed to be interviewed about it on Manchester radio by the novelist Elizabeth Jane Howard. Brian Redhead was also involved.

'The programme was about people who had just published books,' says Doreen. 'There was a young girl of about fifteen, Liz and some others. Liz came to stay with us because we were then living in Nottinghamshire. I'd persuaded her to do it and had to drive her over to the studios. She was *determined* not to go. It was spite. We stopped at a friend's on the way . . . had champagne, that helped. Elizabeth Jane Howard was very nice to us . . . met us, etc. Foolishly though she gave us lunch in the staff canteen. Well . . . sandwiches like *that*. It was a bit silly of her, and Liz was terribly rude about it . . . She was awful on the programme . . . sounded like a bad-tempered school ma'am and said she never wanted to do it again. I said, "Liz, I'm terribly sorry."

' "That was awful, wasn't it?"

'I said, "Yes." '

Elizabeth's style of public performance did not improve with the increase of her reputation; with age it became worse. Her first and only appearance on television came about only a few years before her death, when she agreed, very reluctantly, to be interviewed by the wine writer Jancis Robinson. The resulting programme was a disaster, and Elizabeth came across as a woman of most unsympathetic mien. Nevertheless, for the present Elizabeth's poor radio performance was to have little effect on the reception of *French Provincial Cooking*. It was a great success. Charles Pick, then co-managing director at Michael Joseph, recalled to the author a dinner with Allen Lane, founder of Penguin, at which he said, 'You've published a wonderful book.'

At the end of 1960 Elizabeth gave up her column for *Vogue* and, with enormous relief, also left the *Sunday Times*. She had appreciated the intelligent and patient editing of Leonard Russell, but could no longer support the bullying and tyranny of her immediate editor, Ernestine Carter. Elizabeth had some time previously become friends with a bright young journalist, Alix Coleman, who successfully persuaded her to move to a paper apparently inappropriate as a vehicle for Elizabeth David's melodious patrician voice. This was the *Sunday Dispatch*, to which Alix Coleman herself had recently moved after being subjected to regular persecution by Ernestine Carter at *The Sunday Times*. She told the author:

> Ernestine was terrible. The first time I was summoned to see her my speciality was interviewing. Anybody, from personalities to Barnardo's children. My pieces went down well so Ernestine called me in and told me I was doing too many interviews and that I'd have to cut them down. She would cut my copy mercilessly. If she thought someone was doing well she would stop them doing it. I left because of her. Margaret Costa took over from Elizabeth. Elizabeth told her that Ernestine was poisonous and she would be well advised to keep away, but Margaret thought she could manage. A couple of weeks later Liz told me that Margaret had telephoned her to say: 'You were wrong about Ernestine. She's much worse than you said.'
>
> Anyway, I left because of Ernestine. Anne Edwards was now the women's page editor on the *Sunday Dispatch* and I told her about Elizabeth; Walter Hayes the editor wanted Elizabeth and we managed to get her for the paper.

Later, in *An Omelette and a Glass of Wine*, Elizabeth herself wrote: 'In 1961, freed from the *Sunday Times* and the monthly stints for the Condé Nast magazines, I worked for a time for the moribund *Sunday Dispatch* and wrote my first contribution for the *Spectator* and, unexpectedly perhaps, thoroughly enjoyed writing for both publications.' Her articles for the *Sunday Dispatch* were as close as Elizabeth came in her writing to the opposite end of the social spectrum from the fashionably tasteful confines of *Vogue* and the intellectually more prestigious *Spectator*.

The *Dispatch* was the Sunday paper of the *Daily Mail*. It was 'an earlier version of the *Sun*. With sleaze, girls, actresses and illustrated serialized versions of novels,' says Alix Coleman. 'Lord Rothermere had been told to write clean stories so they got us. Anne Edwards and I came from the *Daily Express*, and there was Kate Whitehorn too. With Elizabeth we were supposed to represent quality, style. Elizabeth had suffered so much under Ernestine that she was much more malleable now. She'd learnt a lot because of the *Sunday Times*.'

And again we see Elizabeth's ability to cross the social divide as few of her contemporaries or friends could do. Her patrician voice is put aside and, alongside pictures of Marilyn Monroe in her shapeliest dresses and would-be Brigitte Bardot girls modelling corsets (precursors of 'Page Three'), Elizabeth steps out with a bright, unpatronizing style. She is still her authoritative and sometimes acerbic self but the language is jauntier, more down-to-earth. In short, says Alix Coleman, 'She understood what was required of her. She wrote these beautiful simple recipes' in a clear straightforward style, complemented by equally straightforward incitements to cook well.

Elizabeth's articles were sufficiently autobiographical to keep the gossip column devotees happy: in March 1961 we are told that she has had to refuse the services of her interior designer friend (Anthony Denney) to reorganize her kitchen. She describes it as: 'a rather barn-like room with three outside walls and the fourth entirely taken up by french windows looking out on nothing but a blank wall'. In wishing to 'turn it into a lighter, warmer, more convenient room to work in – and to entertain in . . .' she wants also 'to preserve its character . . . My kitchen's assets are its size . . . and its parquet floor . . . and old English pine dressers I've collected over the years and the massive table 5ft. 6ins x 3ft. 6ins. with a 2in. thick scrubbed wood top which I had made a few months ago to go on an old one I already owned – a magnificent table both to work on and to sit at.' She has modern spotlights set in, 'vital' heating and a new china sink and cupboard underneath. She buys 'a fine, old 19th century pine cupboard . . . to replace that battered old dresser . . . and a hard wood plate and dish-rack which I've had fixed on the wall above one of the draining boards.' (With the exception of the 'ravishing pink called Columbine' with which she warms up the walls – she later called it 'corset pink' – this was very much the way Elizabeth's kitchen remained for many years to come.)

In December Elizabeth was off to stay in Ireland with the intensely sociable painter Derek Hill in his expansive Donegal house, St Columb's. She told Félicité she was collected off the ferry at Belfast by another guest, John Bryson, who was extremely well-connected and never stopped talking. Elizabeth found the swift, friendly service in the Irish shops much to her liking after London; her replacement of a forgotten petticoat 'would have taken me three hours in Harrods – and John Bryson went in to a confectioner's shop to buy sweets for the domestics while I was posting a letter and it was all over in half a minute.'

Elizabeth and Derek Hill had become friends through Lesley O'Malley. In Donegal Derek was blessed for many years with his cook, the late Gracie McDermott, a warm and generous-spirited local woman devoted both to her cooking pots and her employer. He was a discerning and regular traveller and returned from around the world with recipes for her to try. The food at St Columb's was renowned, and Gracie loved the constant round of guests and meals Derek's hospitality entailed. After Christmas Elizabeth was writing to Felicité from her bed, one of her favourite places in which to work, with Derek's huge golden retriever lying in front of her fire. (For years Felicité kept a spaniel upstairs at Halsey Street but Elizabeth's great love was always cats. Her own, Squeaker, had been a present from a litter produced by a cat of Doreen's. Elizabeth was utterly devoted to this cat and often mentioned details for her care whilst away. Squeaker appears in the Beaton photograph on the back cover of *French Provincial Cooking*. After many years Squeaker's death left Elizabeth distraught. 'Oh, she was inconsolable for a time,' says Doreen. 'I was glad I wasn't around when it happened. It would have been too much to bear.')

Elizabeth continues her letter: 'Terrific frost on the ground, and I don't suppose anything will stop Derek having a skating party on the lake if he can possibly organize it in between the lunch, tea, drinks and dinner parties which scarcely cease for an instant . . .' She made several visits to St Columb's; its combination of restfulness, stimulation and good food suited her. She tells Felicité, while fretting about Squeaker, to find 'a whole box full of white wine Veronica has given me, very nice and just the thing for visitors . . . that Muscat is not for every day.'

The quiet luxury of Derek Hill's hospitality was a pleasant relief to her. For the present it suited her, relinquishing the responsibility of having to put 'saucepan to stove'. She was later to use some of Gracie McDermott's recipes, saying that she was 'the greatest natural cook' she had ever met. Gracie herself – photographed each year by

Derek's friend Cecil Beaton when he came to stay – found Elizabeth's books 'a great help to me because she explained things so nice and so beautiful that I was able to follow them'.

Back in London Elizabeth was again at work on pieces for the *Spectator*, a publication for which she truly enjoyed writing. Looking back in *An Omelette and a Glass of Wine*, in 1984, she wrote that: 'they were stimulating years for me. Well, look at the company I found myself in. Katherine Whitehorn, Cyril Ray, Bernard Levin . . . Brian Inglis was my first editor . . . and at the end the lamented Ian McLeod.' In characteristic style, with her compulsion to settle old scores, Elizabeth remarks on the sharp contrast between the late Ernestine Carter's 'cutting shears' and what at the *Spectator* she found to be 'the co-operation, support and on occasions most beneficial editing by Cyril Ray and Katherine Whitehorn'.

The *Spectator* pieces were 'in the main topical . . . all over the place, from reviews of eccentric books . . . to harmless fun at the expense of restaurant guides and the baiting of public relations persons who made imbecile suggestions', to encounters with hitherto unknown foods and 'delicious wines'. Elizabeth's fine-tuned wit and and tendency toward satire were particularly well suited to a magazine such as the *Spectator*. Her protests are therefore disingenuous when she writes that her fun and baiting were 'harmless'. They were no such thing and the furious response which her badinage and satire some-times provoked from those concerned was exactly their purpose: to draw attention to the 'disregard for the authenticity of other people's and indeed our own culinary specialities' and much else here of a second-rate nature to do with food. In a piece called '*Franglais*', written for the magazine in 1965, she gets right under the skin of the differences between the essential Englishness and Frenchness of dishes, via a brilliant anatomy of a revered English (as it turns out, French) accompaniment; Cumberland sauce.

Elizabeth's friend Veronica Nicholson, like several others, believes 'Elizabeth wrote some of her best pieces for the *Spectator*. They were so funny. I've always thought Elizabeth a very good essayist. She couldn't handle a really long piece. In a way her books are bits and pieces. I told her that I had come to that conclusion. I don't know if she was pleased. I said I thought she played a beautiful minuet but not a concerto . . . that she was something like Lamb and Hazlitt and all those lovely writers whom she despised. She wasn't a story-teller.'

Amongst friends she was renowned and amongst enemies (by now she was collecting a fair few) feared for her hatred of anything or anyone with a whiff of pretension about them. Patrick Woodcock asked her to dinner with 'a fat old queen who was very knowledgeable. He came to dinner and Elizabeth said to me afterwards, "Thank you for asking me, Patrick . . . I was pleased to meet that phoney." '

Historical pieces; in a number of cases to prove of considerable significance in Elizabeth's life, and a rash of quirky reviews of eccentric books, were the other topics she dwelt on for the *Spectator*. There were books such as Sir Harry Luke's *The Tenth Muse*, first published by Putnam in 1954. Elizabeth commends the *Muse* and says it has 'the collector's madness . . . Few authors are as modest as Sir Harry Luke . . . and fewer still provide the stimulus, the improbable information [it is replete with extraordinary asides], the travellers' tales, the new visions which to me make his book a true collector's piece.' Luke had been a Governor of Malta and knew Elizabeth's sister Priscilla well. In these post-colonial days his book is a strange bird indeed. We catch a glimpse of the man himself in a photograph, where he sits like an intrepid mouse beside the benevolent giant, Queen of Tonga.

Viola Johnson's husband Arthur had died in 1958 and in 1962 Viola decided to come to England and try her hand at work. Accordingly, she bought a bookshop in Museum Street near the British Museum, whilst living in Sloane Avenue with her son John. Viola and Elizabeth had remained close friends since those days on Capri, and almost every Sunday Elizabeth went to eat lunch with them. John recalls: 'My mother and Elizabeth went on a number of trips around Piedmont and a visit to Venice together in the 1960s. They were an extraordinary pair. My mother became most eccentric, would tell people she was leaving town when she wasn't at all so that she wouldn't be disturbed.' In the autumn of 1963 a trip with Viola to Alba in Italy for the truffle festival, produced the article 'Truflesville

Regis' for the *Spectator*; according to Elizabeth written hurriedly. Viola criticized the Italian spelling mistakes and corrected them for a later reprinting, as she had done so conscientiously for *Italian Food*. Elizabeth's journey to Italy with Viola ended with an inspirational visit to Turin, where she unearthed a little confectioner's shop selling those candied walnuts of obscure and ancient Italian tradition. She carried some triumphantly back home to England.

John Johnson describes how 'The trip to Venice produced risottos from Elizabeth when I'd go round there. Over time they became ever more minimalist, with eventually very little in them. Two peas and one prawn. You know, that sort of thing.'

John meanwhile had decided he wanted to be a bookseller and went to learn with Felicité, now working in another bookshop which she had helped to set up with the owner, John Sandoe, in 1957. Combined with her persistent habit of reading, Felicité's expertise in the buying and selling of books was considerable (she ran the paperback department at Sandoe's) and John recalls her warning him: 'If you work in a bookshop you'll never read a book again.' John ignored the warning and spent several months in the shop with Felicité. 'She wore her hair drawn back, and tweedy skirts and knitted tops. Much more a sensible country look than Elizabeth's. She rode about Chelsea on a bicycle and talked in very precise, clipped tones. She was very protective of her sister. She didn't cook, wasn't interested in it. Felicité was a lovely person. Her attitude to Elizabeth was rather a subservient one.

'A certain Mr Marks bought frequently from the shop, and he often seemed to find things wrong with his purchases and would bring them back. Felicité was always very patient about this and would exchange them. One day something came up about his name and he said to Felicité, "Don't you know who I am?"

'"No."

'"Why, Marks of Marks and Spencer."

'He was so pleased that Felicité had been so civilized without knowing who he was that he immediately asked her to tea at his house. That way they became good friends.'

Elizabeth was also about to make a new friend. Having spent three years as a staff writer for Condé Nast publications, in 1963 the young Hugh Johnson (to become a renowned expert on wine, and later horticulture) took over from André Simon, retiring editor of *Wine and Food*. The Spring issue was the first under Hugh Johnson's auspices with André Simon now Editor in Chief and Harry Yoxall Consultant. In his generous posthumous tribute to Elizabeth Hugh Johnson said: 'I first read her articles in the *Spectator*. . . . "Pale soups the colour of summer frocks," she writes, and the soups, and the mood, stick fast in your memory. I trusted her completely, and I believe that is the secret of her writing. It is transparent; never affected. Her readers cannot doubt for a moment that she is telling the truth. She is a writer who plunges straight in. Time and again I have picked up one of her articles and felt the strong grip that marks the start of a good story.

'And she could be as funny as Stella Gibbons. The first piece in *An Omelette and a Glass of Wine* . . . tells the story of the dire conditions that provoked her to start writing . . . in Ross on Wye in 1947, and Miss D's catastrophic antique shop where the proprietress laid waste her own toppling stock with every clumsy movement; and it still makes me shake with laughter.

'An ambitious editor could not *live* without such ravishing writing. I invaded Halsey Street . . . with little real idea of what I was asking for; just wanting my readers to feel the same exhilaration as I did.'

'Reading the introduction to *French Provincial Cooking* inspired me as a wine writer. I thought: That's how I want to write about wine.'

Hugh wonders why she made him welcome, sat him at her kitchen table and began 'to hypnotize me with the loaf she had just baked, the pale butter that asked for nothing else; the olives, the ungrand but totally vivid glass of wine I had scarcely heard of. Probably out of respect for André [Simon had insisted that Elizabeth be invited to his retirement party], and possibly because *Wine and Food* was a vehicle for longer pieces than the *Spectator*, and for more of the history and literature of cooking which was becoming more and more her passion . . . We got on like a house on fire and before long we were going out to meals together.'

Hugh Johnson was correct in saying that Elizabeth wanted a

venue more amenable to the increasing length and more historical nature of her writing, but he was too modest in saying that she responded to him as she did simply out of respect for André Simon. Elizabeth saw and appreciated his enthusiasm, knowledge and willingness to learn. Her nephew Stephen Grey's assertion that 'Elizabeth didn't like people who didn't know what they were talking about' concurs with the opinion of everyone who knew her. 'She was intimidating to those who didn't.' 'Don't put up with nonsense merchants,' she would say to Stephen. As long as they were sincere and not 'phoney' and had something to offer which interested Elizabeth she was interested and interesting. There was now a growing band of younger devotees who, like Hugh Johnson, became her friends. One who later fell into this category, Alan Davidson, remembers an occasion when he and his wife Jane invited her to lunch with a Billingsgate fishmonger and his wife. 'Elizabeth got on famously with the fishmonger and his wife. They talked about fish, but also about family matters. Elizabeth could be a very sympathetic person; she was very curious about other people's lives.'

Hugh Johnson began his editorship of *Wine and Food* in the Spring of 1963 with a new cover design: huge bright lime-green script on a cream ground. In the very next issue, Summer, he had secured a long article by Elizabeth, entitled 'An Anthology of Ice Creams: these recipes cover briefly the history of ice-cream making, from 1720 to 1963'. This immediately demonstrated Elizabeth's wide knowledge of sources, French and English: Menon, Emy, Hannah Glasse, Alexis Soyer, etc. As Hugh Johnson said, 'She was very accurate . . . the truth was very important.'

Nineteen sixty-three was a particularly hectic year for Elizabeth. In the early spring she had made what turned out to be a disastrous commitment and one from which she fled early, with the help of Veronica Nicholson and her husband John. A rich homosexual, Rex Henry, recently married to a young and beautiful French model, was living in Marrakesh. He wished to entertain on a scale commensurate with his aspirations and employed Elizabeth to teach his cook to produce French cuisine. From the start Elizabeth and Rex Henry miscommunicated. With some apprehension regarding the cooking, she had agreed to stay in this ménage, lodged in her own apartment attached to the luxurious house. She saw the venture as a means of making a good sum of money and getting herself out of England to the sun. She was also curious to look again at the Mediterranean. In part this was out of nostalgia, but intertwined with that was also the urge to observe at first hand again, the kinds of place responsible for what she would eventually describe as 'the English love-affair with Eastern food and Arabian Nights ingredients'.

Morocco, only recently independent of France, was, like Alexandria, a hotch-potch of races: Phoenicians, Romans, Arabs, Jews, Muslims, black Africans, Spaniards, Portuguese, and finally the French; all of whom had left their mark in a country situated in the north-west corner of Africa yet only 8 miles from Europe. For centuries the cities of Morocco had been caught in the hustling economic and cultural Mediterranean cross-fire. Marrakesh . . . with an admixture of ancient custom and modern aspiration, a city of extraordinary beauty and wretched poverty; a city where can be found a dusty clearing at night hung with lamps lighting up the bustle of snake charmers, acrobats, beggars, competing with the call of artisans, water-sellers and food stalls, for the money of passers-by. This is called Djemma el Fna, the 'assembly place of artisans'.

But whether of rich or poor Elizabeth saw little of life outside the kitchen, and the allotted time which she had agreed to devote to her dubious task quickly became an onerous and frustrating burden from which she chafed to be free. She wrote to Felicité saying: 'Don't think I can make my escape until April 4th – from Tangier via Gibraltar – London. They are trying their best to be decent to me, but they are just perfectly awful people.' She knew she should never have gone, and vowed it would be the last time she went against her instincts and undertook any venture just for the sake of getting to the sun. The weather was the most perfect she could remember since Cairo, and she found the country fascinating, but, as she was in the kitchen or the back of a car the whole time, it hardly made any difference. She had not been allowed out to the souk or any shops except the market. The cook was charming, and good, but the task hopeless – her employers wanted elegant international food, composed of ingredients unavailable in Marakesh. (It is in any case unlikely Elizabeth would have agreed to instruct in the preparation of one of

the types of cooking against which she had spent so long reacting.)
Rex Henry refused to listen to anything she told him about cooking
and instead 'talked as if he were in the nineteenth century'.

At the same time Veronica and John had arrived for a holiday to
explore Morocco. 'John didn't want to meet up with Elizabeth, but I
told him it would be impossible not to. We were staying at this large
hotel where one stayed and it was inevitable she would discover we
were there. She couldn't bear it with these people any longer – got
chippy about any possible kind of servant status . . . they had dinners
to which she wasn't invited. They had certain social pretensions,
which annoyed Elizabeth intensely. She begged us to save her, so we
took her off on a journey through the Atlas Mountains for some days.
It was very beautiful and Elizabeth was very obliging. But she did
always have to have a butt. I put her in the front with John and I
was reading out guide books from the back. She would keep making
terrible fun of me . . . quite unfairly . . . I think it was part of her
defences, she simply had to put something up . . .

'We stopped the night at such a beautiful town on the coast,
called Mogador. It was whitewashed, very Arabic-influenced with
those lovely arches and then that French Gauloise blue and then there
was brown. We went round the market. She would have been up at
four if necessary to do something like that. We all loved markets but
John was into a passion to get it over with and Elizabeth was in a
passion to stay. It was so *illuminating* to be there with Elizabeth.
When I came home I made our ridiculous kitchen in St Anne's
Terrace out in these colours. It was Elizabeth really, she had such an
artistic view of things it influenced one.'

Back in England, after three weeks away and recovering from a
complicated bout of flu, Elizabeth wrote in her regular *Spectator* article
about a small and learned publication's attempts to classify and
illustrate the edible fish of Tunisia and the central Mediterranean. She
said that the author, a young diplomat, Alan Davidson, then on a
posting to Tunisia, 'has a gift for conveying memorable information
in a way so effortless that his book makes lively reading for its own
sake.' A colleague of Alan Davidson's at the embassy in Tunis, Roger
Eland, had worked with Elizabeth at the Ministry of Information in

Cairo during the war, and sent her the booklet. Elizabeth's involvement in Alan Davidson's fish interests continued and as he subsequently wrote in his book of culinary essays, *A Kipper With My Tea* (Macmillan, 1988): '. . . years later when it had long been out of print she persuaded her editor, Jill Norman, that it should be turned into a proper book covering the whole Mediterranean.' This was *Mediterranean Seafood* (Penguin, 1972), acclaimed as the most authoritative book yet written on the subject.

Elizabeth later wrote of this period in *Spices, Salt and Aromatics in the English Kitchen*, that she had 'enjoyed my compulsory leisure re-reading old favourites in my cookery library'. Some, like Mrs Leyel's *Gentle Art of Cookery*, 'had been my earliest kitchen companions'. Others such as Lord Bute's *Moorish Recipes* were more recent discoveries of which she had written in 1955, in a review for the *Sunday Times*, 'a lovely little book of Moroccan cookery, beautifully written and illustrated . . . A cookery book concerned more with the authenticity of the dishes than with what the English housewife may make of them is a rarity. We are fortunate to get it. It is a collector's find . . . the fine free style in which the recipes are written and set out are most pleasing, and how elegant are the Moorish cooking pots and serving dishes shown in the illustrations.'

Another far more serious reason for Elizabeth's 'compulsory leisure' was that shortly after her recovery from flu she was taken gravely ill. As Doreen says, 'She had been drinking too much spirits. A while previously Liz and I had had this crazy arrangement whereby I came up from Kent several times a week to help her with her papers and filing. Everything was in a terrible mess. She never threw anything out so there were piles and piles of papers and piles of books. It was simply ghastly, and we didn't get much done. But we had some lovely lunches. So many interesting people passed through. Afterwards I had a job working in the Harrods Food Hall and I'd come round for lunch most days.

'One day I went round routinely and there was Lesley [O'Malley] in a terrible state. Liz was lying there trying and unable to speak . . . she couldn't. It was awful. I got the ambulance and then Lesley and I followed it to the hospital [Edward VII]. It was all very dramatic.

She'd had a stroke. Liz was in the same room as the actress Bebe
Daniels. We would sit there making her [Liz] talk. Anyway she got
better very quickly. After that Liz hardly drank spirits.'

Elizabeth made this distressing event known only to her closest
friends; she didn't want it to jeopardize her reputation for working.
Although it was fairly mild and she quickly recovered she was very
young to have experienced an illness of such potential gravity. At the
time of the stroke she was forty-nine. Afterwards her fear, expressed
to Veronica and Judith years before — 'I don't know what I'd do if I
lost my sense of taste' — was partially realized: she could no longer
properly taste salt. One of her future colleagues, Peter Trier, remembers many occasions when Elizabeth would have him testing dishes
for the salt content. Veronica too, remembers testing many times
Elizabeth's favourite recipe (Suleiman's) for salted almonds. 'There'd
be saucers out for you to try with the food salted to different degrees.'

During the same year, 1963, Elizabeth wrote a new introduction
to *Italian Food* and revised the book for a first Penguin paperback
edition. She says:

> During the last decade provision shops and supermarkets selling
> a high proportion of Italian and imported produce have multi-
> plied. In our big towns new Italian restaurants open almost
> monthly. The Espresso Coffee Bar, phenomenon of the early
> Fifties, has developed into the Roman or Neapolitan-type *tratto-
> ria*, and spreads far beyond the confines of Soho into the outer
> suburbs of London and our great industrial cities and seaports.
> Scarcely a week passes but somebody writes an article in a
> national newspaper or magazine extolling the glories and subtle-
> ties of Italian cooking.

She tells her reader that, added to this, relatively accurate Italian
recipe books pour off the presses. She is nonetheless at pains to point
out that many still do not understand two of the essential virtues of
Italian food: a respect for the seasons around which the cooking
revolves, and the regionalism which still dictates the type and quality
of most of the produce and consequently dishes too.

Having said that reviewers had originally been 'unimaginably kind and welcoming' about the book, she adds that there had also been 'criticisms, queries, and corrections from readers'. Elizabeth's reputation was now sufficiently large for her to have a fairly voluminous postbag. She speaks to her following with these well-chosen words: 'I do not think there is one [letter] which has not been enlightening, constructive, and encouraging . . . It is in view of such criticisms and requests for more detailed explanations, and in the light of ten years further cooking experience, as well as in consideration of conditions much changed . . .' (A number of the criticisms she has in mind are from her friend Viola Johnson who again checked the recipes and corrected more of the Italian. Her son John says, 'Mother never could understand how it was that so many simple mistakes got into the text.') Towards the concluding section Elizabeth writes: 'What I in fact believe is that the English are now more creative and inquiring about cooking than they have ever been before.'

In the autumn Elizabeth appeared in *Wine and Food* again with 'Wardens an Unearthly Savour'. This fascinating piece traces the variety of delightful ways in which pears and quinces have been transformed into sweet dishes for the last 400 years. She once again demonstrates the breadth of her knowledge relating to the history of cookery literature and her discerning qualitative judgements are clearly made from considerable familiarity. 'Among the most interesting fruit recipes to be found in the whole of English cookery are those in Robert May's *Accomplish't Cook* first published in 1660', the year of Charles II's restoration to the throne: tarts, pies, creams, all of quinces, that exquisitely scented golden fruit which so beguiled Elizabeth. More recipes follow for the quince confection so beloved of the Portuguese, Spanish and French; called by the French *cotignac* and by the Spanish *membrillo*.

With quotations from the great French traveller and essayist Michel de Montaigne's *Italian Travel Journal* (a copy was given her the year previously by Veronica) we are reminded of Elizabeth's appreciation of the literature of travel, used since her very first book. And with it she is now consistently reaching further back in time. Montaigne says: 'In the evening Signor Ludovica . . . sent me a present of some boxes of very good quince jelly, scented, and some lemons and some oranges of extraordinary size.' The year is 1581. Elizabeth quotes too the great Massialot on pear compote. Massialot was one of those ferociously determined cooks who, at the close of the seventeenth century, dragged French cuisine out of the Middle Ages and into a new more simplified yet refined culinary aesthetic.

In *Wine and Food*'s Winter issue Elizabeth has 'A Nostrum of Neat's Tongues'. She ranges from the seventeenth to the twentieth century in a résumé of recipes getting the best from a calf's tongue. 'Packed into shallow pots or white-lined terrines and sealed with a layer of clarified butter', this is, she later wrote, 'to my mind the best and most subtle of all English potted meat inventions'. Her recommendations include eating tongue hot with her favourite Cumberland sauce, or potting it in a variety of ways. Under a subsequent recipe, for Lemon Mincemeat, Eliza Acton, a more humble domestic writer than Massialot, is credited by Elizabeth with being 'unsurpassed for her taste, her meticulous instructions (her *Modern Cookery*, 1845, is to my mind unquestionably the finest cookery book every written in the English language)'. In these historical pieces Elizabeth is not just purveying nostalgia. What she consistently gives are usable recipes from the great cookery writers of the past.

Hugh Johnson had rapidly put his mark on the journal of the Wine and Food Society (of which he was Secretary), at first most noticeably in his stimulating layouts and designs. He illustrates the covers and inner pages of *Wine and Food* using reproductions of old still-life paintings, that hitherto almost ignored rich source for the history of food. Elizabeth and Hugh's friendship had quickly developed and he generously gives her credit for inspiring him on both his regular visits to Halsey Street, and their trips to try out new restaurants together. 'We would talk over the covers and illustrations throughout each issue and her great knowledge of art and her passionate interest in design was of immense inspiration and help to me.'

CHAPTER EIGHTEEN

Selling a Dream
(1965–1973)

IN 1958 ALIX Coleman had introduced Elizabeth to a young man who owned a company making copper pans. Among other enterprises Peter Trier also fulfilled the vital service of retinning these pans. Peter Trier described himself thus: 'I was a tinker really.' He sold to many of the reputable retail outlets – John Lewis, Selfridges, the Ferrari Brothers in Wardour Street and Madame Cadec. In 1960 he had also begun importing the French Le Creuset enamelware into England, with considerable success.

'Almost the entire first consignment was bought by Selfridges. The shops had said to us, "It will never go because the English housewife will think it too heavy amongst other things." They were wrong.'

'We had a lot of help from Liz over these things and other ideas. It was she who later got Le Creuset to make the blue and was the first shop to sell it. She was sick of the yellow and when she mooted the idea David Schmitt of Le Creuset asked what kind of blue she suggested, then: "That's the blue I want," and she pointed to a pack of Gauloises lying on the table – the cigarettes she always smoked. No one used that colour then except the Dutch in their black enamelware with the cobalt blue inside it . . .'

When the Le Creuset blue was finally launched in 1967 after two years of procrastination on the manufacturer's part, the French magazine *Marie-Claire* commented, '*C'est la couleur qui fera fureur.*'

'She suggested we should make wooden chopping boards, bowls; should make a mezza-luna chopper. She wanted people to have wooden draining racks, so we had them made and distributed; all these things and more to other companies . . . [Peter's brother Stephen became involved here also.] By then Elizabeth knew her mind and was inclined to be dogmatic, but whatever she said there would be a public following for it. It became obvious that with this enormous clout that her name carried we would have been silly not to have gone with her ideas, the standards she had were so high . . . Liz had been thinking about the idea of setting up a shop for some time, and together I thought we had a lot to offer.'

Elizabeth, like Peter, knew Madame Cadec and her remarkable little shop in Soho, then one of the best and most interesting places in London to buy high-quality kitchenware: utensils, containers, pots and pans of all kinds from France. For those domestic buyers who knew of it Cadec's was invaluable; Madame Cadec was extremely knowledgeable. Among her numerous eccentricities was a practice she commented on to Peter Trier: 'Purchase tax. Oh I don't deal wiz zat orreeble abit.'

Some time after Peter and Elizabeth's thoughts on a shop had begun to take shape, in May 1964, another large shop was opened by someone else on London's Fulham Road to great public acclaim. Called Habitat, almost overnight it became the place where mildly affluent young Londoners found designs for their houses which reflected their belief that they were liberated, yet without having to bankrupt themselves in the process. During the Fifties Terence Conran had developed his ideas about designing furniture and textiles and learnt more about how to sell them. He was above all interested in reaching a wider public than most furniture and fabric companies then did. The Habitat look reflected Conran's interests and influences: a liking for pale Scandinavian woods, natural materials, an Arts and Crafts concentration on good craftsmanship, organized to create design which was both beautiful, functional and affordable. In the kitchenware section of the shop Conran demonstrated his love of the Mediterranean.

Furniture, as one of the costlier types of object made for the home, was sold at that time in the rather hushed and precious atmosphere then considered appropriate for department stores and furniture showrooms. Conran disliked this method and decided that alongside his simple practical furniture and fabrics he would add kitchenware. As kitchenware is cheaper and therefore sells more quickly he believed that this would give the shop a more busy, bustling feel, and help to create a vibrant, instant and stimulating atmosphere. Conran himself had, since his first visits to France and subsequent reading of Elizabeth's books, always loved food and its objects. This addition to his merchandise, like most of what he sold, derived from a personal interest. Never so avant-garde as to be threateningly stylish Habitat radiated an impression of being up to date; it was comfortable and durable too. Some of the objects one could buy in Habitat were obtainable in other shops, but Conran's instincts were masterly in giving his customers not only the things they wanted but also the guidance and the reassurance that this was the way they could put them together. By showing his customers how, he gave them confidence in surroundings which were both modern and not too difficult to emulate. He was a virtuoso at navigation within the English system, and at manipulating it to his advantage; at the same time he contributed to its reform and its mellowing.

Inspired by France itself, by Elizabeth's books and by what Conran had seen at Madame Cadec's in Soho, most of the kitchenware in Habitat came from France. At that time one of the best retailers in Paris was Dehillerin in Les Halles. Here Conran found the tools for the kitchen: knives, mills for pepper and salt, sieves, earthenware bowls and containers, terrines, pots, copper pans. Crockery came from Scandinavia as well as England. A vital feature of the new shop, and one whose originality is difficult to remember because now ubiquitous, was the display of the kitchenware. Conran wanted to replicate something of the feeling of those French ironmongers which had so inspired him ten years earlier, more recently the warehouses too. Consequently he had all the merchandise displayed on deep shelves in the shop itself. Little was stored away in stockrooms behind. All the glasses were out, all the china, all the saucepans. This gave the combined impression of cheerful abundance and the functionality of a warehouse.

Central to the success of all this was that Conran was selling not only objects but a life-style. 'Also', as he told the author, 'Habitat had a fashion connection. It was designed to be constantly changing, with new looks and new ideas. However, classic cookware and furniture was the permanent base of it all.'

Elizabeth was annoyed that the young Conran had pipped her at the post with his kitchen section in Habitat. He knew her socially by now and she felt that he had taken some of her ideas. 'She often referred to it as Shabbycat or Tattycat. I suppose she thought it was a bit vulgar really. But yes, she was quite fond of him as well in a way,' says Stephen Trier's wife Caroline, who worked in Elizabeth's shop for its first two years. Elizabeth need not have felt concerned to undermine Conran's enterprise, however, because in him she had a magnificent disciple. Conran was part of that first, younger post-war generation which had been inspired by and was now proselytizing her ideas. Nevertheless Elizabeth was and would always remain ambivalent about her followers. As a result she was not entirely consistent about what her writing and this new enterprise represented. Conran is generous towards her, though, and prepared to give credit when he says: 'Yes, I was incredibly influenced by Elizabeth.'

Meanwhile, plans had been going ahead in that same year of 1964, for Elizabeth to launch her own shop. Pam Pugh (then Llewelyn) remembers 'a meal at the Chanterelle where we all sat down and decided that we would go ahead with it'.

Before they opened Elizabeth had coaxed and finally persuaded her friend Renée Fedden to join in the venture. Whilst Renée's financial contribution came from her close friend Rosie Peto, Lady Hinchinbrook, Peter Trier's wife Jenny bought the leasehold on a little shop in Bourne Street, off Sloane Square. This was most convenient for Elizabeth in Halsey Street just the other side of the King's Road. The tenants presently in the shop had wanted to purchase it but Elizabeth's enthusiasm had inspired the others to go ahead with the venture. Pamela and Brian Llewelyn were asked if they would consider joining as partners with Renée, and Jenny Trier. 'Elizabeth provided little of the finance, but all the cachet in her name' says Peter Trier. The above-mentioned four and Elizabeth were the directors (Peter, although intimately involved with the enterprise from the beginning, was never one of them).

Peter Trier and Elizabeth went 'in a beat-up old Bedford van on several buying trips to France. She wanted to have her own products in the shop and was prepared to scout the length and breadth of England and France to secure them.' Shops such as Dehillerin in Paris were already of course well known to Elizabeth but she and Peter were in France to discover wholesalers. These they found by asking around and through the connections Elizabeth had already made in France.

'A little factory here, a small pottery there. I can see Liz now, twenty feet up in an old warehouse, picking out old dusty bowls and getting so excited about them. South from Paris and turn left and an old pottery there. Liz went bananas about it. "I've found the real thing," she kept saying.

'The shop was to be a serious kitchen shop. You could call it a grown-up Madam Cadec. We were gradually loading up a ton of big pots on the Jeep [someone else was driving this] and the old Bedford van and lumbered back home with it all. XYZ was her code name for the pottery; she was nervous about us being copied before we began. So we sent back a card saying: "We found XYZ."

'Anything to do with design for Elizabeth was completely handed over to Anthony [Elizabeth's friend Denney, who designed the interior of the shop].'

The shop was neither large, nor in a particularly well-placed position; added to which there was an unsympathetic meter merchant next door. Unlike Conran's Habitat on the corner of Walton Street and Fulham Road Elizabeth's shop could not be viewed to advantage from a distance; but its proximity to Sloane Square and this particular district's potential for customers, a large proportion of whom already owned a number of her books, was not lost on Elizabeth. (At the time her shop opened Elizabeth had revised all her books and published them with Penguin in paperback.)

Anthony Denney's utterly simple shop design succeeded as the perfect backdrop for what Elizabeth and her partners were about to sell. Elizabeth David Ltd reflected the growing contemporary trend for public spaces to become more workmanlike. In keeping with this attitude the aesthetic and spatial possibilities of old warehouses were becoming recognized; picture galleries, for instance, were now regularly sited in this type of building. Aspects of Modernism; its functionalism and clarity of line, had finally become acceptable to more than just the artistic élite.

But Elizabeth herself was not much concerned with trends and estimations. She was driven from within. Although in one sense a natural communicator she was not self-conscious like Terence Conran, did not have his particular sensitivity to the spirit of the age, and seems not to have been much affected by the tumultuous decade of the Sixties. According to *Time* magazine this was the decade of Swinging London, the capital of Pop culture, the Place Where It Was All Happening. At the heart of Pop culture and design was a claim for the value of novelty, for the ephemeral, the temporary, the expendable. The symbols of mass-culture were becoming the new cultural criteria and would increasingly displace the older ideals of 'good taste' and excellence. On the other hand there was tradition, memory, permanence and the élite. Despite her modern-looking shop interior, within this duality Elizabeth was on the side of tradition. The cult of the Mediterranean – Provence, Italy, and the Isles of Greece – is an old English passion; a passion reflecting a profound attraction for tradition and permanence. So also Elizabeth's love of well-matched function and craft – craftmanship *is* tradition and memory – was one long established in England.

One of the most significant purveyors of Pop culture was music, which entirely passed Elizabeth by; as did most other aspects of the movement. However, at the time she was seen as New, and therefore automatically a Good Thing. She did not flaunt her remarkable memory and knowledge of the past, her 'square' High Tory monarchism, or any other unfashionable mental habits.

Elizabeth Good, who had written a preview of Habitat in the recently instituted 'Design for Living' section of the *Sunday Times* the previous year, interviewed Elizabeth the day before Elizabeth David Ltd opened. She is described as 'shy . . . reserved . . . hates being photographed . . . is tall and slim' and her

> style is muted, deceptively off-hand: she tucks her grey silky
> hair behind her ears and the large hornrimmed glasses she
> sometimes wears ride constantly halfway down her small school-

girl nose. Her soft, almost expiring voice is often the vehicle for some pretty lethal comments on her profession. When words fail she resorts to long, effective silences.

Her voice quickens when she talks about cooking and the equipment she will sell . . . Handling each piece with familiar affection, an almost sensuous feeling for textures and shapes . . . she says, 'What I want to sell is traditional French and English cooking utensils and tableware. I want to make this clear. We are trying to get English things as well as French ones. I went to France to look for traditional regional pots, traditional shapes and materials. About 40% of our stock is French.'

Elizabeth Good wrote that the interior by Denney had interpreted Elizabeth's views 'simply and effectively: builders' finishes, black and white [tiled floor], the only colour is a soft blue-grey, the only decoration a leaf motif in cast iron which is used as brackets for cool marble shelves and as a rail to the stairs leading into the cellar.' (The cool shelves had come from Burketts, the recently closed-down high-class fishmonger opposite Harrods.) Denney said, 'I call it a no-decor shop. It's nostalgic, it evokes memories of bakeries, still rooms and larders. Elizabeth herself would not have used the word nostalgic. She called it "very professional looking, very solid. Not grand and not forbidding. I want anyone who passes to feel they can come in and buy a toothpick."'

Notwithstanding the fact that a good fraction of Elizabeth's clientele was quite grand, alongside the toothpicks they would have found the warm browns of traditional French earthenware diables, casseroles, jars, tians, terrines; the yellow and paler creams of glaze and salt-glaze, the steely glint of knives, one for every kitchen task; whisks of willow, spoons of china, wood and metal for cooking, serving; mortars, moulds, mandolins, hachoirs, white china Pillivuyt bowls, ramekins, cocotte dishes and much more, crammed in orderly display on shelves and on the floor; all the perfect little tools for those obscure kitchen tasks at which the French so excelled. Elizabeth Good wrote: 'Together they have brought off a difficult proposition: to make tangible an atmosphere and an attitude.'

Elizabeth David Ltd was quickly copied, and those involved in the management of her shop became even more wary of disclosing vital sources of supply. But others were quick to follow and an English supplier commented later: 'These cooking shops we sell to, they're all copies of hers.'

Peter Trier says: 'A lot of Elizabeth's friends came to the shop, it became a kind of club for her. Several of them worked there too. Those like Joyce Murchie whom Elizabeth had known since Cairo and spent time with in Italy.'

'Joyce was great fun, she was a very social being,' says Caroline Trier. 'She had a small income and didn't really need to work but did it to help Elizabeth out. To the surprise of us all she turned out to be a brilliant saleswoman. She could sell anything to anybody.' Caroline Trier recalls that this prompted one of Elizabeth's bons mots: 'Oh, Joyce could sell an egg-cup to cook a turkey in.'

Part of the reason for Elizabeth's success was that she was not and had never been avant-garde. Instead she represented fashion in the traditional, now almost obsolete sense. At the heart of this tradition was the idea of 'the prevailing customs of the upper classes'; the ruling élite, from which Elizabeth herself sprang. Elizabeth David Ltd was the first specialist kitchen shop in England to foster the ideas she had promulgated for over a decade in her books.

On the day of opening, 1 November 1965, 'You couldn't move in the shop,' says Pamela Pugh. 'Liz had let it slip to some other journalist or someone, anyway the word had got out and other papers had written something up about it as well as *The Times* who was supposed to have the scoop. We were absolutely inundated. We had started the whole thing off in such an amateurish way really that we were taken by surprise at the success of it. After a week our stock was gone. We had been driving over nearly every evening to the warehouse to restock. Our French suppliers were not exactly highpowered or speedy so we had to frantically get more stuff. It was lucky we were so young. It was very exciting and stimulating, you were learning on your feet . . . I remember so well that distinctive and evocative smell in the shop . . . Gauloises, and pâté, and there was always wine around.'

Peter Trier says: 'Liz would bring lunch in a string bag and even if it was just a boiled egg, it would be beautifully cut up with home-

374

made mayonnaise and sprigs of parsley and all beautifully arranged on a white plate.' His sister-in-law Caroline Trier remembers that 'Yes, every day Liz brought in a lunch for us. There was a crate of wine delivered at regular intervals and there was always wine there for lunch. It was Red Lisbon. The stockroom was small and very cramped but one squeezed in. There was one of those old Singer sewing machine bases with a marble top for a table and Liz would beautifully lay out whatever she'd brought for that day. One of us would remain in charge of the shop if someone should come in during the lunch period. We didn't really sit down for it though, just grazed in passing. It was always delicious.'

Elizabeth came into the shop every day and Renée most days too. At any one time there were always one or two people working in the shop helping Elizabeth. She wouldn't always be out front serving customers and spent a certain amount of her time in the back room sorting, organizing stock and orders. Only two months after the shop opened Renée and Robin Fedden separated. 'Elizabeth was whole-heartedly behind Renée on this, she was immensely supportive of her,' says Caroline Trier. At Elizabeth David Ltd it is noteworthy that for the first time in her life Elizabeth was working only with women.

For the next seven years Elizabeth David Ltd was to take up much of Elizabeth's time, and for the first part of that period she did little writing. In the months prior to the opening of the shop, however, she had a flurry of journalistic activity, including several pieces for the newly launched women's magazine *Nova*. *Nova* was subtitled 'A new kind of magazine for the new kind of woman'. With articles on cooking and the home it set out to reflect a new attitude of self-fulfilment before duty. The *Nova* woman apparently cooked more because she enjoyed it than because she had to; a principle to which Elizabeth in her single state could comfortably subscribe.

Another well-established pattern by this period was her division of the day. Since her months in India, and whenever possible before that, Elizabeth's periods of work and rest, reading and writing were not governed by any conventional norm. Up at about five, she would often work from bed with her instant coffee beside her. In the evening if she wasn't seeing anyone she could work late. If there were guests, while smoking, talking, listening, drinking, she usually prepared only one or two dishes. Guests would sometimes be asked to help wash up.

The writer and wine connoisseur Sybille Bedford had met Elizabeth in 1963. 'She wrote me a fan letter and I had written her one, our letters crossed . . . I was then living in the South of France. [Elizabeth had written in her tribute to Norman Douglas that Sybille Bedford, 'that magical writer', had assisted Norman on his cookery book *Venus in the Kitchen*: 'Sybille Bedford's succinct, quiet reveries on her friend are amongst the most perceptive and sensitive.'] When I was to be in England she invited me to dinner in Halsey Street. It was one of those Georgian houses . . . very narrow and when you came in it was made narrower by having bookcases on both sides of the passageway. It was like one of those First World War trenches and they felt as if they were going to fall in on you. The house was stuffed with books and ornaments.'

Hugh Johnson recalls the same impression: 'Bookcases almost blocking the entrance hall, books silting up the sitting room, ziggurats of books on the dresser, the stairs, the bed . . .' Elizabeth kept her full *Oxford English Dictionary*, all fourteen volumes of it, doubling up as a table at the end of her bed.

Sybille Bedford continues: 'Felicité was there that first evening – we later became good friends. After drinks she didn't immediately absent herself and Elizabeth said, "Felicité, I had asked you for drinks not dinner," and she had to remove herself upstairs. That evening I had white Beaujolais for the first time. We went down into the kitchen . . . Everything was open . . . all the shelves . . . the china was white.' (The complete invasion of white was not in fact to occur for another few years, when Elizabeth had grown more purist and got rid of much of her traditional blue and white.)

Sybille Bedford describes the meal as 'simple and delicious. We had kebabs, cheeses and apricots . . . From the beginning we had so much to talk about. Food; we always talked about that. It is very much part of my writing. But much else besides. We talked about painting, Shakespeare. Elizabeth was very erudite, on Shakespeare . . . and poetry. She was such a perfectionist. Elizabeth was someone who was very severe in her standards; she was so amusing, and very unforgiving. She didn't do a prima donna act, she enchanted people. I rose from the table to leave at 1.45 a.m.'

Elizabeth David Ltd was used by a number of friends, such as Sybille Bedford, to illustrate Elizabeth's generosity. 'She was immensely so, to the point of insanity . . . When she liked someone she would give them something, see to one's comforts. She gave me a bottle of La Tour, "Because," she said, "your standards of dinner are so high." I was later given a complement of white china from the shop.'

Doreen Thornton comments: 'Liz had not the slightest idea about money really. She was so generous. Right back when we were young; and she'd say about things, "Oh, put it on my account."

'I'd often come up to London and see her in the shop. There were always friends milling about, as well as those officially there to help. I'd do something to lend a hand, one didn't just stand around. And she'd send me back with armfuls of lovely white things . . .'

'She was so generous materially, but not about people,' says Sybille Bedford. 'She had fallen out with an editor [this refers to the debacle with Macdonald over *Italian Food*] and fifteen years later she had not forgiven him. This trait became worse. Elizabeth was very, very temperamental. She had such an excess of fury.'

It is maintained by all who knew her that Elizabeth was essentially private, hated publicity and wouldn't give interviews. Nonetheless she always kept a sharp eye out for useful publicity, for a new book, or the shop. During the Sixties she actually gave interviews not only to most of the major newspapers, but also to a young journalist, Michael Bateman, for a book he was compiling on the best-known contemporary figures making 'food' their livelihood.

Bateman began his record of the interview: 'There's only room for one at the top and that place is occupied by Elizabeth David . . . For some years now books have been coming out from other writers in which they acknowledge a debt to her and her only. Katherine Whitehorn . . . says she is David inspired . . .' Bateman noticed, like everyone who entered Halsey Street, the tools of her trade which surrounded Elizabeth in such profusion.

Despite some inaccuracies (Elizabeth wrote a sharp letter about him to a friend), Bateman convincingly evokes something of the real

Elizabeth. 'Her books . . . go to America and one by one get translated for the European markets.' Elizabeth says: '*French Provincial Cooking* was a notable flop in the US. I had fan-tas-tic notices in the US. Better than here, so it shows you that notices don't do anything for you. I just don't know the market.' (Despite her great success she always remained at one level quite instinctive and unable to articulate her function. Interspersed with her will to communicate was also a dialogue she was continuing with herself.) By 1965 Elizabeth was reaching a far wider audience than before, with all her books currently published in paperback by Penguin. Since 1963 this was under the auspices of a young editor, Jill Norman, on whose life Elizabeth was to have a great impact.

The following year, 1965, Elizabeth was interviewed by the new editor of *Wine and Food*, Pamela Vandyke Price, who belonged to the younger generation of people under Elizabeth's sway. She described her thus: 'Gioconda of the kitchen, she will smile and talk of other people. Elizabeth says, "Why should anyone want to know about me?"

'"Hundreds of thousands of people want to know about you," I tell her, "because you have made us think differently about food . . . You've sharpened up the standards of restaurants and become compulsive reading for men and women who don't cook at all. . . . It's your ideas, as well as your recipes, that dominate the entertaining of those of us who . . . grew up in the war, and ever since have had to cope singlehanded in the kitchen."

'Elizabeth counters that: "There was already so much wonderful work being done to encourage good cooking. André Simon, Ambrose Heath, Elizabeth Craig – where would any of us be without them?"'

In this same wilful vein, according to Pamela Vandyke Price, when she tries 'to trace her influence among food writers', Elizabeth says, 'For goodness sake, there's too much nonsense written about cookery – they'll be publishing books on Lowestoft cooking or Tunbridge Wells cuisine next.'

Between 1967 and 1969 while the shop took up most of her time, Elizabeth wrote little journalism. Nevertheless, during these years she did write and have printed at her own cost four little booklets which she sold in the shop alongside the rest of her books. A very select collection of paperback cookery books by other authors was also on sale. Elizabeth's booklets are beautifully designed and printed; she was obsessive about every detail as they went through the press. 'She had nightmares. There'd be hell to pay if anything was wrong with that kind of thing,' says John Johnson. The booklets were:

Dried Herbs, Aromatics and Condiments (1967). Elizabeth had 5000 of these printed and they were presented in a herb, spice and condiment pack. After two years the little booklets had sold out and Elizabeth reprinted them.

English Potted Meats and Fish Pastes (1968) was a version of the article done for *Food and Wine* on 'Neat's Tongues'.

The Baking of an English Loaf (1969) appeared in its first guise for *Queen* magazine in December 1968.

Syllabubs and Fruit Fools (1969) was published in the first issue of *Nova* in March 1965.

These were not Elizabeth's first ventures into the genre of pamphlets, and in 1972 she wrote one on *Green Pepper Berries: a New Taste*; she sold these berries, which fascinated her, in the shop. Despite their slightness these little books are interesting, giving eminently useful instruction and information at the same time. Significantly they were the seeds which would germinate and flourish as the works consuming the last years of Elizabeth's life.

In 1969, Anthony Denney married a young woman, Celia Royde-Smith, who had for some time been working in Elizabeth's shop. Elizabeth and Renée, amongst others, were very surprised at the marriage and for some time Elizabeth felt deeply hurt both by Celia and Anthony. In this frame of mind she made that criticism most damning in her vocabulary: 'disloyalty'. (Elizabeth always had difficulty in accepting that those close to her might also wish to lead autonomous lives.) In time Elizabeth forgave Anthony and Celia, as much as she was able, going to stay with them in Spain on more than one occasion. As a result of his enormous earnings Anthony had effectively become a tax exile and moved much of his wealth to Spain, where he bought and restored a farmhouse near Alicante in the south-

east of the country. Here in the mid-1960s, before his marriage to
Celia, Elizabeth had stayed with him and his current boyfriend, an
Australian, afterwards writing about her stay for the *Spectator*.

In 1970, ten years after her last full-length book, Elizabeth brought
out a new publication. This was a synthesis of ideas, which she said
had come to her in a moment of comprehension while re-reading Mrs
Leyel's *Gentle Art of Cookery*, during her extended period of ill-health
in 1963. Elizabeth had realized that her old favourite was 'yet another
manifestation of the English love-affair with Eastern food and Arabian
Nights ingredients ... The train of thought ... is still incomplete,
still no more than a glance into the English preoccupation with the
spices and the scents, the fruit, the flavourings, the sauces and the
condiments of the orient, near and far.' She called this new book
Spices, Salt and Aromatics in the English Kitchen and announced that it
was the first volume in what was to be a series, 'perhaps three volumes
of five, it depends how much time I have, I write terribly slowly ...
Later volumes will deal with bread, yeast, cakes, creams and cheeses
and egg dishes, and meat and game.' Meanwhile, this the first, was
an enlightening little treatise. Oddly, it is the only one of her books
whose title is clumsy in its scansion; a rare occasion when one is
reminded of Elizabeth's 'boredom' with music (in her later life she
owned a television but no stereo system). And even those who know
and admire the book frequently misquote the title, reversing the first
two words to *Salt, Spices* ... instead of *Spices, Salt* ...

A simple description – 'This book offers a sample ... of the
immense number of English spiced and aromatically flavoured dishes'
– is inadequate. In the very first lines, with her accustomed elegance
and mastery of her medium, Elizabeth captures the reader's imagination, evoking the past for us with one of her incantational lists.

> For some two thousand years, English cookery has been
> extremely spice-conscious, not surprisingly to anyone in the least
> familiar with the history of the spice trade in Europe and the
> part played in it, successively, by the Phoenicians, the Romans,
> the Arab conquerors of Spain, the Norman crusaders, the mer-

chants of Venice and Genoa, the religious orders which fostered the arts of healing, medicine and distillery, the Portuguese explorers who opened the sea route to the Indies, the Dutch empire-builders who wrested the spice trade from Portugal, the British East India Company whose merchants in their turn made London for two centuries the greatest spice mart in the world.

She continues with a fine résumé of the usage of spices and flavourings throughout the history of the English kitchen. Elizabeth diverges from the (then) prevailing belief that the traditional English fascination with these things was largely a result of attempts to mask contaminated food, or to enhance 'a monotonous diet of salt meat or boiled fish'. She argues that the reason they have such an honourable place in our cooking tradition was probably because 'the English have a natural taste for highly seasoned foods – as do most northern people – and since trade with the Near East and Southern Europe brought us early in the evolution of our cookery considerable opportunities for indulging the taste, we took to spiced food with an enthusiasm which seems to have been almost equal to that shown by the Romans at the height of their preoccupation with the luxuries of living.'

In 1968 a young woman, Claudia Roden, exiled through political upheaval from her Egyptian homeland and the city of her birth, Cairo, published a beautifully written book entitled *A Book of Middle Eastern Food* (Thomas Nelson). She said it was 'the fruit of nostalgic longing for . . . food that was the constant joy of life in a world so different from the Western one'. In evocative and judicious prose she presented 'humble peasant food, flamboyant Mediterranean dishes, the elaborate . . . as well as the everyday dishes of the middle classes throughout the Middle East'. She has given generous credit to Elizabeth as the person who 'with her brilliance and integrity' inspired her to write when she read her first book. In lifting 'the veil from the food which she [Elizabeth] had learned about when she lived in Cairo, Alexandria and Greece . . . her book of *Mediterranean Food* . . . slightly eased my nostalgic homesickness . . . In the early editions she intimated that there were many more dishes in the Near East which needed to be discovered; that was the spark that fired me.'

Claudia Roden's book was an instant success, and not only

because the late 1960s was a period of fascination with anything 'ethnic'. *A Book of Middle Eastern Food* is a delight to read and inspiring to use, but its degree of success is a partial reflection of those very strands present in English history and the national psyche and which Elizabeth sets out to draw together in her own *Spices, Salt and Aromatics in the English Kitchen*. Elements of Middle Eastern food – as also other aspects of the cultures of the Middle and Far East – had for centuries been brought back as exotic, and made fashionable with the upper classes in Northern Europe. Certainly by the end of the eighteenth and the early nineteenth century the vogue for things Eastern was widespread among the educated classes: one thinks of Edward Fitzgerald's *Omar Khayyam*, Richard Burton's *Arabian Nights*, the collecting of Persian miniatures, and the related vogue for Chinoiserie in house decoration and dress.

Elizabeth herself had personal experience of the East, of course: she had lived several years in Egypt, travelled in the Middle East, for a while in India, and had visited Morocco. Added to this she had an easy familiarity with many of the classic works on the East in her own library, including Doughty's craggy nineteenth-century master-piece, *Arabia Deserta*, and Lord Bute's *Moorish Recipes* (Oliver and Boyd, 1956). To these she brought her now considerable understand-ing of the history of England's food and its dependence on the Middle East and the classical Mediterranean. In the most consistent cel-ebration of English food she had so far undertaken, Elizabeth produces a book which is not a dry historical work but instead fulfils the claim she made for her beloved Mrs Leyel: 'Stimulus, that was the quality . . . provided and in plenty, for she had the gift of making her recipes sound enticing.'

Occasional comments throughout *Spices, Salt and Aromatics in the English Kitchen* clearly illustrate Elizabeth's present preoccupations. When discussing the vexed question of the French influence upon English cooking she says, 'Towards appreciation of these points, increased familiarity with our own cookery history and its literature, so astonishingly rich, varied, and illuminating, would help.' And her own command of this heritage is made abundantly clear. At least by 1958, quite probably earlier (it was first published in 1939), she had become familiar with *The Englishman's Food: Five Centuries of English Diet* by that remarkable, food-loving biochemist J. C. Drummond. During the war Drummond had assisted Lord Woolton in master-minding wartime rationing – 'the best food for bad times' – along sound dietetic principles.

Drummond's book was the most comprehensive study yet under-taken on the history of the English at table. Although the subject is increasingly recognized as a branch of social history, with much primary literature published, *The Englishman's Food* has still not been superseded. Elizabeth rightly called it 'absolutely engrossing . . . an invaluable work of reference', written 'lucidly, with great learning and a nice dry wit'. Related to Drummond's work is another group of books which Elizabeth cites in her bibliography and from which she quotes at length in the body of her book.

As long ago as the 1930s a number of women had begun to collect and write down British regional or folk recipes; somewhat akin to the way in which Cecil Sharpe had made his great collection of the folk music of Great Britain. The aim of these English women was to record and present in a manner commensurate with contem-porary life, traditional cooking before the industrialization of food had 'completely crushed [it] out of existence'. One of the most effective of these women, Florence White, started the English Folk Cookery Association to carry out the task. The Association died with her in 1940 but her book *Good Things in England* (Jonathan Cape, 1932) is a fine testament to her valuable work. Historical collections of English recipes were not new and continued being made; one of the most recent, *English Recipes and Others* (Methuen and Co., 1967) was by the well-known *Daily Express* food columnist Sheila Hutchins, who had a fine collection of old food books. In 1932, however, Florence White had insisted that hers were recipes still being used by living people rather than memories surviving only in books. These were not 'museum pieces' but recipes that had often been in use in people's families 'for over a century. These are so many and so varied that the present volume is merely a small instalment of our kitchen and stillroom riches. England does not know her wealth.' Nor was this written by a zealot provincial. Florence White had trained and worked in France for several years, concluding that 'there is no reason why the famous French cuisine and our fine traditional English cookery should be bitter rivals. Both are absolutely distinctive.'

In 1954, as well as bringing out Elizabeth's *Italian Food*, Macdonald had also published an extraordinary book by a woman called Dorothy Hartley. This was *Food in England*. After studying early manuscripts in the British Library, for many years Hartley had wandered around England (by bicycle) collecting and writing about the pre-industrial customs and crafts of Britain in a voluminous series of books and articles. Despite certain inaccuracies and an inadequate bibliography for tracing sources, *Food in England* is a remarkable, rambling compilation of traditions and practices connected with the making of English food, illustrated with the author's witty and distinctive drawings.

Elizabeth's *Spices, Salt and Aromatics in the English Kitchen* is an extension of this genre. It is a reappraisal of her own knowledge, her sense of belonging, and the deeply deleterious long- and short-term effects of industrialization on our food. Unlike Florence White or Dorothy Hartley, Elizabeth doesn't collect her recipes from living practitioners but uses instead some of the best English cookery books of the last 300 or so years. Her choice of English recipes is quirky and inspiring, with a stimulating selection from so many of the authors made familiar by her articles. Their inclusion springs from beliefs long held by Elizabeth, but only now finding expression in a more expansive form. (Even when generous and encouraging, as Audrey Withers or Hugh Johnson had been, they were still always bound by editorial constraints: a maximum of two or three thousand words.) With typical wit Elizabeth describes how, for example, a simple English butter sauce for fish was gradually transformed out of all recognition and 'we began to confuse good plain cooking with plain bad cooking ... What it did become was billsticker's paste, and on this basis egg sauce, parsley sauce, caper, anchovy, shrimp, mushroom, lobster and some half dozen other perfectly respectable sauces fell toppling to their ruin.' And from this sorry conclusion springs the crucial point of *Spices, Salt and Aromatics*: to restore these sauces, and the whole body of English cookery to its earlier ethos,

Elizabeth believes, 'We need to go back, far back, to the recipes of more than a century ago, to the early and mid nineteenth century, when an authentic and still strong English cooking tradition flourished amid the ravages of the Industrial Revolution.'

We are given two practical, learned and graceful chapters on 'Aromatic Herbs, Dried or Fresh' and 'Spices and Condiments': Allspice, Aniseed, Caraway Seeds, Cardamom, Cayenne, Coriander, Cumin, Mustard Seeds, Nutmeg . . . Peppercorns . . . Poppy Seeds . . . Saffron . . . Salt'. And so on. None of these flavourings is particularly obscure, but amongst the remarkably varied collection of information on their origins there is much good advice on their virtues and the pitfalls of misuse. Elizabeth's own prejudices were always confidently displayed but her nephew Stephen Grey, for whom this book and her next were favourites, maintains: 'Most books have a feeling of what is right or wrong, but Aunt Liza was liberal; in the sense that it is up to you how you want to have your bread. She only sets standards from an historical point of view . . . she never rams things down your throat. The magic was in the stories . . . and then to find out how easy it was was marvellous. But I wouldn't have bothered if I'd had to just read a recipe. You weren't left with much choice after reading it but to get up and make those things.'

Stephen Grey is correct, Elizabeth was most certainly telling readers what they ought to do. Nonetheless, it was done with such subtle persuasion and absolute confidence in her opinions that the reader, by implication a follower, doesn't wish to be thought less tasteful than Elizabeth, so will be at pains to concur.

Elizabeth says:

The use of herbs is very much a matter of association, taste, and prejudice, and cooks whose work I respect recommend a branch or two of rosemary in the dish with veal, chicken and lamb roasts (I prefer branches of wild Provence thyme); others suggest that the meat be spiked with the minutest pieces of dried rosemary and garlic. As for sage, Italian cooks, like ourselves, are fond of it, and use it for a number of veal dishes. To me, it deadens the food with its musty, dried-blood scent. [A lethal

Elizabeth thrust. One has to steel oneself to reach for the jar of sage after this.] Instead of sage, it is worth trying dried mint or basil . . .

To make a bouquet of herbs in leaf form . . . put a teaspoon of mixed basil, marjoram, thyme, savory, with a crumbled bay leaf, in a 4 inch square of muslin. Add three or four whole peppercorns and, if you like, a peeled clove of garlic crushed with a knife. Tie the little bundle with thread . . .

Personally I find the little ritual of preparing herb bouquets one of the minor pleasures of cooking. Nothing would persuade me to relinquish it in favour of a bought bouquet made up in a factory . . . all as like as two – or rather twelve – teabags.

Elizabeth is constantly fighting against mass-production and standardization in all that she does. However instinctive and unarticulated it may have been she understood the dubious benefits of industrialization on the long-term quality of food.

Another chapter devoted to 'Sauces' commences with one of those brilliant pieces of historical unravelling of culinary myths which she was so good at: Elizabeth wades through the quagmire of inaccuracies surrounding the true origins of her favourite, Cumberland sauce, 'the best of all sauces for cold meat . . .' Over twenty pages of 'emulsions sweet and savoury' follow, taken largely from pre-industrial cookery books, written when Elizabeth believed the English still understood the principle which the likes of Prosper Montagné, had also maintained: 'that the basis of all good cooking must be good taste and common sense, and not mere fancy and make belief'. As André Simon says: 'Montagné believed, and never tired of repeating, that sauces and garnishes were not meant to camouflage, cover, or make acceptable . . . their function . . . was to help and not to hide, to add flavour, taste or consistency to the food which they adorned, and to do it discreetly.'

Elizabeth includes recipes from the inimitable seventeenth-century wit, man of letters and proto-scientist Sir Kenelm Digby and his *Closet Opened*; Eliza Acton's *Modern Cookery* of 1845; *A True Gentlewoman's Delight*, the posthumously published cookery book of the seventeenth-century Countess of Kent, to whose book Elizabeth was particularly attached. She quoted from it often and made considerable researches into the life of the Countess, Elizabeth de Grey, sister to the Countess of Arundel. Elizabeth had some time ago fallen for the charms of the spirited Welshwoman Augusta Llanover's *Good Cookery* of 1867 and had written a biographical piece on her for *Wine and Food* in 1965. 'My aim', wrote Lady Llanover, 'has been to preserve or restore all the good old habits of my country, and utterly repudiate all immoral introductions which ruin the health as well as imperil the soul . . .' Wife of a local MP, Benjamin Hall, Augusta was 'formidably industrious, endowed with a high sense of duty towards her dependants and her husband's constituents'. She also

> devoted immense energy to the study of Welsh traditions and agriculture, to local folklore, music, literature, husbandry, cookery and housekeeping. After the death of her husband . . . [it is to Benjamin Hall that Big Ben owes it nickname] Lady Llanover evidently settled down to the writing of her cookery book. We can take it that everything she set down was first-hand, noted from direct observation and practical experience. When she gives recipes for rice bread, barley cakes, leek and plum broth, chicken and leek pie with cream, Welsh salt duck, Gwent short cakes . . . her authority is indisputable . . .

Elizabeth's verdict on Welsh salt duck in *Spices, Salt and Aromatics* is that it produces 'a deliciously flavoured and tender duck; and the melon goes to perfection with cold duck . . . It is fortunate for us that Lady Llanover recorded such recipes . . . for they do not appear in other published works'. Elizabeth is not only here being something of a Welsh Nationalist (she had always loved visiting Wales and undoubtedly became more conscious of her Welsh origins on her father's side as she grew older), it is also a book after her own heart. This is vividly illustrated when Elizabeth tells us that Lady Llanover professed certain beliefs which were anathema to Victorian taste: 'In her repudiation of the marvels of Victorian progress and the products of what she called "mechanical talent" she was also reactionary. Or was she a visionary? To those of us who today yearn increasingly for authenticity and natural food, she appears sometimes to be writing of the 1960s rather than the 1860s.'

Writing five years later in *Spices, Salt and Aromatics* Elizabeth reiterates: 'Now seeking means to combat the Chemical Age, we look to our forebears for help.' This is the repeated battle-cry of the book. She says that she writes 'mainly out of a wish to preserve some memory of the seasonal aspect of fruit and vegetables, before everything green . . . disappears straight into the packet, the dehydrating machine, and the deep freeze.'

In this book Elizabeth is trying to create a present world from the past, and herein lies the difficulty. At the outset, in *Mediterranean Food*, she used quotations from past writers to give depth and context to her representation of a world, but it was a world which still existed in the present. The Middle East, regional France, provincial Italy, were still growing and preparing food using methods often little changed for centuries, sometimes even millennia. For Elizabeth the past gave depth and added meaning to the present, just as it did for the poet T. S. Eliot in his plea for the crucial place of tradition and history in the modern world, and just as it had always done for every culture prior to the relentless West in the twentieth century. In *Spices, Salt and Aromatics* Elizabeth has to overcome the problem that the English world she describes through her recipes can no longer be found in real time. Pre-industrial, agrarian England had paid the price, had been swallowed up 'by the ravages of the Industrial Revolution'. Unlike the Mediterranean countries she had always written about, Britain had sacrificed many of the traditions of a culture rooted to the soil and connected, through continuity, to its past.

In 'Anglo-Indian Cookery' Elizabeth regrets having to record that since the time of her redoubtable and admired nineteenth-century Colonel Kenney-Herbert and his *Culinary Jottings*, little in India had changed. 'The kitchens which I myself had the opportunity of observing in New Delhi were still unbelievably primitive, and the food which came out of them an astonishing mixture of English nannies' puddings, cakes festooned in spectacular spun-sugar work . . .' and so on. It was the Colonel whom she had quoted verbatim in *Summer Cooking* on the making of an omelette. In her comments on him she is clearly identifying: 'Several good cookery books have been written by professional soldiers, and this is perhaps no coincidence. On the whole the most successful books of technical instruction, and this applies as much to cookery as to other subjects, are those . . . [where] . . . the author expresses his views with soldierly precision and is prepared to go to some lengths to defend them.' At the same time Elizabeth believed, as she said of Kenelm Digby's recipes for mead, metheglin, hydromel: 'all the best recipes . . . are runes, litanies, something even of magic spells'.

On 'Cured and Brined Meat' Elizabeth has this to say:

> English food, so extravagantly overpraised by its advocates and so bitterly, and so often rightly, reviled by those who have suffered from British hotel and restaurant catering, is never seen to greater advantage than when it is presented in perfect simplicity, unadorned, and on a rather large scale.
>
> Let us consider some of our genuine English culinary assets. Among the best of them are our cured and salted meats. Hams, gammons, salt silversides and briskets of beef are not . . . so preposterously expensive that only about half of one per cent of the population can ever taste them . . . It is here especially that we get back to cooking in a certain quantity . . .

'Kebab Cookery' tells how to make perfect kebabs derived from 'the Levantine and oriental traditions to which English cookery already owes so much. Khichri is: 'The dish from which the English evolved kedgeree. The original contains no fish, and is simply a mixture of lentils and rice cooked with spices. It is very cheap and filling.'

Those potted meats about which Elizabeth had already written are here repeated and augmented: Prawn Paste, Potted Tongue, Potted Spiced Beef, Pork . . . Served chilled with hot thin toast, these simple and delicious little pots, for hors d'oeuvres and savouries, are quintessentially English and as such are perfect for wintry Sunday morning breakfasts in the country with a fire nearby, good strong coffee and fresh home-made toasted bread.

'Sweet Dishes and Cakes' contains some of the most homely, delicate and luxurious dishes Elizabeth had yet recorded: Almond Rice, and Hot Chestnuts and Prunes from Mrs Leyel; How to Make a Pippin Tart from the Countess of Kent; Thick Perkins, Dark Ginger Cake, 'this excellent recipe . . . from my partner, Renée Fedden'; Chocolate Chinchilla, and here Elizabeth reminds us that the favoured seventeenth-century flavouring for chocolate, newly arrived from the New World, was cinnamon. There is also a Cinnamon Ice Cream.

This ice cream has more recently been taken up by contemporary chefs, one of the many recipes which Elizabeth has not been credited with resurrecting. Good chefs and food writers have always looked at old dishes. Several of the best chefs and writers have had considerable collections of cookery books; but it is only in more recent years that grandiloquent versions, or what amounted to pastiches of old dishes, have sometimes been replaced in England with the original. The drive towards 'authentic' traditonal food, which Elizabeth was responsible for maintaining with *Spices, Salt and Aromatics*, has been little understood by most contemporary chefs. Their food is frequently described as 'authentic', but for many in Britain it is only 'quaint', and will be forgotten at the next turn of fashion. Food has become part of the new leisure; the only time numbers of people turn from versions of fast food and really cook. One is reminded of Elizabeth's criticisms of the English for making an effort only for special occasions and not for every day.

The novelist A. S. Byatt gave *Spices, Salt and Aromatics in the English Kitchen* a perceptive review on its publication, saying:

> She has a sense of facts, of the history and geography of real food, quite divorced from the timeless fantasy and charade which we have whipped up in response to shining machinery and hygenic mass-production, our indiscriminate parade of Granny's old cambric nightdress, shawls and laced boots, cheap Indian bedspreads . . . her stone porringers were used in the seventeenth century and she suggests sensible modern equivalents. She treats the English language with the response she accords to food, and writes with a purely English combination of the flatly Anglo Saxon . . . and the lyrically Romantic . . . The new book com-

bines practical and Romantic in its very subject, the history and illustration of the English addiction to spices and aromatics . . . the romance is English and earthy, solidly established in time and space.

Another favourable reviewer said:

> Provincial France, Italy, the lands bordering the Mediterranean, those were the areas whose food she evoked so eloquently. And when I came to visit them years later . . . Yes it was all as she had said. But English cookery? It seems such an alien field, a vast gastronomic desert of pale blancmanges, stodgy suet puddings and boiled fish – could she do the same for that? The miraculous answer is yes, she can and has.

There were other contemporary writers making claims for the importance of resurrecting old English dishes. Many of these books, however, were either exercises in nostalgia or ultimately too unwieldy and academic to be used as modern cookery manuals. Elizabeth's aversion to inaccuracy, verging on the obsessive, and her profound understanding of the history of her subject led her to avoid either of these pitfalls. For those who were prepared to read carefully, *Spices, Salt and Aromatics in the English Kitchen* was not only inspiring but also useful, with a degree of subtlety not so far seen in her work.

Despite its undoubted merits for the most part the book's reception was not as wholehearted as her previous work had been. This latest message was a difficult one for many of Elizabeth's first followers to accept. For years her writing had inclined the Anglo-Saxons away from their own culinary traditions and taught them to savour instead the food of the sun. In this latest work she was telling them that, at its best – found in recipes from the past – their own tradition had been as rich and rewarding as that of the Mediterranean.

As Elizabeth had so exactly characterized it herself, the 'runes, litanies and magic spells' had always been the unifying force in her writing; the evocation of place, the calling up of atmospheres and conjuring with the words, until her readers were in the place she recalled, ready to experience, however momentarily, a hint of paradise.

These evocations were enhanced by passages from other writers, but the realist in her had always held the whole together with the recipes, the practical realization of those spells. She may have described what was to some the unknown, but there was usually the knowledge that if readers could only get there; get themselves to that obscure corner of Sardinia, Provence, Egypt, they would actually discover the food Elizabeth was describing. In *Spices, Salt and Aromatics*, however, she was attempting something more difficult; she was conjuring with the past. For most of us, to travel in time like this and then to bring back the past into the present, to re-create it, is not as easy as travelling in space. It demands a more imaginative commitment than Elizabeth had so far demanded of her readers and which a number were not prepared to give.

Spices, Salt and Aromatics in the English Kitchen was dedicated to Elizabeth's old friend and present collaborator in the shop, Renée Fedden. In early April of 1970, the year the book was published, Elizabeth had just returned from one of her buying trips abroad. Since Elizabeth David Ltd had opened, she had made this journey once or twice a year usually with Renée. They would return to favoured sources of supply and also search for new ones. One of the results of these journeys was an essay written in 1980, entitled 'Eating out in Provincial France 1965–1977'. Elizabeth sadly but accurately recorded what she saw as a general decline:

> How is it that French restaurant cooking has so notably . . . deteriorated during the past two or three decades? Among [the reasons] I would say the main one has a good deal to do with the conservatism of the French themselves in matters of eating. In the vast majority of French restaurants . . . the order of menu has remained unchanged for fifty years . . . What has suffered from shrinkage is the quality of raw materials, of the cooking skills and also . . . the critical faculties of the customers . . . What has dismayed me as much as anything else has been the complacent attitude of customers and restaurateurs alike.

She says that on her trips for the shop she was there for 'an average of two or three weeks at a time travelling all over the country, staying in different hotels night after night, eating in every type of restaurant from village inns to the occasional . . . three star establishment'. She tells us that they mostly kept away from the tourist haunts, motorways and the tourist season,

> staying often in hotels patronized by commercial travellers.
> During the subsequent three years my visits to France were less
> frequent and less extended and . . . I was free to pick and choose
> . . . restaurants . . . So it is with some experience that I record
> the melancholy fact that during those fifteen years I have eaten
> far worse meals in France, and more expensively . . . than I
> would have believed possible in any civilized country.

She remembers one of the exceptions: 'meals in a pretty and elegant country restaurant' owned by the mère Brazier whose other restaurant, in Lyons, Elizabeth had written about lovingly in *French Provincial Cooking*. This one was up out of the 'notorious fogs of the city . . . and for a time my favourite restaurant in all France . . . alas that it must be written about in the past tense . . . there was a gaiety and a grace about lunches at Col de la Luère which seemed to me to be most essentially French.' She concluded that 'in France these days' culinary experiences of quality are 'more likely to be connected with a picnic than with a meal in a restaurant. Picnics in France combine so many joys . . .'

During this period Elizabeth hints at 'staff problems'. Amongst these problems was a manageress removing things from the shop. More importantly still Elizabeth was beginning to have fundamental disagreements with her partners. For some time the Triers and Llewelyns had been most concerned about profits, telling her that she must be more careful about how and what she sold, but Elizabeth refused to bend.

'Liz wanted the shop to be a little museum, a place saying to people: "This is how you do it." But you couldn't do that without losing enormous amounts of money,' says Peter Trier. 'A big percentage of the stuff in the warehouse over at Vauxhall Bridge was stuff that we had bought and Liz had got fed up with. There'd be something selling well and she'd decide she didn't like it any more, so it would just stay sitting in the warehouse collecting dust. She was always fiddling about with stuff on the shelves. If someone wanted something from the window display they were told to come back in two months when the window display was changed.

'On many occasions I told her that we couldn't go on in the selective way in which we were without the shop folding. She just didn't want to see it . . . the shop was a social centre for Liz . . . It became a kind of club for her friends, that was part of the problem . . . It had such a smart clientèle; younger people like the Dimblebys, the Johnsons [Judy worked there for a time] and others like Peggy Guggenheim, Freya Stark, Princess Margaret and Lord Snowdon. When John and Fanny Craddock came into the shop at the beginning to see what it was about, she hid in the loo; she couldn't stand them. Liz was in the shop so much of her time. For those years it was the centre of her life I think. But one of the overriding things about Liz was that she couldn't stand the average member of the public. She was intolerant of ordinary people. It was an entirely cerebral thing. It wasn't their social background, that didn't matter a bit.'

'Oh, but she could talk to anybody as well,' says Pamela Pugh. 'Yes, people of every type,' says Peter Trier. 'She didn't care as long as there was something they had in common. It could have been anyone. If they were talking about food or anything to do with it – pots, pans, recipes, she would be interested, would be open, would get so involved and stand there talking and listening – she could always listen – and offering advice. Whereas if it was more her contemporaries and she thought they weren't genuine, she wouldn't care who it was, she'd be utterly merciless right there in the shop. She could have been an academic and had the common touch too, that is the rarity. Her meticulous attention to detail overrode the crap. She would say: "That's absolutely crap." She was enormously kind too. When she went on her Paris trips she would always bring me back violet jam because my mother was called Violet. The letter that she wrote when my mother died was absolutely marvellous.'

'At the beginning it was all sweetness and light with everyone,' recalls Doreen Thornton. 'But the trouble was she expected everyone to work with *her* dedication and *her* hours. She had no family commitments like the others did. Renée worked so hard for Elizabeth.'

Renée was in the shop most days and her daughter Frances Fedden who worked for Elizabeth then, told the author of her own and her sister's annoyance at times 'because she [Renée] wouldn't be able to get back home until quite late with the shop keeping her there . . . At 5.30 one wanted to leave work. You wanted to go out, do other things, but Elizabeth found it difficult to understand. You were always being a bit disloyal if you insisted you had to go.'

Gilly Gretton, a young painter who worked in the shop, remembers that: 'One often had to leave late. Not only when the window was being done. Elizabeth was just so dedicated to the shop and her work there that she found it difficult to understand that anyone could want to do anything else . . . It somehow wasn't really like a normal job. You felt part of this endeavour, sometimes kind of whether you liked it or not. But it did make you feel loyal to what the shop represented.'

By 1967 Elizabeth David Ltd had launched a catalogue service and it was clear to the other partners that this wholesale selling was going to be the only way of keeping the business afloat. 'The shop alone wasn't viable, we were unofficially becoming as much a wholesaler, with all the stuff having the Elizabeth David logo on it,' says Pamela Pugh. Renée and a young woman called Antonia Grahame, now spent most of their time over at the warehouse looking after this aspect of the business.

In the summer of 1970, her Kensington house sold, Priscilla had moved back to the country and Wootton, which at Roland's death she would inherit. Roland, eventually a ward of court, had been in a home since 1965, while Wootton was managed by a pilfering cook and general handyman. They were seen off, and during 1969–70 Priscilla renovated the house to something of its former beauty.

In April 1971, after a debilitating illness, Diana had died – for years before her death she had suffered too from that alienating condition, tinnitus. Elizabeth had sometimes spoken and written with impatience of Diana over the years, nevertheless, she and Felicité deeply mourned their beautiful, scatty sister. Elizabeth was initially taken aback when Christopher, Diana's husband, for years Elizabeth's doctor, remarried some months after Diana's death (although she quickly saw how sympathetic was Christopher's new wife). Matters had not been helped by internecine family wrangling over money and property during the course of 1971; finally resolved as a result of Elizabeth's timely and decisive intervention. She had seldom returned to Wootton in the years since leaving it as a girl, but was pleased that her sisters had maintained closer ties with her childhood home. And now Priscilla was châtelaine, the eldest of Rupert's daughters.

In 1971, almost thirty years after she had been forced by circumstance to leave, Stella also returned to Wootton and was installed in a small flat. Since 1962 she had lived in Enfield, on the edge of London. The house was unremarkable except for the fact that it came with a double garden. With the manual assistance of Judith Lassalle's son Patrick, Stella 'made a beautiful English herb garden when hardly anybody else was'. Her daughters tried to persuade Stella to move but she remained adamant in her refusal to do so until she grew too feeble to manage on her own.

By 1972 relations between Elizabeth and the other partners at Elizabeth David Ltd were becoming really strained. To complicate the issue for Elizabeth, always demanding in her expectations of loyalty, it was clear that Renée had some sympathy with the other directors. Peter Trier remembers Renée as 'very quiet, she worked very hard, kept in the background at the shop. She was strong, but not dominatingly so. One or two have called her bossy, but she was a very kind person.' Sybille Bedford, who was like Elizabeth close to Renée, remembers her friend as 'highly intelligent, capable of being emotional; she was thin, severe, haughty, remote. She cooked beautiful Middle Eastern food.'

Negotiations were going ahead to open a branch of the shop in a large store. Elizabeth was reluctant. Peter Trier's analysis of what the shop represented for her — more a kind of permanent social gathering place, with herself as the centre – is correct. Also, notwith-standing her ambivalence about the public, at a level which Elizabeth herself probably did not understand, the shop was for her a way of giving, just as her cooking had always been. Here she was the undoubted magnet for the clients and source of inspiration for the whole enterprise. The underlying message of the shop was Elizabeth's role as teacher: the pots, the tools, the simple gadgets, and finally she herself, were there as purveyors of her message.

Nonetheless for all her shrewdness and professed worldliness Elizabeth was not capable of making a business work enduringly. She had neither the managerial skills nor a good enough appreciation of how others were motivated to continue in any public or impersonal capacity for very long. Stephen Trier, Peter's musician brother, who saw a good deal of her at this period, says: 'Elizabeth had a streak of enormous kindness in her. She could manage while it [the shop] functioned as a club for her but once the others had made it finally clear that it had to work as a business, she couldn't do it.' The problem was insoluble. Elizabeth had succeeded as a brilliant com-municator to large numbers of people with her mass-market publish-ing with Penguin, but here she had to face unique individuals whose ideas didn't coincide with her own. One is reminded of her frustration on the trip to Munich before the war to meet Priscilla, Priscilla's new husband Richard and Felicité. Their opinion of the city hadn't coincided with her own rosy-coloured vision and her anger and frustration were extreme. She hadn't changed very much. Personalities aside, with her books as instructions for the practice, Elizabeth's attitudes regarding quality and design of cooking tools, how they were to be used and the style of the kitchens which housed them, had all been profoundly influenced by her ethos in the last few years. And this was reflected in the myriad kitchen shops which soon opened in the wake of her lead.

Meanwhile at Wootton Stella had grown very frail and in early June 1973 Elizabeth was urgently recalled by Felicité from a visit to Italy. Not long after her return she wrote: 'My mother was very ill and unlikely to recover. So I went down to the country where she lived . . . and spent several hours with her before she died – yesterday afternoon [9th June]. She was nearly 90.'

Soon afterwards Maudie O'Malley wrote to offer Elizabeth her condolences and received this letter in reply:

> My mother really was a very remarkable person although she could be, as you say, alarming – and her personality was so strong that it is very hard to believe that she is no longer here.
>
> I am thankful for her that it is over. She was not happy . . . could not have been, once she had lost her independence, and her garden. Indeed during the past year . . . I knew she felt that there was little point to her existence . . .
>
> It would be futile to pretend that she was a good mother in the conventional sense but what extraordinary qualities she had in other ways – none of us, sadly, had inherited her genius for gardening, but . . . all our surroundings, came in some way or other from her. Her influence was very strong . . . and it was of course due to the somewhat erratic education and upbringing she gave us that I was able eventually to write my books and create my shop. Félicité asks me to thank you so very much for your letter . . .
>
> With love to you and Peter
>
> > Elizabeth.

Stella was buried in the small churchyard at Folkington close by Wootton, where she had attended services many times with her husband Rupert and small daughters half a century ago. Elizabeth wrote a card to Julia, Priscilla's daughter, thanking her for helping to make the service and wake afterwards at Wootton 'such a remarkable occasion. For that one day, Wootton was once again Stella's domain. Even her vanished garden seemed to live again in the dazzling June sunshine. And Diana wasn't left out.'

By now Elizabeth felt that her strenuously high standards in the shop were being chipped away; compromised for the sake of profit. Her partners said, 'No, we are just trying to survive.'

Elizabeth David Ltd had never really been organized with formal directors' meetings. 'Everyone had basically just made decisions along with Liz. The choices about stuff in the shop had all ultimately been hers,' said Stephen Trier. 'She'd have a turn in the shop. Oh, quite often. She'd say, "God, what are we carrying all this bloody rubbish for," referring to things on the shelves that she'd decided she no longer liked. And it would have to be cleared away into the stockroom and the other stuff would sit at Goading Street [the store under the arches near Vauxhall Bridge]. She would have a caprice in the shop like that. And that's how Elizabeth split from the shop. One day she had a turn and flounced out saying that was it. And it was. That was it. She didn't come back.'

As time passed her self-imposed exile became fixed in Elizabeth's mind as the result of unremittingly horrible circumstances; her principles undermined and compromised by commerce. To friends she was remorseless in her attacks on all but Renée. Elizabeth's fury and despair arose essentially from the realization that she could not maintain the shop as previously. Once her partners finally made her understand that they couldn't continue in the same way for much longer, Elizabeth's attitude to retaining a hold on the shop became more ambivalent. This she admitted to no one else and probably not herself either. 'It came to the point where I thought, "We're just going to lose Jenny's money,"' said Peter Trier.

Elizabeth found it almost impossible to admit error; instead turning her partners into vulgar 'monsters' relieved her from the pressure of taking any personal responsibility for the failure of the shop to make a profit. With her growing inclination towards litigiousness Elizabeth launched herself into the attack, vilifying her ex-partners for the rest of her life; a sad outcome to the years all concerned had devoted to Elizabeth David Ltd.

Elizabeth continued seeing Renée for a few months after severing relations with her other partners, but when Renée became more openly sympathetic to their ideas Elizabeth could not accept this and cut her off too. Indeed, after Renée's 'disloyalty' Elizabeth was implacable and these close friends of thirty years never saw one another again. On 17 January 1974 Elizabeth wrote Renée a letter in which her gratitude does little to temper her damning criticisms. Overshadowed as it is by fury, Elizabeth's judgement is clouded, leaving her uncomprehending of Renée's or the other partners' positions. This miserable state of affairs continued until the end of Elizabeth's life.

Dear Renée,

Don't think, on account of anything I've said in the enclosed communication, that I underestimate your contribution to the business. It was enormous and very important, and I don't think we could have made Elizabeth David Ltd what it *was* without you.

I just feel bitter and sad that my own part in it has been so belittled, and my requests for proper treatment so contemptuously rejected by the company.

You invested your money in my name and its prestige, at least that's what you said at the time. I'm glad that its paid off for you, even if not in a very sensational way. [Renée in fact had little financial reward from ED, Ltd.] Again, it was sad that you grew to resent my name and felt it necessary to participate in the rejection of all that it implied so that the name has become a sham.

                                                            E.D.

Only weeks after her sister Diana's death, in April 1971, Elizabeth had travelled to France with Renée on a pre-planned buying trip for the shop. Following their return in May, Elizabeth wrote Renée a letter whose sentiments serve as an illustration of the depth of their now severed friendship.

Dear Renée,

You will never know how much you have helped me . . . I didn't believe that I could manage the trip at all, and certainly with anyone else but you there could have been no question of my going away. As things turned out I think you were right, and anyway the job had to be done. You have done all the work, all the planning and coping, and at the same time you have comforted me and kept me going and provided many moments when grief was forgotten . . . and like every one of our journeys together this one produced what will prove to be happy memories . . . even sometimes a good meal.

You must be very tired. As I well know from my sessions with poor Diana during the last weeks of her life, sustaining somebody who is in misery is totally exhausting. Your patience and understanding are not gifts for which one can exactly say thank you I suppose. I can say thank you, my love, for using them so wonderfully.

> Elizabeth.

Recalling this period of acrimony and turmoil, Sybille Bedford said of Elizabeth, 'She felt that in Renée all her ideals had been let down . . . the break was definitive. For her it was like a mortal blow . . . Elizabeth's ability to see straight had narrowed over time.'

After another year or so Renée herself retired from working for Elizabeth David Ltd but the shop carried on with Elizabeth's name. She tried her utmost to withdraw from her partners the right to use it; wrote long and emotional letters to friends and sought legal advice on the matter, including asking Veronica Nicholson's solicitor husband John to help. 'But,' said Peter Trier, 'if Liz had been more civilized about the whole thing we'd have let it go. High drama was Liz's thing and no doubt she dined out on it for years afterwards. She could be so destructive if she felt that way inclined . . . Liz made a lot of song and dance about it not being right after she left – "That terrible stuff being sold in my name" – but it wasn't really much changed.'

Peter did not entirely understand Elizabeth's passionate relationship with her name, why should he? It seems quite clear, however, that as someone so preoccupied with controlling the various aspects of her life, Elizabeth's professional name was central to her identity. She felt that in losing control of her name she had lost part of herself. The loss of control in her carefully divided life was something which Elizabeth feared more than almost anything. 'Years later, when we met again,' Peter said, 'she chundered on about it . . . she had an obsession with her name.'

Twelve years later Elizabeth was at a book-signing for her collected journalism, *An Omelette and a Glass of Wine*. Someone there was speaking to Chuck Williams, an American devotee and friend of Elizabeth's who owns an enormously successful group of kitchen supply shops in the United States. Chuck Williams was told about the events which had led Elizabeth to leave her partners in the shop, and that she had not seen any more of them since that time. 'It wasn't that we had said we weren't seeing one another, we just didn't get in touch,' says Peter, who also 'wouldn't stand for crap'. He felt Elizabeth had behaved excessively. Chuck Williams subsequently rang Peter and said, 'What on earth are you doing being so stupid like this?' Peter gave it some thought, 'And I sat down and wrote Elizabeth a letter.' She replied and afterwards he and Elizabeth saw one another regularly. 'When we took up together again I'd take her out. We'd go to places she then liked: Sally Clarke's, Simon Hopkinson at Bibendum . . . others. "You were such shits to me," she'd say more than once. But we weren't, you know. We had to make a living and Liz wasn't interested in that . . .'

At the end of 1973 Elizabeth was in hospital writing in low spirits to Marjorie Lloyd, a friend from the MOI in Cairo, and saying: 'Work progresses hardly at all. Disruptions continual, and swollen legs now joined to neuritic feet with inflamed joints. Temper often inflamed too, on account goings on of E.D. Ltd. Much love E.' Although during this year she was given the André Simon Memorial Award, the first public award made for her writing, her gratification was marred by exhaustion from anger. Time and age had not blessed Elizabeth with greater restraint, nor a more tranquil spirit. She had inherited to the full those relentlessly unforgiving aspects of her grandfather James Gwynne and these became more evident as she ceased to be the femme fatale, now often preferring the company of women.

One example serves to illustrate the intensity and bitterness of her feelings and the remorselessness of her attacks on those with whom she had worked. In one of her annotated first editions of *Spices, Salt and Aromatics in the English Kitchen*, inherited by her great-nephew William Harcourt-Smith, Elizabeth has scored through and made illegible every passage which refers to Elizabeth David Ltd. At the first reprinting and revising of the book in 1973, she was quick to benefit from the opportunity and erased her public connections with the shop by omitting all reference to it in the biographical frontispiece and throughout the rest of the book. In all subsequent publications of this and her other books she articulated her fury with greater force still, by addition of the sentence: 'In 1973 Mrs David severed all connection with the business trading under her name.' A final and perhaps conciliatory point worthy of note: Elizabeth never had the dedication to her estranged friend Renée removed from *Spices, Salt and Aromatics in the English Kitchen.*

CHAPTER NINETEEN

A Mediterranean Passion Cooled
(1973–1977)

ONE OF THE assistants working in Elizabeth David Ltd, April Tanner (later Boyes), had previously trained as a librarian and when she left the shop Elizabeth asked her to help catalogue her books at Halsey Street. Years of collecting had led to such an expansion of her library that it was now 'silted up' into the thousands. Described in some wonderment by friends, the books were everywhere: in piles on tables, chairs, the stairs, and badly needed organizing into some kind of system. April did her tidy and methodical best, and by early 1974 Elizabeth was writing to Alan Davidson that she was 'still working spasmodically on my books'. The situation was made more difficult by the presence in her library/sitting room of almost 'fifteen huge cartons of papers, utensils and oddments' retrieved from the shop. These required sorting, but Elizabeth felt unable to rise to the task at that moment. For years April arrived for part of the week to act as secretary cum general factotum to Elizabeth; driving her to libraries and further afield outside London on many occasions.

In *Spices, Salt and Aromatics in the English Kitchen*, Elizabeth had declared that the book was simply the first volume of a series which was to be nothing less than a thematic history of English food. A notable addition to the field of serious histories of English food had recently been made with *Food and Drink in Britain* (Constable, 1973) by a Brotherton Librarian at Leeds University, C. Anne Wilson. A thoroughly researched book, which Elizabeth called 'admirable', it is nevertheless more history than cookery and not exactly the kind which Elizabeth believed she wanted to write. No one had yet undertaken such a literary and broadly cultural look at the whole subject by theme as she intended, and there was plenty of room for her mammoth projected undertaking. Although one of these themes would eventually take precedence Elizabeth was at present researching on the next two works in tandem. They were to be, first a book on bread in England, the germ of which had been the little booklet written for her shop entitled 'The Baking of an English Loaf'; and next, the 'Creams, Ices, Syllabubs, Trifles' she had referred to in *Spices, Salt and Aromatics*.

Another writer who, like Elizabeth, combined in her work a felicitous mix of literature and history, was the then young (now late) Jane Grigson. By 1974 she had published three well-written books. She was Cambridge-educated and a prize-winning Italianist, whose first book, *Charcuterie and French Pork Cookery* (1967), had been sent to Elizabeth as a typescript by Anthea Joseph of the publishers Michael Joseph. Elizabeth's response was very positive, as she wrote of the book in her own posthumous tribute to Mrs Grigson in 1990:

Here was a writer who could combine a delightful quote from
Chaucer on the subject of a pike galantine with a careful recipe
for a modern chicken and pork version of the same ancient dish,
and who could do so without pedantry or a hint of preciousness.

The year following its publication Elizabeth had proposed Jane Grigson to the *Observer*. Jane's magazine articles gained her a huge following, notable, as Alan Davidson wrote of her in his *Times* obituary:

Because she was above all a friendly author, equipped by both
frame of mind and style of writing to communicate easily with
[the public]. However much she knew about this or that . . . she
never seemed to be talking down to anyone. On the contrary she
is a most companionable presence in the kitchen; often catching
the imagination with a deftly chosen fragment of history or
poetry . . . [Jane was married to the poet Geoffrey Grigson.]
How often have I heard people declare that her recipes are not
just a pleasure to read – they always work!

Jane Grigson had from the first, in the introduction to her *Charcuterie*, declared: 'Nobody can produce a cookery book these days without a deep appreciation of Elizabeth David's work.' In an interview with the author Paul Bailey defines the difference between Elizabeth and Jane Grigson as:

> A very fine one . . . Jane was a scholar of a different mental discipline . . . it was Jane's tone of voice that Elizabeth liked . . . they were both on the same course. Elizabeth writes the more fine porcelain prose. But Jane is no mean writer. She is more robust, she is a more generous spirited creature than Elizabeth. She's not so aloof. But Elizabeth came from a different time, she was so reticent, and that squares with her hiding behind her prose . . . that there is another message there in her work to do with art, and a whole seriousness about life.
>
> Jane said she believed that the reason Elizabeth's writing was so good was because it came from some kind of compulsion. Most people who write about food write about it because there is a lot of money to be made from it . . . particularly nowadays . . . Jane sensed that Elizabeth had had something traumatic happen to her and that she therefore needed to write to express herself. But being an Englishwoman of a certain class and time and having a certain reticence . . . and being someone who appreciated food and had tasted all those flavours abroad . . . what better way to hide her real purpose, which was to express herself in the deepest possible way, than to do it in a scholarly way . . . As she grew older her books became more and more scholarly.

This is perceptive, but can be read as implying a self-knowledge which this author does not believe Elizabeth possessed.

In early 1974 she had not recovered from her self-imposed exile from Elizabeth David Ltd and was at a low ebb. Her health was suffering and she wrote more than one letter which shows clearly her difficulty in mustering her normal enthusiasm. To Alan Davidson she wrote that she had been immobilized for a short while, owing to a persistent ulcer on her right ankle, 'which refused to go away whatever

I do or don't do'. (The effectiveness of antibiotics in treating infection is of course severely limited when combined with alcohol, and this Elizabeth refused to stop consuming.) 'I try to get on with my two books, but without much conviction. I don't really foresee either of them getting finished.'

In February she said to Maudie O'Malley, the painter who had attended Cedric Morris and Lett Haines's art school, that she was 'plodding away at my yeast book, but see no end in sight.' Elizabeth had for the moment lost the will to write, and it was an effort to put pen to paper.

Elizabeth may have felt downhearted and without the will to apply herself, but her disciplined mental exertion had long ago become compulsive, and we see the necessity to immerse herself in her books beginning to provoke stimulating thoughts and ideas.

During this year Jane Grigson brought out her *English Food* (Macmillan, 1974) with its lovely, usable recipes, never in the least misty-eyed or effete. Her lucid introduction is a well-judged balance between past and present, an overview which Elizabeth could not always manage so well. Elizabeth's demon, which had driven her so relentlessly and to such creativeness, had not facilitated an integration of her spirit, already so clear in the young Jane Grigson. The subject, an appreciation of English food from the past, was becoming a popular one, but Jane Grigson's voice on this was amongst the very best in its integrity and unpretentiousness. Her sentiments were entirely understood by Elizabeth, whose creed they perfectly endorsed and who was vitriolic in her condemnation of those who jumped on the bandwagon of 'Ye Olde Englande'. For a description of the very task upon which Elizabeth had launched herself and whose essential nature she didn't always communicate too well, Jane Grigson's introduction to her own book seems entirely appropriate and is here quoted at length.

> The English are a very adaptive people. English cooking . . . is a great deal more varied and delectable than our masochistic temper in this matter allows . . . It is . . . true that a good many things in our marketing system now fight against simple and delicate food. Tomatoes have no taste. The finest flavoured

potatoes are not available in the shops. Vegetables and fruit are seldom fresh ... Cheeses are subdivided and imprisoned in plastic wrapping ... Words such as 'fresh' and 'home made' have been borrowed by commerce to tell lies.

In spite of this the English cook has a wonderful inheritance if she cares to make use of it ... My aim has been to put in dishes of quality ... I have also included a number of Welsh dishes because ... they are linked closely with much English food while retaining a rustic elegance which we have tended to lose ...

There's no avoiding the fact that the best cooking has come down from the top. Or if you don't like the word 'top', then from the skilled, employed by those who could pay and had the time to appreciate quality. In England on the whole the food descends less from a courtly tradition than from the manor houses and rectories and homes of the well to do merchants ... It hands down the impression of the social life of families in which wives and daughters weren't too grand to go into the kitchen and to keep a close eye on the vegetable garden and the dairy ...

One thing to note is that the great English cookery writers, from Hannah Glasse to Elizabeth David, have most often been women, in contrast to the French ... Our classical tradition has been domestic, with the domestic virtues of quiet enjoyment and generosity. Whatever happened when the great mass centres developed in the nineteenth century, English cookery books of the eighteenth century to early Victorian times had been written from an understanding of good food and good eating, a concern for quality.

This piece conveys with grace and apparent effortlessness, some essential features of English social history. Despite subsequent pessimism about the future of England's table, Jane Grigson echoed Elizabeth's beliefs when she wrote that: 'I finished *English Food* full of hope. In discovering at least something of our tradition for myself, I began to see that we did have a treasury to be exploited ...'

Elizabeth was also labouring: burrowing, searching, sifting, synthesizing, in order to illustrate for her readers just that 'treasury' to which Jane Grigson refers. She had long ago realized the importance of England's culinary past, represented in the present only by books. With the help of writers like Kenelm Digby, Elizabeth Countess of Kent, Robert May, Hannah Glasse, the Ladies Llanover and Clark of Tillypronie, her beloved Eliza Acton and many more besides, Elizabeth was continuing her task, begun with *Spices, Salt and Aromatics in the English Kitchen*, of creating a new world. Just as Jane Grigson did not deal in nostalgia, neither was Elizabeth's writing about the past ever quaint. She had too much integrity and knew too much of England's past either to prettify or trivialize it.

Jill Norman, her editor at Penguin, was a new friend whom few of her older ones met socially with Elizabeth more than in passing. With Elizabeth's present book Jill Norman's position of support as editor and friend was at times to be crucial over the next few years. This included a number of trips taken together, foraging for information and corroboration. By happy coincidence Jill's husband, Paul Bremen, was an antiquarian book dealer, specializing in early manuscripts and incunabula. This association of interests accorded with Elizabeth's own growing obsession.

With the successive reissue of Elizabeth's earlier books by Penguin in recent years, Jill's input had necessarily been a modest one; Elizabeth made revisions (always meticulously up to date) and revised or rewrote her introductions to the original hardbacks, and Jill Norman simply checked over the process. With *English Bread and Yeast Cookery* (Allen Lane, 1977) the position was different.

For some time Jill had been commissioning original Penguin books and taking more editorial responsibility for them. One of these was Alan Davidson's first book, *Mediterranean Seafood*; at Elizabeth's suggestion commissioned by Jill. 'She worked with me for the entire book, she was a very good editor,' says Alan, now himself a publisher and an acclaimed author of several more books. Elizabeth felt the same about Jill's contribution to her present book, *English Bread and Yeast Cookery*, where her editorial influence was significant.

Meanwhile April Boyes continued with her cataloguing of Elizabeth's library – against Elizabeth's wishes she had pencilled shelf-marks on the books. She also drove Elizabeth on regular errands of research inside and outside London; the Guildhall Library, within the ancient City Square Mile, was an important source of material. If April dropped Elizabeth off in the morning rather than staying to help her she would be reminded to put the wine to keep cool in the pond in the little garden behind the library. At about two o'clock when Elizabeth had finished they would spread out a blanket on the grass, fish the cooled wine out of the water and take their picnic lunch in this incongruous little haven with the roar of traffic and the bustle of commerce just beyond the shielding walls.

'She was coming in and out then, often with Mrs Boyes,' says Irene Gilchrist, the Principal Reference Librarian at the Library. 'It was clear that she wasn't well. When the air became too much for her she would go and sit on the library steps, giving the City police quite a turn . . . Mrs David had already used the library before 1974 . . . In her writing it's clear she was only interested in history inasmuch as it could serve a purpose . . . She always respected the staff here, she looked up things herself. She did demand respect though, it was never put into words . . . I did feel she had a certain arrogance. We would see her several times in a few weeks and then not for months and months.'

Elizabeth's working practices were now settled into a pattern which did not vary much until her death. Writing to Marjorie Lloyd in 1975, she asks her: 'to come round for a glass or two of wine or a picnic-type lunch. (I've all but given up eating in the evenings and try not to drink more than a glass or two of wine, so that I can get to bed early and can then start work early – also I'm trying to make drastic cuts in smoking – it's not only the ridiculous waste of money, but I've been coughing so badly, all self-inflicted.) . . . My book plods on. It has become a burden and I am determined to get it over with very soon. But there's quite a bit still to do.'

There *was* still a great deal to do but Elizabeth's working regime rarely held to the one described above. She often laboured until very late into the night. Sybille Bedford lived nearby and, a late person herself, remembers passing on numerous occasions when Elizabeth's light was still burning at two or three o'clock in the morning. Elizabeth would then wake early, often work from bed, have lunch at home or sometimes out – if with a friend probably long and bibulously – then sleep for the latter part of the afternoon. The cycle would then repeat itself with work late into the night. Nothing changed outwardly as Elizabeth worked her way through her book, except that over these years she became more difficult to please, more acerbic in her condemnation of those of whom she disapproved. (Robert Carrier, for instance, whose ideas for his successful kitchenshop Elizabeth believed had come entirely from her own, she called 'the thief'. It rankled that he even wrapped his kitchenware in black tissue paper as she had done in Elizabeth David Ltd.) As a consequence of voicing her disapproval Elizabeth was not without enemies.

Beside the predictable calcification of someone of Elizabeth's temperament, a much more important final shift of emphasis was taking place in Elizabeth's writing. A change is already noticeable in *Spices, Salt and Aromatics in the English Kitchen*, a delightful little book whose sources are clearly and avowedly historical. With *English Bread and Yeast Cookery* the orientation is now unmistakable.

In Elizabeth's most intense journalistic phase, through the late Fifties and into the mid-Sixties, she applied her formidable intelligence to aspects of the world which she had hitherto ignored. The small man, increasingly threatened by the large corporations, had been consistently championed in England by a small group of writers such as Jane Grigson. It was so obvious as to be hardly worth saying that, in general, good food and cooking tended to go with a multitude of independent, small-scale centres of activity. This view was implicit in all of Elizabeth's work, but in *English Bread and Yeast Cookery* she addresses these themes with unrelenting vigour:

> What is utterly dismaying is the mess our milling and baking concerns succeed in making with the dearly bought grain that goes into their grist. Quite simply it is wasted on a nation which cares so little about the quality of its bread that it has allowed itself to be mesmerised into buying the equivalent of eight and a quarter million large white factory-made loaves every day of the year.

Elsewhere Elizabeth notes from an *Assessment of the British Bread Industry*, carried out in 1974, that: 'British bread is the most chemically treated in Europe.'

Concurrently with these practical concerns which rightly infused the book, Elizabeth was also launching herself into themes of a far grander nature. 1973 had been both her sixtieth year and the year of her mother's death. By nature an artist, like many such, however, with the writing of *English Bread and Yeast Cookery* Elizabeth 'builded better than she knew'. Clearly not entirely conscious of the personal significance of her labours, throughout this exceptional book she is seeking to describe what enduringly exists. This she achieves by linking herself with something more real and permanent than that first wishful, nostalgic, Romantic-escapist vision in *Mediterranean Food*. After the solid, integrated craftsmanship and restrained discipline of *Italian Food*; the beautiful, studied and mature gathering together of her years of thought on France in *French Provincial Cooking*, in *English Bread and Yeast Cookery* Elizabeth at last brings to a halt her lifetime of escape.

A moving leitmotif of this magisterial work is Elizabeth's wrestling with growing old; facing up to the terrors of mortality and the ineradicable human yearning for its opposite. The themes over which she ranges are often so deep and rich, so remarkably varied, that the book becomes impossible to paraphrase adequately. Because it is not a simple work whose themes are immediately available, their very weight proved a stumbling block for many readers, and as a consequence few have read it all the way through. Its many-layered historical approach does not facilitate appreciation by being dipped into nor, with its 547 pages, is reading at one sitting very likely. Above all *English Bread and Yeast Cookery* is something to return to when there is an odd quiet hour to spare, in a spirit of dedication and with time for rumination. The advice Elizabeth had quoted long ago from that little book *Home Baked*, which had so inspired her: 'All that bread needs is time and warmth,' is entirely appropriate for the reading of her own book. She need only have added: 'And a willingness to experiment.' For such readers the rewards will be manifold.

English Bread and Yeast Cookery is divided into two parts: Part I is a *History and Background*, while Part II gives the *Recipes*. Part I describes the varieties of grain past and present used for the milling of flour. Elizabeth tells us about the milling and the flour itself; the leaven, yeast, salt and flavourings, the remarkable variety of bread ovens, the bread factories, the commonplace and quaint names and the shapes of buns, cakes, loaves, and much else besides. In Part II she states bluntly that the recipe for French bread from the eminent seventeenth-century English cook Robert May, 'is extremely simple, a total refutation – there are many others in this book – of the belief too hastily assumed by home economists, cookery journalists and cookery-book reviewers, that any recipe earlier than Mrs Beeton is impracticable today'.

Setting down the anatomy of English recipes, Elizabeth traces the development of the old ones. Sometimes she concludes with her own modifications to the myriad baps and rolls, manchets and payndemayns, crumpets and muffins, pancakes and oatcakes, dumplings and doughnuts, regional yeast cakes and spiced fruit breads.

As Elizabeth traces the histories of the materials and methods for making the innumerable varieties of bread, her book fairly resounds with quotation. In writing of bread, whose ancient craft and mysteries are interwoven with so many of the enduring myths and symbols of mankind, her thoughts turn again and again to English tradition and its practices. She speaks of:

> The ancient rituals of ploughing and sowing and reaping, the gruelling work at harvest time, the thanksgivings and feasting when the corn was safely gathered in, the allusions . . . to the millstreams running dry so that no grain could be ground, the tales of dishonest millers, the portrayals of the poor humble gleaners bent double over their task of scratching the few last ears of wheat from the cornfields after the landlord's grain had been harvested – all these are more or less familiar to us through the works of our poets and writers. From William Langland to Shakespeare, from Chaucer to John Bunyan . . . from the Jacobean translators of the Bible to the eighteenth-century Parson Woodforde, all and scores more, travellers, diarists . . . have in some way recorded the year's cycle of growing and harvesting.

In a long letter to Veronica Nicholson Elizabeth writes at length of her attempts, through her readings of the Bible, to unravel the problem of the words leaven and yeast. She admits that her knowledge of the Bible was rather shaky, and hopes to be able to complete this book without having to quote it. She begins her letter in annoyance, but the subject soon claims her, provoking a disquisition; the germ of which became, in her book, one of the most varied and interesting passages yet written on that elusive substance, yeast. It commences here in her letter to Veronica with a beautiful introductory passage: 'In Chaucer's England one of the names for yeast or barm was Goddis-Goode "bicause it cometh of the grete grace of God." These words imply a blessing. To me that is just what it is. It is also mysterious, magical . . . this substance which performs the ever-recurring leavening miracle . . .' And it is worthy of note in the writing of *English Bread and Yeast Cookery* how the words mysterious, magical, miracle, recur more than ever before as Elizabeth seeks to understand. 'First, leaven doesn't mean yeast as we understand it – and leaven not yeast is the word used in the Old Revised Version. It was like this. Before the days when yeast, or barm, was isolated as a fermenting agent taken in liquid form from the top of the cask of ale . . .' Elizabeth's explanation of one of the most stirring passages from the Old Testament continues in robustly practical tones. Yet her feeling for the beauty and significance of the words gets the better of her and we see her moved:

> The origin of the Passover was that the Israelites were getting ready to up sticks and get out of Egypt, so Moses told them to throw out their leaven, they couldn't take it with them – all those heavy jars and trekking across the desert – so when they didn't have any leaven they had to do without risen bread and bake just flour and water – biscuit – and ever after they kept the Passover with unleavened bread in memory of that time (I expect I've got all this garbled, it may be more Cecil B. de Mille than the Bible).
>
> I don't know whether St Paul was the first to use leaven as a symbol of corruption, and unleavened bread as one of a return to innocence, anyway that's what he was saying to the Corinthi-

ans. I don't know what they'd done to provoke the diatribe — that chapter is mostly about fornication . . . and in the Old Revised Version reads as if some lunatic sub. had been at work on it. But . . . I don't understand . . . all the references by St Paul to cleaning the leaven of evil, purging is the word used by the old translators who didn't use words for nothing . . . so perhaps there was . . . some way of cleaning a leaven, purging it, renewing it — a purification, a spring cleaning.

In my bible (given to me at my christening) there is a splendid Concordance . . . According to this: 'Leaven is any substance that promotes fermentation. In the N.T. . . . a symbol of silent pervasive influence, usually of that which is corrupt.' Silent pervasive influence is marvellous. Pasteur must have thought something like that when he finally discovered that it was the bloom on the grape which makes the ferment in wine. But I'm sure he didn't think it was corrupt . . . The Jews aren't the only people who are superstitious about it [leaven]. I think the Puritans were anti-leaven, they would be, and at different times I fancy there have been other outbursts against it.

In *English Bread and Yeast Cookery* Elizabeth is not only recalling some good recipes with a few bits of history tacked on, she is attempting to create a world. With the loss of so many traditional practices this is, as we saw in her previous book, *Spices, Salt . . .*, of necessity from the past and its records alone. In the latter years of her life, history became an abiding interest for its own sake, as well as a means to order her own inner chaos. Most importantly it is used as her handmaiden, and she harnesses its battery with exemplary command, to evoke and capture our sympathy and imagination. With our interest and imagination so primed we understand that the recipes are the essential core of the history, the backbone of the very real world she *creates*. In her customary manner Elizabeth enlists others to add weight and lustre to her themes, and the cumulative effect of her quotes, from the far distant to the more recent past, is somehow more powerful than in any of her previous works.

One strand, quietly and consistently present throughout this book, is Elizabeth's easier acceptance of her own Englishness. The authors cited, like the themes, range far and wide over time and place. She quotes from *Centuries of Meditation* by the seventeenth-century cleric and poet Thomas Traherne, in which he wrote that when he was a child it seemed as if 'the corn was orient and immortal wheat, which never should be reaped nor was ever sown. I thought it had stood from everlasting to everlasting.' And Elizabeth adds, 'magical and mysterious words'.

'"My bread is sweet and nourishing, made from my own wheat, ground in my own mill, and baked in my own oven",' wrote Tobias Smollett in *Humphry Clinker*. For the twentieth century Elizabeth has York Ketteridge, quoted from *Five Miles to Bunkum*, as 'a most kind and understanding man who knew about wheats, their differences in height, colour and yield. He would snatch a couple of near-ripened ears, rub them in his horny hands to shed the husks, then blow into his cupped hands to winnow husks from grain. Husks clung to his whiskers as he tossed the grain into his mouth. "Wheat is life, boy. Don't let no silly bugger tell you different."'

George Eliot contemplates watermills in *The Mill on the Floss*: 'The rush of water, and the booming of the mill, bring a dreamy deafness which seems to heighten the peacefulness of the scene. They are like a great curtain of sound, shutting one out from the world beyond. And now there is the thunder of the huge covered wagon coming home with sacks of grain.' And later: 'then there was the smell of hot toast and ale from the kitchen, at the breakfast hour.'

From Henry Mayhew's revelatory study *London Labour and the London Poor* (1861): 'Perhaps no cry — though it is for only one morning — is more familiar to the ears of a Londoner than that of One-penny-two-a-penny, hot cross buns on Good Friday.'

Elizabeth illustrates another archetypal example of Englishness:

> one of our greatest naturalists, Gilbert White of Selborne, on a year's grain growing in Hampshire in the eighteenth century; with their echoes of Shakespeare's 'rich leas of wheat, rye, barley, vetches, oats and pease', these notes evoke a picture most essentially and intensely English. Gilbert White, author of the famous *Natural History of Selborne*, one of that wonderful breed of country parsons who have enriched our literature with their

diaries and their meticulous records – William Harrison of Essex, from whom we learn so much of Tudor England, was another – kept his journals for nearly a quarter of a century, from 1768 to 1793. He noticed and noted everything going on around him. Such details as the exact 'delicate soft tinge of green rye', 'the millers complain for want of water' ... 'Farmer Knight's wheat of a beautiful colour ... Wheat, being secured by the snow, looks finely ... Great rain ... Rock-like clouds. Oats and pease are cutting ... Sweet harvest weather ... Much wheat bound up in the afternoon ... Goldfinch sings. Oats are cutting. ... White dew. Peaches ripen. Barley begins to be cut.'

We read this and remember that Elizabeth was familiar with Gilbert White's home ground from her youthful visits to Uncle Top and Aunt Grace, the Earl and Countess of Selborne. At their home, Blackmoor House, the estate almost bordered on Gilbert White's beautiful pocket of the Sussex–Hampshire borderlands. In her tribute to the great naturalist, as more than once in this book, Elizabeth leads us to a place rich in memories of her childhood and youth. 'The little water mill at Michelham Priory in East Sussex, founded in the thirteenth century, was restored to working order in the mid-seventies. Visitors to the priory can buy the freshly ground flour and see the workings of a small mill much as it was five or six centuries ago.' This was the same Michelham Priory that Elizabeth's grandfather James had restored, and that her mother Stella was given the choice of upon her marriage to James's son, Rupert Gwynne, seventy years before.

Another place of youthful memories and prominent in *English Bread* ... is Wales, where Elizabeth made numerous journeys while writing her book. There she could still find a few small millers from whom one could buy best-quality flour. White Mill was near Carmarthen: 'Mrs Lickley, the miller's wife ... makes her own blend ... and, should there be none ready when you call at the mill, she will blend and pack it for you while you wait. Many a time I have brought White Mill flour back to London with me, and have also used it for bread to be baked in the old brick oven at Ty Isaf' (this was the old farmhouse near Llandeilo belonging to her friend Jean Bolland).

As ever Elizabeth experimented, and for the five years it took her to write the book, she baked constantly until she understood the recipes. She found the experience of using the oven in Jean Bolland's home – trying out recipes older than the dome-shaped brick oven, itself identical in design to those used for centuries – a moving and instructive one.

Lady Llanover, to whose *Good Cookery* practices Elizabeth had become particularly attached to, and whose delicate drawing of bound wheat sheaves she used as endpapers for her book, appears frequently in the numerous recipes from Wales. But perhaps Elizabeth's greatest favourite, the sensible yet 'poetic' Eliza Acton, finally has her day. With regular references and quotes from her eminently usable books, *Modern Cookery for Private Families* (1845) and *The English Bread Book* (1857) Elizabeth reminds us that: 'It is not under 1845 that we find decisive instructions and definite directions for the making of bread and the management of yeast. What a blessing this book must have been to the baffled housekeepers and cooks of the time.'

Elizabeth was always adept at collecting 'loyal subjects', some more 'slave-like than others', as Doreen Thornton put it. While her sister was writing *English Bread and Yeast Cookery* Felicité's role continued, as Elizabeth described in her acknowledgement: 'in a category unique to herself . . . the imaginative finder and provider-in-chief of books for study'. 'Without her remarkable eye for the relevant book I might perhaps have finished writing my own sooner, but I certainly wouldn't have learned or enjoyed so much while I was doing it.' Felicité 'book-scouted' on Elizabeth's behalf not only in John Sandoe's bookshop, where she still worked, but also through the pages of secondhand book catalogues of which she and Elizabeth received a large number. Regarding Felicité's assisting her to learn and enjoy so much, Elizabeth adds that she could say the same of her editor Jill Norman, to whom she dedicated the book. Jill had 'nursed it along chapter by chapter and stage by stage . . . and certainly worked on it as hard as I myself'.

In London and 'further afield' Elizabeth had April Boyes, and for trips to France Elizabeth Savage, both of whom acted as semi-official assistants. Elizabeth's warm thanks in her acknowledgements touchingly reflect these supportive female relationships upon which she was so dependent. 'In Wales Jean Bolland has done the same, driving me to mills, museums, libraries, bakeries, local markets – and as a bonus provided the cleaned-out old brick oven in her own house for me to try my hand at the ancient way of making bread. Nothing could have been more instructive or more enjoyable or indeed more fruitful for this book than my visits – rather prolonged some of them – to South West Wales.'

One of the loyal band of followers, the late Jean Bolland was happy to act as second fiddle, to drive Elizabeth about in the car and have her to stay in her house. Mrs Priscilla Bain described Jean Bolland in a letter to the author: 'As well as being great fun she was a very tolerant and unconcerned person and very restful to be with. In fact – and I say this with affection – she was basically lazy and happiest with the *Times* crossword, a cigarette and coffee or a glass of wine . . . She had a great sense of style and her house . . . always managed to look pretty.' Mrs Bain continued: 'She was pretty chaotic too – untidy, no sense of time – but one forgave her all because she was such fun . . . perhaps the perfect companion for E.D.'

Certainly Elizabeth delighted in her visits to Ty Isaf – another pleasure to be indulged in there was the drive across country for lunch at The Walnut Tree restaurant – and in *English Bread and Yeast Cookery* her enthusiasm for its old farmhouse oven is infectious: 'They are of extraordinarily skilled construction . . . once cleared out one of these old ovens will be ready for firing and for baking just as it was for centuries, before the commercial bakery took over the job of supplying our daily bread.' With this new experience Elizabeth was now particularly alert to the vagaries of baking methods described by Eliza Acton in her *English Bread Book* of 1857:

> It is most of all in many of our villages that better accommodation is required than now exists for baking generally, and for baking bread especially; for great discouragement to the makers often attends the sending it to a common baker's oven, should there chance to be one at hand, which in many instances there is not.

In *A London Family* 1870–1900 (Oxford, 1946) Mrs M. Vivian Hughes recalls that the products of those initially unpopular iron ranges, which had often displaced the old brick ovens, were still, as Elizabeth writes, 'So much better than the London baker's bread that neither she, nor her children as they grew up, ever willingly ate bought bread. A familiar story.' Elizabeth may at times vent too much spleen but her observations on, for example, the inadequacy of the ovens in modern gas and electric cookers, 'which are too small and getting smaller', are surely so familiar to her readers that they must have identified with her protest.

In essence Elizabeth wrote *English Bread and Yeast Cookery* for the ultimate, ideal English reader. Elizabeth here displays all the English sensitivity to the passage of time, to history, to nostalgia. But in this she is neither quaint nor simply writing an antiquarian lament. Her book is more robust than that. As literature, as a work of art, it has none of the inconsistencies or erratic messages of some of her earlier writing. Her command of subject and her powers of exposition have matured and grown, making the book the work of a writer who can do all she once could, but more besides and with greater sureness. Above all, the writing here is not literary. It doesn't seek directly to please the reader but yet will please some discerning readers more than any other of her books.

Throughout her life Elizabeth took up the cudgels against the impoverishment and ugliness of life under puritanism and the industrial system. And in *English Bread and Yeast Cookery* she creates a practical handbook of ways and means to tackle an alternative. This is the most reflective of Elizabeth's books, demonstrating with absolute clarity an interest in knowledge as apart from pure information. It is not really possible to read *Bread . . .* unless one becomes absorbed, and then it compels thought in a way which her other books do not.

Elizabeth here makes her most concerted attempt at coming to grips with the actual world, at suggesting how to bypass the sterilities of modern society. She passionately fights her female corner in the name of effective individual skill and craftsmanship against the proliferating crudities of a desiccating technology. Although she does not overtly relinquish her mentor Norman Douglas and the world he represents, in *Bread . . .* there is none of his disdainful paganism. In this, the last book published in her lifetime, Elizabeth has left something of her Mediterranean self behind. Norman Douglas is displaced by writers intensely representative of the English tradition; the likes of Kenelm Digby, the Countess of Kent, Eliza Acton and Lady Llanover, and these augment the overall intensity and coherence of vision which Elizabeth's book gradually discloses. Together with her scholarship, knowledge and craftsmanship, Elizabeth has lost nothing of her passion, her driving demon. Never quite surfacing, it is nonetheless there, implicit throughout.

An undercurrent running throughout *English Bread and Yeast Cookery* frequently reveals an unmistakably affectionate tone, unusual in Elizabeth's writing. Again untypically, the book encompasses the virtues of homeliness and friendliness, as well as the more spectacular and striking aspects of human nature. To a greater or lesser degree, Elizabeth's Mediterranean books are well-judged mediations between fantasy and reality. Her lyrical passages wring every last drop of colour, texture and atmosphere out of those Mediterranean cameos, yet before the purple has a chance to cloy she moves over to the down-to-earth practicalities of food preparation and cooking. Similarly, in *Bread* . . . the evocation of a past milieu, with all its rituals and traditions, is beautifully done. Before, however, it can become an exercise in antiquarian nostalgia, with quaint spelling and suchlike embellishments, Elizabeth transfers us to the precise methods required to achieve some particular effect in the making of bread, and how this can be adapted to modern conditions. When writing on the Mediterranean she so often had the actual practice before her, and consequently her work was a description, a record of the present. The difficulty Elizabeth faced and overcame in her writing on England was that she almost always had to commence with sources from the past.

Elizabeth's first book, *Mediterranean Food*, in a way half denies the domestic aspect of cooking, or at least vacillates about it, but in *English Bread and Yeast Cookery* there is no such ambivalence. It is a friendly, comfortable book, as in the older sense of the word used in *The Book of Common Prayer*: 'comfortable words . . . those that give strength in time of need'. Perhaps the most moving and significant message at the heart of this singular book is that Elizabeth achieves that rare thing: a celebration of the domestic without denying romance.

English Bread and Yeast Cookery was published in the autumn of 1977 to considerable acclaim and won the prestigious Glenfiddich Trophy for 1978. It was evident, however, that most reviewers, intimidated by the book's size and its author's reputation, gave little more than a cursory glance at some of its obvious themes. Many, such as Hilary Spurling in *The Times*, did not take enough trouble to describe what Elizabeth had achieved. Perhaps this was because they simply had not fully comprehended its magnitude. One of the most perceptive exceptions was Claire Tomalin for the *Sunday Times*. She drew attention to much of the essential matter of the book, saying that Elizabeth had:

> made us nostalgic . . . for worlds most of us could not possibly know. For two and a half decades she has turned our faces away from England. We were a very willing generation to grow greedy and reject our Anglo-Saxon culinary conditions . . . the war and rationing encouraged whole worlds of fantasy about food and travel to flourish in our heads. In the fifties standard English cookery books were still recommending the use of dried eggs and margarine, with a pinch of sage as the most dashing herb on the shelf. Against such a landscape Elizabeth David appeared as liberating and delightful as Homer Lane did to the young Auden. Our eclectic kitchens became the hearts of our houses. Now we are being led to consider our native traditions again.

Tomalin says Elizabeth's motivation was frustration at the standard of 'manufactured' bread and the sense that people might again be 'prepared to spend time baking their own bread'. Her interpretation here is essentially accurate, although with the benefit of hindsight we can see that Elizabeth's motivation was also more complex and varied than this. Tomalin continues, observing that: 'We have lost our traditions here.' But *English Bread and Yeast Cookery* 'has much more than the touch of history and topography that one finds in all good cookbooks. It is a work of devoted scholarship, using all manner of records of the past to re-establish its practice.' She goes on: 'there is a formidable amount of detail involved, and some readers will be impatient to reach Part II . . . where the practical instructions begin. But even if you decide to start the book there, you will find yourself turning back for references and practical advice.'

In interview with Caroline, Terence Conran's then wife, Elizabeth said: 'This started out as a small book and I got more and more deeply enmeshed. My interest in the subject germinated in 1956' – she refers here to the *Spectator* review she had written on the Scurfields' *Home Baked* – '. . . the research was done in libraries here and there . . . I most specifically didn't start out to crusade or to preach . . . but the more I found out, the more impossible I found it to forgive the cynical debauching of our bread. . . . if people want to eat factory bread they can, but they should be told, they should know more. . . . I've enjoyed doing this book so much. I've really behaved like a lunatic, eating yeast pancakes galore – and cakes like Sally Lunns – I love cooking with yeast, it's so easy.'

Elizabeth's originality lay in her ability to synthesize, and in parallel her fine-tuned reflecting of the Zeitgeist was unerring; consequently she was always just that one step ahead of her time. In the 1970s many were already disenchanted with the results of mechanization and would have agreed with Eliza Acton's comment in her *Bread Book* of over 100 years earlier, that English bread was; 'noted both at home and abroad for its want of genuineness, and the faulty mode of its preparation'. In 1977 they went out and bought Elizabeth's book. It sold 15,000 hardback copies in a short time.

Many other studies on the making of bread, from late last century and on into this one, were quoted by Elizabeth: William Jago's exhaustive researches on the principles and technology of breadmaking, John Kirkland's 6-volume *The Modern Baker and Confectioner* (1907), and Walter Banfield's beautifully titled *Manna* (1937) are some of those Elizabeth describes in her acknowledgements as 'splendid works'. Nevertheless, her own book, with its searching scholarship and meticulous attention to detail, its comprehensive, magisterial tone and passionate vision, is unquestionably the greatest book written on the history and practice of breadmaking this century.

In the year of the book's publication, Elizabeth was made a *Chevalier de l'Ordre du Mérite Agricole* by the French. The previous year,

1976, she had been awarded an OBE. On presenting it to her the Queen asked what it was for, to which Elizabeth replied that she wrote cookery books. 'That must be very useful.' And indeed *English Bread and Yeast Cookery* was exactly that.

CHAPTER TWENTY

Ice and Beyond
(1977–1995)

THE ENGLISH PEDIGREE of some of the recipes in *English Bread and Yeast Cookery* is, on first reading, dubious. On further scrutiny their presence is usually merited as imports, which Elizabeth judged popular enough to have installed themselves in the English national repertoire. Now frequently made badly on their home territory they benefit from new instruction (Claire Tomalin's review refers to: 'A mournful chapter on the present . . . decline of traditional French bread'). In an interview Elizabeth made scathing reference to that relentless English practice to which so many of us were subjected in the 1970s: (bad) quiche with everything. Elizabeth says: 'Quiches, quiches everywhere. But they bear no relation to those lovely creamy tarts from Alsace and Lorraine. The pastry is unspeakable in what is laughably called a quiche in this country.'

Included, along with some mordant wit at the expense of the monstrosities offered in its name, is a recipe for the making of a good pizza and its relative, Elizabeth's favourite, the *pissaladière*. She wrote to Priscilla's daughter, Julia, on the eve of her marriage in 1976 with some advice: 'One of the things you need to know in order to feed young persons – and everybody else too – fairly cheaply is how to make a pizza, and coming from that . . . a pizza dough to make all sorts of other good dishes.' Elizabeth had taught Julia's cousin, Johnny Grey, how to do this a year or so earlier: 'Since when I believe he has become the wonder and admiration of his brother's friends' and made huge quantities and froze them successfully. Elizabeth offered to teach Julia, saying it was so easy and satisfactory. The pizzas Elizabeth made were light, unlike the 'repulsive brick things' served in pizza houses or bought frozen. 'And they cost a fraction of what people pay for those con jobs'.

Johnny Grey was, like his aunt, compelled by an interest in design (trained as an architect, he has subsequently become a noted kitchen designer) and spent time during these years talking and listening to Elizabeth. In 1977, on the publication of her bread book, Terence Conran also published a large photograph-filled compendium, *The Kitchen Book*. Incorporating some of the most influential contemporary ideas, Conran's book was very popular, subsequently a valuable fragment of social history. One of the kitchens photographed in the Conran book is Johnny Grey's first attempt; an outrageously impractical neo-gothic reaction against the current vogue for streamlining and uniformity. Another kitchen in the book is an illustration of what was described, with a touch of satire, as Elizabeth David's 'Dream Kitchen'.

In mid-July Elizabeth wrote again to Julia saying that *Bread* was in its final stage. And then she was off again to Wales. In the years of research and work on the book her attachment to Wales had grown sufficiently for her to think seriously of buying a house there. As we have seen, developments in France had disaffected her and she said, 'Too many sad things have happened there. I want a house in Wales with water.' Elizabeth remained captivated by water all her life, its presence proving a spur to some of her most memorable descriptions of place. In April of the following year she thanked Hugh Johnson for presents of his honey on a card depicting an elegant seventeenth-century water mill in delightfully vernacular style. Elizabeth finished her card: 'As for the water mill . . . it's the one I'm looking for . . . Much love E.'

One of the quotes in *English Bread and Yeast Cookery* from M. Vivian Hughes's quietly celebratory autobiography *A London Family*, refers to a tea with relations at the little town of Machynlleth in 1888. Elizabeth's reason for including this quote is undoubtedly as much autobiographical as for its reference to Welsh 'light cakes'. Her own particular memories of Machynlleth and its river valley extended as far back as the Gwynne girls' first idyllic Welsh holiday in the mid-1930s. And we recall that during the war Elizabeth had nostalgically asked Priscilla if she did not remember the little house they had seen on that holiday together. She recalled its position along a path by a river, which ran through the garden, and nearby was an odd-looking sugar loaf hill. 'I have absolutely got to have that house. I don't say I want to live there permanently but I have never ceased regretting that I didn't take it.' This was one of the regions of Wales in which Elizabeth still believed, over forty years later, that she wanted to live. Her dream was never to be realized. She was always concerned about money, but perhaps most importantly the energy, patience and determination required to buy, organize and probably renovate a house so far away from London, was soon to be put in doubt.

Driving back with Johnny Grey from another trip to Wales in the autumn, their car was involved in a major accident. 'It was terrible,' says Hugh Johnson. 'Liz was devastated by it. I don't think she ever really recovered properly.' Apart from broken limbs Elizabeth's right hand was left for a time unusable and her jaw broken, resulting in permanent problems with her teeth. The broken limbs meant that she had to spend three months in London's Lister Hospital and in her own words remain 'effectively out of action for several more'. Friends concur with Hugh Johnson's view that 'Liz never fully recovered physically, but more, I think, it affected her whole psyche. She couldn't have written another popular book after this. She was simply more frail, had less zest for living.' Alan Davidson remarks that 'After *Bread* there *was* a diminuendo.'

Elizabeth was only sixty-four, but she seemed unable to overcome this premature frailty brought about by the car accident. In subsequent years other aspects of her deteriorating health, combined with the increasing tendency to fall and – with osteoporosis – break bones, put her frequently in hospital, sometimes for many weeks at a time. In the London hospitals she frequented, her room with its little fridge was always filled with delicacies and wine; offerings brought by the regular stream of visitors.

Research on the next volume in Elizabeth's grand projected history series was already under way; material had been collected intermittently during the writing of *Bread*. As the years passed, and she became more fascinated by the byways of scholarship, the book's subject grew. Taking on different perspectives and emphases its focus eventually became most concentrated on the use of ice and the creation of ices. The disentanglement of the history of ice was to fill the rest of Elizabeth's life.

Aided in her book-collecting by the indefatigable Felicité, Elizabeth had early decided against the habit of collecting fine first editions in favour of less precious later editions of books. There were two major reasons for this decision. First, it meant that she could afford to buy more, and second, as she wrote in the first issue of Alan and Jane Davidson's journal, *Petits Propos Culinaires* (*PPC*): 'When it comes to cookery books . . . it is a fearful mistake to pay large sums for first editions and neglect later ones, and this applies particularly to works which have had a long life.'

Continuing with this theme, central to her own book-collecting, she wrote that first editions of famous cookery books 'wouldn't be nearly as interesting to serious students of cookery as later ones, in which authors themselves have made revisions, corrected errors, added new recipes, brought cooking methods up to date, and incorporated recently introduced ingredients'. Elizabeth's comments here are entirely valid, but also miss the crucial point about a first edition existing as an intact, fixed piece of history to which readers often feel considerable allegiance, for personal associations as much as for literary value. (This misapprehension on Elizabeth's part occurred again when she later republished, revised and augmented editions of her first four books, and was surprised at the adverse reaction this provoked from some readers.)

For all her capability to communicate in her writing Elizabeth was often unable to comprehend fully what it was she represented for her audience. With *Mediterranean Food* she had communicated, above all, a passionate dream of escape. With *Italian Food* and *French Provincial Cooking* a more sober *modus vivendi* for this dream and its relationship to reality was evolved. Moving on, in this last phase of her life it was the realities of history and tradition and their rightful place and value in the present which she was most concerned to promulgate. Elizabeth had written originally out of a need to express herself and in response to the vicissitudes of her own class and generation, and they had responded with warmth and recognition. Over the years Elizabeth's readership had not only grown it had become more heterogeneous. But for most the things which she represented above all were still a vigorous and sophisticated commendation of simple things: uncomplicated authentic food, combined with escape.

Believing that the 'soul' had gone out of her writing in the later work, some of Elizabeth's earliest followers wanted more of the familiarly evocative recipes and less history. As devotees of her original creed they did not want or expect her to change and were unwilling to follow her along these more thoughtful and demanding routes. This was quite reasonable enough, however, Elizabeth's own course was now ordained. In her pursuit of truth she never ceased to recommend the authentic – this is the essence of her recipes. Nevertheless, in these later years well-structured escape no longer fulfilled her and, if only subconsciously, she was confronting a more austere reality.

During 1978 Elizabeth was revising *English Bread and Yeast Cookery* for the American publisher, trying to answer some of the volume of letters received from her English readers and staying again in Wales. While Felicité had been suffering for some time from various ailments, in August the following year her symptoms intensified and she was taken into hospital. John Johnson drove Elizabeth to visit Felicité and remembers being annoyed with Elizabeth. 'She had some bizarre ideas about what was good food for Felicité, would make these extraordinary rich little dishes all beautifully got up in cloths and things and we'd take them in daily.' Elizabeth's life came to a virtual standstill for Felicité during the most intense period of her illness. Yet despite this concern friends and family were familiar with Felicité's timidity towards Elizabeth, and Elizabeth's neglect and insensitivity regarding her sister's physical and emotional needs. The sisters now rarely entered each other's areas of the house, preferring to communicate by telephone or notes left on the stairs. An anecdote from this period is illuminating. Felicité increasingly felt the cold in her upstairs rooms. Elizabeth had always kept Halsey Street underheated, but the deterioration of Felicité's health made her more susceptible than previously to the cold. Sabrina (Priscilla's elder daughter) bought a heater for Felicité, but everyone's fear of Elizabeth was such that Priscilla had to stand guard while Sabrina hauled the heavy and offending object to a quaking Felicité up above. Then the guilty trio fell on the sofa in relieved laughter as Felicité offered a drink to celebrate their success.

The dynamic of the Gwynne sisters' relationship was, however, too complex to lend itself to judgement on the basis of such neglect alone. These two had shared a house for thirty years – 'leading', as Elizabeth later wrote to Maudie O'Malley, 'our quite separate lives, but of course dependent upon each other for so much'. Despite Felicité's presence upstairs, Elizabeth also felt increasingly alone and isolated with her own pressing fears.

John Johnson recalls two startling examples of these anxieties, about which he was uncomprehending at the time. One evening while talking with Elizabeth after they had visited Felicité in hospital, the conversation had turned to Viola, John's mother, who was now living alone in Greece and about whose welfare they were both concerned. Then, by some underground connection, Elizabeth confessed to John: 'Sometimes at night I find myself screaming out loud.' John was stunned and unable to comment. In recalling this wretched admission he was reminded of an occurrence which at the time had shocked him similarly in its intensity. Some years before Felicité's illness he had been at dinner with Elizabeth in Halsey Street. 'We had probably both drunk a good quantity. Anyway Elizabeth dropped and broke a sugar bowl. It didn't look to me particularly special but nevertheless its breakage provoked in Elizabeth the most terrible reaction. She was absolutely *overcome* with rage and shouted: "Objects are even *more* terrible than people." The shock must have registered on my face because the next day in the bookshop Felicité said rather tentatively, "I understand Elizabeth was a little overwrought last night."'

The following year, Alan Davidson, whose booklet on fish Elizabeth had enthusiastically written about in the *Spectator*, was made Alistair Horne Visiting Fellow at St Antony's College, Oxford, in order to finish the book he was working on at the time. (Alan Davidson's growing expertise on fish had resulted in more publications and in 1975 he left the diplomatic service to write full time.) 'The Dean of the college stopped me one day in the corridor and asked me, "In what way do you propose to make manifest to the other members of the college your presence here and the reason for it?"' Taken aback, Alan asked what he would suggest and was told: 'A seminar.' He decided that as there 'wasn't any provision in the university calendar for food history I would remedy it . . .' He asked Elizabeth, amongst several others, if she would attend. She didn't manage the first two but came to the third where: 'She made highly relevant and pointed contributions about the history of cookery books in England. Her attendance helped to give the thing a lot more impetus and the next one was a full-scale symposium.' This event was the initiation of the international Oxford Symposium on Food and Cookery, now attended from around the world by some of the more thoughtful writers on the subject.

In the same year, by a circuitous set of circumstances, Alan founded, with Jill Norman, Elizabeth and Richard Olney (a mutual friend), a publishing company, Prospect Books, and a journal called *Petits Propos Culinaires* (*PPC*); both of which aimed to publish in-depth articles and books on food and its history. Elizabeth wrote several detailed pieces on her reigning preoccupations in the early numbers of *PPC*. These ranged from a disentanglement of the true authorship of the seventeenth-century Countess of Kent's book to *Banketting Stuff*; *An Eighteenth Century Kitchen Garden at Christmas*; an article on 'a high-summer fête in the gardens of Versailles for Louis XIV in 1668', partly researched by her niece Sabrina Harcourt-Smith, and more on Elizabeth's researches into ice. In thanking Sabrina for her efforts at the Royal Library at Windsor, Elizabeth added that her 'work into the history of ices isn't getting on very fast'. With her thanks came a copy of the relevant *PPC* and the comment: 'an eccentric little publication'.

This and other references clearly reveal Elizabeth's ambivalence regarding this skilfully edited and produced journal, possibly the only publication at that time which would have recognized the importance of her present work. This ambivalence stems from a dilemma which Elizabeth could not solve. Alan Davidson over-modestly credits her essays as the main reason for *PPC*'s immediate success, while the Oxford Symposium also prospered and grew, spawning similar events around the world. Each year 'Elizabeth took a considerable interest in what was going on . . . and felt that the proceedings consituted a major new resource of information about food history. Some of the more recondite contributions particularly struck her,' says Alan. '"Some little known aspects of Trans-Caucasian Mountain Ram cookery". She thought that one was great . . . a really good subject!'

Alan's irony here obscures the fact that his combined efforts have been instrumental in the increasing recognition of food history as an invaluable and almost unexplored area of social history, to which Elizabeth was now dedicated. Paul Bailey, who met Elizabeth in her last years through their mutual friend Jane Grigson, recalls that by the late 1980s she would say to him, 'I don't want to write recipes any more. God, I can't carry on writing them, I've done all that. The excitement of life now is in tracing the texts.' Paul Bailey believes that Elizabeth was saying: 'I want to find out how these things came into being, who thought of them.'

Ten or so years earlier she had met Richard Leech, owner of the Holland Press which published sorely needed facsimile editions of rare and out of print bibliographies relating to food and wine. Richard Leech and Elizabeth began collecting material for a series of books on the Stuarts at table. At the same time Richard and his then wife's friendship with Elizabeth became a source of scholarly and emotional support to her. Richard Leech told the author, 'Elizabeth was really not interested in food by now you know. She would enjoy a pleasant Middle Eastern restaurant, but really didn't make food. At Halsey Street food was just little bits and pieces, but you were always assured of a *good* glass of wine.'

In about 1982 Elizabeth met someone else of likeminded historical interests, adding to her small band of academic devotees. Peter Davidson, a young researcher at Warwick University, discussed with Elizabeth the possibility of their producing an edition of Kenelm Digby's cookery book, *The Closet of the Eminently Learned Kenelm Digby Kt. Opened* (1669). Despite telling Peter that she wished she had had the scholarly training to approach seventeenth-century material with confidence; that she had stumbled into scholarship in her later years and felt disadvantaged having to move forward so slowly checking everything, the idea was that Elizabeth would write a lengthy introduction. 'Yes, she did regard herself as self-taught,' says Paul Bailey. Apropos this preoccupation, Peter Davidson remembers a lunch in London with Elizabeth and Jill Norman. Peter Davidson told the author, 'Mrs David asked about Richard Waller, the seventeenth-century Fellow of the Royal Society, and I knew whatever it was and she turned to Jill in rather a proprietorial way and said, "You see, he *knows*, it's his *world*." (Peter Davidson has recently completed the edition of Digby's famous book with Jane Stevenson for Prospect Books and dedicated the volume to Elizabeth's memory.)

Meanwhile Alan Davidson continued feeding Elizabeth all manner of information on unexplored territory, including some crucial research on a variety of subjects for her ices book in the Bodleian Library. 'Elizabeth had a phenomenal memory,' he says, 'she was alert to every detail. She could quote word for word and if she corrected you she was *always* right.' Her work was now of a clearly academic nature and she especially regretted to Peter Davidson, who 'translated quite a lot of Latin here and there', her ignorance of it. Yet until the end of her life she remained ambivalent about the whole academic enterprise.

She could write irritably to Alan saying that the bibliography for the late Jane Grigson was an editorial mistake because it was 'boring, which Jane never was', and add soon afterwards that she hoped 'no one would even *think* of doing one for me'. Meanwhile her response to other less scholarly members of her profession could be vitriolic if she thought they had got something wrong. She loathed being referred to as 'the doyenne of cookery writers', saying to Paul Bailey, 'Who wants to be the doyenne of *them*?'

In 1979 she was happy to accept an honorary doctorate offered her by the University of Essex. She was perhaps most proud of being made a Fellow of the Royal Society of Literature in 1982 and the recognition as a writer which this conferred. Grey Gowrie told her that he had used her work for his students at Harvard as examples of how to write. 'She appreciated that her books could be used as pieces of writing. She went beyond the bounds of cooking writing. She had pace and rhythm and could be read well out loud. A feel for the physical world is very good in a writer.' Elizabeth accepted willingly the recognition of her literary skills. Where her dilemma lay was over her increasingly scholarly inclinations. Broadly speaking the milieu in which she had grown up esteemed fine literature above 'bookishness'. The traditional notion that literature should be created with inspiration and apparently effortless ease in many ways ran counter to the zeal, precision and analysis necessary for the practice of scholarship. And this latter had increasingly consumed Elizabeth's life.

Notwithstanding these preferences, during the following decade she experienced a diminution of that drive and will-power which were necessary for sifting research material in a consistently disciplined manner. She continued to write articles arising from her researches but the greater stamina required to fashion her boundless research into a book, an extended coherent whole, was elusive. She remained her formidable self, with her memory razor-sharp, however, despite having several of the aforementioned friends prepared to carry out primary research for her, the purpose which had formerly spurred her on was now in decline.

Another of the hazards of ageing, the loss of old friends and relatives, also began to weigh upon her. The painter Lett Haines was first to go, leaving Cedric finally alone, apart from their devoted housekeeper Millie. Felicité wrote a letter of commiseration to Maudie O'Malley, a close friend of the duo at Benton End. Acting for so long as the guardian of Elizabeth's interests, Felicité's own persona appeared to many shadowy by comparison with her passionate sister, yet those who took the trouble to know her soon discovered that she was anything but a mouse; and possessed of a sense of humour too.

'Oh, Felicité had a real twinkle in her eye,' recalls John Johnson. 'She had that slight smile hovering on her lips. The smile of those who have lived an internal life, have been observers and not always spoken as much as listened.' Felicité's path had been determined long ago, in part simply by being born Elizabeth's sister. If this wasn't in any doubt it was confirmed inexorably when she came to live with her. In the following passages to Maudie, Felicité reveals her plight with touching clarity:

'Elizabeth gave me your letter yesterday, for which we both thank you. Am sure she'll write herself before long, but as she's struggling hard with research for next book (or books, am not sure and seems frightfully preoccupied with any number of things) I'm writing in the meantime.

'Wish I could say something constructive about Cedric. I could ... write a great deal on what you said about friends (in inverted commas). Seems to me to be one of the major penalties of having in some way been great or famous . . . or in some way of use to the in no way great or gifted . . . Exploitation in fact. Poor Cedric . . . Terrifying to think of the loneliness of very old age . . . I still totter in three mornings a week to the bookshop, but do little work, as I have truly lost my wits, my balance, my strength and much else besides. Apart from that am trying to eke out extra occupation and finance by copy-typing here at home. Never was my favourite occupation . . .'

One recalls that during all her years at Halsey Street Felicité had continued to type most of Elizabeth's articles and books. She continues: 'Wish I could get about a bit more . . . I hanker for my one time independence. I sold my beloved bicycle a few days ago, finally admitting it seems implausible I'll ever be able to ride it again . . . I greatly envy people like yourself who paint, like Elizabeth who can write. In fact I envy of course anyone who is creative and for whom every day is far too short. Altogether I must admit to a feeling of great desolation . . .'

The following year, 1982, brought the death of the Gwynne sisters' brother-in-law Chris Grey. Elizabeth wrote to Maudie: 'Yes, Chris was our doctor and we have always been very close to him, I have known him since I was twenty when Diana first met him. His death is a crushing blow.' Cedric Morris also died that year and Felicité again wrote to Maudie saying, 'I think of him every day, of course, because of his two pictures (one of Wootton) which give me perpetual delight and solace.' Her own health showed no improvement and she said she 'appears to be an idle old good for nothing'. . . . In the course of this letter she hopes and prays that Maudie's 'home life is more peaceful again. The hazards of married life would I know have always been too much for me. Have never been strong enough to cope with my own dottiness, let alone a husband's or whatever person I'd have committed myself to.' Further on she says, 'The thing I'd most love to be able to do would be to write – not for publishing or anything like that – but just the ability to spin words together to my own satisfaction.' (From early youth Felicité had in fact written a considerable amount of poetry, but obviously not to her satisfaction.) She concludes 'Meanwhile I type Liza's spectacular scholarship and her skill with words. The gods gave *her* all the genius, and had not a vestige to spare for me. You can paint like an angel ... miraculous and haunting pictures, for which I'm insanely envious. Think of being able to write music, poems, books. All I've ever been was ... quite a good bookseller ...'

During the 1980s the small number of admiring younger people who were welcomed into Elizabeth's life and revived some of her enthusiasm for her remaining years included Michael Day, proprietor of what he calls the Huge Cheese Company. Michael is an uncommon man whose air of ingenuousness combines with worldliness, nonetheless underscored by a determined optimism and lack of cynicism. His generosity can be outrageous. He is a gossip. He is also one of those who knows how to entertain as well as to listen, and under the mask of the showman his intuitive sensitivity extends itself to a sympathy with the old. For Elizabeth he took on the role of court jester, thus sometimes lightening her own failing spirit.

I met Felicité first because I used to swap cheese with her for books, and I used to have tea with her and admire her scarves. I was giving a party and I asked her and she asked if she could bring her sister Elizabeth. I didn't know who Elizabeth David was and I hadn't read any of her books ... I asked her and Bernard Levin to come to lunch. John Clements (his brother wrote *Dad's Army*) was there too, in Leyton's Wine Cellars. She wasn't temperamental then. There were about four people who had a key to her front door and I was one of them. I would leave cheese there. I liked her. She used to call me an imbecile. I used to read books to her in Danish and she would laugh and I would fall over. She would say outrageous things. She came with Jane Grigson to the Crystal Room in the Mayfair. We had a competition ... who could get the most time spent on them by a famous chef. At Mosimann's he spent about five minutes flattering Elizabeth and then spent two minutes on me. At Nico Ladenis ... I thought he was a conceited, arrogant man and I said, 'You don't have to buy my cheese.' He wanted Elizabeth to do an introduction to his book and she wouldn't although she did think he was a good chef. Elizabeth could be pretty vicious sometimes.

At the beginning, every fortnight I would go round and we would drink seven or eight glasses of wine. Jeremy (Round) and Lindsey (Bareham) . . . when they got to know her well we would take Elizabeth out together. We were very fond of her. Elizabeth was very observant. She had some Henry Moore prints of sheep on the wall and I took them off the wall and put them under the sofa because I thought I would borrow them . . . She came back into the room and said, 'Michael, where are those prints?' 'Oh, those prints.' And I had to put them back.

She seriously did cook me an omelette with roquefort in it. She wasn't cooking by then. Then we stopped this drinking habit, because it was stupid. We'd take her out to eat instead. She would go to sleep at about 2 a.m. and we'd whisper, 'She's asleep' and she would shout at us, 'No I'm not!' and we'd say, 'Bedtime,' and she'd say, 'No it's not!'

Her top books were *Cold Comfort Farm* and *Wind in the Willows*. She had an impressive ability to put away a lot of drink and still come up with a pretty acid line at the end of it. That was a most endearing quality. If she didn't like you she didn't and that was that. Once or twice she got a bit narky with me. But she could be very charming. She wrote a letter of apology to me saying, 'Sorry I behaved so badly.'

She did get grumpy, but she knew she was behaving badly. I think she pushed it as far as she could to see who would back off and who'd stand up to her. Not that many people did. I got on quite well with her in a strange way. People would come to the door . . . fan club, sycophantic people. The eye contact between us said it all. She'd let them go on for about thirty seconds before she'd hit them with some put-down phrase.

She went in for a sort of testing game. She tested Jeremy Round to see if he did actually know about whatever subject he was talking about. Whether the bread was cooked to this degree, the pasta was made like this or like that. And Jeremy would come back three times as fast as Elizabeth. Hardly anyone could do that. If she was impressed by you that was OK. But for me, being a complete philistine ... someone who enjoyed the fact that I'd never read any of her books ... it was nice to watch and see them. 'Yes I like him because he *can* answer my question. He *does* know.' And if they *didn't* know what they were talking about they were out. She had little time for people who were fools ... except me fortunately. ('But you played the floor as the fool didn't you?' 'Yes, but it was the only one I could play,' and he laughed, 'I didn't know anything about cooking.')

A young woman who did know something about cooking was Lindsey Bareham, then writing the restaurant reviews for *Time Out* magazine. With trepidation she had been introduced to Elizabeth one evening by the proprietor of the Lebanese restaurant in Abingdon Road, the Phoenicia. 'Oh, she loved all those handsome waiters, those liquid brown eyes looking down into hers,' recalls Paul Bailey. 'But she loved the food too. She'd say, "Why do we bother with French food? This is just the best thing. You don't gorge yourself, you just pick and choose." We talked about books, writers we both liked, what was in the air. She liked to be entertained and she did drink a lot and she didn't care.'

To Lindsey Bareham's enormous surprise Elizabeth knew and liked her work. Lindsey asked her out to lunch at the Caprice where Martin Lam was then chef. 'We seemed to have so much to talk about we finally left at 4.30 p.m. You couldn't make sloppy remarks with Elizabeth. She concentrated my mind so much, I found her very stimulating company and very damning about food writers of the time. She said they all had "half-baked ideas" – except Jeremy Round. She did feel that she had set a standard, had done a lot of the research that other people made free with. She always had the latest books, would know what everyone was up to. Not many people in the food world came across her but she was keeping a beady eye on *them*. She was aware of the influence she'd had on food writers in a general way.'

Paul Bailey remarks that Elizabeth's 'influence on writers has been circuitous. She had an ego about her talent, but she did believe in manners. She was very much aware that many people went into food writing for all the wrong reasons. And the most wrong was to make a lot of money quickly. The cleverness of the new writers was that they realized that Elizabeth had touched a nerve ... I feel Elizabeth was one of those writers who was ignorant of her audience. But I don't think she cared. She is one of the few who liked writing and one of the few food writers who has made any impact on *writers*.'

As to the restaurateurs, Lindsey Bareham observes that 'she affected the up and coming restaurateurs, but they gave her credit for it. Martin Lam, Alistair Little, Rowley Leigh, Simon Hopkinson. They were a generation of chefs who appreciated her writing for its own sake as much as the recipes.'

Elizabeth had always gone out to restaurants with friends, but this happened more frequently as she became uninterested or unable to cook herself. One of her favourite chefs, Simon Hopkinson, joined Terence Conran in opening his restaurant, Bibendum, in 1986. Among the first friends to take her there were Hugh and Judy Johnson and to everyone's enormous relief she liked it. Terence Conran's concern to have a lift especially to accommodate the difficulty Elizabeth now experienced in walking was repaid, as she returned often.

Lesley O'Malley had continued living in the basement flat at Halsey Street for many years but it was clear to her family that Elizabeth no longer made her feel so welcome. Elizabeth wanted to make some alterations to the house and Lesley decided to move permanently to her weekend house in Great Missenden in Buckinghamshire. Here she would be closer to her old friend from Cairo, the writer Roald Dahl. She was an entirely loyal friend to Elizabeth and made no word of complaint.

With designs made by Elizabeth's nephew Johnny Grey, the basement at Halsey Street would now be converted into another kitchen. It was intended that this large basement 'with better light than the original kitchen upstairs' would be a study/sitting room/kitchen area for winter use. In fact Elizabeth used the upper kitchen much less after this second one was completed.

During early 1984, with Jill Norman as editor, Elizabeth put together her splendid selection of journalism and other more scholarly pieces written over the last forty or so years and entitled, *An Omelette and a Glass of Wine*. While this was in progress, and continuing her life-long habit of spending several weeks of every year out of England, in February Elizabeth was in Uzès in the South of France with Jean Bolland. Here they were staying in the house of an old friend, Elizabeth's doctor Patrick Woodcock, during his absence for the winter. Elizabeth described the beautiful house and her time in Uzès in an essay in *An Omelette and a Glass of Wine* entitled 'Confort Anglais, French Fare'. The theme: that it was increasingly preferable to eat French food on picnics or by cooking it oneself at home, had been established in 'Eating out in Provincial France 1967–77'. A disillusioned piece on the decline of French restaurants, it was originally written as an introduction to her revised edition of *French Provincial Cooking* for Michael Joseph in 1977. Rejected as too long – probably also regarded by Michael Joseph as too down-beat and not an inducement for sales – Elizabeth had first published it in *PPC* before reprinting it in *An Omelette and a Glass of Wine*.

From Uzès Elizabeth wrote to her niece Sabrina, saying that she'd had a wonderful three weeks, with the days passing at devastating speed. In the Saturday market, selling delectable food, she was able to buy at least fifty different cheeses; the bakery sold seven varieties of brown bread; and the pâté in the charcuterie was delicious. But in the big *supermarché* they sold 'sliced white Mother's Pride type loaves . . . Who buys it . . .?'

Near Uzès lived Elizabeth's old friend Lawrence Durrell. Jean Bolland's friend Mrs Bain remembers that Jean 'would be instructed to do the cooking, being told, for instance: "Lawrence will be coming for lunch today – we will have . . ." Jean, who was pretty imperturbable, said that she was frequently shaking at the knees by the time she had finished.'

In 1979 Jill Norman had set up her own imprint, including on its projected list the most prestigious cookery book writers in England: Elizabeth, Jane Grigson, Alan Davidson and Claudia Roden. In January 1984 Jill Norman had negotiated to move her imprint under the auspices of the publishing house John Hale. However, by July, when Elizabeth had just signed the contract for *An Omelette and a Glass of Wine*, disagreements had arisen and Jill was dismissed from Hale. An appeal against unfair dismissal was brought by Jill and, either through loyalty or her increasing litigiousness, perhaps both,

Elizabeth joined the fray on Jill's behalf in the magazine of the book trade, the *Bookseller*. Statements had to be retracted and a kind of stalemate was reached through the courts.

Not unconnected was the particular ferociousness of Elizabeth's reputation for scorning pretension and inaccuracy, which arose from a genuine distaste for both. Looking behind Elizabeth's projection of herself, one senses that sometimes this otherwise commendable trait arose from a well-submerged lack of confidence. 'There were so many people she didn't approve of,' says Paul Bailey. 'Elizabeth had very strong opinions. There was a very clear borderline of people she didn't like and she wasn't afraid to say so. She didn't like people who didn't write well, opportunists or entrepreneurs. If she could see someone was being pushy she didn't like them.'

A case in point was *The Foodie Handbook* brought out in 1984 by Ann Barr with the journalist Paul Levy. A frenetic, tongue-in-cheek journalistic mix of fact and fashion, the book traced the rise of the current obsession with food, reflected by the coinage of the word 'foodie'. Despite some potentially thought-provoking observations and a collection of mini-biographies of influential figures in the field over the last century or so, it contains inaccuracies and the several different agendas are not all out in the open. On the one hand the reader is apparently beckoned to join the fashionable crowd who 'worship food' and on the other is being sneered at for doing just that.

Elizabeth featured prominently in the book and was incensed, not only at the biographical inaccuracies about herself, but also the general tone. In a long letter about the book to her friend Hugh Johnson, she said she believed that Ann Barr had been 'corralled' into it but regarded Levy as an opportunist. She regretted not emulating Derek Cooper on Radio 4's Food Programme, who had told Levy that if he printed anything about him he would sue. Elizabeth had written a biting piece decrying *The Foodie Handbook* in the *Tatler*, in response to which she said she had had a number of appreciative letters. She was not an advisable enemy.

An Omelette and a Glass of Wine included the brilliant piece 'John Wesley's Eye', in which Elizabeth had (partially) described her first attempts at writing, in reaction to the culinary horrors of post-war England. Among the other essays are tributes to some of those who had influenced her, in particular Norman Douglas. In 'Have It Your Own Way' she cites his dictum: 'Do as you please, and send everybody to Hell, and take the consequences. Damned good Rule of Life.' With this Elizabeth makes oblique reference to Charles Gibson Cowan and her projected escape with him to the Greek islands during the war. She tells us that Norman Douglas's intention had been to 'jolt me out of an entanglement which, as he could see . . . had already become a burden to me. And the gentleman concerned was not very much to his liking.

'"You are leaving with him because you think it your duty . . . Stay here with me. Let him make do without you."

'"I can't, Norman. I have to go."

'"Have it your own way, my dear, have it your own way."

'Had I listened to Norman's advice I should have been saved a deal of trouble. Also, I should not, perhaps, have seen Greece and the islands, not spent the war years working in Alexandria and Cairo, not have married and gone to India, not have returned to England, not become involved in the painful business of learning to write about food and cookery . . . Was he right? . . . Does it matter? I did what I pleased at the time. I took the consequences . . .'

Other essays in *An Omelette and a Glass of Wine* were some of the best from her *Spectator* years. Despite its illustrations, the book was hugely successful and went quickly into paperback.

Sending a copy to Maudie O'Malley soon after its publication in the autumn of 1984, Elizabeth recalled the recent funeral service of her cousin Archie Gordon which Maudie had been unable to attend. 'Quentin's address splendid. He revealed that Archie's predecessor in the job of producing policitians for broadcasting had been "a very different personage; his name was Guy Burgess". If we hadn't been in Church Q. would have had a big ovation.' Archie, the fifth Marquis of Aberdeen, had been a close friend of Cedric Morris and Lett Haines, and Elizabeth tells Maudie: 'I was so sad that when the Cedric and Lett shows opened I couldn't get to either of the parties. At the time I was suffering from a horrible affliction – my legs covered in sores, and I could hardly get my shoes on . . . so I missed all my old friends. I *did* manage to get to the Cedric show in its last week at the Tate. I thought it was splendid, and the catalogue brilliantly done by Richard Morphet.'

Elizabeth's love of painting – she was particularly appreciative of still-lifes – was by no means confined to those with which she had some personal connection. She tells Maudie that the previous evening she had been to 'a special viewing of the Fantin Latours . . .' organized by the NACF. Amongst some very beautiful pictures was one of her favourites, a perfectly plain white cup and saucer with spoon. Its companion piece, a little white candlestick, was also there.

Her following had for a number of years extended beyond Europe to the United States and Australia, but she had never visited either country. Hugh Johnson was instrumental in effecting a change. Elizabeth's old friend Gerald Asher had for some time been living in California. Hugh Johnson says of Asher that: 'In the sixties he was the most informative and forward-looking wine merchant in England, importing small quantities of then little known bottles into this country.' Asher had left England in 1970 and, with the help of his well-written wine articles for the prestigious American *Gourmet* magazine had established himself as one of the luminaries of the Californian wine trade.

He and Elizabeth remained friends and Asher sent her admirers from the States. Hitherto unsuccessful in persuading her to visit him there, Hugh Johnson swung the balance. 'I thought California an exciting place to be. I told Liz that she must go and visit Gerald. I was sure she'd love it once she got there.' Accordingly, in the spring of 1981 Elizabeth made her first visit. She had long been a friend of James Beard, grand old man of the American culinary world; now under Gerald Asher's wing she was fêted by a new and enthusiastic group. Taken on journeys into the country, on picnics of exquisite preparation, she ate and drank in San Francisco's most interesting restaurants, visited unusual food shops – a Lebanese one particularly seduced her with its powerful aromas of spices, while the apricot paste for summer drinks evoked memories of Egypt many years before. Other shops were selling beautiful kitchenware, whose inspiration had been Elizabeth's books and her own shop; and in still others there were the secondhand books she could not live without.

Elizabeth liked California; its museums, food, wine and good restaurants. Some of these, such as the celebrated Chez Panisse and Zuni, attribute their very existence to the inspiration of her books.

Back in England, in June Elizabeth wrote to Sabrina telling her that her kitchen was now operational again, 'rather too much so, in fact'; she had been repaying hospitality received during her holiday in San Francisco, 'and the stream of Americans continues until August'.

Elizabeth returned every year to San Francisco to stay with Gerald Asher, for a month or more, until 1991 when ill-health made it impossible. One person who is conspicuously absent from Elizabeth's acquaintanceship in America – and for that matter by mention in her books – is M. F. K. Fisher, the only other writer on food of Elizabeth's generation whose prose was consistently as felicitous as hers, quite a number would say more so. Perhaps professional jealousy prevented Elizabeth from suggesting such a meeting, or Fisher's venerated literary position meant that Elizabeth's American friends did not know her. Whatever the reason, the two women's respective iconic positions would no doubt have made friendship impossible.

While her sister's opportunities for reviving visits abroad continued, Felicité's life became more constrained as her health deteriorated still further. Although the cause of her symptoms was for sometime in debate, she was eventually diagnosed with encarditis, inflammation of the nerve-endings of the heart. In March of 1986, when her heart could take no more, Felicité died. Her death left Elizabeth alone and desolate. Their niece Sabrina, Felicité's goddaughter and executrix, remembers a frantic journey back from Holland at the end of which she arrived just too late. 'Jean [the housekeeper] and Aunt Liza were there. It was awful. Liza was utterly distraught. She just couldn't cope.' With the help of April Boyes Sabrina began to organize what had to be done. Felicité was buried in the peaceful little Sussex churchyard close by where their parents, Rupert and Stella, already lay.

Elizabeth wrote after the funeral to Maudie O'Malley: 'Thank you so much for the lovely flowers you sent . . . Poor Felicité, she was so courageous but she had no luck. A recent although short bout of illness looked like leaving her further impaired physically and mentally, and I don't see how she could have coped with much more

444

infirmity so one must accept that her quick end was really merciful, and good for her that she was at home . . . not in hospital.

'I can't quite imagine how I will manage in this house without Felicité. We had shared it for thirty-four years . . . but of course dependent upon each other for so much.' Elizabeth wrote to Alan Davidson, grateful for his condolences, again expressing something of her loss: 'Thank you also for your letter about Felicité. Without her this house is inexpressibly sad.'

Visiting during this period, Lindsey Bareham located the happier facets of 'this house' created by Elizabeth's presence and the setting she had created:

> Lovely things. Books everywhere, pictures, china, glass, wonderful earthenware pots and bowls, wonderful old storecupboards, no mixers anywhere; the kitchen Greek powder blue, the huge kitchen table with that low lamp you kept on knocking into, she always seemed to have a wind-up timer and an egg-timer on the go. Up the stairs and in Elizabeth's bedroom there were still more books and lovely pictures, and that huge four-poster bed. I don't know how she got in and out of it, it was just *covered* with papers and books, always sprouting yellow stickers. She had steps down from the bed and a tiny fridge next to it. Her dressing-room, her bathroom, her scarves and gloves and blouses hanging everywhere; lovely simple clothes. It was artistic, bohemian. It was also a terribly feminine room. I loved the atmosphere. I went to the house soon after she had died and it was so noticeable that she wasn't there. I have *never* been so struck by a presence as I was by Elizabeth's. It was quite remarkable.

Not long after Felicité's death Elizabeth contracted tuberculosis and was in hospital. Once again friends came to visit, to encourage and restore her. Poor Elizabeth's habit of falling and breaking bones had already established hospital sojourns as a ritual element of her calendar. With lunches in restaurants impossible, some friends brought picnic lunches to share with her. One of these was Janet Clarke, a cookery book dealer from whom Elizabeth had bought for several years. Janet's authority on her subject and capacity for warmth endeared her to Elizabeth, and professional transactions had developed into friendship. 'Elizabeth always looked lovely sitting up in her white cotton nightgowns. She had her hairdresser come in regularly too. Her appearance *was* important to her. When she kept breaking things in those last years most of the time she wasn't actually ill. She simply had to stay there because she shouldn't walk and move herself about. So she worked and was surrounded by flowers and her books and carried on as normal as possible.' (It was to Janet, confiding in Elizabeth about a painful affair in which the man was married, that Elizabeth had said, 'But the best ones always are my dear. The best ones always are.')

Writing in the spring of 1987 to alter an arrangement to meet Sabrina and Priscilla, necessitated by having to 'go through page designs & pictures, captions etc, for the new edition of *Italian Food*', Elizabeth refers to 'so much time in hospital in the last year'. Indeed a good part of the work on *Italian Food* was done while there. Writing to Sabrina in January of the following year she wonders 'how your Christmas was. Fairly exhausting I expect.' (Sabrina by this time had three growing boys to look after.) Elizabeth continues emptily: '*I* don't do much, other than limp up and down my stairs, and waste a lot of time revising old books, wishing they had been better written in the first place . . . Lots of love Aunt Liza.'

Despite writing several articles and more than one learned introduction for others' books subsequent to the publication of *An Omelette and a Glass of Wine*, Elizabeth was conscious both that the material in her latest book was not original and that work on her ices book was not progressing with any coherence. Her regrets that her earlier books weren't 'better written in the first place' were understandable, she was reflecting with more than a quarter of a century of writing separating her from them. Besides Elizabeth herself was frequently not the best judge of where her originality lay. The knowledge that she had not written a new book since *English Bread and Yeast Cookery* must have been galling to her; particularly during 1987 and 1988 while she made those extended versions of her 'old books', done in the days when her purpose was so much clearer.

With minor revisions to the text these new editions were produced in large, luxurious format, each one being augmented by reproductions of old paintings; much in the way Elizabeth had customarily quoted from other writers to create a *mise en scène* for her work. Despite all the work *Mediterranean Food*, *French Country Cooking* and *Summer Cooking*, through no fault of Elizabeth's, are not very absorbing. Their presentation reflects the glossy cookery book as coffee-table-entertainment syndrome, even down to the questionable practice of reproducing the presenting celebrity's signature on the cover. Elizabeth must have balked at that. Despite some good pictures these sleek modern packages are somehow remarkable only for their dampening of each book's original and pervasive spirit: a sense of authority in combination with an irrepressible vitality, freshness and simplicity. Dr Johnson's line from *The Rambler*, 'The love of life is necessary to the vigorous prosecution of any undertaking,' catches something of the essential Elizabeth. It is sadly absent here.

The one exception in these re-editions is *Italian Food*. Writing appreciatively in 1988 to Alan Davidson about a good review in *PPC* of the re-edition of *Italian Food*, Elizabeth was irritated that some other 'critics have been very hostile . . . mainly it would seem, on the grounds that the book has been around a long time and that I have no right to change its image now'. With *Italian Food*, the first of her re-editions, she certainly had changed its image. But here she need not have felt despondent about 'wasting time'. It is a fine book. As well as consolidating all previous revisions, she had added a new introduction, a 'brief new chapter on Italian wines . . . expanded lists of Italian cookery books, of guides to food and wine in Italy, and of relevant reference books'; all these were filled with fascinating commentary. She had enlarged the chapter on ices with interesting aspects of her recent research and, finally, included 'a selection from the accounts written by the scores of English and French visitors to Italy from the end of the fifteen century down to the 1980s'. Since the first publication of *Italian Food* in 1954, Elizabeth's understanding of the cultural significance of travel literature had reached quite a different plane and she cites some of the finest writers of the genre. We remember that almost all travellers made their way to Italy for the remains of its Classical past and as the cradle of its resurgence. Linked to this and in keeping with historians in other fields, throughout the new book Elizabeth's fuller appreciation of the crucial influence the

Italian Renaissance exerted for centuries upon European nations, is abundantly clear.

Italian Food not only has an engrossing text, it is also enhanced by its illustrations. Elizabeth knew she had riches from Italy at her disposal, with the tradition of still lifes of food reaching as far back as the Romans. After a lapse of centuries, in the late sixteenth century, with painters like Caravaggio, Italy was the first country where still lifes once again began to appear; not only as details in other paintings, but as a genre of their own. And in *Italian Food* Elizabeth gives us a selection of some of the most beautiful of them all: Roman mosaics and frescoes, fifteenth-century miniatures and frescoes, paintings by Caravaggio, Vincenzo Campi, Giovanni Recco, Veronese and the Caracci, and on through the eighteenth and nineteenth centuries until Renato Guttuso in the twentieth. Elizabeth was interested in still lifes both as works of art and as vital historical records of how things had actually looked. The art historian Michael Helston, who mounted *Painting in Spain in the Later Eighteenth Century* at the National Gallery in 1989, was asked to take Elizabeth round the exhibition. He remembers: 'She was fascinated with the great Luis Melendez. She seemed to have a remarkable knowledge of everything going on in those wonderful still-lifes of food.'

In remaking *Italian Food* Elizabeth was really trying to forge it into a many-layered thing on a par with *English Bread and Yeast Cookery*. That was not possible. It was as if with the revised *Italian Food* she had travelled back almost to where she had begun; back to those days with Norman Douglas and her passionate and instinctive response to the ancient in the modern Mediterranean. But that bore only partial resemblance to this measured and authoritative appreciation permeated by her present absorption in history, and a deeper understanding of Italy's roots in its ancient Mediterranean past.

In recalling her final years Doreen Thornton describes Elizabeth's sense of isolation: 'Latterly it was so hard. She grew very quiet, didn't speak so much. She was *such* a good friend, but I was getting deaf, and she would whisper on the phone. She *would* quarrel with her best friends and became more and more businesslike with them. People like Renée. Then she became lonely for friends she knew well, though she knew a lot of people. They weren't all real friends. It was awful, she'd ring and say to me, "*Can't* you come up, Doreen?"' (But Doreen lived in Sussex and the trip was as difficult for her as for Elizabeth.)

'The last time I saw her she said to me, "I want to die, Doreen."
'"You can't, Liz, you've got to finish your ice book."
'"I *have* finished it."'

And Doreen did not then know that this was not true. Realizing that Elizabeth was unable to complete it, Jill Norman had come to Halsey Street and taken the manuscript away.

After a stroke Elizabeth died at home on 22 May 1992. At seventy-nine her unquiet spirit was finally laid to rest.

Postscript

ELIZABETH HAD denounced most contemporary writing on food as 'pretentious' and 'precious' and declared that it was never her intention to produce such an effect as she had: 'and I'm not sure that I like it or the intensity and self-consciousness that goes with it.' In the days after her death on 22 May 1992, the obituaries nevertheless sounded with superlatives in her praise: 'Keeper of the National Palate', The Woman Who Changed the Face of Middle Class Kitchens', 'An Authentic Miracle Worker . . .' In September of that year a memorial service held at St Martin-in-the-Fields brought a large gathering of friends, followers and a few enemies – united at least in their tribute to the significance of Elizabeth's legacy.

Elizabeth's will had originally left Felicité the chief beneficiary of her estate, but in the years following her sister's death Elizabeth exerted to the full her ability to manipulate and made successive codicils to the document. To the chagrin of certain other members of her family, with the exception of a few small bequests, she eventually made over almost her entire estate to her third eldest nephew, Stephen Grey, who had gone to live in Australia several years before. Elizabeth's munificence to Stephen Grey extended to the royalties on most of her published books. The rest she left to Stephen's brother Johnny. Continuing in devisive mode, Elizabeth gave the copyright for her works to her literary executor, Jill Norman, knowing that the Greys must seek her permission to reprint and consequently receive royalties on Elizabeth's books. Jill Norman herself was left a small number of books by Elizabeth. She is, nevertheless, able to exercise the entitlement of the copyright holder to ask fees from those seeking to publish any of Elizabeth's works.

Not long before her death Elizabeth gave her favourite painting, Cedric Morris's *The Eggs*, to the Tate Gallery. To the National Portrait Gallery she left the Ambrose McEvoy portrait of her as a girl, the Adrian Daintrey portrait, the drawing by John Ward and the Egyptian portrait photograph of her taken shortly before her marriage. The National Portrait Gallery accepted the photograph and the John Ward but rejected the McEvoy and Daintrey. The McEvoy remains in Stephen Grey's possession.

Elizabeth stipulated that the Warburg Institute, London University, could choose what they wanted from her large library of culinary and related books. The Warburg was an appropriate resting place in Elizabeth's particular case as its *raison d'être* is the study of the history of the Classical tradition and Mediterranean culture. A number of books went to family and friends. About 2000 other culinary books were offered for a large sum by Jill Norman to the London Guildhall Library, which already houses the greater part of another important cookery library, the late Jane Grigson's. Elizabeth's books are still in store awaiting cataloguing. The task will not be an easy one as most of them were bristling with the yellow Post-it stickers she used for annotations and notes. However, even if they are, remarkably, still not available to the public, at least the books are together. The card index which April Boyes made of Elizabeth's books was not completed when she retired from working for her ten or so years before Elizabeth's death, and during which time she continued buying books. With no bibliography of her library made before its dispersal, a crucial aspect of Elizabeth's tastes and working methods is sadly lost to history.

Following the apportioning of spoils from her house, Phillips were instructed by Stephen Grey to auction off the remnants in February 1994. This included the kitchen table (by now famous as her writing desk) as tempting bait, with 200 or so books and other odds and ends to be sold as Elizabeth David memorabilia. Phillips had underestimated the drawing power of their sale. The auction room was large, but not nearly large enough. With no places left even for standing room, over 100 more potential buyers were forced to send in their bids from queues running down the corridors. Members of Elizabeth's family, friends — those left out of the will — and devotees waited in anticipation.

Television and journalists' cameras flashed and whirred and as the sale finally commenced the tension was extraordinary. Despite a rather inadequate catalogue the lots became collectors' items, even before the last one went under the hammer. Phillips had calculated the lots should reach about £20,000 in all. By the end of the afternoon relic-hunters had driven the total up to £45,000. After fierce bidding Prue Leith of Leith's Cookery School was applauded as she won the kitchen-writing table. Wooden spoons in an earthenware jar went for over £300. A scrapbook containing cards from friends such as Lawrence Durrell, and coloured sketches by the illustrator of Elizabeth's earliest books, John Minton, were estimated at £100–£200: they fetched over £800.

The manuscript of the ices book over which Elizabeth had laboured for more than ten years, remained unfinished at her death. The task of putting together and editing the notes was completed by Jill Norman, who published the book as *The Harvest of The Cold Months* in 1994. It would be reasonable to assume that Elizabeth had hung on to this last book for so long because she was hampered by ill-health, and her illnesses *were* debilitating. Most significantly she had lost her particular sense of intellectual energy and drive. Her objectives were also obscured by having become entangled in the web of scholarship — perhaps antiquarianism is a better description of her late inclinations.

Harvest of the Cold Months charts the history of man's exploitation of the preserving and pleasurable properties of ice. It travels far beyond Elizabeth's initial idea of a history of ices, creams and fruit fools, initiated by her little booklet on syllabubs and fruit fools in 1969. Instead she became fascinated by ice and everything with which it was associated.

Elizabeth describes how ice was first harvested and stored to cool food and drink, then frozen, flavoured to eat as sorbets and ice-creams, eventually recognized as an invaluable preservative and, finally, created artificially. Travel literature is appropriately plundered by her as a rich source of information, making this book the first social history relating to culinary matters which does so with such thoroughness and authority. Descriptions of the extraordinary early methods of collection and manufacture of natural ice and its uses are exhaustively traced from China through India, Persia and eventually to Europe. By the late sixteenth century wealthy Florentines commonly kept ice stores for snow-chilled wine and beverages. Astounding ice sculptures were regularly incorporated into dazzling spectacles laid out at ceremonial banquets. The ruling Medici family excelled at this, using the talents of gifted artists such as the great sculptor Buontalenti to create unparalleled displays of opulence. This was only one early aspect of a craze which, despite almost unanimous medical condemnation, was to hold Europe in its grip for centuries.

This most perishable and valuable of commodities was transported across land and sea, sometimes thousands of miles, often withstanding attack by thieves. Fortunes were made – spectacularly so by Americans in the nineteenth century – and lost. Late seventeenth-century Europe saw ice commonly used by rich and poor alike. England joined in the vogue relatively late on, but by the end of the eighteenth century rival London confectioners bid to outdo one another in the magnificence of their glacial luxuries.

It is abundantly clear that a great deal of painstaking research went into Elizabeth's final opus, and much of the material is fascinating. There are glimpses of her familiar style – terse, lively and sardonic – but a welter of detail sometimes obscures the narrative and threatens to overwhelm the reader with the worthiness of a doctoral thesis. Jill Norman put Elizabeth's notes together having (apparently) made the decision to edit little, to respect the integrity of the original text. Although this was, arguably, a praiseworthy decision it did little for Elizabeth's posthumous reputation, and we witness her indulging in the minutiae of scholarship.

The manuscript she left behind was too long and *Harvest of the Cold Months* needs pruning; references in the text are not always accurate; the index is inadequate and, extraordinarily for a book such as this, there is no bibliography. In the light of Elizabeth's increasingly scholarly bias this is not mere carping, for it is clear she now wanted her work to be judged on its academic merits. On the grounds that she was entitled to change, this was perfectly reasonable. Nevertheless, *Harvest of the Cold Months* would inevitably appeal to a much smaller, more specialized audience and Elizabeth's wider following was unenthusiastic. Some may not have read every page of *English Bread and Yeast Cookery*, but who does not respond to the pull of identification with its subject? In *Harvest of the Cold Months*, neither subject nor style are as sympathetic and it is not a great success.

To live one must eat, and frequently. Food is fuel, but also so much more than fuel. It is custom, routine, conviviality, and is saturated with feeling and association. A cuisine, a way of cooking, is a way of life, and from it springs an abundance of words, metaphors and modes of thought; it is one of the major dimensions of human existence.

Many will consider that Elizabeth, more than any other person during the last 100 years, influenced and altered perceptions of food and culinary practices in England and beyond. Born at the end of La Belle Epoque, in her early aesthetic education she was immensely privileged, surrounded by a flowering of artistic knowledge and commitment. In her emotional life she was not so fortunate; for all her privilege she was even deprived in some respects – many working-class girls had things much better in their childhood. It was not until her mid-thirties that Elizabeth found her vocation as missionary to the Anglo-Saxon Barbarians, preaching the Gospel of the Mediterranean, the Gospel of rational hedonism, in lyrical prose of outstanding power and beauty.

Elizabeth continued to develop over several decades and gradually came to understand that the malaise she had spent so long describing went even deeper than she had thought. But she discovered that there were buried treasures within her own English tradition, if only you were prepared to dig. With this her last message she had fulfilled her great potential, leaving behind a legacy of writing which was at once inspiring and illuminating.

Sources

APART FROM A very small number of essays, publications devoted to Elizabeth David's life and writings have so far been confined to journalism. A posthumous selection of her writings, the recent *South Wind Through the Kitchen: The Best of Elizabeth David* (ed. Jill Norman), includes some cautious reminiscence from some of those who knew her. Although it is incorrect to say that Elizabeth never gave interviews, most of these contain some fundamental inaccuracies – as she wrote to Hugh Johnson: 'You know Hugh I expect that by the time you are as old as I am there will be a lot of myths attached to you, and you'll remember how it's been for me' – and can only be used with some caution.

In her own writing there is a certain amount of autobiographical information, but again caution is necessary. Elizabeth was scrupulously accurate when it came to her recipes, but a master at putting together ambiguous information about herself. Occasionally she was quite simply inaccurate or she was obscuring the facts.

Her attitude to a biography was similarly unclear; it was generally believed that she was vehemently against one. However, she spoke to at least two friends, about them taking on the task, although it came to nothing. The crux of the matter was really that Elizabeth (understandably) wanted control over what was said about her as much as not wanting anything said at all.

The published sources consulted included Elizabeth's articles spread throughout the many publications for which she wrote. Among these were *Vogue*, *Harpers Bazaar*, *House and Garden*, the *Spectator*, the *Food and Wine Quarterly*, the *Sunday Sketch*, the *Sunday Times*, *Go*, the

Compleat Imbiber, Harrods News, Nova, Housewife, the *Observer.* There were also the little booklets written for Le Creuset and Saccone and Speed, and those published by herself between 1968 and 1969. Other sources were the small number of serious essays devoted to her, family papers, numerous letters to and from Elizabeth, and interviews and correspondence between myself and those who knew her. A bibliography is given at the end of this book which includes some of the texts relating to wider themes than Elizabeth's personal life.

After reflection, in the interests of privacy, but without misrepresenting the essential history of Elizabeth's life, it was decided to omit the occasional name or detail. For want of space other unpublished material, and much from interviews is also, sadly, here left unrecorded. The spelling and punctuation of quoted letters has generally been left as the original.

Bibliography

BOOKS BY ELIZABETH DAVID

FIRST PUBLICATIONS only are listed below. However, with the exception of *An Omelette and a Glass of Wine*, Elizabeth revised and in several cases wrote new introductions for later editions. Most of the publications she wrote for are listed throughout the text.

A Book of Mediterranean Food, John Lehmann, 1950
French Country Cooking, John Lehmann, 1951
Italian Food, Macdonald, 1954
Summer Cooking, Museum Press, 1955
French Provincial Cooking, Michael Joseph, 1960
Spices, Salt and Aromatics in the English Kitchen, Penguin Books, 1970
English Bread and Yeast Cookery, Allen Lane, 1977
An Omelette and a Glass of Wine, Jill Norman at Robert Hale, 1984
Harvest of the Cold Months, Michael Joseph, 1994

Acton, Eliza, *Modern Cookery for Private Families*, Longman, Brown, Green and Longman, 1845
    The English Bread Book, 1857; reprinted Southover Press, 1990
Acton, Harold, *More Memoirs of an Aesthete*, Methuen, 1970
Alexander, Michael, *Delhi and Agra*, Macmillan, 1987
Barr, Ann and Levy, Paul, *The Foodie Handbook*, Ebury Press, 1984
Bateman, Michael, *Cooking People*, Leslie Frewin, 1966
Beck, S., Bertholle, L. and Child, Julia, *Mastering the Art of French Cooking*, 1961; Cassell, 1963

Bedford, Sybille, *The Sudden View: A Mexican Journey*, Victor Gollancz, 1953

Bitting, Katherine, G., *Gastronomic Bibliography*, 1939; reprinted Holland Press, 1981

Borrow, George, *Lavengro*, 1851; 6th edn, 1900

Boulestin, Marcel, *Simple French Cooking for English Homes*, Heinemann, 1923
> *Having Crossed the Channel*, Heinemann, 1934
> *Myself My Two Countries*, Cassell, 1936

Burnett, John, *Plenty and Want*, Thomas Nelson, 1966

Caesar, Adrian, *Dividing Lines: Poetry, Class and Ideology in the 1930s*, Manchester University Press, 1991

Carpenter, Humphrey, *The Brideshead Generation*, Weidenfeld and Nicolson, 1989

Castelvetro, G. (trans. Gillian Riley), *The Fruit, Herbs and Vegetables of Italy*, Viking, 1989

Chaney Dr Edward, *Quo Vadis? Travel As Education and The Impact of Italy in the Sixteenth Century*, Frank Cass, 1998

Clark, Lady C., *The Cookery Book of Lady Clark of Tillypronie*, 1909; reprinted Southover Press, 1994

Connolly, Cyril, *The Rock Pool*, Obelisk Press, 1936

Conran, Terence, *The Kitchen Book*, Mitchell Beazley, 1977

Cooper, A., *Cairo in the War*, Hamish Hamilton, 1989

Correnti, Pino, *La Gastronomia nella Storia e nella Vita del Popolo Siciliana*, Milan, 1971

Cuisenier, Jean, *Les Français et La Table*, Editions de la Réunion des Musées Nationaux, 1985

Curnonsky, *Traditional Recipes of the Provinces of France* (trans. and ed. Edwin Lavin), W. H. Allen, 1961

Dale, Frances and Craddock, John, *Around Britain with Bon Viveur*, John Lehmann, 1952

Davidson, Alan, *Mediterranean Seafood*, Penguin, 1972
> *A Kipper With My Tea: Selected Food Essays*, Macmillan, 1988.
See in particular, *An Omelette and a Glass of Wine*

Davidson, Alan and Jane (eds), *Petits Propos Culinaires*, Prospect Books, 1979–1997. See in particular essays on and by E.D.

Davies, W. H. *Autobiography of a Super-Tramp*, 1908; reprinted Jonathan Cape, 1921

Dawson, Thomas, *The Good Housewife's Jewell*, London, 1585; reprinted Teatrum Orbis Terrarum, 1977

Dods, Mistress Margaret, *The Cook and Housewife's Manual*, Edinburgh, 1826

Douglas, Norman, *Siren Land*, J. M. Dent, 1911
    Old Calabria, Secker and Warburg, 1915
    South Wind, Secker and Warburg, 1917
    How About Europe? Secker and Warburg, 1930
    Looking Back, Secker and Warburg, 1933
    Together, 1923, Penguin, 1945
    Late Harvest, Lindsay Drummond, 1946
    Venus in the Kitchen, Heinemann, 1952

Douglas-Home, Jessica, *Violet*, Harvill Press, 1996

Driver, Christopher, *The British at Table 1940–1980*, Chatto and Windus, 1983

Drummond, J. C. and Wilbraham, Anne, *The Englishman's Food: Five Centuries of English Diet*, Jonathan Cape, 1939

Dudley, Georgina, Countess of Dudley, *The Dudley Cookery Book*, Edward Arnold, 1909

Durrell, Lawrence, *The Alexandria Quartet* (single volume edn.), Faber and Faber, 1962
    Spirit of Place, Letters and Essays on Travel (ed. Alan G. Thomas), Faber and Faber, 1969

Eliot, T. S. *Selected Essays*, 1932; 3rd edn., Faber and Faber, 1951

Escoffier, A., *Ma Cuisine*, 1934; republished (trans. Vyvyan Holland), Paul Hamlyn, 1965

Farr, Dennis, *English Art 1870–1940*, Oxford, 1978

Fedden, Robin, *Personal Landscape, An Anthology of Exile*, Editions Poetry London, 1945
    Personal Landscape, Turret Books, 1966

Fedden, Romilly, *Food and Other Frailties*, Seeley Service, London, 1948

Fermor, Patrick Leigh, *A Time of Gifts*, John Murray, 1977

Fielding, Xan, *Hide and Seek*, Secker and Warburg, 1954

Fiennes, Celia, *The Journeys of Celia Fiennes* (ed. C. Morris), Cresset Press, 1947

Fisher, M. F. K., *With Bold Knife and Fork*, Chatto and Windus, 1983

Ford, Ford Madox, *A Mirror to France*, Duckworth, 1926
    Provence, J. B. Lippincott, 1935

Freeman, Sarah, *Isabella and Sam: The Story of Mrs. Beeton*, Victor Gollancz, 1977

Fussell, Paul, *Abroad*, Oxford University Press, 1980

Gibson Cowan, Charles, *Loud Report*, Michael Joseph, 1938
    The Voyage of the Evelyn Hope, Cresset Press,1946

Glasse, Hannah, *The Art of Cookery Made Plain and Easy*, London, 1747; 5th edn, 1755

Gray, Patience and Boyd, Primrose, *Plat du Jour*, Penguin, 1957

Grigson, Jane, *Good Things*, Michael Joseph, 1971
    English Food, Macmillan, 1974

Hartley, Dorothy, *The Countryman's England*, Batsford, 1935
    Food in England, Macdonald, 1954

Heath, Ambrose, *Good Food*, Faber and Faber, 1932
    Kitchen Front Recipes, London, 1941

Holloway, Martin, *Norman Douglas*, Secker and Warburg, 1976

Hope, Annette, *Londoners' Larder*, Mainstream Publishing, 1990

Hutchins, Sheila, *English Recipes and Others*, Methuen, 1967

Jago, William, *The Technology of Breadmaking*, 1911; revised edn, The Northern Publishing Co., 1921

Jenkins, Alan, *The Thirties*, Stein and Day, 1976

Johnson, James, *A Hundred Years Eating*, Gill and Macmillan, 1977

Kent, Countess Elizabeth of, *A True Gentlewoman's Delight*, London, 1653

Kirkland, John, *The Modern Baker and Confectioner and Caterer*, 1907; revised edn (4 vols), Gresham, 1927

Lassalle, George, *The Fish in My Life*, Macmillan, 1989

Lassels, Richard, *The Voyage of Italy: Or a Compleat Journey Through Italy*, Paris, 1670; 2nd edn, London, 1698

Lewis, Lesley, *The Private Life of a Country House*, David and Charles, 1980

Leyel, Mrs C. F. and Hartley, Olga, *The Gentle Art of Cookery*, Chatto and Windus, 1925

Llanover, Lady Augusta, *Good Cookery*, London, 1867

Luke, Sir Harry, *The Tenth Muse*, Putnam, 1954

Lutyens, Mary, *Edwin Lutyens*, John Murray, 1980

Lyall, Archibald, *The Companion Guide to the South of France*, Collins, 1963

Maclean, Virginia, *A Short-Title Catalogue of Household and Cookery Books Published in the English Tongue, 1701–1800*, Prospect Books 1981

Manning, Olivia, *The Levant Trilogy*, single volume edition, Penguin, 1982

Markham, Gervase, *The English Housewife*, London, 1615

May, Robert, *The Accomplisht Cook*, London, 1660

McNeill, F. Marian, *The Scots Kitchen*, Blackie, 1929

Mennell, Stephen, *All Manners of Food*, Blackwell, 1985

Money, James, *Capri: The Enchanted Isle*, Hamish Hamilton, 1986

Montagne, Prosper, *Larousse Gastronomique*, Libraire Larousse, 1938; republished Paul Hamlyn, 1962

Montague, C. E., *Fiery Particles*, in particular the story *Honours Easy*, 1923, Chatto and Windus 1928

Montaigne, Michel de, *The Complete Works of Montaigne, Essays, Travel Journals, Letters* (trans. Donald Frame), Hamish Hamilton, 1965

Morphet, Richard, *Cedric Morris*, Tate Gallery, 1984

Morphy, Countess Marcelle, *Picnic Snacks*, Eldon Press, 1933

Morton, H. V., *A Traveller in Southern Italy*, Methuen, 1969

Orwell, Sonia (ed.), *The Collected Essays, Journalism and Letters of George Orwell*, Penguin, 1970

Oxford Symposium On Food and Cookery, Proceedings (ed. Harlan Walker), Prospect Books, 1989–97

Oxford, A. W., *English Cookery Books to the Year 1850*, 1913; reprinted by the Holland Press, 1977

Plat, Sir Hugh, *Delights For Ladies*, London, 1600; republished, Crosby, Lockwood and Son, 1948

Poems from the Desert, George Harrap, 1944

Pomiane, Edouard de, *Cooking With Pomiane* (trans. Peggy Benton), Bruno Cassirer, 1962

Ray, Cyril, *The Complete Imbiber*, 1956–71, various issues

Ray, Elizabeth (ed., with an intro. by E. David), *The Best of Eliza Acton*, Longman, 1968

Ridley, Ursula, (ed.), *The Life and Letters of Cecilia Ridley*, The Spredden Press, 1990

Roden, Claudia, *A Book of Middle Eastern Food*, Thomas Nelson, 1968

Root, Waverly, *The Food of Italy*, 1971; reprinted by Vintage Books, 1977

Ross, Janet, *Leaves From Our Tuscan Kitchen*, J. M. Dent, 1908

Rundell, Maria, *A New System of Cookery*, London, 1806

Shand, Philip Morton, *A Book of Food*, Jonathan Cape, 1927

Simeti, Mary Taylor, *Sicilian Food*, Random Century, 1989

Simon, André, *Food*, Burke Publishing, 1949

  By Request an Autobiography, The Wine and Food Society 1957

Sissons, Michael and French, Philip (eds), *The Age of Austerity*, Hodder, 1963

Sitwell, Osbert, *Left Hand Right Hand*, autobiographical volumes, Macmillan, 1945–48

Smollett, Tobias, *Travels Through France and Italy*, 1771

Spalding, Frances, *British Art Since 1900*, Thames and Hudson, 1986

Spry, Constance and Hume, Rosemary, *The Constance Spry Cookery Book*, J. M. Dent, 1956

Spurling, Hilary, *Elinor Fettiplace's Receipt Book*, Salamander, 1986

Stewart, I. McD.G., *The Struggle For Crete*, Oxford University Press, 1966

Stobart, Tom, *Herbs, Spices and Flavourings*, David and Charles, 1970

Sysonby, Lady Ria, *Lady Sysonby's Cookbook*, Putnam, 1935

Theroux, Paul, *The Pillars of Hercules*, Hamish Hamilton, 1995

Touring Club Italiano, *Guida Gastronomica d'Italia*, 1931; reprinted 1951

Waddell, Helen, *The Wandering Scholars*, Constable, 1927

Waugh, Evelyn, *Officers and Gentlemen*, Chapman and Hall, 1955

Westbury, Lord, *Handlist of Italian Cookery Books*, Leo Olschki, 1963

Wheaton, Barbara Ketcham, *Savouring the Past, the French Kitchen and Table from 1300 to 1789*, Chatto and Windus, 1983

Wheeler, David (ed.), *Convivium*, vol. 1, no. 1, Spring 1993

White, Florence, *Good Things in England*, Jonathan Cape, 1932

White, Gilbert, *Gilbert White's Journals*, Routledge, 1931; reprinted David and Charles, 1970

Wickes, George (ed.), *Lawrence Durrell and Henry Miller: A Private Correspondence*, Faber and Faber, 1963

Wilson C. Anne, *Food and Drink in Britain*, Constable, 1973
    (ed.), 'The Appetite and the Eye' and 'Banqueting Stuffe', papers from the 1st and 2nd Leeds Symposia on Food History, Edinburgh University Press, 1986 and 1991

Wine and Food Quarterly (ed.) André Simon, subsequently by Hugh Johnson, Pamela Vandyke Price, etc.

Withers, Audrey, *Life Span*, Peter Owen, 1994

Index

ONE STOP Customer Care

The One Stop Series

Series editor: David Martin, FCIS, FIPD, FCB
                Buddenbrook Consultancy

A series of practical, user-friendly yet authoritative titles designed to provide a one stop guide to key topics in business administration.

Other books in the series to date include:

David Martin	*One Stop Company Secretary*
David Martin	*One Stop Personnel*
Jeremy Stranks	*One Stop Health and Safety*
John Wyborn	*One Stop Contracts*
David Martin	*One Stop Property*
Harris Rosenberg	*One Stop Finance*
Robert Leach	*One Stop Payroll*
David Martin/ John Wyborn	*One Stop Negotiation*

1998 Titles

David Martin	*One Stop Communication*
Karen Huntingford	*One Stop Insurance*
Robin Ellison	*One Stop Pensions*
Patrick Forsyth	*One Stop Marketing*

ONE STOP
Customer care

DAVID MARTIN

ICSA Publishing
The Official Publishing Company of
The Institute of Chartered Secretaries and Administrators

in association with

Prentice Hall Europe

London New York Toronto Sydney Tokyo Singapore
Madrid Mexico City Munich Paris

First published 1998 by
ICSA Publishing Limited
Campus 400, Maylands Avenue
Hemel Hempstead
Hertfordshire, HP2 7EZ

Typeset in 10/12.5 pt Meridien with Frutiger Light
by Hart McLeod, Cambridge

Printed and bound in Great Britain
by MPG Books Ltd, Bodmin, Cornwall

British Library Cataloguing in Publication Data

A catalogue record for this book is available from
the British Library

ISBN: 1–860–72065–X

1 2 3 4 5 02 01 00 99 98

Contents

CONTENTS

Preface

Stating the obvious

Most organisations are suppliers with virtually identical aims – making money which they achieve only by 'supplying' satisfactorily. The customers they supply are the ultimate arbiters of the attainment of their aims. If suppliers satisfy their customers all the time, their successes are virtually guaranteed.

Customer care has two main functions:

- to ensure that we satisfy (in the widest sense of the word) the customer in developing, presenting and supplying our products, and

- to ensure that should there be defects in any of those operations swift and positive action is taken to rectify the position.

These functions are inextricably linked since unless we achieve the latter we can never attain the former.

The reality?

Whilst some may find my opening paragraph simplistic and obvious – which indeed it should be – experience indicates that such contentions fail to penetrate the intelligence of many responsible for the success of their organisations. When challenged on this some will attempt to blame those at the sharp end. But this is rubbish – it can never be their responsibility. The responsibility for customer care is a priority – indeed *the* priority – of the Board and cannot be delegated. Research summarised below indicates that although many Boards subscribe to the 'priority of the customer' few spend any time actually listening to them. Presumably they prefer to rely on second-hand data – reports, information and even hearsay (all of which can be misconstructed, misinterpreted and misconstrued) – anything, in fact, rather than dealing directly with those who pay their salaries.

If this aspect of business (that is, caring for those who provide the resources on which the future of the organisation depends) is not addressed, then the problems of disappointed customers becoming demanding complainants will plague our organisations, wasting our time, diluting our resources and dissipating our efforts in the process. Further, as research demonstrates, failure to deal effectively with disappointed customers can cost our organisations dearly. As many as 80% of dissatisfied customers will not repurchase from their supplier, whilst one leading UK company states that a person with a bad experience is likely to inform up to 17 other potential customers. Conversely, where complaints are dealt with satisfactorily, over 80% will repurchase and will also spread the good news, acting as unpaid promotion agents.

The approach

This book uses short, true case studies to illustrate the practical suggestions and recommendations included. The examples demonstrate bad practices as well as good, on the premise that it is sometimes easier to learn from our mistakes than our successes. Using the expanded index format leads to a certain amount of repetition but this is deliberate in order that each item can be dealt with holistically. The terms 'supplier' and 'product' are intended to cover the whole range of organisations that sell, and the items, services, advice and so on, that they supply respectively.

The case studies illustrate practices and also draw conclusions why particular approaches did or did not work, although such lessons and inferences drawn therefrom should only ever be used as guides. 'Circumstances do alter cases' and this is never more true than in attempting to deal with customers and their problems.

Flexibility and consistency

Often of course there can be more than one possible solution, and in training those whom we require to deal with customers we need to:

- adopt parameters that illustrate the manner in which we wish to do business without restricting their flexibility or innovation

- provide guidelines under which they can 'do a deal' and thus cater for the non-standard problem, rather than hard and fast rules, and

- allow discretion to manoeuvre rather than impose narrow limits of action which may otherwise hamper common sense reactions.

The conclusions which are drawn from the case studies and recommendations put forward are intended not as a complete answer to a problem – indeed there may be no 'right' answer. The aim is to provide suggestions that will enable us to have a greater control over the way in which we provide customer care.

Sadly, good quality customer care and service tends to be the exception rather than the rule in the UK. If we do not provide this, then, as the competitive 1990s draw to a close and the new millennium dawns, it may be impossible to escape the almost inevitable reaction of such attitudes – our customers voting for our competitors with their feet and with their wallets.

Whilst what seems to be a minority, are able to deal with such matters and care for their customers positively from the outset (an attitude which must surely provide a sound investment in future business) the majority seem not to bother. Their approach seems to be that yesterday's and today's customers are unimportant since there is always another customer tomorrow. This may be so, but the cost of attracting and servicing tomorrow's customer may be five times that of retaining the existing customer. It may also be the case that we are protected since our competitors are also pretty poor at customer care and their disappointed customers come to us. This is a dangerous complacency, and it would be preferable to seize the opportunity to be better than them – thereby gaining a competitive edge.

The Central London Training and Enterprise Council conducted a survey in 1997 and discovered that just over half the organisations asked, carried out customer care training and half of them intended to increase such spending. Of the 40% of respondents who do not carry out such training 34% stated they had no intention of introducing it.

If this were not a poor enough commitment to those without whom an organisation cannot survive, it is compounded by research from P.Four, the strategic marketing consultancy. Their findings were that although 70% of those questioned felt that customer focus was the first or second priority for their organisation less than 25% thought that time spent with customers was important. Over 75% thought that attaining new business was an important way of measuring the effectiveness of management, despite the adverse multiplier factor mentioned above. That factor would seem to indicate that 'retaining existing customers' would be a far more cost-effective measure of management's effectiveness.

Customer care is not difficult – but it is absolutely priceless if we want our organisations to have a soundly-based future.

David M. Martin
Buddenbrook
March 1998

Active listening

Introduction

In a report in the monthly journal of the Institute of Directors in October 1997, Chief Executive of 'Investors in People', Mary Chapman, commented that boredom and frustration at work was 'widespread' and is 'often the result of an employee's lack of involvement with the company's goals and a feeling that their ideas are not wanted'. Whilst this should be of considerable concern to employers in terms of their relationship with their employees, it is critical in terms of the potential problems it could create should such demotivated employees be required to interface with those without whom the supplier cannot cease to exist – its customers – and particularly those with problems, concerns or complaints. The key to successful customer care and to COMPLAINT CONVERSION is listening to the messages (said and unsaid) generated by the customers and responding positively – if only to protect the business from the subsequent and repeated adverse comments of such disaffected customers. Suppliers need to ensure that their own staff are treated positively if customers are to be similarly treated. Indeed, only if employees feel they are treated well and their concerns listened to are they likely to listen to and treat their employer's customers well. If the reverse is true many employees' attitude could be 'if that's the way they want it I can be just as awkward'.

At the root cause of many relationships (both the organisation with its INTERNAL CUSTOMERS and those employee–customers with the external customers) is often a basic problem of communication. In many instances this is because the true meaning of communication is not understood, the descriptions 'information' and 'communication' being used as if they were interchangeable which is far from the case.

Information is not communication

Sender	I	F	C
Data encoded	N	E	O
Transmitted	F	E	M
Received	O	D	M
Decoded	R		U
	M	B	N
Recipient	A	A	I
Received	T		C
Decoded	I	C	A
Comprehension	O		T
Clarification	N	K	I
			O
			N

Message appreciation

Research indicates that when two parties are face to face, the words they utter comprise only around 7% of the complete message being conveyed. The overwhelming mass of signals regarding their words (and the meaning the speaker intended to give to those words) is derived from

- tone, language, inflexion of the sounds received, and
- the manner in which the words are delivered, that is the body language of the speaker (which itself can be affected by the body language of the listener).

Interpretation of the intended sense can be hampered should the words and the silent messages be in contradiction.

Example

If one speaker, smiling broadly, says to another, however menacing the tone (for example in banter or response to a not serious insult) 'I am going to kill you', it is unlikely that the listener will take the meaning of the words seriously. Conversely if the same listener was confronted alone on a dark night by a masked man wielding a knife saying the same words but in virtually the same menacing tone, it would be hardly surprising if his comprehension of the words wasn't somewhat different.

The message is simple – yet surprisingly often, and in many walks of life, overlooked. If we are trying to start a communicative process (which means that we wish to encourage feedback and response otherwise we are simply providing information and not attempting to communicate at all) then we need to be prepared to listen to and appreciate the real messages provided by that feedback and response – nowhere is this more critical an endeavour than in interfacing with our

- internal customers without whom nothing can happen in our business, or our
- external customers without whom we have no business.

In fact, even though there may have been no thought given to ensuring the recipient could understand the message in the way intended, when the parties are face to face the chances of true communication may still be high. If there is misunderstanding one party can ask for clarification from the other and the responses (both words and body language) may provide additional guidance to the level of comprehension.

However, when the parties are remote and the communication medium is not 'face-to-face-verbal' but written (either in hardcopy or by electronic connection) the likelihood of shared understanding is made immeasurably harder. Tone, inflexion, facial expression and other indicators are lost and all that replaces them are words which can mean very different things to different people – and can generate unexpected reactions.

Constructing the right message

Before any consideration of the feedback (which is essential before true communication is effected) we need to ensure that the message we intend to deliver is absolutely correct. 'Correct' in this context means

- that it reflects what we really wish to say,
- that the language and words used are correct, and,
- that our message is couched in language and format that is appropriate to (that is, 'can be clearly understood by') the target audience.

The need to provide the right message in the right way can be encapsulated in the prime guidance to all who seek to communicate (which basically means everybody): **'if the reader or listener does not understand the message as was intended – the responsibility is that of the writer or speaker'.**

The obvious truth of this statement (again in practice often overlooked) is that the whole reason for writing or speaking should be so that the receiver can understand what the sender wishes to say. Sadly it seems that in a number of instances the writer or speaker thinks only in terms of what he or she wishes to say and the interests of the target of the message are sublimated to that preference. Nowhere is this more likely to lead to

3

misunderstandings and resentment than in dealing with customers with complaints – the golden rule is to listen carefully and actively and to let them speak as much as possible. In doing so the supplier is restoring control to them which they will feel they lost when the products, services or whatever, in which they had invested did not live up to their expectations.

The effect

The danger of not constructing the right message, or of constructing the right message but then not transmitting it accurately, or of constructing and transmitting it accurately but then not listening actively to the response, is that we can be trapped into assuming that we understand what our target audience are thinking or saying which in turn can lead us into misconceptions and false assumptions. In some instances this process is totally ignored and an arrogant assumption is made that the originator knows and understands what the target audience's views are or what their response will be. Whilst on occasion a correct assumption can be made, it is a high-risk policy, basically since any organisation or originator which does not listen to the views of their target audience can be trapped into making incorrect decisions thereby alienating them.

Case study: Unelected

The scale of the defeat of the Conservative Party in the General Election of 1997 surprised many people. Yet this should not have been the case since the view was widespread amongst its own supporters (its customers) that those in charge of the party were either not reflecting or not listening to (or both) their views. Over a number of years of local elections the Party's 'grassroots' support had been whittled away and it seemed little attention was being paid to trying to restore these foundations. If people are ignored or their views not taken into account it is hardly surprising if they withdraw support. (In that instance their plight was exacerbated by the fact that their opponents were listening very carefully and apparently responding in terms of policy commitment to the wishes expressed by those customers.)

Note: *Such an attitude is not rare. In a 1997 survey, consultancy P.Four discovered that although 70% of managers rated customer focus as their organisation's prime or secondary priority, less than 25% thought management hours spent with customers were important. Reconciling these two results is difficult to say the least although it may reveal why real customer care in the UK is, with a few notable exceptions, of poor quality.*

The benefits

The benefit of listening to and providing an active communication with our customers is that we will have an insight into what they require – a route by which our organisation is more likely to be able to survive tomorrow. The only way in which we can tap into this data source is by a commitment to a positive customer care programme which should encompass

- recognition of the value of customers, their views, complaints and observations

- adherence to procedures and processes that welcome comment and contact from, and encourage communication with customers

- facilities that make it easy for customer feedback to be captured and processed

- being seen to be listening to customers no matter what they say (rather than as some suppliers do, ignoring their customers with a breathtaking ARROGANCE)

- treating customers when complaining about a product as positively as they are treated when considering their purchase, and

- ensuring all employees understand and adhere to such a commitment at all times.

Case study: Abbey habit

Survey after survey has revealed that generally customers have a low opinion of traditional banks. Particularly galling to many customers is the habit of many bank staff taking breaks at what may be the only time that most customers can visit them – between 12.30 and 2.00 p.m. In a major advertising campaign in early 1998, Abbey National (which before becoming a public company and a bank was a building society – a movement which traditionally seems to have been more aware of customer requirements) stated that it was committed to providing adequate staffing when it was convenient to the customers rather than convenient to the bank. This is customer care in action.

Postscript

The rapid development of loyalty cards in the UK is an example of suppliers attempting to 'get close to' their customers and using technology to achieve that aim, with the considerable benefit of being able to engender customer commitment to their brand/stores and so on in the process. Following considerable planning Tesco launched its Clubcard and within six weeks had acquired 5,000,000 members. Not only does the company now know who its (probably) most loyal customers are, but it will increasingly build considerable knowledge of their purchasing patterns. Further, by analysing the data that the card generates groups can be focused and targeted. Similar tactics have now been adopted by other leading retailers – Sainsbury, Boots, and W H Smiths to name but a few. However there is little point in trying to generate customer loyalty by the introduction of such sophisticated means unless the basic reaction to customer problems is also positive.

Arrogance

Introduction

Running a wealth-creating organisation takes confidence, confidence tends to aid success, and success to breed success. There is nothing wrong with these attributes – indeed in the UK it might be better for us if we as a nation felt more comfortable about showing pride in what we have achieved rather than at times denigrating successes. However, such a self-effacing attitude is infinitely preferable to an over-confidence leading to corporate arrogance – a belief that everything one does is right (and the views of anyone else are of no account) which can in turn lead to a feeling that there is no need to listen to anyone, customers included.

There are numerous examples of both executives and organisations becoming so over-confident and convinced of their own opinions that they come to believe that neither they nor their organisation can do no wrong. If such an attitude exists amongst the top management of an organisation it may be mirrored by junior staff. If they in turn display such an attitude to their customers it is unlikely to do anything but generate irritation. In a letter from one of the UK's largest banks, a Customer Relations Manager wrote 'we have overall responsibility in this department for the level of service provided by the Bank'. It may be that this was sloppy letter drafting but it displays a totally flawed arrogance – the true responsibility for the level of service provided by the bank rests solely and squarely on the shoulders of the members of the Board. Delegating such a fundamental aspect of their responsibilities reflects the dichotomy disclosed by the survey P.Four referred to in ACTIVE LISTENING – namely, that customer service is a priority but there is no need to listen to customers!

Board responsibility

The Chinese have a saying that 'the fish rots from the head' – if the head is rotting then everything rots. If there are problems in an organisation – the responsibility for dealing with them rests with those at the top and only those at the top can correct them. In turn they can only correct them if they know what is going on throughout the organisation and in the minds of their customers. To do this the Board needs to ensure that it (that is, the Board or a senior manager at that level) is in direct contact with the sharp end rather than receiving all its information second hand from those whose interests may be threatened unless the true position is filtered out. Conduits between Board and those at the sharp end and the customers with whom they interface are essential. But for this to be effective it is vital that those at the top admit they do not have all the answers and can, as we all do, learn every day.

Case study: Overconfidence = arrogance

In the late 1980s/early 1990s the Insurance industry were allowed to market personal pensions, the original intent of which was to provide a vehicle by which high-fliers who were unlikely to remain with one or two employers during their career could obtain a pension which was tied to them rather than to their employer. Despite those involved in company schemes warning those in employment that their safest route was to remain within an occupational pension scheme, many who did not fall into the 'high flier/mover' category at all, were persuaded to opt out of their occupational scheme by glossy and persuasive marketing aids and some fast talking representatives who were motivated more by their commission than by consideration of whether the package was appropriate for the 'punters' despite the latter being their customers and deserving of better advice. Few insurance companies were immune to the attractions of selling personal pensions and some of the largest came in for considerable criticism.

In late 1997 the Financial Services Authority castigated one of the largest – the Prudential – for a 'deep-seated and long standing failure in management' since it failed to control the sales force that missold many such pensions. The *Daily Telegraph* singled out the Prudential's former Chief Executive, Mick Newmarch, for having a 'contempt for regulation (which) permeated right down to the salesmen, some of whom put profitability first and looking after the customer a distant second'. These comments are particularly ironic (and sad) given the Prudential's reputation which had been built on over 100 years of personal and tailored service to its policyholders – indeed this personal attention aimed at providing services ideally suited to its policyholders was the very foundation of its current wealth and size.

Creating an environment

The point we should consider here, is not so much the mis-selling of pensions, appalling though that was, as the fact that it was the arrogance of those in control – the belief they knew better than those who sought to regulate their activities, which spread to those at the sharp end and imbued this over-confidence. In then dealing with their customers, it is unsurprising if some representatives, full of this corporate confidence, in turn oversold the goods they had on offer. At the sharp end individual greed for increased earnings in some cases subsumed the professionalism of selling the right product but it was corporate greed to gain as large a share as possible of the personal pension market which created an environment where those at the sharp end were encouraged to act accordingly.

Case study: Overselling

One long-time policy holder with the Prudential who had just become self-employed wanted to set up a personal pension. Despite being one of the target audience for which personal pensions were ideally fashioned, he still encountered problems. He was told categorically during the selling process that it was possible to vary the manner of contribution from a yearly lump sum to regular monthly amounts, but when he attempted to do this it caused considerable confusion which took over four years to sort out to his satisfaction. Fortunately the new management at the Prudential seem to have recognised the problem and to be taking corrective action.

Insurance companies caught in the kind of high public profile problem referred to above may be big enough to admit their mistakes and strong enough to be able to withstand the fines and costs of rectification involved – as well as the damage to their reputations. Not all organisations are so fortunate. Perhaps the best known display of corporate arrogance occurred when Gerald Ratner, then the Chairman of one of the UK's biggest and most successful jewellery chains, in making a speech to the Institute of Directors, referred to some of the products his shops sold as 'crap'. It may have been meant as a joke but many of his customers felt that he was insulting and patronising them by inferring that they would and did buy virtually worthless items. Within a few months the company's share price plummeted from 177p to 8p, Ratner had to resign as Chairman and later as Director, many of the shops were sold and the remainder of the chain had to change their trading name and the company its corporate name. The golden rule in customer care is that 'Customers and their views should never – ever – be taken for granted'. Indeed we could encapsulate this guidance in the phrase *'patronise your customers and ultimately they will not patronise your products'.*

A failure to appreciate that demand and reputation can be fickle friends has been the death of many organisations. The only way to combat any complacency or arrogance is to ensure there are real links between

- top end (decision takers)
- sharp end (decision implementers) and
- power end ('buy or not' decision makers).

Those best placed to report on the market and its needs and preferences are employees at the sharp end but the Board needs to ensure they have been properly briefed and fully understand the aims, policies and attitudes of the Board.

Customers have a habit of showing the organisation that thinks it knows it all, that in fact it had imperfect perception. Reputations (and demand) can take years to create and seconds to lose. The use of CARELINES, customer care and MARKET RESEARCH, not just on the products but also on the perception of the organisation, can be valuable.

Case study: *Qui s'excuse, s'accuse*

A customer had received poor, even amateurish, service from two employees at the branch of a clearing bank where he had been a customer for over 20 years. At the same time (but presumably by coincidence) he received a personally addressed letter from the Managing Director of the bank enclosing a questionnaire concerning his perception of customer services provided by the bank. Rather than complete the questionnaire which was couched in general terms he decided to reply by means of a personal letter to the MD explaining his concerns.

He received replies from the customer services department and his own branch. He replied to the branch letter pointing out that in response to a personal letter from the MD he had replied personally to the MD but no response had been received from him. Obviously this was fed back since he then received another letter from the Manager of Customer Relations which read '[the MD] is not generally able to reply personally to correspondence as he does spend a large part of his time away from the office meeting business groups and branch managers'.

The customer replied that

- he hoped the MD would be busy but if he generated personal letters in his own name it created an expectation of personal attention,

- it was difficult to see what could be more important to a Managing Director than a personal interface with at least one of his customers, and

- the MD might gain a better perception of his role if he read the P.Four research.

Basic reminders

Possibly the most valuable advice for Boards tempted to believe that they have all the answers and have no need to research or listen to the market is to remember Oliver Cromwell's plea to the General Assembly of the Church of Scotland: 'I beseech you in the bowels of Christ think it possible you may be mistaken' – and to take action accordingly.

We might also heed the example of Imperial Rome. When riding in a chariot through the streets and receiving the adulation of thousands of citizens cheering the news of another victory, behind the triumphant Caesar would stand an ordinary citizen whispering in his ear 'Remember Caesar thou are mortal'.

Thinking it possible that we might be wrong does not mean lacking confidence in what we are doing, merely a caution to take nothing for granted and advice that we should always be checking to ensure we have got it right, and indeed checking personally.

No one should assume they know what their customers think – that is corporate and managerial arrogance. We need to find out – or else we fail to do so. Fail the customers and ultimately the business will fail.

Postscript

It is not just wealth-creating organisations that can become arrogant. Wealth-consuming organisations can also be arrogant which adds insult to injury considering that those suffering the insult are often those providing the salaries of the arrogant. In January 1998 a code was issued requiring bureaucrats employed by the European Union to deal courteously with telephone calls and promptly with correspondence so that all enquiries from the public (who of course actually foot the bill for this bloated organisation) are treated 'competently'. During 1997 there were nearly 1,200 complaints lodged with the EU Ombudsman – mostly complaining about highhandedness of the bureaucrats. In addition officials will be prohibited from accepting free holidays and gifts of anything more than 'symbolic' value, which presumably have been offered in the past to try to obtain decent service!

Introduction

'I don't need anyone to survey my customers, I know they are all satisfied since we get no complaints' said the Chairman. This was puzzling since having used some of the products I had not been particularly impressed with the quality or reliability and could not believe that others would not have found them unacceptable. In discussing this with a colleague who knew of the company it transpired that he had bought one of their products, been dissatisfied with it and attempted to lodge a mild complaint with the company. However the reaction from the sales department (there was no customer care or even complaints department) was so offhand and unhelpful he had given up, thrown the product away and replaced it with a competitive product. A subsequent test phone call disclosed a similar response. The product was eminently substitutable and the company spent considerable amounts on advertising. An analysis of customer accounts revealed that few repeated their orders, and when a sample of non-repeating customers were contacted, widespread dissatisfaction was discovered. To his credit, the Chairman changed his attitude when told the facts. He set up a customer care department, complaints were dealt with positively, their nature was recorded and analysed (see DARN), and a base of repeat customers was gradually developed. This allowed a reduction in marketing expenditure which more than compensated for the cost of handling the complaints positively.

Avoiding misconceptions

Like all management problems it is essential to obtain some facts – and preferably all of them – before making a decision. Unlike many management problems the facts that are needed in order to make the appropriate decision are contained in the minds and perceptions of the customers who very often may not be directly accessible to the supplier. However, it is the perceptions of our customers that we most need to access and adopting the initial 'ostrich' pose of the Chairman referred to in the introduction is the antithesis of what is required. Accordingly the whole ethos of the organisation needs to be geared to encouraging customers to advise the supplier of their views – both positive and negative. In this we need to try to stress the positive nature of the process – and one way of doing this is to completely avoid the use of the word 'complaint' itself.

'Complaining' has a number of unfortunate connotations – all of which are emotive and negative. One suffers from 'a complaint' in medical terms, and as a customer making a 'complaint' may be seen as 'protesting', 'moaning' or 'griping' (which has a further link to an unwanted medical condition). Inherent in 'complaining' may be the complainant's self-perception that they are at a disadvantage and one that few suppliers will want to know about. They may fear they will be viewed by the supplier as an outcast – one who is trying to disturb the status quo. They know that many organisations will regard their complaint as an allegation of 'fault' and that some will suspect that they are 'trying it on'. The challenge for the supplier is to remove all these negative 'messages' and to create an environment that is positive, wants to know of its mistakes and is willing to learn from them.

Customer concern

A complaint is actually the last of a first series of occurrences, and hopefully the first of a second series (namely, the process by which the supplier seeks to recover its position). The first process can be summarised as

1. awareness of the product (advertising, display, word of mouth, and so on),

2. understanding its purpose (specification, brochure, point of sale material, packaging, and so on),

3. appreciating price and value (comparison with competitors, previous models and so on),

4. deciding to buy (manner treated by assistant, supplier and so on),

5. use,

6. discovering that there is a fault (for example, does not perform what is claimed in the specification, brochure and so on), and

7. deciding to raise the query with the supplier.

During the first three of these steps the customer is absorbing information about the product which enable him or her to assess whether to exercise customer CHOICE and buy the product. There are a number of instances here, where the supplier's attitude to customer concerns can be presented and then re-emphasised to prospective purchasers. Thus from the outset the supplier can take the initiative and stress that, for example:

'the only way in which we wish to carry on our business is in the confident assurance that customers are satisfied. In the event that anything is not as the customer perceived before purchase, we want to hear of this and to this end, here is the freephone telephone number of our customer care team who really want to hear from you and will do their best to rectify any problems.'

Not only should this encourage customers to lodge concerns it is also a valuable marketing message – not least that the supplier has confidence both in the product and in their ability to handle concerns positively. It is also a complete commitment which if not fulfilled could create a considerable backlash.

The problem with many products and with most services is that the packaging which could carry wording reinforcing the above message may be thrown away and the message forgotten. Inscribing the message (or simply the customer care telephone number) on the product may counter this. Where products are of some value it may also be possible to record personal details so that they can be direct mailed with other offers – the document incorporating the original message.

Ideally nothing should be a bar to the customer registering a concern. Thus a 24-hour-a-day, 7-days-a-week, freephone telephone service could be provided. Increasingly there are moves to 24-hour business. Some organisations in banking, food retailing, fuel retailing, remote/mail/media ordering and other areas now operate on such a continuous basis. Thus a manned 24-hour-a-day telephone number is not unusual. If the phone cannot be manned on this basis, at least an answerphone service could be provided. The semiotic message being conveyed is that the supplier is so concerned at the customer's concerns that they are prepared to listen on a 24-hour-a-day basis. In addition American research indicates that when a supplier provides a freephone number for customer concerns, 86% of consumers believe that the products are 'quality' and the supplier has faith in their product – literally 'we believe it will do what we say but if for any reason it doesn't we want to hear about it and (by implication) do something about it'.

Obviously when the customer does ring it is essential that they are dealt with positively (see CALL HANDLING).

Basically the aim should be to acquire a reputation that tells everyone that here is a supplier that practises what it believes regarding customer concerns; that although some customers will undoubtedly attempt to exploit the system, most will respect the effort being put in to provide a positive customer care policy and practice and will respond accordingly. The rationale of the Marks & Spencer customer relationship is 'we are a supplier that provides quality – in our food and clothing, in the presentation of our stores, in the service of our staff and in our attitude to our customers and their concerns'. Such an attitude must work or M & S would not be as generally rated as Britain's most respected and successful retailer.

Building a data base

When a customer rings with a concern the supplier gains information – personal data where perhaps they only knew numbers before. Not only have they such data but they know it is derived from a person who is already a customer. Provided their encounter was concluded reasonably positively the customer could be subsequently contacted and the opportunity used for

- checking whether the customer repeats their purchase,

- asking whether they are aware (or want to be aware) of new products,

- enquiring whether they would be prepared to complete a questionnaire and/or answer some market research questions,

- checking how they felt their concern/complaint was handled, and so on.

Care needs to be exercised in using personal data, and the latest legal position regarding storage and usage of personal data also needs to be checked. If it is decided to try to use this approach, the customer should be asked whether they object.

The views of those that do object must be respected but the number may be surprisingly few particularly if some recognition is made of their assistance.

Technology can also provide our database for an audit and basic customer care without the customer even being aware of it. Loyalty cards now used by a considerable number of leading multiple retailers have been promoted on the basis of rewarding customers' purchases by 'giving away' products or cash in exchange for the points registered on the card. However, the most intelligent of these cards provides the store with detailed insight into the shopping habits of its most stable customer base. From this data the store can

- build promotions,

- discern which products generate repeat purchases, and which do not (which if such information is repeated widely must raise questions concerning the product without any complaint being registered),

- generate reports and analysis, and so on.

Testing the market

Market research is entitled to a book on its own and can only be briefly referred to here, but generally the proactive supplier that seeks out and repeatedly checks the views of its customers is at least likely to protect its position than one that uses the 'ostrich tactic' of the Chairman in the Introduction. Asking questions may condition the respondent. Some will provide answers that they think the questioner wishes to hear, others can deliberately distort the information, and still more may have 'axes to grind' and will thus slant their response. However, skilled compilers of such questions can combat this by the use of check questions. Providing a random (and large enough) sample is used the effect of such maverick responses can be discounted.

Postscript

One of the seminar and conference providers for whom I give presentations requests all delegates to complete a critique of each speaker and the whole event. There are usually five categories ranging from Poor to Excellent. However, in analysing the replies, unless there are a large number in either of the extreme columns these entries are ignored and the middle three results considered in more depth. Experience has shown that some delegates can be less discerning and provide high marks ('the halo effect') whilst others who may simply dislike the style (or something as basic as the dessert offered at lunch) can provide low marks ('putting the boot in'). To quote Abraham Lincoln – the trick is to 'please most of the people most of the time' which will probably have been the case provided most ticks are in the middle or higher of the middle three columns.

Basic principles

Introduction

In essence there should be little about dealing with customers and particularly customers that have concerns or problems, that is either difficult or in any way different from dealing with any other management problem, except that

- since we are dealing entirely with people and their problems the challenges may be somewhat more varied, and
- since we are dealing with those who for one reason or another are disappointed in our organisation the discussion may become emotive.

Like other management problems we need to

- identify the challenges,
- seek to avoid the incidence of the encounters that otherwise we must resolve, and
- recognise and always remember our ultimate aim (not forgetting the fact that such aim(s) may differ from that of the person(s) with whom we will be interfacing).

However, in addition we may need to

- realise that we and our customer may have different standards which need to be reconciled, and not least
- consider the changing face of consumer demands and expectations.

The basic principles that follow are itemised here although they are separately developed as part of other concepts later.

Identifying the challenges

It is entirely unrealistic to expect that the average organisation can completely eliminate mistakes, errors, missed deadlines, poor quality, and so on. 'To err is human' and whilst not attempting to use this as an excuse, we must accept the almost inevitable truth of the phrase. This would seem to indicate that during every stage of the operation to achieve sales there will be times when things will not go according to plan. Very often this will be our responsibility as a supplier – which should immediately create a demand for action to correct the shortcoming. Indeed we might go a step further and state that whilst we will always aim at achieving perfection and that this should be everyone's aim, realistically we can expect (say) 2–3% of our sales to be the subject of such a shortcoming or concern. Regular auditing of concerns may enable us to refine this figure which we may find exceeds our profit margin. This may help put the challenge into perspective – not so much a negative 'how can we minimise customer dissatisfaction' but a more positive 'what's it worth to protect a figure equivalent to that of our profit margin, by satisfying those who would otherwise be dissatisfied'. With tight demand and competitive trade, retaining existing customers must be a priority.

After all, those that already buy from us have

- been attracted to our product sufficiently to buy,
- knowledge of us, our products and services, and
- belief and confidence that what they are buying is worth their investment.

The longer we can retain customers the greater the time and number of purchases over which can be spread the 'cost' of acquiring them. If we retain all our customers in theory, we need spend nothing to attract new customers to maintain the status quo. If we still spend such sums, the expenditure can be most effective since it can be focused to add new customers to our customer base. Conversely if we lose 10% of our customers each year then quite swiftly our whole customer base will be lost. Realistically the organisation would probably have ceased trading by about the fourth year of such non-replenished losses. Retaining satisfied customers requires an investment in customer commitment and care far less costly than customer replacement.

Avoiding the incidence

Whilst customer dissatisfaction can be caused by a faulty product, poor service or late delivery, such failings can be swiftly eradicated by prompt and positive action. In this way any complaint is minimised and contained. What really annoys customers is not so much that a fault has occurred (since most people accept that, with the best will in the world and the highest standards, mistakes can and do happen), but a failure to

- accept the fault,
- treat the complaint seriously and urgently, and
- provide adequate restitution.

Case study: Papering over the cracks

The consumer had bought a number of rolls of wallcovering and started decorating with them. Having put up three lengths she noticed that there was a repeating flaw in the paper. She returned to the store and pointed this out – not only did the store replace all the rolls with a different batch but also they gave her a credit for one roll to cover the cost of her special journey to return the covering.

> **Key technique**
>
> Recognition that a purchaser may be put to some inconvenience in order to attempt rectification of a problem which, whilst it may not be the fault of the supplier, is certainly their responsibility; this should be a priority.

Whilst it may have been impossible for the retailer to avoid the incidence of the problem in the above case study, the application of a policy of proper recompense can not only defuse the situation but generate a satisfied customer who may well tell several others of the experience. Indeed having been treated 'right' research indicates that most customers will remain loyal despite having suffered a problem.

Recognise the aims

The aim of most suppliers is to make a profit and in this regard having to provide replacement product or compensation incurs a cost which could be said to detract from such an aim. Conversely the aim of the disappointed customer is either to obtain a product that works as it was understood it would at the time of purchase or to be put in the position they occupied before they invested their money.

However, these apparently diametrically opposing aims of the two parties are reconcilable since proper treatment of the disappointed customer may well result in that person becoming a loyal and repeating customer – and even an unpaid sales representative for the organisation. Someone who feels they have been well treated often tells up to six others – a situation which can only benefit the organisation as it may create new sales. Conversely the person who is badly treated by the organisation may also talk widely of their experience (to possibly as many as 20 others) – all to the potential detriment of future sales.

Differing standards

On occasion there will be a difference of opinion regarding the standards to be expected of a product, service or whatever. Nowhere is this more likely to occur than in the selling of holidays. Inevitably the brochure copywriter will attempt to make the resort, the location or the entire package as attractive as possible. Whilst there is an element of 'buyer beware' in placing an order for such a service the supplier needs to ensure that the impression created is reasonable and not 'hyped'. Where the standard expected by the purchaser is not met by the product there can be a genuine difference of opinion regarding the reasonableness of any complaint. As far as the supplier is concerned it is possible for some purchasers to take advantage of any perceived generosity and, perhaps understandably, entrenched positions can be taken up. Conversely the supplier may feel that being seen not to argue but instead to compensate in such instances may be a valuable investment in reputation and future marketing (actual or latent). After all this is the policy on which much of the success of the UK's premier retailer – Marks & Spencer – is built. If such an encounter has a public profile, despite the subject matter possibly being a complaint, the 'message' should be one of confidence that at least if there are problems they are likely to be dealt with positively.

The changing face of consumer demand

Perhaps as recently as the 1960s most consumers tended to accept what they got. There were few laws to protect their rights and interests and indeed the innate reserve of the British tended to mean that dissatisfied customers 'didn't complain' – but simply voted with their feet. Travel to countries where service is a quality in which suppliers take a pride, an awareness of the demands made by other races both in their own countries and in the UK, as well as developing consumer protection legislation and a far greater awareness of 'consumer rights' means that UK consumers are no longer prepared to accept what they are given if they feel that what they are given is

- substandard,
- not in accordance with previously advertised levels of performance, or
- simply unacceptable.

Suppliers who ignore the above, do so at their peril. If they are prepared (and can afford) to invest constantly in attracting new customers they may survive, but if their business has lower margins where customer retention is important, or they value and wish to use their reputation to good effect then full account needs to be taken of growing customer power. In short organisations can ignore the views of the consumer, and some do, but to do so is to run the risk of a shrinking customer base, or heavy and costly investment to replace those lost.

Organisation and responsibility

Within most organisations four facets/departments/responsibilities interface with the customer:

- those who market the organisation (corporate public relations),

- those who market the product (marketing department),

- those who sell the products or services (the sales organisation), and

- those who field the problems that some customers experience with faulty products or services. Such a department should be called the customer care organisation rather than the customer complaints department which provides the wrong impression for all involved, not least those who work there.

Whilst many organisations may link their sales and customer care functions, few seem to link all four – or at least the marketing and/or public relations and customer care departments. Yet this seems to be an obvious move not least since the public relations department seeks to create an image. If this is not borne out by the performance, quality, reliability and so on, of the products and the way complaints are handled, the credibility of the whole organisation (and not least the messages disseminated by the corporate and products public relations departments) may be suspect. If, however, the public relations and customer care departments work closely together then:

- for those attempting to create an image the reality of the situation is obvious which may temper any over-enthusiastic claims,

- whilst for those fielding the complaints the reality of the image that is being attempted should leaven their approach to more closely resemble such precepts.

In addition to these the customer has available a more unified and believable message.

Postscript

Ideally the description 'complainant' or 'complaining customer' should be avoided. It may be preferable either to refer to them as customers with problems (but even this is a misnomer as the problem really belongs to the supplier) or simply 'disappointed customers' which is a more accurate description of their position. Use of such a description may also convey to those dealing with them the obligation placed on them to recover the position. In addition using the description 'invested' may engender a greater awareness of the disappointment of the customer when the product or service fails to live up to their expectations.

Call centres

Call centres

Introduction

Until recently if a customer wanted to check a rail timetable, speak to their bank, register a complaint about a product or even give praise for something a supplier had performed well, they spoke directly to the station, branch or supplier's office. It was then realised that a vast proportion of such calls wanted similar responses – in most cases the provision of fairly straightforward information to the caller, in others an opportunity for the caller to give information, and in some but probably relatively few to require a reaction. It seemed logical therefore to set up dedicated facilities where all such calls for (say) a group of 20 bank branches, or the CARELINES for several suppliers, or the timetable information for a number of the privatised rail networks (which is a type of HELP DESK) could be received and answered by people specifically trained to deal with such enquiries. The concept of the call centre was born. In the UK we lead Europe, if not the World, in the use of such centres, as out of Europe's 2,000 centres just under 1,500 are in the UK with a 10% annual increase forecast. The movement of personnel is considerable since they already employ around 250,000 – a figure which is expected to quadruple by the year 2000.

Set up

Essentially a call centre is a telephone switchboard with a large number of lines and an equally large number of operators manning them. The centre can either be dedicated to a sole supplier (for example the centres set up by a group of branches in the same bank) or be a shared facility (a 'call centre hotel' serving several clients – a system favoured in Belgium). In such a facility a variety of organisations 'rent' the service and receive a dedicated number. When a customer or client calls what they believe to be the organisation, the call will be handled according to the number dialled, for example if the number was 0800 501 XXX it would indicate it was a call for 'Blogg' and can be answered by an operator knowledgeable about Blogg's products. If however the number 0800 502 XXX was dialled the call would be for 'Smiths' and be answered accordingly. So sophisticated are some call centres that they can handle overseas calls and again by virtue of the number dialled the operator can answer in the language of the caller which, apart from anything else, demonstrates a real commitment to customer ease and satisfaction. Call centre hotel facilities can also be used as a form of talking 'Yellow Pages' where consumers and suppliers can be put in contact with one another.

Here, however, we are concerned with the dedicated call centres which so far have been used mainly by the financial services sector and particularly banks.

Routine enquiries

Most of the enquiries to local branches tend to be fairly routine, yet the time spent answering such calls, inevitably received randomly means that the attention to other work is disrupted and, at least in theory, the establishment of each branch needs to reflect these time demands. Some staff are able to deal with customer queries better than others, but the random nature of receipt of such calls means that anyone could be required to answer them and inevitably, particularly when the workload on other matters is high, there may be a tendency to 'guess' a response in order to be rid of the caller. The trouble with guesses, like assumptions, is that an considerable majority are false.

Case study: Wrong guess

The customer operated a number of accounts with one of the top four UK clearing banks from which bankers' orders were paid. He wrote to the bank cancelling an order made from one of these accounts and specifying all relevant details. Some weeks later he was horrified to receive from his insurers a note that as he had missed paying a premium, one of his life policies was being suspended. He contacted the bank and explained the situation.

'I expect they (that is, the Insurer) have lost it' (**Guess 1**) was the initial reply from a young clerk obviously irritated at needing to break off from other work to deal with such a query.

'I think that's unlikely – don't you think you should check to see if you paid it first?'

'Oh OK – I'll ring you back.'

Forty-eight hours later when no call had been received the customer rang the bank again.

'No we didn't pay that premium – we cancelled it in accordance with your instructions.'

'What instructions?'

'The instructions you sent us some weeks ago.'

'I think you will find if you check that what you have done is to cancel the wrong premium from the wrong account.'

'No we haven't done that.' (**Guess 2**)

'I'm sorry but you must have done – it's the only explanation.'

'No that's impossible.' (**Guess 3**)

'OK – please send me statements on all my accounts today.'

When the statements arrived they showed plainly that indeed the wrong premium from the wrong account had been cancelled. The customer wrote pointing out that although he accepted mistakes could happen the original and perhaps understandable mistake had been compounded since

- the clerk concerned had been offhand,

- he had not bothered to check the details,

- he had suggested the customer take action to correct a mistake caused by the bank's own inefficiency,

- he had not rung back when he said he would, and

- rather than checking, had guessed (or even lied) into the bargain.

Eventually the bank paid £50 compensation for the combined incidents.

Key techniques

Guess 1 How on earth can he know this unless he checks first to see that the Bank has sent it? His prime consideration should have been to apologise and, if the data weren't immediately available, to have said he would ring back – and then made sure he did so.

Guess 2 A call fielded by someone as inexperienced or as apparently untrained who is inclined to guess rather than find out, can only create more problems than the original.

Guess 3 Unless he checks how can he make this statement?

Understandably it can be annoying to be interrupted and distracted from other duties. Such a break in concentration can lead to both irritation (as evidenced in the above case study) and to a potential for mistakes (in both the work interrupted and the new query posed). Further if the service is to be provided in-branch then everyone who may field a call needs to be trained in all aspects of the work and in dealing with customers. Setting up a call centre means that there should be little need to train general bank staff to answer such queries. All the resources previously spread thinly can be concentrated on the call centre staff. Intensive training in all aspects of the business as well as customer care telephone techniques can be given and in addition senior support staff be made available to deal with particular problems.

In addition by using computerised systems the information on the caller can be brought onto a screen in front of the employee thus setting the scene for the generation of some rapport between the caller and the recipient.

Such a system has obvious advantages. As well as the above, having a specially trained staff should mean that the length of each call should be shorter, the type of action (or inaction) that creates such calls can be logged more easily, and there is greater scope for covering sickness and absence.

However it also has the disadvantage that the caller is not speaking to a person actually at their branch but to someone who is remote from the branch (as is the caller) and who may never have seen either the branch or its personnel.

Case study: Progress?

The customer had operated two accounts at the central London branch of a clearing bank for many years. When he came to check his current statement he found there was a sheet missing between the last he had received and the new sheet. He rang the telephone number but was told by a recorded announcement that the number had been changed. A number was given at an exchange he did not recognise although he was told he would only be charged at a local call rate.

He rang the new number and it was answered by a woman with a lilting Welsh accent. He explained the problem and she promised to order him a copy statement which he was told would take around a week. Ten days later when it had not arrived he rang the number which again was answered by an operator with a Welsh accent. Again he explained the position but the employee could find no record of the statement being ordered. Accordingly he asked for it to be ordered again but as the call was ending asked for the location of the person to whom he was speaking – 'South Wales' he was told.

After another week he still had not received the statement and sent a letter of complaint to the branch. A manager rang and apologised for the delay. During the call the customer asked for the telephone number of the branch – he was given the number in Wales. 'But that is not your number – that's the number of a call centre – if I want to speak to my branch I want to go through to someone actually there who works on my accounts.'

This case study encapsulates a number of problems with call centres:

1. They are physically remote from the branch/business on whose behalf they speak and it is not surprising if they have little commitment to the customers (although most call centres can now accommodate this by transferring calls to the branch).

2. Each time a call is made it is likely that a different person will answer, and thus accountability may be reduced. It does not seem possible yet to ask to speak to a particular employee – indeed this would probably reduce the effectiveness of the system as calls could start to queue for the most effective operators.

3. Essentially the operators are 'bound' to their phones and screens for their shift. It must be difficult to remain bright and positive in such circumstances as there is little to link caller and operator (the link is the branch from which both are remote). As a result annual staff turnover in such facilities tends to be high – over 100% is reported in some instances. (In many ways those working on such lines can be compared to manual workers on a production line incapable of being stopped – not all can handle this pressure.)

4. At some times (for example, lunchtimes, Monday morning) there are peaks of calls and there has to be a flexibility that allows increased numbers of operators to be available at these times to ensure callers do not wait too long for their call to be answered, since if they do it defeats part of the basis for setting up the call centre in the first place.

Setting up

Suppliers considering setting up a call centre need to address these problems or the perceived solution could pose problems more severe than the original difficulty. The effect of a call centre may be to save money in branches – the purpose should be to provide a better customer service. The interrelationship between these two challenges needs to be considered since if the former is given a priority the latter may suffer. But some companies are able to get it right. Diana Wright, the *Sunday Times* Personal Finance Editor, referred to a reader's letter praising the excellent service given by one of the largest telephone banking operations, and commented that she had heard nothing but good about First Direct's telephone banking operation.

Postscript

Research carried out by First Direct indicates that 94% of its customers believe its service to be superior to that of traditional banks. As a telephone bank, all the employees need to be trained as would those working in call centres, thus First Direct requires its personnel to complete an eight week induction programme before anyone is allowed to take their first call. A third of its customers join because of personal recommendations – proving, if proof were needed, the value of the investment of providing good customer care. That additional third of new customers cost nothing to acquire other than the good service being given to others who then 'sold' the service for the bank.

Call handling

Introduction

Telephones are very convenient devices. They enable us without thinking to place ourselves in almost instant contact with people who can be many miles away. That's the advantage. The disadvantage is that having a device that provides such instant access can mean that we call without thinking – or at least without thinking sufficiently or planning what we want and what we are going to say. If we do call without a plan then it may be no surprise if the call itself is ineffective or less effective than we might wish. American research indicates that callers remember only around 11% of a phone conversation. Inevitably the impact of such a conversation is likely to be much less than were we face to face. After all in the average face-to-face conversation words are only 7% of the content – 38% of the message comes from tone and 55% from body language. In a telephonic conversation most of the power of the body language is lost which thus loses over half the impact of the message – and thus of the recipient's memory of them. However, increasingly the phone is being used to promulgate and chase concerns and complaints. Indeed many organisations are encouraging this development since

- it tends to be cheaper to process phone calls than letters,

- personal contact can avoid the creation of entrenched positions which careless choice of words in letters can create, and

- a solution may be found more informally and more swiftly through direct interface.

The danger is that due attention may not be given to assimilating the messages that callers wish to convey – in this the onus is on the organisation to ensure that they fully understand the message being conveyed and attempt to determine a solution.

Telephiles and telephobes

In the 1990s the Henley Forecasting Group carried out a study which discovered that nearly 50% of the UK population are prepared to use the phone and are confident in their use of it to carry on business. They described these consumers as 'telephiles'. Conversely only 16% are 'telephobes' – people who use the phone as little as possible. The remainder of the population don't necessarily enjoy using the phone but are prepared to do so. Thus a substantial proportion of the population is becoming increasingly proficient in and confident about their use of the phone. Indeed one has only to listen to local and national radio to realise how familiar the phone is becoming as a general communication medium – and how well most can organise their thoughts so that they can put across a cogent argument. Perhaps because this is so, there appear to be an ever-increasing number of programmes which encourage (indeed depend for their existence) on listeners phoning in to put forward their points of view. Such a trend can only encourage greater confidence in and use of the phone even though, in December 1997, a Cable & Wireless survey disclosed that most people still prefer to complain face to face – perhaps because they know how much easier it is for the other party to be evasive and even to lie convincingly on the phone!

As part of ongoing research during regular seminars around the UK on communication-based subjects, I asked delegates to indicate if they liked dealing with difficult or awkward matters over the telephone (such as, responding to and explaining complex matters). Only around 100 (out of over 1,000) stated that they did and, when they were questioned, all confirmed that their approach was to prepare carefully for the encounters before placing the calls. In most cases this involved making detailed notes of all aspects of the subject (and even counter-arguments and their own possible responses).

Fielding the call

From research carried out in connection with the setting up of CARELINES it seems that providing a route by which a customer can connect directly with someone able to do something (if only listen and take note) about the matter that concerns them (whether to praise or complain) opens what can be a valuable customer conduit which can be used for a variety of purposes. Inevitably, since in the UK we tend to praise too infrequently and criticise too readily, the majority of such calls will concern complaints. Indeed the editor of *This Week* writing in December 1997 recalled that during his time in Fleet Street 'the only time I ever remember hearing from readers was when they had something to complain about'. If this is so we have already gained valuable information – providing a customer conduit will encourage customer complaints to be made – although it may also encourage positive comments. It should be obvious that we need to plan accordingly. The operative words in the first sentence of this paragraph are 'connect directly'.

If we are raising the expectations of our customers that by ringing a number someone will be able to help them with their problem the person who answers the phone must be in that position. Before the phone rings they will need to be aware of

- potential problems and how to react to them,

- how to channel the enquiry to the correct source of help if they cannot help directly,

- products and service information – and the most up-to-date position on them,

- the organisation philosophy concerning customer service and care,

- the limits of their own authority to deal, and

- how and when to refer the matter to higher authority.

To be able to provide this instant response, specially to the 'odd' or particularly awkward complaint requires a training investment in all those responsible for the service. This can be costly since such training (particularly in product information) cannot be completed once – it needs to be ongoing. However, providing a quality response at this level may well save considerable costs and the time of more senior personnel should an enquiry not be satisfied here.

Some outline guidelines for providing such a service are set out below but it should be noted that in providing this list the principles of COMPLAINT CONVERSION have been adopted – that is, it has been assumed that this process is in being and those fielding the calls have already been through such training. To assist in internal 'selling' of the concept reasons for the inclusion of items have also been provided.

Checklist: Customer call fielding

1. *A manual freephone system will be provided.*

- Properly staffed so that callers do not have to queue) this will be more expensive than an automatic 'message response and recording' system. However, research carried out by National Opinion Polls showed that the third most highly rated irritant was 'companies where the telephone is answered by recorded messages'. Such systems have a caller 'slam down' rate of 67%! If you want callers to ring, and providing a customer careline raises the expectation that you do, providing a system where the ire of two-thirds of the callers is immediately raised seems illogical to say the least.

- Similarly not providing a freephone system passes a hidden message to the customer with a complaint – 'not only have we let you down

33

regarding the product but also you will have to pay to tell us about it'. Many customers already annoyed by being let down by the product or service will regard this as unwarranted ARROGANCE. A complaint embodies not simply dissatisfaction with the supplier but also some elements of self-dissatisfaction in that many purchasers feel they have been taken for a 'mug' or conned. These initial dissatisfactions can only be aggravated if they have also to pay for the call. The annoyance thus generated can make the opening exchanges become subject to unnecessary aggravation.

2.   *All calls will be answered by the third ring.*

If automatic answering systems are the third highest irritant, organisations which fail to answer their phone promptly must be in the top ten. Once again a slow response raises aggravation – no call charges may be running but the customer's time is still being wasted.

3.   *The initial response will be positive and welcoming.*

An initial greeting such as 'Good morning, Bloggs Customer Care service, Miss [name] speaking, how can I help you?' said in a bright, enthusiastic tone as if the call were the first of the day helps set the scene. Personalising the response may help defuse some aggravation whilst the last phrase indicates that, at least in theory, the recipient of the call is listening and keen to help.

   Guidance as to the tone to be used is essential – 38% of a face-to-face message is drawn from the tone of the voice, but in a telephone conversation, visual body language being absent, tone assumes a much greater percentage of the message being conveyed – 86% has been suggested. The sentence cited above could be said in a flat bored voice which would not only totally belie the words, but would also convey to the listener that there is no real commitment to the process. Similarly an unenthusiastic response conveys an impression of unprofessionalism totally at odds with any implied content – hypocrisy rules!

4.   *The customer will not, without their agreement, be asked to hold on, or to leave a message.*

The ideal is to restore choice to a customer – the choice they possessed before they purchased the product. Allowing a customer to decide what to do gives them power which may help assuage irritation or anger. Being told to leave a message negates the concept that the customer should be able to obtain action when they called – without being deferred.

5. *The customer will be listened to without interruption or contradiction.*

Using encouraging phrases such as 'I see', 'Mmm', 'Do go on' and so forth help the caller along and indicate the recipient is prepared to listen patiently. Some people experience problems expressing themselves clearly. However, interrupting to ask questions or correct false impressions at this initial stage may either confuse or irritate, or confuse, *and* irritate. Letting people 'get their ire off their chest' whilst listening in a supportive way can help defuse aggravation, provide some information and may give a guide as to what it is that they actually want.

6. *Notes will be made of everything said.*

Although these notes may not provide the whole story, being able later to say 'I think you said that...' will convey to the caller the attention given to their comments right from the start. The provision of information even in a jumbled way should simplify the later data collection.

7. *The customer will be identified.*

If the customer has not already given their name, ask for it and then use it during the subsequent conversation where this seems appropriate (it should be used naturally but not to excess).Personalising the conversation in this way should create an empathy and can help pacify and/or mollify customers. Creating an empathy provides the message 'together let's solve this problem'.

8. *The facts will be checked.*

Once the customer has finished their initial comments state 'Yes I see, now can I quickly check that I've got the facts correctly noted so that I can see if we can help solve this problem' and ask the questions on the checklist.

Saying 'Yes' indicates positive action – anything else lacks this 'let's move this forward' implication. The words 'quickly' 'help' and 'solve' are also very positive and indicate to the caller that progress – and speedy progress at that – is likely to occur. If such reactions do not occur the expectations thus generated could backfire!

The items on the checklist needing completion could include

• the name, address and telephone number of the caller.

If a freephone number is not provided it could be helpful to suggest that the organisation rings them back to 'save your cost'. Providing the ring back is carried out immediately or at a time convenient to and agreed with the customer, again the customer's irritation is being pacified.

- the exact model, number, reference, price, and so on,
- the place where bought, and
- the exact defect.

The employee needs instant access to the marketing information, product specification and so on, to be able to judge whether the complaint concerns non-performance of what was claimed or has been used for a purpose for which it was not designed.

- as assessment of what the customer wants.

There is no doubt that some claims are entirely false (see ROBUST DEFENCES) and some customers attempt to defraud the supplier. Unfortunately, knowing this, suppliers can be tempted to take a jaundiced view of all customer claims. In fact false claims probably account for less than 10% of all complaints and to judge the other 90% by the behaviour of the 10% is inherently unsound.

Case study: Premier attention

Arguably the UK's premier retailer and one with a world-wide reputation, Marks & Spencer has built that reputation not only on providing reliable value (of product, service, courtesy, and so on) but also on their policy of providing a refund or replacement in respect of goods that are unwanted (let alone those that are faulty). Inevitably such a policy is open to abuse. However the value of the goodwill created by such a practice must far outweigh the losses incurred by such abuse.

In a few cases all the customer may require is an acknowledgement of error and an apology. In such cases an instant verbal apology should be given. Ideally this should be backed by a written apology and it may assist to provide some small gift in recognition of the aggravation caused. If replacement of the product is called for, this should be arranged speedily. What all disappointed customers want is acknowledgement of fault and speedy resolution.

The words 'I'm sorry' convey messages out of all proportion to their size and cost. Not only do they indicate contrition, but also they create an empathy between the two parties which can defuse most situations. Many people find it difficult to maintain their anger if the other party is apologising.

9. *The problem in hand will be concentrated on.*

At all times concentrate on what the customer is saying. On no account allow yourself to be distracted by a person or event or attempt to do other things. The fact that you are doing something else can be conveyed to the customer and this in turn will indicate that you may not be giving the problem as much attention as they expect – adding insult to injury. It can also lead to mistakes.

Case study: Bad manners = bad work

The customer in the building society always tried to avoid being served by one assistant. She was pleasant enough but had a habit of carrying on a conversation with her colleagues whilst completing his business, which he found rude. On one occasion she omitted to credit one of a number of cheques to his account and he commented that had she paid more attention to what she was doing rather than chatting to her colleague this might have been avoided. Her reply was somewhat flippant which was unfortunate as not only was the customer a shareholder but also he knew the Deputy Chairman of the company personally. The tendency to chat was soon stopped.

Key technique

Many of those who deal with customers and consumers seem to lack training in basic manners and politeness and also make the assumption that such people know less than they do about the organisation. This is a dangerous assumption – you never know who you are serving or whom they know.

---

10. *The complaint will be resolved by providing the customer with choice.*

Before a customer buys a product they have choice – the choice of retaining their money or parting with it in exchange for a product. These customers lose that choice if the product is faulty – their considered investment has bought them faulty product. In satisfying their complaint it is important to try to return original choice to them. Hence rather than saying 'we will replace the product within 48 hours' it may be preferable to state 'the best solution may be for us to replace the product within 48 hours unless you would prefer something else?'. This returns choice to the customer. They have the implied option of a refund should they ask for this which experience indicates most don't – they simply want a product that works. Giving them an option places them (almost) in the position they occupied initially.

Introduction

A careline is a telephone service provided for and advertised to customers with the invitation that they should use the facility to call the supplier when they have anything to say about it – whether good or bad. The theory (borne out in practice) is that if customers are provided with a telephone number and invited to voice their views on a variety of subjects, then

- the main thrust of any antipathy they feel may be dissipated (since they have a route for their concerns),

- rapport and/or understanding (on both sides) may be attained, and

- above all, valuable and free (other than the costs involved in fielding the calls) feedback is obtained.

The value of the careline system is thus not just that the ire of disaffected customers may be dissipated, but also that it is an inexpensive form of market research. It can also provide a most valuable form of customer communication – not only can the supplier discover what the customer thinks of them, their products and their service, but also careful questioning may discern a demand for new products and spin-offs.

Administration

A careline requires a dedicated telephone number, manned at all times by person(s) of sufficient seniority, training and knowledge that they can

- deal competently with every enquiry,

- answer every question or know who can answer it,

- make and implement decisions if necessary that may entail paying compensation or making rectification, and

- deal with each caller in a tactful, sympathetic yet firm manner without becoming flustered or annoyed despite what can be considerable antipathy and even anger. The precepts set out in CALL HANDLING all apply but in addition those manning a careline should be prepared to develop suitable conversations to try to carry out a limited amount of market research.

Thus to the list of 'how to do it' in CALL HANDLING we could add the following:

Checklist: Market research

If a complaint conversation is proceeding positively, and where the customer has rung to praise or congratulate the supplier, check:

1. *Product likes* – the preferences of the customer as to size, colour, composition, price, presentation and so on, of the product.

2. *Product dislikes* – any dislikes of the items set out above with any reasons.

3. *Range knowledge* – the customer's knowledge of the supplier's other products. If such products are unknown, a brief résumé should be offered with an invitation to send a brochure or arrange a representative's visit. Neither should be forced on the customer – this must be the choice of the customer and this should be stated clearly. Only if the customer states that they want either should arrangements be made.

   Note: Research indicates that many people find it hard to say no despite this being their preference. Putting them under pressure to take a brochure can inhibit further contact from them and anyone they tell of the experience.

4. *Encouraging suggestions* – encourage customers to make suggestions concerning products and so on. This flatters them and creates a rapport with them (and those they tell of the experience) and may actually lead to new products or spin-offs. Even if this is unlikely it may confirm the potential demand for (or resistance to) products already under way.

Case study: Not the real thing

Coca-Cola includes a freephone telephone number on its soft drinks packaging and receives an average of just under 3,000 calls per week which raise all sorts of points, although only around 10% are complaints. The company believes that its careline acts as an excellent filter to indicate if there are going to be widespread problems – with which it can then deal; as well as being a very good way of gauging interest in new products. When Coca-Cola introduced 'New Coke' its careline was inundated with complaints from its customers, most of whom did not like the new recipe and wanted the original product back. To the company's credit it responded immediately and reinstated the previous recipe. Had the careline not existed no outlet would have been provided for these comments, sales could have dropped alarmingly possibly without immediate explanation.

Note: *The New Coke experience should be a salutary lesson for those who believe implicitly in market research. After all, the acceptability of the new recipe had been extensively researched yet it was only the careline that provided the real thing – at least as far as customers' views were concerned.*

5. *Generating new business* – one never knows what contacts the caller has. ARROGANCE can lead many suppliers into the assumption that the customer is a one-off who can 'take the product or leave it'. This however can waste opportunities since few customers exist in a vacuum and informing callers of other products that are available, whilst these may not be of interest to the caller, may be of interest to their contacts or friends.

Case study: Spin off demand

A national paper featured a product designed to help sleeplessness. Seeking an additional Christmas present a customer rang the number only to be told that such had been the interest generated by the article that all supplies had been exhausted. However the helpful employee of the supplier asked for the customer's telephone number and in fact rang back twice to advise on progress regarding the supplies eventually obtaining both supplies and an order the value of which was less than £20. In passing however the supplier suggested their brochure was sent since they had a range of other products. The customer was uninterested in the other products but passed the catalogue on to a friend who ran a hairdressing salon who did use similar products to those featured. As a result the salon placed an initial order in excess of £100 and repeat orders have followed.

Note: *This checklist is provided as a base only. The supplier's own market research discipline should be able to customise requirements which should be regularly updated to ensure topicality.*

Additional uses

Carelines can also be used to allow members of the public to 'report' poor service. Thus displaying a careline number on organisation vehicles with an invitation to others to ring the number if they feel the driving of the organisation vehicle leaves something to be desired allows other road users an opportunity to 'vent their spleen' in such circumstances. In fact several of the organisations that operate such a system report that they have had very few calls – in the main they feel the fact that their own drivers know they can be reported acts as a spur or reminder to them to drive with consideration for other road users.

Indeed simply stating a careline number indicates to other road users (who could of course be customers of the supplier operating the lorry) the organisation's commitment to value and quality.

Case study: Carelines in use

Mars Confectionery have operated carelines for some time and now receive a very high number of calls every hour. The tenor of most calls is very positive although some callers do use the freephone number purely as an opportunity to talk to another person, whilst a tiny proportion take the opportunity of being abusive. Mars employees conduct a mini research survey on every caller and, by taking their personal details generate a mailing list of those who state that they like Mars products.

In phoning to congratulate the company on its new 'Celebrations' assortment (mini versions of its most popular bar lines in bite sized pieces, individually wrapped in a presentation box) a customer made the suggestion that he was surprised that the company did not sell the bite sized pieces in separate boxes. Within a few weeks such products were available. No doubt the company were already working on the idea, and no doubt other callers may have made the same point but at least it confirmed the company's view of potential demand.

BurgerKing, the fast food chain, wishing to move away from a system whereby every customer letter had to be answered by letter, encourages customers to use a careline by displaying its contact number not only in-store, but even on the customer's till receipts. In dealing with the calls the company is able to derive considerable assistance in the development of its service and products.

(See also HELP DESKS.)

Uncaring and unlistening

Despite the evidence that carelines are good for customers, good for business and good for the development of business, the head of a company providing such a service commented in a *Sunday Times* interview 'the single most important factor preventing the spread of carelines in the UK is a lack of appreciation by senior managers of the importance of providing answers to customer queries'. It is difficult to see what can be more important to the continuation of the organisation than dealing with and listening to its customers but this may reflect the conclusion of the P.Four survey of customer care attitudes – that what suppliers say they do and what they do are two very different things.

Unless an organisation listens to its customers it is likely to lose them as its perception of what they want could swiftly become dated. Leading consultants Price Waterhouse discovered in a survey of the top 200 UK companies that losing existing customers costs British industry around £100 billion each year – which coincidentally is about the same amount as they spend on marketing and sales helping (at least in part) to replace such lost sales.

In the UK only 22% of consumer goods' producers use careline numbers, whereas in the USA 83% of consumer goods (including all household goods) carry careline numbers.

Backlash

The use of a careline can however encourage calls of which a proportion will be hoax, useless, or even insulting and vicious. Counselling and training needs to be given to staff to try and help them cope with these kinds of calls. The response to calls which are abusive should be that the call is being tape-recorded and the number traced. This is relatively easy now and even if the caller has blocked access to their number details of the calls are available to the police.

Where threats or foul language are used and, despite requests to moderate their language, the caller persists, they should be advised that they are committing an offence and details may be passed to the police for investigation. Under the Telecommunications Act 1984 'a person who by means of a public communication system, sends a message or other matter that is … menacing, or … causes annoyance' is guilty of an offence and can be fined on conviction.

Postscript

Although there may be a logic in separating CALL CENTRES for customers with concerns or complaints from CARELINES for those with general comments, it may be thought beneficial to channel both types of call through the same department. At least then those manning the call centre lines will not feel that they are 'always dealing with complaints' but may find greater job satisfaction with a mix of calls. In turn this may reduce the high level of labour turnover experienced in call centres.

Choice restoration

Introduction

When considering the purchase of a product or service the consumer has and can exercise their individual choice – essentially the choice to spend and purchase or not to spend. In exchanging money for goods or services the consumer judges that the goods are worth the investment. If the goods turn out to be faulty, or not to the standard expected, or the service is inadequate, not only is that consumer's perception of the company damaged, but his or her own self-esteem, since he or she made the judgement to buy, is damaged. In addition, and vitally important, **the customer has lost the essence of purchasing – that is, choice**. No longer does the customer have the capacity to buy or not to buy, or to buy an alternative product. He or she is locked in to the faulty product and the inherent power of the consumer – the choice to buy or not to buy – is denied. Further, inherent in the purchase of a product or acceptance of a service is an underlying presumption that the supplier will keep the 'promise' of the purchase or supply (see KEEPING PROMISES).

When considering items that fail to live up to the expectation or implied promise of value, not only has the customer lost out in cash terms (their investment has proved valueless), they may also feel that they have lost in that they feel cheated in losing the choice they once had. The loss of choice means that there has been a power transfer from purchaser to supplier. Before the purchase the customer was in control and at that point the supplier needed the customer. After the purchase, when assets have been exchanged, the supplier no longer needs the purchaser who becomes, to some extent 'powerless'. This combination

- of an inherent promise being broken,
- of a blow being dealt to the customer's self-respect, and
- the feeling of relative impotence where once there was power,

can be powerful motivators to ensure swift reinstatement of the status quo, and, should perceived losses have been incurred, adequate recompense. Put more bluntly, the customer will want to get their choice back – and if this is mishandled may well wish to 'get their own back'. This may not be very mature but it is understandable and is a powerful motivator. Such feelings should be anticipated by suppliers.

Recognition of appropriate standards or expectations

'Hype' is short for hyperbole. Although it is often regarded as being 'puff' or 'advertising blurb' which shows a product or service in the best light to encourage sales, its real meaning is 'a statement which exaggerates and is not meant to be taken literally'. In that definition the operative word is 'not'. However, in marketing products and services these days, 'hype' does tend to be used to some degree and in some cases to too great a degree. Whilst most consumers will expect there to be some exaggeration in advertisements, suppliers need to take care to avoid 'over hyping', so that greater expectations of worth or quality are created than those that can reasonably be delivered. If an organisation does indulge in this, then it should expect

- a greater number of disappointed customers,

- considerably enhanced difficulties in trying to satisfy them not least since the customer choice has been lost on a false premise, and

- customers perceiving the product to be of greater value than has turned out to be the case and consequent problems adjusting expectations to reality.

Returning choice

Where choice has been lost the inevitable result will be the consumer requiring the supplier to return to him or her the original position of choice. When the customer complains, he or she is not only notifying that a faulty product has been received, but also that the original position of choice has been lost and in return now needs a further choice. In reacting to the complaint the supplier should consider how best to achieve this requirement, without however making the decision for the customer. Although such action can be seen as returning choice, in a way it negates this since any decision made for the customer denies him or her choice – no matter how well intentioned. Thus if a customer has a faulty product, the immediate reaction may be to offer to replace it, which it would appear, at least initially, should satisfy (and probably will in most cases). The problem is that the history of the product (at least as far as that customer is concerned) may not be conducive to the consumer having confidence in it. Whilst being prepared to give the item another chance, in many ways the customer may feel the only true restoration of choice is by obtaining a refund. The supplier may be unwilling to provide this although an alternative may be to provide a credit note or vouchers which can be exchanged for other products. This should be acceptable provided there is at least a reasonable choice of other products. However, the following points could be considered:

1. In the product being faulty the consumer has lost not just the item, but has suffered inconvenience and the time registering the complaint. An assessment of recompense should bear this in mind and thus any credit should reflect some, albeit minor, enhancement for inconvenience. Further enhancement may be required if, to return the faulty item and/or to obtain the value of the credit, unnecessary travel costs were incurred.

2. Credit notes or vouchers should be unrestricted in time so that the customer is not put under pressure to exercise his or her restored choice of purchasing power.

3. If a replacement product is offered and agreed then the exchange should be carried out at the cost of the supplier. Asking the consumer to travel to collect in order to rectify a supplier mistake simply adds insult to injury – although obviously if the customer offers to do this it could be accepted.

Case study: Furnish me with the costs

A customer placed an order for around £5,000 worth of furniture. He had calculated the approximate cost in advance but when he came to sign the order the retailer calculated it as £4,600. The customer queried this indicating he thought it should be more but the assistant checked it and assured him it was correct. Since there was an offer of free credit, the purchase was achieved by the customer paying a 20% deposit and signing a credit agreement for the balance.

A few days later the store phoned him to say that they had discovered a mistake and the price should have been nearly £400 more. They suggested he return to the shop and sign a new agreement.

'Ignoring the time element that's a round trip of 30 miles – who is going to pay for that so something which is not only your mistake, but one which I queried at the time is rectified?' he asked. Eventually it was agreed that the store would give him a £20 voucher when he called in to rectify the paperwork. Subsequently, since the voucher could not compensate for his lost time, he suggested rather than do that he send the store a cheque for the balance needed and they still send him a voucher since they would be receiving 80% of the cost up front rather than under the credit agreement.

'In your own interests get the basics right'

Often the main stumbling block in agreeing recompense or restitution is a lack of appreciation of, and sometimes a complete refusal to even consider, the viewpoint of the customer – the person without whom the supplier cannot exist. The assistant telephoning the customer in the above case study made an assumption – that because the customer had made a purchase at their store they could 'drop in when convenient'. Too often assumptions like this are made without any reason – forgetting the adage 'assume' makes an 'ass' of 'u' and 'me'! There was no excuse for the above assumption since the assistant had the address of the customer when telephoning, yet did not, at least initially, consider the inconvenience to which the customer was being put in order to rectify a mistake not of the customer's own making. True, the assistant agreed to his suggestion of recompense but it would have been infinitely better had the assistant initiated the suggestion. What was evident was a lack of care for the customer's concerns – a practice which is surprisingly widespread considering that trade is not generally buoyant and substitute suppliers abound in many instances.

In many of the case studies cited in this book, disappointed customers were not particularly demanding or even aggressive – they merely put forward their views with the purpose of recovering the choice they once had, only to have their viewpoint or rights abused to the point where goodwill evaporated. In such instances the organisations not only fail to be proactive in restoring choice but actually *create* assertive, even aggressive, customers, wasting their own resources and damaging their reputation in the process. It is difficult to see why they adopt this strategy since it seems to provide neither party with a 'win' and has the potential to ensure both 'lose'.

Postscript

Research indicates that when customers' problems are treated constructively and they feel they have been well treated over 80% are likely to be repeat customers. By restoring choice to such customers they then tend to exercise their choice in favour of the same supplier. Denying choice restoration is extremely unlikely to generate repeat custom. Choice restoration may thus be best regarded as an investment in future custom.

Clangers

Introduction

There are probably few members of the human race that have not made a mistake or dropped a 'clanger' at some time in their life. Similar misfortunes will befall most organisations in selling their products and in their relations with their customers – but almost inevitably the incidence of occurrence will increase if those organisations are

- not well organised in the first place,
- not prepared to deal with the likelihood of mistakes being made and needing rectification, and
- not perceptive and aware enough to develop flexible responses when such mistakes occur.

Very often the response tends to be the standard – even if the problem is anything but standard. The only result of using standard responses to non-standard problems is to aggravate an already difficult encounter.

Be prepared

In the following case study a great deal of time and cost could have been saved had the organisation recognised and appreciated the effect on customers of them changing without notice a commitment entered into in good faith. Such commitment was a legal contract, the terms of which cannot be unilaterally altered by one party. Having decided to alter arrangements (which with notification and honouring of existing contracts would have probably been acceptable to most customers) the next challenge to be addressed was to ensure that those with such contracts were dealt with on an 'exception basis' – they would have an unusual problem which required specific one-off handling.

Case study: Procedural straitjacket

The customer had a domestic appliance on which they had taken out a service contract with the manufacturer. The appliance developed a fault,

51

but when the customer rang the telephone number provided on the service contract she was referred to another number with a different company. (**Clang 1**)

The customer rang the second number and was offered a visit five days later, although her service contract (with the original company) promised a 48 hour call and (**Clang 2**) also specified that the time for the repair was to be designated by the customer – 'including weekends'. Quoting this wording was however brushed aside by the off-hand telesales staff, despite three phone calls trying to quote her contract terms. (**Clang 3**)

'The computer does not recognise the terms you are referring to – so the earliest available call is on Monday' was the only response. (**Clang 4**)

Eventually a message was left on the customer's answerphone offering a Saturday service provided she rang back to confirm she would be available at any time. On ringing back (**Clang 5**) no one knew anything about the Saturday offer and the customer was back to the 'it's Monday or nothing' routine. At this the customer's patience broke and she demanded to be put through to a more senior person. This request was refused. (**Clang 6**)

The customer stated that unless she was put through to someone senior in the organisation she would put the phone down and her next call would be to the local Trading Standards officer. She was put through to a supervisor who again accessed the computer and was told 'We've got you booked for Monday.' (**Clang 7**)

Learning the lessons

Had this encounter not happened as recounted above one might think it was a classic script for a 'How not to do it' training session or a television farce. We can identify no less than 7 clangers (and lessons) in this brief exchange:

1. The company had failed to notify the change of contact office and/or telephone number to the customer despite there being a legally binding contract. Whilst one can appreciate that individual notification could be costly there was a perfectly easy way of achieving the same end – an automatic switching device to re-route calls made to the old number directly to the new. In addition the consumer is hardly going to be best pleased at having to dial a second number knowing that they've already wasted the cost of one call. This initial irritation could have been avoided by making the (at least) second number (and ideally both) freephone.

2. Legally contracts can only be varied with the agreement of both parties. Increasingly consumers are aware of their rights – indeed, since 1 July 1995, all terms with consumers must be in plain English and unfair terms can be rejected by consumers piecemeal (that is, they can remove one term from the contract even though the others could continue in force). Such a development opens the organisation to immediate criticism and puts it in the wrong particularly as publicity could be given to the incident. Thus all those dealing with such enquiries need to be trained to listen carefully to the customer and be prepared (and authorised) to offer non-standard service where the circumstances dictate.

3. Customer service must encompass customer care. 'Care' in this instance involves listening to the customer. Obviously a mistake of omission had occurred – the computer system has not been programmed to recognise other (or older) contract terms. This may be understandable – even excusable. But what is neither understandable nor excusable is the casual dismissal of what the customer is saying. Standard responses do not adequately deal with non-standard enquiries.

4. Staff need to be told that efficient as they are, computer systems are not infallible – indeed they can only ever be as reliable as the staff who programmed them. The computer may not be able to make a mistake, but the human being working it certainly can. Blind reliance on the technology demonstrates a dangerous naïveté – 'GIGO rules OK'. ('GIGO' being short for 'garbage in, garbage out'.) Staff need to be trained to spot and deal with non-standard enquiries.

5. Again the customer is bearing the cost of the call which simply adds aggravation to an increasingly angry encounter. The provision of a freephone number would have avoided at least this minor irritation.

6. Callers were given only the telesales service telephone number. The operators could not normally refer to higher authority. It seemed that only by becoming very angry and using threats that such reference was possible. In other words the way the system was set up actually encouraged increasingly aggravated calls which is in no one's interest. Whether in a manual or automatic answering system (and particularly in the latter) there should always be a route to more senior staff who are more likely to be able to recognise and deal with the non-standard enquiry.

7. Referral of a call to higher authority should entail briefing the fielder of the call with a synopsis of the background to the call. This would enable a fresh start to be made which despite all that has gone before, might

defuse an increasingly explosive situation. Senior staff should be aware that if a customer has been referred to them there is a potentially serious problem which needs to be handled carefully.

Note: *The consumer was so annoyed at the treatment received and recounted above that she contacted the Managing Director of the organisation and eventually negotiated an ex gratia payment in excess of £100 – inadequate service can be costly.*

A different scenario

The following case study bears some similarities to the one above in that the interests of the consumer were apparently intended to be completely sublimated to those of the organisation despite the fact that satisfying the consumer was stated to be one of the organisation's aims.

Case study: Hot air

Under a contract the supplier was required to conduct an annual service of the customer's heating boiler. Since nothing had been heard from them the customer rang the company (at his expense) to make an appointment which was not only arranged over a subsequent phone call but also confirmed in writing some weeks before the date agreed. At 4.45 p.m. on the date set for the service since no one had appeared, and the consumer had wasted a day waiting, the consumer rang the supplier and, after some delay, was told that due to 'emergencies' all servicing had been cancelled for that day and another day had to be arranged. On enquiring whether such a rearranged appointment could be confirmed the consumer was told that should emergencies occur again then such a 'routine' call could again be deferred. (**Clang 1**)

The consumer decided to lodge a complaint regarding this and wrote to the Managing Director at the registered office address shown on the letterhead. A letter of apology was received from a Planning Manager (at a different address) (**Clang 2**). The Manager apologised stating that what had occurred was exceptional and the company normally gave 24 hours' notice of a cancellation. The letter also stated that the consumer was being sent £10 compensation. The consumer replied that to offer £10 for the waste of a complete day was derisory and queried the rationale behind cancelling appointments for (presumably) a number of people with confirmed dates given the costs and dislocation involved. (**Clang 3**)

The Manager then stated that the amount offered was 'fair and reasonable' when the supplier had to cancel a previously arranged appointment; to which the consumer replied that the appointment had not been cancelled by the supplier, no notice whatever had been given and it was only because he had phoned at 4.45 p.m. that he had discovered that no one would be attending on a date of which written confirmation had been received. In closing he gave the Manager seven days to disclose the name and address of the company's Managing Director. Very swiftly a reply offering a further £60 compensation was received in a letter which also disclosed that the Managing Director was at the address originally written to. (**Clang 4**)

Reviewing the clangers

1. The logic behind reducing staffing to such a level that should emergencies occur (which presumably occurs fairly often) a large number of calls need to be rescheduled (and compensation paid to those suffering the postponements) is totally baffling. In no way can it constitute customer care. This is corporate ARROGANCE at its worst – the semiotic message is that the customer's interests count for nothing.

2. When a letter is addressed to a named office holder it would seem courteous (and somewhat disarming) for that office holder to at least acknowledge the letter even if it is only to state it has been passed to a named individual for attention. This demonstration of customer respect has the added dimension of the senior person 'owning' the problem – and of the junior person knowing their actions may be checked.

3. The hidden message inferred in offering £10 for a wasted day is that the consumer's time was worth only £10 simply adds insult to injury. When the demand was made for a senior person's name to deal with the matter the immediate upgrading of the amount to £60 not only made a fairer offer but seems incidentally to confirm the supplier's agreement to the customer's description of the first offer as being derisory. One wonders what charge the company would have considered had the customer cancelled without notice?

4. The confirmation that the Managing Director worked at the address originally contacted yet no answer was received from him demonstrates once again the lip service that many companies pay to customer care. As previously suggested the responsibility for customer care lies firmly with directors – very often those who take the greatest steps to ensure they hide from their customers.

Postscript

In its corporate documentation the supplier in question states that 'we aim to be a world class energy company ... by ... satisfying our customers' wishes for excellent quality of service and outstanding value'. This does not seem to be borne out at the sharp end and one has to question whether the corporate public relations people are in contact with the reality of the situation. Unless senior management demonstrate their commitment to 'excellent ... service' (which by not acknowledging the customer's letter the Managing Director failed to do) there is little likelihood of adequate commitment and performance at more junior levels. The 'easy way out' is too convenient an alternative.

Complaint conversion

<table>
<tr><td>

Introduction

The real challenge with disappointed customers and those with concerns is to convert customers with complaints into compliant customers. To do so all we need to do is to alter the perspective (and position) of the 'i'. The 'i' meant here is not only the letter in the two words but also the 'individual' (the customer) and their 'interests' which need to be treated with 'integrity'. However, before we can convert complaints we need to ensure that we encourage their notification – not as a means for conflict but because we can learn from them. Indeed if we wish to survive, we *should* wish to hear from the non-compliant as their constructive comments may enable us to improve/rectify errors. If, using their feedback, we can improve so that we satisfy the most demanding customer, then satisfying the others should be simple.

Failing to encourage complaints means we have

- no information as to why we did not satisfy that customer (which may mean we will continue to lose others who won't bother to tell us of their displeasure but will vote with their feet),

- lost a customer who could have given us valuable information about the perception of our business and our products in the marketplace, and

- now need to replace that customer simply to maintain the status quo of our business (which can be a costly exercise).

Above all we will have

- aided our competitors who will be only too pleased to accept our disappointed customers as their additional customers.

</td></tr>
</table>

'Go west young man'

Traditionally the American attitude to service custom and customers differs considerably from that of the UK. Consumer and market power, the need to satisfy, and the real and constant competition makes American suppliers far more aware of the need to serve the customer. 'Serve' is used here in the widest meaning of the word and not as in some areas of UK business,

57

conjuring incorrect and inappropriate images of 'subserviency' and perhaps because of this, in some instances, tending to be resisted. Because we are an island race, geographically and historically separated from our continent and by language from our nearest neighbours, and by oceans from those countries that use our language, this has perhaps led us to become insular in our attitude. Most of our suppliers tend to be relatively small, competing for the most part with other relatively small suppliers. As we try to compete in world markets, we find ourselves in competition with much larger rivals some of whom will be setting standards which we must emulate, in markets where consumers expect high standards. Only if we can match or exceed those requirements will we win – or even survive. (See EMULATING COMPETITORS.)

Complaints welcome here...

There is an additional value in companies making a positive effort to encourage customers to notify them when there is a problem. Not only are they then learning what their customers feel about them and their products, but they are also drawing the sting of such complaints at the first instance. This tends to be the normal manner of approach in parts of Europe and in the USA. However, in many instances in the UK, customer service and the satisfaction of complaints is not given such positive response. Since the average consumer knows that if a complaint is raised the expected reaction will often be defensive, and that because it may be necessary to fight to gain rectification of the 'damage', many duck the challenge and vote with their feet – passing their custom to an alternative supplier. Realisation that only a small percentage of those who may be dissatisfied will actually voice such concern is extremely important, as notified complaints may be indicative of a far more widespread problem. If we have such a problem we need to know about it – and fast if we are to protect our customer base. In the USA research carried out by the Technical Assistance and Research Program for the White House Office of Consumer Affairs discovered that businesses do not hear from 96% of dissatisfied customers and that for every complaint received a further 26 customers have problems of which six are likely to be serious.

Conversion

Research also indicates that customers who are treated badly by a supplier when they have a complaint can tell up to 20 other potential customers and that 91% of retail customers will not return to a shop if service is really bad. Conversely research indicates that where a customer has a complaint which is handled well by the supplier 82% of such initially disappointed customers will repurchase. Indeed by handling the matter well not only can we retain four-fifths of the original complainants but also we may ensure that those now-satisfied customers are likely to tell up to another 6–8 potential customers – compliant fans indeed. This is how reputations can be made or lost – like ripples on a pond – we must not assume in dealing with a customer we are dealing with a single entity.

Complaint conversion requires a positive approach which can only emanate from the top, decision-making level of the supplier. Unless the Board are committed to the precept it cannot work. Indeed before the adoption of a policy in interfacing with customers the Board needs to adopt a similar commitment to the treatment of those whom they require to deal with the customers – their own employees. Unless employees feel confident in their own treatment by the supplier they are extremely unlikely to deal positively with customers. (See ACTIVE LISTENING and INTERNAL CUSTOMERS.)

XYZ Company Ltd

Customer Complaints Conversion (CCC)

Policy

Our operation is geared to satisfying our customers since it is only through satisfying them and more of them that we can pay for everything on which we spend company money, including of course our own wages. The customer is vital to our organisation's survival and this should never be forgotten.

It is our policy to positively encourage contact with customers so that:

1. The company obtains feedback from the marketplace – since unless we know precisely how the marketplace views our products we cannot develop and improve them.

2. Problems and queries related to our products and services are brought to the company's attention for swift rectification.

3 Positive customer satisfaction is generated with both our products and our after-sales service.

4. To ensure the above, we have adopted the approach of Customer Complaints Conversion (CCC) which we require all employees to adopt positively and with ZELOSO.

5. Using CCC we aim to convert customers with complaints into compliant customers who will not only buy again from us but have their confidence in us and our products restored so that they will recommend us to others.

---

6. CCC has several functions
   - to create a rapport with the customer and marketplace,
   - to discover the true nature of problems,
   - to discuss/decide any contribution to any loss suffered or other recompense,
   - to attempt to retain the customer for repeat sales,
   - to preserve the company's reputation, and
   - to consider whether it is necessary to implement any design changes as a result of the information generated.

Practice

1. *Training*. Every employee who may come into contact with customers will attend the CCC training course before being placed in the position of customer-interface. Such training will include product and organisation familiarisation, principles of customer care and negotiation, inter-personal skills (including dealing with customers), guidance on levels of authority and so on.

2. *Initiation period*. Having completed the course an employee will remain under the guidance of a supervisor who will be able to provide advice and guidance during an initial period of work.

3. *Refresher*. Every six months thereafter all CCC department personnel will attend a refresher course.

4. *New products*. All CCC personnel will receive briefing on all aspects of every new product, and will be provided with technical data, brochures and so on, to ensure they become conversant with the item.

5. *Senior control*. [Name of nominee preferably at Board level] will be responsible for the programme and for reviewing all complaints for possible product/provision/service review and improvement.

Senior personnel involvement

Making a senior person responsible for the programme is essential since only if a lead is provided from the top will

- employees' views of the importance of the system be reinforced,

- sufficient authority to ensure appropriate treatment (particularly where compensation is required) be available, and

- the real perceptions held by customers of the supplier and its products be available at the level capable of making decisions concerning them.

All too often complaints with potentially serious implications are handled at a too junior level by employees who, however well-meaning, may not realise such implications and can commit their organisation to a course of action (or inaction) which could prove very costly – in time, money or reputation.

Case study: The customer bites back

This was the second order placed by the customer. The first had been a somewhat rushed order for Christmas gifts and the second (delivered late despite a reasonable delivery time being specified by the customer) was in response to a discount flier the company had produced to try and generate trade in the low demand part of the year. Following its standard practice, the company had produced and invoiced 10% over the number of items ordered. The customer telephoned to query this.

'I am very surprised to see that the order which I requested for delivery by 1st April was delivered late without any apology and in addition you have charged me for overs.'

'That is in accordance with our standard conditions of trade shown on our catalogue – I'll send you a copy.' (**Clang 1**)

After receiving the catalogue, the customer telephoned again.

'I queried your charging for the overs on my second order, and the late delivery, and you have sent me your catalogue. However, I would point out that your discount flier makes no reference to any such conditions. In addition, you have ignored the fact that the order was delivered late, even though I had stressed in my order that the date was critical, and you did not query it on your 'Acknowledgement of Order' form. Further, in rereading through the catalogue you have sent me, I have also realised that you overcharged me for my first order last Christmas, as you charged for the overprinting which is not referred to as being a charge for the goods I ordered.' (**Clang 2**)

The reply came swiftly from a 'customer complaints' department: 'We are sorry to hear you are unhappy with the company. (**Clang 3a**) Our offer sheet was rushed out and we overlooked the requirement to refer to our terms, and we will be mindful of this in future to avoid any such remote misunderstandings. (**Clang 3b**) You are also correct in identifying a discrepancy in our catalogue. Unfortunately this was noticed after the printing had been completed, but it was felt that all our customers would appreciate that even though it does not state this, the additional charge would apply. (**Clang 3c**)

We feel it is unreasonable of you to stress this point. (**Clang 3d**) We hope that with this explanation you will feel more sympathetic towards us and the efforts we make on behalf of all our customers. (**Clang 3e**)

Key techniques

Clang 1. Treating a genuine customer query in this dismissive way, as well as ignoring one of the points raised, merely stores up trouble for the future. Here, had the supplier realised there was a problem with the terms, it could have offered a credit note for the overs and saved itself the £50 eventually deducted from the outstanding invoice by the customer.

Clang 2. Further it was only the irritation caused by the dismissive approach which was the direct cause of the customer investigating further. Now the company had to either try to justify the three matters, or to negotiate (rather than impose) a solution.

Clang 3. This dismissive response seeks refuge from the facts in unnecessary and totally 'flowery' wording, the effect of which is merely irritating. Plain language without jargon, flattery or complex phrases is preferable and more effective. In addition the comments slide round the facts – the customer had a genuine grievance which, despite all the words, has not actually been answered. He was not unhappy with the company (**3a**), but he is unhappy with its unprofessional service, particularly as he is being forced to waste time trying to sort out the effects of its mistakes. This makes the last comment (**3e**) utterly illogical. Since it is the customer who has suffered – why should the company expect sympathy? By its own admissions, the company is in the wrong in each case.

Clang 4. Throughout the encounter the company failed to appreciate its goal and lost sight of the desired result. The result should have been satisfaction of the customer when raising a legitimate matter of concern, and avoidance of a returned and wasted order. A more positive approach initially would have saved a great deal of time, trouble and eventually a deduction of funds.

Postscript

So annoyed was the customer that on receiving the company's brochure for gifts for the following Christmas, and finding the same mistake repeated, he reported the company to the local trading standards office who then investigated the whole administration of the company's mail order operation at considerable inconvenience to their business. The matter was reported in the local paper and picked up nationally.

The episode could have been avoided with a simple apology, never offered, for the late arrival of the items, and credits of the overs and overcharged printing – a total cost of under £30.

DARN

Introduction

The relationship between supplier and customer could be compared to a piece of weave or fabric, and a faulty product generating a complaint to the appearance of a hole in the weave/fabric of their relationship. If the user of the fabric takes no positive action the hole can grow wider, but, with action to 'patch things up', the hole can be mended. In needlework this process is 'darning' – an attempt to repair the hole and to try and make the whole as good as new. An expert seamstress plying her needle carefully can indeed make the repaired item look as good as it was originally even though it will be generally known that there was a hole there. Indeed so clever may be the repair process that the owner may wish to demonstrate to others the expertise employed in the renovation. In a similar way good work by customer care staff may be able to generate a pride in the customer such that he or she boasts of the efforts made by the supplier to repair the damage.

DARNing

DARN is simply a part pun and part mnemonic which stands for Discovery, Apology, Rectification and Novation which identifies the four stages of the process by which we hope to repair the sales 'fabric', restore choice to the customer and rebuild the confidence in the product and/or the supplier once evidenced by the customer buying the product.

1. By listening hard and asking open questions we seek to get the facts down so that we can **D**iscover and identify the problem experienced by the caller.

2. Assuming this indicates that we as the supplier (in the widest sense of the word) are at fault (and even if we are not or the possibility of fault is unclear) this should generate at a very early stage an **A**pology. Apologising is an extremely valuable weapon in the customer care armoury. It costs nothing and providing it is sincerely offered can often draw the sting from many complaint encounters. Whereas people can lose their temper when faced with intransigence, when the other

party is apologising most people warm to them and lose much of their propensity to anger. It can be difficult to maintain anger or annoyance when the other party seems genuinely sorry and is, apparently, trying to rectify the matter.

3. This brings us to the next stage in the process – **R**ectification. Since the supplier is at fault (and even if sometimes we are not, it may be counterproductive to argue) we need to make amends in some way. In this, using the telephone to deal (and in reality 'do a deal') with the caller can be very useful since we are not committing ourselves to paper and no evidence will exist for use as a precedent.

Case study: Doing a deal

The holidaymakers had hired a canal boat for a holiday in France. The boat, which was glowingly described in the brochure, turned out to be somewhat less reliable in reality. It leaked constantly so that the bilge pump was always at work – creating a noise that could be clearly heard at night when the family members were trying to sleep. It also repeatedly broke down, meaning that instead of cruising, the holidaymakers were forced to wait for a mechanic to reach them on at least three occasions. This wasted part of their holiday, severely curtailed their range and thus their enjoyment of the holiday. Since the mechanic commented that 'it was always happening with these boats' the holidaymakers felt this to be unacceptable.

On return the problem was put to the cruise company which initially dismissed the complaint out of hand. Since it seemed to the holidaymaker that the company had made no effort to understand either the loss caused by the breakdowns or the spoiling effect this known unreliability had had on their (and presumably other people's) holidays – he wrote to the Chairman.

The following Sunday morning he was impressed to receive a telephone call from the Chairman who, having first enquired if he minded him phoning on a Sunday and dealing with the problem over the phone, apologised not only for the unreliability of the boat but also for the dismissive way his initial letters had been treated. The Chairman went on to ask how they could put the damage right and it was agreed that a discount on a future holiday with the company would be appropriate.

Key technique

There were a number of advantages to the company in this method of handling the problem:

1. A personal telephone call showed how seriously the company regarded the problem which had developed from an inappropriate response to the original reasonable complaint.

2. The fact that it was the Chairman himself who made the call on what would normally be regarded as a non-working day added solace to the 'injury' caused by the initial dismissive reaction. The company was seen to have 'put itself out', compensating in some degree for the way the holidaymakers had been 'put out' by the breakdowns.

3. The positive effect of the Chairman's initiative had a disproportionate public relations value to the costs involved. The Chairman probably realised the potential downside should adverse publicity be given to the situation – a dimension which seemed to have escaped his colleague.

4. The fact that a deal was done over the phone meant as far as the company was concerned there was nothing in writing which could be quoted back to them as a basis for trying to increase an amount agreed or used as a precedent by others.

5. A deal was agreed between principals without what could have developed into a long-winded (and costly) correspondence which could have had the effect of further polarising viewpoints.

Remedial action:

1. Train and empower customer care employees to view complaints as the customer views them and to suggest flexible solutions to problems either themselves or by referral to supervision.

2. Try to do the deal verbally – it saves time and avoids the permanence of print.

4. Finally the darning process ends with **N**ovation which is concerned with the changes we may need to make to the product, process, system, administration or whatever, which has been shown to be faulty. It may be that an analysis of complaints can aid the development of whatever it is that is at fault – which is part of the theory behind the use of CARELINES.

For this reason, as well as to provide a check on quality control, details of all complaints should be regularly reviewed by senior management. If data on such problems is not reviewed and acted upon, there is little likelihood that common problems will be rectified and the incidence of complaints will almost certainly increase, at the expense of the organisation's reputation. Unless the supplier records and considers the complaints, much of the positive benefit of these encounters can be lost.

Avoiding the filter

Often complaints are regarded as 'nuisance' events, dealt with 'hurriedly' at a low level in the organisation and there is no effort made to record or cross-reference the points made. Further in some instances junior management deliberately conceal complaints from senior management since they feel they may reflect badly on them. The fact that this may be true is even more reason for senior management to ensure that they do discover the real position regarding customer satisfaction and, more importantly, dissatisfaction. For this reason a procedure such as the following may be advisable.

Complaint review procedure

1. All complaints will be recorded in a (computerised/manual) record file giving details of (for example) date, customer details, product/service complained of, solution proposed, other comments and so on.

2. All complaints will be coded to determine whether they arose from: faulty product, faulty service, late delivery, poor service, rude service, failure to comply with specification, unreasonable customer, and others. (This needs to be customised as necessary.)

3. Failure to record and code details of a customer complaint is regarded as misconduct and will render the person responsible subject to the disciplinary procedure.

4. At the end of each month the record for the previous period will be assembled and submitted to director who will review the encounters and take such action as may be necessary to avoid repetitions, improve the manner of dealing, rectify ongoing problems and so on.

5. At the end of each half year the previous six months' complaints will be reanalysed and listed under each fault heading. This analysis will be submitted to the Board with a report from the Director responsible indicating the action that was (and is being) taken (and when) to rectify

all faults (particularly any that are repetitive). Such reports will be compared with those submitted previously to ensure that progress is being made with all but especially the most common faults.

6. All those involved in product design, production, marketing, selling, and servicing as well as the customer care department will be advised of the Board's requirements with the names of those responsible and a date by which time improvements must be effected. An estimate of the cost of the complaints and of dealing with them will be included. A statement of the trend of complaints (i.e. whether the incidence is rising, static or falling) will be provided.

7. A brief résumé of the report provided under 6 above will be given to all other employees to underline the need for everyone to appreciate that everything they do at work has only one point – to satisfy the customer.

The advantage of such a system is that:

- Those making decisions about the production and marketing of goods (and services) will have available real response from the sharp end – discerning customers. Provided they wish their organisation to survive they can devise a strategy to rectify the situation.

- Those responsible for the faults are identified in order that they can learn and rectify.

- People are made accountable. If people are left unaccountable it is all too easy to 'pass the buck' meanwhile nothing is done to actually rectify the complaint.

Case study : Unenlightened

The householder lived in a long dark road in which there were relatively few houses and only a few street lights. During road works the light opposite his house failed. After a few weeks when nothing had been done to repair it, he notified the Council and was thanked for his interest. A month later the light was still unrepaired. He rang again and was told that it was 'OK because we have told the electricity company who carry out these repairs for us'.

A month later the light was still dark and another lamp further along the road had also failed. He rang the Council again. This time the response was a little peeved: 'Yes we know – it's being done – we've told the electricity company.'

'You told me that last month but nothing has happened – it may be their role to repair but it is your role to make sure they do. Pretty soon the dark evenings will be with us and this road will be dangerous.'

A month later the situation was still the same and the householder wrote to the Council pointing out that part of the Council Tax he paid was for road lighting which had not been provided for the best part of four months. The only response was the same 'but we have acted we have told the electricity company'. The householder pointed out that this was merely an abdication of responsibility – action was required not an ineffective procedure. He contacted the Chief Executive and the light was repaired within 10 days.

- Pressure is created to try to eliminate faulty products and services.

- Those not directly responsible can appreciate the incidence and cost of complaints and may be able to appreciate how essential it is for work to be carried out as accurately as possible.

Case study : 3,000 salespersons

The director was concerned at the incidence of complaints and the problems of poor quality, high waste and inefficiency. As part of an ongoing employee communications package he suggested to all employees that (a) they all think of themselves as sales representatives and tackle their work accordingly, and (b) that unless the products on which they were working were bought by a customer, eventually jobs were at stake. Analysis of production in the year following this and endorsing messages, showed that returns fell from 10% of output to 4%, wastage was cut to under 5% and a survey of customer satisfaction showed a considerable increase.

Postscript

Organisations often say that they want to 'eliminate complaints'. Apart from probably being an impossible dream this conveys totally the wrong impression – as they should want to hear *all* complaints. What they should be seeking to eliminate is the *source* of the complaints – which they can only do if they do hear and record them all. Stressing this may help put the challenge into a proper perspective.

Dealing

Introduction

Often demanding encounters generated by customer disappointments are caused as much by entrenched attitudes or misconceptions as by the original fault. However if the supplier's representative keeps an open mind, endeavours to restore choice to the customer and tries to bring the encounter to a mutually acceptable conclusion entrenched attitudes may be avoided and there is a possibility that the parties can 'do a deal'. There is nothing to be gained by the supplier refusing to negotiate. Such a stance simply risks the encounter becoming a confrontation, often with the potential to move into the public arena which could have damaging effects on the reputation of the supplier.

Doing a deal

'Dealers' need to keep an open mind, to avoid starting the encounter with any prejudices, or preconceptions. In this way the discussion can at least commence with some degree of clarity. However 'dealers' also need to try using their perception or understanding to put themselves in the customer's place and see things through their eyes in order to understand *their* attitude. In *The Water Babies*, Charles Kingsley refers to the 'loveliest fairy in the world and her name is Mrs Doasyouwouldbedoneby'. If we treat others as, were we in the same position ourselves, we would wish to be treated, then we should be able to understand the other party's viewpoint more readily, and we may also be able to understand their concern or even anger at the way they perceive they have been let down. Taking this view we should improve the chances of our being able to conclude the encounter in a positive, and mutually satisfactory, manner. For this reason we need to ensure that there is a similarity of outlook of those responding to those complaining. In the case study in 'DARN' the Director who dealt with the original complaint was totally unable to see the problem through the eyes of the holidaymakers – indeed he made no effort to do this. His single reaction and aim was to defend what the holidaymakers regarded as an indefensible position. That the boat had broken down was not at issue – it had and was accepted as a fact. The point at issue was the equally weighted fact that the result of this had been to impair the enjoyment of the customers' holiday. Instead of sailing unfettered along French canals, on three days out of seven they had to wait for a mechanic to repair their ailing craft. Inevitably this restricted the area they could cover during the holiday – a clear case of expectations being raised only to be dashed in the execution of the contract. Trying to defend such a situation made the supplier look stupid as well as incompetent (in terms of failing to ensure the boats they hired were capable of performing reasonably satisfactorily for seven days). The situation was recovered by the Chairman who realised

- that his company's position was untenable,

- that the reputation he had striven for many years to create was at risk (national media – both newspapers and the increasing number of television holiday programmes – would seize on such a story with relish), and

- that a deal had to be done to try to recover the position.

Making a phone call – particularly on what would normally be regarded as a non-working day – gave considerable satisfaction to the holidaymaker and added solace to the 'injury' caused by the initial dismissive reaction. The company was seen to have 'put itself out', compensating in some degree for the way the holidaymakers had been 'put out' by the breakdowns. Further the fact that a deal was done over the phone meant as far as the company was concerned there was nothing in writing which could be quoted back to them as a basis for trying to increase the amount or used as a precedent by others.

Lessons – and dangers

In this encounter the Chairman took an initiative and a suggested a flexible solution. Such ORIGINALITY can be a powerful weapon in concluding a deal and if it is possible to train and empower customer care employees to suggest flexible solutions to problems either themselves or by referral to supervision, this may enable more encounters to be resolved at an early stage.

Case study: Creditable performance

Because she was going on holiday and would be away when her credit card statement was due to arrive and would be due for payment, the customer telephoned the card company to ask what the outstanding balance would be on the statement due to be despatched the day after she left. She was given a figure which she found somewhat more than her own estimation but nevertheless paid the full amount.

On her return from holiday some weeks later she found that the figure outstanding shown on the statement was considerably less than she had been told and thus she had overpaid the company. The excess figure was represented by purchases made after the statement cut-off date which she had deliberately timed so that she gained the maximum credit.

She telephoned the credit card company who firstly stated that there was nothing they could (they meant 'would') do. She persisted, stating that she had been misled and the effect was that money which could have been earning interest had been in the possession of the credit card company for an additional six weeks quite unnecessarily. Eventually the credit card company asked her what she wanted. She replied that the minimum she required was interest on the lost money and accepted a credit of £25.

The person dealing with her complaint at the credit card company had sufficient authority to do a deal which allowed the encounter to be settled swiftly and by phone.

Doing the deal verbally saves time and avoids the permanence of print. However care needs to be taken so that those doing the deals have a clear understanding of their range of authority and know when to pass the matter to a more senior level.

Getting a good deal

In seeking to come to a swift conclusion it must not be overlooked that trying to conclude a disagreement by correspondence is far more difficult than doing so either face to face or on the telephone. When words are reduced to black and white text they lose all tone and inflexion, and can acquire a stilted formality. Conversely the tones and inflexions we use when speaking, both soften and give otherwise 'hidden' meanings to their literal meanings. Further, when writing we have to use words which may have different and unwanted meanings to different people which can create or compound misunderstandings. Put simply – one cannot ask questions of, or gain elucidation from, a piece of paper. There can also be a tendency, in composing a letter, to become 'carried away' with the 'correctness' of our views and case (another reason for leaving a draft of a letter for later reconsideration before despatch). In a conversation, our flow would be interrupted, either by voice or by bodily reaction, and such interruption might give us cause to think again and possibly modify our response. This does not happen when we write – we cannot determine or even second guess how exactly our words will be taken. Finally, writing has a permanence which a conversation does not. In the first case study referred to above, the Chairman seeking to do a deal over the phone had a number of advantages over his colleague who had answered by letter:

1. He could tell by the tone and attitude of the holidaymaker if he was likely to be amenable to a swift deal (or if it was likely to be achieved).

2. He could check out the facts and gain an impression of the strength of the case being made and of the annoyance of the customer.

3. He could float ideas across during the conversation with a reasonable degree of confidence that much would not be recalled accurately and, if difficulties developed, could even be denied.

4. He could try to conclude a deal without any written offer being made.

5. He could use verbal pressure to gain agreement.

In fact the conversation was more the result of an instinctive reaction – genuine sympathy for a holiday somewhat spoiled and a wish to agree some recompense swiftly. Obviously this deal was made relatively easy for the Chairman to complete in view of his complete authority. However this should not necessarily be a barrier to a person of lower rank – all that is required is to set the limits within which they can operate but to stress that they may need to be flexible with out-of-the-ordinary cases (that is, not to apply standard responses to non-standard situations).

Written dealing

In contrast, the situation outlined below shows how polarisation can occur when a dispute that could have been solved by telephone or personal visit was instead mishandled by post.

Case study: Meeting better than writing

A customer had a major query with a building society's product and service and had written to the local branch to gain information and redress. Over the following two months a number of letters were exchanged, the situation being made worse by the branch making a number of further minor errors which only served to aggravate what was already a difficult situation.

Inadequate and insufficient explanations were provided and eventually the customer involved the Head Office at Board level. As a result a further three-way correspondence ensued which again went on for several weeks.

When the situation was sorted to some extent, even after compensation was paid, the customer was left feeling that he had been inefficiently and poorly treated. In terms of customer care this was hardly an encouraging outcome, whilst in terms of potential adverse publicity it was dangerous.

Key technique

A meeting between the customer and a senior person in the company who could have investigated the original problem, and the subsequent mistakes the society had caused, checked all the details, agreed action and ensured proper restitution, might have achieved a better and swifter solution.

In this instance such a meeting would have had the advantage of the recognition of body language, was unlikely to have degenerated into dispute and would have had the advantage of not providing a written record of the maladministration. The time invested in such a meeting would have avoided the potential downside as well as the resources consumed in a lengthy and at times acrimonious correspondence which reflected well on no one, least of all the building society, for which one would think a sound customer-orientated image was essential.

Remedial action:

Adopt as policy that if a problem cannot be resolved by initial letter a telephone call or visit from a senior member of staff should be used to attempt to gain resolution.

Postscript

It should not be overlooked that when a deal is done by phone, the two parties are in direct contact. Provided there is a reasonable rapport it may be possible to structure the deal involving an additional or new product. For example, in the instance of the spoiled boat holiday the choice offered to the customer was either a cash refund or an enhanced sum of another holiday. In an encounter concerning a faulty electrical drill the offer made over the phone was a trade-in of the faulty item plus an allowance for inconvenience against a more powerful model. In both instances the customer had choice and in both alternative products were made available. Indeed when fielding a complaint over the phone there is little to stop the supplier trying, if the circumstances are appropriate, to market other goods!

E-mail

Introduction

The ability to use electronic transmission to convey a letter or note has for some time been transforming many of the ways in which we have traditionally done business – and is likely to generate substantial long-term changes as its use widens. E-mail is fast, reasonably reliable and since the item can be printed, enables the recipient to retain a hard copy of what is essentially an intangible exchange.

Like all innovations however there are problems associated with the use of this new medium for communication and, particularly when interfacing with customers (both internal and external), it may be appropriate to provide some guidance. One can expect to see e-mail used for an increasing number of exchanges in the same way as once the telephone took over from letters. The transfer from written letter to verbal telephone call gained the parties the chance of considerably better communication in that tone and emphasis were added to the information being transmitted. In moving from verbal telephone to electronic mail the situation is completely reversed – and indeed since e-mail transmissions tend not to receive the same amount of consideration and redrafting usually given to letters, the situation may actually be worse.

Contracting

Traditionally contracts have been entered into by a process of negotiation ultimately leading to a situation, usually evidenced by a form of words, which is acceptable to both parties. Where each party has its own standard terms this process can be lengthy – drawn out by what can be called a 'battle of the terms'. During this period negotiations take place with each party trying to obtain agreement to as many of its own standard terms as possible perhaps having to agree to some terms of the other side before a complete set, acceptable to both parties, is arrived at. Normally this 'battle' will be evidenced by letters so that in the event of later disagreement as to what was agreed, reference can be made to the process and the correspondence. In other words the creation of the contract between the parties is usually obvious and hard copies exist of the stages.

The danger with communicating via e-mail is that either a contractual position between the parties can be created unwittingly, or if there is intent to create a contract not all the terms that might normally have been agreed are incorporated (or there is an element of doubt between the parties whether such terms – and/or which version of them – are incorporated or not). Like the telephone, e-mail is essentially informal in nature and used informally, but unlike the telephone permanent records available to the parties (via the records of the service providers) exist of what was 'said'. It can be difficult (though admittedly not impossible as there could be witnesses at least to one end of the conversation) to 'prove' what was said during a telephone exchange and still more difficult (without a tape-recording) to prove the existence of a verbal contract. However, with the benefit of hardcopy evidence of what was 'said' in an e-mail exchange, any contractual link may become somewhat easier to prove. Although the parties may not view their exchange equally – during what one party may regard as an informal outline of a potential link, the other may be expecting that the exchange itself is semi-contractual – this may not necessarily be apparent from the messages. If the party treating the matter as an informal exchange does not consider the construction and import of the messages carefully, a contract could be created.

Case study: I didn't mean that

The supplier was in e-mail contact with a customer with whom business had been completed in the past and the following exchange took place:

Customer: Earliest quote needed for price/delivery for 10,000, 20,000 and 50,000 widgets.

Supplier: Widgets 10k January £20,000, 20k £38,000, 50k £94,000.

Customer: State colours available.

Supplier: Green January, Blue, Red in addition.

Customer: Order confirmed 50,000 Red widgets for £94,000 reference XYZ123.

Supplier: Rec'd your e-mail dated XXX and order XYZ123.

The supplier actually meant that they could supply 10,000 green widgets in January, but other quantities/colours could not be delivered until later. In sending the last message the supplier didn't want to let on that it might be difficult to meet the January delivery for red widgets. In the meantime he would check to see what could be arranged. The customer however, since the supplier had not rejected what he felt was an order, assumed the order was accepted and went ahead on the basis the delivery was assured.

The situation in the above case study is a simplification of a transaction which was eventually sorted out not least since the parties had an ongoing relationship which neither wished to upset. However, because e-mail messages tend to be informal and truncated (rather than formal and composed in a traditional format in a letter which may pass through a number of drafts) situations can be left open to misinterpretation – and even to dissent and argument which regardless of the outcome, can cause waste and loss – not least of customer goodwill, and potentially the customer.

It may be advisable to set up a programme within the computer so that on any occasion that e-mails are being exchanged, a standard wording is incorporated. This could indicate that

- no contract must or can come into existence by means of such interface,

- the contents of all e-mail messages are subject to the preparation and exchange of a written contract,

- e-mail exchanges are expression of intent in good faith and should not be regarded as binding, and

- full terms need to be agreed prior to any contract coming into effect.

It might also be advisable to include further standard messages such as

- the contents of all e-mails are composed on behalf of the employing organisation (in order to attempt to protect the personal position of senders,

- the e-mail system must only be used for legitimate business information, and

- the display of the legally required data of companies (country of registration, and registered name, number and office) on all such messages.

Libel

Further danger of the use of the system exists in the possibility of third parties being able to see comments made between two users believing their exchange to be confidential. If such comments, for example about a third party, are 'broadcast' in this way the third party might well have an action for libel against the users – or more likely, since the employees themselves may not have available the resources for compensation likely to be able to satisfy someone libelled, an action could be brought against their employer. This scenario has already occurred, with Norwich Union paying Western

Provident, £450,000 in an out-of-court settlement after employees of Norwich Union cast doubts about Western Provident's financial stability in a number of e-mail messages. (It should not be overlooked that although users may think that their e-mails disappear unless the recipient prints them off, this is not so with e-mails sent via the Internet since the service provider can keep the messages for two years and the police have rights to access them.)

Procedure

It may be advisable to adopt a procedure or policy such as in the following example.

Example: Use of e-mail

1. E-mail should be used primarily to distribute/update information, confirm arrangements, confirm meetings and so on. although as an exception they can be used to leave messages where the recipient is not available and the message can await their return.

2. Whilst e-mails can be used to outline the terms and details of a proposed contractual relationship, the medium should not be used to conclude a contract and it must be made clear that no contract exists until and unless terms are agreed between the parties in written form.

3. E-mails should not be used as substitution for face-to-face or telephone conversation.

4. On no account should the system be used for vindictive, harassing, discriminatory or abusive comment or criticism of anyone, whether the target, another employee or any third party. Any person in receipt of an item which they feel should have been prohibited by this clause should produce the item to [name]. Any person proved to have deliberately sent an item prohibited by this clause will be deemed guilty of gross misconduct and will be dealt with under the disciplinary procedure accordingly.

5. Users of the system should appreciate that untrue and/or careless comments concerning a third party could lead to action for libel. The making of such comments should be avoided.

6. All messages and so on should be clear and unambiguous and coded from five star to no star in order of priority. Whilst it is fully appreciated that the system lends itself to informality and brevity, clarity is preferable.

7. An outgoing e-mail message should be treated as if it were a hard copy letter and drafted and checked in the same way.

8. No response to an e-mail message should ever be sent in haste, anger or hostility.

Postscript

E-mails have been used for bullying, harassment and sexual and racial discrimination. Providers of the service should ensure that such interfaces, particularly when being used as a communication process with the organisation's internal customers:

*   are outlawed and prohibited,

*   that penalties for such use are severe, and

*   that the system is regularly policed.

In addition confidential reporting and counselling should be provided for victims.

Emulating competitors

Introduction

The concept of emulating competitors (or benchmarking as it is perhaps more conveniently known) could be said to be one of laziness in origination since it merely uses another organisation's standards of quality care and so on, as the standard for the subject organisation. However, compliance with such standards may require considerable effort since it requires the organisation to take all the steps necessary in order to attain the adopted standards. Basically decision-makers determine to adopt the standards, or a proportion of the level of the standards, set by (for example) the market leaders in their particular sector. Thus they might decide that Bloggs are the market leaders in their segment and they will endeavour to match them in every aspect of the provision of product or service. Alternatively they may feel that there is no way that they can compete on price but will endeavour to attain Bloggs' standards on quality, reliability, after-sales service and so on. As a concept it is widely used in the USA where it has been credited with being one of the main reasons why there has historically been a perception of better standards of customer care and quality being given to customers in America – although sadly there is evidence that such high standards are being eroded.

Competition

As a commitment, emulating has the considerable advantage that it forces a supplier to compare itself with those who seek to put it out of business. Although it may be somewhat unfashionable to describe an organisation's competitors' aims as being to put the organisation out of business, viewing them in this light should focus attention on the need to ensure the organisation does everything that will attract and retain its customers since allowing them to be poached by competitors has a double impact on the organisation – not only does it lose sales but their competitors gain them. Benchmarking could also be said to encourage commitment to the concept – 'if you can't lick 'em, join 'em'. Our competitors may not perform better than we do in every area. But to try to preserve our position, if we can improve where our performance is worse than them, whilst maintaining our position on those things we do better than them, then we may gain an edge. If not then we may find the terms of trade turn against us.

Case study: Don't make them like we make them

Traditionally, when it came to buying a car, Americans simply 'bought American' and although a few foreign manufacturers managed to penetrate the American home market, mostly the vehicle trade was driven in the reverse direction with American cars finding their way into most countries in the world. However when import barriers against Japanese cars were lifted, the American public found that these new imports provided better value, performance and all round quality than many of their home produced models. Swiftly Japanese cars producers seized a large slice of the US car market. There was only one way to combat the threat – US manufacturers had to improve their standards to match.

Key technique

Comparing one's own performance against that of the best 'producer' in the marketplace and achieving such standards, should entail being in tune with the most demanding customers' expectations. Maintaining this level of performance in turn should reduce complaint incidence.

'Rubbishing the opposition' is quite a widespread attitude. But even if the opposition is not up to our standards, there is little point in doing this – rather it would seem advisable to concentrate our efforts on exploiting the competitive edge that it would appear their poor performance gives us. Indeed highlighting it may bring it to their attention – and to its resolution. Denigrating the opposition can generate a feeling of superiority – and potentially lead to complacency and ARROGANCE. Generally however competitors should be respected, or at least given credence, particularly if they then start nibbling away at our market and our sales – they must have got something right which we have not.

Case study: Tables turned

Gaskell & Chambers once had a virtual monopoly in all kinds of bar and drinks equipment. It had relatively few competitors until a company formed by an immigrant engineer arrived on the scene. The attitude of some of the long-serving employees was that the new company could be ignored as they knew little about traditional items and had concentrated on refrigeration and derivative products. The Senior Sales Director was concerned however since, after an uncertain start, the newcomer began to have an effect on sales. His concern was ignored and no spirit of deter- mination could be engendered to take on and defeat this newcomer. Two years later the newcomer launched a successful takeover bid and Gaskell & Chambers (which had been established for over 70 years) disappeared.

A policy commitment

Elsewhere in this book are suggested policies and procedures for the practicalities of dealing with customers. However, it may be advisable, particularly if trying to emulate the market leader, for us to create an appropriate ethos within the organisation by means of a policy commitment.

XYZ Company Ltd

Customer Relationship Policy

As a wealth-creating organisation our aim is to make a profit by producing products and/or services which have a value to our customers. Organisations do not stand still – they either expand and prosper, or contract and ultimately go out of business. We wish to expand and thus need to be able to satisfy more customers each year, or at least to create more sales to our existing customers each year. To achieve either (and ideally we wish to achieve both) we need to satisfy those customers with the best value, quality, delivery, and so on, and expect all employees to bear the following commitment in mind at all times:

1. We commit ourselves to produce quality/value products available at the time required by the customer where such a time can be reasonably achieved by the organisation.

2. Our aim is to satisfy the customer on the first occasion to such an extent that they will wish to repurchase. At each repurchase our aim is to satisfy them to at least the standard, and ideally better than the standard they were satisfied to on the first occasion.

3. Repeat business is vital to our organisation and we will strive to match and beat the best operator in our business in terms of value, quality, service and dependability.

---

4. In the event that a problem arises with a product, we will endeavour to deal with such a problem objectively and positively, with the aim of both solving the problem and converting a dissatisfied customer into a satisfied one.

5. All concerns and complaints, no matter what the source or basis, will be treated with courtesy and a positive attitude. This is so even if it means compensating a customer where there is perceived to be no genuine complaint, or where the complaint seems to be exaggerated.

6. Customer visitors will be treated courteously and, provided the time is appropriate, invited to tour the premises (except for any parts of the operation from time to time considered as sensitive or secret, which will be suitably protected).

7. All letters received from customers will be reviewed and answered in person by a Board level executive and such action as necessary will be actioned by that person.

8. All directors will spend an average of one day in every four weeks in personal contact with customers.

Repeating the business

Purchasing (particularly in retailing) is all about creating habits. Human beings are creatures of habit – not least since most of us find it easier to continue doing something which is familiar than to do something for the first time. Customers are affected by this propensity to adopt habits and will tend to repeat what they have done before – even in the High Street walking in virtually the same path and visiting the same stores each time they shop. The fact that customers do follow habits and exhibit what we can call 'consumer inertia' provides a considerable advantage to a supplier since repeat customers will normally be half-committed already. All that is needed is to provide at least the service/quality/value provided last time and we should be able to repeat the sale. This should be regarded as a minimum commitment as inevitably our competitors will be attempting to make our customers change their habits – thus we cannot afford to be complacent.

Case study: Hypocrites

Most organisations shown the policy and paragraph immediately above will reply that they are principles which in outline if not in detail, they hold good and already observe. In fact reality indicates that this is not so – particularly amongst the UK's largest companies. This is odd since it is the largest who should have the greatest commitment as they have the most to lose – when you are at the top the only way is down. In 1997 P.Four Consultancy carried out a major survey of customer care in the UK and came to the conclusion that the often much-vaunted commitment to customer care was actually 'only skin deep'. Many of these businesses are not at all keen on managers spending time with customers. Although 70% of those asked thought that customer focus was their organisation's first or second priority, less than 25% of those interviewed thought customer interface time was important. It is difficult to understand how these two statistics can be reconciled.

The P.Four survey also disclosed that 75% of those surveyed thought that acquiring new business was an important measurement of management performance. Statistics from entirely unrelated surveys demonstrate that UK business spends as much on acquiring new customers as it loses by failing to ensure existing customers repeat-purchase. It would seem that customer retention statistics might be a more valuable criteria to measure management performance. However, since marketing and endeavouring to attract new business may be more appealing and fun than simply ensuring existing customers are resupplied, often the latter does not gain the attention it should receive thus engendering waste of resources and impairing profitability.

Customer retention

Customer retention, as a specific commitment or part of the process of emulating competitors is a lesson which many small organisations readily recognise, but perhaps that is because their owners/directors tend to be far more in touch with their customers and more personally aware of the importance of their retention. Small organisations tend to benefit from what we could call 'entrepreneurial hands-on direction'. It appears that the larger the organisation, then the greater the danger of salaried directors losing touch with their customers. The advantages of keeping in personal contact with customers are considerable. Such contact provides

- those who direct the organisation with reaction 'from the horse's mouth' rather than receiving it second-hand, via possibly 'filtered' or censored reports,

- a valuable insight into the way those at the sharp end are performing (it may also give them a morale boost that someone at the top is interested in how they perform),

- a perception of the organisation by the customer, again on a direct and unreported basis, and

- a way of checking how the organisation compares with its competitors against whom it is, whether it commits to it or not, benchmarked by the customers.

Finally, the ability to bend the ear of a director could be a most effective method of customer retention.

Postscript

It can of course be an expensive investment attempting to match the requirements of the 'best of the bunch'. Disneyworld is located near the swamps of Florida yet very few visitors ever suffer the discomfort of mosquito bites. When this was queried the casual answer was that there were no mosquitoes since trucks circle the Magic Kingdom throughout each night spraying the whole area with insect repellent. Customer care in the real sense of the word and at its excellent best!

Financial aspects

Introduction

Making those involved in customer care, customer service, and/or public relations aware of the financial effects that inadequate service or attention on their part can cause may help focus their attention and place their role in perspective. Other than monopolies few organisations can take their customers for granted. There are usually alternative suppliers and service providers only too willing to take our place and our trade if it proves to be inadequate in some way or service is unacceptable. Very often the return on an organisation's investment is quite low – the profit figure may be less than 10%. This does not leave much of a margin for error.

The financial facts of life

Making the following sequence of data available to customer care staff may assist placing their important role in full perspective:

The profit/cost relationship

If a supplier is making 10% profit on its sales every £10 of extra sales adds only £1 to the profit. Conversely, every £1 saved from its expenditure means it needs to generate £10 less sales to achieve the same profit:

(i)   Sales £100 less costs £90 = £10 profit
(ii) Sales £110 less costs £99 = £11 profit
(iii) Sales £100 less costs £89 = £11 profit.

With the level of profit return on sales in (i), to increase profits the choice needs to be made between increasing sales by 10% as in (ii) (which might have the effect of increasing costs in proportion – as assumed here) or reducing costs by £1 as in (iii). Sales may be hard to come by and in any event may not be entirely under our control, whereas our costs are. Savings on costs and waste may be the easier option. So by saving £1 on our costs we can, if we wish, avoid the need to find £10 of sales, and our sales target is unchanged. Retaining our existing customers saves us needing to replace them with new customers – which would increase our costs.

Massaging the figures – 1

There is a further dimension to this since if we can shave 10% off our costs and maintain our sales we can virtually double our profit

(i) Sales £100 less costs £90 = £10 profit
(ii) Sales £100 less costs (£90 minus 10%) £81 = £19 profit.

Massaging the figures – 2

Taking the above a stage further we can really make things happen if we can shave our costs by 10% *and* increase our sales by 10%.

(i) Sales £100 less costs £90 = £10 profit
(ii) Sales (up 10%) £110 less costs (minus 10%) £81 = £29 profit.

However, in playing with the above figures, each assume either that our customer base is static or increasing. If the customer base is decreasing most organisations will either

• increase some promotional costs to try to minimise the decrease in the existing customer base, or

• invest in increasing the customer base to gain new customers. If this is happening, the figures could run as follows:

(i) Sales £100 less costs £90 = £10 profit

(ii) Assume a loss of 1% of sales: Sales £99 less costs (say) £91 = £8 profit

(iii) If a further loss of 1% is incurred and marketing is again increased to try to attract new customers: Sales £98 less costs £92 = £6 profit

(iv) If this scenario is continued, then by year 5 or 6 (or even earlier in some cases) the organisation will be loss making.

Generating repeat customers

Hard-nosed suppliers who need only one interface with their customers can perhaps be understood (although not excused) if they do not treat customers complaining of broken promises, with concern and a constructive approach. Many suppliers however need not just one interface with a customer but repeat business from them. This is particularly true in today's trading climate when many trades are experiencing restricted demand and facing strong competition. In such circumstances retaining existing customers should be a priority. After all, those that already buy have knowledge of the products and services, which supports a belief and confidence that what they are buying is worth their investment – that is, they have a belief that the product's implied promise has been kept. The longer period over which customers can be retained, the greater the time and number of purchases over which can be spread the 'cost' of acquiring them. In theory, if all customers are retained, nothing need be invested to attract new customers in order to maintain the status quo. Conversely if 10% of the customer base is lost each year then, if not replenished the business will probably fail due to lack of cash by the fourth or fifth year.

Cost of customer replacement

Replacing 10% of our customer base each year may not be deemed to be too difficult a task but if customers are dissatisfied with the product's performance or with the service they receive, or with the way in which their problems are considered and treated, customer replacement costs can rise steeply. In a survey of the top 200 UK companies, consultants Price Waterhouse found that barely 10% analyse how many customers they lose each year, and yet the firm estimated that customer defection loses British industry around £100 billion each year, whilst a similar amount is spent on marketing, sales and distribution expenses. Retaining satisfied customers requires an investment in customer commitment and care far less costly (about one-fifth has been estimated) than customer replacement. In most cases completely replacing the complained of product is likely to be less expensive than sourcing a replacement customer.

However, losing those that you have acquired by such investment merely as a result of poor customer attention is the most costly process of all.

Case study: Care-less

The family had been going to the hotel regularly. On their last visit, however, they were given a very substandard room (recently recommissioned after a period of disuse). It was obvious that the high standards of service and food provided by the previous owners, had been discarded by the new owners. Prices had increased whereas standards of service had plummeted and the attitude of most of the new short-service staff that had replaced the former long-service staff was offhand and casual. In discussing this with other guests it became clear that they had similar opinions and did not intend returning.

In complaining of this deterioration of the value being given, despite the regular national press advertisement continuing to indicate that the previous service and standards would be available, the former guest pointed out that many of the failings were not cost- but standard-related, and, since the hotel had numerous competitors in the immediate vicinity, there was an urgent need for a re-think to avoid a complete loss of business.

Key technique

Establishing a 'requirement for success' criterion may be helpful. Here, that criteria was the retention of repeat custom and/or the achievement of a high room occupancy figure. Attraction of new and additional guests was also important and could have a considerable effect on the profit earned, but the retention of former guests to create the foundation on which additional sales could be built was critical. As the family were regular guests, consideration should have been given to ensuring they were given a room at least as good as that previously used, since if other aspects were at least bearable they might have rebooked. New guests, with no experience of what had been provided before, might have been a better choice as occupants of the recommissioned poorer quality room.

In failing to concentrate on the basics, the management had created a situation that encouraged complaint – costly to deal with, and dangerous to their ongoing reputation.

Customer retention

Writing in the *Harvard Business Review* in early 1993, Frederick Reichheld, Director of Consultancy at Bain & Company, underlined the need to retain as much of the customer base as possible as is exemplified in the above case study, with the comment 'customer loyalty appears to be the only way to achieve sustainably superior profits'. He used as an example the life assurance business stating that a 5% increase in customer retention has the effect of lowering costs per policy by 18% – which is no small amount of cost in any business. Similarly MBNA, an American credit card company found that a 5% rise in customer loyalty led to a 60% increase in profits after five years.

Twenty-first century consumers

The days when loyalty could be relied upon as an assured 'continuing customer base' no longer exist for most organisations. Price, service and value for money tend now to be king. If supplier B is now perceived to provide better value then the customer may well decide to give their custom to B rather than A, previously their 'favoured supplier'. In late 1997 market researchers NOP disclosed that some of the highest spenders were fully prepared to 'churn' their suppliers immediately they were dissatisfied with anything – and to change again if necessary. Some of the various reasons for changing were analysed as

- service mistakes – 44%,
- indifference, rudeness, ill-informed service – 34%,
- poor response to complaints – 17%.

All of which factors are entirely under the control of the supplier. When those who changed suppliers were asked whether anything was done about their defection, it emerged that in 73% of the instances, the suppliers knew of it but did nothing about it, although 35% of the defectors could have been retained as customers if only an apology had been offered and 82% said they would have remained customers had there simply been better customer service.

Incredibly it seems that many suppliers do not understand that when a promise has been broken, or expectations are unfulfilled or damaged, an apology can rectify the situation in over a third of the cases, not only removing the problem but also, and in many ways, far more importantly, avoiding the investment needed to generate a replacement.

Postscript

The above seeks to put into perspective the cost-benefit relationship of customer care/retention and could form the basis of training for customer care staff. Perhaps somewhat cynically, given that research indicates that as many as 40% of directors do not understand the monthly management accounts produced for their organisations it might be advisable if those in charge of organisations were also briefed in such fundamentals. The cost of actually dealing with complaints/concerns/replacements should also be considered as it is in ULTIMATE AIM.

Guarantees

Introduction

The dictionary defines a guarantee as a 'written or other undertaking to answer for the performance of an obligation' – an explanation with which most customers will readily identify. The very fact that a supplier is prepared to provide a guarantee should be a valuable means of reassuring the customer that should any problems develop with the product or service they have chosen to acquire, the supplier will be ready to indemnify them in some way – by restitution of the price paid, by the substitution of a replacement product, or by some other recompense.

There are a variety of 'consumer assurances' loosely called guarantees which include

- Price promises such as the John Lewis Partnership's famous 'never knowingly undersold' claim which guarantees to the customer that if they can find the item being sold at a lower price then JLP will reduce the price paid for their item to match the lower price. (Other suppliers, particularly retailers, have adopted a similar promise.)

- The add-on 'service guarantees' sold at a price additional to the product to provide insurance cover should the product default for (usually) up to three years. (In fact this is not so much a guarantee as an additional charge for the product. If this is not the case then it begs the question of whether the supplier is implying that they expect the product they are selling to fail to perform within a fairly short time!)

- The more common guarantee of performance usually subject to a range of circumstances or provisions or conditions, and

- Specifications with which products being supplied are expected to comply which may be generated either by commercial customers or suppliers. These may spell out details of required recompense regarding replacement, compensation and so on, should they fail to meet the specification set.

Provision

Most reputable suppliers provide guarantees and should these be insufficient the UK law provides a legal framework to protect consumers. Fortunately the days when the old Latin tag 'caveat emptor' – let the buyer beware – governed trade and left the purchaser virtually without any protection have long since passed. 'Caveat emptor' may have originally provided a spur to innovation and investment in new products and processes but it had the unacceptable side-effect of providing a wonderful screen for the unscrupulous suppliers. In effect it gave them virtually a free hand to supply inferior goods without come back. At the time that the tag came into use, if sword makers in ancient Rome sold a defective sword to a soldier which failed to perform, the customer was probably in no fit state to claim. Sadly some suppliers still try to operate in such a way, or more subtly to frame their guarantees to appear to give protection when they do no such thing. This is a high risk strategy since stating that there is a guarantee and then providing one creates (even raises) the expectations of the product by the purchaser. These expectations are that

- the item will perform to the level claimed. Almost inevitably this will create in the customer's mind the feeling 'obviously they think it's good and will perform to that level as they are prepared to give a guarantee', and

- performance of restitution in the apparently unlikely event that the product fails. Again this creates a feeling of 'comfort' in the purchaser's mind.

In purchasing from an establishment rather than an itinerant there is a further 'comfort' factor – that the supplier's investment in the outlet provides some 'guarantee of stability' or permanence – they are likely to be here 'tomorrow'.

Having created these expectations, whether implicit or explicit, if the product then fails and the guarantee is required to be implemented, but when it is, it also fails, the disillusion and frustration of the customer can be severe. In fact the reaction may be far more severe because expectations have been raised, than would have been the case had no such promises been made. Failure of the 'guarantees' in such circumstances can only add insult to injury to the customer and generate an encounter in which anger can overtake irritation. Anger can be a potent force acting against the interests of the supplier particularly in relation to the publicity that can be given to the encounter.

Case study: Out of time

In November the consumer bought an electrical item as a Christmas present and stated this at the time to the assistant. A guarantee card was stamped and inserted into the packing of the electrical item. The customer added some wrapping paper to her purchase, both items, amongst others, being shown on her bill. Immediately after Christmas, the first time the item was used, it malfunctioned. The consumer, somewhat embarrassed by having the gift returned by the relative to whom it had been given, returned to the store only to be greeted by the statement:

'I'm sorry but this item is only guaranteed for one month from date of purchase.'

'That's absurd, it was bought in November as a Christmas present – as well you know since we discussed its purpose at the time and I even bought wrapping paper for it. If you only guarantee it for one month that means that the guarantee had already expired before the box was opened and the product's life even started.'

'I'm sorry but that's what the guarantee says – look it's here in black and white.'

'It may be but it's a pointless and totally worthless guarantee and one which does not reflect well on the reputation of this company. In any event once you stamped it you put it into the box and sellotaped it shut so I had no chance to read it. The next time it was opened was when my relative unwrapped it at Christmas – I must insist you replace this item.'

The encounter, in the store, became increasingly heated with other customers as interested onlookers. Eventually the store did replace the item, retreating in the face of common sense from their original stand. To their credit they also altered their guarantee soon afterwards, lengthening the coverage to a year and in addition making the phrasing more user-friendly. They also displayed notices outlining such terms.

Framing the wording

Under the Unfair Terms in Consumer Contracts Regulations, the terms of trade governing a contract with a consumer must be fair and in clear English. Both before and since the implementation of these Regulations many suppliers have adapted and rewritten their terms so that they comply with the new requirements and their terms can be read with ease and swift comprehension by the 'ordinary man on the Clapham omnibus' (Lord

Denning's famous definition of the 'person in the street'). But translating legal jargon into plain English does not of itself provide a clear and usable guarantee. What is required is a plain statement setting out what the supplier is prepared to do should the product or service default or not conform in some way to its stated purpose.

Thus the guarantee should state

- the name, address, telephone/fax/e-mail numbers of the supplier,

- the name of the department/person to be contacted in the event of problems/concerns,

- recommended times of contact,

- the time limit of the guarantee (which should be reasonable), and

- any other limitations to which the guarantee is subject.

The other limitations that may need to be applied might concern usage, manner of claiming and so on. Unless these – or indeed any other terms – are quite straightforward, it may be advisable to state them clearly and prominently since if the customer reads the guarantee this may draw their attention to the limitations and may pre-empt a later argument. To ensure that both parties do understand the situation correctly it may also be helpful to run through the main points of the guarantee (or to display them clearly) at the point of sale. It might then be difficult for the customer to claim lack of understanding of the term.

Service guarantees

In recent years when trade has grown so much more competitive and prices have needed to reflect this, the custom has grown of offering insurance or service guarantees at a price additional to the price of the item. So great has been the selling power of these and so valuable a contribution to trade, that the profit from the sale of such 'add ons' comprised the whole of a recent year's profits of one major electrical retailer. In itself this perhaps indicates that such service guarantees are overpriced although the counter position to that may be that if their sales value was not available the prices of the goods themselves would need to increase. However, as far as the customer is concerned care needs to be taken. Obviously for a complex product worth over £1,000, paying just over £20 for a three-year service guarantee may be viable and potentially valuable although most items are covered for the first year in any event. However, for low priced items it is an expensive form of insurance. In some cases the service guarantee offered actually costs more than the product being covered which must be a nonsense. This is exacerbated with some products where improving technology means their retail price is actually decreasing and ignores the underlying implication that the store feels the products might fail fairly quickly!

Case study: Misdirection

The assistant tried very hard to sell the customer a three-year service guarantee for £24 (later reduced to £20) on a product just bought for £99 in Dixons. The customer replied that he was not interested since the product guarantee was for the first 12 months by which time the item would have lost part of its current value and to pay £20 for an item then worth, say, £75 (in the second year and even less in the third) did not seem to be a good deal – at least not for him (it may have been a good deal for the store and for the assistant who no doubt received a commission on every service guarantee sold).

> *Note:* *So intent was the assistant on trying to sell the deal that he overlooked the fact that the remote control handset was not included within the packaging of the item. Rectification of this error later caused considerable toing and froing as the customer had to telephone the shop on three occasions to try to obtain one. On each occasion the manager said he would ring back – on no occasion did he do so.*

On his second visit to the shop, after a wait (mainly caused by the manager being interrupted to deal with other queries whilst trying to find it) the control was produced. One would have thought that as a gesture the batteries required to operate it would have been given to the customer – but no.

The Sunday Times featured the same store in a report of a customer who lost data stored in a computerised personal organiser when the batteries ran out and the back-up battery was found to have been installed incorrectly. Stating that the store had installed the back-up battery incorrectly, the customer claimed £100 compensation and was given a voucher for £25. Appealing to the Chairman's office had little effect since referring to the fact that the customer had had to spend considerable time re-entering the data, his office suggested she could have minimised her losses by entering the data 'in her spare time'!

Operation

Customers can perhaps be forgiven for losing their temper swiftly when seeking to ensure a supplier fulfils the promise made in the guarantee because experience indicates that in some instances (unfortunately not rare) suppliers will try to avoid meeting or complying with the expectation of performance they have created.

That this is so has led some suppliers to try to underline their guarantees and to reassure their customers that concerns will be dealt with positively. Thus the Thresher Wine Store chain states in its 'Wine Buyers' Guarantee': 'If for any reason you are not COMPLETELY SATISFIED with, or have not enjoyed a wine from our range, we want to know. Please bring it back and we will replace it – NO QUIBBLE!' The capital letters attempt to indicate the commitment to what should appear to most to be a very reassuring guarantee. If suppliers wish to reassure their customers a form of wording such as Thresher's use should be considered – providing always that the supplier intends to live up to the expectation.

Postscript

Suppliers can perhaps be forgiven for being strict concerning the interpretation and implementation of their guarantee since there is no doubt that some customers will 'try it on'. However, care needs to be taken as otherwise they may finish up treating the honest majority in a way perhaps more fitting for the dishonest few. In many ways it may be simpler to honour the guarantee in all but the most blatant cases – it will certainly save time and may also avoid the damaging confrontations referred to in the above case studies. The motto 'pay up and look big' may be apposite – bearing in mind the considerable costs that can be incurred in disputing a guarantee claim and the potential adverse publicity of a disappointed customer telling others. In truth 'hell hath no fury like a disappointed customer'.

Help desks

Introduction

Help desks fulfil similar roles to CALL CENTRES and CARELINES. The essential difference is that whereas a call centre will tend to deal with routine information based requests, and a careline with complaints, concerns and/or compliments, a help desk tends to field more complex queries which may require

- longer calls,
- greater in-depth knowledge of a particular process or product and its capability (and limitations), and
- guidance as to operation of a product.

According to a report in the *Financial Times* of January 1998, help desks have a 'dowdy image' which through increased use of technology and better training is now being dispelled. The *FT* stated that as an industry help desks were worth $460 million in 1997 – a market expected to grow to $1 billion by the year 2000.

Customer support

Many customers who buy complex equipment – such as the computer on which I am writing this book – like to feel that they can master the item on their own. With truly user-friendly equipment and handbooks, this may be so. Where it is not, or where the process develops a fault or they cannot make progress, the provision of a help desk may well enable them to move on without needing to call in a service engineer or expert to help them find the solution. Inevitably this is a valuable benefit to the customer and nowadays few packages of this kind of equipment are sold without the provision of this kind of help desk. There are advantages to both supplier and customer:

- The help desk can record all the queries which may in turn demonstrate a need for attention in particular areas where information is insufficient or even inaccurate. Guidance literature can be progressively updated to address the points raised.

- Provided the desk is properly manned by trained and expert personnel a consistent response can be provided to all callers.

- The desk becomes part of the product and the rapport between customer and those on the desk can develop. Thus not only can questions be answered or queries satisfied, but also the marketing of additional or new products or services to what may be the exact market aimed at, can be undertaken.

- Being able to discuss a problem with someone who knows and understands the difficulty relieves the customer of frustration and can be highly valued by them.

- Sales staff are also supported since they can also use the help desk should they have a query. For field staff working on their own this could provide a boost to morale and confidence when attempting to sell.

- The provision of a help desk may itself help sell more products.

Case study: Help as investment

Nintendo, the computer games specialist, spends over £100,000 a year running its telephone helpline. Despite such a service being more related to providing assistance to players of its games, rather than dealing with more general product queries and complaint, it is possible that were it not for the existence of such lines some of its customers might have relieved their frustration by ceasing to buy its products. If so the expenditure of £100,000 (itself tiny compared with the cost of advertising its products) pales into insignificance.

Internal help desks

The last item under the advantages for a help desk links with the concept of the provision of internal help desks, and some organisations that initially developed the concept 'facing outwards' to deal with customers swiftly realised the value of using the same concept internally since most departments are customers of other departments and may themselves be suppliers to others. Too often mistakes are caused by staff needing to take decisions on matters on which they are unsure simply because there is no one to provide support for them. Ideally their manager should be providing this support as it is one of the five principles of good management – Listen, Encourage, Advise, Delegate and Support (the initial letters forming the mnemonic LEADS) – but if not, then a help desk can at least provide reassurance. An additional advantage of operating internal help desks is that it creates a 'customer' culture – namely, that we are all simultaneously customers and suppliers. This in turn may help create the culture or approach of 'doasyouwouldbedoneby' – implying that if we are treated poorly by a help desk we should know how we as a customer felt the next time we need to act as supplier. Similar advantages to those identified with an external help desk apply although care needs to be taken when problems are identified internally to ensure that they are allowed to be discussed and are not covered up by those responsible. If they are allowed to be covered up then the credibility of the help desk will be threatened. Research carried out by GE Information Services (part of the General Electric Group) indicates that as many as a third of the queries fielded by the Information Technology help desks that they provide for clients are related to the customer not understanding their equipment – which should immediately indicate a need for greater training and better explanatory documentation.

Staffing

The creation of a help desk, whether external or internal, creates an expectation in the mind of the customer – that 'here is a source from which I can obtain advice'. Creating an expectation means that we need to deliver. Failing to deliver having created the expectation is worse than not creating the service in the first place. Thus those that staff help desks need considerable and on-going training in

- the technicalities of the subject matter,

- all new developments as they happen to ensure knowledge is always up to date,

- effective and user-friendly communication skills (not least how to listen actively to ensure the answer they give is to the question asked), and

- how to deal sympathetically and helpfully with the callers.

With complex products or services, or a large range, it is extremely unlikely that one person can assimilate and control the amount of information needed to answer all calls and thus there may need to be an allocation of responsibilities between several personnel. In that case it will be necessary to filter the calls initially and then to route them to whoever is specialising in that particular product. Alternatively it may be necessary to use a pyramid approach whereby as the calls become more and more complex they are moved from the base of the pyramid to its apex (in knowledge terms). With more complex questions it may be necessary for the customer to be called back and if so commitments as to time and so on need to be given and adhered to.

Further, those providing the service at the 'sharp end' (that is, answering the calls) need themselves to be supported and so they may require back up from experts specialising in particular aspects of the products. Such experts should be able to be accessed immediately for external help desks. Such immediate access (which may tend to be expensive) may not be as essential for internal help desks but should be available, say (depending on the product), within the working day. If this is not the case the credibility of the service may be undermined. Providing access to experts regardless of the source of the problem means that the organisation of the whole business needs to be carefully and clearly delineated. If sources of information, reporting structures and so on, are unclear then it is unlikely the system can work effectively.

This does not mean that help desks should simply act as a sounding board or advice provision. As Richard Dodd of Siemens stated in the *FT* report referred to above 'the help-desk [is a] service centre which acts as a one-stop shop for all our customers' requirements. This can vary from simple problem solving to the provision of add-on services. We believe in delivering the complete solution. Service desks will become more and more proactive in identifying and spotting trends for their clients. It will not be all about problem-solving.'

Learning from the data

The questions asked and the answers sourced provide a valuable data bank for the organisation and although answers should be passed to the customer at all speed, a copy of both question and answer should be kept in two forms

- as additional data available to the call desk operator so that if the same question is posed, the data is immediately available, and

- as a means of identifying areas in which attention needs to be given to designing the problems out or providing customer information which should avoid the question needing to be asked.

Hardware

The essential characteristic of a help desk (apart from training the operators) is a high standard of technology providing quality telephony giving clear sound for both parties, an ability to hold and switch calls plus immediate access to the customer and product details via computer screens. Where a proportion of the queries are relatively routine it may be helpful to provide an automatic answering system whereby the caller can access certain information via their own telephone number pad. However, operator access should be provided for those using the automatic system.

Marketing strategy

Where a customer has purchased a product or service and has a problem, the absence of any help to that person when they request it will tend to antagonise them greatly (and research indicates they may tell as many as 20 other potential customers of their bad experience). Conversely providing help (particularly when this is achieved in a specially friendly and positive manner) to a person in need tends to create a rapport between customer and supplier and may well create a bond generating the likelihood of repeat purchases or at least recommendations to others. It is unlikely that there can be a better (or cheaper) form of marketing than by personal recommendation of a satisfied customer. To obtain the best involves total commitment by those involved.

Case study: Smooth motoring

Car manufacturer Vauxhall has operated a customer assistance centre for nearly 10 years. It receives around 30,000 calls per month and deals with around 3,000 items of correspondence. Customer relations manager after sales, David Hyde, comments 'The staff are totally dedicated to a closed loop resolution process ensuring that every enquiry or complaint … is dealt with in a manner that the customer becomes totally enthusiastic about Vauxhall. Teams of consumer affairs consultants provide contact continuously between the hours of 8 a.m. and 6 p.m. and at peak times these hours are extended to meet the demand.'

Postscript

Many car drivers tend to stick to the same manufacturer even though they may vary the model – another example of the human predilection for habits. One leading manufacturer calculated recently that over a lifetime a committed purchaser could spend over £400,000 on a series of models. Providing a help desk merely to assist in the creation of a strong rapport with that kind of a customer, let alone as a means of assisting less committed customers, would appear to be a sound investment.

Internal customers

Introduction

In mentioning the word 'customers' most people will immediately think of an outsider paying for products or services that a supplier generates. However, very often the relationship is cyclical – in that we all tend to be both customers and suppliers in a variety of relationships. In the average organisation any departmental arrangement of services creates many internal relationships of customers and suppliers and most situations where one department is both simultaneously. Research indicates that although the vast proportion of suppliers rate 'customer service' very highly when questioned, in fact reality indicates that in many cases this is little more than a public relations claim and customers' requirements tend not to be given the priority one would expect for the means by which the organisation survives. If this is the case as far as external customers (without whom the organisation cannot survive) are concerned, the situation concerning the regard given internal customers (without whom the organisation cannot operate) may be worse. Sadly in many such organisations this does tend to be the case and corporate hypocrisy comes into play again with claims that 'our employees are our greatest asset' being made in Annual Reports whilst simultaneously employees are treated as little more than payroll numbers.

Praise me, scold me but never ignore me

The above phrase sums up the requirement of many employees. They like being praised – indeed who does not – and will accept being disciplined for non or poor performance, provided it is carried out in a fair way with due respect for the individual. What few employees will accept is being ignored, patronised or overlooked. A supplier's internal customers can have a vital effect on the organisation as can the attitude of the external customers – and the attitude of the former can well create the attitude of the latter. Take away the external customers and the organisation will atrophy. Take away the internal customers (or just their goodwill) and similarly the organisation will fail. In fact of course if the internal customers do not perform, the external customers will not have the opportunity to exercise their choice. There is no organisation yet invented that can achieve anything without the performance of its internal customers. Indeed the best customer care and service can only be provided by those who are themselves customers and understand the way in which most people wish to be treated. External customer care is unlikely to be effective and convincing unless those who provide the service are well-motivated, in tune with their employer's aims, and themselves feel that they are well-treated.

Management

Customer care is concerned with managing the customer–supplier relationship and the customer–product relationship. Equally, internal customer care is concerned with managing the people that can provide these services. Correctly managed they may be able to be enthused and motivated to do their best for the customers and ultimately for the supplier – their employer which again means for themselves. What we need is to ensure that our internal customers are properly managed – or do we? In a number of seminars concerned with management I asked delegates to determine five characteristics of a good manager. After a little prompting and a certain amount of creativity with descriptions we usually managed to assemble the following list

- Listen – as in ACTIVE LISTENING; what was meant was having the time to listen to the words and the perception to realise what lay behind them. Inevitably this will lead to better two-way communication. In a survey by American business research organisation The Conference Board, 80% of employees ranked two-way communication as either very important or important in what they wanted from their work. This requirement was placed second in a list of preference behind 'interesting, challenging work'. Secure employment was ranked fifth.

- Encourage – to be available to give praise when a job was well done and to prompt employees to move forward when sometimes they might lack the confidence to do so. Research indicates that as many as 50% of employees are able to perform at a level one above that at which they are performing. Sadly many such employees rather than being encouraged are actually held back by their so-called managers.

- Advise – to be available to help guide employees through their tasks, explain problems, and so on.

- Delegate – the comment above regarding employees being able to perform at higher levels is bound up with the propensity of the manager to delegate or not (see below).

- Support – which entails being available to assist employees with problems whether work related or not. The provision of support is vital in terms of those manning customer service desks (see JOB ATTRIBUTES).

Quite deliberately the initial letters of these five attributes create the mnemonic LEADS which, it is suggested, is what management should be doing all the time (but which experience indicates it often does not). This widespread lack of commitment to building and leading teams seems strange since only by ensuring that their employees, their team members, do what they need them to do, and do it willingly, is a manager likely to ensure that they achieve the tasks they have been set. In addition it is a truism that when there is a team and good team spirit, performance can be greater; the output of a team can be greater than the sum of the outputs of the individual members – literally Together Everyone Achieves More. As Trevor Bailey, one of England's best test cricket players, said 'good captains [leaders] tend to make good players [employees] rise above themselves'. Praise and encouragement are powerful motivators and are most effective when contributed in person rather than in writing, on a computer screen or via some other impersonal format.

If we want those who report to us to serve our customers well (and this means harnessing the efforts of every employee) then we need

- to acknowledge their achievements – praise as long as it is sincere is an extremely effective means of motivation, with the added benefit that it costs nothing,

- to monitor and demonstrate progress – if we praise progress, when there is no progress, the need for effort is obvious and most people will accept fair encouragement and constructive criticism,

- to share the preferred tasks and the awkward tasks, so that all members of the team take their turn at both,

- to ensure the leader does his/her fair share of any awkward tasks – leading from the front is a powerful motivator,

- to encourage team members to discuss their concerns and problems, and

- to encourage everyone to look for opportunities in problems, in short to think positively.

If all our internal customers are subject to this process their commitment should be considerable and most should demonstrate the same commitment to serving the external customers.

Delegation

Much of the perception of the treatment of internal customers will be concerned with the willingness of the organisation in general and its managers in particular to encourage employees by delegating tasks to them in order that they can develop their skills to the mutual benefit of organisation and employee. In the following checklist are set out guidelines to assist management to bring about an effective delegation.

Checklist: Guidelines for effective delegation

1. Assess (on an ongoing basis) all employees for capability and willingness to assume a greater workload.

2. Establish precisely the duties, responsibilities *and* authority that are to be delegated.

3. Check whether the employee is likely to be able to assume the extra duties delineated immediately or needs training, or a delay before taking over such duties.

4. Delegate only to those able (and willing) to carry out the work, and to accept greater responsibility. This will mean discussing the proposal and the implications of items 1, 2 and 3 above with them to gain their input and agreement.

5. Brief and train the delegate to carry out the work. This may mean providing external training as well as internal support and advice.

6. Advise all involved of the delegation. Everyone concerned should know of the move in order to ensure that any additional responsibility and control is widely recognised.

7. Provide time, support and guidance for the delegate on an ongoing and regular basis so that the employee knows that support is available whilst growing into the role.

8. Avoid any destruction of confidence by undercutting the authority of the employee assuming greater responsibility. In the event of any undercutting of authority the delegation is likely to be ineffective and the employee may be in a worse position than before the proposal was accepted.

9. Regularly review progress and accomplishments – supporting where necessary, bearing in mind that most of us take some time to grow into a new role.

10. Motivate and *never* denigrate.

Empowerment

The modern word for the above approach is empowerment which should not simply be regarded as an effective means of staff motivation. A survey (*1998 Empowerment Audit*) by consultants Bourton (formerly Ingersoll Engineers) discovered that 'empowerment' works financially as well as motivationally. The research indicated that those companies which forsook the traditional type of management which issued orders and expected them to be obeyed without question did not fare as well as those with a more modern outlook and ethos. Those organisations which empowered their employees and encouraged a participative style of management in which employees' views were sought and suggestions acted upon, were twice as likely to be ranked highly on a financial return basis as the others. For example, 43% of top performing companies (in terms of return on capital) scored highly for empowerment.

PIE making

The aim of generating a better team spirit is primarily the creation of a feeling whereby the individual identifies with the whole; a feeling which can only be generated when there is a feeling of mutual trust and understanding – which should be a prime aim of the whole management process. A by-product of identification with the whole and of the creation of mutual trust and understanding, should be a simultaneous creation of a feeling of pride in the endeavour. This is valuable, since not only does it tend to generate real commitment to the organisation and its products, but also employees who are proud of what they and their organisation achieve tend to become the best ambassadors for their product or service. To generate pride, we need to create enthusiasm, and to generate enthusiasm we need to inspire the workforce. One wonders if the Virgin Group of companies would be anywhere near as successful as they are were it not for the charismatic and infectious enthusiasm of their founder, Richard Branson (repeatedly named in countrywide seminars as someone that most delegates regarded as an effective leader).

The relationship between these three factors – pride, inspiration and enthusiasm – is all important for the successful supplier and the successful generating of sound customer relationships and service. Since one tends to generate the other they are best depicted as a circle – that is, a figure without end. It is certainly true that nothing succeeds like success.

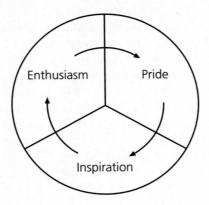

The PIE

Postscript

The role of management should be to help people succeed – and if management realises this and abides by its obligations then internal customers should be well-motivated and confident. If those who deal with external customers are so treated they should be able perform their tasks with enthusiasm and understanding.

Job attributes

Introduction

Inevitably many of the requirements for those charged with the task of dealing with customer queries, concerns and complaints will vary according to the specific requirements of the organisations. Some key attributes however are common to all – but if experience is anything to go by seem relatively rare. In general the attributes which should be common to all revolve around the need for those dealing with customer care to be totally knowledgeable of

- the products, services, and so on, with which their organisation is dealing,
- their organisation's terms, procedures, and policies, and
- the requirements of the customer.

In addition, those who operate best in this area are those able to guess or perceive the motivation of the customer.

The latter requires skills that may be more inherent in the personality of the employee than generated by a training programme although such skills can be developed by training. These personal skills (which are interdependent and tend to overlap) can be summarised as Sincerity, Empathy, Recognition, Vision and Enthusiasm or SERVE – a most apt mnemonic in the circumstances.

Sincerity

'If you can fake sincerity, my son, then you have got it made' runs the advice from an old-hand sales representative to a trainee rep. It may be sound advice since in the customer concerns scenario the customer that believes that those concerns are receiving sincere efforts to assist, will tend to warm to, and feel a rapport with that person which can have the effect of reducing any anger or vexation at the cause of the interface. In no way is this meant to be an encouragement to be insincere. Any suspicion of such an attitude would be counterproductive, it would compound and intensify any aggrieved feeling due to the original problem – annoyance could turn swiftly to TEMPER, as insult would be seen to have been added to injury.

What is necessary is either true sincerity or the appearance of sincerity. Although it is perfectly possible (and should be the aim) for each customer of a small organisation to be treated personally and with sincerity, with an organisation of any size, this may be difficult. The advantage the small organisation has is that those dealing with customers tend to understand the necessity to retain them in order to survive – in his book *Consumer Behaviour* (1997, Prentice Hall) Professor Robert East of Kingston Business School estimates that the cost of obtaining a new customer is five times the cost of keeping an existing one. The larger the organisation, the greater the gap can be between those who understand such a financial equation and those dealing with the problems. Further it is easier to be sincere with a person you know as a customer than one who is only an account number. Nevertheless creating the appearance of sincerity can work with the largest organisations – all that is needed is top level commitment.

Case study: Missed date

The customer had ordered a bouquet of flowers for delivery on St Valentine's Day. The reaction of the operator, when the customer reported their non-arrival on the day, could not have been more sincere. She fully appreciated that their delivery a day late would ruin the effect. But then one tends to expect that reaction from a company like Marks & Spencer, which not only rearranged the delivery but also refunded the full cost.

The suggestion of 'faking sincerity' may appear somewhat inapposite but will certainly be more acceptable for most people than rudeness or indifference. Speaking at the British Psychological Society's annual occupational conference in January 1998, Sandi Mann of the University of Salford indicated that most UK consumers preferred the 'have a nice day' type of customer communication to downright rudeness or indifference. As one American commentator once said 'I would prefer someone to say "have a nice day" however insincerely, to someone saying "sod off" in complete sincerity'. Whilst this may work with external customers it would be unwise to use it internally as the survey disclosed that most people were not tolerant of faking within the workplace. The classic mistake would be to attempt to give praise without sincerity, which, if suspected, will be worse than if nothing had been said.

Empathy

The dictionary defines 'empathy' as 'the power of projecting one's personality into (and so fully comprehending) the object of the contemplation'. The operative word here may be 'so', since it is the act of projection that allows us to comprehend the other side's views more completely. If respondents to customers with concerns have empathy with those voicing those concerns then greater understanding will result and conflict can be averted in many cases. In essence 'empathy' should enable us to see how the other person sees things – and to understand their attitude, motivation and so on. Empathy is most easily evidenced by demonstrating that one has time to listen to another's problems (the approach adopted by caring organisations such as the Samaritans). Thus by taking the trouble to actively listen to and make a note of the concern, that alone, without any further action, may actually be sufficient to 'draw the sting' of the complaint. Then without any corrective action, it may be possible to put a problem into perspective – although it must be the perspective of the customer rather than the organisation. A refusal to accept the terms of the complaint at all merely evidences a complete lack of empathy (as well as sincerity, since inevitably they are linked) and will merely serve to inflame what may already be a contentious issue.

Case study: Listening improves quality

There had been a number of complaints regarding the quality and choice of the food available in the staff restaurant over a number of years. The newly appointed Personnel Manager became aware of these and invited two of the chief protagonists of the complaints to come and see her to discuss the matter.

'I understand you are very concerned about the restaurant.'

'You bet we are – we've been on about the quality and poor choice for ages but no one takes any notice and nothing gets done.'

'I see, well as you know I'm new, so if you can bear repeating all the problems I will certainly consider them and see if we can meet at least some of your complaints. I must first say that I am very concerned about the restaurant since its finances are in my budget and we do not seem to be getting value for the money we are investing.'

The complaining employees outlined the main causes of their concern during a fairly long meeting, and in turn the Personnel Manager set out the problems the company was experiencing with the financing. It was agreed that a Catering Committee should be set up to consider ways and means of improving the situation. Before it convened for the first time, and before any action had been taken regarding the complaints, one of the complainants sought the Personnel Manager to thank her for the improvements that had already been put into operation.

> **Key technique**
>
> Listening constructively, and to some degree sympathetically, to complaints rather than dismissing them out of hand created a situation where it seemed to the employees that improvements had already been effected! Subsequently considerable improvements were made and a regular process of price increases was introduced to bring the subsidy back under control. Even though this raised the costs to the employees, because the initiative had been seized and those affected were involved and 'owned' the situation, the 'reduce the subsidy' policy was accepted without problem. The fact that improvements were also introduced as promised obviously helped later acceptance.

Recognition

'Recognition' or perhaps more accurately 'perception' tends to be more of a personal gift than an attribute that can be learned, basically since it tends to rely on intuition. In this context it is an intuitive recognition of what is going on in the attitude and mind of the other party – in this it could be considered similar to 'empathy' but perhaps goes one stage further. Empathy means relating to, and demonstrating the act of 'relating to', the other party, whereas perception involves discerning motives, objectives and purpose without necessarily making the other party aware that this process of assessment is taking place. Inevitably some perceptions will be incorrect – not least as sometimes the perceiver will not be in possession of all the facts. Thus an essential part of 'perceiving' will depend on the collation of as much information as possible (it should not be overlooked that during an encounter, demonstrating a wish to discover all the information should itself indicate sincerity and empathy).

Truly perceptive people can achieve a high degree of accuracy in recognising and assessing the requirements of those with whom they come into contact – an ideal attribute for dealing with customers with concerns. Experience of previous incidents and reactions can assist but since all people are different the essential ingredient is to keep an open mind.

Vision

As Jonathan Swift said, 'vision is the art of seeing things invisible' and in this context has similar impact to that suggested for recognition or perception. Viewing the interface and the problem through the eyes of the customer is vital for all responsible for customer care. In this the guiding indicator might be an invention of another author – Charles Kingsley – who in *The Water Babies* created the 'loveliest fairy in the world – Mrs Doasyouwouldbedoneby', thereby inferring that treating other people as you would wish yourself to be treated is all important. Obviously the way those customers are to be treated needs to be determined by the organisation first and foremost, but in this as in so much else in caring for customers, the tone of voice, and enthusiasm and willingness to 'sort out the problem' are essential.

Enthusiasm

To some extent this attribute is dealt with in ZELOSO as a summary of all that is needed to deal with customer care with the most positive attitude. However that section emphasises the need for organisations to be enthusiastic in their corporate commitment to customer care whereas here we are concerned to try to ensure that those actually interfacing with customers are enthusiastic. Like the need to evince sincerity on an ongoing basis this can be difficult to achieve but the customer care phone operator, or customer service desk assistant, who greets the next client as the 47th of the day with a tired and resigned 'Yes?' (rather than an enthusiastic 'Good afternoon, sir, I'm John, how can I help you?', as if the caller was the first, and most important, caller of the day), is creating a negative reaction in the customer that can only bode poorly for the organisation. The caller is an existing customer – if we fail to retain him it will cost five times as much to find a replacement customer. It is worth the investment of an enthusiastic operator to try to avoid such a cost. Operators might also be reminded that repeat customers account for 90% of an organisation's profits.

It can be difficult to sound sincere with the 47th concerned customer – but it is essential that this should be attempted and, at least in the majority of instances, achieved. Similarly those responsible need to try and pitch the tone of their voice with sincerity to avoid sounding like a 'tape-recorded' and totally disinterested voice. Standard phrases need to be said with enthusiasm and meant with sincerity.

Personal problems

Underlying all the above requirements is perhaps the need for those who field customer concerns and seek to provide customer care to have patience and tolerance. Inevitably this can be difficult should the person themselves be suffering from problems of their own. Whilst not impossible it will require considerable strength of character to deal patiently with what are seen as (and, perhaps by comparison are) relatively minor and unimportant problems of customers when facing a personal crisis or trauma. It is estimated that around 40% of employees are experiencing personal problems at any one time. Of these around 25% (thus 10% of the total) will be experiencing serious problems – serious sickness, bereavement, marital or partnership difficulties, and so on. The thought that at any one time around 10% of the employees attempting to deal with a disappointed but otherwise reasonable customer (let alone someone determined to be awkward) could themselves be under considerable strain and stress should give those responsible food for thought. Those dealing with customer interface should be encouraged to advise their employer if they have problems. Ideally confidential counselling should be provided and the employee moved to work which potentially poses less severe problems.

Postscript

In organising a seminar on Customer Care in early 1998, the Institute of Directors stated that 'in a typical medium sized company, bad customer service can result in lost revenues of £1.8 billion over five years and lost profit of £267 million'. Those who feel that investing in finding, training and supporting the right people to man their customer service desks thereby helping retain customers rather than lose them, might be somewhat re-assured that the inevitable costs of such actions could have a considerable pay back.

Keeping promises

Introduction

Since the earliest days of trade, suppliers have extolled the virtues of their products and/or services to prospective customers. This may be acceptable even, in some cases, to the extent of suppressing minor adverse factors. However since the earliest itinerant mendicant marketed an unusual coloured liquid as the cure-all 'elixir of life', there has been a tendency to oversell or overhype products. In former days, the likelihood of the supplier facing retribution from customers disappointed that the claims made for the product have not been fulfilled might have been slight. Nowadays not only are most purveyors traceable and thus able to be made accountable, but also legislation, publicity and public opinion can be marshalled to effect considerable sanctions against such flights of fancy. Nevertheless 'overhyping' still takes place as does the almost unintentional practice of creating expectations or inferring promises which cannot be substantiated. Further, consumers are increasingly knowledgeable about their rights and able and willing to attempt to enforce such rights – in short they expect the promises made which encouraged them to part with their money to be honoured.

Raising expectations

In the case study recounted in NEGOTIATION much of the problem that had to be dealt with by the staff on the shopfloor was caused by the telephonist's remark that the item could be replaced. Immediately such a statement was made, it raised an expectation in the mind of the customer who had been prepared to return the item to the manufacturer himself. Had she stated the policy was to ensure the item was repaired, no such expectation would have been raised. In that case the customer might still have had a justifiable argument that whilst the item was being repaired he should be loaned a replacement but he would not have been faced with a flat contradiction of what had seemed to him to be an implied promise and commitment to replace. There the supplier made the situation worse for themselves by breaking their own promise.

Case study: Expensive breach of contract

One of the main reasons for the householders taking out a service contract with a supplier was the promise which headed the service agreement: '48 hour breakdown service – attendance in evenings and/or at weekends if required'.

Both partners being at business during the day, the offer of evening or weekend attendance was vitally important and they signed up. The appliance broke down on Wednesday, a call was made on Thursday and an offer of a Tuesday morning attendance was made.

'But that's five days away – you state 48 hour attendance.'

'Yes but we don't count the day you ring or the day of the visit – or Saturday or Sunday.' (**Clang 1**)

'But it doesn't say that here – in fact it says that evening and/or weekend attendance is offered if required.'

'Oh we stopped that. We found out it was too expensive – everyone wanted weekend attendance and our engineers didn't have much to do during the week.' (**Clang 2**)

The ensuing dispute was also expensive for the supplier who eventually had to refund the entire subscription for the original service, grant a free subscription to the reduced service and contribute £200 to the costs of the customers – all payments in respect of broken promises.

Reviewing the clangers

1. This may be understandable but to most reasonable people 48 hours means two days, and two days from Thursday is Saturday. If this is not what is meant then the supplier not only has an obligation to state that, but also by not stating it creates circumstances which will inevitably lead to argument and disillusionment at the failure to meet the expectation raised.

2. Customers are not mind readers – they are parties to contracts which one party cannot unilaterally change. If changes are required then there is an obligation to notify the other party and to give them an opportunity to terminate the contract since what is now on offer is not what they accepted in the first place.

The irony in this example is that the supplier had a clear opportunity to make money. Increasingly our society requires both partners in the relationship to work full-time, meaning that there is an increased pressure for weekend and evening attendance by any sort of home service provider.

If that is what the customers need then that is what they should get. The reasonable response from the supplier is that it will be more expensive to provide such a service and to state the cost. If these alternatives are provided, the essential ingredient – customer choice – is available. The fact that such choice has a price tag is unarguable.

Case study: No exit

The blurb from the direct mail retailer trumpeted long and wide about its new computerised customer service system which would enable customers to phone orders on a 24-hour basis.

One month the customer received an indication that a payment on his behalf had been refused by the bank. Since there was no reason for this he used the computerised system to try to discover the problem. However, although the system had the capacity to check orders, to take and cancel orders, to check balances due and so forth, there was no capacity that would enable the customer to pose questions, leave a message or simply speak to a human being.

Accordingly he wrote to the company not only posing the question but pointing out that the new much vaunted customer service system had a number of flaws that needed attention. He received no reply. So disillusioned was he with this non-service that he used the vaunted computerised service once more – to cancel his membership.

Hype not

'Hype' is often used as a description of marketing blurbs or sales brochures without realising its true meaning. It is an abbreviation of the word 'hyperbole' which means 'an exaggerated statement not meant to be taken literally'. Given such a definition it is no exaggeration to suggest that 'hype' should play no part whatever in the marketing of goods or services. It is because the inclusion of hype can lead to the creation of so many problems in customer care that the suggestion is made elsewhere in this book that there should be a lively interface between marketing, public relations and customer care departments.

Commitment

In endeavouring to provide a good customer care strategy, suppliers need to apply strict rules regarding descriptions of products and services – in short what is promised should be supportable. Their watchword should be 'if we cannot support a statement, don't make it'. Thus there is little point in affirming in the Aims or Mission Statement of the organisation that 'at all times customers come first and we will always ensure they are provided with prompt attention, complete courtesy and will always be satisfied', if the phone in the customer care department is never answered in under 3 minutes, if the treatment that callers receive is offhand and casual and that a defensive attitude is always assumed when complaints or concerns are notified.

Commitments are relatively easy to stipulate – particularly by those who are far removed from the sharp end dealing. If the Board creates and adopts rules, it needs to ensure that those rules and procedures backing them are adhered to and that generally everyone does comply with the principles they have espoused. Gaining adherence may be far more difficult to ensure, particularly if the product or service is sold by those whose income is dependent upon their sales figures. A recent European survey suggested that there was a fairly widespread belief that British salespeople will say anything to obtain an order and there is no doubt there are numerous examples of this problem. The scandal of the marketing and selling of personal pensions in the late 1980s and early 1990s demonstrates that even in the financial services sector, salespeople were not immune from overhyping and overselling their product – or of selling plainly inappropriate products to some customers. Indeed it is interesting to note that employees of Marks & Spencer (regarded as one of the most reputable and dependable traders in the UK – a reputation which has taken years to build) who sell their financial services products are paid salaries only – there is no commission and hence far less pressure to sell an inappropriate package to a consumer.

Where sales are being made to corporate clients rather than consumers it may be easier to control the 'promises' made as very often the deal will be evidenced by a contract. The advantage of a contract is that the terms can be delineated – and may even be specially agreed between the parties. The disadvantage is that agreeing the terms may take considerable time and indeed a 'contract terms war' may develop during which both sides try to ensure that their terms control the contract to the exclusion of those of the other party – but at least most of the factors that can affect the contract should be explored.

Glossary

When parties are agreeing a contract it may be beneficial to develop a glossary so that words used are defined and/or explained and neither party can later suggest that they were disadvantaged because they didn't understand the meaning the other gave to such words. Whilst providing a glossary may not be applicable in contracting with consumers, legislation (Unfair Terms in Consumer Contracts Regulations 1994) now requires that all terms in such contracts must be in plain English and certain (administrative) terms must in addition be 'fair'. This at least should ensure that those that comply make their terms clear which itself could lead to checks being made that promises that cannot be substantiated are not being implied.

Case study: No meeting of minds

Two parties to a proposed agreement were discussing their relative viewpoints regarding what they wanted to achieve. One was an old timer (OT), the other an ambitious go-getter (AGG).

AGG: Tell me, Ted, where are you coming from?

OT: Eh?

AGG: Well what's your remit?

OT: Eh?

AGG: What are your terms of reference?

OT: Eh?

AGG: What are you trying to achieve here?

OT (relieved): Oh that's what you mean – why didn't you say so… ?

What may be crystal clear to us, can be so much gobbledegook to others.

Creating hostages to fortune

This is not meant to imply that promises should never be given but that the wise will try to avoid making themselves hostages to fortune. Rarely is everything entirely under one's own control – there are usually a number of factors over which we may have no control. However your customer has only one interface – you. The customer is not interested that your supplier has had a fire and won't deliver to you until tomorrow, or that your computer is down and the expert can't get there until later, or whatever – as far as the customer is concerned you said a delivery would be made at such and such a time and that time has passed.

Postscript

Murphy's first law states that 'if it can go wrong it will', whilst his second law states that 'if it can't go wrong it will'. Meanwhile O'Reilly also has a law which states that Murphy is an optimist! The salutary lessons:

- promise to deliver only what you are certain you can deliver, and
- leave some leeway so that you have room to manoeuvre.

When drafting weekly paid contracts of employment I always advise clients to state 'payment will be made each week by Friday'. One said 'Why not put "on Thursday" since we always pay on Thursday'. I replied that it simply gave a little leeway in case something went wrong. A few months later their computer had a glitch, the payroll could not be generated on Thursday but by working throughout the night they managed to work everything out manually by the Friday. Some employees were inconvenienced but there could be no real come back since the contracts said 'by Friday'.

Loyalty

Introduction

Research indicates that it costs five times as much to source a replacement customer as it does to retain an existing one. The Institute of Directors stated in early 1998 that 90% of the average UK company's profits are derived from repeat business – that is from existing customers 'repeat buying'. Inevitably customers will only buy again if they are satisfied – with the quality, price, service or whatever they received first time around. This does not mean that customers need perfection in order to 'repeat buy'. Provided any problems are dealt with to their satisfaction (that is, swiftly, without dispute and positively), over 80% of customers who have suffered from the effects of mistakes are still likely to 'repeat buy'. Conversely one must assume that if mistakes are not rectified to the satisfaction of such customers, there is a danger that not only will they not 'repeat buy' but also that they could spread disaffection amongst a number (up to 20) of other potential (or existing) purchasers. It would seem logical as well as being economically sound to try to ensure the loyalty of as many as possible of one's customers – and with the profits derived therefrom, invest in extending the customer base.

The ties that bind

In the boom years of the 1980s attention was paid by relatively few to the concept of customer loyalty – there was little perceived necessity since customer demand was high. The recession of the early 1990s (which some commentators are suggesting could be repeated around the turn of the century) brought about a much reduced level of demand in the UK – so reduced indeed it has been estimated that the previous levels of retail trade are not likely to be regained until the first decade of the twenty-first century. With such a scenario it should be obvious that 'hanging on' to the existing customer base is all important – as both a defensive and offensive strategy. Innumerable retail and other organisations have introduced loyalty cards and schemes which reward the customers that 'stick with them'. In many ways this seems to emulate

- the concept of trading stamps in the 1960s and 1970s when eventually so many organisations were offering them that their point in attracting trade to a particular client was lost, or

- the 'fuel wars' of the same period when virtually every garage was offering wine glasses or tokens, with virtually the same result.

Both these and the current clutch of loyalty cards work on the basis of encouraging purchases at that rather than another unit thus transferring demand from one to another organisation. In the current climate when consumers are actively seeking 'value for money' some means of retaining loyalty may be essential. However, value involves not only price and free gifts but also service and quality.

Case study: Rewarding service

The customer had used the same garage for servicing and repairs for over 20 years. One Christmas he had a problem with the windscreen wipers and rang the garage which, since he needed the car for a business trip, needed to be solved immediately. He rang the garage but received a somewhat offhand reply. He rang the service department of another local garage. Despite it being the first day back after the Christmas break the second garage offered to inspect the problem the same day, whilst warning the customer that if serious damage had occurred they could not effect the repair for eight days. On arrival at the garage a mechanic was pulled off another job to inspect the problem and within five minutes had eradicated it. The garage would not accept any payment. The customer decided to change his servicing garage.

Investing for future sales

Writing in the *Harvard Business Review* in early 1993, Frederick Reichheld, Director of Consultancy at Bain & Company, stated 'customer loyalty appears to be the only way to achieve sustainably superior profits'. Robert LaBant, Senior Vice-President (Sales and Marketing) of IBM North America, commented that 'every percentage point in customer satisfaction scores translates into a gain (or a loss) of $500 million in sales over 5 years'. $100 million each year is a great deal of extra sales value to gain – and a horrible amount to lose – so encouraging loyalty is worth a great deal of effort but requires customer-friendly or customer-value policies and procedures emanating from the Board.

However, plans to try to 'buy' loyalty need careful consideration not just in purpose, but above all in terms of their practicality and a full appreciation of what they entail.

Case study: Losers – and winners

In the mid-1990s household electrical manufacturer Hoover made headline news following the offer of (at least as it appeared to most customers) free flights if a consumer purchased a product. The subsequent high profile media attention when consumers demanded the company honour its promises, meant that the company was forced to do so – but at considerable expense.

Boots offered a voucher for school computers with every £5 spent. This was deemed by many customers to be too poor an exchange value and many were discarded – thus not reaching the schools collecting them. The schools complained since the numbers of vouchers they collected were often insufficient to allow them to obtain the equipment and Boots were forced to double the value of the vouchers to extricate the company whilst preserving some prestige.

Conversely the Air Miles campaign which has been adopted by many retailers, and which in many ways matches the Green Shield stamps idea, has been widely accepted by UK consumers. It is estimated that 10% of the UK population collect Air Miles although it must be queried whether, with such a large number of outlets providing them, their availability can guarantee any real loyalty to a particular outlet.

Twenty-first century consumers

The days when loyalty could be relied upon as an assured 'continuing customer base' are no longer in being for most organisations. Price and service tend now to be king. If supplier B is now perceived to provide better value (in the widest sense of the word) then the customer may well decide to give their custom to B rather than A, previously their 'favoured supplier'. The statistics quoted in FINANCIAL ASPECTS regarding the preparedness of customers to churn their suppliers and the casual, indifferent way many are treated by suppliers make sobering reading particularly when it is realised that 35% of dissatisfied customers who voted with their feet could have been retained as customers if only an apology had been offered.

Incredibly it seems that many suppliers do not understand that customer loyalty is dependent not just on quality and price but also on meeting commitments previously given or inferred.

Case study: What price service?

The Director of a small consultancy business used two local businesses –
also relatively small – a business supplies organisation and a taxi service.
Repeatedly via mail and telephone he received offers of lower price
stationery and business supplies and lower journey charges. He always
rejected these and when this was queried his reply was that the businesses
he currently patronised had given him good service over the years – they
had a good working relationship and if there were ever any difficulties the
personal aspect of the relationships meant there was personal service to
assist.

On contemplating buying a small computer, the price in a high street chain
store was quoted as £35 more than the best price offered by the business
supplies organisation. Despite this he still bought from the small business
supplies organisation commenting – 'he needs my business more than the
high street store needs my business – if something goes wrong, who am I
likely to obtain better service from?'

Snowballing

The point the Director made in the above case study of the relative value of
the offered trade is enhanced when one considers the effect of repeat
business. What would be a one-off purchase to the high street store would
be one in a series of orders for the business suppliers. It is well worth
looking after (even taking a small loss on an occasional order) a regular
customer since repeat orders do tend to mount up. This concept of the
continuum of order placing needs to be fully appreciated by those handling
consumer relations. Carl Sewell is well-known as both an exponent of the
need for sound consumer relations (he co-wrote *The Golden Rules of Customer
Care*, Business Books) and for running a Cadillac dealership in Texas. He
commented, 'Once you realise that a sale is not a one-off transaction then
it makes sense to keep the customer happy'. Sewell calculates that even
though each sale or service may be relatively small in value over a lifetime
a customer could spend over $330,000. If one regards the customer as a
$330,000 customer rather than a (this time) $99 customer it tends to put
things in a different perspective. Similarly in the case of the two small UK
businesses, although each order placed by the consultancy was worth only
an average of £300, with 9 or 10 orders a year, in 10 years of business the
business supplies organisation had received around £30,000 worth of
orders.

Whilst loyalty cards have the advantage of apparently offering the loyal
customers a 'bonus' or free gift, usually once predetermined levels of

expenditure have been attained (although whether there is a real 'bonus' must be questionable since ultimately the customer must pay for everything), perhaps their underlying value will be the information they will provide on shopping patterns and preferences of customers. If the sponsoring organisations can determine exactly what is preferred by customers it may be able to slant its business in a way that helps retain the customer base and encourages repeat business. Rapport of supply and demand will then be achieved which in turn can only assist the development and cultivation of customer loyalty. The phrase 'I am committed to this store because it provides exactly what I want' is the one such organisations wish to hear, rather than 'I shop at this store because it is convenient (or cheap or gives me "free" gifts)'. Passing trade can be valuable but there is always a danger that trade will literally pass rather than shop.

Soft focus

The above is perhaps somewhat hard-nosed in that it concentrates mainly on the cash effects. However, inherent in the foregoing are the values of developing what we can call the 'soft' skills – quality and service. No matter how valuable a discount or keen a price, if the service is unacceptable to the customer, ultimately many may decide to take their custom elsewhere. If the only tie is 'price' this can work effectively for a time, but should another supplier become available at roughly the same price there may then be nothing left which can retain their custom. Customers are not always logical.

The customer is always right

This Rule 1 catchphrase (and its alternative Rule 2 – 'if the customer is wrong see Rule 1') is mentioned elsewhere but nowhere does it have more significance than in attempting to encourage customer loyalty. If the customer has evinced a concern or experienced a problem, properly applied COMPLAINT CONVERSION can engender loyalty where mere insistence on terms or ignoring the second half of Rule 2 can only encourage a dispute following which, regardless of who wins, future loyalty may be jeopardised.

Case study: Rule 2 applies

In *Customer Service for Dummies* (IDG Books), Karen Leland and Keith Bailey refer to an incident in Hong Kong where a businessman opening a new office was undercharged by $4,500 when settling his hotel bill. He claimed his expenses from his employer before the mistake was realised and understandably was considerably embarrassed (since he felt his company might not wish to entertain a second 'balancing charge') when the hotel contacted him and attempted to levy the missing amount. Eventually they asked him what he wanted them to do. He replied 'forget it' and to their credit they did. Their adherence to Rule 2 paid off however when the businessman opened his company's new office and proceeded to use the hotel for in excess of $100,000 repeat business. Effectively they bought some very valuable ongoing loyalty.

Postscript

In the last case study, the hotel could have insisted on payment of the missing amount – after all it was a considerable sum. No doubt there would have ensued a potentially awkward confrontation perhaps involving lawyers on both sides. Almost inevitably the hotel would have needed to have negotiated on the sum outstanding and in addition would bear the time and money cost of the argument. Far better to accept the effect of their own mistake and to invest in what they might hope for as future trade.

Market research

Introduction

Where separate disciplines exist within an organisation consideration should be given to linking the customer care and public relations (and/or marketing) operations to ensure that the latter, responsible for promoting the public image of the organisation and/or its products, have a 'hands on' feel for the problems encountered at the sharp end – particularly any disappointed expectations. In a similar way there should be at least a link between the responsibilities of the market research department and the customer care facility. Indeed if the supplier encourages its customers to contact it (using freephone CARELINES, positive complaints procedures and so on) in many ways their comments can become some of the most valuable market research available to the supplier. The following provides an outline guide to the subject from the viewpoint of customer care only. The attention of the reader is drawn to Patrick Forsyth's book in this series, *One Stop Marketing*, which provides more detail on the development and use of market research.

Missing opportunities

Many suppliers complain that they simply cannot afford market research, completely overlooking the fact that if the customer care system is set up properly (namely, so that customers are encouraged to convey their views to the supplier and such views are listened to actively and objectively) a mass of information (freely given for the most part) can be made available to those required to take marketing decisions. Unfortunately those that receive the messages are often not of sufficient seniority to appreciate the import of the data being provided and if there is no procedure to enable the data to be captured for later review the value of the encounter is lost. For this reason it may be helpful, if, as well as ensuring details of all problems are recorded, senior personnel occasionally sit in with those fielding such calls in order to gain a first-hand view of the encounters and the messages underlying them.

Case study: Missed

The customer had a legitimate complaint of an ongoing nature against a building society/bank. As part of an ongoing strategy she was sent a customer service questionnaire, but preferring to lodge a complaint in a more focused and formal way she wrote to the Chief Executive. No reply emanated from that dignitary, although a reply which failed to deal satisfactorily with any of the problems raised was received from a junior supervisor. The customer tried again to gain some feedback from the Chief Executive but again the approach was rebuffed with the excuse that the CE was 'far too busy with customer groups' to bother with individual customers! This seems a wonderful missed opportunity – a captive customer prepared, very enthusiastic and committed to the subject, having written a letter rather than just ticked boxes in a questionnaire, to discuss real concerns, problems and opportunities.

Structured market research

Market research exists to assist the supplier and their advisers

- discovering the size and composition of the market for a particular product,

- checking the demand for and adherence to competitive products and the relationship with own product,

- monitoring the effectiveness of sales promotion techniques and campaigns, and

- testing market reaction to new ideas.

The active nature of the verbs used to introduce the suggested key purposes seek to underline the need for such activities to be ongoing. The above four main objectives can be redefined into a number of subsidiary aims and purposes.

Case study: The benefits

Linda Galvin, Field Director of Research Services Ltd (contact 0181 861 8015), one of the top six UK market research companies, states that suppliers use market research interviews and questionnaires for several reasons, including

---

1. where a launch of a new product is envisaged – to gauge market potential and acceptability,

2. to gauge the positioning/required appeal of a new product,

3. to assess competitive standards where there are alternative products,

4. to check the recognition and perception of the image of a product or service,

5. to assess the perceptions of the service on offer,

6. to determine whether a product (existing or prospective) has a competitive edge,

7. to check whether the consumer feels they have received value for money (and if not why not),

8. to query and identify the reason(s) for a consumer buying an alternative product,

9. to check the penetration and/or success of an advertising or promotional campaign, and

10. to determine whether a promotion has reached and/or is likely to attract the target audience.

RSL's computerised Capibus project allows subscriber clients to be given instant access to the views of the man and woman in the street (quite literally as interviews of respondents specified in terms of age, sex, socioeconomic factors, are conducted in the street) about their products, services, value and so on. Such data can be captured weekly if required enabling suppliers to monitor trends and developments and, if necessary to react very quickly thereto, not least since the interviewers' computers are modem linked to RSL's central computer system. Thus the results of the research can be made available within hours of the interviews taking place.

Creating the right image

To avoid complacency, which can lead to ARROGANCE, suppliers should be anxious to know how the marketplace in general, and consumers in particular, view them and their products on an ongoing basis. By gaining feedback alterations can be made so that the created image is the required image. On occasions, however, even the best intentions and images can create problems.

Case study: Right ad in the right place?

In a run down and inner city area with poor housing and exceptionally high unemployment, an advert for personal savings appeared featuring an idyllic country cottage over the caption containing a message to the effect that if people saved with the company they could retire to such a cottage. The advertisement remained in pristine condition for about two hours before graffiti reading 'we should be so lucky' was added to it.

Secret testers

Another form of market research can be conducted by employing a supplier's own employees (or an outside body) to pretend to be a customer in order to check the service, attitude and procedure provided. Very often the main purpose is to check on cash handling procedures but all aspects of the service being provided can be investigated from the viewpoint of the customer. This is particularly important as far as public sector bodies are concerned where quality management, because of the size of the undertaking, may be spread more thinly. During the final stages of preparing this book, I had to telephone four public bodies – the Inland Revenue, the Department of Social Security (two offices), and the Probate Registry. In most cases I had to dial two or three times, no one answered the phone in under a minute and in one case it took over five minutes before anyone deigned to pick up a phone.

In addition, senior staff of many retail chains make random and unexpected visits to stores – sometimes finding surprising results.

Case study: Caught you!

The director was making a random visit to a series of shops operated by his company. In one he found that certain products seemed very overstocked. Subsequent checking by field staff discovered a fiddle in operation whereby the manager was buying stolen goods and displaying them in the shop and then pocketing the money thereby generated.

Not only do such random visits provide a means of spotting such activities, but also the visits can act as a deterrent. In addition it provides senior staff with an insight into sharp end activity both of their own staff – and of customers.

Top management commitment

In this as in so many other areas what is needed is top management commitment. If senior management insist that

- customers are listened to when they talk and especially when they complain,

- there is constant checking of the image and appeal of the organisation and its products in the marketplace,

- the comparison of the service and/or products provided is constantly compared with market leaders (or the perceived differential with the next product is maintained or increased and so on

then service to the customer and subsequent care are assured. If such top management commitment (sincere and consistent) is not present the service depends upon the individual attitude (good or bad) of individuals down the chain.

Case study: Remembering the customer

AMP is the world's largest maker of electrical connectors – essential components of most items of electrical equipment. When the company holds planning and management meetings, as well as the human delegates in attendance a cardboard cut-out of a person is propped into a chair. The cut-out represents the customer and if ever the meeting runs into a stalemate or dispute, the cut-out comes into its own and the meeting is invited to consider 'what would the customer say?'. The company maintains that this is an effective way of reminding those who need to take decisions, just whose interests need to be placed foremost.

Postscript

Much of the thrust of market research is to endeavour to discover what customers think. However, to some extent the astute supplier may be able to condition (even manipulate) such thinking – particularly with a new product that has certain characteristics not previously available. Experienced suppliers will already have a sound idea of what the market likes and wants and in many ways the research may actually be, at least in part, a defence mechanism to ensure that the thoughts, hunches and beliefs of the supplier are confirmed. The one essential is an open mind since some products that had the total commitment of the supplier have been flops, and some where the supplier and the market research indicated success have been failures (see the New Coke case study in CARELINES). It could be said that there are three essentials in conducting market research – check, check and check again (and a fourth: listen to the customers actively).

Negotiation

Introduction

Negotiation is a skill which we each start using when very young. The baby soon learns that when it cries there will be a reaction of a cuddle, warmth, or food – attention of some kind. Unfortunately such simplistic 'prompt and response' techniques work for a relatively short period and may, even at that age, if used too often have a reaction completely the opposite of what we require! Unfortunately this is true in later life – whilst books may counsel those making complaints to be reasonable and measured in tone, since this may work more effectively than the baby's scream, in many cases such reasonableness may be exploited and taken for granted. When this occurs some complainants may go away (not necessarily satisfied) – others may resort to the equivalent of the baby's scream and negotiation in such a scenario may be reduced to the survival of the most strong-willed as opinions on both sides become more entrenched.

In dealing with customers and trying to develop positive customer care, organisations are essentially negotiating with their customers. There is an understandable temptation to 'see' customers as a homogeneous mass ('our customer base') but this is one thing they are not – customers are individual people (or, if corporate bodies, are represented by individuals) and as such, customer care and negotiation is all about understanding people, their motivations, their goals and their pressures. Sadly there are no rules that can guarantee success in dealing with these individuals – what will work for one may fail another – and perhaps the most important rule worth remembering in negotiating with customers is to **treat each case afresh despite superficial similarities**. Those who try to force individuals into categories, and treat them accordingly, may create more problems than they solve.

Preparation

Like any other encounter in negotiating we need to consider what it is we are trying to do in order to maximise our chances of a successful outcome and minimise our risks of failure. However 'outcome' and 'failure' are somewhat emotive words and need to be carefully determined and delineated.

In theory we should

- understand what we are about. For the supplier this means fielding a problem and (assuming this is the strategy) attempting to convert a problem into a solution satisfactory to both sides. This means we need to determine our desired result. Our short-term response may be to 'get this complainer off my back' – although if this is really the attitude to its customers which are its lifeblood (which incredibly seems to be the case in many of the case studies recounted in this book), then our organisation may not have the luxury of developing a long-term response. Ideally the desired result should be: 'we (as well as our customer) have a problem here, we need to deal with this problem and obtain benefit from the encounter by determining what we can learn from it'.

- prepare our case. For the customer this will entail putting forward certain facts supporting their complaint or problem; for the organisation this will entail having details of the specification of the product, what it has said it will (and will not) do, details of changes to the product (to ensure both parties are discussing the same model and its characteristics) and so on.

- listen to what the other party is saying. In this the onus is very much on the supplier to listen carefully to the complaint. Too often an answer is provided to a comment or question that has not been put simply because the listener has not listened carefully enough to the point being made. In some cases the point will not be made clearly and again the onus is on the supplier to attempt to discover the facts. This will entail asking open questions.

In practice the steps set out in the following checklist may be helpful.

Checklist: Negotiation principles

1. Establish all the facts in order to arrive at an initial view – listen carefully and non-judgementally to the comments. Ask questions that will define the problem and the customer's requirements.

2. Try to determine exactly what is the other party's view.

3. Accept there are two sides to every story and that the other party may hold different views even for apparently illogical reasons.

4. Research the background of the other party and endeavour to assess their manner of approach. Having access to customer records can be advantageous. If the person is a regular customer and this is the first incidence of complaint, the manner of approach may be somewhat different to a regular customer who has a record of constant complaint.

5. Give weight and credence to the views of the other side. Dismissing their views out of hand is likely to provoke a negative backlash. Giving serious credence to the other's views and comments, used with discretion, can be very compelling.

6. Sublimate your own prime preferences to achieve consensus and assess whether there is a substitutional solution acceptable to both. Such 'British compromises' at least may have the advantage of allowing things to progress.

7. Try to make constant movements towards the desired result, ensuring that a flexible approach is adopted and that an entrenched position does not close off possible progress towards the ideal or substitutional end.

8. Be ready to compromise, it may not be ideal but at least it may enable progress to continue.

BATNA

The BATNA acronym stands for 'best alternative to a negotiated settlement' and reflects the need to be flexible. Often in negotiation a situation develops where the supplier, despite feeling the customer may not have as strong a case as they believe, realises that despite negotiation there is no alternative but to concede. In fact it may be that despite needing to agree to demands in the short-term, there is a longer-term advantage that could be derived.

Case study: Giving in gracefully

The customer had bought an electrical appliance which had proved to be erratically faulty. On telephoning the store, he was told that should he bring the appliance back, it would be replaced. On taking it to the store, however, and informing an assistant of this arrangement, the assistant dealt the item two or three hefty slaps with his hand and indicated that if the customer left it, it would be repaired – a process which would take some weeks. (**Clang 1**)

The customer replied that was not what he had been promised on the phone the day before and, having seen his electrical purchase dealt with in such a way he was not at all happy about having it repaired by the store! Indeed since the fault was erratic he failed to see the point of the assistant's action. (**Clang 2**)

He asked to see the Manager, but instead a Supervisor was called:

'Good morning, sir, what seems to be the problem?'

'Basically this product is only a month old and is intermittently faulty. I rang to find out what I should do – return it direct to the manufacturer or to you – and was told to bring it in and you would replace it. Your assistant hit it several times and told me it can be repaired which would take some weeks. I find this entirely unsatisfactory.'

'Well that is our policy, sir.'

'But it is not what it says on your guarantee – it says here you will replace any items found to be faulty within three months of purchase.'

'I am afraid that is not our current guarantee, sir.' (**Clang 3**)

'But it's the one you supplied with this product – it says here, under your company's name, that you will replace. I was told on the phone you would replace and I have brought it in – making a special 20-mile journey – to arrange that replacement.'

'I see – could I show that guarantee to the Manager, sir?'

The Supervisor took the guarantee and went to see the Manager – not returning for 10 minutes.

'I am sorry, sir, the Manager is not around and I can't find anyone to give me a decision.' (**Clang 4**)

'With all due respect that is not my fault – I have made a special trip here, following phoning you for advice yesterday. I must insist you replace this faulty item, or I will have to take this matter up with the Trading Standards Officer and, since I am a shareholder, with your Board of Directors.'

'Can I try again to see if I can contact the Manager.' (**Clang 5**)

Key techniques

1. This encounter took place on the shop floor surrounded by customers, several of whom not only saw the item being manhandled by the assistant which was hardly a good recommendation for the way the store treated its products, but then hung around to hear the rest of the event, in one or two cases giving moral and very vocal support to the customer.

2. The customer understood – and had explained – that the purpose of his visit was to gain a replacement (see KEEPING PROMISES) not to have the item repaired (and thereby lose its use for some weeks).

3. Whilst a swift solution to the situation could have worked, indeed could have been good public relations for the onlookers, it might have been better for the Supervisor to have tried to move the encounter to a more private place. By raising his voice the customer could involve other customers in the dialogue and create additional pressure on the store staff.

    Further this is another example of the need to get the TERMS of business right:

    • had the correct guarantee been provided, the case of the customer would have been severely weakened, whilst

    • had the telephonist given the correct advice (and thereby not raised expectations) the encounter might either have been avoided or been far less demanding and confrontational.

4. You can cover a great deal of a relatively small store in 10 minutes and it defies belief that it took all this time to find that the Manager was not around.

5. Whilst it is difficult to judge whether the Supervisor had made the decision on her own, or whether management reversed its instructions to her, and whether it was just coincidence that the customer had announced that he was a shareholder or not, the customer achieved his desired result. The same can hardly be said for the retailer – the hiatus was witnessed by several customers and there was potential damage to the reputation of this national chain. The patience and professionalism of the Supervisor was its one saving grace.

Ultimately there must have been a realisation that regardless of the strength of the customer's case there was no way in which negotiation was going to achieve a solution satisfactory to the customer other than replacement. In the circumstances the store saved face (and perhaps went some way to preserving its reputation) in the eyes of the customer and those others in earshot by replacing the item.

Postscript

The strategies and tactics that can be adopted in a process of negotiation are addressed more fully in *One Stop Negotiation* (Martin and Wyborn, ICSA Publishing, 1997). Here it was only the considerable pressure exerted by the customer that forced a reasonable response. This was despite the fact that their telephonist had to some extent pre-empted their scope for alternative actions. Had such an indication not been given and the assistant been trained in dealing with such a situation, a swift recovery could have taken place when the customer pointed out that if it was sent away for repair the store should offer a replacement for use in the meantime. The customer might have responded by pointing out that he would still have to drive 20 miles to exchange the items when the original was returned repaired but this problem could have been negotiated away with the offer of a voucher to cover the petrol cost. Even then the customer could have pointed out it would be inconvenient in time for him to make the trip so a voucher of greater value than a 'petrol cost' would be needed. A compromise solution might have been arranged which is always a possibility when there is a flexible approach. Here it was the 'broken promise' and the inflexibility that caused the worst of the argument in a potentially damaging place.

Originality

Introduction

Although 'man is a creature of habit' as consumers we do like 'something new'. We stick with the same brand or the same item for a number of years, realising only if we see a photo of how our favourite product looked some years ago that the design, shape and so on may have changed almost without our being aware of the changes. Compare the front page of the current edition of *The Times* to the front page of the same paper 20 years ago; although it is essentially the 'same' paper, that initial aspect (vital for customer attraction) has changed beyond recognition. Where once text filled the entire page with an almost complete absence of headlines, illustrations and photos, the current front page contains a meld of such characteristics in a far more 'relaxed' style reflecting changed (and changing) public tastes.

Appeal

Taste and public opinion are subject to constant change, and suppliers need to ensure their products reflect such patterns. How a supplier deals with customer enquiries, concerns, or the everyday interface can also change and an original approach can mark the supplier out as having 'something special' to say.

Case study: It's a pleasure

Wishing to set a standard of employee, customer, neighbour and supplier and shareholder relationships, the newly appointed Chairman devised the phrase 'It's a pleasure' and stipulated that it was to be a pleasure for all those with whom the company related to do business with it. Procedures were adopted and attitudes changed so that there was a real and practical effect to the adoption of the commitment embodied in the phrase. This extended to the retail units using the phrase whenever a customer said 'Thank you'. When subsequently a takeover bid was launched for the company, the Board was able to stress that during the bid it was essential that the commitment to all that was inherent in the use of the phrase should continue. Thanks to the preparatory work and the ethos that had been created, during the difficult and stressful nine weeks that the bid lasted, customer relationships were never higher and complaints never lower.

Commitment

To attain positive customer service and care requires commitment – essentially of those at the sharp end who actually interface with the customers. However, their commitment can only be a reflection of the commitment of the decision-making body of the supplier. Unless there is top level commitment few employees further down the line will have any and those that do have (from training elsewhere or their own natural enthusiasm) may soon lose it as, without regeneration and support, their motivation will wane. The problem is that to continue to maintain high standards of commitment requires constant attention at the highest level and an insistence that standards will not slip. Ironically such a commitment which should help provide a high standard of customer care is so rare that when it is encountered it seems to be original instead of the customary response we should expect.

Case study: A rich seam

Richer Sounds is a relatively small, but fast growing company, that readily acknowledges that it receives many of its best ideas from its staff. Thus, amongst many other ideas, employees have suggested

- a discount scheme which had the effect of boosting sales tenfold, and

- a policy of telephoning customers to check that they were happy with a repair service and so on.

Key technique

The response of customers receiving a call checking that they were satisfied with a service can only be imagined given that many repairers may try to avoid seeing previous customers in case the repaired fault has repeated or another developed! Whatever Richer is doing it seems to work – it is reported to have the highest sales per square foot in the world.

'Grit your teeth and listen'

It may come as a surprise to some management, not used to listening, that they do not have the monopoly of good ideas. Indeed who should know better the problems and difficulties of performing a job than the job holder – yet often when there are changes they are the last to know or be involved. Encouraging employees, through suggestion schemes or less formal means, to put forward money saving or product enhancing ideas can tap a rich vein of suggestions as well as motivating those employees and encouraging their commitment to the company and to its customers. Suggestions do not always relate to new products or means of supplying or promoting them – or emanate via a formal scheme. Provided the supplier is prepared to invest in employees it is interesting to see what can develop.

Case study: Up the pole

Pacific Power and Light is a power supply company which operates in some rough weather conditions in north-west America. In many of the mountainous areas power is transmitted on overhead lines which often break under the weight of accumulated ice formed by the freezing of the constant snow. The method of avoiding breakages was to send linesmen along the line with poles constantly knocking the snow off before it froze. Several brainstorming sessions with the linesmen were held to try and solve this problem, during one of which a linesman complained that the previous week he had been chased by a bear. The suggestion was then made that if they could get the bears to climb the poles the weight of the animal would shake the snow off the lines, and another suggestion that if they put honey pots on top of the poles that would induce the bears to climb. The problem of how to place the honey pots on top of the pole then arose and the use of a helicopter was suggested. Cutting across this fanciful and increasingly risible idea came the notion that the downdraft from the helicopter rotors would itself remove the snow before it froze. Nowadays PP&L use the downdraft from overflying helicopters to clear the lines.

Key technique

Perhaps only a few companies would have allowed a meeting of their staff, addressing the serious problem of change needed to maintain customer services, to stray to the fanciful tangent of encouraging bears to go after honey pots at the top of power poles, and yet it was only because they had gone through that idea that the eventual solution was discovered. Perhaps the solution, adopted by Richer Sounds for example, is not to take things too seriously in order to encourage originality.

Inspiration

Where there have been problems very often, even assuming a positive response, rectification is achieved in a traditional 'replacement or recompense' manner. Whilst adequate and acceptable in its own way, the company that can be original in such a situation can create a valuable public relations exercise.

Case study: It's good to talk – and to listen

The small business owner was dismayed to learn only a short time after her telephone number had been altered by the addition of an initial digit that not only was the number to be changed again, at relatively short notice, by the addition of a further initial digit but also she was to have a completely new exchange number. In addition BT could not state the exact day on which the changes would occur. Her business depended on contacts, including a substantial number of telephone calls from abroad often from those unable to speak good English. She complained to BT but was told that the three months' notice of intent was 'adequate' but no exact date could be given until 'later'. She responded by stating that although the local BT office might know much of its business it knew nothing of hers. She had already placed advertisements in foreign papers with the old number and would now incur costs in making alterations but would still not be able to quote a definite changeover date. In addition the provision of a recorded redirecting message offered by BT for only six months following the change was insufficient for her business. The local office were not helpful.

Being a shareholder the businesswoman decided to write to the Chairman of BT outlining her concerns not only at the lack of notice of the change and the short redirection service but also at the poor attitude to customers with problems. Much to her surprise she was contacted by phone by someone from the 'Chairman's office' who not only took all the details but also promised to contact the local office.

Initially the local office confirmed that the redirection service would be extended for 15 months and was soon able to quote, at least to her, a confirmed changeover date. Nearer that date she was surprised to be invited by the local office to see the actual exchange changeover and to attend the 'celebratory' breakfast (the changeover was at 6.00 a.m.).

Increasingly there is choice of telephone providers so even a quasi-monopolistic organisation such as BT needs to provide decent service. With organisations operating where there are many alternatives, decent service, positive response and originality should be the essential watchword of the organisation. Compare the approaches of the two hotels featured in the following case study – which would you frequent again?

Case study: Poles apart

John Green, Senior Lecturer at Coventry University, tells the story of his stay at a hotel in San Francisco where his slumber was disturbed late at night by a rowdy party of children. He asked the Duty Manager the following morning if anything could be done to avoid this in future. The response from the Duty Manager was a promise to take positive action and a reduction in Mr Green's bill by $100. (An original and very memorable approach.)

A party resident in the Holliers Hotel on the Isle of Wight found their slumber disturbed by a very loud disco for non-residents. On phoning the duty manager the guest was asked rudely, 'Well what do you want me to do about it?' (An unoriginal – particularly for the UK – but still memorable approach.)

The head of the Marriott hotel chain states that customer care is all about '50,000 moments of truth a day'. This is the number of times a day that he estimates guests staying in Marriott hotels worldwide test the chain's customer care techniques.

Quality

Nowadays we hear a great deal about the quality initiative and the quality standard and many organisations have subscribed to such standards and proudly proclaim the fact that they are 'quality standard' approved. Sadly in many cases it seems the paper standard may have been achieved whilst the actual standard still languishes. Other companies predate these paper qualifications and manage to achieve and maintain both high standards and consistent and original service.

Postscript

The intervention of senior management (such as occurred in the BT case study above) can often rescue a poor situation which has been created by more junior staff. Originality in response can be a valuable additional means of recovering customer commitment. What is needed is such top level commitment, leadership and insistence on standards at all times. When top management's goals and standards are unclear, individuals at any level may superimpose their own – a very unsafe foundation for any policy.

Product recall

Introduction

Even organisations that take the utmost care in production and/or presentation of products occasionally find the need to publicly advertise the fact that there is a fault in such product in order to try to recover them to destroy and/or replace them, or to carry out modifications and/or alterations to rectify the problem. The problem seems to be on the increase – *The 1997 Review of Crisis and Risk Management* (Infoplan International, Fleet Street, London) reported in late 1997 that product recalls had increased by 300% in the two years since 1995 with damaged, dangerous or contaminated products the main causes. One of the authors commented that whereas previously suppliers had tended to play down recalls, hiding notices at the foot of newspapers' pages, the current vogue was to blazon the advertisement: 'The message seems to be getting through that the consequence of not coming clean about a problem that affects your consumers is far more dire than simple honesty.'

Previously it seems that consideration of the inherent challenge in a product recall operation may (and has in a number of instances) encourage the supplier to attempt to cover up the event. Apart from being irresponsible, this is extremely foolish for the reasons set out below. With the move to an increasingly litigious society, refusing to acknowledge a problem and take adequate steps to correct it could aggravate any claim for damages. Indeed since the number of organisations prepared to advertise nationally and widely in order to recover faulty goods is increasing rapidly, there is an argument for believing that consumers will expect a certain number of requests for recall and not think such action to be too much out of the ordinary – thus the perceived adverse publicity may be minimised although it must be stressed that it depends how open, honest and prepared to make amends a supplier is.

Procedure

Determining whether there needs to be a product recall encompasses three distinct aspects – discovery, assessment of consequences and recovery. The three aspects may overlap and for that reason one team (it is suggested that around seven people is the ideal composition for most recall teams) should be charged with dealing with all the challenges. As with other types of crisis it can help if the supplier is prepared for the eventuality and has a contingency plan already in being. This will enable clear thinking to be undertaken and alternative strategies considered at length when those responsible are not under pressure to act or react immediately. If the supplier produces consumer items and/or has a high profile, preparedness of this kind, is essential.

Discovery

Discovery of faults may emanate mainly from customers and thus there is an onus on the supplier to ensure that there are adequate reporting and analysing procedures so that such reports are

- taken seriously,
- cross-referenced to demonstrate trends,
- inspected by senior management and/or technical staff who can appreciate the implications of a reported difficulty, and
- assessed in terms of determining which productive unit was responsible for the item so that particular and focused corrective action can be taken as required.

Case study: Air problem

The consumer, somewhat shaken, drove to his local servicing garage by forcing the airbag which had inflated without warning, away from his view. The garage could not determine why the airbag should have inflated but since they were under instructions from the manufacturer to report any odd occurrences with the new model passed a report to the manufacturer. Since this was not the first report they had received of such an occurrence, the manufacturer investigated and as a result had to recall all the models of a particular series for modifications to the airbag inflation procedure.

Note: *This was a somewhat low-key method of advice of a problem compared to that which for example occurred with the Mercedes A class car which turned over during an 'elk' test (used to test the car's reaction to fierce consecutive and opposite direction swings or swerves). The test – and the car turning over – was shown a number of times on national television. With Mercedes' reputation and its instant announcement that it was redesigning the car (the test occurred just before the launch) perhaps not too much damage was done to its reputation – other smaller organisations might not be so lucky.*

Assessed for consequences

Objective consideration needs to be given to the problem. For example:

- what is the size of the problem; has the regular monitoring of customer complaints or concerns previously identified a problem?

- is the fault identified likely to affect the whole batch, the whole output from one factory, the whole of a (week's/month's) production from many sources?

- what is the reason for the fault; is it internal or external; is it fundamental or cosmetic, does it involve consumer safety?

- what is the likely financial cost (under older product liability insurance covers recall might, at least to a limited extent, be covered but modern policies tend to exclude recall)?

The likely consequences can affect the consumer, the organisation and regulatory bodies overseeing the actions of the supplier. In turn each of these can be further subdivided. Thus the effect on the consumer could be

- injury or potential injury,

- claim for damages and/or general loss,

- lack of confidence in the supplier, and

- encouragement to 'blacken the name' of the supplier if the position is not handled carefully or, indeed any combination of these four.

The effect on the supplier could be to require

- expenditure and time generating returns and dealing with recompense and replacement,

- investment in research and/or alteration of procedures to design out the fault,

- investment of costs of positive promotion to offset the reputation damage and/or to reassure consumer of other products produced by it,

- possible action against a third party supplier or fabricator, and so on.

As far as regulatory bodies are concerned problems generated by one operator could stimulate investigation of others operating with similar products in the same industry but against whom no problems have yet arisen. (This was essentially the case with the overselling of personal pensions in the UK where problems surfacing as a result of one supplier eventually provoked an enquiry – of several years' duration – of the whole industry – see ARROGANCE.)

Recovery

Obviously recovery can only commence when the problem has been identified and any continuation eradicated. Once this has been achieved the supplier may need to commence a complete marketing campaign as if for a new product launch – which in a way is what is occurring. Where there have been safety implications such a launch needs to address the solution of the safety problems as much as the good points of the product. Assuming the recovery cycle has been successful it will still be necessary to monitor the product since experience suggests that lightning can strike twice and similar problems can resurface despite everyone's best endeavours.

Practical steps

On identifying a problem, the responsible supplier could perhaps adopt a seven-point plan:

1. Be prepared.

2. Show concern for the problem.

3. Demonstrate commitment to a solution.

4. Refuse to compromise safety.

5. Come clean to all customers (and others).

6. Provide updates to keep everyone advised of the problem – and progress on the solution.

7. Plan to try to avoid a repeat – whilst anticipating this might occur (that is, reverting to item 1 above).

Case study: Anything but plain sailing

The refit of a high profile cruise ship fell behind target. As a result when the time came for the first post-refit cruise to America the ship could only sail by taking with it many of the fitters and tradespeople who carried on working around the passengers. Cancelling the cruise would have cost the company a considerable amount in compensation and would have attracted comments and adverse publicity but this would have only been a fraction of the compensation it had to pay, and would probably have suffered only a fraction of the media attention it received when the full story broke. Many of the passengers took video recordings of the work and the state of cabins, public areas and so on – and not least the dangerous state of many parts of the ship and made these available to the national media.

Key technique

It might have been far preferable to have contacted all the passengers a few days before the departure date offering (for example) full refund of the amount they had paid plus free tickets on a replacement cruise and then to have issued a press release announcing that the refit had been delayed and that the organisation had taken those steps. Everyone knows that problems occur and had the cruise ship owners been seen to have acted positively, decisively and with a proper perception of the interests of others (that is, the customers on whose satisfaction their reputation and continuation of operations depend) could have won plaudits rather than the eventual and deserved brickbats for failing to take action.

Dangerous cover up

Whilst the temptation to suppress the information may be considerable, this is unwise since almost inevitably (either by investigative journalism, interest of consumers' programmes or one or more affected consumers determined to give the matter publicity) the fault will be discovered and it will be far more damaging for it to become known that the supplier knew but did nothing about it.

Also, provided adequate restitution is made for inconvenience and/or recompense (if the product cannot be repaired or replaced) the adverse effect of the incident may be minimised. Conversely if the public discover that their confidence has been taken for granted or, still worse, their safety has been compromised there can be a severe backlash.

Case study: Owning up works – 1

In *Talking Straight* (Sidgwick and Jackson, 1988) Lee Iacocca, the man credited with having saved the Chrysler Corporation from liquidation, recounts that the organisation was selling cars that it knew had a fault as a result of some malpractice. Eventually the fault and, more damagingly, the fact that the organisation knew of the fault became public knowledge – research indicated that 55% of the public thought the company were 'bad boys'. Chrysler decided to run an advertising campaign admitting their mistake and making the promise that it wouldn't be repeated. From a

---

survey carried out it was clear that the public liked the fact that they were owning up – a new survey found 67% in favour of the company, a massive about-turn of public attitude.

Case study: Owning up works – 2

In 1994 the high profile Pentium processor was found to have a flaw in the 'floating-point divide'. Initially there was some disagreement concerning the responsibility for the flaw but eventually Intel, the originators of the processor, accepted full responsibility by using full page advertisements which not only invited all users of computers suffering from the flaw to exchange their processor for a new version but was also signed by the President and Chief Executive Officer, the Executive Vice-President and the Chairman of the Board.

Postscript

It has often been said that there is no such thing as bad publicity and although most suppliers would prefer to avoid publicity of this nature, handled well good might come out of the problem. In late 1991 Smith Kline Beecham were the target of alleged tampering of bottles of Lucozade by the Animal Liberation Front. The company removed 5 million bottles of Lucozade from stores and replaced the product with tamper proof seals. It also set up a careline to handle customer concerns and dealt with over 1,500 calls – only one of which was from a customer complaining of feeling ill.

Even interfacings caused by such problems provide an opportunity for the supplier to 'talk' directly to its customers. Depending upon the circumstances, this may give it an opportunity to apologise, to attempt to restore its reputation and may even provide an opportunity to sell more/alternative products.

Queuebusting

Introduction

The British have a reputation for being good 'queuers'. Travellers in other parts of the world may recognise that although this is not invariably the case, very often the British are patient (perhaps too patient in the same way that they have historically been too quiet when required to accept poor service) to a degree that would not be acceptable in most other countries. This being so there is an inherent danger in taking such patience, reticence and forbearance for granted to the extent of exploiting it. This occurs in many instances – for example when supermarkets and banks provide too few outlets to provide or take money, when telesales operations require callers to waste their time in their call 'stacking' systems, or when emergency services close roads leaving many stuck in jams. Few may object to the latter situation particularly when caused by an accident – whilst we may grumble at the delay most will willingly grant a priority to the emergency services. However when it seems that there is simply an arrogant attitude to customers – namely, that they can wait, wasting their time, until we find it convenient to deal with their business (which is actually our business) – few would blame such customers if they prefer to take their (that is 'our') business elsewhere.

Waiting irritates

Modern life is lived at an unprecedented pace. Whether it is right for this to be so or not is irrelevant – it is simply a statement of fact and it needs to be realised. It also needs to be accepted that the pace is likely to increase still further. Living life at a fast pace means that individuals are placed under pressure – greater pressure than hitherto – and consequently anything which hinders their progress is likely to cause far more irritation than would be the case if they were not under such pressure. Getting caught in a queue, when under pressure to cope with a number of other priorities, can cause considerable frustration – often taken out on those least responsible.

> **Case study: Happy New Year**
>
> In shopping in a national chain store over the New Year break the customer noticed several instances where other customers were arguing with the assistants operating tills, whilst the standards of hygiene, service and provision of crockery and cutlery in the in-store restaurant were very poor. On offering a shareholder credit card to pay, the cashier suggested the customer might like to take up with the Board why insufficient staff had been provided for what was a very busy time of the year. So great was the pressure on the staff who were on duty, and so many were the instances of arguments generated by customers needing to be kept waiting for an inordinately long time, that some of the staff walked out thus making the situation even worse. The chain store later reported that it had experienced a 'profitable New Year trading period'. No doubt it had, but their customers might be correct in assessing such increased profitability had been at the expense of the provision of decent service.

Reducing the wait

Some suppliers, realising that customers can become irritated if forced to wait too long have developed a system of 'queuebusting' whereby experienced staff are held in reserve ready to 'attack' the delays causing the queue. In supermarkets this can entail staff assisting customers packing goods and transporting them away or even opening more checkouts. Whilst such efforts may be fairly minimal at least those customers who see the process in action will appreciate that something is being done. Similarly customers of Abbey National will no doubt welcome their commitment to provide increased numbers of cashiers at lunchtime – the very time when not only will many of their customers wish to visit their branches, but also a time when those customers will be under pressure to carry out a number of tasks in a short time. (It is interesting that since the Abbey National's announcement, Halifax have announced that they are opening on Sunday. It seems at last the financial services sector are realising they need to be open at times when their customers can easily get to them, rather than when most are working themselves.)

If these queuebusting facilities are not provided there must be a likelihood that customers will choose alternatives to avoid the wait. For customers of Abbey National, the alternative could be banking by telephone – which would not only lose them a customer's deposited funds but also the possibility of selling them other products seen or referred to during their visit.

Paying for not queuing

For supermarkets and other retail trades, the alternative to queue time could be electronic shopping backed by personal delivery. Obviously this could involve a payment but such is the dislike of queuing for long periods of some customers that they may be prepared to pay to avoid the incidence. Indeed it is possible that electronic shopping, whereby the viewer 'sees' a virtual reality representation of a shop, or simply the goods available via a screen displayed catalogue, and makes a selection from the comfort of their home, could generate extra sales. Not only is the customer saving the time and costs travelling to the shop, but also the fact that there is no need to transport the items to car or public transport and thence to home may be sufficient incentive to tempt them to increase their purchases.

Case study: Personal shoppers

Dressed in 'striking blue uniforms', a team of middle-aged assistants started conducting personal shopping for customers of the supermarket chain Somerfield in January 1998 at their store in Chippenham. The customers select the goods they require from a catalogue displaying over 3,000 items; the orders are transmitted to the store where the personal shoppers carry out the physical 'shop'. The orders are then delivered to the customer's home. Market research company Mintel report that two-thirds of customers have expressed an interest in such schemes.

Note : *If a catalogue of 3,000 items seems somewhat 'restrictive' it should be realised that to many shoppers, too much choice is as irritating as too little. In America, market pollsters FBC Research International reported that 80% of those they asked stated that many of the so-called 'new' products on display in the average store looked and performed like old ones whilst 70% stated that they preferred the 'old days' when there was less choice and thus fewer decisions to be made. Similar results were obtained from British shoppers. Over 1,000 new lines reach supermarket shelves each month and whilst 90% of new items fail within six months, this leaves around 15% additional products to consider each year. Increased choice does not necessarily lead to an increase in trade. Some shoppers are fazed by additional choice whereas others fall back on tried and tested favourites.*

Time will tell whether this form of shopping will catch on but it certainly seems likely that a sizeable minority of consumers could well be tempted to shop in this fashion regardless of whether there is a charge for delivery or not. Indeed the possibility of gaining additional trade and pure competition may swiftly force abandonment of any suggestion of delivery charge. The first chain to offer free delivery will inevitably gain trade.

Electronic queuing

Whilst many will be prepared to wait patiently in a physical queue (perhaps because they can see movement) many callers refuse to queue electronically (that is, by waiting in a telephone call stacking system) where the 'slam down' factor is over 60%. Where the business is essentially mail order (when the customer's trade or enquiry is generated by means of an advertisement in national media) it seems the height of folly not to provide adequate means whereby an order can be placed swiftly. The solutions are relatively easy – what is needed is a realisation of the reactions of the customer and not the convenience of the supplier.

Case study: Never thought of that

The prospective customer rang a mail order service to place an order. He was answered by a computerised call system which gave him no human contact option merely a choice of 'order placing', 'customer service' or 'returns'. Selecting 'order placing' he was told by a recorded voice how much his custom was valued and that he was in a stacking system and was currently eighth in the queue. Muttering that he didn't see how they could value him much if they wanted him to wait whilst seven others were dealt with, nevertheless he waited and two minutes later had made it to sixth in the queue at which point he gave up. Although the number was a freephone, he refused to waste further time waiting.

He suggested to the Managing Director that they might consider using

- a computerised ordering system whereby the computer could generate questions which the customer could answer using the telephone buttons, or

- an answer machine facility where details of the required order and personal details of the caller, method of payment and so on (all of which could be included in the original advertisement so the customer would know what to expect and be prepared) could be recorded with a note of the customer's own telephone number in case of any difficulty.

He suggested that alternatively they consider increasing the number of telephone lines and operators. After all if that many calls were being received it seemed the campaign was generating considerable interest and presumably profit.

Robust defences

Introduction

Most of the recommended practices in this book are geared to the need to provide customers with the respect to which they are entitled as the providers of the means by which everything the organisation needs is sourced. However, it is undoubtedly the case that some customers will seek to take advantage of such positive attitudes and to benefit from them. The incidence of false and even fraudulent claims is perhaps low in most instances but it does exist and suitable responses need to be generated to be able to deal with it. It has been estimated that between 1% and 2% of customers will try to cheat suppliers. There may be little point in attempting to eradicate this fact of economic life and it may be more effective to accept it as a charge which needs to be built into the prices charged. Irritating though it may be to know that these kinds of baseless claims are being made, this is no reason for regarding all customers with concerns as if they were of such a nature. Nevertheless at times robust defences may be necessary.

Checking the facts

The surest method of resisting false claims is by being able to demonstrate the facts of the case, showing that these do not support the contentions now being made. Thus the initial response must be the same as to all genuine claims – a willingness to help, a need to sort out the problem but a requirement that to do either requires facts to be collated and checked. Unfortunately the activities of some organisations lend themselves to abuse and it may be difficult for those that have to deal with complainants (particularly where these are aggressive) not to adopt a jaundiced attitude. Fortunately in some instances the customer is so intent on pursuing their claim their own vehemence can provide a clue to the possibility that the claim may not be entirely legitimate.

Case study: 'The lady doth protest too much, methinks'

In October, several weeks after the agency had supplied an au pair to a family they informed the agency that she was unsatisfactory as she had been stealing. In the circumstances, in the interests of good customer relationships, the agency agreed to find them a free replacement, even though under its terms it had no obligation to do so. The family stated that they did not want a replacement until the New Year and accordingly the agency made the necessary arrangements. Two days after the new au pair arrived in January the family rang the agency.

'This girl is absolutely useless.'

'I'm sorry to hear that – what's the problem?'

'She is useless around the house, dreadful with the children and she hardly speaks any English.'

'But that's why she has come to England – to learn the language. We did stress her English was poor. I can't understand why she should have any difficulty with the children – she is the eldest of eight children and has had plenty of experience dealing with her siblings.'

'I don't care about that – you have supplied someone who is no good at all to me. I want her replaced.'

'Don't you think you are being a little premature – it is quite an upheaval for her coming here, it's bound to take time for her to settle down with a new family. Don't you think you should give her a little time and help?'

'No – it's totally unacceptable. She's useless and so is your service – I want a replacement immediately.'

'But...'

'Immediately do you hear, or I shall be taking this matter further.'

Key technique

Despite the vehemence facts must still be checked – indeed it is essential in such an instance since bluster can be used to try to confuse the supplier and gain agreement to the required course of action. Here, as part of its process of seeking out the facts the agency discovered that the previous au pair had not been stealing, that she had been perfectly happy with the family and had not left them until just before Christmas and then only at their suggestion since they had a replacement coming in January! The family had concocted the story to avoid paying a fee for a replacement. However since the replacement was not of the same calibre as the girl they had let go, their fury knew no bounds. In fact whichever party uses vehemence, anger or a loss of temper, the likelihood of the other agreeing to their requirements must be diminished. Human nature being what it is, very often the reaction to demand is denial whereas the reaction to request may be acquiescence.

Unfortunately some organisations' activities lend themselves to customer abuse and even downright fraud so it is perhaps understandable if they are more cautious, even intrusive in seeking to discover the facts. Insurance companies are often seen as 'fair game' by the unscrupulous, and even some of those who consider themselves utterly honest discard such morals when completing an insurance claim form and either gild or falsify their claim.

Insurance fraud is widespread and is running at an annual figure of around £400,000,000. To combat this, the insurance industry has set up CLUE – a linked computerised system that allows subscribers to cross-check information on all household insurance claims. Claimants have their details checked out via computer screens, and, if found to have claimed fraudulently, are blacklisted. Initially the system handled only household claims but it has been reported that it is being extended to motor and other covers. Having said that, in many respects the industry has only itself to blame for being regarded as 'fair game' – the overselling of inappropriate pension policies has hardly endeared them to their target audience. Complaints against the insurance industry have risen by over 40% since 1992 and pensions overselling has led to governmental intervention and fines being imposed. When in the wrong, robust defences are of little use and positive (and above all swift) care is essential. J Sainsbury, having adopted a generous policy of giving recompense to all complaining customers and subsequently finding evidence of abuse of the system, have invested in computerised cross-checking to enable them to identify those that abuse such generosity.

The customer is wrong

The number 1 rule of customer care is 'the customer is always right' and the number 2 rule is 'if the customer is wrong see rule number 1'. This is sound in the vast majority of cases, even where there is a suspicion that what the customer contends may not be entirely correct or reasonable, since often the time and aggravation involved in resisting a doubtful claim may cost more than agreeing to replace (or to reinstate, as applicable). There may be a precedent created by the act for others, but if records are kept and cross-referenced it may be possible to challenge future claims from the same source.

However there are occasions when the customer is wrong – indeed as Alan Sugar, founder of Amstrad Computers, once stated 'the customer isn't always right and I'm not afraid to tell them so from time to time'. Customer care means treating customers correctly, fairly and politely – it does not mean the supplier's capitulation!

Case study: Rowing cross the Mersey

In late 1997 BBC television featured a series of half-hour programmes on the real time happenings at the Adelphi Hotel, Liverpool. Purists no doubt gasped in horror at some of the 'techniques' (although 'lack of' the same might be a better description) used by the management, displayed during this 'fly on the wall' series. Indeed it was difficult to imagine how teamwork was possible in an environment where confrontations, loss of temper and browbeating seemed to be the order of the day – at least as far as the employees were concerned.

The treatment of some of the hotel's customers seemed equally robust, although it must be said that on most occasions it may have been deserved. Strident demands that guests not bring takeaway food into a hotel can hardly be criticised although the fact that this was loudly and very publicly effected in the middle of the hotel lobby rather than tactfully and in a more private place might cause an aggressive response which would be in no one's interest. A refusal, when the hotel was completely full due to the cancellation of the Grand National following a bomb scare, to honour a reservation made but not confirmed by the required time was perhaps understandable. Again however more sympathy might have been accorded this guest who claimed he had been unable to return to the hotel in time to register simply because of the traffic chaos caused by the same bomb scare. At least an offer of ringing another hotel to try to find a room could have been made – the treatment he received was hardly likely to engender LOYALTY.

On the other hand one must presume that the hotel knows its clientele – and its staff – and knows and understands the fact that some will take liberties. Perhaps a robust approach is essential in such circumstances and such a location (Liverpool – which is after all known for its outspokenness and strident humour) and perhaps the lesson to be learned is that there can be no single hard and fast approach and flexibility is essential. The fact remains regardless of opinions of the 'right' approach, the Adelphi claims that since the television series its bookings have increased by 20%. Whatever the reason those extra guests have decided to frequent the Adelphi, it can hardly be bad for its business although one hopes that their reception and treatment will be a little more tactful than some of those featured!

Postscript

As someone committed to positive and constructive internal and external customer care because it can be a potent force to enhance an organisation's reputation (or a potentially lethal adverse reaction), it is sometimes irksome to realise that there is no such thing as bad publicity. During the Adelphi series the *Mail on Sunday* asked a hotel inspector to test the Adelphi. He did not rate it highly – scoring it only 25 out of a possible 70. When he asked to see the General Manager there was a confrontation which ended by him being ordered out of the hotel in a similar fashion to others during the series – surely this must count as too robust a defence! The other irony is that apparently for all their robust treatment, the employees tend to stick with the employer as labour turnover is low.

Introduction

Those required to deal with customer care and to convert complainants into satisfied and repeat customers need every assistance and comprehensive training to ensure the policy adopted and required to be implemented is promulgated in practice. Whilst there is no doubt that potential 'handlers' can (and should) be trained to provide the service and attention at the level and with the approach determined by the organisation, it helps if such people can approach the job with an inherent liking for people ('warts and all') and a positive desire to help them resolve their problems.

The right approach

Unless the person responding to the initial application by the customer, whether by phone, in person or in writing, does so positively the chances of a successful resolution are immediately diminished. The 'offhand' response can only raise the ire of most who are only making the contact because the organisation has 'let them down' and removed their choice. They should have the absolute right in such circumstances to expect a positive, helpful, and even conciliatory approach – and one that reflects the interest and view of the customer. Can it really be appropriate for one of the UK's leading holiday companies to offer £400 compensation to a couple who entirely through the fault of the company found themselves on the wrong cruise and unable to disembark? Such an attitude totally belies customer care and satisfaction. The minimum offered should have been a replacement cruise to the correct destination – anything less was an abuse of the company's dominant position in the market.

Case study: Lack of vision

Responding to an advertisement for folding glasses in the national press, the customer telephoned an order paying by credit card. Nothing was heard for eight weeks although the amount was debited from the credit card account.

On telephoning the company, the bored voice of a young girl mumbled the question 'Was the magnification 3 dioptres?' The would-be customer confirmed this was so, and was then told that in that case they were still expecting a delivery 'very soon'. The customer enquired in that case why had the credit card account been debited six weeks previously.

'That's for security – we can't leave cheques lying around here.'

'But this was a Visa debit not a cheque.'

Silence.

Since at this point not a single word of apology for the delay had been offered the consumer cancelled the order. Even in doing that, 'bored voice' had to be reminded that as well as the customer's name and address they would want the Visa account details in order to make a refund.

Result: One lost order, one set of costs with no revenue, one dissatisfied would-be customer and one potentially adverse public relations sore.

Remedial action:

1. Ensure all telesales personnel are monitored for helpfulness and customer care.
2. Always apologise (even where unnecessary) as it aids rapport.
3. Be alert and understand the customer's viewpoint.

In fact this company redeemed itself by means of a personally-telephoned apology from the Managing Director who undertook to ensure such a poor advertisement for his company was not repeated. 'Bored voice' herself should not be blamed out of hand as obviously she may not have had the benefit of a proper training programme, or, if she had, her performance was not being monitored by supervision. Having said that, one would have thought that simple basic courtesy – namely, inherent good manners – could have overcome this problem encounter. Indeed it could be said that the current trend in the UK to poor customer service relates very much to declining standards of manners.

It is perhaps worth considering an alternative scenario:

'Bloggs Mail Order company – Jackie speaking – can I help you?'

'I placed an order on 24th August, have heard nothing and find you have already debited my Visa account with the cost.'

'Could I have your name, sir, and details of the product you ordered?'

'Mr Wilson and the order was for a pair of triple-magnification folding spectacles.'

'Oh I am so sorry, Mr Wilson, we had such a demand as a result of that advertisement that we used all our ready stock and our reserve stock and are waiting for the replacement stock which should be in any day now.'

'Well why have you debited my Visa account?'

'That's for security reasons. Usually we aim to despatch the goods within seven days of making the debit but this time we got caught out by the demand. I am so sorry you have been kept waiting but we should be able to despatch the glasses within the next seven days, or else we can refund your Visa account today – whichever you would prefer.'

Key techniques

1. Using her own name as well as that of the customer personalises the encounter and helps create a rapport between assistant and customer.

2. A crisp business-like response provides an impression of efficiency.

3. The obvious knowledge of the reason for the problem also aids rapport with the customer. Nothing irritates customers more than to raise a problem and find that the other person knows nothing of it, and it is impossible to be put through to someone who does. Ignorance of those charged with customer care aggravates frustration and demands.

4. Apologising does help mollify most complainants – it is easy to be angry if the other person is angry but far more difficult if they are sympathetic and apologise.

5. Offering the customer the choice of money back or waiting a little longer returns to the customer control of the encounter. If this had been the instant response, in all probability the order would not have been cancelled and despite the original discourtesy, the sale would have been preserved.

Introducing SARAH

The principles of good customer relationships and care are dealt with at length as part of various techniques and approaches elsewhere in this book but can be very briefly summed up in the process described by the mnemonic SARAH. SARAH is a friendly and helpful export from the USA and, although she was originated for use more in selling, her principles apply equally to customer interfacing. SARAH has five key aspects – the initials of her name.

S

Stop talking and **S**mile: if the supplier's employee is talking, then the customer cannot be heard and neither can their complaint, comment or suggestion. Nothing is guaranteed to annoy a customer more than for the other party to keep talking, preventing them explaining or stating what they wish to say. It seems that an attempt is being made to 'talk out' the subject matter. As the Greek philosopher Zeto of Citium said, 'the reason we have two ears but only one tongue is that we should listen twice as much as we talk' – if only this were true there might be better understanding of customers' concerns and a more realistic response.

In addition a ready smile may disarm all but the most committed complainers. Indeed in body language terms a smile tends to generate a return smile, or at the very least can be regarded as an inviting sign – an indication that in registering a concern, at least the initial reaction is likely to be positive. Of one thing the supplier can be sure, if the customers are smiling then it is unlikely that they are also going to be complaining. In the mid-1990s, German airline Lufthansa ran a successful advertising campaign. Full page advertisements recited four key stages in the development of the airline finishing with the copy 'The future? Our most important objective remains unchanged. Your smile.' If your customers are smiling it should indicate satisfaction.

A

Adopt active listening: the corollary to ceasing to talk is to listen more. This means much more than just hearing what is said. Hearing is purely a mechanical act, whereas listening entails active consideration of what is both said and left unsaid. This may mean needing to ask questions or making comments to discover facts – but above all it means carefully listening to the answers and what is not said. The questions need to be open, non-judgemental and tactful, for example

- 'When you plugged it in, did anything happen at all?' rather than 'Are you sure you plugged it in?'

- 'Did you find anything difficult about following the instructions?' rather than 'Did you read the instructions?' (or even worse but often said 'I bet you didn't bother to read the instructions, did you', almost as if the customer was in the dock in court!)

- 'These items can be difficult to handle, can't they?' rather than 'Are you sure you didn't drop it?' and so on.

R

Reflect content or feeling: to show that the supplier has understood what the customer has said they should repeat key sentences or comments in their own words. This has three advantages:

- it helps fix the details of the problem in the mind of the supplier,

- it helps check that what has been received by the supplier was what was meant by the customer, and

- it engenders a rapport between the two which could be used as a base for a settlement.

For example, 'To make sure I fully understand the problem can I just check that I have all the details...' and 'Let's make sure I have this down exactly as it happened'. The benefit here is that the inference of joint action to solve a problem is being suggested – the customer is being invited to participate in the recording and (again by inference) the solving.

A

Act with empathy: this entails showing that the employee understands and appreciates the feelings and motivation of the customer – in other words the problem must be seen through the eyes of the customer not through the eyes of the organisation.

Case study: Are we seeing things in the same way?

The BBC *Watchdog* programme features many examples of incidents which we can tactfully describe as inadequate customer care. In one case a couple had booked a two-week cruise on the River Po in Italy. Unfortunately due to heavy rain the Po was running at a too high a level and although the couple spent the whole time on the cruise boat it remained securely moored to the quayside throughout. When the couple complained, the travel company's response was that they felt they had fulfilled the contract. The travel company's perception of 'satisfying the contract' seemed to be based on the fact that the accommodation, food and so on had been provided on the boat featured in the brochure. However, the couple's (not unreasonable) perception in booking a cruise was that the boat would move, so that they could see the area they had chosen – the beautiful Po valley. Whilst the accommodation, food and so on, were an integral part of the holiday, the key was movement of the boat and the chance to see the sights. Obviously the travel company could not be held liable for the height of the river but surely and morally one would have expected them to make some gesture of recompense – if only a repeat holiday at a discounted price (which has the advantage of giving something which is of greater value to the customer than it actually costs the organisation).

Key technique

If empathy and perception are lacking, customers will conclude that they are wasting their time as the organisation does not really care about their views, being blinkered to its own tunnel vision.

This kind of attitude exemplifies the description 'package' in the holiday – except that it is the customer who is regarded as the package rather than the various arrangements.

H

Handle the subject matter with care: most complaints concern over-charging, faulty products or services, or a failure to meet a deadline. These are real problems and the customer is very much the injured party. The organisation has responsibility to correct, and possibly compensate and any deal to satisfy or rectify should be conducted in that light.

Postscript

Lacking a smile, keeping talking, not listening, not checking meanings, not empathising and not seeing the matter from the point of view of the other party can only ever have one result – a lack of customer care and the creation of a situation likely to lead to confrontation. Ironically this kind of scenario is all too common – but whom does it benefit?

Service

Introduction

In a book on customer care divided (to try and make it user-friendly and accessible for our customers) into an index format, it would seem illogical not to include a section on service. It may seem ironic that this section is the shortest in the book even though it addresses two of the most important aspects of customer care:

1. If suppliers provide good service (in the widest sense of that word) then most customers will be cared for in the way they wish. Conversely if service is inadequate in any way such care will not be available – and neither ultimately may the customer be for any repeat business.

2. That the key to good service is commitment and consistency. If good service is achieved on a random basis the customer has no guarantee what type of service they will get. Only if they are confident that every time the same level of service and care will be achieved and that the supplier is committed to answering their needs can we claim to give good service.

The brevity of this section is deliberate in that all the other sections concentrate on and take for granted aspects of this one essential characteristic of customer care. If commitment to consistent standards of service is lacking then there is little point anyone reading the remaining sections.

Definition

There is a misunderstanding in the UK, which is surprisingly widespread, that confuses the provision of 'service' with a requirement to be 'servile' and there is also reticence about providing what in other countries (the USA being a particularly pertinent example) would be regarded as basic everyday service. This may be a hangover from the days of wealthy families using servants, and of a time when being 'in service' involved the relationship of master and servant.

As the twenty-first century dawns this misinterpretation can exist no longer. The provision of service does not require the provider to be subservient – to grovel in an obsequious way like Charles Dickens' repellent Uriah Heap. Those who provide good service have every right to be proud (and to take a pride in) what they do without in any way feeling inferior to those that they serve. In the same way that all of us are at sometime both suppliers and customers, equally we are all at some time both providers and users of service. Giving good service (and if it is not good then it cannot be service) can be an end in itself.

Expectations

A further aspect of the problem is that what some regard as acceptable service may be unacceptable to others – a fact that may depend more on the customer's own expectations than the service provider's ability to deliver. The result can only be a mismatch of expectations. This mismatch often results from another widespread tendency to 'trade down' and deliver to the lowest demand level. Whilst this may provide an easy solution to the service provider it can give an unacceptably low level of service to those who have standards above such lowest level. The service provider may complain that they cannot afford to provide a 'higher' level of service – in which case they have no one but themselves to blame if they disappoint a proportion of their customers. A few may voice their protest but by far the greatest number will stay silent and vote with their feet, turning themselves into ex-customers. Research indicates that only 1 in 26 dissatisfied customers will voice their concerns. The others choose alternative suppliers requiring the supplier to re-invest in replacing them – an investment which if made in their staff and procedures could have ensured the satisfaction and retention of far more customers.

The benefits of trading up

Without seeking to achieve the unreasonable, suppliers should aim to provide a standard which is at least above average. The advantages should be obvious – those that would be satisfied with something less will be more than satisfied, whilst those that would not be satisfied with anything less should be satisfied. There may still be some for whom the standard is insufficient but the supplier may feel that their demands are unreasonable and realistically the attainment of 'pleasing most of the people most of the time' is sufficient.

Case study: Closed for business

Lloyds Bank plc ran a television advert in the mid-1990s advertising that whenever there was a queue for a branch cashiers' attention, another window would be opened and for a time this policy worked well – even though inevitably the service was constrained by the total number of service positions available. This was a sound although apparently shortlived commitment – what is required is commitment to providing such service each and every time the customer visits a branch. Inevitably it has a cost.

Whilst the British are known to be good and patient at queuing, most people dislike needing to wait for attention more than two or three minutes. The really irritating habit is for customers to find that there are only a few positions open at lunchtime which anyone should be able to predict will cover most branches' peak customer demand. Banks, post offices and building societies are particularly susceptible to this practice which in reality is an abuse of their quasi-monopolistic positions. How pleasing it is, in the interests of the provision of good service to customers, to see Abbey National pledging itself in a national advertising campaign in early 1998 to provide an adequate number of cashiers at lunchtime, that is, to provide the service its customers require.

Standard letters

Introduction

If not using a CARELINE or CALL CENTRE which can deal with many customer concerns in a relatively formal and instant way, many suppliers will be forced to respond via the traditional letter format. To try to reduce the time taken in composing letters (and hopefully ensuring they are produced in a correct form – with accurate spelling and grammar – which sadly is not always the case), many will endeavour to produce standard letters dealing with most enquiries. Whilst having a number of advantages, not least that the formats can be held on a computer and with a little input can be personalised, there are also disadvantages if the system is not handled with care and attention to the real question being posed.

Coverage

In *Putting it Across* (Michael Joseph, 1993) Angela Heylin suggests that most letters can be divided into the following 11 types (plus reminders)

- Yes
- Sorry
- Thank you
- I want
- Maybe – tell me more
- Congratulations

- Can you
- Buy my
- No
- Help
- Let me explain

If this is so (and having tried analysing my post for a few days it does seem to work) it certainly suggests that the majority of the postbag can be dealt with by using variations of 11 standard letters of response. However, the contrary is also true – a minority of the letters cannot (and thus should not) be answered by using a standard letter. When devising a bank of standard letters to be used in response to customers, suppliers need to stress that standard letters should only ever be used when the matter raised is standard. It is irritating to receive a letter that deals with a concern which is not the one that was raised. Reliance on standard letters can create a laziness and an encouragement to use them even where the circumstances do not fit the answer.

Case study: Pointless

A monopolistic landlord had a large number of outlets leased or let to a range of businesses and individuals. One long-term lessee was somewhat bemused and not a little irritated to receive the following letter:

Covenant enforcement

You have been found to be in breach of the terms of the Tenancy Agreement. Please remove all stickers/posters displayed on the windows/doors and unit front. The unit should then be redecorated in appropriate colours where necessary. Retail goods on display must be well presented and the area kept clean and tidy at all times. I hereby give you four weeks in which to comply with this Notice. Otherwise I will have no alternative but to take further action on this matter.

The lessee had previously enjoyed a good working arrangement with the landlord, paying the rent on time, and could have been excused for responding robustly to both the content and the tone of this ill-thought out missive. Firstly there is a difference between a 'tenancy agreement' and the lease which governed the relationship here. Secondly although the lease contained various covenants there was no prohibition on the display of posters in the windows. Thirdly the responsibility for the tidiness of the shop was that of the lessee and it was kept tidy – whereas the area outside the shop (the responsibility of the landlord) was often untidy.

When the lessee challenged the letter he was told that – it was a 'standard letter' to all holders of tenancy agreements (not the case here),

- it referred to instances where posters, and so on, had been attached to the exterior of premises (not the case here),

- it was a written confirmation of previously made verbal comments (not the case here), and

- the redecoration referred to the possibility that in removing exterior posters, paintwork could be damaged and should be repaired (which is not what the wording says at all).

Corporate ARROGANCE here allowed the conceit that one standard letter, written in a brusque, even offensive, style could cover a multitude of different cases. Here it served only to irritate a responsible lessee and to reflect poorly on the organisation that could allow such an ill-conceived communication to be sent.

One can understand that the above problem might have been caused by the inexperience of the writer but its effect was to denigrate the whole organisation.

Precautions

In using standard letters responding to customers (indeed in any area of use) great care needs to be exercised to ensure that

* the situation being addressed really is standard,

* the standard letter is appropriate,

* the tone used is appropriate, and

* the answer given is positive and can be defended should publicity be given to it.

To ensure this is so it might be helpful for the organisation to lay down guidelines for use by those who write on its behalf.

Checklist: Guidelines for letter-writing

1. All letters are to be written on organisation letterheads using the standard layout [specified].

2. Only those of [status] or above are entitled to write on behalf of the organisation.

3. Attention is drawn to the bank of standard letters which can be used either as drafted or as a base, subject to alteration in individual instances. On no account should a standard letter be used where the circumstances are not exactly the same as those laid down in the introduction to each letter. Where circumstances are different, appropriate alterations must be made to the standard letter or else an original letter should be drafted.

4. All letters should be drafted with respect for the other party. In the event that a letter needs to be sent which robustly responds to criticism

by them or refuses to agree to recompense and so on, in respect of a complaint, such a letter must only be sent after approval by [specify] and in the exact form so approved.

5. The following points should be considered by every letter writer before a letter is sent:

(a) what is my desired result with this letter, that is, what am I trying to achieve?

(b) does my letter actually deal with the point identified in (a)?

(c) is my letter as clear as I can make it and will it be understood *in the way I have intended* by the recipient?

(d) can I reduce the length of my letter, make it clearer, remove jargon?

(e) could I make it shorter without losing clarity?

(f) what reaction is there likely to be to this letter – and is that the reaction I want?

6. No letter should be despatched without being 'spell checked' on a word processor. In the event of the author being unsure about the grammar used, this should be checked with [name].

7. All communications sent by electronic means should comply with the foregoing (particularly 4 above). Ideally an electronic communication with a third party should be viewed by another employee before sending.

8. Copies of all letters other than routine reminders should be placed in an individual's 'Reminder' file so that a central record exists of outstanding matters and suitable reminders can be generated after an appropriate time.

9. All letters of complaint against the organisation must be channelled through [name] although replies which must also be approved by [name] may be signed by the original person dealing with the matter.

Automatic aggravation

Many systems are now based on computer programs which can automatically generate standard letters. One area for the useful application of this is in credit control. However, such systems need to be made subject to human control if they are not to aggravate a customer unnecessarily.

Case study: Lack of control

The business purchased a selection of items on a regular basis from a supplier. Whilst most were fine, one batch of a particular item was faulty and the customer, who had already ordered a further batch of a different item, telephoned his concern and it was agreed the items would be collected and a credit note issued.

Delivery and invoicing of the other items was effected but still no collection had been made of the faulty items nor had any credit note been issued. The business reminded the supplier of the situation and ordered a further alternative batch of products which again were delivered and invoiced. Still no collection/credit had been effected.

The business ordered a third alternative batch and again reminded the supplier that collection/credit was outstanding. These items were delivered and invoiced.

Using standard, computer produced letters, the supplier started chasing urgently for payment of the three alternative items. Twice the business faxed back the reminder with notes stating he wanted to settle all three accounts but first wanted the faulty goods collected and a credit issued. Whilst a phone call ensued stating that collection would take place, further reminders chasing payment were received at regular intervals. Eventually the business sent a fax to the supplier stating that unless the credit was issued within seven days the orders for the three alternative items would be cancelled and the supplier could collect them all.

Postscript

Receipt of non-applicable or 'senseless' (in the context that the content lacks common sense) standard letters can swiftly destroy a customer–supplier relationship. They should be used with discretion and always made subject to human control before issue.

Temper

Introduction

Communication between two or more parties can only take place where there is a meeting of minds and anything that impedes this meeting can impede the communication flow. Inevitably when customer and supplier consider a complaint their two views, at least initially, may be opposed to one another. If this encounter is not handled positively and swiftly, it will be easy for it to develop into a confrontational event when one, probably the customer, or even both parties (if the supplier's representative is insufficiently controlled or patient) lose their tempers ('a brief lunacy' as the poet Horace called it). Whilst the adage 'lose your temper, lose the argument' may hold true, this may be of little interest to a person already aggravated by what they view as intransigence or inadequate service – or both.

Raising temper

Those charged with customer care or fielding disappointed customers' calls (by telephone or visit) will almost certainly at some time have to deal with someone who has lost their temper. Since little progress can be made whilst someone is seized by temper the first aim may be to try to dispel the temper, although this is easier to state than it is to achieve.

Whilst suggestions are made below for ways of calming temper it may be appropriate firstly to try to identify ways in which the temper of a customer can be generated.

Temper-generating situations

1. Generating expectations which are then not fulfilled which can also be termed the opposite of KEEPING PROMISES. It may be better to say 'I'm sorry this will take at least a week to repair' and then provide the repaired item within four days, than to say 'This will only take two or three days' and then take four days.

2. Lying. Liars need excellent memories – those who lie tend to be found

179

out because lies (which need inventing) can be more difficult to recall than the truth.

3. Being patronising, ignoring or being rude to customers. A study of poor customer relations indicates that very often the root cause is a lack of reasonable manners.

4. Opting out of the situation. 'Don't blame me, I just work here' is a common attitude even if the words are not said. Treat enough customers in this way and soon the problem will disappear as there won't be any work.

5. 'Going through the motions' – the attitude that the words are being said so that is all that is needed. The encounter lacks enthusiasm or even commitment.

6. Undue waiting and/or being ignored. Many people have busy lives and resent being forced to wait – particularly if the cause is faulty product or service from the supplier.

7. Incompetent employees. This may not be the employee's fault, but it is certainly the supplier's responsibility to place positive, alert, helpful employees in such a high profile situation.

8. Those who are unable to prioritise. In the case study recounted in GUARANTEES, the manager compounded the rest of the shop's poor performance but stopping to deal with problems raised by other staff members on his way to and from the stockroom to fetch the remote control – all the time leaving the customer (whom they had let down) waiting!

Controlling temper

It can be extremely difficult to calm someone seized by temper particularly as in some instances the real emotion may actually only be part of the reaction and there may be some element of play acting for effect.

Checklist: Dealing with temper

1. Remain calm at all times. Once two tempers clash then it is unlikely that any consensus will emerge, and the situation will almost certainly degenerate. Inevitably dealing with situations where the other party is behaving in a difficult manner can create a situation where it can be difficult for a supplier's representative to 'keep their cool'. Retaining one's patience is essential if one is to continue trying to provide customer care.

Case study: Just the job

One of the recent 'fly on the wall' documentaries by the BBC featured a number of ordinary employees doing what many might regard as extraordinary jobs at Heathrow Airport. Inevitably in dealing with large numbers of people in a stressful situation, tempers can flare swiftly and situations get out of hand. One of the 'stars' of the *Airport* series, turned out to be Jeremy Spake who is the Check-in Supervisor for the Russian airline Aeroflot. In a series of aggravating situations he was seen coping with (for example):

- an orchestra demanding to take all their instruments on the plane as hand luggage,

- players of the same orchestra disappearing when take-off was only 25 minutes away, and

- the conductor losing his baton and the flautist losing his flute.

The fact that few spoke English and thus he was relied upon to speak Russian added to the traumatic situation which most people would find impossible. However, Jeremy's attitude was calm – 'I love all my passengers dearly and anyway it's all part of a day's work'. He went on to comment that 'I face abuse every single day. People call me all the names under the sun, but I keep smiling – it's like water off a duck's back.'

It is that kind of 'unflappability' that is essential when dealing with temper, stress and aggression.

---

2. Try and remind those apparently losing control that nothing will be gained by a loss of temper. Indeed losing one's temper can probably only damage one's case. The problem is that such rational and calm comment can actually further inflame some people who almost desire their opponent to join them in the 'showdown' – 'I've lost my temper, why haven't you?' may run their theme. Indeed some seem to enjoy confrontation – it may even be that they enjoy the rush of adrenalin that can occur when temper is lost and a verbal 'fight' ensues.

3. Note facts or opposing views uttered in temper without immediately commenting. Commenting hastily may merely inflame the situation, whilst the longer the other party can talk without being challenged, the more they may be able to reduce the pressure they feel. It is essential to try to ensure that all contributors speak separately and wait, without interrupting, until the other has finished. If temper is being used for effect, allowing the other party to speak uninterrupted may also help

defuse this aspect of the problem since they may start to exhaust all their arguments. In any event they should disclose what is annoying them.

Case study: 'And?'

A famous actress was once confronted in her dressing room by an erstwhile fan who was incensed by something she had done or said (or was reported to have done or said). He berated her without letting her say anything for about a minute. At a pause she mildly said

'And...'

The fan continued his diatribe, often repeating himself, until he again paused for breath and again she commented softly

'And...'

but the fan had had enough and rushed out of the room.

---

4.   Asking neutral questions to try to uncover as much of the case, or cause of concern, as possible may help, simply from the genuine interest apparently being evinced.

5.   When the encounter is between the two parties face to face, it may help by offering to adjourn or providing refreshments. The provision of refreshments can both buy time and calm everyone down.

6.   Where the encounter is by phone, offering to ring back 'after I've been able to check the facts our end' at an agreed time may assist since if the ring back does not occur for an hour or so, there is a considerable chance that the caller's temper will have subsided.

7.   On resumption or after any flow of temper has ceased, if no adjournment is possible, recheck and correct the facts as already discovered and noted. This should enable a more accurate résumé of the dispute to be prepared. Further, since time will have passed since the original outburst, a more objective view may be obtained.

8.   In making a decision under pressure, care should be taken to avoid making precedents and thus decisions should be of an interim nature pending final clarification and/or approval and possible confirmation in writing. If this is agreed then the confirmation should be given very swiftly.

Postscript

Temper in customer confrontations is widespread. The Retail Consortium recorded 9,000 instances of violence against employees in retailing in 1997. Under increasingly stringent legislation, employers could be held liable if they are not proactive in protecting their employees. Requiring employees to resist customer claims could be held to be a case of the employer creating a situation where the employee could by hurt. An angry person's brain generates activity in the amygdala which swamps the rational side of the brain thus negating its rational logical reasoning. Dealing with anger should entail attempting to calm the other person with neutral comments and action thus allowing them time so that their 'angry amygdala' can cease its activities allowing more rational thought to control the encounter. Some Californians keep a finger on their pulse during an argument. Once their pulse increases by 10 or more they call for a break to allow them time to 'regain their cool'.

Terms

Introduction

The subject of most disappointed consumers' encounters tends to be a failure of a product, the failure of a service or the failure of a product or service to perform to the level expected. Such encounters are probably the most numerous. However, others that will occur may relate more to difficulties between, say, corporate customers and corporate suppliers. In these instances (as well as in some consumer instances) the problems are more likely to be related to the contract terms. If there is a contract dispute, the first question that may need to be asked is 'what did the parties agree?'. The whole point of framing and agreeing terms is so that should problems arise, the parties' respective positions will be known so that the question of any restitution can be determined. If this is the point of the terms, it should indicate that understanding the terms at the outset is all important.

Getting the basics right

Nowhere is it more important to be aware of the terms than if it is wished to resist claims robustly. If the supplier knows (and can show) they are in the right and the customer 'knows' (or can be made aware) that they are in the wrong this places the supplier in a strong position. Insufficient attention to the terms can only lead to situations where a robust defence is difficult to mount. Terms need the following characteristics.

Terms need to be written and read. Terms should be framed using decent everyday English, particularly if dealing with private consumers who cannot be expected to understand the pseudo-legalistic phraseology often used. This is not just sound commercial practice, it is a legal requirement under the European Union Unfair Terms in Consumer Contracts regulations which require terms to be subject to two rules:

- core terms (the essential factors of the contract) must be in plain English, and

- other terms must be in plain English *and* be fair.

Terms need to be brought to the attention of the customer. Provided the supplier can prove the customer knew the terms (and they are fair) before the contract was entered into it should be difficult for the customer to base any complaint if the supplier has complied with the terms. Conversely, if a customer complains about a widget that was bought three weeks ago, and in purported answer is shown for the first time a set of terms in complex language in which lies buried a comment that states the expected life of the widget is 96 hours from purchase, it is unlikely that the customer will be satisfied or consider that the supplier has acted fairly.

Terms need to be known and understood by the employees of the supplier.

Case study: Arguing on the wrong foot

Having advertised regularly in a magazine for some years, the agency was advised that the owners of the magazine had changed. Subsequently, with trade being badly affected by the UK recession, the agency decided to suspend advertising for two issues and received the following reply:

'We note that you wish to suspend your advertising. Since you are cancelling your advertisement, I must advise you that there will be a cancellation charge and in addition, you will be required to repay your series discount.' (**Clang 1**)

In telephoning to query this, the conversation ran as follows:

'But we have never agreed any terms with your company.'

'Yes you have – the terms state that late cancellation leads to a 25% charge and cancellation of a series leads to repayment of the series discount.'

'I am sorry but I must disagree – you are referring, incorrectly, to the terms issued by your predecessors. No terms have been issued by your company.' (**Clang 2**)

'For the pittance of commission I am paid I am not going to provide new terms for the one instance where an absence of goodwill leads to this kind of problem.' (**Clang 3**)

'That is completely irrelevant. Normally this would be a question of contractual commitments, but in this case there is no formal contract. However, leaving this aside, even if we accept your predecessor's terms, they do not set out the charges as you have indicated. Only if there is late cancellation is there a charge, and although one understandably loses the series discount, those terms do not indicate that the customer must repay the discount obtained earlier.'

'You have cancelled late.'

'I am sorry, but I cannot accept that – we told you of our decision more than six weeks before publication date.'

'We need to know six weeks before copy date.' (**Clang 4**)

'But that is not what your predecessor's terms state – they refer to six weeks before "publication date". I gave you notice over three months before one, and over six months before the other publication date.'

'Well we rely on the goodwill of our customers and I don't accept this kind of close analysis of terms.' (**Clang 5**)

'But the terms govern the contract, and besides it was your analysis of those terms which led to this discussion. That analysis was totally incorrect – hence our querying it. I repeat that we gave several months' notice of suspension of our advert, having advertised every quarter in your magazine for several years. As a customer of some long standing I feel we are entitled to better consideration than that evidenced by this conversation.'

Key techniques

1. This can hardly be accepted as the best method of starting a communication with a long-term advertiser and customer (even if the supplier were in the right).

2. The employee is attempting a robust defence without even having available the terms on which her arguments are based. Had she checked and discovered that no terms had been issued it just might have suggested a different approach.

3. Angry frustration may be understandable, but it is not going to solve the problem but merely make the situation worse. Seeking to obtain sympathy as a technique seems curious, but is surprisingly widespread. It is rarely effective, often being regarded as a sign of weakness.

4. Now the employee seems to be making up rules, or seeking to apply internal requirements to a customer who is ignorant of such requirements. A robust defence is impossible in such circumstances.

5. Seeking to base a case on terms is admirable but if the terms have not been issued and/or are unknown to the other party not only can they not be relied upon but also the fact that this is being attempted in such circumstances is likely only to aggravate the customer.

Orders taken by supplier agents (salespersons, representatives and so on, should be subject to the requirements set out in the following checklist.

Checklist: Effective terms

1. Representatives (and/or agents) must comply with the agreed journey-plan and submit their call report schedule within five days of the end of each accounting period.

2. Deviation from price list values may only be allowed with the prior written authority of [name of authority]. (Note 1)

3. Details of proposed orders being variations from the standard list, showing number of units, delivery date, and so on, must be submitted to [name] who will advise whether the variation can be produced and, if so, the price/delivery to be quoted. (Note 2)

4. Comprehensive details on the company's official order form must be shown. The customer must confirm the order by signature and retain a duplicate copy. The status of the signatory should be checked to ensure he/she has appropriate authority. (Note 3)

5. Orders below the minimum order level [specify: cash/product numbers] will only be accepted on the basis of a pro forma invoice (that is, payment being made with the order) which will bear a minimum handling/delivery charge. (Note 4)

6. Orders from new customers will be accepted, but not processed until receipt of two satisfactory trade references, and credit clearance.

7. Sales staff are expected to liaise with Credit Control to set a level of trade which seems reasonable given the customer's financial standing. Orders in excess of this level may only be accepted with the prior written authority of [name].

8. Journey cycles and terms of trade means payment for an order placed in month X should have been received by the next call but one. Finance department will advise if this is not the case so that the representative/agent can investigate the position.

9. Subsequent orders will not be processed until payment is received. The order acknowledgement will bear a warning that repeated poor payment will lead to a requirement to use the pro forma system or to a suspension of supplies.

10. If difficulties are experienced with payment, visits by sales and credit control staff will be made.

11. If it seems that a customer is in financial difficulties this fact should be brought to the attention of [name]. (Note 5)

12. Terms need to be carefully delineated, regularly updated and brought to the attention of the customer, either prior to the effective date (where a change has been implemented) or on the first placing of an order. (Note 6)

Key techniques

1. Orders that deviate from price lists, apart from involving the possibility of destroying margins, can generate disputes where customer A, paying the full price, discovers customer B is gaining the benefit of an advantageous price. Logical reasons for the difference are essential to combat the inevitable complaint.

2. Similarly, variations from the standard product, which are likely to be more apparent than an advantageous price, may not only reduce profitability but also prompt demands from other customers for similar bespoke products or even for a price reduction for taking the standard product.

3. & 4. Most supplier–customer disputes revolve around costs and charges. It is essential that the whole basis of the order and its authority is clear from the start.

5. Early notification of this event may enable action to be taken at an early stage to avoid the worst effects.

6. Notifying and keeping the customer updated regarding terms and changes should avoid complaints of the 'I didn't know' variety.

Commercial contracts

Whilst there are a number of Acts protecting the rights of consumers or private individuals there is less legislation affecting the position where both parties are corporate entities although legislation is currently being drafted to allow interest to be charged when invoices are paid late. Whilst many such contractual relationships can be regarded as the meeting of two opposing 'camps', increasingly the realisation that supplier and corporate customer are actually in a partnership in which both have something to gain is gathering widespread acceptance.

Case study: BP best practice

BP Exploration Europe is one company that has adopted the concept of best practice, together with its suppliers since they are in partnership and have mutual interests. In BP's 'alliances' initiative the company and a number of its suppliers generate a tendering process which selects contractors who are then available to BP for advice on the contract terms, risks involved, costs and so on. As a result of this process which encompasses an agreement regarding the sharing between the partners in the alliance of any savings made as a result of such co-operation, BP claims to have been able to reduce expected costs on major capital projects. In many cases the saving has been as much as 25% of the projected cost and since the suppliers share in this saving in addition to the profit they make on the contracts allocated, it is a win:win situation for both parties.

Postscript

If terms are kept simple, clear and visible many conflicts concerning them can either be avoided or possibly reduced in scale. Often however terms are printed in feint and tiny (virtually unreadable) type giving the impression that

- the supplier does not really want the customer to read their terms, and

- because they are in small type the supplier has something to hide.

Interestingly pawnbrokers, whose customers are private consumers are legally prohibited from using small print in their agreements to try to ensure that their customers always know the terms under which they do business.

Ultimate aim

Introduction

When immersed in dealing with customers or providing a customer care regime some representatives of suppliers seem to find it difficult to remember the ultimate aim of the process. Yet such ultimate aim is relatively simple and can be expressed in five parts:

1. To try to convert a dissatisfied or disappointed customer into a satisfied or mollified one.

2. To try to ensure that the customer is retained as a likely repeat customer.

3. To ensure the reputation of the supplier will not be damaged as a result of the encounter.

4. To ensure that potential costs of the encounter are minimised.

5. To operate effectively and efficiently.

Complaint conversion

This first aim is the subject of a separate section in the book. As that section suggests, it requires the supplier to take action that will accept the problem as its own, consider the requirements of the customer and make recompense as near as possible to that required by the customer, as is as feasible to attempt – all within a reasonable time scale since customer dissatisfaction with the process of recompense will resume growth if rectification is not attained within (say) five days.

Gaining a repeat customer

Research indicates that provided a customer's complaint is owned by the supplier, apologised for and dealt with to their satisfaction within a short time span, over 80% of previously dissatisfied or disappointed customers will be repeat customers. There are three important factors here – that the supplier will own the problem as theirs (not the customer's), that an apology is given (this is vitally important since not only is it difficult to maintain irritation and/or anger when someone is apologising but also apologising underlines the ownership of the problem – 'this is our fault and we are sorry'), and that the matter is speedily resolved.

Protecting positions

Many employees of suppliers (as well as some suppliers themselves) fail to appreciate that some of those with whom they deal may have power, influence, and position that can either damage their own position or that of the supplier. In many ways an attitude which fails to appreciate this is another example of corporate ARROGANCE – in this respect the belief that the supplier is right (even if not) and the customer is wrong and of no importance since 'there are another 100 or so behind him as alternatives and what can he do anyway?'

Case study: Who?

The supplier had let the customer down badly and when this was pointed out, first of all refused to accept that the error was their fault, although this was absolutely clear from the evidence which was incontrovertible. When they reluctantly accepted the error as their own, they then 'dragged their feet' concerning restitution of the loss suffered by their customer. Eventually an agreement was made although at that late stage the customer, despite having been proved right had not received an apology. So annoyed was he at the lack of positive customer care that as part of his last letter he revealed that not only was he a shareholder in the supplier but their deputy chairman was a former colleague and he had contacts in the national press who would welcome details of the encounter as part of a campaign they were running on poor service. By almost immediate reply came a letter from a more senior manager apologising for the dispute and the poor quality of treatment and so on, and offering recompense – anything it seemed that would either stop the matter going further or show the local staff in a better light should it do so.

Controlling costs

Dealing with complaints and restitution (that is, converting complainants into satisfied customers) can be expensive – albeit only a fifth as expensive as replacing that customer with a new customer. Assessing the cost of dealing with customer concerns can help place the matter (such as, the failure of service, quality, performance or specification) in perspective. Appreciating that such costs tend to rise the longer the matter subsists without agreement is also important. The following analysis can serve as a means of calculating the costs and of stressing the need to try to effect a resolution swiftly.

Company name _____ Complaint Ref _____	Costs
Customer details Name _____ Address _____ Tel. no. _____ Ref._____	Basic
Product details Description _____ Reference number _____ Purchased _____	Reputation
Complaint details Advised on (date)_____ By Person / Telephone / Letter / Other (specify)_____ Nature _____ Restitution required _____	Aggravation
Action details Investigation _____ Supplier / Engineer comments _____ Customer comments _____ Other _____	Time Travel Admin.
Restitution details Suggestions _____ Accepted _____ Authority _____	Recompense
Rectification required Specify _____ Action by (state name/position and date required) _____ **Total error rectification cost**	Improvement
Reported to Board (date) _____ Approved _____ (Initial)	

Explanatory notes

The assessment of the various categories of costs highlighted by such a form is set out below. Figures have been inserted for the purpose of example. Some of these may seem high but research indicates they are not unrealistic.

Basic: Every complaint wastes resources before it is recognised as such and should bear a charge of (say)... **£50**

Reputation: The fact that there is a complaint against the organisation damages our reputation, and entails using expense in restoring our good name. A notional charge needs to be allocated to each complaint. This is for individual consideration and may depend on the seriousness of the complaint. For the sake of the example... **£100**

Aggravation: Each day that the complaint is unresolved aggravates the complainant to the extent that further and more public notification of the complaint may been gendered. A daily charge of at least £15 should be made. If we assume the complaint will take 20 days... **£300**

Time, Travel and Administration: Complaints absorb management time – and if not resolved swiftly and competently tend to absorb time of more senior management. Allowing for all oncosts and benefits as well as salary, the charge for the Chief Executive could total £2 per minute, with proportionately less for more junior personnel. We will take an average charge of £1 per minute and assume that it takes around 180 minutes to deal with the average complaint... **£180**
(Note that this assumes a reasonably swift settlement. If there is a dispute this figure could be considerably increased.)

All travel costs need to be reflected should an on-site inspection be required or the customer need to travel to the organisation. In addition, letter writing, telephone, computer input, as well as all oncosts involved (heating, lighting) should be costed against the complaint. All are being incurred whilst the organisation is dealing with a complaint and not furthering its business. For an average complaint... **£60**

Recompense: Obviously this depends on the product or service under complaint, but on the basis that most people will not complain about something worth less than (say) £20 that could be a minimum figure... **£20**

This gives a total cost to be borne by the supplier of... **£710**

Such a cost speaks for itself and the fact that many of these costs are hidden should be no consolation.

Operating effectively

For any organisation to be able to operate effectively it needs to be able to spend as much management time concentrating on running and developing the wealth creating side of the business. Customer complaints (whilst it is important they are notified and dealt with) detract from this aim other than providing a possible means of promoting other products. Attempting to avoid the incidence of problems must therefore be a sound philosophy.

Case study: Clarity pre-empts arguments

In taking over an agency which provided temporary staff to private customers, the new owner was concerned to note the number of arguments that had developed concerning the terms of the agency in general and the guarantee regarding replacement in the event staff did not complete their booked term in particular. He altered the documentation so that everything was user-friendly and altered the procedures so that clients were required to sign an undertaking which confirmed that they had read and understood the terms before they could register with the agency and receive any details. This procedure was required on each occasion that repeat business was commissioned – thus protecting the agency should other terms have been altered since the previous booking.

The requirement of clients to sign the undertaking was made an inviolable rule. Later when there were any disputes and clients attempted to claim for an inappropriate operation of the guarantee using either the 'I didn't receive the terms' or the 'I wasn't able to read/understand this' excuses, the signed copy of the undertaking could be produced. In most cases this tended to bring any confrontation or dispute to a swift end. In many cases this was tempered by some allowance against a repeat fee in the interests of good supplier–client relationships but the important factor was that the supplier's case stood on firm ground and any allowance could be seen as a 'gift' from the agency.

Postscript

The above form allows for consideration of rectification of errors so that, should the complaint be likely to recur, advance action can be taken, whilst it also calls for the Board to authorise the action, not so much for the actual granting of authority to commit resources to the problem, as to ensure the party likely to take action is advised of the problems arising. In turn this may help the Board stress the ultimate aim of achieving customer satisfaction either when there are no problems but especially when there are problems. Allowing the customer to 'win' (or feel they win) a little is a sound tactic. Generally people resent losing but value a bargain. Giving a little when not forced to do so allows both sides to win and the customer to think well of the supplier.

Variation of terms

Introduction

The principles that a supplier should draft clear terms and promulgate them openly as a strategy to minimise the effect of later dispute revolving round the principles under which business was conducted are set out in TERMS. In that section reference was made to the need to try to avoid varying terms. There are two main reasons for this:

- if variations are made on a regular basis it may be very difficult to keep track of the position, and

- if not thought through variations can have a deleterious effect on the supplier, adding uncosted expenditure and time to the productive process.

Thus considerable restrictions should be placed on those who accept orders before they are able to vary terms. However this will not necessarily stop customers taking steps so that they 'vary' the terms regardless of the wishes of the supplier. Nowhere is this probably more widespread than in customers taking an excess of credit.

Thus sometimes a customer–supplier conflict does not concern the customer recording a claim over faulty goods or services so much as the organisation initiating the interface because the customer has not paid. Unfortunately, despite the legitimacy of the action, this can result in the loss of customer goodwill – hence the principles of customer care should not be overlooked in dealing with what may be a far more delicate subject than fielding the backlash from a faulty product.

Planning

As indicated elsewhere what is essential is that these problems are planned for from commencement of business. The process of credit control should concentrate on planning to collect payment before the due date primarily, even though much of its thrust may be required where payment is delayed. Procedures and practices that will enable credit control to closely monitor the position and attempt to restrict the elbowroom that might otherwise be allowed to debtors need to be set up. Sound systems, well-drafted and communicated TERMS, staff training and making everyone (including potential transgressors) aware that there is a vigorous policy which seeks to ensure that everyone pays promptly can assist in creating an awareness that delays are unacceptable and very much the exception.

Delaying tactics

Inevitably a customer's business is only worth having if ultimately one is paid for the work. The operative word there is 'ultimately' since although most UK debtors do pay, some also tend to extend the payment period considerably, illegally and with possible dire results to their creditor. The creditor's problems may be compounded by an unwillingness to have recourse to legal sanctions as these may involve the loss of future business from the source. The incidence of such problems can be reduced by setting the scene correctly.

Case study: Ineffective undertaking

In making arrangements for a funeral the owner was chatting to the family and, perhaps to soften the encounter, was telling them of problems he experienced in collecting the costs from previous clients. Apparently he was owed accounts from six clients for over four years. On reading the agreement which he prepared for them, the family realised that nowhere on the contract itself, which they were required to sign, did it state the name of the business, its address or telephone number.

Although no doubt the undertaker would have been able to prove his debt in the Court, it would have made such an endeavour far easier to accomplish if in the contract itself the names of both parties were clearly set out – together with the terms of payment (which were also missing). Failure to attend to such basic matters can make the subsequent control of credit far more difficult.

Checklist: Credit terms

1. Ensure terms and payment basis (strictly in accordance with terms of business) are shown clearly on quote (which itself should bear the names of the parties). This means that from the inception the debtor should be left in no doubt as to the terms of trade. If in addition the fact that the terms of trade are strictly policed is understood it may help set the scene for later chasing.

2. Parties' names, terms and payment basis details should be repeated in the invoice – again with an indication that the terms are expected to be strictly adhered to and only if this is so will future/larger orders be accepted.

3. Restrict size of orders until completion of [defined period] satisfactory trading/payment at lower levels.

4. Include retention of title clause in terms.*

5. Ensure payment terms are adhered to strictly, and that all customers know extensions of credit are not permitted.

6. If reciprocal trading takes place, stipulate that any debt owing by the business to the customer, will be offset against any monies owed to the business by the customer.*

7. Charge interest on late payment.*

8. State that the customer will be recharged with any amounts levied by bankers for dealing with dishonoured cheques.*

9. Lay down strict procedures for guidance of credit control personnel, ensure adherence, and grant authority to threaten sanctions where necessary.

10. Credit control staff should be trained to be assertive, to chase for payment regularly and to visit awkward customers.

11. Ensure collection staff are trained to negotiate – and to bargain.

12. Stipulate that in the event of action being needed to be taken to recover, all costs incurred will also be due.*

13. Set up automatic procedure to action claims (such as, via the County Court).

Items marked * should be incorporated in the terms of business, which themselves need to be written and widely promulgated.

Checklist: Invoicing and credit control

1. Invoices will be sent at the same time as delivery of goods/services or completion of orders. Uncompleted orders should be avoided, since the non-completion of the order may mean the invoice cannot be served and the payment period cannot commence.

2. Second class post will be used. As the invoice will not be paid for over a month why pay for 'first class' service?

3. Payment terms are end of month following invoice date. Every effort should be made to despatch orders with invoices before the end of each month.

4. Payment terms cannot be extended other than by prior written authority of the Board only.

5. Seven days before the due date, a statement will be sent requesting prompt payment.

6. Two days after the due date, finance/credit control will check any reason for delay. If an acceptable reason is given set further time for chasing.

7. If an unacceptable reason is given for non-payment, a chasing letter (first class or faxed) is sent stating that unless payment is made by return, the matter will be passed to solicitors and costs will be charged.

8. Two days later, request solicitors to commence action. (There are a number of computerised packages for this purpose. These operate on a fail safe basis – that is, they automatically generate the next stage of chasing unless action is taken.

9. Claim should include the original debt, costs of collection, including solicitors' costs, plus interest on the amount due for the time overdue (which should be made clear in the terms – see above).

Key techniques

1. If the customer knows when he or she will be invoiced, how this will happen and when the amount is due, the customer's ability to evade due payment legitimately, and to generate confrontation is limited.

2. Firm control over payment terms and the procedure, as well as regular chasing should aid recovery.

3. Making notes of all that is said will build a file on the process, thus enabling the supplier to confirm or deny earlier statements.

4. When payments 'on account', or which do not seem to relate to particular invoices are made, check with the debtor what invoices are being paid.

5. Record all telephone calls and agreements in writing and where there has been a verbal agreement record this and send the other party a copy.

6. All discussion including telephone calls should have a clear purpose and advance consideration of alternative outcomes and any action required as a result.

7. Ensure there is active liaison between sales and credit control.

Postscript

The simplest rule to apply when considering the prospect of varying terms is **don't do it**. Realistically however it may be essential to allow a variation. Whilst conflicts and disagreements over terms are usually resolvable, in many cases this may need recourse to the courts and the main winners may well prove to be members of the legal profession. It may be far better to try and avoid the incidence by laying down the ground rules, and communicating them to those involved right from the outset. This will not necessarily resolve all incidents but may help avoid some.

Winning through face to face

Introduction

Most 'post purchase' encounters with customers, particularly those with complaints, tend to take place via electronic means (for example, telephone, fax, e-mail) or via written means (for example, letter, memo). However in dealing with INTERNAL CUSTOMERS and in some trades (such as, retail) face-to-face encounters will be common. In many ways these can be more difficult to handle, particularly if they are awkward (after all one can always ignore a letter or put the phone down if a customer becomes too irate) since the complainant is there in person as large as life. Indeed if the encounter takes place in a public place, the customer might well exploit this additional dimension since it may work in their favour (as was the case in the encounter set out in NEGOTIATION).

However, true communication (that is, the two-way process) is most likely to occur when the parties are face to face, so, if it can be arranged, such an encounter may stand the best chance of success – one where both parties win.

Tactics

The following tactics are examples of those that can be employed.

Personalise the encounter

Provide your name and take (and use) the customer's name.

Smile

A smile should encourage the other party to relax. Many people view lodging a complaint with some trepidation and expect an aggressive response – unfortunately experience indicates that very often their expectations are fulfilled. Being greeted by a smiling face should help allay such concerns as well as aiding the flow of information which is the first step towards finding a solution. In terms of customer care and complaint conversion smiling has other advantages:

- it is difficult to be rude to someone who is smiling and trying to be helpful,

- the effect of the smile can be disarming and it can be hard to avoid smiling back,

- the smile can also indicate an apparent concern to ensure things are rectified. Often complaints are aggravated simply because an off-hand response indicates to the customer that there is a total lack of real concern for their problem, and

- a smile lays the foundation for empathy and understanding between the parties.

Very often customer care facilities are staffed by women which may be advantageous since in general women find it easier to smile than men. Generating a return smile may also assist the supplier's representative in gauging what it is that the customer wants. Research carried out at Cambridge University in 1997 indicates that simply by looking at photographs of the eyes, many adults could tell if they belonged to those who were worried, angry, scheming, decisive, arrogant or in a number of other mental states. In addition women were better than men at determining the appropriate mental states – in tests they tended to correctly ascertain the mental states in 22 out of 25 instances.

It is even possible to gain rapport by smiling when on the phone. The smile relaxes the muscles and this will have a similar effect on the voice tone – the listener will be able to 'hear' the smile.

Conversely there may be occasions when a smile may be entirely inappropriate. For example, if face to face with an internal customer and giving them some bad news (for example, that they are about to be made redundant), starting the encounter with a broad smile would hardly be appropriate or wise.

Pay attention at all times

If other matters – for example, breaking off the conversation to take a telephone call, speaking to visitors, and so on – are allowed to interrupt the discussion an additional semiotic message is conveyed. In that instance, the following words may not be said but they are certainly implied – 'your complaint (problem, grievance, appeal or whatever is not as important as these other matters'. In such circumstances it is hardly surprising if aggravation and annoyance is generated.

For this reason it is preferable if an encounter can take place where interruptions are unlikely to occur – for example a special meeting room to which access can be restricted except in emergency and where there is no phone or other means of intrusion. It may also be advisable to remove any clock as even glancing at a clock can convey a message (not necessarily accurately) that the person doing so wishes that the encounter was at an end or is taking too much time. If the person needs to know the time, it may be best for them to move their wristwatch to under their wrist as it can be easier to view the dial unobtrusively, although any effort to curtail the discussion may, unless there has been a settlement acceptable to the customer, be counter-productive.

Don't fidget

Yawning and/or fidgeting sends the message to the other party – 'this is a waste of my time, I'd sooner be elsewhere'. Whilst the latter might be the case, and even understandable, communicating this to the customer is not only rude but foolhardy as once again it can polarise attitudes and aggravate the whole situation. The point that 'without our customers there is no point to our employment' might be a suitable catch phrase to have printed across the top of the notebook or encounter résumé pad to be used by those fielding such encounters.

Keep your body language under control

Non-verbal body language accounts for 93% of the message in face-to-face communication so the expression on your face, the way you sit, the way you listen all send messages to the other party. To ensure positive messages are sent the supplier needs to be encouraging at all times, to lean forward (possibly making notes), to nod occasionally, and at all times to be (and be seen to be) attentive. Leaning back, closing one's eyes, yawning and sighing will all be seen as negative messages.

Case study: Don't bother

The tribunal case had little value and seemed to have been brought as an attempt to extract some money for nuisance value. After the evidence the applicant's barrister was invited to make closing submissions. He spoke for 50 minutes. After about 15 minutes he started to repeat himself and to veer away from the evidence that had been presented. Progressively the members of the tribunal stopped taking notes, capped their pens and started quietly shuffling their papers into folders. Oblivious of the messages being conveyed that they had heard enough (which seemed crystal clear to his opponents) he ploughed on for a further half hour. The tribunal retired for only a few minutes before announcing that the applicant's case had failed – a message clearly conveyed by their actions some time earlier.

Seat everyone

Aggression and aggressive behaviour can be difficult to achieve when one is seated – but much easier when one is standing. The act of sitting encourages one to be comfortable – whilst the act of standing requires more exertion and is less comfortable particularly if one is kept standing for some time. The development of making the accommodation in football stadia all-seated results from awareness that the propensity to violence is reduced when people are seated.

Offering a seat demonstrates a concern to put the person at their ease which itself can work towards creating a rapport and empathy between the parties. Thus, seating opponents should relax the parties and reduce the possibility of aggravation.

Serve refreshments

Whilst it will not always be possible or desirable to serve refreshments, the act has a multiple advantage. It is a neutral act, although it indicates a concern for the other party's wellbeing and also creates rapport by virtue of the shared experience. Further the fact that the organisation is playing host may give it a slight edge in the rest of the encounter – at least it will indicate from the outset that the supplier is prepared to listen simply by the fact that they have taken 'time out' for the purpose.

Be accountable

In the past it was often the case, particularly in contacting public sector and large private organisations, that the person responding would refuse to be identified. This shield of anonymity was frustrating to the caller for two reasons: firstly because it was an obvious way of avoiding accountability, and secondly because, since the original contact was unknown, there was no way of ensuring a further conversation took place with a person conversant with the facts of the case. Fortunately this practice is fast disappearing. Effective complaint solution is best served by those responsible being identified by giving a name in any letter and over the phone, and by giving a name and having a name badge in face-to-face encounters.

Don't keep people waiting

Obviously this is difficult in the case of chance visitors, but even then there should be a minimum delay before he or she is seen. If a delay is unavoidable then they should be invited to take a seat, provided with literature and possibly refreshments. Such courteous treatment may well aid a softening of any adversarial attitude. If an appointment is made, then, other than in the most extreme situation, the supplier should be there at the time stated. Keeping people waiting, particularly without apology or information merely stores up resentment that may find an outlet in a determination to be even more awkward than hitherto the case. If there are delays then not only should an apology be made and an explanation offered, but also the customer should be given the choice of cancelling the appointment, and setting another or waiting for a further stated time. Again, the strategy restores choice to the customer to help defuse difficult situations.

In addition knowing the expected length of the delay can help.

Case study: Knowing shortens the delay

London Transport are installing 'time before the next train's arrival' indicators on their stations. The odd thing is that many commuters comment that knowing how long they have to wait for their train seems to shorten the perceived waiting time. In some way it may be felt that this restores choice to the consumer – that is, they can either wait for the time advised or find alternative means of transportation.

Always tell the truth

It is said that liars must have good memories – either that or they must make comprehensive notes and keep them safely. The trouble with telling lies is that they have a habit of backfiring as very often the truth comes out, which can be damaging to the instigator of the lie. In such circumstances any chance of a rapport or respect will have been lost and the likelihood of the dispute being settled amicably is also made more difficult. The telling of lies is particularly aggravating to the recipient of the deception as he may feel that the organisation must regard him as a fool, capable of being easily duped by a lie. Organisations that perceive their customers in this light can lose credibility.

Create empathy or understanding

Most complaint encounters can only be aggravated by a supplier attempting to defend their position. It is usually more constructive (and probably a sound way of shortening the encounter) if the supplier makes efforts to understand the customer's viewpoint and position and to attempt to deal with the problem from that viewpoint. Given the known difficulties that face-to-face encounters pose to customers, those that do so must be recognised as people most likely to press home their comments and least likely to be dissuaded from so doing. 'I see what you mean', 'I do understand how you feel', 'Yes I can appreciate that', all help create empathy and rapport. Further the creation of such a link may help the customer moderate their initial demand whereas a defensive stance may well aggravate their views.

Don't patronise your customer

If you do they will not patronise your products. The use of jargon or technical language is not helpful to moving the encounter towards a solution. Using jargon which the other party cannot understand is lazy (since the opportunity is not taken to explain the matter properly), defensive (since it can imply that the supplier is attempting to 'blind the customer with science'), or patronising (since it implies to the customer that they are in some way inferior, or possess a level of knowledge which is inferior, to the supplier). The latter is almost certainly true – but irrelevant. I cannot tell whether the mechanic that services my car has performed the job well or not, but if it does not perform I need the position rectified. I am not really interested in whether the 'differential gear's sprocket has been dislodged from the casing' – what I want to know is whether it can be put right, when, for how much, how long the repair will take and whether there is any alternative.

Don't promise what you cannot deliver – but do deliver what you have promised

Most customers want a solution and want it fast. If promises are made then they must be sustained, otherwise the result will be worse than the original problem.

Re-create a positive relationship between customer and supplier

Once they had a relationship that was positive – the customer valued the product and bought it and, if everything went well, would value the supplier. However, if the product is faulty or not up to expectations the relationship is damaged and needs repair. Properly repaired it could turn out to be stronger than was initially the case and the customer could become a firm advocate of the product and the attitude, but if the repair is bungled then 'hell hath no fury like a customer scorned'.

Case study: A gold plated clanger

In *A Complaint is a Gift* (Berrett-Koehler, San Francisco, 1996), Janelle Barlow and Claus Moller recount the tale of Jeremy Dorosin of California who bought two espresso machines from Starbucks. He was not given a free half-pound of coffee which was normally given with the purchase of the machines, one of which he claimed also malfunctioned. He gained no satisfaction from the company and commenced a high profile campaign against the company, even taking out advertisements in the *Wall Street Journal*. As a result he appeared on CBS Evening News and the story was featured in the *New York Times* – and all for the lack of a half-pound of coffee.

Winning

Avoiding and dealing with demanding customers is essentially concerned with detail – with the desire to get it right first time. Customer and supplier form, or should form, a mutually dependent partnership. Only if this is the case, and is understood by all involved to be the case, will we both minimise the incident of complaints and be able to deal with them effectively. Further, this is not something which we can strive for and achieve once and then forget, since

- it is ongoing and constant,
- it needs to be repetitive, and
- it needs to form habits.

Postscript

Bill Shankly, the one-time Manager of Liverpool Football Club, which during his managership was the best team in the game, once said: 'when you get up you must have the intent to do the best you can that day, and the following day when you get up you have to have the intent to do the best you could that day, and so on – you must give of your best every day'. Those that have to deal with customer complaints and problems need this kind of attitude as well as a realisation, which must come and can only come from the top management of the company, that their businesses can only succeed to their full potential, and indeed may otherwise be unable to survive, if everyone has a commitment to

- customer concern, care and respect,

- providing service and response in the way we would like to be served and responded to, and

- solving problems courteously, tactfully and swiftly, always bearing in mind that the best way of dealing with complaining customers is to avoid creating them in the first place.

Tom Peters, the American management guru, identified as winning companies those that

- were willing to flatter their customers,

- were conscious of the importance of service, and

- had a high degree of responsiveness to the market.

Telephone complaints

Here are some 'don'ts' when dealing with telephone complaints (with some suggested 'do's':

1. Don't let the telephone ring – it should be answered swiftly.

2. Don't omit the flexibility of access to a human being if using a computerised answering service – some questions will be non-standard and not 'fit' the alternatives offered.

3. Don't sound bored, offhand, rude or tired when answering the call – say who you are and offer to help in a bright, enthusiastic voice.

4. Don't be offhand with callers – they are customers who at the end of the day pay your wages.

5. Don't say 'hang on' when answering the phone. If you are already on a call and a second call comes in then excuse yourself to the first caller ('excuse me a moment – would you mind hanging on whilst I answer this call – thank you') and say to the second caller 'Thank you for calling [name], I'm [name] but I am answering another call right now'. Then either 'I'll come back to you in just a moment', or 'if you would like to give me your telephone number and I'll call you back immediately'.

6. Don't forget to ask who you are speaking to and to use their name. Personalising the encounter can help reduce anger so use your own name as well.

7. Don't say 'I don't know' (or worse 'I dunno'). Obviously there will be occasions when you may not know the answer. Instead say, 'Yes I see that is a problem and we need an answer. I would like to check with [name or position] and come back to you – could you give me your number to avoid you hanging on?'

8. Don't give any indication that the customer is a nuisance for calling. If they have a complaint their only reason for making the call is to advise the supplier of a problem – our response should be to imply that we are only here to help them achieve a resolution of that problem.

9. Don't say or imply that the customer is wrong or doesn't know what he or she is talking about. If you don't believe what they are saying, be noncommittal but take notes of everything that is said.

10. Don't say or infer that what the customer is asking for cannot be done, for example, 'No we cannot do that'. The use of the negative can anger many people particularly if they are already feeling let down by the organisation. Far better to say, 'Yes I can see the problem, the difficulty is that…'. At least the initial response is positive and the underlying impression is that of forming a partnership to sort out the problem.

11. Don't begin any sentence with 'No' – it probably isn't true anyway since, most things provided, there is intent. In any event 'no' tends to imply that you want the conversation to end which is the last thing the caller wants until he or she has received satisfaction.

12 Don't be ingratiating or obsequious. Callers do not want servility, they want service delivered professionally – with ZELOSO.

13. Don't knock or denigrate the products. Even if it is the 30th call that day complaining about a malperforming widget, it is the only problem to the caller and should be treated as the first of the day. If the caller says 'you must have had other complaints about these products', reply 'I'm not sure – in any event what matters is that we sort out the problem you have had with yours, isn't it?'

14. Don't use jargon or technical language unless the customer uses it first.

15. Don't forget to apologise. Even though you may imply an apology it can rile many people if you (that is, the organisation) do not use the words 'I am sorry'.

16. Don't lose your temper even though the customer may lose theirs. Remaining cool can be difficult as some customers will deliberately try to make you lose your temper knowing the old saying 'he who loses his temper loses the argument'.

17. Don't shout or raise your voice even though the caller is shouting or raising his/her voice. In fact it may be effective to deliberately lower your voice thus making it difficult for the caller to hear you. This will force the caller to stop, draw breath and listen simply to keep the conversation going.

18. Don't state that you must transfer the customer to someone else without gaining agreement to the transfer. The customer must feel he/she has some choice and control over the matter.

19. Don't transfer a caller without making sure the person concerned is available and on the line and knows the problem so as to respond positively.

20. Don't denigrate the caller's position. If the caller says he or she is a Doctor, Professor, Major, or whatever, use the title. The courtesy may help defuse their ire.

21. Don't do or say anything that is at variance with the organisation's aims or mission statement. If your attitude is not in accordance with its philosophy, the customer can use this to indicate hypocrisy.

22. Don't lie or attempt to bluff your way out of a situation. Lies can be uncovered and bluffs can be called. In both instances the result will be worse than the original situation. If you don't know, don't say 'I don't know' but do say 'I'm sorry, I am not sure I am the best person to help with that query, I think it might be better if I got [name] to talk to you about it.'

23. Don't promise what you know cannot be achieved. If you know getting a replacement widget will take two weeks there is no point in promising instant delivery. All this will do is to add to the customer's anger when let down again. Far better to say 'I am sorry, I am afraid we are having a little difficulty with our suppliers of widgets – it may be eight to twelve days before we can send you a replacement but I'll put priority on your order.'

24. Don't imply it's not your fault. Objectively no one may be able to say it is your fault but as far as this conversation goes, you are the organisation, the problem is certainly the organisation's fault and responsibility and you are the person charged with sorting it out.

25. Don't imply that you are having a bad day. You may be, but that's nothing whatever to do with the caller – he is having a bad day since he has parted with hard-earned cash and has only a faulty product to show for it.

26. Don't do the job unless you welcome the chance to deal with difficult people positively. If you do not 'suffer fools gladly' then this work may not be for you.

Written complaints

There is no doubt that using the telephone to lodge complaints is increasingly popular since it does have the benefit of the customer voicing a complaint to a representative of the organisation, and using tone and even forceful language can stress the need for action. Nevertheless, setting down a complaint in writing does have the advantage that the customer has a written record of what was said. Should there be no reply, a file can swiftly be built of efforts made to make the claim, which if there is no response may form the basis of a legal action. Of course it may be more expensive to deal with written claims, although there is no reason why a written complaint should not be given a telephone response – as indeed was the situation during the case study related in DEALING where the Chairman of the company rescued his company from adverse publicity for its responsibility for a spoiled holiday and for not dealing positively with the complaint originally.

The following are things to avoid, and how to avoid them, when dealing with written complaints.

1. Don't ignore the letter. Customers who write have had to put themselves out far more than telephone callers. In addition if the letter is clearly and well written, almost certainly it means that the writer 'knows the ropes' concerning complaining and will not allow the matter to die.

2. Don't deal with the matter using a standard letter. Even if the complaint is a standard one, the fact that a standard letter is available indicates that the organisation may have a great number of complaints which is hardly a good advertisement.

3. Don't delay in sending an acknowledgement. Customers with involved complaints may well understand that it could take some time for the organisation to deal with their problem. This they can forgive – what they may be less prepared to forgive is the organisation apparently ignoring them. A simple card stating 'We are sorry to learn of your problem. We are investigating and will contact you again by [date]' is all that is required. Having given a date for a future contact such contact should be made even if it is a further stalling letter.

4. Don't be offhand in drafting a reply. All such an attitude can create is resentment and will aggravate the situation.

5. Don't avoid saying 'sorry'. An apology (apparently sincerely expressed and meant) can have an effect on the complainant out of all proportion to the cost of the words – and anyway words cost nothing.

6. Don't be miserly in response. The customer has not only suffered in terms of having a faulty product, he/she has also taken time to record the problems and send an analysis to the organisation. Replacement of the product should be augmented by recognition of these ancillary costs involved. Sending a small gift in addition to a replacement product can regain goodwill.

7. Don't pick holes in the comments made by the customer. The desired result of the organisation should be to try and convert a complaining customer into a satisfied potential repeat customer, scoring points. Referring to 'your undated letter', 'your misspelled missive', 'your unsigned note', or whatever, only serves to irritate the customer – after all the presentation is irrelevant, what matters is its substance.

8. Don't use weasel language which evades the point. If an apology is required – give it fulsomely and properly. Stating 'I was sorry to learn of your dissatisfaction' slides round the matter unsatisfactorily – the fact that the writer is sorry about the customer's dissatisfaction is irrelevant and may merely seek to annoy the customer further. The writer almost seems to imply that the customer has in some way injured him or her. What should have been said is 'I am sorry our widget was not delivered in the condition either you or we expect' – which indicates that the organisation 'owns' the problem.

9. Don't avoid accountability. Whether or not the organisation made the product, or part of it is irrelevant. What matters is that to the customer the organisation is the one with which the deal was done – the party that accepted the customer's money. Legally the organisation may have a right of recourse against the supplier but that is irrelevant to the customer. Indeed the cost of an extended argument, potentially legal action and the damage to reputation seem high prices to pay for defending what most would regard as an untenable position.

Case study: Whose fault?

'Not our fault' is perhaps the easiest line for a supplier to trot out when a complaint is lodged – to which on many occasions the response may be 'perhaps so, but it *is* your responsibility'. The holidaymaker and his family stayed for a week at Easter in a self-catering apartment in Majorca. It was unseasonably cold and although the brochure had indicated that the rooms were centrally heated the heating was not on and the holiday was marred by this. As the holidaymaker commented, 'I don't expect to pay over a £100 a day to stay in a fridge'. At first the holiday company tried to avoid liability stating that the heating was provided by the hotel and had not been available as the system was broken. Eventually however it was forced to pay over £200 to the holidaymaker. Arguing the case did little for its reputation – particularly since the holidaymaker made sure as many people as possible knew of the problem.

10. Don't 'duck' any, or 'cherry pick' only some, of the matters raised. Nothing is guaranteed to raise the irritation factor more than to find the response to a complaint is that the writer ignores some of the matters and focuses on others where perhaps the supplier may have some reasonable defence. Dealing with everything 'warts and all' may be difficult, particularly if there is a lot to apologise for, but at least it may gain some respect. Avoiding issues in the hope that they will 'go away' is a high-risk tactic. Whilst some will give up at this point, those that don't will be the most determined and the 'fobbing off' will simply add to their ire. In addition the evasion can only show the organisation in a bad light.

11. Don't try to lie your way out of the problem. Liars have to have good memories and if the organisation is caught out in a lie, having already been caught out in supplying a faulty product, it further damages its reputation and enhances the customer's case for adequate recompense.

Case study: Liar

The customer placed an order for a three-piece suite stipulating that it should be like the one in the store but not that model since it had a flaw. He chased for delivery a number of times and eventually the suite was delivered. However, he immediately wrote to the company stating that in contradiction of his order they had not supplied a suite from the factory but the display model from the shop.

The shop replied that this was not so – the model supplied was an ex-factory model.

The customer replied with a letter to the Managing Director enclosing a copy of the store's letter and a copy of the sale ticket which had been attached to the suite proving that it had been in the store!

12. Don't assume customers are fools. Whilst some may be – so too are some of those that work for organisations. Patronising customers is

dangerous, one never knows how much they know – or what proof they have.

13. Don't assume that customers do not know their rights and/or how to prosecute those rights. An increasing number of consumers know their way around and know how to exercise their rights and bring pressure to bear on the supplier.

14. Don't assume you can fool all of the people all of the time. Some of the people may be able to be fooled for some of the time but if they discover they have been fooled the result can be worse than the original position. In addition trying to promote such an attitude reflects very poorly on the organisation.

15. Don't feel you know all the answers. No one does – be prepared to consider the matter objectively and indeed to treat the customer as you would wish to be treated yourself were the roles reversed.

16. Don't assume the customer shares your low view of your organisation. The customer judges that the organisation can provide value. Denigration reflects as badly on the customer as it does on the speaker and the organisation. It will not calm the customer and can cause further irritation.

17. Don't expect the customer to show sympathy for you. The fact that the supplier has problems is accepted but is nothing to do with the customer – all they want is satisfaction which is what they thought they would get when they originally parted with cash, in return for a product which has now not lived up to expectations.

Ten pet hates

During 1997, Professor Leonard Berry, of Marketing at Texas University, asked his students to carry out a three-week research project. During that period they recorded what occurred during every 'service encounter'. Despite widespread perception that standards of service tend to be high in the USA, the results from this survey led him to conclude that there is currently a 'customer respect deficit'. In presenting at a conference to US retailers and bankers he concluded that the top ten pet hates of American consumers are

1. being lied to,

2. assuming customers are stupid or dishonest and treating them harshly,

3. not KEEPING PROMISES,

4. using the 'I just work here' excuse,

5. being kept waiting too long,

6. being given an automatic response (that is, the impersonal response without any eye contact),

7. being given the silent treatment,

8. suppliers' employees being non-proactive (namely, not making any effort to assist customers),

9. employees giving the impression 'lights on but no one at home' (these are the clueless who make no attempt to obtain the answers to a customer's questions), and

10. employees' misplaced priorities (such as those who chat to each other rather than serve the customer).

X is for Xmas (and also unknown)

Consider the following case study and attempt to determine the errors made by the supplier (answers in ZELOSO).

Case study: Post early for Christmas

The customer wanted a mail order item for a Christmas present and rang the number advertised in the national paper. He stressed that he only wanted the item if they would guarantee the item would arrive in plenty of time for Christmas. This was promised – indeed it would be sent within two weeks.

Nearly four weeks later (on 19 December) when there was still no sign of the item and as time was now very short, he rang the number again. A recording answered and gave him the choice of dialling 1 for orders or 2 for queries. He pressed 2 and heard a further voice stating his call would be answered soon. Over the next 10 minutes he heard several times an announcement stating the operators were busy but he would be dealt with soon. He was also informed he was eighth in a queue! The queue did not seem to move since after a further five minutes the voices stopped interrupting the muzak and it seemed the system had broken down.

He disconnected and rang an alternative number – it was engaged. He tried pressing 5 so that the number would ring him when unengaged but a BT voice said the ringback was not available on that number. He tried the original number again and this time after waiting a further five minutes was answered by an offhand operator.

'Good morning [it was 4 p.m.] or is it good afternoon?'

'It feels like good evening – do you know I have been trying to get through for nearly 20 minutes?'

'We're very busy.'

'I would like to know why an order I placed nearly four weeks ago has not arrived.'

'Could you give me your name and postcode ...' The details of address etc. were exchanged. 'Hang on, I'll just check ...'

The caller – at his cost still – waited for a further 2–3 minutes, then...

'That product was despatched on 15 December.'

'Will it get here in time for Christmas as I was promised?'

'It should do.'

The call, which did not provide a great deal of reassurance, lasted only a tenth of the time it had taken to get someone to answer the phone.

Postscript

Although the item did arrive in time for Christmas, the way in which the enquiry was handled hardly encouraged the customer to consider placing a further order with the company.

Your views – not mine

Introduction

In considering a customer complaint and request for restoration of choice, very often a classic mistake is made: the supplier substitutes their views of the situation and thus their choice or attitude for that of the customer. Almost inevitably there will be some divergence of views between the parties but if there is to be a consensus, the views of the supplier may need to be sublimated for those of the customer – or at least some mutually acceptable compromise reached.

Whilst this may be easy to determine on an ad hoc basis it may be more difficult on a general basis unless steps have been taken to attempt to discover what people think. To effect this it may be appropriate to try to discern customer views, either by ongoing dialogue or by conducting a survey of customers and/or prospective customers. Inevitably the number of customers needing to be canvassed will tend to determine whether a personal interface (either face to face or by telephone) or one effected by means of a written questionnaire will be appropriate. Generally it may be possible to gain a better insight via personal interface although the results could be skewed by the forthright views of relatively few, whereas a perhaps shallower overview from a large number may be able to provide a more accurate guide to the views of the majority.

Why ask?

This question can be answered in two parts. Firstly, so that the enquiring supplier gains customers' views of their products and particularly new products. Thus, introducing their 1998 survey, the National Shoppers' Survey organisation stated: 'If shoppers don't like a product, [suppliers] lose money ... eight out of ten new products actually fail in the shops ... so it is important for firms to know what customers ... actually prefer'. As Coca-Cola discovered despite all the market research they had carried out with their new recipe for 'Coke' it was the customer comments on its CARELINE (*after* the launch) that gave them the most accurate guide to what the market wanted – which was *not* the new recipe. Secondly, to gain views on the standard of services provided on an ongoing basis.

Asking the right questions

Many companies are now taking advantage of the expanding industry of MARKET RESEARCH companies (or even their own internal research departments) to survey their customers on a regular basis usually using a questionnaire or a question-and-answer session. In this respect one tends to get what one pays for. Asking customers to complete a questionnaire is relatively cheap but the information may be skewed and suspect (although this can be overcome at least in part by ensuring the sample is large so that the effect of 'mavericks' is diluted). If carrying out face-to-face surveys instant responses can be captured which may be more likely to be the truth.

Providing either means is used on an ongoing basis, considerable insight should be generated into the perception of the organisation by its target audience. However, all questions need careful composition since immediately one starts asking questions one tends to condition the respondent and unless check questions are inserted the results can be skewed by respondents either

• not being entirely truthful in their answers, or

• answering in the way they feel the questioner may want an answer, or

• accentuating their replies because they have a particular 'axe to grind'.

Professional questionnaire compilers can minimise the effect of this kind of 'false' response and those wishing to undertake such a survey may be best advised (even if ultimately they wish to use and apply their own questionnaire) to commission a professional company to effect such work. Research Services Ltd (see MARKET RESEARCH) state that it is important to 'bury' the main subject of the questionnaire amongst more general questions so that any 'hothouse' effect is dissipated. Most compilers of questionnaires try to compensate for the fact that respondents do manufacture their answers by inserting camouflage (and check) questions which, because a lie (or simply an exaggeration) is more difficult to remember than the truth, may be answered differently, indicating that the answer to the original questions may be suspect.

Generating expectations

Embarking on a commitment to invite comment on a service or product can create the expectation that improvements will be made (or shortcomings eradicated) or even, if invited on a more personal basis, that some action will occur as a result. Failing to meet such expectations may result in a situation worse than had the offer not been made in the first place.

Case study: Adding insult to injury

The holiday company advertised in its brochure that at the end of every holiday it invited all holidaymakers to complete a questionnaire on its service, arrangements and so on. This point was emphasised by the Director responsible in a personally addressed letter (accompanying the questionnaire) which emphasised how much he wanted to receive and read their comments. The family spent some time completing the questionnaire but since part of their holiday had been far from satisfactory they also composed a lengthy letter setting out their concerns over shortcomings and failures to meet the standard and/or provide facilities described in the brochure – all of which were the responsibility of the company.

No reply having been received within a month, a reminder was sent. This generated a reply but one which, rather than apologising for the perceived shortcomings, took issue with every point made (despite the fact that many were incontrovertible) and in effect dismissed the matters raised (and in so doing patronised a loyal customer).

Since the holidaymaker was a shareholder in the company, he felt so annoyed that he wrote a personal letter to the Chairman pointing out that this exchange was totally at odds with the commitment of the company because

- the original letter had been ignored,

- the matters raised had been dismissed in a cavalier, patronising fashion, and above all

- what the holidaymaker thought was important and vital to the company (namely, the views of the customer) had been sublimated to those of the Director.

A sequence of events and attitudes which, when the company was on record as stating that it wanted to hear from customers, merely added insult to injury. Virtually by return came a holding letter apologising and indicating that a full investigation was proceeding and a week later came a letter acknowledging the truth of the complaints and offering a cheque for around 15% of the total holiday cost.

Key techniques

1. The customer accepted, pointing out that, whilst as a holidaymaker he found the offered deal satisfactory, as a shareholder he was not at all happy that a letter outlining a number of complaints had not received proper consideration, and that those responsible needed to be educated to understand that such incompetence could easily lose customers, thus threatening its own profitability. In addition the company appeared to be ready to ignore the considered and objective views of a customer who had no reason to 'do it down', being also a shareholder, who had indicated areas where the company was potentially legally liable.

2. Adopt care guidelines as follows:

   (a) All correspondence to be acknowledged within 24 hours (vital with this kind of personal service organisation) and answered within 15 days.

   (b) Non-standard replies to questionnaires to be passed to manager for attention immediately.

   (c) Positive comments to be made. There is little point disputing opinions – the supplier invited them so there is an onus on them to accept them, whether they like them or not. Disputing customers' opinions, which the supplier solicited, adds insult to injury and continues the aggravation. Far better to apologise and simply state – 'how can we recover the situation?' (virtually regardless of who is 'right').

Note: *If customers are viewed as the 'package' in the package holiday it is hardly surprising if complaints ensue, particularly since such suppliers sell a 'dream' and the two parties' perception of that dream may be somewhat different.*

Unrecognised images

Organisations sometimes overlook that fact that at every stage of their operation the opportunity exists to conduct random qualitative market research. Often however the opportunity is not seized – indeed not only is it not seized but also a negative image can be created, whereby the prospective customer may receive an underlying message that their views are not really wanted or important.

Case study: Slow service

On behalf of the *Sunday Times*, a correspondent wrote to 65 leading UK companies and public bodies. 'Full replies came back in anything from three to 49 days and varied from prompt, charming and informative to late, curt and rude. Nine have yet to write back despite a reminder.'

Key techniques

1. In the article, Vincent Mitchell, Lecturer in Marketing at the University of Manchester, stated that the way an organisation deals with its correspondence reveals a lot about how it is run and their views on customers and outsiders: 'How they reply is indicative of the way they view their marketplace, and an indication of the philosophy of the company.'

2. The organisations that responded in a 'late, curt and rude' manner seem to be unaware that customer, public, and shareholder relations are a vital part of their operation and reflect how well or, in their case, how poorly they regard the customer and such outsiders: 'Sometimes one almost feels ashamed at having disturbed their apparently preferred hermit-like existence.'

3. The enquiries were in no way demanding. Ignoring them, or answering them in a rude or curt manner, is one of the best ways of ensuring that the next contact is indeed a demanding one – dealing with which could be costly. Aggression tends to generate aggression.

4. The fact that the organisations had been contacted generated a research opportunity. Informal (or even formal) contact from the supplier inviting comments on a range of subjects or perceptions of the organisation could have been invited – at very little cost.

Remedial action:

1. Adopt as a company policy the rule that all items of correspondence will be acknowledged within 24 hours and answered, where necessary, within 15 working days.

2 Devise a questionnaire concerning knowledge of the organisation and its products/services and send it to all such unprompted contacts. After all, if the contact wants a favour from the supplier, why not, when granting it, ask for one in return?

Creating a 'demanding' customer

There are several instances of poor complaint/concern/enquiry reaction highlighted in this book. In them, those who were simply customers with problems were giving (free, gratis and for nothing) the suppliers the benefit of their directly reported views. Despite this in many cases they were converted into demanding and difficult customers purely because of an inadequate initial reaction from the supplier. The fact that this needless aggravation of a situation is totally self-defeating seems to escape the attention of the suppliers' representatives involved. The inadequate reactions involved have included:

- poor response,
- late response,
- dogmatic reaction,
- failure to appreciate the other side's viewpoint,
- unthinking response,
- patronising response,

and so on.

Not only could all of these have been easily avoided and the initial problems solved with relatively little attention, but the failure to solve the problem in the early stages, led, in most cases to a situation where the encounter became far more difficult, consumed far more resources, including both time and money, and, very often resulted in a potentially reputation-damaging conflict. The fact that customers do talk to other customers simply does not seem to occur to many of those who have responsibility for dealing with such problems. Whilst a failure to do a deal at an early stage for fear of precedent-creation can be understood, all too often what transpired had nothing to do with that and was more related to inadequate systems, inadequate training and inadequate respect for the vital importance of the customer – and their views.

Postscript

The situation is aggravated in many instances since some of the suppliers who argued the most were actually those who at least in 'lip service' terms state that they want to hear the views of their customers. If they make such a statement then the very least they should do is to listen. If you do not really want to hear the views of your customers don't waste their time, and don't risk their ire by inviting them to comment and then either ignoring them or rejecting the comments you sought!

Zeloso

Introduction

Z stands for Zeloso – or 'with fervour'. In seeking to provide customer care both organisation and employees need to be enthusiastic. This is not simply because it will show the organisation in a better light, but also because it may be essential for the survival of the organisation in the harder competitive times that we may be facing. In *Managing to Survive*, former head of ICI, Sir John Harvey Jones, makes the point that he 'believes the 1990s are going to punish those who do not think about [their] problems. Your business is only as good as your customer base.' If Sir John is correct (and there is every reason to believe him and little reason to argue against such an authority) and the 1990s are going to punish the thoughtless, then the twenty-first century is also waiting to exact its toll on the unwary. Those who wish to survive past the second millennium will need to address their customers' needs and demands with considerable attention – and some *zeloso* will not come amiss.

Acting proactively

This is not as difficult as it at first sounds since the major part of the problem we can avoid by simply hanging on to the customers we have – even if they have cause to complain. If complainers are dealt with courteously (or at least in the way that they would expect), with respect and above all speedily, most can become committed and long-term customers. Charles Weiser, head of customer relations at British Airways, endorses this point. He suggests a four-point plan to convert complaining into repeating customers which can be summarised as follows:

1. Apologise and 'own' the problem. Complainers do not care whose fault it was – what they want is action and rectification.

2. Do something – and do it quickly. Initial satisfaction that something is being done, dips if customers feel they have to wait more than five days – and is destroyed if they have to ring or write again.

3. Assure customers that the problem is being sorted. Those who are asked to deal with complaints must be fully aware of all that is going on – and

particularly of changes in the products and services. (They should also be enthusiastic about their role in rectifying problems.)

4. Phone them back (or write back) quickly – most customers appreciate personal service. A phone call can be more personal than a letter.

Honour underpins business

In 1997 the Institute of Directors launched a campaign which will bridge the two centuries. The 10-year HUB (honour underpins business) campaign aims to help transform public perceptions of business and the fundamental contribution that business makes to the UK's prosperity and freedom. The perceptions that the public have of an organisation depend very much on

- the values that each organisation are seen to embrace,

- the messages that the organisation conveys – whether explicit or implicit, and

- the treatment they (as well as those they know or read or hear about) receive from the organisation.

Twenty-first century consumers will be far more streetwise and perceptive than their twentieth-century counterparts. Further there is a continuing and growing trend to grant more and more protections and rights to consumers at a time when demand (at least domestic demand) may not be growing as quickly – or even, in some cases, at all. In such a scenario ensuring the right and consistent messages are disseminated is essential for survival.

The last postscript: X is for Xmas

In X FILE we asked readers to try to spot the number of errors made by the mail order organisation. Here's our list:

- Having taken an order and promised despatch within 14 days, no advice was given to the customer that this had not been achieved (even though his credit card account was debited immediately the order was taken).

- In receiving the call (for which the customer paid) no human alternative to the recording was offered – yet this was a non-standard query.

- No opportunity was provided to the customer to leave a message which, whilst it would have cost the supplier a short call in response, would have saved the customer time waiting whilst the answer was discovered.

- Knowing the position in the queue does provide information but to most people the fact that one is eighth in the queue merely confirms an early suspicion that the supplier has no respect for their customers (otherwise they would provide more operators to field the calls at what was obviously a busy time).

- The ring back facility is useful since it saves everyone's time so why was it not available? It would also have transferred the cost of making the call from customer to where it belonged – with the supplier.

- The lack of enthusiasm for the encounter was quite marked yet for all the operator knew the call could have been from a new customer.

- The fact that the supplier was busy was actually in their favour – presumably trade was brisk. If they feel that to be a problem, that is their lookout – in any event it is not the customer's problem. Going for the sympathy vote is rarely successful.

- No apology was offered for having kept the customer waiting.

- No apology was offered for not complying with the original promise of despatch within 14 days.

- No choice was offered regarding keeping the customer waiting again.

- No apology was offered for the delay when the employee returned.

- No thanks were offered for the call.

- No apology was offered for the need to make the call.

That's 13 errors in a relatively short call – and there are probably one or two more. In short, however, the employee evinced no *zeloso* – in fact she had a total lack of enthusiasm for her role. As a direct result it would be unlikely if the customer had any *zeloso* for using them again!